GCSE AQA B: Science in Context
Core Science
The Revision Guide

This book is for anyone doing **GCSE AQA B Core Science**.

GCSE Science is all about **understanding how science works**.
And not only that — understanding it well enough to be able to **question** what you hear on TV and read in the papers.

But you can't do that without a fair chunk of **background knowledge**. Hmm, tricky.

Happily this CGP book includes all the **science facts** you need to learn, and shows you how they work in the **real world**. And in true CGP style, we've explained it all as **clearly and concisely** as possible.

It's also got some daft bits in to try and make the whole experience at least vaguely entertaining for you.

What you need to learn

This book is suitable for both Foundation Tier and Higher Tier students.
Some material is needed for Higher Tier only — we've clearly marked this in green boxes.

The Higher Tier questions in the book are also printed in green.

Contents

How Science Works

The Scientific Process ... 1
Your Data's Got To be Good ... 2
Bias and Issues Created by Science ... 3
Designing Investigations ... 4
Collecting Data ... 6
Processing and Presenting Data ... 7
Presenting Data ... 8
Drawing Conclusions ... 9
Controlled Assessment ... 10

Section 1.1 — My Wider World

The Universe ... 11
The Origin of the Universe ... 12
The Earth's Structure ... 13
The Earth's Atmosphere ... 14
Atoms ... 15
The Periodic Table ... 16
Electron Shells ... 17
Compounds, Mixtures and Formulas ... 18
Balancing Equations ... 19
Useful Chemicals From The Ground ... 20
Getting Metals From Rocks ... 21
Impacts of Metal Extraction ... 22
Resources From The Air ... 23
Economics of Chemical Production ... 24
Revision Summary for Section 1.1 ... 25

Section 1.2 — Life On Our Planet

Classification ... 26
Competition and Distribution ... 27
Adaptations in Animals ... 28
Adaptations in Plants and Microorganisms ... 29
Evolution ... 30
Plant Growth ... 31
Food Chains and Nutrient Cycling ... 32
Energy Transfer ... 33
Pyramids of Biomass and Number ... 34
The Carbon Cycle ... 35
Revision Summary for Section 1.2 ... 36

Section 2.1 — My Family

The Nervous System ... 37
Reflexes ... 38
Hearing ... 39
Homeostasis ... 40
Hormones and Blood Sugar ... 41
Chemicals and Hazards ... 42
Acids and Alkalis ... 43
Reactions of Acids ... 44
Indigestion Tablets and Drug Testing ... 45
Genes and Chromosomes ... 46
Variation in Plants and Animals ... 47
Alleles and Genetic Disorders ... 48
Treating Genetic Disorders ... 49
Revision Summary for Section 2.1 ... 50

Section 2.2 — My Home

Limestone ... 51
Metals ... 52
Polymers ... 53
Ceramics ... 54
Composites ... 55
Choosing Materials for a Product ... 56
Fuels from Crude Oil ... 57
Problems with Fuels from Crude Oil ... 58
Alternatives to Fossil Fuels ... 59
Comparing Energy Resources ... 63
Generating Electricity ... 64
Supplying Electricity ... 65
Revision Summary for Section 2.2 ... 66

Section 2.3 — My Property

Calculating Power and Current ... 67
Calculating Energy Use and Costs ... 68
Efficiency ... 69
Energy Labels ... 70
Sankey Diagrams ... 71
Electromagnetic Waves ... 72
The Wave Equation ... 73
Uses of Radio Waves and Microwaves ... 74
Uses of Infrared, Ultraviolet and Visible Light ... 75
Dangers of Electromagnetic Radiation ... 76
Revision Summary for Section 2.3 ... 77

Section 3.1 — Improving Health and Wellbeing

Microorganisms and Disease ... 78
The Body's Defence Systems ... 79
Vaccination ... 80
Use of Drugs to Treat Disease ... 81
Antibiotic Resistance and Drug Testing ... 82
Recreational Drugs ... 83
Medical Uses of Radiation ... 85
Radiation Safety Precautions and Ethics ... 86
Revision Summary for Section 3.1 ... 87

Section 3.2 — Developing and Improving Products

Electroplating ... 88
Uses and Risks of Electroplating ... 89
New Products ... 90
More New Products ... 91
Selective Breeding ... 92
Tissue Culture and Cloning ... 93
Genetic Engineering ... 94
Revision Summary for Section 3.2 ... 95

Section 3.3 — Environmental Concerns

Greenhouse Gases ... 96
Global Warming and the Kyoto Agreement ... 97
Pollution ... 98
Pollution and Indicator Species ... 99
Waste Disposal and Plastics ... 100
Heat Loss in the Home ... 101
Reducing Heat Loss in the Home ... 102
Pollutants in the Home ... 103
Domestic Boilers ... 104
Revision Summary for Section 3.3 ... 105

Index ... 106
Answers ... 108

Published by CGP

From original material by Richard Parsons.

Editors:
Luke Antieul, Ellen Bowness, Katherine Craig, Emma Elder, Edmund Robinson, Hayley Thompson, Karen Wells.

ISBN: 978 1 84762 600 4

With thanks to Barrie Crowther, Ian Francis and Glenn Rogers for the proofreading.
With thanks to Laura Stoney for the copyright research.
With thanks to iStockphoto.com for permission to reproduce the photograph used on page 72.

Pages 42, 50, 65, 89 and 103 contain public sector information published by the Health and Safety Executive and licensed under the Open Government Licence v1.0.

Energy Efficiency Label on page 70 © European Union, 1995-2010.

Every effort has been made to locate copyright holders and obtain permission to reproduce sources. For those sources where it has been difficult to trace the originator of the work, we would be grateful for information. If any copyright holder would like us to make an amendment to the acknowledgements, please notify us and we will gladly update the book at the next reprint. Thank you.

Groovy website: www.cgpbooks.co.uk

Printed by Elanders Ltd, Newcastle upon Tyne.
Jolly bits of clipart from CorelDRAW®

The Scientific Process

For your exams and your controlled assessment, you need to know about how the world of science works.

Science is All About Testing Hypotheses

Scientists make an observation.

1) Scientists OBSERVE (look at) something they don't understand, e.g. an illness.
2) They come up with a possible explanation for what they've observed.
3) This explanation is called a HYPOTHESIS.

They test their hypothesis.

4) Next, they test whether the hypothesis is right or not.
5) They do this by making a PREDICTION — a statement based on the hypothesis that can be tested.
6) They then TEST this prediction by carrying out experiments.
7) If their prediction is right, this is EVIDENCE that their hypothesis might be right too.

Other scientists test the explanation too.

8) Other scientists carry out more experiments to test the hypothesis.
9) Sometimes these scientists will find more evidence that the hypothesis is RIGHT.
10) Sometimes they'll find evidence that shows the hypothesis is WRONG.

The explanation is accepted or rejected.

11) If all the evidence that's been found supports the hypothesis, it becomes an ACCEPTED THEORY and goes into textbooks for people to learn.
12) If the evidence shows that the hypothesis is wrong, scientists must:
    - Change the hypothesis, OR
    - Come up with a new hypothesis.

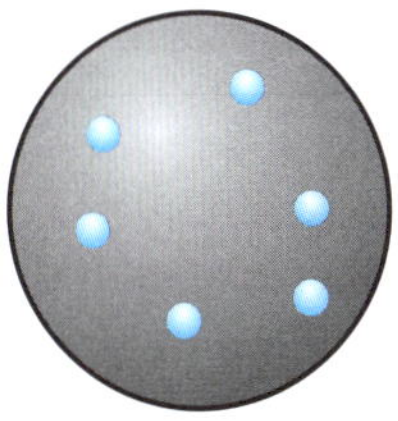

About 100 years ago, we thought atoms looked like this.

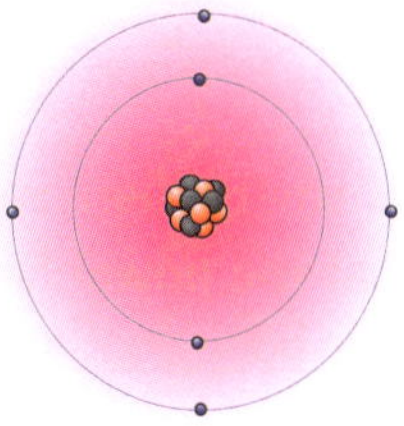

Then we thought they looked like this.

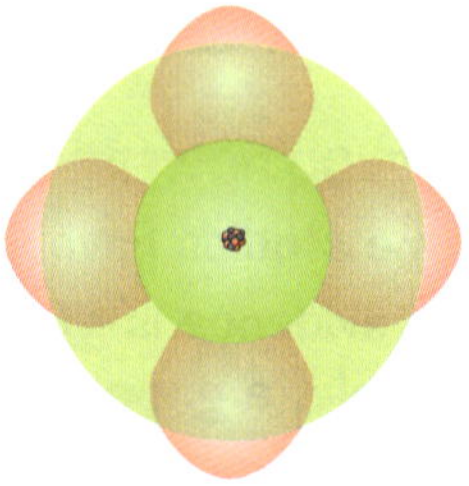

Now we think it's more like this.

You expect me to believe that — then show me the evidence...

If scientists think something is true, they need to produce evidence to convince others — it's all part of testing a hypothesis. Along the way some hypotheses will be disproved (shown not to be true).

Your Data's Got To be Good

Evidence is the key to science — but not all evidence is good...

Lab Experiments and Studies Are Better Than Rumour

See page 4 for more about fair tests and variables.

1) Laboratory experiments are great. A lab is the easiest place to control the variables in your experiment. This makes it easier to carry out a FAIR TEST.
2) For things that you can't study in a lab (e.g. climate) you carry out scientific studies. In studies, you control as many of the variables as possible.
3) Old wives' tales and rumours are NOT scientific. Without any evidence, they're just opinions.

The Bigger the Sample Size the Better

1) Sample size is how many things you test in an experiment or study, e.g. 500 people or 20 types of metal.
2) The bigger the sample size the better — to reduce the chance of any weird results.
3) But scientists have to be realistic when choosing how big their sample should be. E.g. if you were studying how lifestyle affects weight it'd be great to study everyone in the UK (a huge sample), but it'd take ages and cost loads.

Evidence Needs to be Reliable

Reliable evidence comes from experiments that give the same data:

- each time the experiment is repeated
- each time the experiment is reproduced (copied) by other scientists.

RELIABLE means that the data can be repeated, and reproduced by others.

EXAMPLE: In 1989, two scientists claimed that they'd produced 'cold fusion' (the energy source of the Sun). Other scientists couldn't get the same results though — they weren't reliable.

Evidence Also Needs to Be Valid

VALID means that the data is reliable AND answers the original question.

EXAMPLE: DO POWER LINES CAUSE CANCER?

- Some studies have found that in areas where there were power lines, more children had cancer.
- This evidence is NOT enough to say that the power lines CAUSE cancer. Other explanations might be possible, e.g. power lines are often near busy roads, so the areas tested could contain different levels of pollution from traffic.
- So these studies don't show a definite link and so don't answer the original question.

RRRR — Remember, Reliable means Repeatable and Reproducible...

So. Now you know loads about evidence. The fun doesn't stop here though — there's more on the next page.

Bias and Issues Created by Science

It isn't all fun and games in the world of science — there are some problems...

Scientific Evidence can be Biased

1) People who want to make a point can sometimes present data in a biased way — i.e. in a way that's meant to affect how other people think.
2) There are all sorts of reasons why people might want to do this — for example...
   - Scientists might want to keep the company that's paying for the research happy. (If the company's not happy they might not pay for any more research.)
   - Governments might want to persuade voters to vote for them.
   - Companies might want to make their products sound better.

Scientific Developments are Great, but they can Raise Issues

Scientific knowledge increases by doing experiments. This knowledge leads to scientific developments, e.g. new technology or new advice. These developments can create issues though. For example:

Economic (money) issues:

Governments can't always afford to do things scientists recommend, e.g. spend money on green energy sources.

Social (people) issues:

Decisions based on scientific evidence affect people — e.g. should alcohol be banned (to prevent health problems)?

Ethical (moral) issues:

There are a lot of things science has made possible, but should we do them? E.g. clone humans, develop better nuclear weapons.

Environmental issues:

Nuclear power helps us produce more energy — but some people think it causes too many environmental problems.

Some Questions are Unanswered by Science — Some are Unanswerable

1) At the moment scientists don't agree on some things, e.g. what the universe is made of.
2) This is because there isn't enough reliable and valid evidence.
3) But eventually, we probably will be able to answer these questions once and for all.
4) All we need is more evidence.
5) But the question of whether something is ethically right or wrong can't ever be answered by more experiments. There is no "right" or "wrong" answer.
6) The best we can do is make a decision that most people are more or less happy to live by.

CGP make the best revision guides — nope, no bias here...

Spotting biased evidence isn't the easiest thing in the world — ask yourself, 'Will the scientist gain something (or lose something)?' If they might it's possible that the evidence could be biased.

Designing Investigations

You need to know a shed load about investigations for your controlled assessment and all your exams. Investigations include experiments and studies. The next six pages take you from start to finish. Enjoy.

Investigations Produce Evidence to Support or Disprove a Hypothesis

1) When scientists observe something they come up with a hypothesis to explain it (see page 1).
2) To decide whether a hypothesis is correct or not you need to do an investigation to gather some evidence.
3) The first step is to use the hypothesis to come up with a prediction — a statement about what you think will happen that you can test.
4) For example, if your hypothesis is:

   "Spots are caused by picking your nose too much."

   Then your prediction might be:

   "People who pick their nose more often will have more spots."

Sometimes a hypothesis and a prediction are the same thing.

5) Investigations are used to see if there are patterns or relationships between two variables (see below).
6) The investigation has to be a FAIR TEST to make sure the evidence is reliable and valid...

See page 2 for more on reliability and validity.

To Make an Investigation a Fair Test You Have to Control the Variables

Investigations that you plan should always be a fair test.

1) In a lab experiment you usually change one thing (a variable) and measure how it affects another thing (another variable).

   EXAMPLE: you might change only the temperature of a reaction and measure how it affects the rate of reaction.

2) Everything else that could affect the results needs to stay the same. Then you know that the thing you're changing is the only thing that's affecting the results.

   EXAMPLE continued: you need to keep the pH the same. If you don't, you won't know if any change in the rate of reaction is caused by the change in temperature, or the change in pH.

3) The variable that you CHANGE is called the INDEPENDENT variable.
4) The variable that's MEASURED is called the DEPENDENT variable.
5) The variables that you keep the same are called control variables.

EXAMPLE continued:
Independent = temperature
Dependent = rate of reaction
Control = pH

Designing Investigations

Trial Runs Help Figure out the Range and Interval of Variable Values

1) A trial run is a quick version of your experiment.
2) Trial runs help you work out whether your plan is right or not — you might decide to make some changes after trying out your method.
3) They're used to figure out the range of values (the highest and lowest value) for the variable you're changing (the independent variable).
4) And they're used to figure out the interval (gaps) between the values too.

Rate of reaction example from previous page continued:

- You might do trial runs at 10, 20, 30, 40 and 50 °C. If there was no reaction at 10 or 50 °C, you might narrow the range to 20-40 °C.
- If using 10 °C intervals gives you a big change in rate of reaction you might decide to use 5 °C intervals, e.g. 20, 25, 30, 35...

5) Trial runs can also help you figure out how many times the experiment has to be repeated to get reliable results. E.g. if you repeat it three times and the results are all similar, then three repeats is enough.

It Can Be Hard to Control the Variables in a Study

1) You have to control all the variables in a study or it won't be a fair test (just like in a lab experiment).
2) Sometimes though, this is really hard — so you have to use a control group to help.
3) A control group is group of whatever you're studying (e.g. plants) that's kept under the same conditions as the group in the experiment. However, the control group doesn't have anything done to it.

EXAMPLE:

- If you're studying the effect of pesticides (pest killer) on plant growth, pesticide is put on one field but not another field (the control field).
- Both fields contain the same plants and get the same weather conditions.
- The control field is there so that you can check it's the pesticide causing the results — not the weather.

Investigations Can be Hazardous

1) A hazard is something that could cause harm.
2) Hazards include things like microorganisms (e.g. bacteria), chemicals, electricity and fire.
3) Scientists need to manage the risk of hazards by doing things to reduce them. For example:

- If you're using a Bunsen burner, stand it on a heat-proof mat.
- This will reduce the risk of starting a fire.

You won't get a trial run at the exam, so get learnin'...

All this info needs to be firmly lodged in your memory. Learn the names of the different variables — if you remember that the variable you chaNge is called the iNdependent variable, you can figure out the other ones.

Collecting Data

It's good if you can design an investigation that people will praise for years to come.
But you'll also need to get your hands mucky and collect some data.

Your Data Should be as Reliable, Accurate and Precise as Possible

1) To make your results more reliable, you should repeat each reading at least three times. Then you can calculate the mean (average) — see next page.
2) Checking your results match with secondary sources (e.g. other studies) also makes your data more reliable.
3) Your data also needs to be ACCURATE. Accurate results are those that are really close to the true answer.
4) Your data also needs to be PRECISE. Precise results are ones that are really similar to the mean.

Repeat	Data set 1	Data set 2
1	12	11
2	14	18
3	13	10
Mean	13	13

Data set 1 is more precise than data set 2.

The Equipment Used has to be Right for the Job

1) You need to make sure you choose the right equipment.
2) For example, the measuring equipment you use has to be able to accurately measure the chemicals you're using. If you need to measure out 11 ml of a liquid, use a measuring cylinder that can measure to 1 ml, not 5 or 10 ml.
3) The smallest change a measuring instrument can detect is called its RESOLUTION. E.g. some mass balances have a resolution of 1 g, some have a resolution of 0.1 g.
4) Equipment needs to be CALIBRATED (set up properly) so that your data is more accurate. E.g. mass balances need to be set to zero before you start weighing things.

Errors can Pop Up if You're Not Careful

1) The results of your experiment will always vary a bit.
2) Sometimes, errors will be made. If the same error is made every time, it's called a SYSTEMATIC ERROR.
3) If a systematic error is caused by using equipment that isn't calibrated properly it's called a ZERO ERROR.

Errors can Affect Your Results

1) Sometimes you get a result that doesn't seem to fit in with the rest at all.
2) These results are called ANOMALOUS RESULTS.
3) You should investigate them and try to work out what happened.
4) If you can work out what happened (e.g. you measured something wrong) you can ignore them when processing your results.

Park	Number of pigeons	Number of crazy tramps
A	28	1
B	42	2
C	1127	0

Anomalous result

Zero error — sounds like a Bruce Willis film...

Weirdly, data can be really precise but not very accurate, e.g. a fancy piece of lab equipment might give results that are precise, but if it's not calibrated properly those results won't be accurate.

Processing and Presenting Data

The fun doesn't stop once you've collected your data — it then needs to be processed and presented...

Data Needs to be Organised

1) Data that's been collected needs to be organised so it can be processed later on.
2) Tables are dead useful for organising data.
3) You should always make sure that each column has a heading and that you've included the units.

Test tube	Repeat 1 (ml)	Repeat 2 (ml)	Repeat 3 (ml)
A	28	37	32
B	47	51	60
C	68	72	70

You Might Have to Process Your Data

1) When you've done repeats of an experiment you should always calculate the MEAN (average).
2) To calculate the mean ADD TOGETHER all the data values. Then DIVIDE by the total number of data values.
3) You might also need to calculate the RANGE (how spread out the data is).
4) To do this find the LARGEST number and SUBTRACT the SMALLEST number from it.

Ignore anomalous results when calculating these.

EXAMPLE:

Test tube	Repeat 1 (g)	Repeat 2 (g)	Repeat 3 (g)	Mean (g)	Range (g)
A	28	37	32	(28 + 37 + 32) ÷ 3 = 32.3	37 – 28 = 9
B	47	51	60	(47 + 51 + 60) ÷ 3 = 52.7	60 – 47 = 13
C	68	72	70	(68 + 72 + 70) ÷ 3 = 70.0	72 – 68 = 4

If Your Data Comes in Categories, Present it in a Bar Chart

1) If the independent variable comes in clear categories (e.g. blood types, metals) you should use a bar chart to display the data.
2) There are some golden rules you need to follow for drawing bar charts:

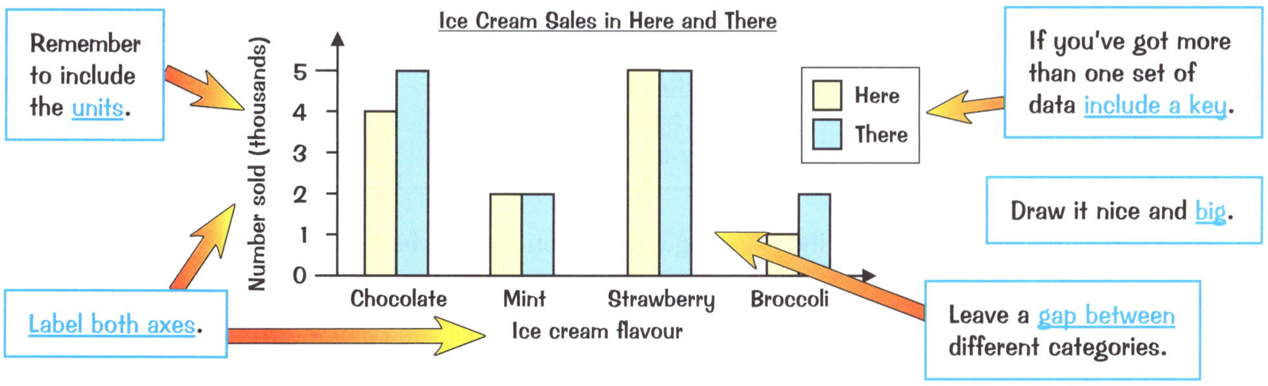

Here's a tip from me — never present data as a Mother's Day gift...

Examiners are a bit picky when it comes to bar charts — if you don't draw them properly they won't be happy. Also, double check any mean or range calculations you do, just to be sure you've got them right.

Presenting Data

Scientists just love presenting data as line graphs (weirdos)...

If Your Data Covers a Range of Values, Plot a Line Graph

If the independent variable can have any value within a range (e.g. length, volume, temperature) you should use a line graph to display the data.

Remember to include the units.

Put the dependent variable (the thing you measure) on the y-axis (the one at the side).

Label both axes.

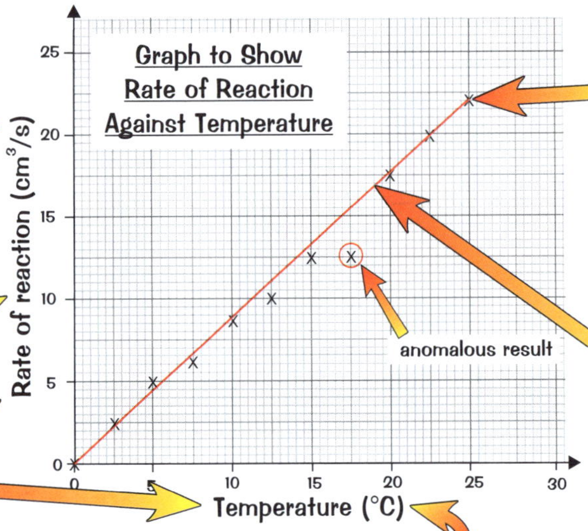

To plot the points, use a sharp pencil and make a neat little cross (don't do blobs).

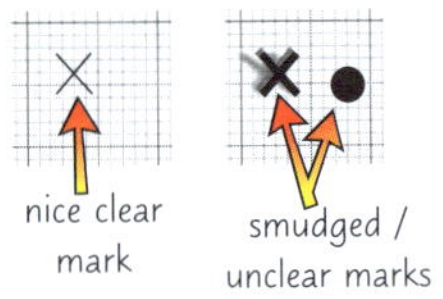

Don't join the dots up. You need to draw a line of best fit (or a curve of best fit). Try to draw the line through or as near to as many points as possible. Ignore anomalous results.

Put the independent variable (the thing you change) on the x-axis (the bottom one).

Line Graphs Can Show Patterns in Data

1) Line graphs are used to show the relationship between two variables (just like other graphs).
2) The relationship between two variables is called a CORRELATION:

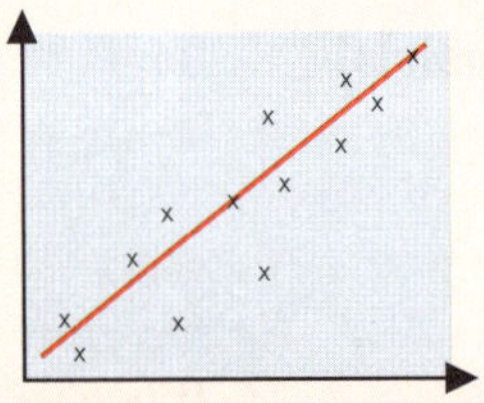

POSITIVE correlation — as one variable increases the other increases.

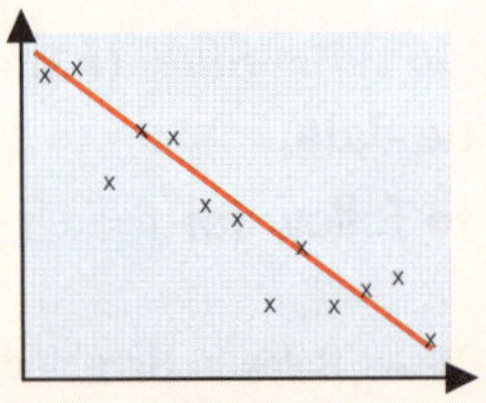

NEGATIVE correlation — as one variable increases the other decreases.

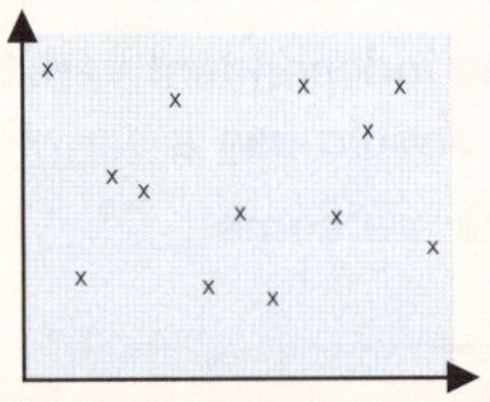

NO correlation — there's no relationship between the two variables.

3) You need to be able to describe the following patterns on line graphs too:

LINEAR — the graph is a straight line.

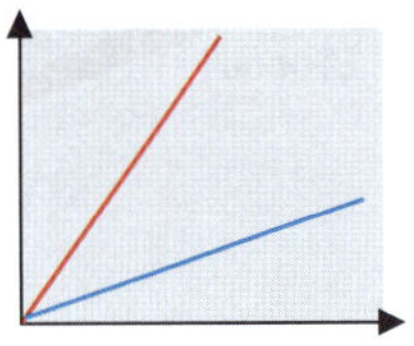

DIRECTLY PROPORTIONAL — the graph is a straight line where both variables increase (or decrease) in the same ratio.

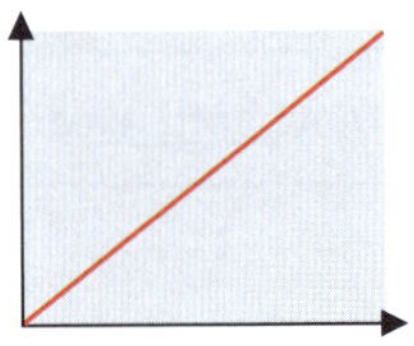

There's a positive correlation between revision and boredom...

...but there's also a positive correlation between revision and getting a better mark in the exam. Cover the page and write down the six things you need to remember when drawing line graphs. No sneaky peeking either — I saw you.

Drawing Conclusions

Congratulations — you've made it to the final step of an investigation — drawing conclusions.

You Can Only Conclude What the Data Shows and NO MORE

1) To come to a conclusion, look at your data and say what pattern you see.

EXAMPLE: The table on the right shows the heights of pea plant seedlings grown for three weeks with different fertilisers.

Fertiliser	Mean growth / mm
A	13.5
B	19.5
No fertiliser	5.5

CONCLUSION: Fertiliser B makes pea plant seedlings grow taller over a three week period than fertiliser A.

2) It's important that the conclusion matches the data it based on — it shouldn't go any further.

EXAMPLE continued: You can't conclude that fertiliser B makes any other type of plant grow taller than fertiliser A — the results could be totally different.

3) You also need to be able to use your results to justify your conclusion (i.e. back it up).

EXAMPLE continued: Fertiliser B made the pea plants grow 6 mm more on average than fertiliser A.

Correlation DOESN'T Always Mean Cause

1) If two things are correlated, there's a relationship between them — see the previous page.
2) But a correlation DOESN'T ALWAYS mean that a change in one variable is CAUSING the change in the other.
3) There are THREE possible reasons for a correlation:

1 CHANCE

2 LINKED BY A 3rd VARIABLE

3 CAUSE

4) 'Linked by a 3rd variable' just means that there's another factor involved.

E.g. there's a correlation between water temperature and shark attacks. They're linked by a third variable — the number of people swimming (more people swim when the water's hotter, which means you get more shark attacks).

I conclude that this page is a bit dull...

In the exams you could be given a conclusion and asked whether some data supports it — so make sure you understand how far conclusions can go.

Controlled Assessment

You'll probably carry out a few investigations as you go through the course. But at some point you'll have to do the one that counts... the controlled assessment. Here's a bit about it...

There are Three Parts to the Controlled Assessment

1 Research and Planning

For the first part of your investigation, you'll be given a topic to investigate. Then you'll have to:

1) Research a real-life application for your investigation. E.g. investigating the effectiveness of different enzymes in breaking down food stains on clothes would be important for washing powder manufacturers. You'll need to:
   - Look at a range of different sources (e.g. books, the internet).
   - Refer to at least three sources when you write up your report.
2) Plan your investigation. Make sure you think about:
   - What equipment you're going to use (and why that equipment is right for the job).
   - What measurements you're going to take of the dependent variable.
   - What range of values and interval you will use for the independent variable.
   - What variables you're going to control (and how you're going to do it).
   - How many times you're going to repeat the experiment.
3) Work out what all the hazards involved in the investigation are, and say how you'll reduce them.

See pages 4-6 for more on this stuff.

2 Collecting and Recording Data

For this part of the investigation, you'll have to:

1) Carry out the experiment as carefully and accurately as possible.
2) Record the data in a table.
3) Spot any anomalous results and try to explain them (see page 6).

An evaluation is where you say what was good and what was bad about something you did.

3 Data Processing, Analysis and Evaluation

The third part of the investigation involves processing the data and analysing it (looking for patterns in it). Then you'll have to evaluate the method you used. You'll also be given some secondary data (data collected by other people) that you'll need to process and analyse along with your own. You'll need to:

1) Process (e.g. using a bit of maths) and present (e.g. using graphs) all the data.
2) Analyse the data to find any patterns (see page 8).
3) Write conclusions for both the primary data and the secondary data (see page 9). Make sure you back them up with your own scientific knowledge.
4) Evaluate the methods you used to collect the data and the quality of the data that was collected.
5) Say how sure you are about your conclusions.
6) Make suggestions for how the method you used could be improved to get better quality data. You'll also need to say why your suggestions would be an improvement.

Read this through and your assessment will be well under control...

You could use this page like a tick list for the controlled assessment — to make sure you don't forget anything.

The Universe

People once thought Earth was the centre of the Universe and everything else revolved around it. Now we know that's a load of codswallop...

Our Solar System is made up of the Sun and Eight Planets

Our solar system consists of the Sun and eight planets circling around it:

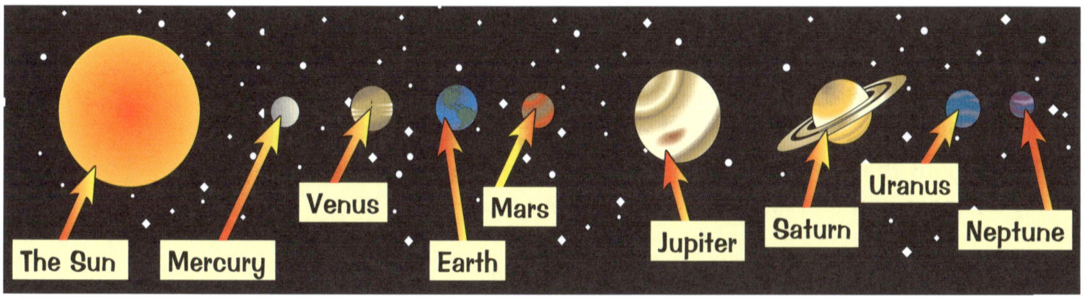

Our Solar System is in the Milky Way Galaxy

1) Our Sun is just one of many billions of stars which form the Milky Way galaxy.
2) Our Sun is about halfway along one of the spiral arms of the Milky Way.

3) Billions of galaxies make up the Universe.
4) The Universe is mostly empty space and is really really BIG.

Scientists Can Use Telescopes to Study the Universe

Telescopes are used to figure out what the Universe is like and how it's changing. There are lots of different types of telescopes — some are on Earth and others are stuck up in space (e.g. on satellites). Choosing which one to use depends on what you want to look at:

1) Optical telescopes detect visible light.
2) Radio telescopes detect longer wavelength radio waves.
3) X-ray telescopes detect X-rays (I know, it's surprising).

The atmosphere can affect how well telescopes work. For example, light pollution (e.g. from street lights), cloud cover and atmospheric distortion can affect the images from optical telescopes. X-ray telescopes have to be up in space as the Earth's atmosphere absorbs X-rays.

We're on a spiral arm — no wonder I feel like I'm going round in circles...

If aliens do exist then I don't think we should worry too much about a big invasion. Getting to Earth is going to take them a very long time and without a decent sat nav they'll probably get lost on the way. Unless of course they have amazing space-based telescopes — in which case they could be watching you right now...

The Origin of the Universe

So you already know that the Universe is a pretty big place. Well, it turns out it's getting even bigger.

Light is a Type of Wave

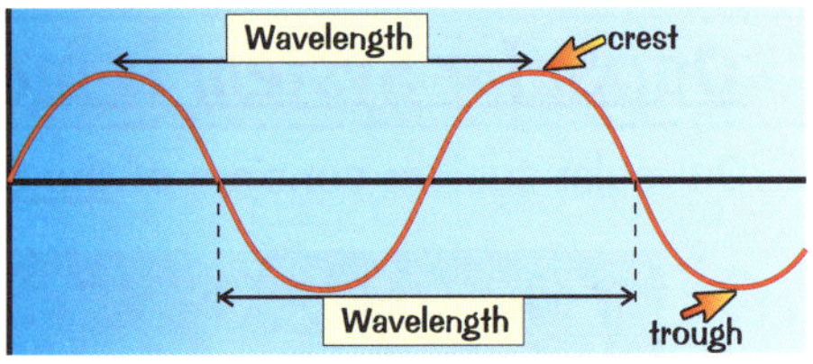

1) Light (and sound) always travel in waves.
2) The wavelength is the length of a full wave, e.g. from crest to crest.
3) The frequency is the number of complete waves that pass a certain point each second.
4) If the object making a wave is moving, the wavelength and frequency of the wave will seem different. This is called the Doppler effect.
5) For example, think about the vrrroomm from a racing car — the engine sounds lower-pitched when the car's gone past you and is moving away from you:

Light from Other Galaxies is Red-shifted

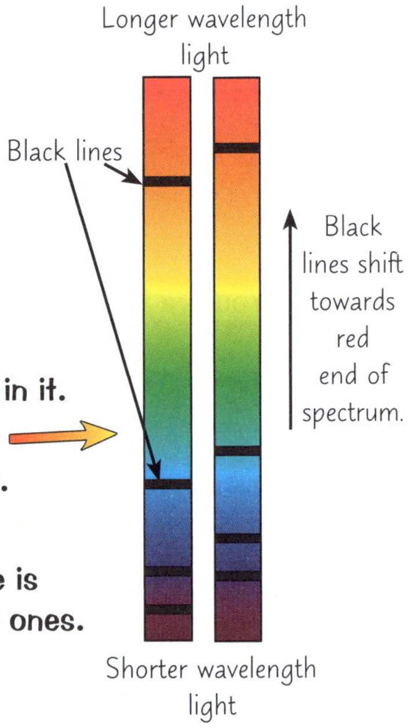

1) We can look at the light from stars and galaxies.
2) When light passes through a prism, it splits into its different colours and wavelengths and produces a rainbow. This is called a spectrum.
3) Scientists do a similar thing with the light from stars.
4) When light from a star is split into a spectrum, there's a pattern of black lines in it.
5) But when you look at stars and galaxies that are further away, the black lines are in a different place — they're shifted towards the red end of the spectrum.
6) The light seems to have a longer wavelength — it's known as red-shift.
7) This is evidence that galaxies are moving away from us and the whole Universe is expanding. Galaxies further away are moving away from us faster than nearer ones.

The Big Bang Theory — the Universe is Expanding

1) Right now, all the galaxies seem to be moving apart at great speed. But something must have got them going in the first place. That 'something' was probably a big explosion — the Big Bang...
2) This theory suggests that all the matter (material) and energy in the Universe must have been squashed into a very small space. Then it exploded and started getting bigger. It's still getting bigger now.

In the beginning, there was — well, it's so hard to tell...

'How it all began' is quite a tricky problem. Among scientists, the theory of a 'Big Bang' to get things started is now generally accepted, because that's what the evidence suggests. Make sure you learn this page inside out and you know how the red-shift evidence supports the Big Bang theory. Then, feel your brain magically expand.

The Earth's Structure

No one accepted the theory of plate tectonics for ages. Almost everyone does now. How times change.

The Earth Has a Crust, Mantle and Core

The Earth is almost spherical and it has a layered structure, a bit like a Scotch egg. Or a peach.

1) The bit we live on, the crust, is very thin.
2) Below that is the mantle. The mantle can flow very slowly.
3) Within the mantle, radioactive decay takes place. This produces lots of heat, which causes the mantle to flow in convection currents.
4) At the centre of the Earth is the core.
5) The Earth is surrounded by the atmosphere (see next page).

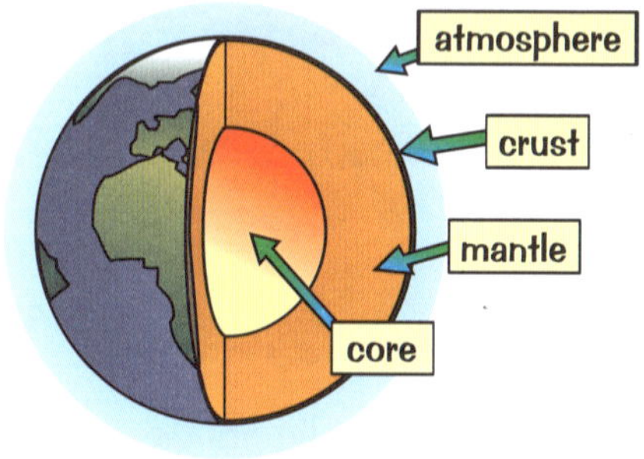

The Earth's Surface is Made Up of Tectonic Plates

1) The crust and the upper part of the mantle are cracked into a number of large pieces called tectonic plates. These are a bit like big rafts that 'float' on the mantle.
2) The convection currents in the mantle cause the plates to move around slowly — usually only a few centimetres per year.
3) Sometimes the plates move very suddenly, causing an earthquake.
4) Volcanoes often form where two tectonic plates meet. Plate movement can cause the volcanoes to erupt.

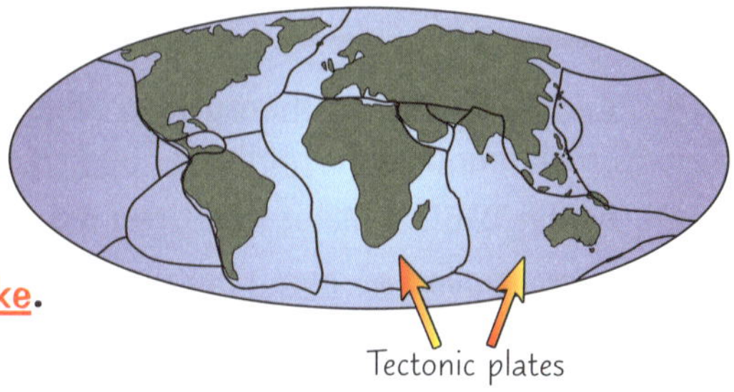

Scientists Can't Predict Earthquakes and Volcanic Eruptions

1) Tectonic plates can stay still for a while and then suddenly lurch forwards. It's impossible to predict exactly when they'll move.
2) Scientists are trying to find out if there are any clues that an earthquake might happen soon — things like strain in underground rocks. Even with these clues they'll only be able to say an earthquake's likely to happen, not exactly when it'll happen.
3) There are some clues that a volcano might erupt soon. Before an eruption, molten (liquid) rock rises up near the surface, causing the ground to bulge a bit. This causes mini-earthquakes near the volcano.
4) But sometimes molten rock cools down instead of erupting. So mini-earthquakes can be a false alarm.

Core blimey, earthquakes are such jerks...

I don't know about you but I find it hard to imagine what the Earth is really like under my feet. In fact, it makes my head hurt a bit. Anyway, it's a good idea to learn the diagram of the Earth's structure off by heart so you can draw it in an exam. You also need to know what tectonic plates are and why they move about.

The Earth's Atmosphere

The atmosphere is all the air between the ground and space. Here's where the gases in the air came from...

The Earth's Atmosphere has Changed Over Billions of Years

1) After the Earth was first formed, its surface was molten (runny) for many millions of years.
2) Eventually it cooled and a thin crust formed.
3) There were lots of volcanoes that kept erupting and releasing loads of carbon dioxide (CO_2), nitrogen and steam (water vapour). We think this is how the oceans and atmosphere formed.
4) According to this theory, the early atmosphere was probably mostly CO_2 (with hardly any oxygen).
5) The steam eventually condensed to form the oceans.
6) A bit later, plants and algae started to grow.
7) They removed CO_2 from the air and produced oxygen by photosynthesis.
8) When the plants died and were buried, they turned into rocks and fossil fuels. The carbon dioxide they had taken in from the air became 'locked up' in the ground.
9) The level of CO_2 in the atmosphere is much lower now.

Condensed means turning from a gas into a liquid.

Higher

- According to this theory (see above), the early atmosphere was mostly CO_2, but there were also small amounts of methane, hydrogen and ammonia.
- In the 1950s, Miller and Urey did an experiment to find if life could have evolved from this chemical mix.
- They applied an electrical discharge to this mix of gases to simulate ultraviolet radiation from the Sun.
- They found that some organic molecules that are essential for life were made, but not as many as are on Earth. This suggests that the theory could be along the right lines, but isn't quite right.

Higher

Greenhouse Gases in the Atmosphere Keep Earth Warm

1) The temperature of the Earth is a balance between the heat it gets from the Sun and the heat it sends back out into space.
2) Gases in the atmosphere form an insulating layer. These are called "greenhouse gases" — they keep the Earth's temperature stable and warm enough to support life.
3) Greenhouse gases allow short wave radiation from the Sun to pass through the atmosphere and warm the Earth's surface.
4) The Earth gives out heat as long wave radiation. Greenhouse gases absorb most of this heat and send some of it back towards Earth.
5) Methane and carbon dioxide are examples of greenhouse gases.

Greenhouse gases — more than just a gardener who had beans for breakfast...

Ah, greenhouse gases. I don't know what we would be without them — apart from very, very cold of course. They're like an invisible front door that traps most of the heat trying to escape, and keeps us all toasty.

Atoms

Atoms are the tiny building blocks that make up everything in the Universe. Anything from your gran to a cabbage to a cowpat is made up of them. So, introducing the atom... drum roll please...

Atoms have a Small Nucleus Surrounded by Electrons

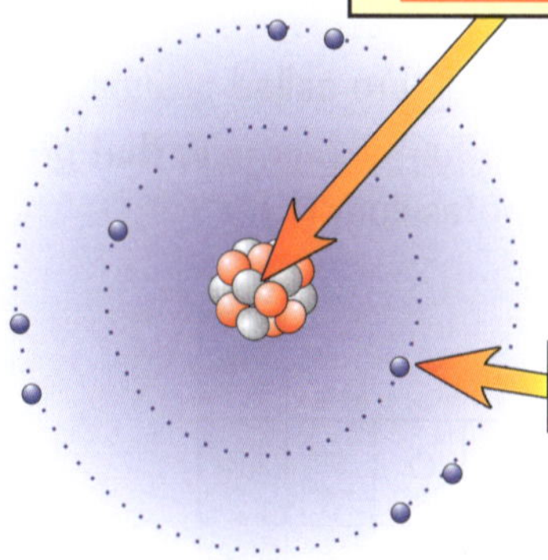

The Nucleus

1) It's in the middle of the atom.
2) It contains protons and neutrons.
3) Protons are positively charged.
4) Neutrons have no charge (they're neutral).
5) So the nucleus has a positive charge overall because of the protons.

The Electrons

1) Move around the nucleus.
2) They're negatively charged.
3) They occupy shells around the nucleus.

Atoms can Form Ions or Molecules

1) Atoms have the same number of protons and electrons so they have no charge overall. (The negative charge on the electrons cancels out the positive charge on the protons.)
2) Sometimes an atom loses or gains electrons.
3) When this happens the proton and electron charges are no longer equal, so the atom becomes charged. It's then called an ion.
4) A molecule is made when two or more atoms join together. E.g. two hydrogen atoms may join with one oxygen atom to make a molecule of water.

Elements Have One Type of Atom Only

1) If a substance only contains one type of atom it's called an element.
2) For example, chlorine gas (Cl_2), hydrogen gas (H_2), nitrogen gas (N_2) and oxygen gas (O_2) are all elements.
3) The atom which makes up the element can be represented by a one or two letter symbol. There are some you need to learn:

Aluminium — Al	Copper — Cu	Iron — Fe	Potassium — K
Argon — Ar	Fluorine — F	Magnesium — Mg	Silicon — Si
Beryllium — Be	Gold — Au	Neon — Ne	Silver — Ag
Boron — B	Helium — He	Nickel — Ni	Sodium — Na
Calcium — Ca	Hydrogen — H	Nitrogen — N	Sulfur — S
Carbon — C	Lead — Pb	Oxygen — O	Zinc — Zn
Chlorine — Cl	Lithium — Li	Phosphorus — P	

Losing electrons — probably something worth keeping an ion...

When it comes to atoms, you have to think tiny. Really tiny. An atom might measure 0.1 nanometres across — that's 0.0000000001 metres, or a hundred-millionth of a centimetre. That's pretty small.

The Periodic Table

You may be thinking that the periodic table sounds like a piece of old-fashioned furniture. Actually, it's a dead useful tool for organising all of those pesky elements...

The Periodic Table Puts Elements with Similar Properties Together

1) The elements are laid out in the table (from left to right) in order of increasing atomic number.
2) Metals are found to the left and non-metals to the right.
3) Elements with similar properties are put into columns. These vertical columns are called groups.
4) If you know the properties of one element, you can predict properties of other elements in that group. For example, the Group I elements include lithium (Li), sodium (Na) and potassium (K). They're all metals and they all react with water in the same way.

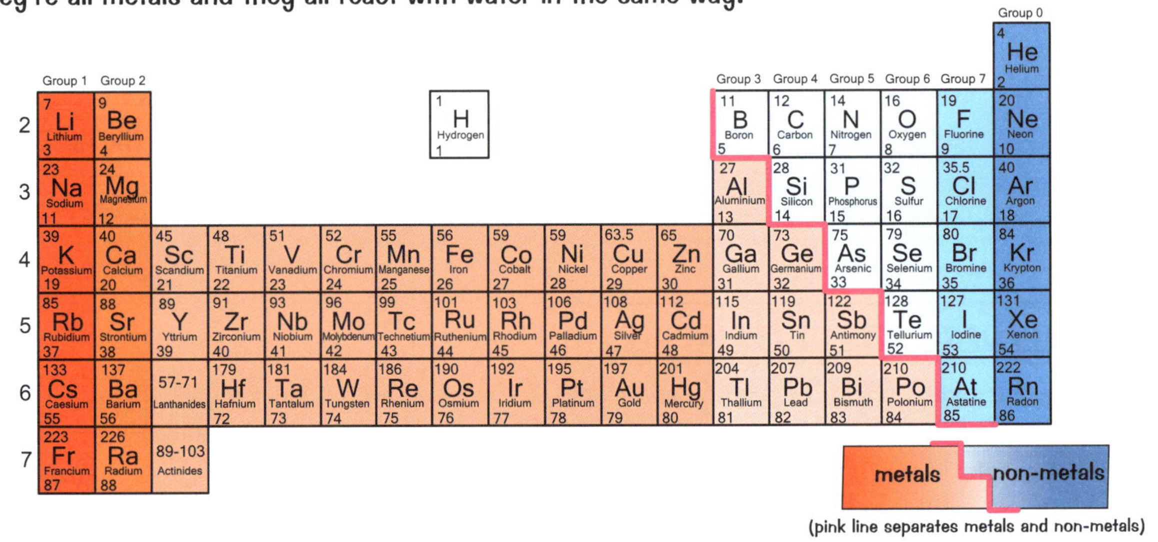

Atomic Number and Mass Number Describe an Atom

These two numbers tell you how many protons, neutrons and electrons are in an atom.

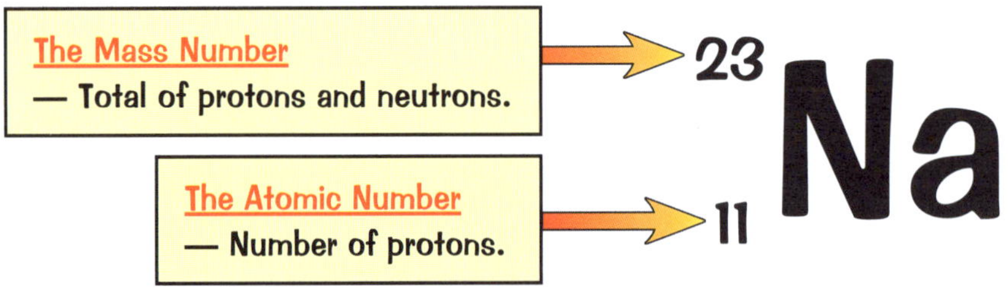

1) The atomic number tells you how many protons there are. Don't forget that in an atom the number of protons and electrons are the same — so this is also the number of electrons.
2) Atoms of the same element all have the same number of protons. Atoms of different elements will have different numbers of protons.
3) To get the number of neutrons, just subtract the atomic number from the mass number.
4) The mass number is always the biggest number.

I love the periodic table — I'm in my element...

Save yourself from a mass of confusion by getting your head around the atomic and mass numbers. You'd feel pretty silly if you were asked in the exam for the number of protons in an atom and didn't know. Even more so because the answer is staring right at you. Learning this page real good should sort you out.

Electron Shells

Electrons can't just be simple and hang around in the nucleus. Nope, they have to be different.

Electron Shell Rules:

1) Electrons always sit in shells.
2) The shells nearest the nucleus are always filled first.
3) Only a certain number of electrons are allowed in each shell:
   1st shell: 2   2nd Shell: 8   3rd Shell: 8
4) Atoms are much "happier" when they have full electron shells.
5) In most atoms the outer shell isn't full — this makes the atom "want" to react.

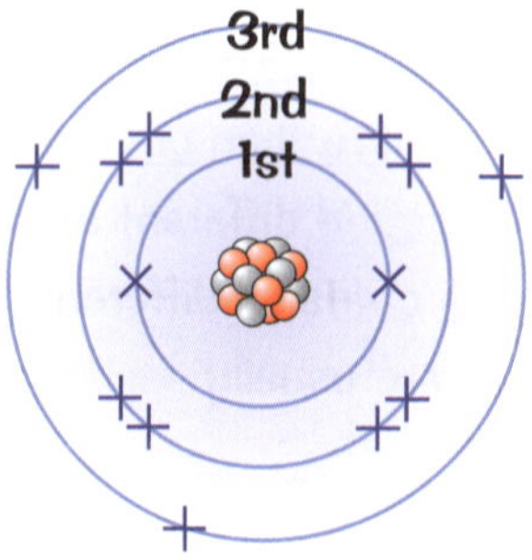

3rd shell still filling

Follow the Rules to Work Out Electron Structures

You need to know the electron structures of the first 20 elements. But they're not too hard to work out. For a quick example, take nitrogen. Follow the steps...

1) The periodic table tells us nitrogen has seven protons... So it must have seven electrons.
2) Follow the 'Electron Shell Rules' above. The first shell can only take 2 electrons and the second shell can take a maximum of 8 electrons.
3) So the electron structure for nitrogen must be 2, 5.
4) Now you try it for argon.

The periodic table has a big gap here where the transition metals fit in on row four.

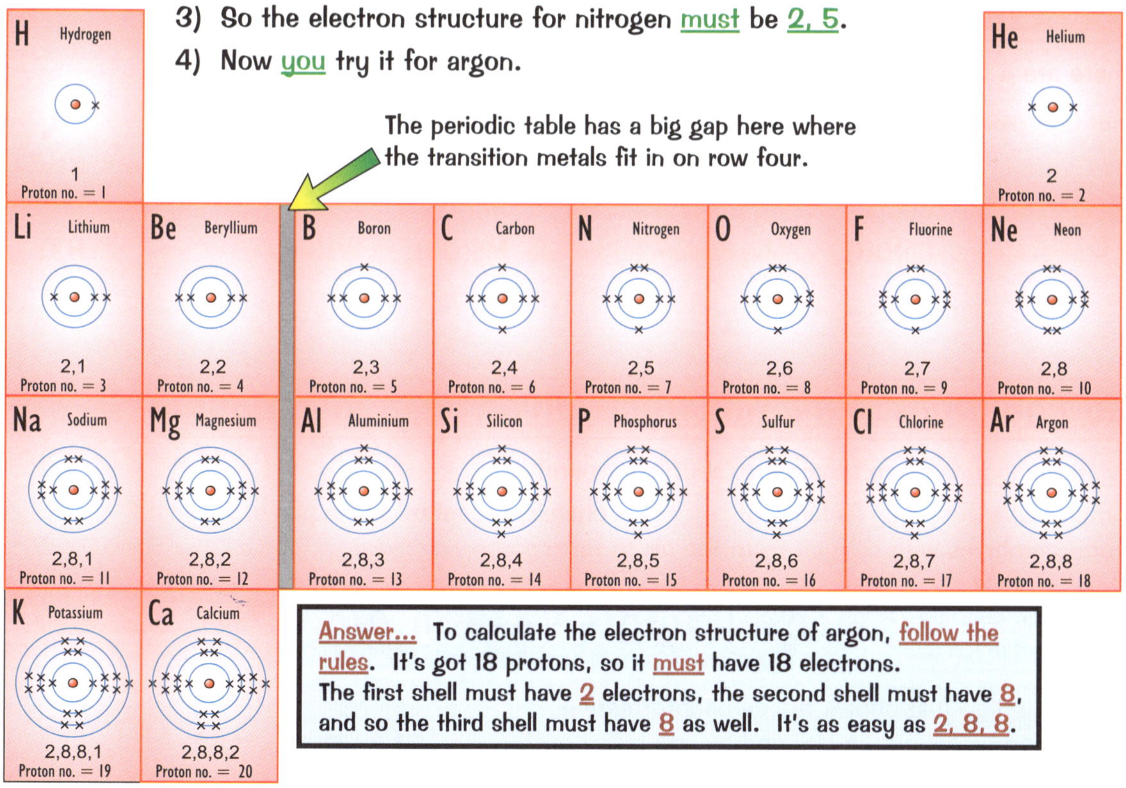

Answer... To calculate the electron structure of argon, follow the rules. It's got 18 protons, so it must have 18 electrons. The first shell must have 2 electrons, the second shell must have 8, and so the third shell must have 8 as well. It's as easy as 2, 8, 8.

One little duck and two fat ladies — 2, 8, 8...

You need to know enough about electron shells to draw out that whole diagram at the bottom of the page without looking at it. Obviously, you don't have to learn each element separately — just learn the pattern. Cover the page: using a periodic table, find the atom with the electron configuration 2, 8, 6.

Compounds, Mixtures and Formulas

The real fun begins when elements make mixtures or compounds...

Compounds and Mixtures Contain Different Types of Atom

1) If there's more than one type of atom, e.g. copper and oxygen, it's either a mixture or a compound.
2) In a compound different atoms have bonded together chemically, e.g. salt is Na and Cl bonded together.
3) A mixture contains different substances that are not chemically bonded together, e.g. rock salt (page 20).
4) Mixtures are usually easier to separate than compounds.

A Formula Shows What Atoms are in a Compound

1) Carbon dioxide is a compound — it's made up of carbon atoms and oxygen atoms bonded together.

Here you go... a molecule of carbon dioxide — one carbon atom and two oxygen atoms.

2) Using chemical symbols, carbon dioxide would be: CO_2

One carbon atom

Two atoms of oxygen

You Need to Know the Formulas of Some Compounds

I'm afraid there are a few that you need to learn:

Aluminium hydroxide	$Al(OH)_3$	Calcium oxide	CaO	Methane	CH_4
Ammonia	NH_3	Carbon dioxide	CO_2	Sodium bicarbonate	$NaHCO_3$
Calcium carbonate	$CaCO_3$	Hydrogen chloride	HCl	Sodium chloride	$NaCl$
Calcium hydroxide	$Ca(OH)_2$	Magnesium hydroxide	$Mg(OH)_2$	Water	H_2O

Chemical Equations Show the Atoms Involved in Reactions

1) A chemical reaction is when atoms are 'shuffled around'.
2) For example, when you burn a lump of carbon, a chemical reaction takes place. The carbon combines with oxygen from the air to form carbon dioxide:

An atom of carbon combines with two atoms of oxygen...

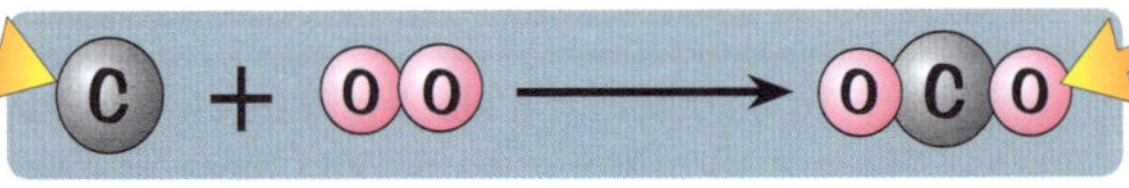

...and forms a molecule of carbon dioxide.

3) A chemical equation just shows the same information about a reaction — 'what goes in' and 'what comes out'.

$$C + O_2 \longrightarrow CO_2$$

4) The things on the left-hand side of the equation are reactants. These react to form the things on the right-hand side of the equation — the products.
5) The properties of the products are different from those of the reactants.

H_2O, CO_2, DVD, FBI, GSOH...

All those lovely compounds you have to learn are products of chemical reactions. And equations are just a pretty neat way of showing what's going on. The reactants on the left react to make the products on the right.

Balancing Equations

Right, that's chemical equations sorted — I'm off. Oh, hang on — we still need to balance some of them...

Atoms Aren't Lost or Made in Chemical Reactions

1) During chemical reactions no atoms are lost or gained. You'll have the same atoms at the end of a chemical reaction as you had at the start. They're just arranged differently.
2) Balanced symbol equations show how the arrangement of the atoms changes during the reaction. For example:

Word equation:	Magnesium	+	Oxygen	$\rightarrow$	Magnesium oxide
Balanced symbol equation:	$2Mg$	+	O_2	$\rightarrow$	$2MgO$

3) As the atoms stay the same, the mass of the reactants equals the mass of the products.
4) For example, if you know that 6 g of magnesium was reacted with oxygen to give 10 g of magnesium oxide you could work out that the mass of oxygen was 4 g (10 g – 6 g = 4 g).

Balancing the Equation — Match Them Up One by One

1) There has to be the same number of atoms of each element on both sides of the equation.
2) You can balance the equation by putting numbers in front of the formulas where needed. Take this equation for reacting sulfuric acid (H_2SO_4) with sodium hydroxide (NaOH):

$$H_2SO_4 + NaOH \rightarrow Na_2SO_4 + H_2O$$

3) The formulas are all correct but the numbers of some atoms don't match up on both sides. E.g. there are three hydrogen atoms (H) on the left, but only two on the right.
4) You can't change formulas like H_2O to H_3O. You can only put numbers in front of them.

Higher

Method: Balance Just ONE Type of Atom at a Time

1) Find an element that doesn't balance and pencil in a number to try and sort it out.
2) This may create another imbalance — if so, just pencil in another number and see where that gets you.
3) Carry on chasing unbalanced elements and it'll sort itself out pretty quickly.

For example — in the equation above there are three H atoms on the left but only two on the right.

1) The only thing you can do about that is make it $2H_2O$ instead of just H_2O:

$$H_2SO_4 + NaOH \rightarrow Na_2SO_4 + 2H_2O$$

2) But we now have too many H atoms and O atoms on the right. To balance that up you could try putting 2NaOH on the left-hand side:

$$H_2SO_4 + 2NaOH \rightarrow Na_2SO_4 + 2H_2O$$

3) That's sorted it — everything balances. In the end the Na just sorted itself out.

Higher

Balancing equations — weigh it up in your mind...

A number in front of a formula applies to the entire formula. So, $3Na_2SO_4$ means three lots of Na_2SO_4. The little numbers in the middle or at the end of a formula only apply to the atom or brackets immediately before. So the 4 in Na_2SO_4 just means 4 O's, not 4 S's.

Useful Chemicals From The Ground

Lots of the useful materials we use every day come from the ground.
Some can just be dug up and used — others need to be processed to get exactly what we need...

Some Materials Can be Used Straight From the Ground

1) A lot of the materials we use are found in the ground.
2) These materials can be taken from the ground by quarrying or mining.
3) Some can be used straight from the ground, e.g. gold, sulfur, limestone and marble.

Rock Salt Needs to be Refined...

1) Rock salt is a mixture of salt (sodium chloride) and sand. It can be used for de-icing roads — the salt melts the ice and the sand provides grip.
2) The salt in rock salt also has other uses — so the sand is often filtered out of the salt-sand mixture to leave refined salt:
   - The rock salt is mixed with water so the salt dissolves.
   - The sand is filtered out.
   - The salt and water solution is heated.
   - The water evaporates off.
   - Dry salt (refined salt) is left at the end.
3) Salt refined from rock salt can be used to flavour food.

If you're asked in the exam how to separate materials in the lab, make sure you say what apparatus you'd use — e.g. beaker, filter paper, Bunsen burner.

...As Does Crude Oil

1) Crude oil is extracted from the ground by drilling.
2) It's a fossil fuel — it's made from the buried remains of plants and animals over millions of years.
3) Crude oil is a mixture of hydrocarbons — these are molecules made up of just hydrogen and carbon.
4) Different sized hydrocarbons make up the different fractions (fuels) in crude oil.
5) These fractions can be separated by fractional distillation:

- The crude oil is piped in at the bottom of the fractionating column and heated up.
- The fuels evaporate (turn to gas) and rise up the column.
- Different fuels condense (turn to liquid) at different temperatures and can be collected.

6) The shorter the hydrocarbon molecules, the lower the boiling point of the fraction. The boiling point is the temperature at which the liquid fuels turn into gas.
7) The longer the molecules, the more viscous (gloopy and thick) the fraction is.

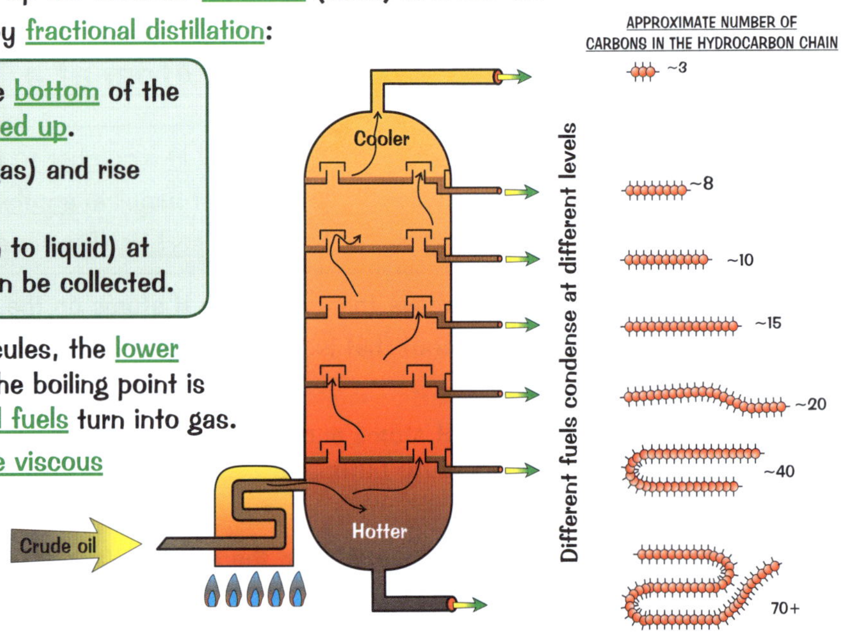

What's black, slippery and tells dirty jokes...

... crude oil... ahem. Right. Some substances are useful in the form you find them. You just dig them out, give them a bit of a spit and polish, and Bob's your uncle: St Paul's Cathedral. Well, almost. Others need a bit of jiggery-pokery before they're ready to use. You wouldn't want sand mixed in with the salt on your chips...

Getting Metals From Rocks

The two main methods of metal extraction are reaction with carbon or carbon monoxide, and electrolysis.

Ores Contain Enough Metal to Make Extraction Worthwhile

1) A metal ore is a rock which contains enough metal to make extraction from the ore worthwhile.
2) Often, the metal is bonded to oxygen — the ore is an oxide of the metal.

Metal ores are compounds (see page 18).

Some Metals Can be Extracted by Reduction with Carbon

Some metals can be extracted by heating with carbon or carbon monoxide (the fancy name for this is reduction). Reduction simply means that the oxygen is removed — this makes it a 'pure' metal.

1) Carbon and carbon monoxide are reducing agents (they take the oxygen away from the metal).
2) This only works for metals that are less reactive than carbon though, e.g. lead and iron.

Lead oxide (PbO)

Lead oxide can be heated with either carbon or carbon monoxide to make pure lead:

lead oxide + carbon → lead + carbon dioxide $2PbO + C \rightarrow 2Pb + CO_2$

lead oxide + carbon monoxide → lead + carbon dioxide $PbO + CO \rightarrow Pb + CO_2$

If you're doing higher, you need to be able to balance these equations.

Iron oxide (Fe_2O_3)

Iron oxide is reduced by carbon monoxide to produce pure iron:

1) Coke (carbon) is burnt to produce carbon dioxide:

   carbon + oxygen → carbon dioxide $C + O_2 \rightarrow CO_2$

2) The CO_2 then reacts with more coke to produce carbon monoxide:

   carbon dioxide + coke (carbon) → carbon monoxide $CO_2 + C \rightarrow 2CO$

3) The iron oxide is heated and reacts with the carbon monoxide. It's reduced to produce pure iron. At the same time, the carbon monoxide is oxidised (gains oxygen) to form carbon dioxide:

   iron oxide + carbon monoxide → iron + carbon dioxide $Fe_2O_3 + 3CO \rightarrow 2Fe + 3CO_2$

Electrolysis Can be Used to Extract Metals

1) Metals that are more reactive than carbon are more difficult to extract — they can't be extracted by reduction with carbon or carbon monoxide.
2) So, electrolysis is used to extract metals that are more reactive than carbon.
3) This method breaks down the ores using electricity. This separates the metal from the other elements in the ore.
4) For electrolysis to work, the ore needs to be molten (liquid).
5) For example, electrolysis is used to separate aluminium from molten aluminium oxide.
6) Lots of electricity is needed to extract the metal. This makes electrolysis an expensive process.

Two metal oxides I know used to date — they ended up separating...

Extracting metals from ores isn't cheap. You have to pay for equipment, energy and labour. It's only worth extracting the metal if it's not going to be too expensive. There's not a lot else to say — apart from learn this page.

Impacts of Metal Extraction

Just imagine if all knives and forks were made of plastic and not metal — there'd be prongs snapping all over the place at dinner time. But, getting at metals uses a lot of energy and can be bad for the environment.

Metal Extraction Has Pros and Cons

People have to balance the social, economic and environmental effects of mining metal ores.

Mining ores can be bad:

1) Mining makes lots of noise in quiet scenic areas.
2) It makes huge ugly holes that change the landscape.
3) Building a mine destroys the habitats of animals and birds.
4) The stuff being mined needs to be transported away from the mine — usually in lorries. This causes more noise and pollution.
5) Deep mine shafts can also be dangerous for a long time after the mine has been left.
6) Metal ores are a finite resource. Once you've dug them all up there's no more.

Mining metal ores is good because:

1) Useful products can be made using the metal that is mined and extracted.
2) It provides local people with jobs and brings money into the area.

Phytomining Can be Used to Clean Up After Mining

1) Coal and metal mines that are no longer used can be cleaned up. For example, mining may leave behind bits of metal such as cadmium, nickel or cobalt in the soil.
2) These metals can be recovered from the soil by phytomining.
3) Phytomining uses plants to take up the metals from the soil using their roots. The metals build up in their leaves.
4) The plants can be harvested, dried and burnt in a furnace. The metals can be collected from the ash.
5) The plants must be able to live in the nasty conditions. Brassicas (a plant group including cabbages and sprouts — yum) are often used.

The humble sprout.
Also comes in cobalt flavour.

At last — a reason for sprouts to exist...

I guess it doesn't come as a huge surprise that building a massive mine is going to create a few problems. But, the value of the material from the mine usually outweighs any problems. These days there are rules that make sure the land is left safe when a mine closes. And that can only be a good thing.

Resources From The Air

The air isn't just for breathing — it turns out it contains loads of useful gases...

Higher

Air is a Mixture of Gases

1) Air makes up the atmosphere. It's mostly made up of nitrogen, oxygen and argon.
2) It also contains small amounts of carbon dioxide and other gases (e.g. helium), as well as water vapour.

Air Can be Fractionally Distilled

Because the gases in air have different boiling points we can split it up to get separate gases for use in industry. This is done using fractional distillation:

1) Air is filtered to remove dust.
2) It's then cooled to around –200 °C and becomes a liquid.
3) During cooling, water vapour condenses and is removed.
4) Carbon dioxide freezes and is removed.
5) The liquefied air then enters the fractionating column and is heated slowly.
6) The remaining gases all have different boiling points so leave the fractionating column at different levels.
7) Oxygen and argon come out together so another column is used to separate them.

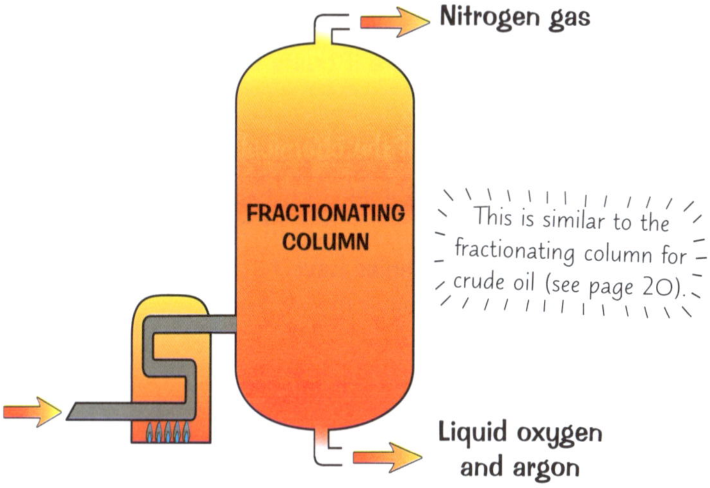

Helium can't be produced by fractionally distilling air. Instead, you get it by fractionally distilling natural gas.

The Products have Many Everyday Uses

The gases we get from air have loads of important uses:

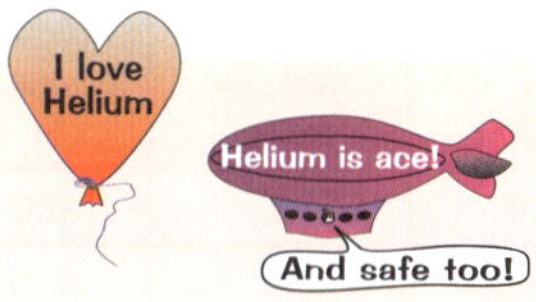

HELIUM is used in airships and party balloons.
Helium has a lower density than air — so it makes balloons float.
And it's a lot safer to use than hydrogen, which can catch fire.

ARGON is used in filament lamps (light bulbs). It provides an unreactive atmosphere which stops the very hot filament from burning away. It's also used in electrical discharge tubes — which are used to make fluorescent lights.

NITROGEN GAS is used to make ammonia (NH_3).
Ammonia is then used to make fertilisers, which help plants grow.

Fractional distillation — sounds like a load of hot air to me...

Yep, fractional distillation isn't just for crude oil. Hopefully you've noticed that this process is pretty similar to the one used for crude oil. And the different bits we get at the end are just as useful. Make sure that you know which gas is used for what — cover, scribble and check. Do this as many times as it takes...

Economics of Chemical Production

There's a lot more to producing chemicals than mixing a load of stuff in a bucket...

There's Lots to Think About When Producing Chemicals

1) Chemical companies need to think about the cost (economics) of making their products.
2) They also have to make sure they work as safely as possible.

Economics

1) Buying the raw materials needed to make a product can be expensive.
2) The company needs to produce as much product as possible from these materials.
3) It's possible to work out how much of each reactant is needed to produce a certain amount of product.
4) You don't want to use too much of a reactant because that creates waste, and waste costs money.
5) Some reactions need to take place at a high temperature. These will use lots of energy so will be very expensive to run.
6) The more it costs to make a product, the less profit a company will make.

Safety

1) Lots of the chemicals that are used in reactions are dangerous.
2) So it's important to limit the amounts that are being stored and used in reactions. Using too much of certain materials (e.g. explosive chemicals) could be dangerous.
3) Companies have to assess who is in any danger at any stage of the process. They have to lower the risk and tell chemists how to work safely.

Choosing the Right Process Isn't Easy

You might be asked to interpret data about different manufacturing processes in the exam.
There are lots of different factors to think about when choosing which manufacturing process is best.
For example, you need to consider costs, the amount of waste produced, and the amount of product etc.

EXAMPLE: Three different processes (A, B and C) can be used to make a product. Which one is best?

1) Process A has the lowest running and raw materials costs. But it produces loads of waste which could cost a lot of money to remove safely.
2) Process B produces the most product but has high costs. However, it doesn't produce as much waste as Process A.
3) Process C has the highest running costs and produces the lowest amount of product. But it produces hardly any waste, which is a benefit for the company.

Process	Raw materials cost (£m)	Running costs (£m)	Waste produced (tonnes)	Product (tonnes)
A	20	11	9	550
B	32	15	3	600
C	27	18	1	480

Whichever process you pick, remember to give reasons for your choice.

Choose the right process — or it'll cost you...

Thinking about the way things are made isn't just important for chemical companies. This could be something for people buying the product to think about as well. The cheapest product may not always be the best — it may have been made in a way that uses loads of energy and produces lots of harmful waste.

Revision Summary for Section 1.1

Phew — you've reached the end of the section. If it's all gone to plan you now know lots about the world around you and how it provides us with the things we use every day. Before you race on though, I've got some questions for you to try. If you can't answer them all, you need to go back and learn the stuff again. Then come back and give them another go.

1) List the eight planets that make up our solar system.
2) Name three types of telescope used to observe the Universe. What does each one detect?
3) What do red-shift observations tell us about the Universe?
4) Describe the 'Big Bang' theory for the origin of the Universe.
5) Draw a diagram of the structure of the Earth.
6) What causes the movement of tectonic plates?
7) Briefly describe how the Earth's atmosphere developed over time.
8) Describe the Miller and Urey experiment carried out in the 1950s.
9) How do greenhouse gases affect the Earth's temperature?
10) Sketch an atom. Label the nucleus and the electrons.
11) List the chemical symbols for magnesium, argon, silicon and iron.
12) What do the mass number and atomic number represent?
13)* The element boron is written as $^{11}_{5}B$.
    a) How many neutrons does an atom of this element contain?
    b) How many electrons does a boron atom have?
14) How many electrons can occupy: a) the first shell in an atom? b) the third shell?
15) What is the electron structure of chlorine (atomic number = 17)?
16) What is the difference between a mixture and a compound?
17) a) What is the chemical formula for methane?
    b) Which compound has the formula $Ca(OH)_2$?
18)* Balance this equation: $CaCO_3 + HCl \longrightarrow CaCl_2 + H_2O + CO_2$
19) Give two examples of materials that are found in the ground ready to use.
20) How are the different fuels separated from crude oil?
21) What is a metal ore?
22) Write down the three word equations for the reduction of iron oxide with coke.
23) Give three reasons why mining is bad for the environment.
24) Describe how phytomining is used to clean up metal mines.
25) What property of gases in the air means we can separate them using fractional distillation?
26) Give one use for each of helium, argon and nitrogen.
27) Why is it important for chemical companies to work out how much raw material to use in a chemical reaction?

* Answers on page 108

Classification

The Earth is brimming with more life forms than you can count. In fact, there are so many kinds of life that studying them all would be a nightmare if we didn't use a classification system to make it easier...

Classification is Organising Living Organisms into Groups

1) Organisms that have similar physical characteristics are classified into groups. For example, bats and humans have a similar bone pattern in their arms. The classification system reflects these similarities.
2) Living things are divided into kingdoms (e.g. the plant kingdom and the animal kingdom):
   - Members of the plant kingdom make their own food by photosynthesis, but can't move around.
   - Members of the animal kingdom can't make their own food, but they can move around.
3) Kingdoms are split up into smaller and smaller groups.
4) An example of one of these smaller groups is a genus — a group of closely-related species.
5) A species is a group of closely-related organisms who can breed to produce fertile offspring (children).

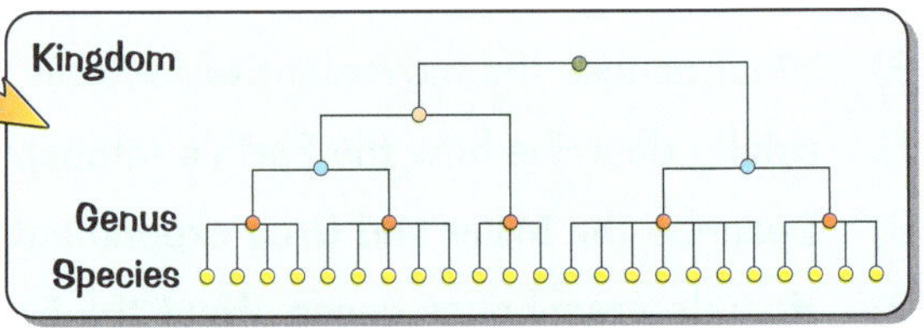

6) Every species has a two-part name. The first part refers to the genus that the organism belongs to and the second part refers to the species. E.g. humans are called *Homo sapiens*. '*Homo*' is the genus we belong to and '*sapiens*' is our species.
7) Classifying and naming organisms like this makes it less confusing where common names mean different things in different places. For example, in the UK and USA there are birds called a "robin" — but they're not the same species. Scientists use the species name so people will know which robin they mean.

The Way We Classify Organisms Has Changed

1) The first classification systems had just two kingdoms.
2) However, developments in science (e.g. microscopy) showed that not all organisms fitted neatly into these groups.
3) So, gradually new systems of classification (models) have been developed.
4) Nowadays, organisms are often classified by a five-kingdom model based on their physical characteristics.
5) An even newer model has been suggested though. This system has three domains (main groups). In this model, organisms are classified by their genes and cell structure.
6) As scientists learn more about how organisms are related, it's likely that changes to the classification systems will be made or new classification models will be developed.

Dullus revisium — the scientific name for revision...

Parents can be pretty mean when it comes to naming their kids — but no one's as evil as a scientist. It takes a special kind of cruelty to name something as cute as a hedgehog *Erinaceus europaeus*. Sounds like a disease.

Competition and Distribution

It doesn't matter whether you're a snake, a sprout or a student — you still need stuff like food and water to survive. And it's a tough world out there — sometimes there isn't enough to go around...

Organisms Need a Supply of Materials to Survive

Organisms get the things they need to survive from their surroundings and from other organisms.

Organisms that Need the Same Resources will Compete

1) Sometimes there aren't enough resources to go around — so organisms have to compete for them.
2) This can happen between members of the same species.

For example, conker trees that grow close together will compete for water and nutrients from the soil, and for sunlight.

3) Competition can also happen between members of different species.

For example, red and grey squirrels compete for the same food.

The Distribution of Organisms is Affected by Many Factors

Distribution means where an organism lives in an environment. It's affected by many things:

1) Organisms need resources to survive, so they can only be found where those resources are. For example, plants need sunlight so they won't be found in places like caves.
2) But fewer organisms live in areas where they're out-competed. For example, few red squirrels live in areas where there are grey squirrels, because the grey squirrels are better at getting the resources they both need to survive.
3) Plants and animals also need the right environmental conditions to survive, e.g. the right temperature. They'll only live where the conditions are right. For example, few plants live in the Arctic because it's too cold.
4) Organisms are less likely to live in areas where there are lots of predators.

I compete with my brother for the front seat of the car...

In the exam you might get asked about the distribution of any animals or plants. Just think about what the organisms need to survive. And remember, if there aren't enough resources then there's going to be competition.

Adaptations in Animals

The reason why there's such a mind-blowing variety of life is because over millions of year organisms have changed to become better at living in their environments — like in deserts, the Arctic and schools...

Adaptations Help Organisms to Survive

1) Adaptations are the features that organisms have that make them better suited to their environment.
2) Organisms that are better adapted to their environment are better able to survive.
3) Animals can be adapted to their environment in many ways — here are some examples:

The Camel — Adapted for Hot, Dry Desert Conditions

They have a really large surface area and a small volume, so they lose body heat very easily.

They have long eyelashes to stop sand getting in their eyes.

Camels save water. They produce very small amounts of strong urine and they don't sweat much.

Apart from the humps, the rest of the body only has a thin layer of body fat, so it isn't insulated — and this helps them lose heat.

Camels keep nearly all of their body fat in their humps. They use the fat for energy on long journeys where there's no food.

The Polar Bear — Adapted for Cold Arctic Conditions

Their thick hairy coat provides insulation — it helps keep the body heat in.

Polar bears have a large and compact (i.e. rounded) shape, including dinky little ears. This means they have a small surface area and a large volume — and this reduces heat loss.

They've got big feet to spread their weight on snow and ice.

The fur on the soles of their paws helps them grip the snow and ice. It also keeps the heat in.

They have a thick layer of blubber for insulation and also to survive when there's not much food.

It's beyond me how a polar bear can bear the polar conditions...

The wolf in Little Red Riding Hood had some great adaptations for eating children — big eyes for seeing, big ears for hearing and big sharp teeth for biting. The one adaptation it was missing was an axe-proof body.

Adaptations in Plants and Microorganisms

We're not done with adaptation just yet — you also need to know a bit about how plants and microorganisms are adapted to survive in the environments where they live...

Desert Plants Have Adapted to Having Little Water

Cacti have a small surface area and a large volume. This helps to reduce water loss.

Some cacti have shallow roots that are spread out over a large area. This means they can absorb water quickly when it rains. Others have deep roots so they can reach underground water.

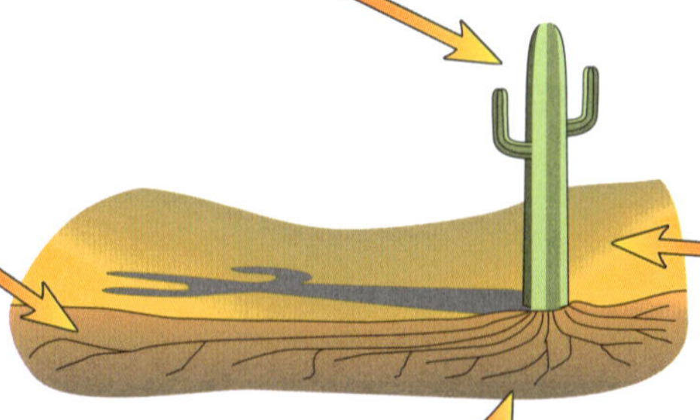

Plants lose water vapour from the surface of their leaves. So cacti have spines instead of leaves to reduce water loss.

A cactus is able to store lots of water in its thick stem.

Some Microorganisms Have Adapted to Extreme Environments

Some microorganisms are known as extremophiles because they're adapted to live in seriously extreme conditions. For example:

Bacteria are microorganisms.

Some microorganisms are adapted to survive in environments that have chemicals which make them so dangerous most other organisms can't live there (e.g. the Dead Sea).

Some microorganisms are adapted to live in really cold places, like the Arctic.

Some types of microorganism are adapted to places where there's not much water.

There are microorganisms that are adapted to live in really hot environments, like inside underwater volcanic vents.

Cactus adaptation — it's a spiky issue...

Right, so basically organisms are adapted to the places where they live. A lot of this involves being good at keeping or losing heat (animals) and water (plants and animals). Microorganisms are adapted as well, but they can live in environments that are so extremely dangerous even I'd be afraid to go there, like under my bed...

Evolution

All the life on Earth today evolved from simple organisms to be adapted to survive in different environments. Species are still evolving right now. I'm sure you're dying to hear all about it...

The Theory of Evolution is Cool

1) All the animals and plants on Earth gradually 'evolved' over billions of years, rather than just suddenly popping into existence. Makes sense.
2) Life on Earth began as simple organisms from which all the more complex organisms evolved. And it only took 3 billion years.
3) Scientists can study fossils to find evidence for evolution.

Evolution Happens by Natural Selection

Genes are instructions that control your body's physical characteristics — like whether you have blue or brown eyes.

Natural selection works like this...

1) Individuals within a species are all slightly different because of the differences in their genes, e.g. some rabbits have big ears and some have small ones.
2) Individuals with characteristics that make them better adapted to the environment have a better chance of survival.
3) This means they're more likely to breed successfully. E.g. big-eared rabbits are more likely to hear a fox sneaking up on them, and so they're more likely to live and have millions of babies. Small-eared rabbits are more likely to end up as fox food.

4) So, the genes that cause the useful characteristics are more likely to be passed on to the next generation. E.g. after a while, all the baby rabbits are born with big ears.

So All Organisms are Related... even if Only Distantly

Studying the similarities and differences between organisms can help us to understand things like:

1) How all living things are related (evolutionary relationships).
   - Species that look alike and live in similar habitats are usually closely related, e.g. whales and dolphins.
   - How organisms are related can be shown using evolutionary trees.
   - The more recent the common ancestor (relative), the more closely related the two species.
2) How they interact with each other (ecological relationships). For example, species that look alike and live in the same habitat might compete for the same resources, e.g. dolphins and sharks might both hunt herring.

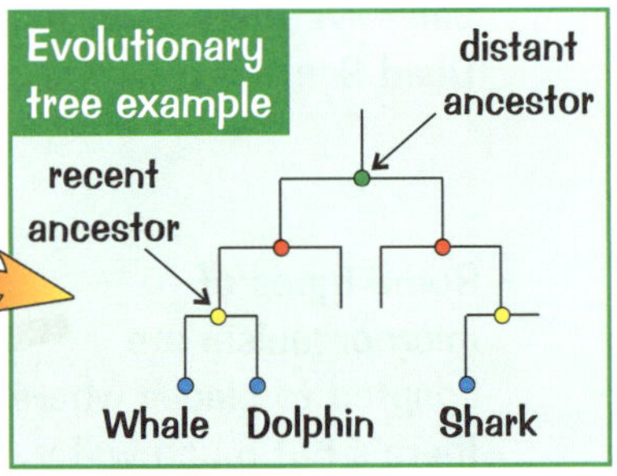

Whales and dolphins have a recent common ancestor so are closely related. They're both more distantly related to sharks.

"Natural selection" — sounds like vegan chocolates...

Natural selection's all about the organisms with the best characteristics surviving to pass on their genes so that the whole species ends up adapted to its environment. It doesn't happen overnight though.

Plant Growth

There's a huge variety of plant life on Earth. You need to know about things that affect their growth. Unlucky.

Many Factors Affect the Growth of Plants

LIGHT — Plants need light for photosynthesis — without it, they can't make the glucose they need for energy and growth. The growth of a plant in response to light is called phototropism.

GRAVITY — A plant's shoots grow up and its roots grow down because of gravity. This helps make the plant stable and gives it a better chance of finding water and nutrients. The growth of a plant in response to gravity is called gravitropism.

TEMPERATURE — Plants grow faster when it's warm because the reactions for photosynthesis happen faster. But if it gets too hot or too cold growth will slow.

DAY LENGTH — In the summer days are longer and there are more hours of sunshine than in the winter. This gives plants more time for photosynthesis so they grow faster.

Auxins are Plant Growth Hormones

1) Auxins are plant hormones that control the growth of shoots and roots.
2) Auxin is produced in the tips of shoots and roots.
3) Extra auxin has different effects in the shoots and roots — it speeds up growth in the shoots, but slows growth in the roots.
4) Auxins are involved in the responses of plants to light and gravity.

Auxins Change the Direction of Root and Shoot Growth

Root or shoot growth can also be called elongation.

Light

When a shoot or root tip is exposed to light, more auxin builds up on the side that's in the shade than the side that's in the light. This has different effects in the shoots and roots:

1) In shoots this makes the cells grow faster on the shaded side, so the shoot bends towards the light.
2) In roots, this makes the cells grow more slowly on the shaded side, so the root bends towards the dark.

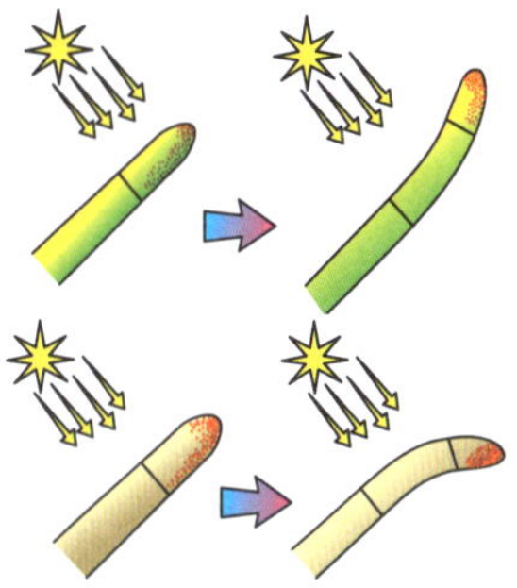

Gravity

When a root or shoot grows sideways, gravity causes more auxin to build up on the lower side — but again, it has different effects in shoots and roots:

1) In shoots, the lower side grows faster, bending the shoot upwards.
2) In roots, the lower side grows slower, bending the root downwards.

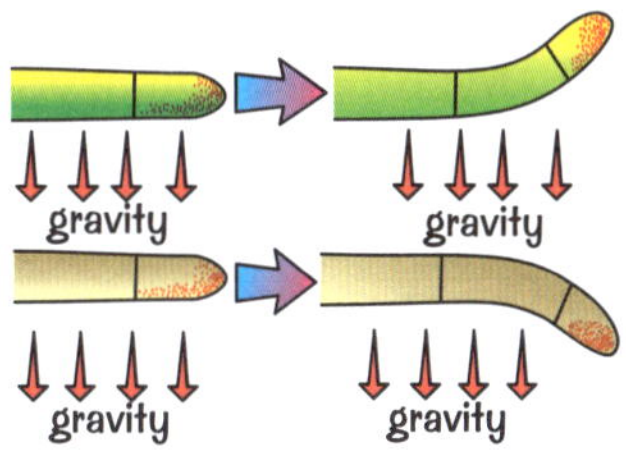

Plants need a place in the Sun — next to the TV listings perhaps...

Learn the page. Learn the whole darn page. There's no getting out of it folks.

Food Chains and Nutrient Cycling

Everything in life is linked together — mostly because organisms tend to eat each other. And when organisms die, the nutrients in their bodies are broken down and recycled to be used again. Sounds disgusting...

Food Chains Show What is Eaten by What

1) All the organisms that live in an environment, along with stuff like water, sunlight and air, make up an ecosystem.
2) All the ecosystems on the planet make up the biosphere.
3) Energy enters the biosphere from the Sun.
4) Plants convert the Sun's energy into chemical energy by using it to make food during photosynthesis.
5) This energy is stored as biomass (living material).
6) The biomass (and so the energy) move through the food chain as animals eat the plants and each other:

Producer, e.g. carrot plants — all plants are producers.

Primary consumer, e.g. rabbit — this is an animal that eats producers (plants).

Secondary consumer, e.g. fox — an animal that eats primary consumers.

7) So food chains show the flow of energy and biomass from the producer to the consumers.
8) Each stage in a food chain (e.g. producer) is called a trophic level.
9) Food webs are made up of several food chains, and show how they're linked together.

Primary consumers are also sometimes called herbivores, and secondary consumers are called carnivores.

Elements are Recycled Back to the Start of the Food Chain by Decay

1) Living things are made of materials they take from their environment.
2) Plants take elements like carbon, oxygen, hydrogen and nitrogen from the soil or the air.
3) They turn these elements into plant material.
4) This then passes through the food chain as animals eat the plants and each other.
5) These elements are returned to the environment by microorganisms called decomposers.
6) They break down dead organisms and waste products, returning the elements to the soil.
7) Microorganisms work best in warm, moist conditions (and some need plenty of oxygen).
8) This means that all the important elements are recycled — they're returned to the soil or air, ready to be used by new plants and put back into the food chain again.

There's loads of info about how carbon is recycled on page 35.

Sausages — my favourite kind of food chain...

As weird as it might sound, all plants and animals are energy stores — energy from the Sun is locked up as chemicals in their bodies. Oh, and don't forget to use the fancy term for living material in the exam — 'biomass'.

Energy Transfer

I'm not going to lie to you — that *is* maths at the bottom of the page. But don't let that put you off. Energy is lost as you move along a food chain, and it's just a fancy way of showing how much.

All That Energy Just Disappears Somehow

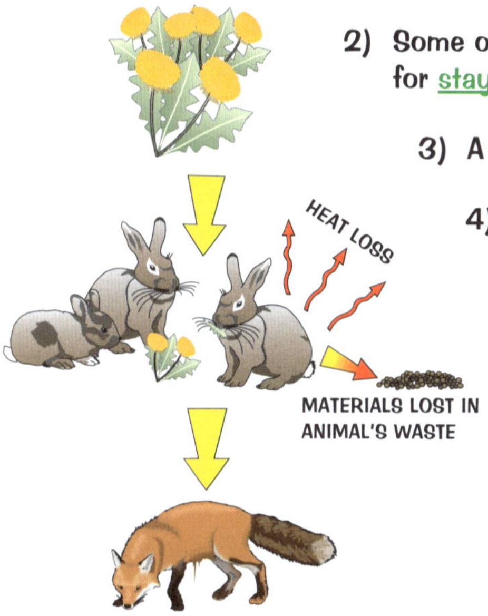

1) Material and energy are lost (transferred to the environment) at each stage of a food chain.
2) Some of the energy is lost because biomass is broken down to release energy for staying alive. The process that does this is called respiration.
3) A lot of the energy is lost as heat.
4) Material and energy are also lost from the food chain because some bits can't be digested, e.g. bones. They pass through the organism and come out as faeces (droppings).
5) Energy is also lost when organisms die — energy passes to the microorganisms that decompose the dead remains.
6) You hardly ever get food chains with more than about five trophic levels. So much energy is lost at each stage that there's not enough left to support more organisms after four or five stages.

You Need to be Able to Interpret Data on Energy Flow

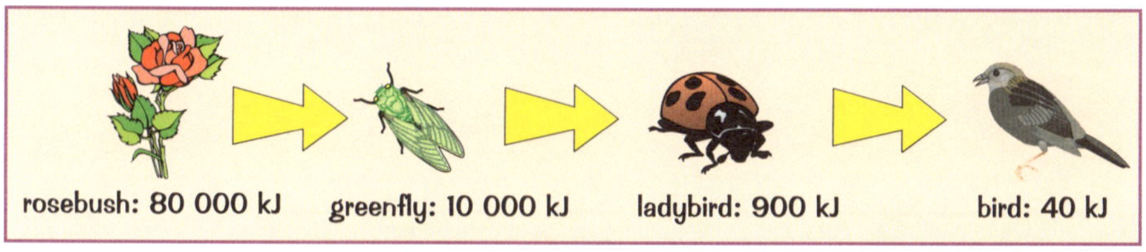

'kJ' stands for 'kilojoule' — a unit of energy.

1) The numbers show the amount of energy stored in each type of organism.
2) You can work out how much energy has been lost by taking away the amount of energy stored in an organism from the energy stored in what it ate. Like this:

energy lost between rosebush and greenfly = 80 000 kJ — 10 000 kJ = 70 000 kJ lost

3) You can also calculate the efficiency of energy transfer — this just means how good it is at passing on energy from one level to the next.

$$\text{efficiency} = \frac{\text{energy stored in the animal}}{\text{energy stored in what the animal ate}} \times 100\%$$

4) So the efficiency of the energy transfer between the first and second trophic level is:

$$\text{efficiency} = \frac{10\,000 \text{ kJ (the greenfly)}}{80\,000 \text{ kJ (the rosebush)}} \times 100\% = 12.5\% \text{ efficient}$$

So when revising, put the fire on and don't take loo breaks...

No, I'm being silly, go if you have to — we're talking in general terms about food webs here. Working out energy transfer isn't the most interesting thing in the world, but it could pick you up a few marks in the exam. Groovy.

Pyramids of Biomass and Number

Every time you move up a level in a food chain, you lose biomass — and because scientists have nothing better to do, they like to show this by drawing pyramids. Will the excitement never end...

Pyramids of Biomass Show Mass

1) Biomass is the fancy word for living material.
2) A pyramid of biomass shows the mass of the organisms at each trophic level in a food chain. Like this:

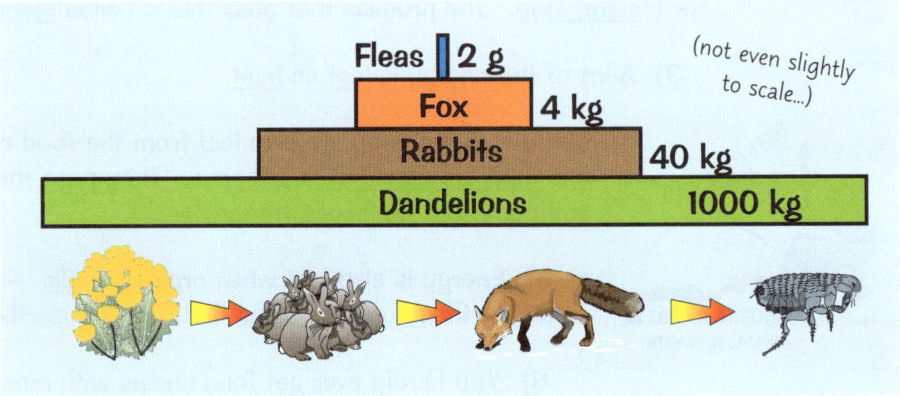

3) If you weighed them, all the dandelions would have a big biomass and the hundreds of fleas would have a very small biomass.
4) Each time you go up one level, the mass of organisms goes down. It takes a lot of food from the level below to keep any one animal alive.
5) Biomass pyramids are always a pyramid shape.
6) Don't forget that if you get a question on biomass in the exam you need to include the units.

Pyramids of Number Show the Number of Organisms

1) There are also pyramids of number.
2) These show the number of organisms at each level.
3) Usually, numbers fall as you go up the food chain.
4) Sometimes they're not pyramid-shaped though, e.g. this pyramid of numbers shows that there are more fleas than foxes, but together their biomass is much smaller than the fox's.

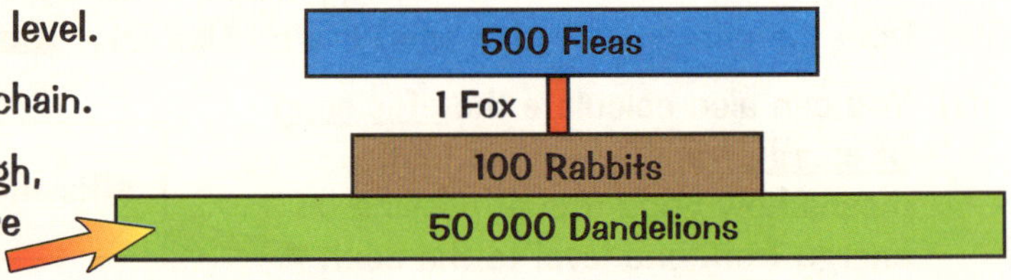

Constructing pyramids is a breeze — just ask the Egyptians...

If you have to construct a pyramid, check it's to scale. E.g. if one square = 10 units, 5 units of fox biomass would be half a square, but 500 units of dandelion biomass would need a 50 square block (e.g. 5 × 10 squares).

The Carbon Cycle

And last but not least, I bring you... how carbon gets recycled. Oh come on — it could be worse (it could be physics).

The Carbon Cycle Shows How Carbon is Recycled

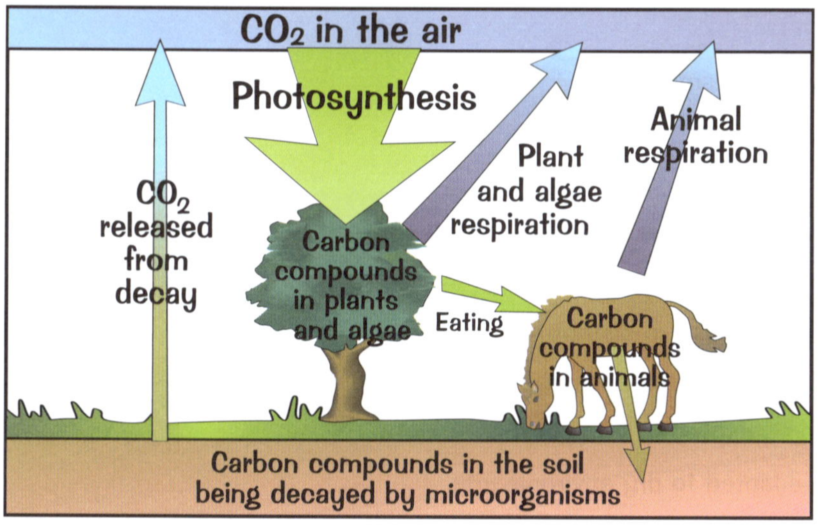

1) There's only one arrow going down from the atmosphere. The whole thing is "powered" by photosynthesis.
2) CO_2 is removed by green plants and algae and used to make carbohydrates, fats and proteins. At the same time, oxygen is released.
3) Some of the CO_2 is returned to the atmosphere when the plants and algae respire. During respiration, oxygen is taken in.
4) Some of the carbon becomes part of the carbohydrates, fats and proteins in the animals when the plants are eaten.
5) Some of the CO_2 is returned to the atmosphere when the animals respire.
6) When plants and animals die, other animals and microorganisms feed on their remains. When these organisms respire, CO_2 is returned to the atmosphere.
7) Animals also produce waste. This too is broken down by microorganisms.
8) Sometimes when organisms die their remains turn into fossil fuels. This stores the carbon. When the fuels are burnt, the carbon is released back into the atmosphere as CO_2.
9) So the carbon is constantly being cycled — from the air, through food chains and eventually back out into the air again.

Carbon Can Be Turned Into Limestone

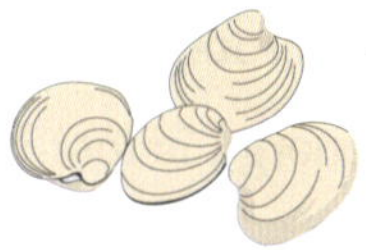

Plankton are tiny organisms that live in the sea.

1) Carbon dioxide can dissolve in the sea.
2) Some of the organisms that live in the sea use the carbon dioxide to make shells and bones, e.g. plankton and coral.
3) When these organisms die, their remains fall to the sea floor.
4) Over really long periods of time the shells and bones of dead marine animals form limestone rocks (calcium carbonate). The carbon from the organisms gets stored in the limestone.
5) The organisms that limestone is made from live in warm, tropical, shallow oceans — so the amount of limestone that's formed depends on how much there is of this type of environment.

What goes around comes around...

The amount of CO_2 produced should balance the amount of CO_2 absorbed by plants. But at the moment the level of CO_2 is increasing. There are two main reasons for this — we're burning loads of fossil fuels (which produces CO_2) and cutting down loads of trees (which then can't absorb CO_2).

Revision Summary for Section 1.2

And where do you think you're going? It's no use just reading through and thinking you've got it all — this stuff will only stick in your head if you've learnt it properly. And that's what these questions are for. I won't pretend they'll be easy — they're not meant to be, but all the information's in the section somewhere. Have a go at all the questions, then if there are any you can't answer, go back, look stuff up and try again. Enjoy...

1) Name two different kingdoms of living organisms.
2) Why is classification of organisms important?
3) Give three resources that are needed by: a) plants, b) animals.
4) Name two organisms that compete with each other. What resources do they compete for?
5) What is meant by the distribution of an organism?
6) Describe two things that affect how organisms are distributed.
7) Describe four ways in which a desert animal may be adapted to its environment.
8) Describe four ways that polar bears are adapted to living in the Arctic.
9) Describe four ways desert plants are adapted to dry environments.
10) What is an extremophile? Give two environments where extremophiles can be found.
11) Describe how natural selection works.
12) What do evolutionary trees show?
13) Define phototropism and gravitropism.
14) Name a hormone that controls plant growth.
15) Explain how hormones cause plant shoots to grow towards light.
16) Where does the energy in a food chain come from?
17) In a food chain would a carrot plant be a producer, primary consumer or secondary consumer?
18) What is each stage in a food chain called?
19) What is the name of the microorganisms that recycle nutrients back to the start of a food chain by decomposition?
20) What conditions do microorganisms need to work best?
21) Give two ways that energy is lost from a food chain.
22) Why do you rarely get more than five trophic levels in a food chain?
23) What is the equation for calculating the efficiency of energy transfer between stages in a food chain?
24) What does a pyramid of biomass show?
25) What does a pyramid of number show?
26) Name two types of organism that remove carbon dioxide from the atmosphere.
27) Describe three ways carbon leaves a food chain and returns to the atmosphere.
28) Describe how carbon gets turned into limestone.

The Nervous System

Welcome to Section 2.1. First thing on the menu is a page about the nervous system. The nervous system is what lets you react to what goes on around you, so you'd find life tough without it.

Sense Organs Contain Receptors That Detect Stimuli

Receptors are groups of cells that are sensitive to a stimulus such as light or heat. There are five different sense organs, which all contain different receptors.

1) Eyes — Light receptors.

2) Ears — Sound receptors.

3) Nose — Smell receptors.

4) Tongue — Taste receptors.

5) Skin — Touch and heat receptors.

Parts of the Nervous System

Central Nervous System (CNS)

Consists of the brain and spinal cord only.

Motor Neurones

The cells that carry signals from the CNS to the effectors. Lots of neurones form a bundle to make up a nerve.

Effectors

All your muscles and glands, which respond to nervous impulses.

Sensory neurones

The cells that carry signals from the receptors in the sense organs to the CNS.

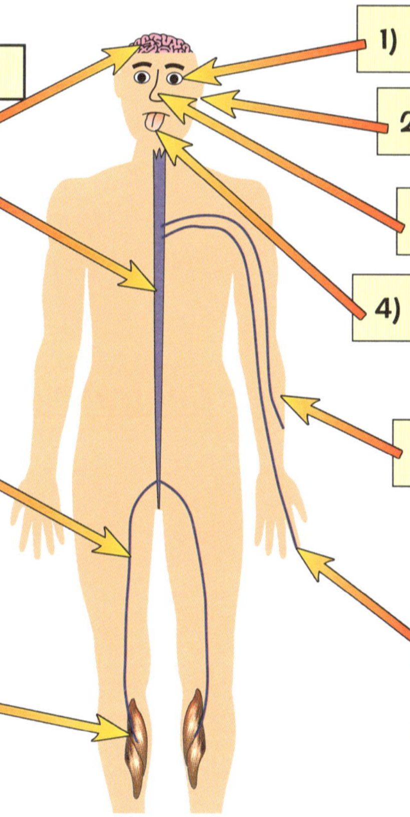

The Central Nervous System (CNS) Coordinates Information

The nervous system uses nerves to communicate information quickly all around the body.

Here's what happens:

1) A stimulus is detected by receptors in a sense organ.
2) This information travels along sensory neurones to the CNS.
3) The CNS is like the control centre of your nervous system. Its job is to COORDINATE all the information and decide what needs to be done.
4) The CNS will send information to the relevant effector (muscle or gland) along motor neurones. The effector will then respond.

Hurrah for sense organs — without them you couldn't revise...

Well, maybe not hurrah then. In a single cubic centimetre of your brain you can have well over 50 million nerve cells. Each one of these exciting little cells can communicate with thousands of other nerve cells to process information from the receptors — and you thought computers were impressive.

Reflexes

Your brain can decide how to respond to a stimulus pretty quickly.
But sometimes, waiting for your brain to make a decision is just too slow. That's why you have reflexes.

Reflexes Help Prevent Injury

1) Reflex actions are really quick, automatic responses to certain stimuli. This means you react to something without having to think about it.
2) Reflexes make it less likely you'll be injured.
3) For example, if someone shines a bright light in your eyes, your pupils react by becoming smaller so that less light gets into the eye — this stops it getting damaged.
4) A reflex arc is the pathway information takes from a receptor (e.g. your eye) to an effector (e.g. muscles that control your pupil).

The Reflex Arc Goes Through the Central Nervous System

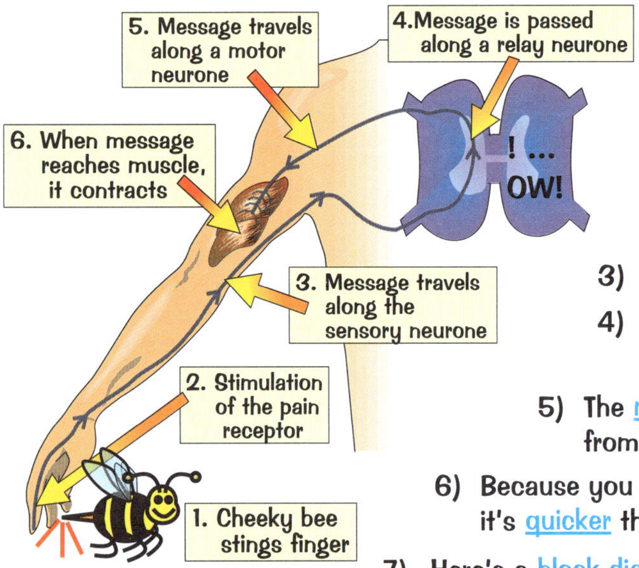

1) When a stimulus (e.g. a painful bee sting) is detected by receptors (e.g. in your skin), impulses are sent along a sensory neurone to the CNS.
2) In the CNS the sensory neurone passes on the message to another type of neurone — a relay neurone.
3) Relay neurones pass on the impulses to a motor neurone.
4) The impulses then travel along the motor neurone to the effector (in this example it's a muscle).
5) The muscle then contracts and moves your hand away from the bee.
6) Because you don't have to think about the response (which takes time) it's quicker than normal responses.
7) Here's a block diagram of a reflex arc — it's another way of looking at what happens.

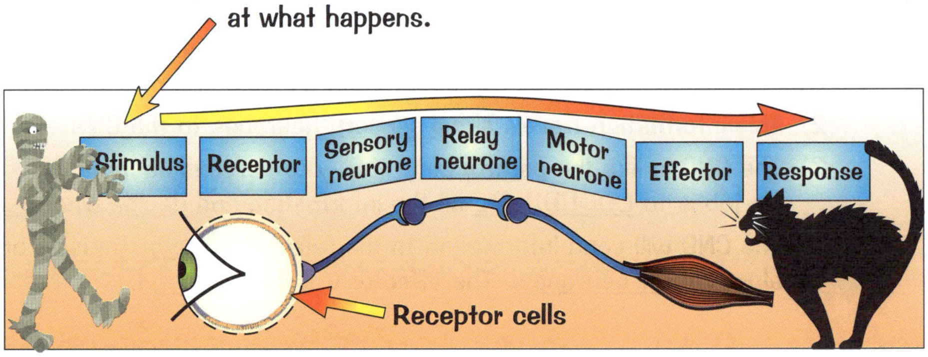

Don't get all twitchy — just learn it...

Reflexes are pretty awesome things. It's like when a doctor taps your knee with a hammer and your leg seems to kick by itself — that's actually your body reacting without you even having to think about it.

Hearing

Thanks to your ears picking up sound waves you can listen to music, but you can also hear your mum shouting. You need to be careful, though — loud noises can damage your ears. So next time your mum bellows that you're playing ABBA too loud, she might just be on to something...

Our Ears Detect Longitudinal Waves

1) Sound waves are caused by vibrating objects.
2) These vibrations make the particles in the air move backwards and forwards.
3) The vibrations are known as longitudinal waves.
4) Sometimes the sound waves will reach someone's ear, at which point the person might hear it.

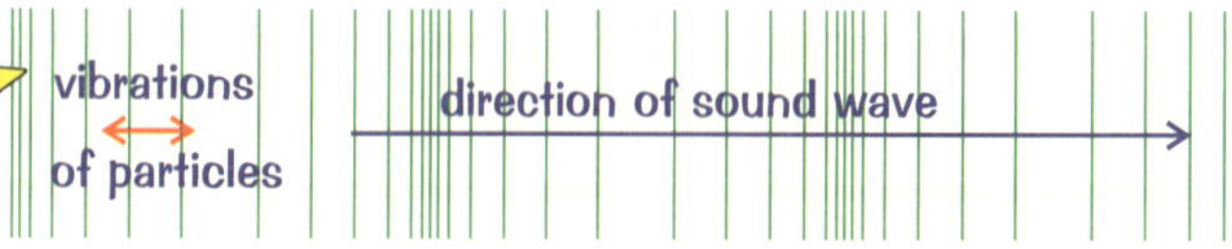

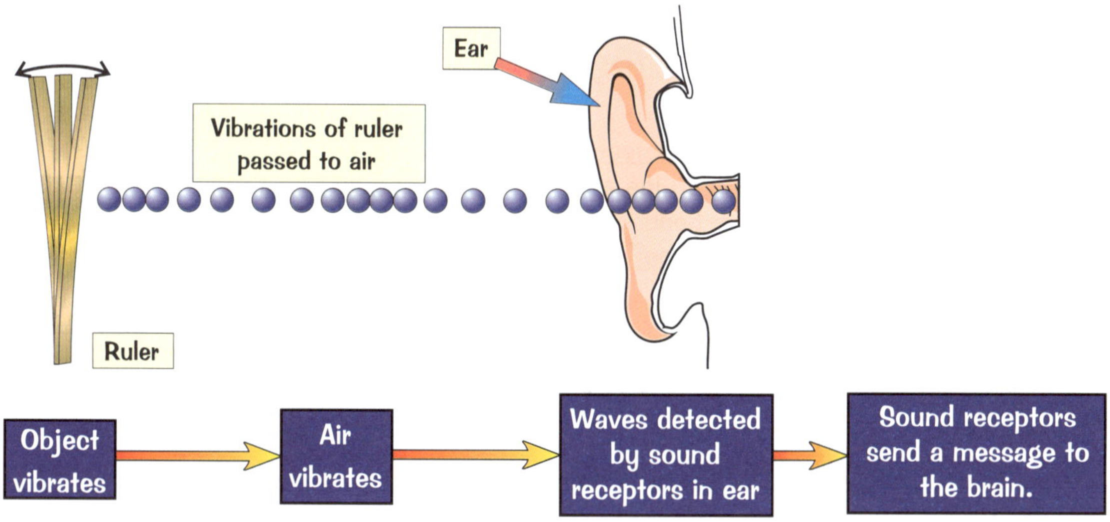

Loud Noise can be a Bad Thing

1) The frequency of a wave is the number of waves per second. One wave per second is one hertz (Hz).
2) The human ear is capable of hearing sounds with frequencies between 20 Hz and 20 000 Hz.
3) The loudness of noise is measured in decibels (dB).
4) Your hearing can be damaged by loud noises. For example, noisy machinery or very loud music from MP3 players and nightclubs can damage your hearing.
5) Here are some examples of how noisy stuff is:

Sounds at 90 dB or more can damage your hearing.

EXAMPLE	LOUDNESS
TV	Around 60 dB
Normal conversation	60-70 dB
Traffic on a busy road	80-90 dB
Pneumatic drill	120 dB
Jet engine	140 dB

Soooometiiiiimes, everybody hertz...

So that was hearing. And what a wonder it was. It might not be as amazing as ABBA, but you need to make sure you've got all this info fixed in your brain — you might just have to write about it in the exam.

Homeostasis

Homeostasis involves balancing body functions to maintain a 'constant internal environment'. Smashing.

Homeostasis is Keeping a Constant Internal Environment

1) Conditions in your body need to be kept steady so that cells can work properly.
2) This means balancing inputs (stuff going into your body) with outputs (stuff leaving).
3) For example, your body needs to be kept at a constant temperature — you need to get rid of excess body heat when you're hot, but hold onto heat when you're cold.

Higher

4) The body has different control systems to keep different things steady.
5) All the control systems use a mechanism called negative feedback.
6) Negative feedback happens between the effector and the receptor of the control system.
7) If the internal environment changes, it's detected by the receptor. A response is triggered by the effector to counteract the change. E.g. a rise in body temperature causes a response that lowers body temperature.
8) This means that the internal environment tends to stay around a norm — the level where the cells work best.

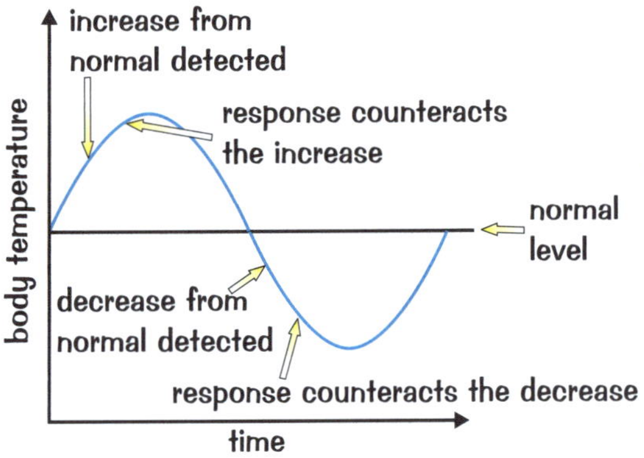

Higher

Body Temperature is Controlled by the Brain

1) There's a thermoregulatory centre in the brain which acts as your own personal thermostat.
2) To keep your body at the right temperature, it does these things:

When You're TOO HOT:

1) Your body makes lots of sweat — when it evaporates it transfers heat to the environment, cooling you down.
2) The blood vessels that supply the skin capillaries dilate (get wider). This allows more blood to flow near the surface, so it can lose more heat into the surroundings.

Skin capillaries are tiny blood vessels close to the surface of the skin.

When You're TOO COLD:

1) Your body makes very little sweat.

2) The blood vessels that supply the skin capillaries constrict (get narrow). This means that less heat can be lost from the blood to the surroundings, as less blood can flow near the surface of the skin.

If you do enough revision, you can avoid negative feedback...

So there you have it. Learn this and the next time you forget your anti-perspirant after P.E. you'll know all about how sweating helps to keep your inside conditions nice and constant. It won't stop your mates avoiding you, but you can't have everything — and at least knowing about it might pick you up some marks in the exam.

Hormones and Blood Sugar

Hormones are nifty little things that are used to pass information around your body — and some control stuff like the amount of sugar in your blood...

Hormones are Chemical Messengers Sent in the Blood

1) Hormones are chemicals made in glands. The glands secrete (release) hormones straight into the blood. The blood then carries the hormones all over the body.
2) They only affect particular organs, called target organs.
3) Hormones cause slow changes within the body, e.g. they control growth and development.

Insulin is a Hormone that Controls Blood Sugar Levels

1) Insulin is made in the pancreas. It controls how much sugar there is in your blood.
2) Eating carbohydrate foods puts a lot of glucose into the blood.
3) The normal working of cells removes glucose from the blood.
4) Doing exercise takes out loads of glucose from the blood.
5) To keep the level of glucose in the blood constant there has to be a way to remove glucose from the blood. And this is it:

If something is insoluble it means it won't dissolve, e.g. in water or blood.

glucose too high → Pancreas detects glucose gain in blood → Pancreas makes and releases insulin → Glucose removed from blood by liver and stored as insoluble glycogen in the liver or muscles → Blood glucose level correct

Higher

Glucose can also be added to the blood if the level drops:

glucose too low → Pancreas detects glucose loss in blood → Pancreas makes and releases glucagon → Glucose added to blood by liver (converted back from stored glycogen) → Blood glucose level correct

Higher

Diabetes — When the Body Can't Control Blood Sugar Levels

Diabetes is a disorder where the level of blood glucose isn't controlled. This means that a person's blood sugar can rise to a level that can kill them. There are two types:

TYPE 1 DIABETES

1) This is where the pancreas can't make any insulin (or enough insulin).
2) It's controlled by injecting insulin into the blood at mealtimes.
3) It's sometimes called insulin-dependent diabetes.

TYPE 2 DIABETES

1) This is where the target organs don't respond to insulin.
2) It can be caused by lifestyle — for example, it's more common in people who are obese, smoke and don't get enough exercise.
3) It can be controlled by a change in lifestyle — e.g. getting more exercise and avoiding foods high in sugar.
4) More and more people are getting Type 2 diabetes. This means the NHS has to treat more people — and this costs more money.

My blood sugar feels low after that — pass the biscuits...

Diabetics can check their blood sugar using a glucose-monitoring device. This is a little hand-held machine. They prick their finger to get a drop of blood for the machine to check. Handy.

Chemicals and Hazards

Chemical reactions keep your body working, but in the lab chemicals can be dangerous and explosive.

You Need to Learn the Common Hazard Symbols

Lots of chemicals can be dangerous in some way. These hazard symbols might just save you.

You Might Find These Symbols on Common Acids and Bases

Corrosive
Attacks and destroys living tissues, including eyes and skin.

Toxic
Can cause death either by swallowing, breathing in, or absorption through the skin.

Harmful
Like toxic but not quite as dangerous.

Irritant
Not corrosive but can cause reddening or blistering of the skin.

How to reduce the hazards:

- Wear safety goggles, gloves and a lab coat.
- Don't eat or drink in the lab.
- Wash your hands after doing experiments.

You should follow this advice when dealing with all chemicals in the lab — including the ones below.

You Might Find These Symbols on Other Chemicals

Oxidising
Provides oxygen which allows other materials to burn more fiercely. E.g. liquid oxygen.
Reducing the hazard: Keep away from naked flames.

Highly Flammable
Catches fire easily. E.g. petrol.
Reducing the hazard: Keep away from naked flames.

Radioactive
Releases radioactive particles or rays (see page 85). E.g. uranium.
Reducing the hazard: Keep the source in a sealed lead-lined container when it's not in use. Hold the source with tongs and keep it away from the body.

Exam papers are an irritant — but they're not actually harmful...

Working with chemicals in the lab is good fun — but don't forget that the lab is full of hazards and that if you're messing about (this includes squirting each other with pipettes) then someone might get hurt. If you follow the instructions properly and handle all the chemicals and equipment sensibly, then you should stay in one piece...

Acids and Alkalis

Acids and alkalis are dead useful — they pop up at home, in school labs and even inside you...

The pH Scale and Universal Indicator

1) The pH scale goes from 0 to 14.
2) The strongest acid has pH 0 and the strongest alkali has pH 14.
3) A neutral substance has pH 7 (e.g. pure water).

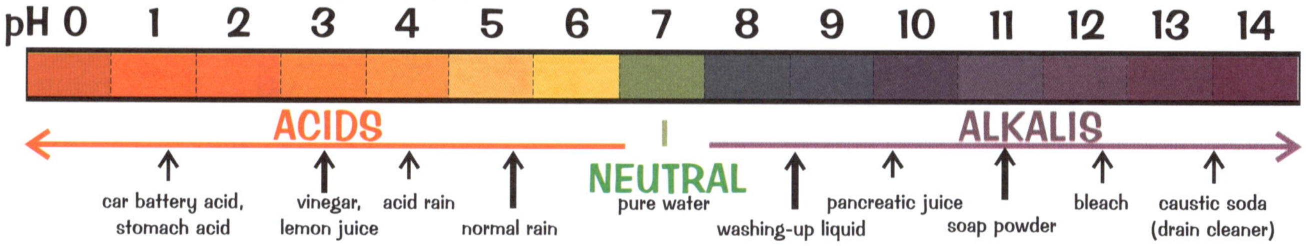

An Indicator is Just a Dye That Changes Colour

1) The indicator changes colour depending on whether it's above or below a certain pH.
2) Universal indicator is a common indicator, which gives the colours shown above.
3) It's very useful for estimating the pH of a solution.

Reactions Between Acids and Alkalis Make Salts

When a substance dissolves in water it forms a solution.

An ACID is a substance with a pH less than 7.
Acids form hydrogen ions (H^+) in water — it's the H^+ ions that make the solution acidic.

An ALKALI is a substance with a pH more than 7.
Alkalis form hydroxide ions (OH^-) in water — it's the OH^- ions that make the solution alkaline.

The reaction between acids and alkalis is called neutralisation. Make sure you learn it:

$$\text{acid} + \text{alkali} \rightarrow \text{salt} + \text{water}$$

When an acid and an alkali neutralise each other, the products are neutral, i.e. they have a pH of 7.

Higher

Neutralisation can also be seen in terms of H^+ and OH^- ions like this, so learn it too:

'aq' means 'in water'
'l' means 'liquid'

$$H^+_{(aq)} + OH^-_{(aq)} \rightarrow H_2O_{(l)}$$

Higher

Interesting(ish) fact — your skin is slightly acidic (pH 5.5)...

There's no getting away from acids and bases in Chemistry, or even in real life. They're everywhere — acids are found in loads of foods (e.g. vinegar and fruit) and alkalis help make things like soap.

Reactions of Acids

Acids can be neutralised by oxides, hydroxides and carbonates. Here's a whole page about what happens...

Metal Oxides and Metal Hydroxides are Alkalis

1) Some metal oxides and metal hydroxides dissolve in water. These soluble compounds are alkalis.
2) Metal oxides and metal hydroxides react with acids to form a salt and water.

Acid + Metal Oxide → Salt + Water

Acid + Metal Hydroxide → Salt + Water

(These are neutralisation reactions of course)

The Combination of Metal and Acid Decides the Salt

All these reactions follow the same pattern — so once you know it, you should always be able to work out the products from the reactants.

Hydrochloric acid	+	Copper oxide	→	Copper chloride	+	water
Hydrochloric acid	+	Sodium hydroxide	→	Sodium chloride	+	water
Sulfuric acid	+	Zinc oxide	→	Zinc sulfate	+	water
Sulfuric acid	+	Sodium hydroxide	→	Sodium sulfate	+	water
Nitric acid	+	Magnesium oxide	→	Magnesium nitrate	+	water
Nitric acid	+	Potassium hydroxide	→	Potassium nitrate	+	water

Metal Carbonates give Salt + Water + Carbon Dioxide

Carbonates give off carbon dioxide when they react with acids.

Acid + Metal Carbonate → Salt + Water + Carbon Dioxide

Here are two examples. (Notice how the equations are quite similar.)

E.g. Hydrochloric acid + sodium carbonate → sodium chloride + water + carbon dioxide
Hydrochloric acid + calcium carbonate → calcium chloride + water + carbon dioxide

I just love acid-plus-metal hydroxide-minus-water and vinegar crisps...

They're my favourites. There are quite a few scary-looking equations here, but don't panic. The patterns are pretty clear — so once you've learnt a couple you should find the rest a lot easier (what a relief).

Indigestion Tablets and Drug Testing

If you've ever had heartburn, you'll know how important the stuff on this page is...

Heartburn Tablets Neutralise Hydrochloric Acid

1) The stomach produces hydrochloric acid (HCl) to help with digestion. The enzymes that break down food in the stomach work best in an acidic environment.
2) Having acid in the stomach also helps to kill bacteria — making it less likely that you'll get food poisoning.
3) Heartburn and nausea (feeling sick) is caused by too much hydrochloric acid in the stomach.
4) Antacid tablets contain bases (e.g. sodium bicarbonate, magnesium hydroxide, calcium carbonate and aluminium hydroxide).
5) They neutralise the excess acid and make you feel better.
6) More effective antacid tablets neutralise more stomach acid.

You can work out the equations for the neutralisation reactions using the patterns you learnt on page 44.

Medical Drugs are Tested Before They're Sold

1. All drugs, including indigestion tablets, need to be tested before they can be used. Drugs are first developed by testing on human tissues in the lab.
2. The next step is to develop and test the drug using live animals.
3. Then the drug's tested on healthy human volunteers to find out whether there are any side effects.
4. If the drug doesn't have too many side effects it's then tested on patients.

1) Drug testing on humans and animals raises lots of issues.
2) Some people think that testing on animals is the best way to check if drugs are safe. But others think it's cruel because the drug may harm the animals. Here are some arguments for and against animal testing:

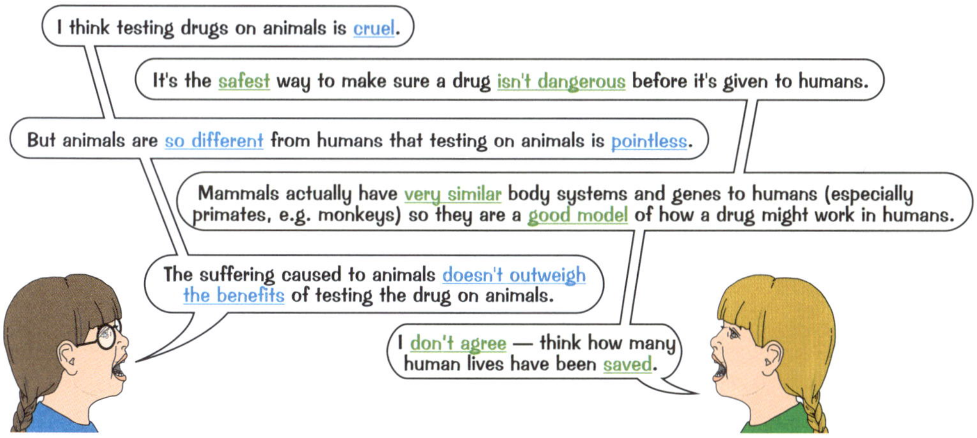

3) When drugs are tested on humans they can still have negative effects, e.g. side effects not seen in animals.
4) When the drug is tested on patients, its effects are compared with people who aren't taking the drug. Some think it's wrong that those people aren't allowed to take drugs that may save their life.

Heartburn — why do you miss when my baby kisses me?

As soon as they develop a drug that teaches you GCSE Science I'll be out of a job, and you'll be pretty happy. It's probably not going to happen between now and your exams though, so maybe — just to be safe — you should learn this the normal way. Cover it up, write down what you remember and check what you missed.

Genes and Chromosomes

Cells are the building blocks of your body. They contain the code that controls your physical characteristics — like whether you have blonde or black hair, the voice of a songbird or one that can crack concrete...

Animal Cells have Three Main Parts

There are three parts of an animal cell that you need to know about:

1) NUCLEUS
Contains genetic material that controls the activities of the cell.

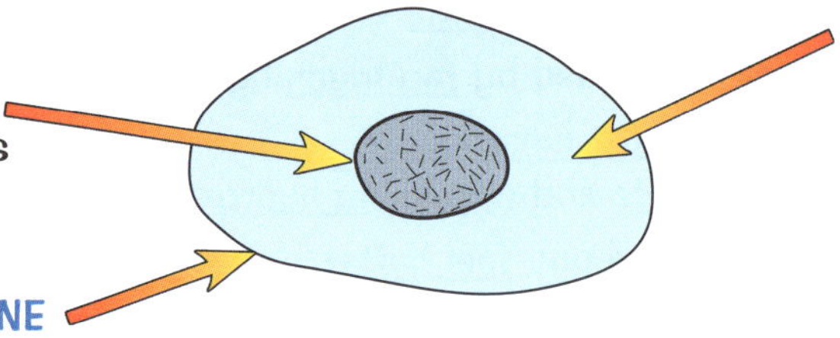

2) CYTOPLASM
A gel-like substance where most of the chemical reactions happen.

3) CELL MEMBRANE
Holds the cell together and controls what goes in and out.

You Need to Know What Chromosomes and Genes Are

Whether you're talking about animals or plants, this basic stuff about genes is pretty much the same...

1) Genetic information in the nucleus is carried as chromosomes.

2) Chromosomes usually come in pairs. For example, the human cell nucleus contains 23 pairs of chromosomes.

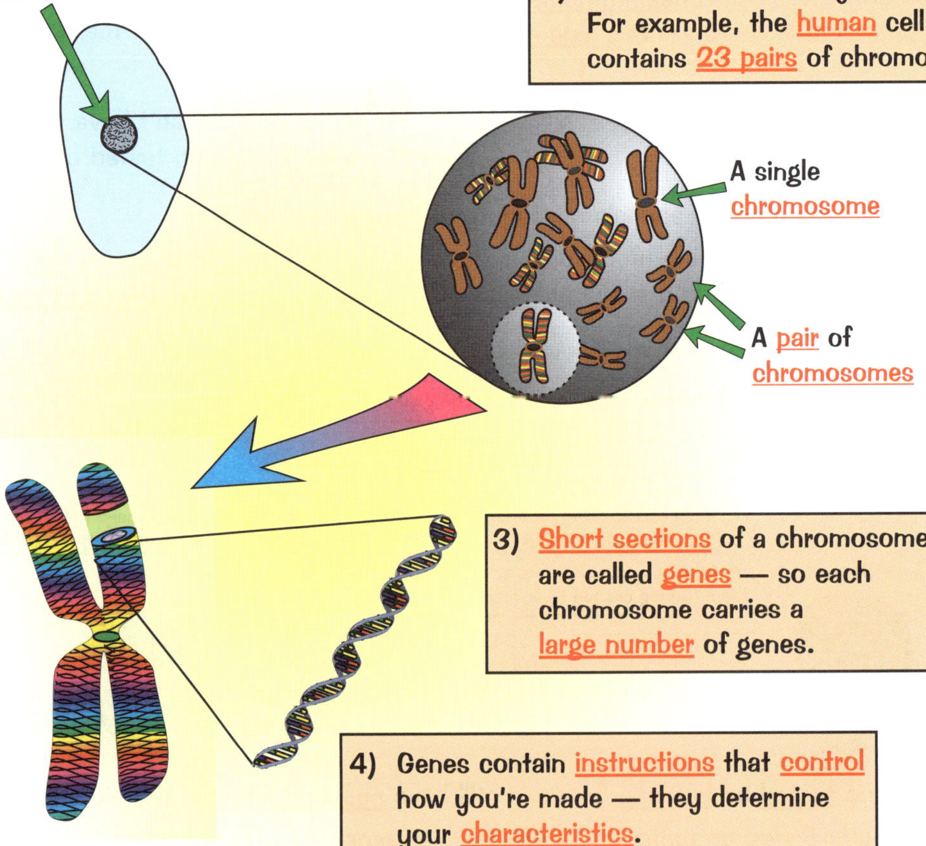

3) Short sections of a chromosome are called genes — so each chromosome carries a large number of genes.

4) Genes contain instructions that control how you're made — they determine your characteristics.

It's hard being a gene — so much to remember...

You, me and that dying plant in the corner all have cells that contain chromosomes and genes. Get your head around what they are — it's the first step in understanding nearly everything that goes on in your body.

Variation in Plants and Animals

You'll probably have noticed that not all people are identical. There are reasons for this.

Organisms of the Same Species Have Differences

1) Members of the same species look at least slightly different — e.g. in a crowd of people there'll be different hair colours, nose shapes and heights, etc.
2) These differences are called the variation within a species.
3) There are two causes of variation: genes and the environment.

Different Genes Cause Variation

1) Organisms inherit genes from their parents.
2) Most animals (and a lot of plants) get some genes from the mother and some from the father.
3) This combination of genes from two parents causes genetic variation.
4) Some characteristics are determined only by genes (e.g. a plant's flower colour, an animal's eye colour).

The Environment Also Causes Variation

1) The environment an organism lives and grows in also causes differences between members of the same species.
2) This is called environmental variation.

   For example, it can cover anything from having yellow leaves to getting a suntan to dyeing your hair purple.

A plant grown on a nice sunny windowsill would have lots of green leaves.

The same plant grown in darkness would grow tall and spindly and have yellow leaves — these are environmental variations.

Most Characteristics are Due to Genes AND the Environment

1) Most characteristics (e.g. body weight, height, skin colour, etc.) are determined by a mixture of genetic and environmental factors.
2) For example, the maximum height that an animal or plant could grow to is determined by its genes. But whether it actually grows that tall depends on its environment (e.g. how much food it gets).

Environmental variation — like sun and scattered showers...

So, you're partly the way you are because of the genes you got from your parents. But you can't blame it all on them — your environment has an effect too. So actually what's made you unique is both. Groovy.

Alleles and Genetic Disorders

You inherit things like lovely blue eyes and a big nose from your parents — but that's not all you can inherit...

Different Versions of Genes are Called Alleles

1) Your cells have two of each chromosome (see page 46). This means there are two of each gene.
2) Each gene can exist in different forms called alleles.
3) The different alleles cause different versions of a characteristic (e.g. blue eyes vs brown eyes). However, only one version of the characteristic will show up.
4) You can have one or two types of allele for each characteristic.
5) Alleles can be dominant or recessive — the dominant allele will always show up if it's present. So:
   - If you have two dominant alleles, or one dominant and one recessive allele, the characteristic caused by the dominant allele will show up.
   - If you have two recessive alleles, the recessive characteristic will show up.

Genetic Disorders are Caused by Faulty Alleles

Some disorders are caused by faulty alleles — and these can be inherited. Here are some examples...

1) Cystic fibrosis causes the body to make thick sticky mucus in the air passages and digestive system.
2) Polydactyly causes people to have extra toes or fingers.
3) Sickle-cell anaemia changes the shape of red blood cells so they can't carry as much oxygen as normal.
4) Haemophilia stops blood from clotting properly so even small cuts can kill.

The Likelihood of Genetic Disorders can be Predicted

1) Punnett squares can help you figure out how likely it is that two parents will have a child with a genetic disorder. They're basically just grids — so don't panic.
2) Letters are used to represent alleles. Capital letters are used for dominant alleles (e.g. 'S') and small letters for recessive alleles (e.g. 's').

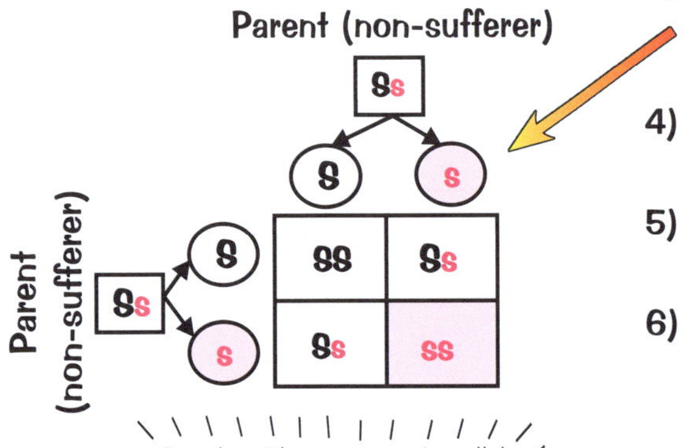

People with one recessive allele for a genetic disorder are called carriers. In this example both parents are carriers.

3) This example shows sickle-cell anaemia. A person will only suffer from sickle-cell anaemia if they have two recessive alleles (ss).
4) Here, each parent has one dominant normal blood cell allele (S) and one recessive sickle-cell allele (s).
5) You line up one parent's alleles down the side and the other parent's across the top.
6) Then you pair up the alleles in the Punnett square to see the different possible combinations of alleles the children might inherit.
7) In this example there's a one in four chance a child will have sickle-cell anaemia (ss).

We know of over 4000 different genetic disorders...

Alleles are just different versions of the same gene — and sometimes an allele is faulty and causes a genetic disorder. But we can predict the chances of getting some disorders, and some can even be treated...

Treating Genetic Disorders

So genetic disorders can be pretty nasty. But there may be a solution — there's been loads of research into the causes and the treatment of genetic diseases, so they could soon be a thing of the past...

It's Possible to Screen for Genetic Disorders

1) We can screen (test) the genes of adults, foetuses and embryos to see if they have a genetic disorder.
   - Adults might choose to be screened before having children to see if they're a carrier for a disorder.
   - Foetuses (unborn babies) are commonly screened for diseases such as cystic fibrosis.
   - Embryos are screened during IVF treatments so that the healthiest (most likely to survive) can be implanted into the mother.
2) However, genetic screening can raise a lot of issues. For example:

ADULT

1) If a person knows they carry the allele for a genetic disorder, it may affect whether they choose to have children.
2) If a person finds out they're going to get ill in the future, it can be hard for them to deal with.
3) If a test showed that someone was likely to get ill, it may stop them being able to get health and life insurance.

FOETUS

1) If a parent finds out their unborn baby has a genetic disorder, they may feel they can't cope or the child will suffer too much.
2) They may decide to have an abortion.

EMBRYO

1) During IVF, the embryos can be tested for genetic disorders.
2) If an embryo tests positive, the parents may have to choose whether to implant the embryo or destroy it.

Gene Therapy Could be Used to Treat Genetic Disorders

1) Gene therapy is a new, experimental treatment for genetic disorders.
2) A new, working version of a faulty gene is inserted into a patient's cells.
3) These cells would then be able to work properly and the symptoms would disappear.
4) For example, scientists are currently trying to cure cystic fibrosis with gene therapy:

> A working copy of the gene can be inserted into the cells in the airways. Trials have been done to test the gene therapy on patients. However, the new copy of the gene only worked for a short while.

5) So, gene therapy still needs a lot of research and testing.

Gene therapy — talk things through with Dr Levi...

Gene therapy is a bit of an ethical minefield. It throws up all sorts of questions, like exactly what should be classed as a 'disorder' that needs fixing. Many people would argue that treating cystic fibrosis is a good thing, but what about high blood pressure, or mad, curly hair, or a really odd laugh... where does it stop?

Revision Summary for Section 2.1

Phew — finally, the end of that section. It was a bit of a tough one — lots of complex ideas, but hopefully it all made sense. Time to find out anyway. Have a go at these questions — if there are any you get wrong or can't answer just go back and reread the page, then come back and have another go.

1) List the five sense organs.
2) Where would you find the following receptors in a human: a) smell, b) taste, c) light, d) touch, e) sound?
3) Where do motor neurones carry signals to?
4) What is the purpose of a reflex action?
5) Describe the pathway of a reflex arc from stimulus to response.
6) Explain how a flicked ruler can be heard.
7) What unit is used to measure loudness?
8) What is homeostasis?
9) How does constriction of blood vessels help keep you warm?
10) What is a hormone?
11) Where is insulin made?
12) What is diabetes? What's the difference between Type 1 and Type 2 diabetes?
13) What does this symbol mean? →

14) What type of ions are always present in: a) acids and b) alkalis?
15) What is neutralisation? Write down the general equation for neutralisation.
16) Complete the word equation for this neutralisation: Hydrochloric acid + copper oxide →
17)* Balance the following equation, showing sodium carbonate neutralising hydrochloric acid.
$HCl + Na_2CO_3 \rightarrow NaCl + H_2O + CO_2$
18) What symptoms do antacid tablets treat? How do they work?
19) List the main stages in testing a new drug.
20) Name the three main parts of an animal cell.
21) Where in a cell would you find chromosomes?
22) What are genes?
23) Name an animal characteristic that is determined only by genes.
24) Name an animal characteristic that is determined by a mixture of genes and the environment.
25) What is meant by the terms dominant allele and recessive allele?
26) Name two disorders that can be genetically inherited.
27)* A faulty version of a gene causes a genetic disorder. The faulty allele (B) is dominant and the normal allele (b) is recessive. One parent is a sufferer (Bb) and the other parent is a non-sufferer (bb). Draw a Punnett square to show how likely it is that their child will be a sufferer.
28) What is genetic screening?
29) How does gene therapy work?

*Answers on page 108.

Limestone

Limestone is great. It can be used for building stuff or it can be fiddled about with to make loads of useful products. For example, it's used to make mortar, cement, concrete and even glass. I told you that it's great.

Limestone is Used as a Building Material

1) Limestone is quarried (dug) out of the ground.
2) This can cause the same problems as mining metals (see page 22).
3) It's great for making into blocks for building with. Fine old buildings like cathedrals are often made purely from limestone blocks. It's also used for statues.
4) Limestone can also be crushed up into chippings and used in road surfacing.

St Paul's cathedral is made out of limestone.

Limestone is Mainly Calcium Carbonate

1) Limestone is mainly made up of calcium carbonate — $CaCO_3$.
2) When it's heated it breaks down to make calcium oxide (quicklime) and carbon dioxide.

calcium carbonate (limestone) → calcium oxide (quicklime) + carbon dioxide

$$CaCO_3 \rightarrow CaO + CO_2$$

Quicklime Reacts with Water to Produce Slaked Lime

When you add water to quicklime you get slaked lime. Slaked lime is actually calcium hydroxide.

quicklime + water → slaked lime

$$CaO + H_2O \rightarrow Ca(OH)_2$$

Slaked lime can be used in construction to make lime putty, which is used for plastering walls.

Limestone is Used to Make Other Useful Things Too

1) Powdered limestone is heated in a kiln (big oven) with powdered clay to make cement.

2) Cement can be mixed with sand and water to make mortar. Mortar is the stuff you stick bricks together with.
3) Or you can mix cement with sand, water and gravel to make concrete.
4) And believe it or not — limestone is also used to make glass. You just heat it with sand and sodium carbonate until it melts.
5) Concrete, cement and glass are all used as building materials.

Tough revision here — this stuff's rock hard...

Wow. It sounds like you can make pretty much anything with limestone. Fred Flintstone managed to make his car wheels and bowling balls out of rock, although I'm not 100% certain if it was limestone.

Metals

Rocks like limestone aren't the only useful materials for building. Nope, metals come in pretty handy too. There are lots of different ones and they have different properties — so are useful for different things...

Metals are Strong and Bendy and They're Great Conductors

All metals have some fairly similar basic properties:

1) STRONG — they're good for holding weight.
2) HARD — they don't break easily.
3) MALLEABLE — they can be bent or hammered into different shapes.
4) CONDUCTORS — they're great conductors of heat and electricity.
5) RESISTANT TO CORROSION — they don't break down easily.
6) DUCTILE — they can be drawn out into thin wires.

Strong metals often have high tensile strength — this means it takes a lot of force to break them.

Different Metals have Different Properties

Lead

1) Malleable — it can be moulded into shape.
2) Unreactive — it doesn't corrode.

Lead is moulded around the joins in a roof (e.g. where the chimney joins on) to form a waterproof seal — this is called flashing.

Iron / Steel

1) Very strong — it has a high tensile strength.
2) Cheap to produce.
3) Rusts very easily.

Steel is used for its strength to make supporting structures and fixings, e.g. screws and bolts.

Copper

1) Malleable — it can be made into sheets and pipes.
2) Ductile — it can be made into wires.
3) Strong.
4) Excellent conductor of electricity.
5) High melting point — so it can cope well with high temperatures.
6) Doesn't corrode with water.

Copper is ideal for water pipes and hot water tanks. It doesn't corrode like iron, or melt like some plastics. Very pure copper is used to make the wires in electrical circuits.

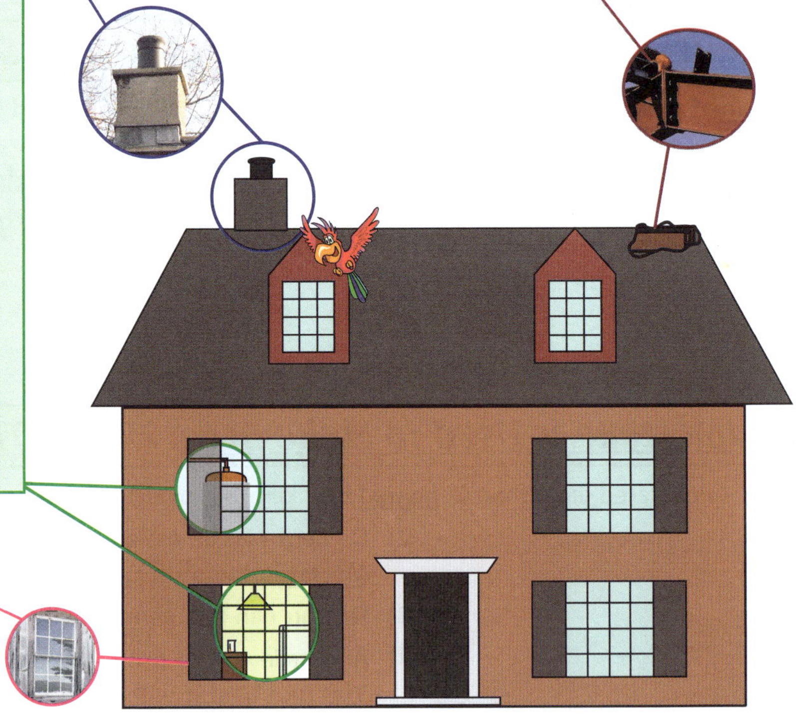

Aluminium

1) Lightweight.
2) Strong.
3) Malleable.
4) Resistant to corrosion.

Aluminium is used for window frames.

Metals are also used by orchestras — they're great conductors...

You wouldn't want to use steel to seal gaps in your roof. A couple of decent rain showers and you'd just have a pretty little pile of rust and a wet carpet. You need to match uses to properties.

Polymers

The plastics we use in day-to-day life are all polymers. They're pretty useful — you can keep things in them, wear them, carry things in them or use them to build with. And they all began life as crude oil...

Chemicals from Crude Oil can be Used to Make Polymers

1) Polymers are long-chain molecules.
2) They're made by joining together lots of small molecules. These are called monomers.
3) Crude oil contains lots of small molecules that can be used to make polymers.
4) The process of making them is called polymerisation (surprising that...).
5) For example, ethene is a monomer. It joins with lots of other ethene molecules to make polyethene.

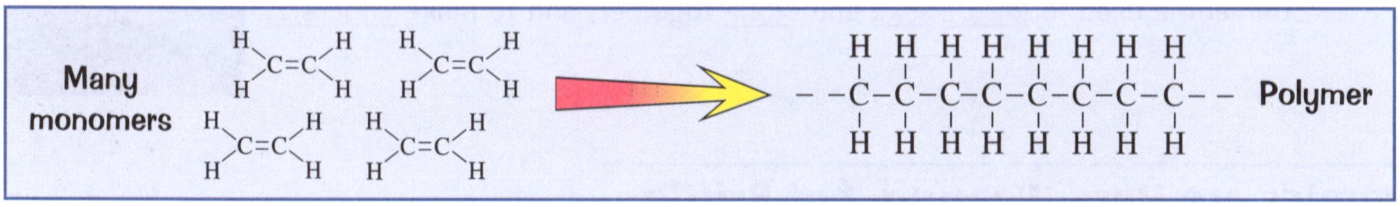

6) Polyethene is used in construction, and so are some other polymers, e.g. polystyrene, polypropene and PVC.

Polymers' Properties Decide What They're Used For

Different polymers have different physical properties. This makes them suited for different uses.

1) WATERPROOF — Polymers don't let water leak through so they're used to make cups and bottles. They're also used in construction for pipes and guttering.
2) FLEXIBILITY — some polymers are pretty bendy and stretchy. Polyethene is flexible so is good for plastic bags and squeezy bottles.
3) LOW MELTING POINT — some polymers have a low melting point so they're no good for anything that'll get very hot, e.g. a kettle. When melted, polymers can easily be moulded into different shapes.

4) POOR CONDUCTORS OF HEAT — polymers are good insulators — they generally don't conduct heat well. E.g. they're great for things like coffee cups and pan handles — they won't allow the heat to burn your hands.

5) POOR CONDUCTORS OF ELECTRICITY — polymers don't let electricity flow through them. So, handily, they can be used as electric wire insulation — the electric current can't travel through the insulation, just down the wire, so it's safe for you to handle.
6) RESISTANT TO CORROSION — polymers don't break down easily. This means they can be used for containers to store corrosive chemicals, e.g. bleach bottles. But, if a polymer ends up in a landfill it won't rot away so could be there for thousands of years.

Plastic pans — not such a great idea...

Polymers are everywhere and have loads of different uses. They're poor conductors of heat so are used for the casings of hot things like hair dryers. Very useful — unless you're Homer Simpson or Patrick Stewart...

Ceramics

People have been making and using ceramics for thousands of years, e.g. pottery and glass are ceramics. Today ceramics are used loads in construction.

Ceramics are Materials Made by Heating

1) POTTERY and PORCELAIN — made by heating clay. Clay can be moulded into any shape you like. It can be glazed to add colours or patterns.
2) GLASS — made by heating sand with other chemicals. It's transparent and can be made into any shape, including flat sheets.
3) CEMENT — made by heating limestone with clay. Cement is used to stick bricks and stone together, and to make concrete.

Ceramics are Hard-Wearing, but Brittle

Properties of ceramics:

1) HARD-WEARING — they don't scratch easily.
2) HIGH MELTING POINT — they're heat-resistant and also fire-resistant.
3) INERT — they don't corrode or react with chemicals.
4) BRITTLE — they aren't very flexible and break easily.

They're Useful for Building Houses and Serving Food

These properties make ceramics useful for loads of building materials and household things...

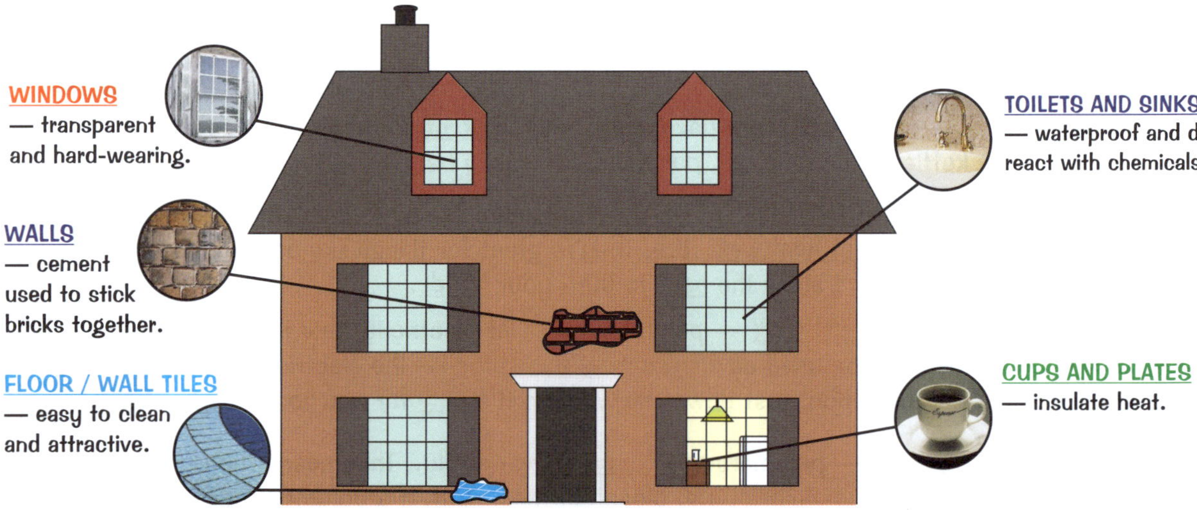

The properties of ceramics make them really useful in industry too:

1) As they have high melting points ceramics are useful for lining big industrial furnaces.
2) They don't conduct electricity so can also be used as insulators on power lines.

So be careful with your mum's best china...

...it smashes easily, but more importantly she'll probably kill you.

Ceramics don't burn, melt, rot, rust or get eaten by termites, which is handy really. The only downside is they're easily broken or smashed — so keep your cricket balls and clumsy hands away from them.

Composites

Once upon a time someone took a carrot and a cake. They stuck them together to make a tasty new creation. The same can be done to two or more materials to make new super useful construction materials...

Composites Combine the Properties of Two or More Materials

1) Manufacturers and designers can't always find one material that has all the properties they need.
2) A mixture of two materials often provides the solution — these mixtures are called COMPOSITES.
3) The properties of a composite are a combination of the properties of the materials it's made from.
4) Some examples of composites are:

FIBREGLASS

1) Fibreglass is plastic reinforced by small fibres of glass.
2) This makes it stronger than plastic but not as brittle as glass.
3) It can also be moulded into different shapes.
4) It's used to make things like baths.

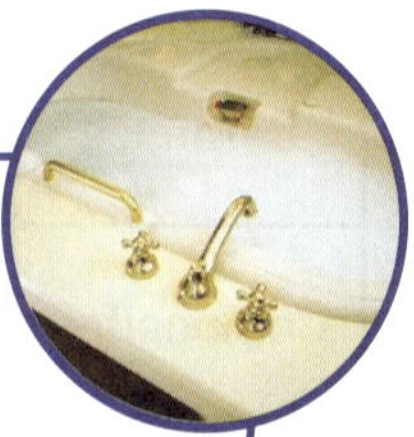

PLYWOOD / MDF

1) These are materials made out of bits of wood stuck together with glue.
2) Plywood is thin sheets of wood glued and stacked together.
3) MDF (medium-density fibreboard) is made of wood fibres stuck together.
4) Plywood and MDF are strong and making them is pretty cheap.
5) They're used loads in furniture and flooring.

REINFORCED CONCRETE

1) This is concrete made stronger by adding rods of metal — usually steel.
2) The concrete provides the basic strength while the metal stops the whole thing bending or stretching.
3) This composite is very strong — making it an ideal material for constructing buildings.

Two materials went on holiday — they stayed on a compo-site...

If you have two pretty useful materials then combining them together could make one very useful material. The properties of composites come from the properties of these components, e.g. mint choc chip ice cream is so tasty because it combines crunchy chocolate bits with minty fresh ice cream. Mmmm.

Choosing Materials for a Product

With so many different materials to choose from it's hard to decide which one is best for a job.

Knowing the Properties of Materials Will Help You Decide

Here are some of the good (and not so good) properties of manufactured materials:

Material	Advantages	Disadvantages
Metals	Strong and hard Conduct heat and electricity	Some are heavy (e.g. steel) Some are expensive (e.g. gold) Some corrode (e.g. iron)
Polymers	Cheap and light	Non-renewable Non-biodegradable
Ceramics	Hard-wearing Insulate heat and electricity	Brittle
Composites	Strong Flexible	Some are non-renewable Some are non-biodegradable

Non-renewable means the material will run out one day. Non-biodegradable means it won't break down.

You can Choose from Modern or Traditional Building Materials

1) When constructing a building you can choose from traditional or more modern building materials. Traditional building materials tend to be naturally occurring, e.g. wood and stone, and modern ones are usually man-made, e.g. polymers, ceramics and composites.
2) Traditional materials are often more sustainable than modern ones — this means that using them doesn't hurt the environment as much and they won't run out.
3) If you're asked in the exam to pick between them don't just say, 'Modern materials are always way better than traditional ones'. Modern materials have advantages over traditional materials, but they also have disadvantages. Here are a few examples:

Steel or wooden frames?
Steel frames are stronger than wooden ones, but they're non-biodegradable and often don't look as nice.

Fibreglass or straw bale insulation?
Straw can be placed inside walls to keep houses warm. This is cheaper than fibreglass insulation and more sustainable. But it's a fire risk and may also rot over time.

Brick or cob walls?
Cob is made up mostly of clay, sand and water.
It's cheap and good for the environment.
Bricks are much stronger, but they're more expensive.

4) So the material you choose depends on what properties you want.
E.g. if you're rebuilding an old farmhouse you'll probably use wood beams to match what's already there. But a block of high-rise flats would need to have much stronger steel beams.

I was going to make a joke about cob walls, but it was just too corny...

Sustainable building is pretty important. Using materials which don't hurt the environment is great, but this doesn't always make the best building. There's a reason tower blocks aren't made from bales of straw.

Fuels from Crude Oil

Fuels are dead important for our everyday lives. They're needed for making toast, staying warm and getting your parents' old car going.

Lots of Fuels Come from Crude Oil

1) Crude oil is a fossil fuel.
2) Fossil fuels are hydrocarbons (see page 20).
   Hydrocarbons contain only hydrogen and carbon atoms.
3) Here are some examples of fossil fuels:
   - Petrol and diesel — used as fuel in cars, buses and trains.
   - Kerosene (also known as paraffin) — used as fuel for aeroplanes.
   - Natural gas and heating oil — used in homes to provide central heating and fuel for cooking.
4) Different fuels have a different energy content.
5) Energy content is the amount of energy given out when 1 kg of fuel or 1 litre of fuel is burnt.
6) But there are other things to consider when choosing a fuel.
   For example, hydrogen fuel has a higher energy content than fossil fuels but storing it's tricky — it's a gas so it needs lots of space. Petrol and diesel are liquids so we can store more in the same amount of space.

You can compare the energy contents of different fuels by burning them to heat a volume of water. Fuel with a higher energy content will increase the temperature of the water more.

Hydrocarbons Release Energy When They Burn

If you're doing the higher exam paper, you may be asked to balance the symbol equations.

1) When hydrocarbons burn in plenty of oxygen, energy is released as heat. This is the equation for the reaction:

$$\text{hydrocarbon} + \text{oxygen} \rightarrow \text{carbon dioxide} + \text{water} \quad (+\ \text{heat energy})$$

$$\text{e.g. } C_5H_{12} + 8O_2 \rightarrow 5CO_2 + 6H_2O$$

2) Shorter hydrocarbons are more volatile (form a vapour more easily) so are easier to ignite.
3) There's a basic pattern for the combustion of hydrocarbon fuels:
   - The number of oxygen atoms needed depends on the size of the hydrocarbon molecule.
   - The bigger the molecule, the more carbon and hydrogen there is...
   - ...and so the more oxygen you need for combustion..
   - ...and the more carbon dioxide and water you end up with in total after the reaction.
4) **Most hydrocarbons in crude oil have the general formula C_nH_{2n+2}.**

   You can use this to work out the chemical formula for any hydrocarbon molecule if you know a bit about it. For example, a molecule in petrol has 8 carbon atoms. This means n=8 so its formula must be C_8H_{18} — (H is [2 × 8] + 2 = 18).

Learn this lot till your head is fuel — or oil be after you...

The good thing about hydrocarbons is that the clue's in the name — they're made of hydrogen and carbon — and nothing else. The equations aren't too scary either — the products are always carbon dioxide and water (and energy). And the bigger the hydrocarbon, the more water and carbon dioxide you make.

Problems with Fuels from Crude Oil

Nothing as amazingly useful as crude oil would be without its problems. No, that'd be too good to be true.

Crude Oil is Non-Renewable — it's Running Out

1) Crude oil is pretty crucial to everyday life. But the supplies we use don't replace themselves.
2) This makes crude oil a non-renewable fuel. There's a finite (set) amount — one day it will run out.
3) So, scientists are developing renewable energy sources — ones that won't run out, e.g. solar power and wind power.

Burning Fossil Fuels Releases Pollution

1) Power stations burn huge amounts of fossil fuels to make electricity. Cars also burn a lot of fossil fuels.
2) When fossil fuels are burnt they release:
   - water vapour.
   - carbon dioxide — this causes global warming (see below).
   - sulfur dioxide (if there are bits of sulfur in the fuel) — this causes acid rain.
   - carbon monoxide (a poisonous gas) and soot if there's not enough oxygen for the fuel to burn properly.

More Carbon Dioxide is Causing Global Warming

1) The level of carbon dioxide in the atmosphere is increasing — mostly because of the large amounts of fossil fuels humans burn.
2) Scientists agree that this extra carbon dioxide is causing the temperature of the Earth to increase. This is known as global warming.
3) This warming could cause big changes in climate and weather patterns all over the world. Flooding due to the polar ice caps melting might happen too.

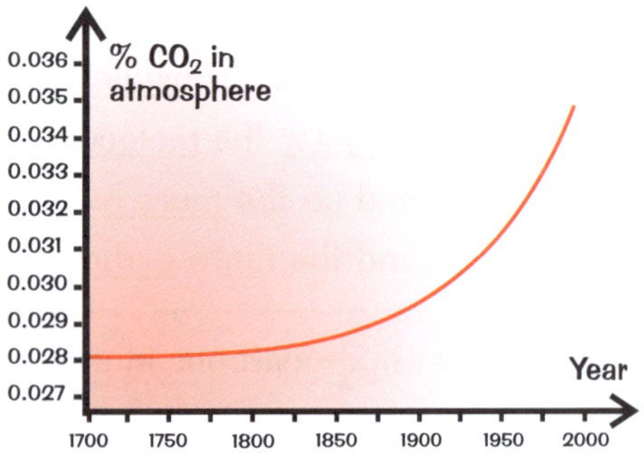

There's more about global warming in Unit 3 — page 97.

Need an icebreaker? Try global warming...

Crude oil is really important to our lives, but it causes a few problems. Burning it sends lots of nasty gases into the atmosphere and it's causing global warming. There are also problems with moving it around — e.g. oil spills can happen if a tanker crashes. This can be a disaster for the local environment — lots of animals can be poisoned by the oil and die. These are heavy prices to pay, but at the moment we rely on crude oil.

Alternatives to Fossil Fuels

Alternative energy isn't just for hippies. Many see renewable fuels as the only way to stop global warming. But, they do have some disadvantages...

Renewable Energy Sources Will Never Run Out

Renewable energy sources can be used instead of fossil fuels. The renewables are:
1) Wave 2) Tidal 3) Wind 4) Hydroelectric 5) Solar 6) Geothermal 7) Biomass

- These will never run out.
- Most of them do damage the environment, but in less nasty ways than non-renewables.
- But some provide less energy than non-renewables and some are unreliable because they depend on the weather.

Wave Power — Lots of Little Wave Converters

1) Wave generators can be located around the coast.
2) As waves come in to the shore the water moves up and down — this pushes air through a turbine which drives a generator.
3) There's no pollution. The main problems are spoiling the view and being a hazard to boats.
4) They're fairly unreliable though — waves tend to die out when the wind drops.
5) Setting them up is expensive but you don't have to pay much to keep them running — there are no fuel costs.

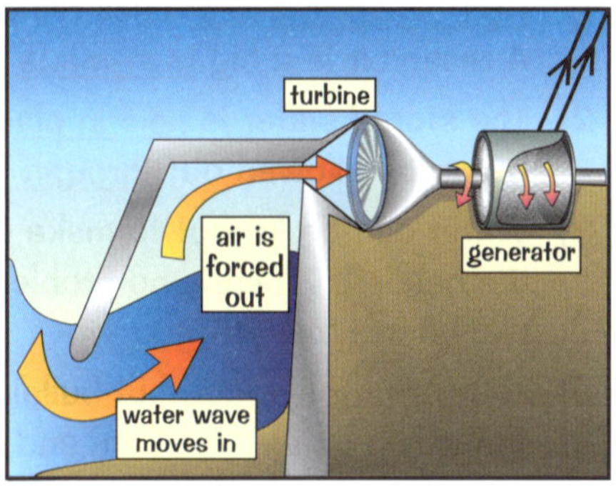

Tidal Barrages — Using Water and Tides

1) Tidal barrages are big dams built across river estuaries. An estuary is the part of the river where it meets the sea. As they're at the coast they have tides as well.
2) There are turbines inside the barrages — these can be turned to generate electricity.
3) As the tide comes in it fills up the estuary. When the tide goes out, the water passes through turbines and makes electricity.

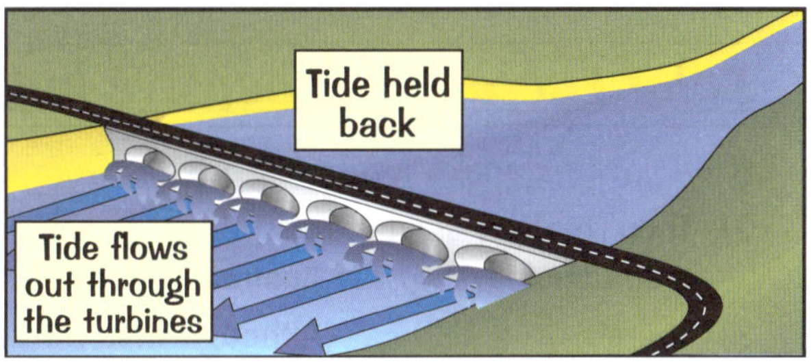

4) Tides are pretty reliable — they happen twice a day without fail. But the height of the tide can change — lower tides will provide less energy.
5) There's no pollution. The main problems are blocking the path for boats and spoiling the view. They also change the habitat of the wildlife, e.g. sea creatures and beasties who live in the sand.
6) Building the barrages is pretty expensive. But they don't need any fuel and keeping them going is cheap.
7) Tidal barrages can only be built in a few of the most suitable estuaries.

Renewable energy — wave goodbye to fossil fuels...

It's really important that you know the big big differences between tidal power and wave power. Yes, they both use salty sea water, but are pretty different apart from that. Make sure you remember this for the exam — you could be throwing away some easy marks if you get the two mixed up.

Alternatives to Fossil Fuels

Waves and tides aren't the only sources of renewable energy — here are another three for your enjoyment...

Wind Power — Lots of Little Wind Turbines

1) Lots of wind turbines are put up in windy places — like on hills or round coasts.
2) Wind turns the blades, which turn a generator inside the turbine.
3) There's no pollution (except for a little bit when they're made).
4) But there are problems. You need about 5000 wind turbines to replace one coal-fired power station. They don't look very nice and can be noisy, which is bad for people living nearby. There's no power when the wind stops.

Hydroelectricity — Reliable but Damages the Environment

1) Hydroelectric power uses rainwater which is caught and stored in a reservoir. A reservoir is a big man-made lake.
2) The stored water is held in place by a big dam. It can be allowed out through turbines.
3) Water can be let out to make electricity whenever it's needed. There's no problem with reliability except in times of drought.
4) There's no pollution, but building a reservoir floods the valley behind the dam and can be bad for the environment. Some species may lose their habitat.
5) At the start costs are high, but there's no fuel and very low running costs.

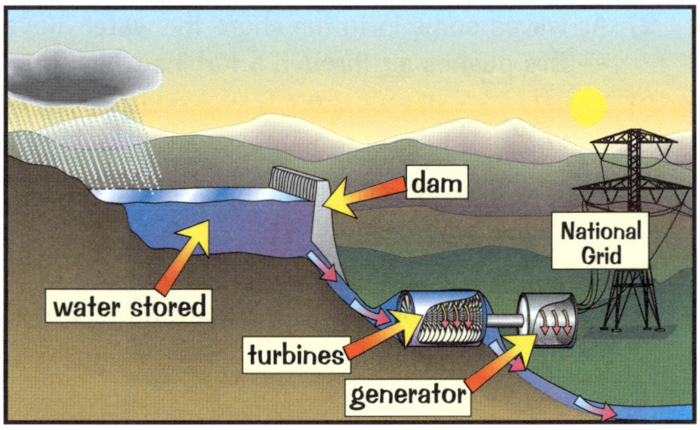

Solar Energy — Expensive but No Environmental Damage

1) Solar cells make electricity directly from sunlight.
2) They're often used in remote places where there's not much choice, e.g. the Australian outback.
3) There's no pollution. (Although they do use quite a lot of energy to make in the first place.)
4) In sunny countries solar power is a very reliable source of energy — but only in the daytime. Solar power can still be used even in cloudy countries like Britain.
5) They cost a lot to put in but after that the energy is free and they cost almost nothing to keep going.

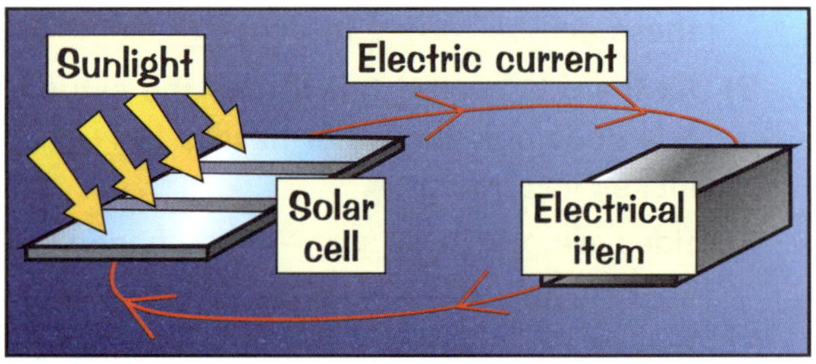

The hydroelectric power you're supplying — it's electrifying...

The big advantage of renewable power is that it doesn't increase the CO_2 level in the atmosphere. Like all good things in life, they also have a number of disadvantages, such as unreliability and environmental damage. The exam could ask you to compare fossil fuels and renewable sources — make sure you know the pros and cons.

Alternatives to Fossil Fuels

Well, who'd know it — there's yet more energy lurking about in piles of rubbish and deep underground.

Geothermal Energy — Heat from Underground

1) Geothermal energy comes from heat underground.
2) The energy can only be used in some places.
3) Water is pumped down to hot rocks and comes back as steam to drive a generator.
4) This gives us brilliant free energy, which doesn't really hurt the environment at all.
5) The main problem is the cost of drilling down to the hot rocks.
6) At the moment there are very few places where we can use geothermal energy.

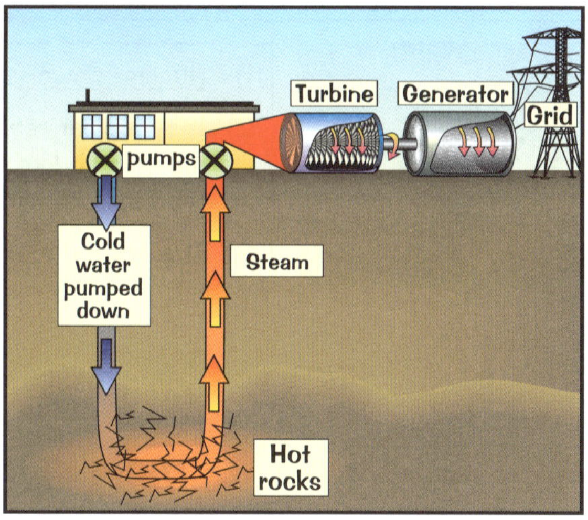

Biomass is Waste That Can be Burnt — Plant Waste and Animal Poo

1) Biomass is the general term for all sorts of organic 'stuff' that can be burnt to make electricity. This can be anything from farm waste, animal droppings and landfill rubbish to specially-grown forests that are replanted when the wood is used.
2) The waste material is burnt in power stations to drive turbines and produce electricity.
3) Burning the waste produces CO_2, which is bad for the environment.
4) But, the plants that grew to produce the waste (or to feed the animals that made the dung) would have absorbed CO_2 from the atmosphere as they were growing.
5) So no extra CO_2 is added to the atmosphere when the biomass is burnt.
6) Set-up and fuel costs are often low, since the fuel is usually waste.

Plant material...

...rubbish...

...and poo.

Where there's muck there's gas...

A dung-fired power station opened in Devon in 2002, using animal manure from nearby farms to produce methane. The methane was burnt to produce electricity, and the process also provided hot water for the surrounding area and organic fertiliser to be sold back to the farms. All clever stuff.

Alternatives to Fossil Fuels

As well as renewable sources there's also a non-renewable alternative to fossil fuels — nuclear. It's a clean and easily available source of power. But it has plenty of problems...

Nuclear Energy Comes from Nuclear Fission

1) Nuclear power stations are powered by nuclear reactors.
2) In a nuclear reactor the 'fuel' is uranium or plutonium. The 'fuel' isn't burnt in air like fossil fuels are. Instead the 'fuel' atoms are split up — this is known as nuclear fission. This releases heat energy.
3) This energy is used to heat water, which drives a steam turbine.

Nuclear Power Stations Don't Emit CO_2...

1) One of the biggest problems with fossil fuels is that they give out carbon dioxide as they burn.
2) Carbon dioxide adds to the greenhouse effect, causing global warming (see page 97).
3) Nuclear power stations produce no CO_2, though there are other environmental problems (see below).
4) It's non-renewable but there's enough fuel to last hundreds of years, making it a more long-term solution than fossil fuels.

...but Radioactive Waste is an Environmental Risk

Nuclear power is clean but the nuclear waste is very dangerous and difficult to get rid of safely.

1) Nuclear power produces radioactive waste. This waste gives off radiation. This can be very dangerous for humans.
2) The level of radiation will eventually fall to a safe level.
3) However, the waste can be dangerous for thousands of years. This is why nuclear waste needs to be stored safely.
4) Storage depends on the type of waste — some types of waste are more dangerous than others. E.g. used fuel rods have to be cooled in water before being sealed in glass blocks and buried underground. But gloves or clothing used in a lab are fairly safe.

Nuclear — think that's the name of my face wash...

With fossil fuels running out and renewables unable to meet all our energy needs, nuclear could be the only decent option for the future. That doesn't mean everyone has to like it though — many people disagree with nuclear power because of the environmental damage and the possibility of an explosion.

Comparing Energy Resources

Just in case you haven't quite had enough on the different types of energy resources, here's another page on it. There shouldn't be too much that comes as a shock to you on this page — it's more like a bit of a summary of the last four pages to help you put it all together and see the bigger picture.

Environmental Issues

- If there's a fuel involved, there'll be waste pollution and you'll be using up resources.
- If it relies on the weather, it's often got to be in an exposed place where it sticks out like a sore thumb.

Visual Pollution
Coal, Oil, Gas, Nuclear, Tidal, Waves, Wind, Hydroelectric

Atmospheric Pollution
e.g. Coal, Oil, Gas

Other Problems
Nuclear (dangerous waste, explosions, contamination), Hydroelectric (dams bursting)

Using Up Resources
Coal, Oil, Gas, Nuclear

Noise Pollution
Coal, Oil, Gas, Nuclear, Wind

Disruption of Leisure Activities (e.g. boating)
Waves, Tidal

Disruption of Habitats
Hydroelectric, Tidal

Reliability Issues

- All the non-renewables are reliable energy providers (until they run out).
- Many of the renewable sources rely on the weather. This can be a problem in places like the UK which have unreliable weather.
- The exception is tidal power.

Set-Up Costs

- Renewable resources often need bigger power stations than non-renewables — the bigger the power station, the more expensive.
- Nuclear reactors and hydroelectric dams also need to be very carefully designed to make them safe, which bumps up the cost.

Fuel Costs

- Producing energy from non-renewable sources needs lots of fuel, which is expensive.
- This is because it costs a lot to get the fuel out of the ground and transport it to the power station.
- Renewables don't need any fuel (except biomass). So there's no cost to worry about.

Running Costs

- Renewables usually have the lowest running costs as they keep themselves going.
- Big non-renewable power stations are more expensive to keep going as the fuel is always being burnt. They have to employ lots of people to make sure everything keeps working OK. Getting rid of waste products safely costs a lot — especially nuclear waste.

The biggest problem is we need too much electricity...

It'd be lovely if we could get rid of all the polluting power stations and replace them with clean, green power sources, just like that... but it's not quite that simple. Renewable energy has its problems too, and probably couldn't power the whole country without having a wind farm in everyone's backyard.

Generating Electricity

As you've seen, there are loads of different types of fuels out there and they're a great source of energy for us. But just how do we make really useful electricity from this energy, you ask. Read on...

Most Power Stations Use Steam to Drive a Turbine

1) When we burn fossil fuels (coal, oil and natural gas) they release energy. This energy can be used to generate electricity for our homes.
2) Big power stations all work on the same principle — using steam to turn a turbine.
3) Here's how electricity is generated in a power station:

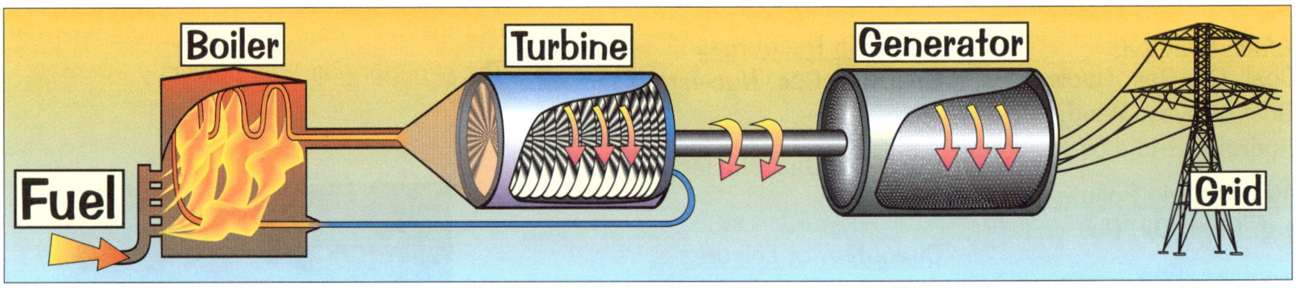

Fuel is burnt and the heat given out is used to boil water. → Steam from the boiling water is used to turn a turbine. → The turbine rotates a generator to create electricity.

4) Nuclear power stations work in pretty much the same way. Except at the beginning a reactor is used to generate heat instead of a boiler.

Electricity Gets Around via the National Grid

1) The National Grid is the network of pylons and cables that covers the whole of Britain.
2) The National Grid takes electrical energy from the power stations to everywhere it's needed, like homes and industry.
3) It means power can be generated anywhere on the grid, and then be supplied anywhere else on the grid.

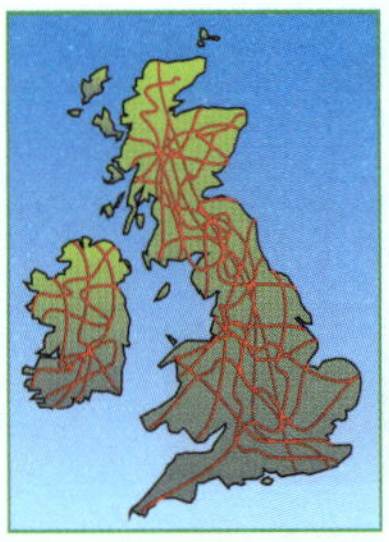

S-team drives a turbine, the A-team drove a van...

The way we make electricity today uses the same idea as steam engines — heating water to make steam which is used to turn the wheels. Steam engines were invented way before you and I were born, in the 17th century. It's amazing that using steam like this is so important today — bet you can't think of many other things that have lasted that long (apart from maybe forks and Bruce Forsyth).

Supplying Electricity

Pumping electricity around the country is best done at high voltage.
That's why it's a bad idea to go climbing all over electricity pylons.

Electricity is Transformed to High Voltage Before Distribution

1) To distribute (move) a lot of electrical power, you either need a high voltage or a high current. But... a higher current makes the cables get hot, which is a waste of all that energy.

2) It's much cheaper to raise ('step-up') the voltage. A step-up transformer is used to boost the voltage before the electricity is sent around the country.

3) Moving the electricity at high voltage means you need big pylons with huge insulators.

4) The voltage has to be 'stepped down' to safe levels that can be used in homes. So, there are local step-down transformers all around towns.

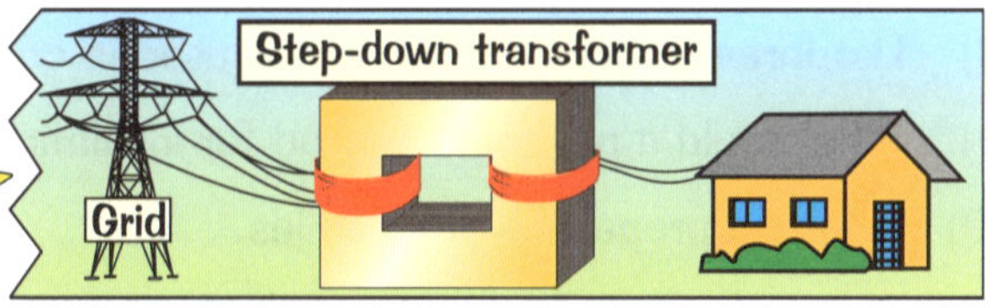

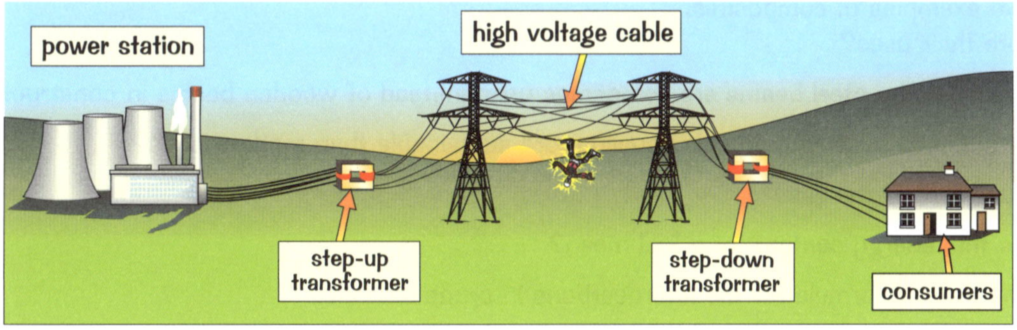

There are Problems with Moving Such Huge Amounts of Energy

1) Even at high voltages, electricity distribution isn't very efficient, so power losses are high.

2) The high voltage is a risk to people — e.g. flying a kite into a power line in the rain could be fatal.

3) Building power lines is pretty bad for the environment. The lines have to be fairly direct so may have to be built through forests and scenic areas.

4) Some people are worried about the effects on the long-term health of people living near power lines. Links with leukaemia (a disease of the blood) have been suggested — but this hasn't been proved.

Revising electricity — great for keeping up with current affairs...

Once you've generated all that electricity, you don't want to waste it by heating up miles of power cables when you're distributing it. So make the voltage high and people in Land's End can still boil the kettle. Problem solved.

Revision Summary for Section 2.2

Aha, here we are again — the end of a section. Hopefully this one wasn't too bad. We've been through loads of different materials and their uses and then ended up looking at lots of renewable and non-renewable power sources. You know the drill by now — here are lots of questions to test yourself with. Don't avoid them if you don't know the answer — go back and learn the stuff and then come back and have another go.

1) What is the formula for the main chemical in limestone?
2) How is quicklime made?
3) What's the chemical name of slaked lime and how is it made?
4) Name three building materials made from limestone.
5) Give three properties that most metals have in common.
6) Why is copper used for making hot water pipes?
7) What is a monomer?
8) List three examples of polymers used in construction.
9) Why would a polymer be good for insulating electrical wires?
10) Give two properties of ceramics.
11) Give two uses of ceramics in the home.
12) a) Give two examples of composites.
    b) What are their uses?
13) Give one reason why steel beams are sometimes used instead of wooden beams in construction.
14) Why are traditional building materials usually more sustainable than modern ones?
15) Give one use for natural gas.
16) What does the 'energy content' of a fuel mean?
17) What is the general formula for the hydrocarbons in crude oil?
18)* Write a balanced symbol equation for the complete combustion of C_7H_{16}.
19) Briefly explain why crude oil is a non-renewable fuel.
20) Explain why burning fossil fuels is causing global warming.
21) Give one advantage and one disadvantage of:
    a) wave power, b) tidal power, c) hydroelectric power, d) solar power, e) energy from biomass.
22) Explain how wind power can be used to generate electricity.
23) Explain how geothermal energy is produced.
24) What is the name of the process for producing energy from nuclear fuels?
25) Why must nuclear waste be disposed of properly?
26) Why are non-renewable sources of energy usually more reliable than renewable ones?
27) Briefly describe how a typical power station generates electricity.
28) How does electricity get from a power station to where it's needed?
29) Explain how 'step-up' and 'step-down' transformers are used in the distribution of electricity.
30) Give one environmental problem of using high voltage power lines to move electricity.

*Answer on page 108

Calculating Power and Current

This section's about your property — think of it as a scientific guide to your home. What could be better...

An Appliance Forms Part of a Circuit

1) When you plug an appliance (e.g. a kettle) into a wall socket, you're connecting it to the mains electricity supply.
2) The 'pins' on the plug are now connected to wires which run through the walls to the point where the electricity supply comes into your house.
3) This makes an electrical circuit a bit like the one shown below. (It's not exactly like this, but you don't have to worry about the details.)

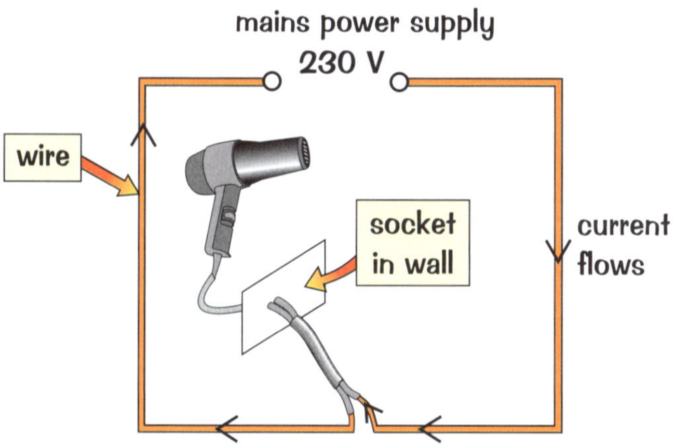

4) When you switch the appliance on, all the bits of wire are connected up. An electric current flows round the circuit and through your appliance. This current is measured in units called amps, A.

A current is a flow of electrical charges.

5) Current is 'pushed' around the circuit by the power supply. This 'push' is called the potential difference (or voltage) of the supply. Potential difference is measured in volts, V.

Power Depends on Potential Difference and Current

1) The power of an appliance is how quickly it transfers (uses) electrical energy (see p. 68 for more on this).
2) Power depends on the potential difference of the supply and the size of the current flowing.
3) Power has units of watts, W.
4) You can calculate the power used by an electrical appliance using this formula:

POWER (watts) = POTENTIAL DIFFERENCE (volts) × CURRENT (amps)

EXAMPLE:

James puts the kettle on.
The potential difference of the mains supply is 230 V.
The current flowing in the circuit is 9 A. Calculate the power used.

ANSWER: Power = Potential Difference × Current = 230 × 9 = 2070 W.

Circuit training — keep fit while you learn...

Mains electricity is great — you just plug in, switch on and there it is... it's almost magical. Never stick your magic wand in a socket, though. Instead, learn about power, potential difference and current — much safer.

Calculating Energy Use and Costs

When you pay an electricity bill, it's the energy your appliances have used that you're paying for.

Power is Energy Used Per Second

1) Energy is normally measured in units of joules, J.
2) The power of an appliance tells you how many joules of electrical energy it transfers (uses) per second.

$$\text{POWER (in W)} = \frac{\text{ENERGY TRANSFERRED (in J)}}{\text{TIME (in s)}}$$

So, 1 watt = 1 joule/second

EXAMPLE: A drill transfers 24 kJ of electrical energy in 1 minute.
Calculate the power of the drill (in watts).

ANSWER: Energy needs to be in joules. 1 kJ = 1000 J, so 24 kJ = 24 000 J.
Time needs to be in seconds. 1 minute = 60 s.
Now use the formula. Power = 24 000 J ÷ 60 s = 400 W.

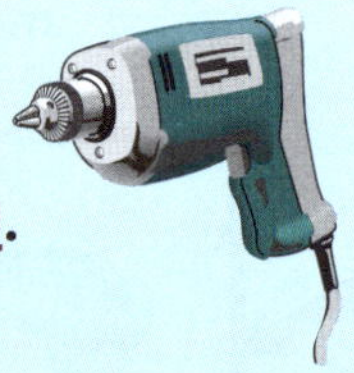

3) If you're looking at more powerful appliances over longer periods of time you should use kilowatts (kW) instead of watts, kilowatt-hours (kWh) instead of joules and hours instead of seconds. (See below.)

Kilowatt-hours (kWh) are "UNITS" of Energy

1) A kilowatt-hour is the amount of electrical energy used by a 1 kW appliance left on for 1 hour.
1 kWh is one unit of electricity.
2) Your electricity meter records how much energy you use in units of kilowatt-hours.

Your electricity meter will look something like this: 00054622 kWh

It shows the total number of units (kWh) used since the meter was fitted. You have to be able to read them for your exam — this one reads 5462 kWh.

The red number shows tenths of a kWh — you can ignore that when you're reading the meter.

3) The energy an appliance uses depends on its power and the time it's on for. Here's the formula for it:

$$\underset{\text{(in kWh)}}{\text{ENERGY UNITS}} = \underset{\text{(in kW)}}{\text{POWER}} \times \underset{\text{(in hours)}}{\text{TIME}}$$

With this one, it's really important to get the units right.

4) If you know how much energy an appliance has used, you can calculate how much that energy costs:

$$\text{Total Cost} = \text{Number of kWh} \times \text{Cost per kWh}$$

EXAMPLE: An electricity supplier charges 12p per kWh.
Find the cost of having an 8.5 kW shower on for 15 minutes.

ANSWER: Energy = Power × Time = 8.5 kW × 0.25 h = 2.125 kWh.
Cost = Number of kWh × Cost per kWh = 2.125 × 12p = 25.5p.

Transfer energy quickly — eat a cream cake then sprint for two hours...

You've probably noticed that there's more than one equation to work out power — you're right, but you've still got to learn them all. Not much fun I'm afraid, but once you know the formulas, physics will seem a lot easier.

Efficiency

If you're an efficient student, you'll learn the greatest amount of information with the least amount of effort...

Appliances Always Waste Some Energy

1) Useful appliances are only useful because they convert energy from one form to another.

   E.g. a kitchen blender converts electrical energy into kinetic (movement) energy.

2) The total energy output is always the same as the energy input, but only some of the output energy is useful.

   So for every joule of electrical energy you put into your blender you'll only get a small amount of it converted into useful kinetic energy.

3) This is because some of the input energy is always lost or wasted, often as heat.

   In the blender example, the rest of the electrical energy is converted into heat and sound energy. This is wasted energy.

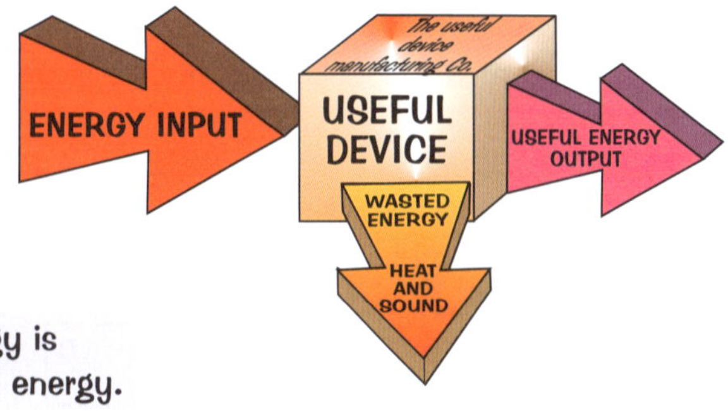

More Efficient Appliances Waste Less Energy

The efficiency of an appliance is defined in two ways:

$$\text{EFFICIENCY} = \frac{\text{USEFUL ENERGY OUT}}{\text{TOTAL ENERGY IN}} \quad \text{OR} \quad \text{EFFICIENCY} = \frac{\text{USEFUL POWER OUT}}{\text{TOTAL POWER IN}}$$

1) To work out the efficiency of an appliance, first find out the total energy or power supplied to the appliance.
2) Then find how much useful energy or power the appliance gives out. The question might tell you this directly, or it might tell you how much is wasted.
3) Then just divide the smaller number by the bigger one to get a value for efficiency somewhere between 0 and 1.
4) If your number is bigger than 1, you've done the division upside down.
5) You can convert the efficiency to a percentage, by multiplying it by 100. E.g. 0.6 = 60%.
6) More efficient appliances waste less energy. If the energy comes from fossil fuels, this is good news for the environment (see page 58).

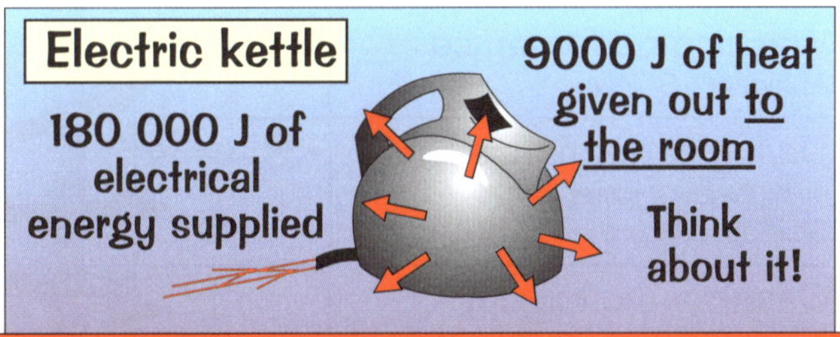

$$\text{Efficiency} = \frac{\text{Useful Energy Out}}{\text{Total Energy In}} = \frac{171\,000}{180\,000} = 0.95$$

Efficiency = pages learned ÷ cups of tea made...

Maybe I'll just go and pop the kettle on — purely for scientific reasons, of course. Whoops — it seems I've ended up pouring hot water all over that tea bag. Oh well, it'd be a shame to waste that lovely tea now...

Energy Labels

The bad news is this is one of the dullest topics in the book. Unfortunately it's also really important, so you're just going to have to grin and bear it, I'm afraid. The good news is there's only one page on it...

Some Household Appliances Have to Have Energy Labels

1) All 'white goods' (things like fridges, washing machines and dishwashers) that are sold in the European Union (EU) have to have an EU Energy Label on them.
2) The labels clearly show the energy consumption and efficiency of each machine.
3) Customers can use the information on these labels to compare different machines and decide which one to buy.
4) Have a look at the label below. It's for a washing machine, but you'll find similar ones on all white goods.

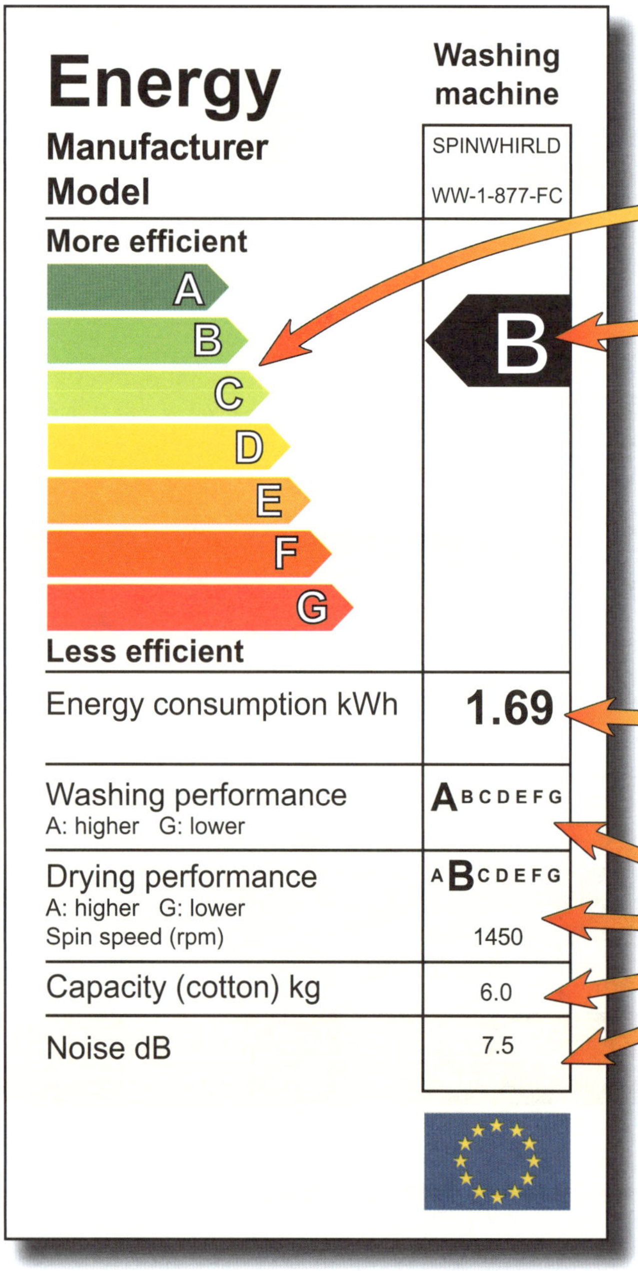

1) These colourful bands represent the seven classes of energy efficiency.
2) Class 'A' is the most efficient and class 'G' is the least efficient.
3) The big letter in the black box shows the energy efficiency rating for this appliance.
4) Some modern appliances that are very efficient are awarded A+ and A++ ratings.
5) The labels allow customers to be able to compare similar appliances with just a quick glance.

- This box tells you how much energy the appliance uses.
- The higher this number is, the more the appliance will cost to run.

The other boxes on the label contain a few other bits of information — they're different for each type of appliance.

My Uncle Alan's washing performance is poor...

Well, that wasn't actually too bad. It's probably not a page that's going to change your life or make you decide on a career in science, but it will help you in your GCSEs and it might even help you buy a fridge one day. Running energy efficient appliances is good for the environment as well as your bank balance, so everyone wins.

Sankey Diagrams

This is another opportunity for a MATHS question. Don't panic though — it's pretty straightforward...

The Thickness of the Arrow Represents the Amount of Energy

1) Sankey diagrams make it easy to see how much energy is being transferred by an electrical appliance into useful forms, and how much is being wasted.
2) Each arrow on the diagram shows a different type of energy transferred by the appliance.
3) The thicker the arrow, the more energy it represents.
4) You can have either a rough sketch or a properly detailed diagram (where the width of each arrow shows exactly how much energy is transferred).

Example — TV:

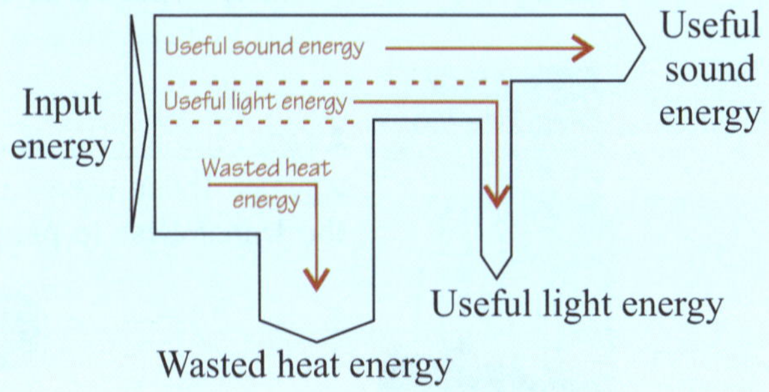

Here's an Example of a Sankey Diagram for a Simple Motor

HERE'S THE SKETCH VERSION:

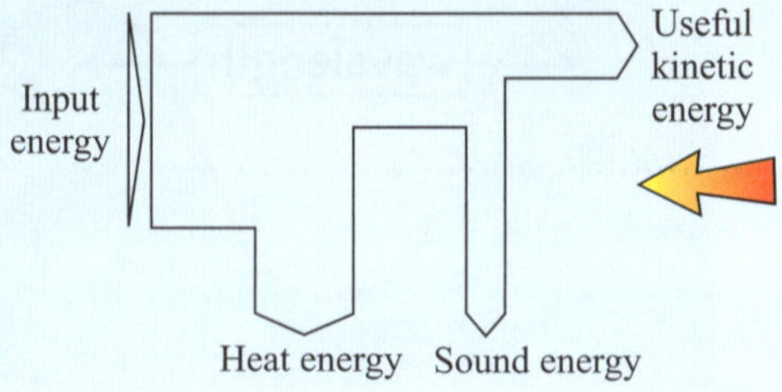

You don't know the actual amounts, but you can see that most of the energy is being wasted, and that it's mostly wasted as heat.

With sketches like this, you might be asked to compare two different devices and say which is more efficient — so look for the one with the thicker useful energy arrow(s).

HERE'S THE MORE DETAILED VERSION:

100 J is 20 squares wide...

...so each square represents 100 ÷ 20 = 5 J.

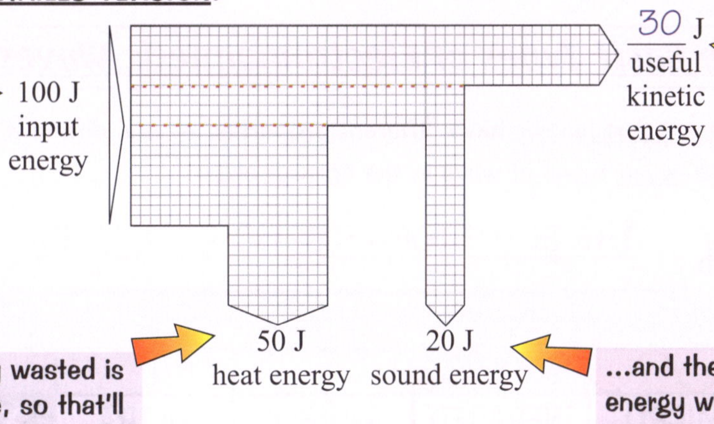

And the useful kinetic energy will be 6 × 5 = 30 J.

The heat energy wasted is 10 squares wide, so that'll be 10 × 5 = 50 J...

...and the sound energy will be 4 × 5 = 20 J.

With these Sankey diagrams an exam question might ask you to fill in one of the numbers or work out the efficiency of the appliance (see page 69). Efficiency is easy enough if you can work out the numbers.

Skankey diagrams — to represent the smelliness of your socks...

If they ask you to draw your own Sankey diagram in the exam, and don't give you the figures, a sketch is all they'll expect. Just give a rough idea of where the energy goes. E.g. a lightbulb turns most of the input energy into heat, and only a small proportion goes to useful light energy.

Electromagnetic Waves

Electromagnetic radiation is things like light and X-rays. It's made up of waves and is a bit odd, frankly.

Waves Transfer Energy but NOT Matter

Electromagnetic waves (EM waves) transfer energy from one place to another without moving any matter (stuff). They're all over the place:

A radio transmitter is a source of radio waves. These waves carry energy from the transmitter to people's radio aerials.

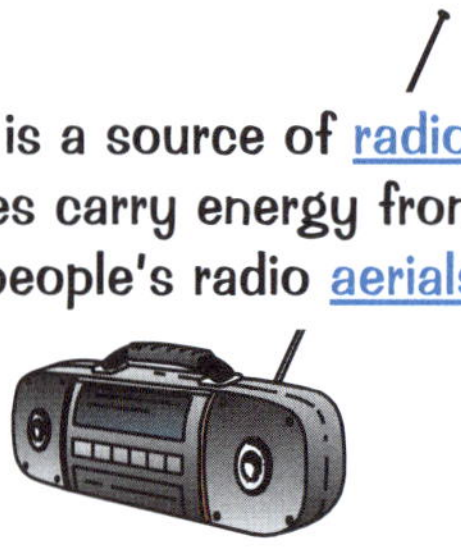

All Waves Have a Few Basic Features That You Need to Know About

1) WAVELENGTH is the distance from one peak to the next. It can be measured in metres, mm or any other unit of length.
2) FREQUENCY is the number of waves that the source produces per second. (A source is anything that produces waves — e.g. a radio transmitter.)
3) Frequency is measured in hertz (Hz). 1 Hz = 1 wave per second.

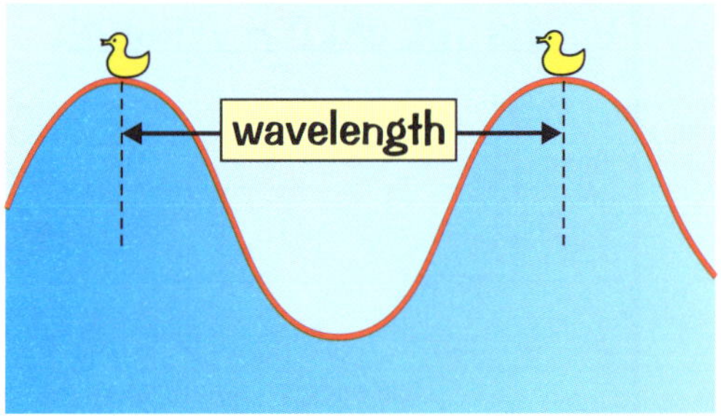

There are Seven Basic Types of Electromagnetic Waves

1) EM waves with different frequencies have different properties — and different uses.
2) You need to know all seven types of wave in the correct order:

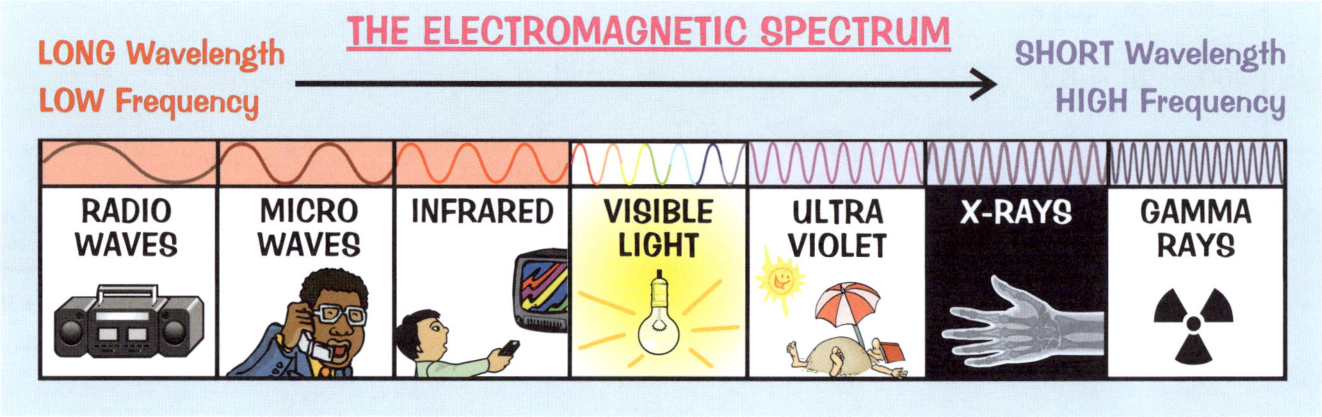

EM Waves — not so much fun for paddling in...

The wavelength and frequency of EM waves are related — the higher the frequency of a wave, the shorter the wavelength. (You can see this in the diagram of the electromagnetic spectrum above.)

The Wave Equation

Like with all great topics in physics, there's an equation you need to know. Sorry.
You'll be thanking me when it comes up in the exam though and you know exactly what to do. Honest...

Wave Velocity = Frequency × Wavelength

Just think of velocity as a posh word for speed.

You need to learn this equation — and practise using it.

VELOCITY = FREQUENCY × WAVELENGTH
(m/s) (Hz) (m)

EXAMPLE:

QUESTION: Eva is building a sandcastle. She estimates that 2 waves pass her sandcastle each second, and that the crests of the waves are 12 cm apart.
Calculate the velocity, in metres per second, of the waves passing Eva's sandcastle.

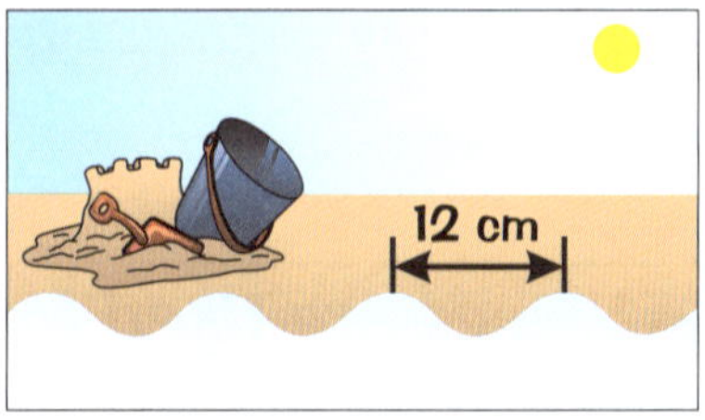

ANSWER: 2 waves pass per second — so the frequency is 2 Hz (hertz).
Don't forget to change the 12 cm to metres first (12 cm = 0.12 m).
Velocity = Frequency × Wavelength = 2 × 0.12 = 0.24 m/s.

Making sure that you've got the right units is really important.

Some Units Can be a Bit Awkward

1) Waves often have high frequencies which are given in awkward units like kHz or MHz, rather than nice straightforward Hz. So make sure you learn this:

1 kHz (kilohertz) = 1000 Hz

1 MHz (1 megahertz) = 1 000 000 Hz

EXAMPLE:

QUESTION: A wave has a frequency of 8.7 kHz and a wavelength of 3.25 m. Find its velocity.

ANSWER: You need to convert the units first: 8.7 kHz = 8700 Hz...
So Velocity = Frequency × Wavelength = 8700 × 3.25 = 28 275 m/s.

Higher

2) Sadly, big numbers like 900 000 000 (900 MHz) won't fit into some calculators.
3) You might have to enter them in standard form. E.g. 900 000 000 = 9×10^8, so press [9] [EXP] [8].
(Your calculator might have a different button for standard form — if you don't know, find out...)

I think I need to stop revising — my brain MHz...

When I first saw this page I was hoping to see something along the lines of '3 friends + 1 meet up = 12 waves'. No such luck. Oh well — I suppose that 'other' wave equation will have to do. Make sure you're happy enough switching between units like centimetres, metres and kilometres and hertz, kilohertz and megahertz.

Uses of Radio Waves and Microwaves

Because different EM waves have different properties, we use them for different things.

EM Waves with Different Properties Have Different Uses

1) When EM waves hit a substance, three things can happen. The waves might:
   - be transmitted — just pass through the substance, like light through glass
   - be reflected — bounce back, like light off a mirror
   - be absorbed — the wave's energy is transferred to the substance, like microwaves heating food.
2) High-frequency EM waves are absorbed quite a bit by the Earth's atmosphere.
3) That's why we use low-frequency waves for sending communication signals over long distances.

Radio Waves are Used for Radio and TV Signals

1) There's a range of wavelengths within the 'radio' part of the spectrum.
2) Radio waves can be transmitted round the world in different ways, depending on their wavelengths. (Remember, shorter wavelengths mean higher frequencies.)

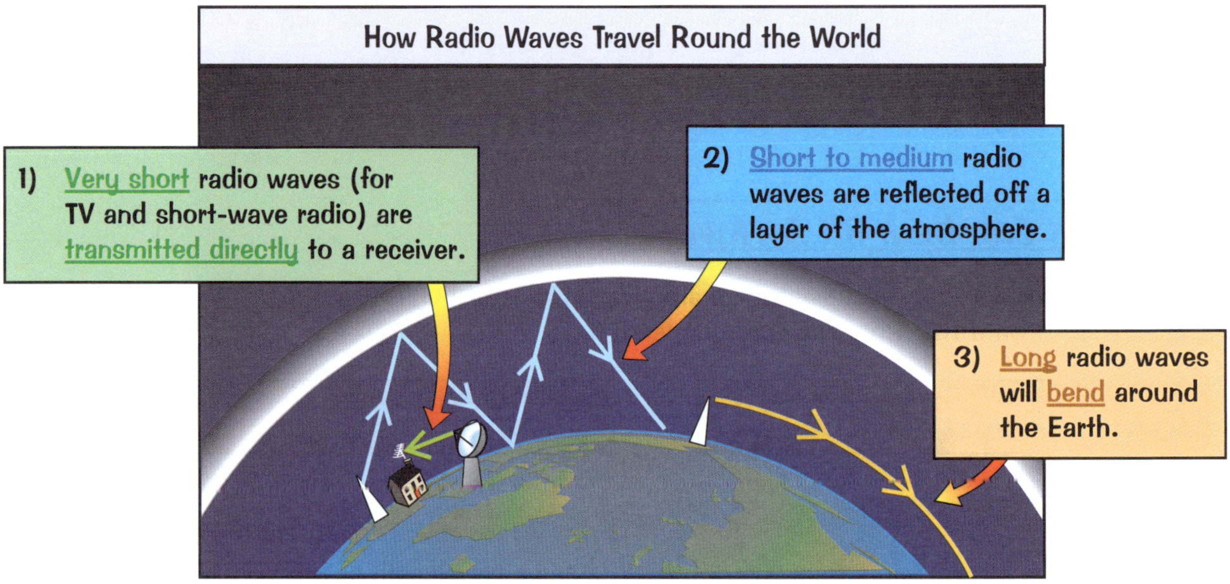

Microwaves are Used in Communications and Cooking

1) Mobile phones connect to the network by sending and receiving microwaves to and from phone masts.
2) Microwaves are able to pass through the Earth's atmosphere so can be used to send data between the Earth and satellites orbiting it. This includes sending satellite TV signals.
3) Some microwaves are absorbed by water molecules. This is how microwave ovens work — the microwaves transfer their energy to the water molecules, which vibrate and heat up the food.

Microwaves — when the Queen can't really be bothered...

Remember, electromagnetic waves come in many different frequencies (and wavelengths) and they behave differently in different substances. That's why EM waves have such a wide range of uses — radio and microwaves for communication, light for seeing things, X-rays for, well, X-rays. Good eh.

Uses of Infrared, Ultraviolet and Visible Light

Visible light's great for seeing things, but there are other types which are also pretty handy.

Infrared is Used for Very Short-Range Communication

Infrared waves are used in remote controls, e.g. for TVs and DVD players.

1) An infrared signal transmits instructions from the control to the appliance.
2) Infrared waves are quickly absorbed by most materials. That's why TV remote controls only work if there's nothing blocking the path between them and the TV.

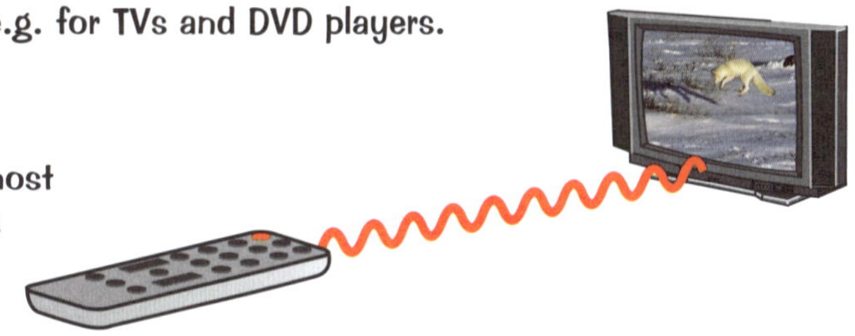

Fibreoptic Cables Carry Visible Light

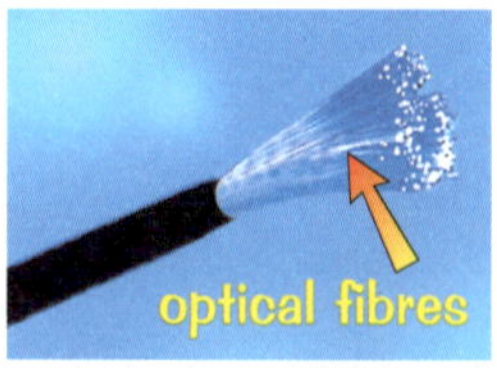

1) One fibreoptic cable contains a bundle of many individual optical fibres.
2) Optical fibres can carry signals over long distances using visible light (see below).
3) The light can be used as a way to transfer data. For example, broadband internet uses fibreoptic cables to carry data (huge amounts of it) as pulses of light.

The diagram shows a single optical fibre.
This is how it carries signals:

1) Visible light enters one end of the fibre.
2) It bounces off the sides of the fibre over and over again...
3) ...until it comes out at the other end.

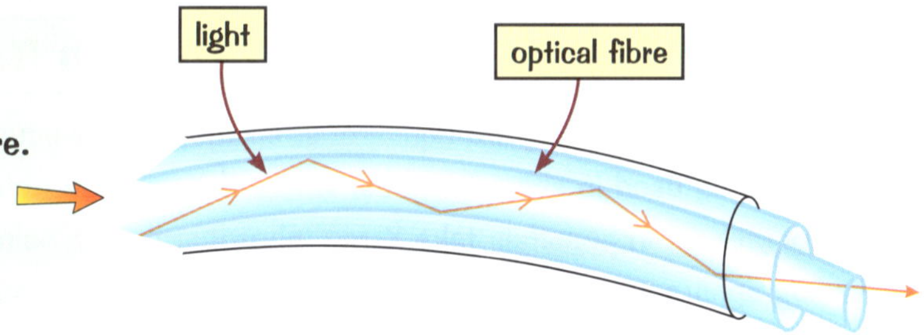

Sun Beds Use Ultraviolet (UV) Light

1) Sun tanning beds work by using UV radiation that's similar to sunlight.
2) So lying in a sun bed is just like lying in the sun, and affects your skin in the same ways too.
3) People use sun beds to make their skin darker.

Fibreoptics — cables with a high bran content...

Optical fibres have many important uses — telephone networks and cable TV for starters (the 'cable' in cable TV is a fibreoptic cable). They're also used in endoscopes — the tuby things doctors sometimes use to see inside a patient's body without cutting big holes. Oh, and in fake plastic Christmas trees.

Dangers of Electromagnetic Radiation

It's a mean old world out there — and there are all sorts of EM waves out to get you...

Some EM Waves Can be Harmful to People

Generally, the higher frequency (so more energy) an EM wave has, the more harm it can do in your body.

RADIO WAVES	As far as we know, radio waves just pass through the body harmlessly.
MICROWAVES	Some wavelengths of microwaves are absorbed by water. If that happens in your body, it heats your living cells up — which could be bad for you. To stop this from happening, microwave ovens have special shields to stop the waves from escaping.
INFRARED	A large dose of infrared could cause burns or heatstroke.
VISIBLE LIGHT	Visible light isn't harmful unless it's really bright. E.g. people who work with powerful lasers (very strong light beams) need to wear eye protection.
ULTRAVIOLET	Ultraviolet is pretty dangerous — it can cause skin cancer. That's why it's a bad idea to use UV sunbeds all the time.
GAMMA / X-RAYS	X-rays and gamma rays are more dangerous still. They can both cause cancers.

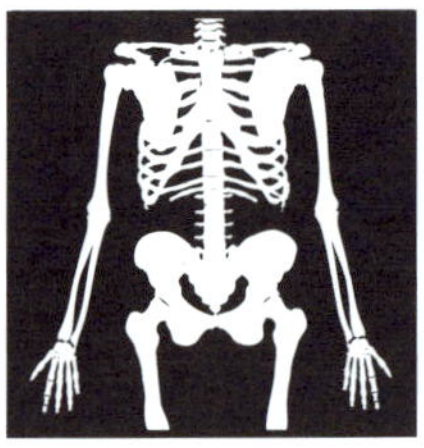

X-Rays and Gamma Rays Aren't Used in Homes

1) X-rays and gamma rays are dangerous, so they're not usually used in the home.
2) They're only used in specialist jobs, where they can be controlled and used safely.
3) Radiographers in hospitals take X-ray 'photographs' to help doctors diagnose broken bones.
4) Radiographers wear lead aprons and stand behind a lead screen to protect themselves from the X-rays.
5) Gamma rays are used for radiotherapy in hospitals. They're carefully fired at cancer cells to destroy them.

Evidence of Danger Has to be Balanced Against Usefulness

Decisions about how and where to use EM radiation are made based on evidence of the dangers.

- For example, microwaves are used for communication devices all the time (see p. 74).
- However, microwaves can heat up water molecules. Because of this, some people think using your mobile a lot, or living near a mast, could damage your health and increase the risk of brain tumours.
- But at the moment there isn't any evidence to prove this.
- So, people carry on using mobiles because they're useful.

For long-distance calls, always shout loudly into the phone...

There's no point worrying too much about the risks of 'modern technology'. It's better to use your mobile phone to call 999 in an emergency than to let your house burn down while you run two miles to the nearest phone box, because you're worried about the possible health risks of microwaves on your brain.

Revision Summary for Section 2.3

If you know what's good for you, you'll be ready to tackle this page. You should know the drill by now. Have a go at as many of the questions as you can. If you struggle on any then have another flick over the pages you're stuck on and give the questions another go. It's not much fun, but it's the best way to find out how much you know, and what topics you still need to spend a bit of time on. 3... 2... 1... GO.

1) Give the units of:
   a) current,
   b) potential difference.
2)* Calculate the power of a circuit if the current flowing is 12 A and the potential difference of the mains supply is 230 V. Don't forget to include the units in your answer.
3)* A hair dryer uses 45 kJ of electrical energy in 1 minute. Calculate the power of this appliance, including the units.
4)* Find the cost of using an electric heater with a power of 3 kW for 45 minutes, if the electricity supplier charges 8p per kWh.
5) Write the two formulas that can be used to calculate the efficiency of an electrical appliance.
6)* A lamp uses 50 J of electrical energy to produce 4 J of light energy. Calculate its efficiency.
7)* What is the efficiency of a motor that converts 100 J of electrical energy into 70 J of useful energy?
8) How might EU Energy Labels be useful to someone buying a household appliance?
9)* Sketch a Sankey diagram to represent an electric toothbrush.
10) Electromagnetic waves don't carry any matter. What do they carry?
11) Draw a diagram showing what wavelength means.
12) Define frequency.
13) What are the units of frequency?
14) Write out the electromagnetic spectrum, putting the lowest frequency waves on the left.
15) Write down the equation that links wavelength, frequency and velocity.
16)* Find the velocity of a wave with frequency 50 kHz and wavelength 0.3 cm.
17) Explain how radio waves allow us to communicate over long distances.
18) What kind of EM waves are emitted by mobile phones?
19) What kind of EM waves are emitted by TV remote controls?
20) Explain why a TV remote control won't work if you're hiding behind the sofa when you try to use it.
21) What is: a) a fibreoptic cable, b) an optical fibre?
22) What kind of EM waves are used in optical fibres?
23) Name one use of UV radiation.
24) What kinds of EM waves are generally the most harmful in the human body? Explain why.
25) How do radio waves affect the human body?
26) What happens to the cells in your body if they absorb microwave radiation?
27) How dangerous are the EM waves emitted by remote controls for DVD players?
28) Explain why using sunbeds for long periods of time is unwise.
29) Which types of EM radiation are known to cause cancer? How are these types of radiation used?

* Answers on page 108.

Microorganisms and Disease

Microorganisms are organisms that are microscopic (unsurprisingly). There are 'good' ones and there are 'bad' ones, which cause horrid diseases that make you really ill. Here's a page about the bad ones...

Infectious Diseases are Caused by Pathogens

1) Pathogens are microorganisms that cause disease.
2) Human pathogens can reproduce very fast inside the body — they love the warm conditions.
3) Pathogens include some bacteria and all viruses.

Some Bacteria Produce Poisons

1) Bacteria can make you feel ill by producing toxins (poisons).
2) Diseases caused by bacteria include tuberculosis, cholera, typhoid (a lung disease) and food poisoning.

Viruses Damage Your Cells

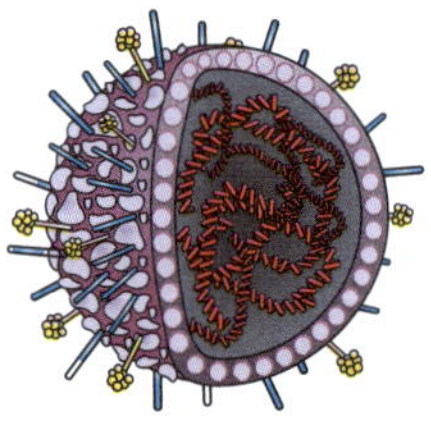

A horrid virus

1) Viruses invade your cells and produce many copies of themselves. The cells will usually then burst, releasing all the new viruses. This cell damage is what makes you feel ill.
2) Diseases caused by viruses include influenza (flu), measles, mumps, rubella and polio.

Infectious Diseases can be Caught in Different Ways

1) Pathogens enter the body in these four ways:
   - through the RESPIRATORY system — you breathe them in. E.g. flu viruses.
   - through the DIGESTIVE system — from food that's 'gone off'. E.g. *E. coli* bacteria.
   - through WOUNDS in the skin. E.g. tetanus.
   - by SEXUAL TRANSMISSION. E.g. HIV.
2) So you can catch infectious diseases from unhygienic conditions (e.g. dirty drinking water) or by contact with an infected person.

Unhygienic conditions — dirty kitchens, students' bedrooms...

There are about 10 times more bacterial cells in your body than there are human cells... which is a weird thought. Don't panic though — most of them won't do you any harm at all. Not like the nasty fellas on this page.

The Body's Defence Systems

Your body has two main lines of defence against microorganisms — 1) stopping the little nasties from getting in, and 2) destroying them if they do manage to get past the first line of defence.

Many Things Stop Microbes Getting In

1) Your skin, plus hairs and mucus in your respiratory tract (breathing pipework), stop a lot of microbes getting inside your body.
2) Small fragments of cells (called platelets) help your blood clot quickly to seal wounds. This prevents microorganisms getting into the body through cuts.

The Immune System Attacks Microorganisms that Do Get In

The most important part of your immune system is the white blood cells. They travel around in your blood, patrolling for microbes. When they come across an invading microbe they have two lines of attack:

1. Consuming Them

White blood cells called phagocytes engulf (surround) foreign cells and digest them.

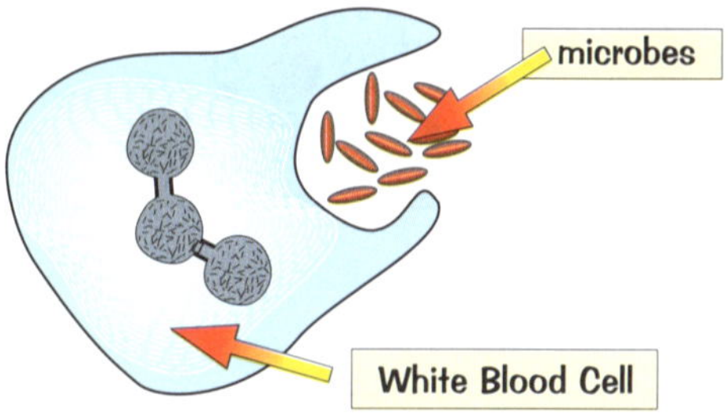

2. Producing Antibodies

1) Every invading pathogen has unique molecules on its surface. These are called antigens.
2) When white blood cells called lymphocytes come across foreign antigens (i.e. ones they don't recognise), they'll start to produce molecules called antibodies.
3) These lock on to and kill the invading pathogens.
4) They're specific to that type of antigen and won't lock on to any others.
5) Antibodies are then produced quickly and flow all round the body to kill all similar bacteria or viruses.
6) If the person is infected with the same pathogen again the white blood cells will rapidly produce the antibodies to kill it — the person is naturally immune to that pathogen.

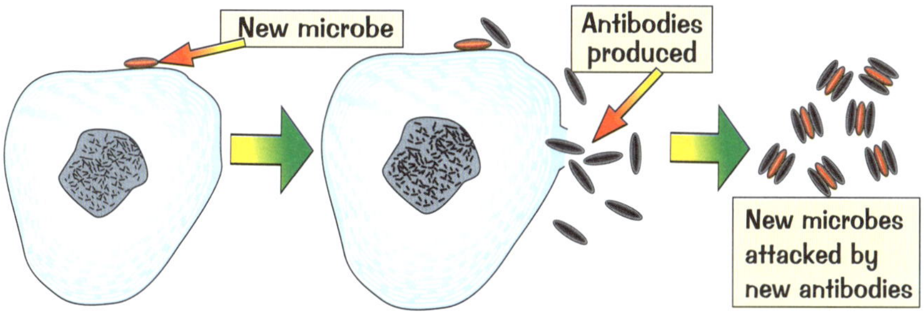

Fight disease — blow your nose with boxing gloves...

There are a few tricky words on this page — and it's quite easy to get them mixed up. And you don't want to do that. So, double check that you know what lymphocytes, phagocytes, antigens and antibodies are.

Vaccination

The body is pretty good at fending off pathogens — but some infections can be pretty serious and can kill you. Scientists have developed a way to protect against some of these infections — it's called vaccination.

Vaccinations Help to Prevent Disease

You can be vaccinated against some diseases, e.g. polio, tuberculosis, measles, mumps and rubella. Here's how it works:

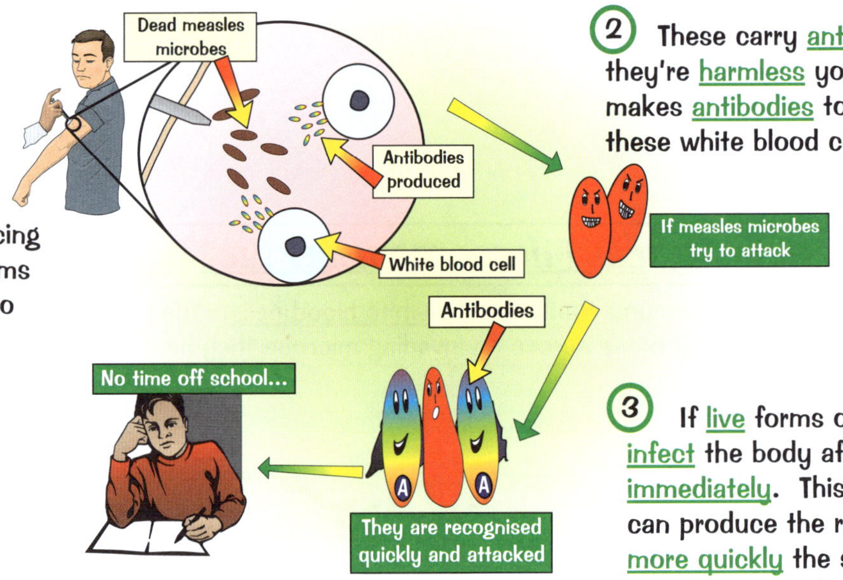

1. Vaccination involves introducing mild or dead forms of pathogens into the body.
2. These carry antigens, so even though they're harmless your white blood cells makes antibodies to attack them. Some of these white blood cells survive in the body.
3. If live forms of the same pathogens infect the body after that, they'll be killed immediately. This is because your body can produce the right antibodies much more quickly the second time around. These destroy the bacteria or virus and stop the disease developing.

1) Vaccines have helped control lots of infectious diseases that were once common in the UK (e.g. whooping cough, TB, tetanus...).
2) And if an outbreak does occur, vaccines can slow down or stop the spread.
3) When enough people are immune to a disease, there'll be very few people who can still catch the disease. This makes it very difficult for the disease to spread and it dies out.
4) The population is then said to have 'herd immunity' (even though some of the people aren't immune).

Vaccines are Very Safe — But There is Some Risk

1) There can be disadvantages to being vaccinated.
2) Some people have nasty side effects (e.g. swelling or fever).
3) But bad reactions are very rare and side effects aren't usually very serious — vaccines are very safe.

Prevention is better than cure...

In the exam you might be asked to interpret a graph of vaccine uptake and disease occurrence (how often it happens). Don't panic — just take each line on the graph in turn and explain what happens to it, e.g. whether it goes up, or down, or stays level. You might also have to interpret data — it's the same deal, just look for the trends.

Use of Drugs to Treat Disease

There are tons of different types of drugs — and some are very handy for stopping sneezes.

Drugs can be Used to Treat Disease

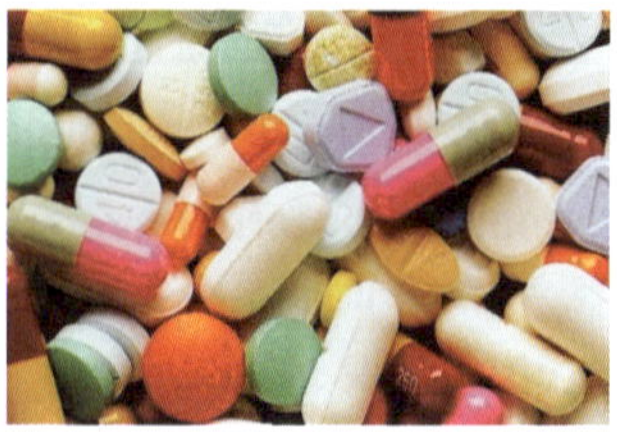

Two drugs you might have heard of are:

- Aspirin — an anti-inflammatory (it stops swelling).
- Penicillin — an antibiotic (it kills bacteria).

Some Drugs Tackle the Symptoms of an Illness

1) Painkillers (e.g. aspirin and paracetamol) are drugs that relieve pain.
2) They don't actually tackle the cause of the pain (e.g. disease or injury) — they just help to reduce the symptoms.
3) Other drugs that just reduce symptoms are sleeping tablets, antidepressants and treatments for high blood pressure.
4) If people use symptom-relieving drugs too much they can become addicted (see p. 83), or their bodies get used to the drugs and they have less effect.

Symptoms are physical signs of illness, e.g. sneezing or headaches.

Other Drugs can Cure Illness

1) Some drugs actually cure illness rather than just reducing the symptoms.
2) For example, antibiotics (e.g. penicillin) actually kill the bacteria causing the problem.
3) By killing the bacteria the disease can be cured.
4) Antibiotics kill most bacteria but they don't destroy viruses.

Drugs can be Personalised

1) Some people react differently to different drug treatments because of their genes.
2) Scientists are trying to design personalised drugs. This will mean that doctors can make sure a person gets the best possible treatment and won't react badly to the drugs.
3) Drug personalisation has its own issues though. Doctors need to carry out lots of genetic testing before they begin. This makes personalisation very expensive.

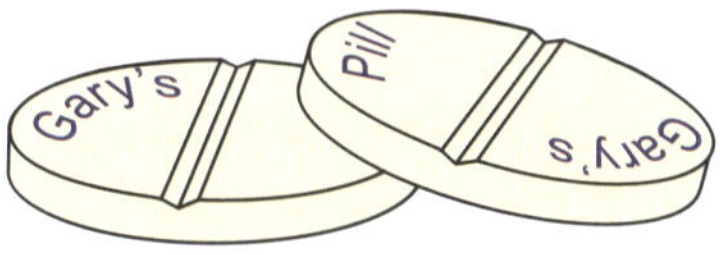

I wish my cough mixture could be personalised to taste like popcorn...

This might all seem a bit obvious but you might get asked about it — at least it's a fairly easy page to learn. Make sure you can give examples of drugs — that way you can show off to the examiner that you know exactly what you're on about (and they'll have to give you lots of marks for being such a genius).

Antibiotic Resistance and Drug Testing

Antibiotic resistance might sound dull — but it's something that can cause lots of problems...

Bacteria Can Become Resistant to Antibiotics

1) Antibiotics kill bacteria (see page 81).
2) However, some bacteria have become resistant to (are not killed by) antibiotics. E.g. MRSA (methicillin-resistant *Staphylococcus aureus*) is resistant to the powerful antibiotic methicillin.
3) Resistance to antibiotics can develop in bacteria spontaneously (by chance) due to random mutations.
4) Resistant strains can cause infections that are impossible (or very hard) to treat with antibiotics.
5) Over-prescribing antibiotics (using them too much) makes it more likely that resistance will develop.
6) People have to be treated with special antibiotics that the bacteria are not resistant to. They may also have to be hospitalised. Therefore, antibiotic resistance costs the NHS a lot of money.

Mutations are changes in genes.

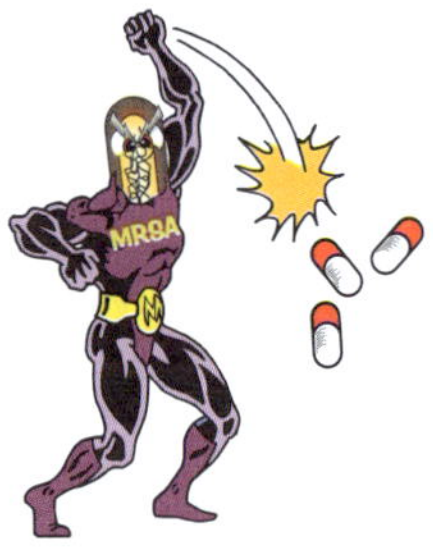

Higher

Here's How Resistant Strains Develop:

- If you have an infection, some of the pathogens might be resistant to an antibiotic.
- This means that when you treat the infection with the antibiotic, only the non-resistant strains of the pathogen will be killed.
- The individual resistant pathogens will survive and reproduce, and the population of the resistant strain will increase.
- This resistant strain could cause a serious infection that can't be treated by the antibiotic.

Nowadays, doctors don't prescribe antibiotics for infections that aren't very serious — for example, mild throat infections. Hopefully, this will mean that fewer resistant strains will develop.

Higher

Medicines Have to be Tested Before They're Prescribed

1) You've already come across drug testing in Unit 2 (see page 45) but you need to learn it again for this Unit.
2) Remember that before new medicines are used to treat disease, they have to be tested.
3) Medicines have to be tested on cells, tissues, animals, healthy volunteers and patients.
4) The tests on humans are known as clinical trials.
5) If the medicines are safe enough (with no serious side effects) and they work (treat the disease), they can be prescribed to everyone.
6) Even once new medicines are in use, their safety and effectiveness are still monitored.

This page might be a bit testing but you need to know it...

Bacteria that are resistant to all our drugs are a worry. It'll be like going back in time to before antibiotics were discovered. So far new drugs have kept us one step ahead, but it may be a matter of time until the options run out.

Recreational Drugs

Some drugs are used medically (i.e. to treat illness) or recreationally (i.e. for fun). Some drugs are legal, others illegal. They can all cause harm to the body, but some are more harmful than others.

Some Recreational Drugs are Legal...

1) ALCOHOL — Alcohol is found in alcoholic drinks. It affects the nervous system and slows down the body's reactions (see the next page for more).

2) NICOTINE — This is the addictive drug found in cigarettes and tobacco. It's a stimulant — it increases the activity of the brain and makes you feel more alert. See the next page for more.

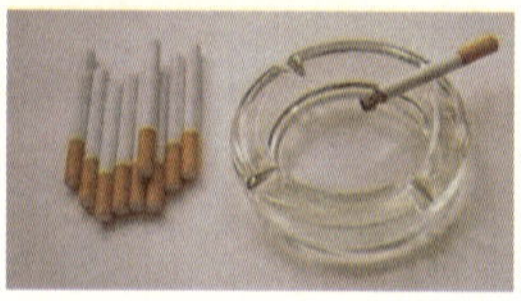

...and Some are Illegal

(without a prescription from your doctor)

1) AMPHETAMINES — Also known as speed. These are stimulant drugs. They make you feel more alert.
2) COCAINE — This is a stimulant — it revs up the nervous system and makes you feel more alert.
3) BARBITURATES — These are medical drugs that are used to help you sleep. They can make you feel like you're drunk.
4) HEROIN — A form of heroin is used in hospitals as a painkiller. But people also use heroin illegally because it makes them 'high'.
5) CANNABIS — Also known as marijuana — it lowers blood pressure and can reduce your ability to concentrate. Like heroin, it makes you feel 'high'.
6) ANTIDEPRESSANTS (without a prescription from your doctor) — These are medical stimulant drugs that are designed to reduce depression.

Lots of Drugs Can Be Addictive and All Can Be Harmful

1) Some people become addicted to drugs — this means they have a physical need for the drug.
2) This is because the drug changes some of the chemical processes in the body.
3) If they don't get the drug they get withdrawal symptoms, e.g. nicotine withdrawal causes headaches.

The misuse of drugs can cause harmful physical and psychological effects. A few examples are:

1) Alcohol in excess causes liver failure and brain damage.
2) Nicotine causes high blood pressure.
3) Cocaine causes an increased risk of heart attack.
4) Stimulants can cause insomnia (when you can't sleep).
5) Sharing needles in heroin use increases the risk of contracting HIV.

Learn all about drugs — and then forget them...

Both legal and illegal drugs can have major impacts on your body, some permanently. The more you take (and the more often you take it) the more likely you are to damage your body.

Recreational Drugs

You might think that just because alcohol and tobacco are legal that they don't do you much harm. Well, think again. They're both dangerous. That's why selling them to young people and advertising them in certain places are banned.

Drinking Alcohol Can Damage the Liver and Brain

1) The main effect of alcohol is to reduce the activity of the nervous system — slowing your reactions.
2) Too much alcohol leads to loss of self-control, unconsciousness and even coma.
3) Alcohol can cause long-term damage. It can damage brain cells, causing a drop in brain function. And too much drinking causes damage to the liver, leading to liver disease.

Smoking Tobacco Can Cause Quite a Few Problems Too

It affects the Circulatory System...

1) Tobacco smoke contains carbon monoxide — this reduces the amount of oxygen the blood can carry.
2) Smoking also causes disease of the heart and blood vessels (leading to heart attacks and strokes).

...and the Respiratory System

1) The smoke and tar from cigarettes damage the lungs (leading to chest infections and diseases like bronchitis).
2) Tobacco smoke contains chemicals that can lead to cancer. Lung cancer is way more common among smokers than non-smokers (see below).
3) And to top it all off, smoking tobacco is addictive — due to the nicotine in tobacco smoke.

Smoking and Lung Cancer are Now Known to be Linked

1) Many years ago, scientists found that cases of lung cancer increased when the number of people smoking increased.
2) In fact, more smokers than non-smokers got lung cancer — but this didn't prove that smoking actually caused lung cancer.
3) Some people argued that there was some other factor that caused lung cancer and made people more likely to smoke.
4) Later research eventually proved that these claims were wrong — smoking does increase the risk of lung cancer.

People have been smoking tobacco for thousands of years...

It's the nicotine in cigarettes that is addictive. Smokers who want to quit can use patches or gum that contain nicotine. This helps them to reduce their withdrawal symptoms whilst they try to break the habit of smoking.

Medical Uses of Radiation

Radiation is a powerful tool. It can be used by doctors to help save people's lives.

There are Three Types of Nuclear Radiation

1) Radioactive sources give out nuclear radiation continuously (all the time).
2) The radiation is 'ionising' — it causes atoms to form ions.
3) This can damage cells and cause cancer.
4) There are three types of nuclear radiation:

Type	Nature	Penetrating Power	Hazards
Alpha (α)	particles	absorbed by paper, skin or a few cm of air	Dangerous if you get it in your body.
Beta (β)	particles	pass through paper and skin but are absorbed by a thin sheet of aluminium	Can penetrate the skin and cause damage. However, it is less ionising than alpha radiation so it doesn't cause as much cell damage when inside the body.
Gamma (γ)	waves	pass through most materials but are absorbed by thick concrete or lead	It can penetrate the skin. However, it passes straight through most tissues so not as dangerous as alpha and beta radiation inside the body.

Radiotherapy is the Treatment of Cancer Using γ-Rays

1) Gamma rays are electromagnetic waves (see page 72). Like all electromagnetic waves, they are transverse waves.
2) Ionising radiation can kill living cells.
3) So gamma rays are used to destroy cancer cells in radiotherapy.
4) Gamma rays can also be used to diagnose cancer:
   - A radioactive tracer is injected into the patient. A tracer is a specially formulated substance that builds up in a particular part of the body (e.g. in a tumour) and gives out gamma rays. Radioactive tracers are sometimes called radiopharmaceuticals.
   - A gamma camera is then used to detect where the tracer travels in the body.
   - This creates an image that can be used to detect where there might be cancer.

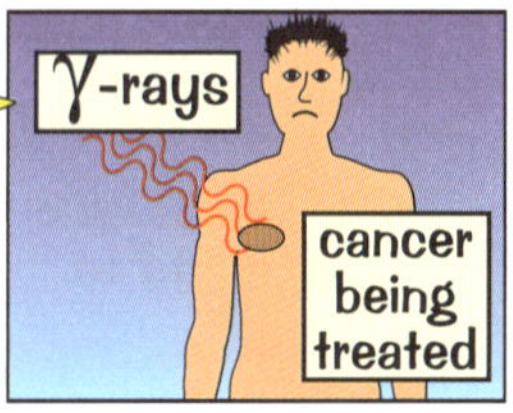

X-Rays are Used in Hospitals to Detect Broken Bones

1) X-rays are also transverse electromagnetic waves.
2) Radiographers in hospitals take X-ray photographs of people to see whether they have broken bones.
3) X-rays pass easily through flesh but not through denser material like bones or metal.

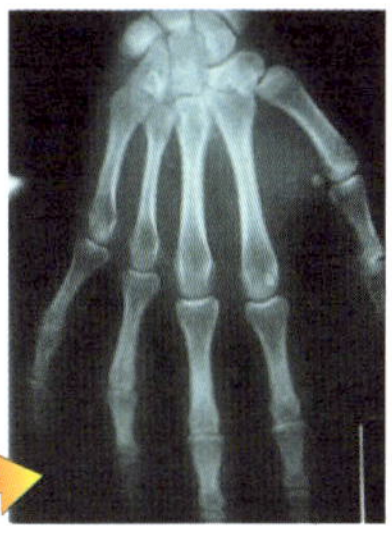

The brighter bits are where fewer X-rays get through to the photographic film.

Listening to The Archers is my idea of radio therapy...

I'm afraid the examiners are more likely to ask you about X-rays than radio shows, so best get learning the stuff on the page. Actually, I wonder if it's possible to take a GCSE in The Archers... I might just go and check.

Radiation Safety Precautions and Ethics

Radioactive materials are used loads in hospitals. But because they can damage the body, people who work with them every day have to be careful they don't end up with three eyes or anything like that...

Working with Radiation can be Dangerous

1) Radioactive substances are used in hospitals for radiotherapy (see previous page).
2) As well as making sure radiation levels are monitored, workers have a few ways to protect themselves:
   - Workers can leave the room when radiation is being used or stand behind a lead or concrete protective screen.
   - Some workers wear special lead-lined aprons.

Workers Wear Film Badges that Measure Radiation

1) People who spend a lot of time working with radioactive materials wear badges that monitor how much radiation they're exposed to.
2) The badge contains a sheet of photographic film (which is sensitive to radiation).
3) The casing of the badge has different 'filters' to block different types of radiation.
4) When the film is developed, it shows how much of each type of radiation the worker has been exposed to.

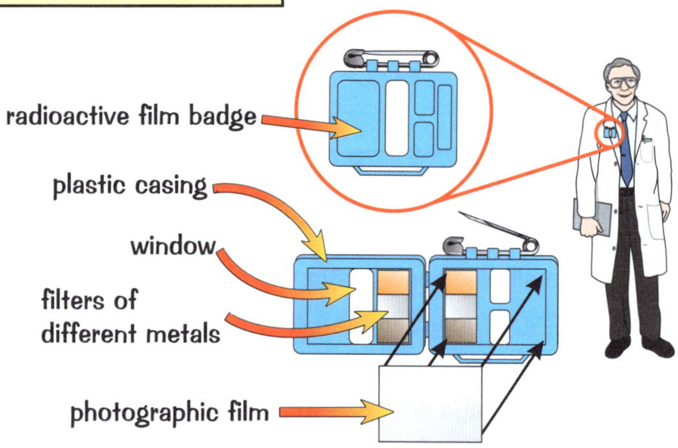

There are Issues Surrounding the Use of Radiation in Medicine

1) Radiotherapy can be used to kill cancer cells.
2) However, there's a very small chance that the ionising radiation could also damage some normal body cells and cause another cancer.
3) Therefore, doctors and patients have to weigh up the pros and cons of using radiotherapy to treat cancer.

I used to wear a film badge to school...

...well I only wore it once and it didn't have filters or photographic film inside — just a picture of that crab from the Little Mermaid that said '9 Today' on it. Needless to say, I didn't have many friends, but when you've got my raw, natural talent for writing such smashing jokes, the cool kids are never far away... (tumbleweed)

Revision Summary for Section 3.1

Surprise surprise: a revision summary at the end of a section. You knew it was coming, you know what you've got to do. Have a crack at the questions and see how you get on. If you get stuck on any come back and try them again after you've had another glance over the section. Time to get going.

1) What are pathogens?
2) How do bacterial pathogens make you feel ill?
3) Give two examples of diseases caused by:
   a) bacteria,
   b) viruses.
4) What are the two main ways infectious diseases can be caught?
5) Describe four ways that pathogens can enter the body.
6) How do platelets help prevent microorganisms getting into the body?
7) What are the two main ways that white blood cells defend the body against microorganisms?
8) Explain how vaccination works.
9) Give one disadvantage of vaccinations.
10) Give an example of a type of drug that relieves symptoms of a disease.
11) Give two problems that can be caused by the over-use of symptom-relieving drugs.
12) Give an example of a type of drug that treats the cause of a disease.
13) What are the benefits of personalising drugs?
14) a) Give one problem with using antibiotics a lot.
    b) Explain how this problem occurs.
15) Why are drugs tested before they are sold?
16) Name two legal and five illegal recreational drugs.
17) What is drug addiction?
18) Give an example of how a drug harms the body.
19) Give two ways in which alcohol damages the body.
20) How does smoking affect:
    a) the circulatory system,
    b) the respiratory system?
21) a) What are the three different types of nuclear radiation?
    b) Name a material that will stop each of them.
22) What disease can ionising radiation cause?
23) Describe how radiotherapy works.
24) What is a radioactive tracer?
25) What are X-rays used to detect?
26) Why do people who work with radioactive materials wear film badges?
27) How do film badges work?

Electroplating

This section's all about how scientists develop and improve things in the world around us. It kicks off with electroplating. It's not as exciting as it sounds. Sorry.

Electroplating is Applying a Metal Coating to an Object

- Electroplating is coating the surface of a metal with another metal.
- Electroplating can also be used to coat other materials that conduct electricity.
- The process uses electrolysis — here's how it works:

1) Electrolysis involves the movement of charged particles in a liquid called an electrolyte.
2) For electroplating, the charged particles are positive metal ions.
3) The electrolyte is a solution of the metal ions used for plating.
4) The ions move between two charged electrodes that are sunk into the electrolyte.

Remember, an ion is a charged atom — it has lost or gained electrons.

EXAMPLE: a brass cup can be electroplated with silver:

CATHODE — this is the negative electrode — it's the object you're going to electroplate.

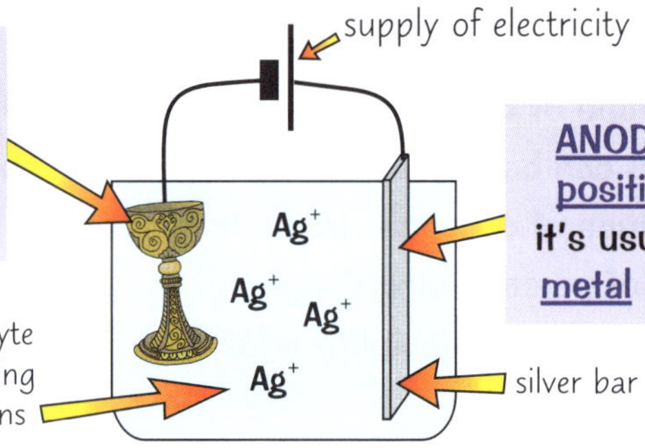

ANODE — this is the positive electrode — it's usually a bar of the metal used for plating.

5) During electrolysis metal from the anode goes into solution (dissolves) and forms metal ions.
6) These metal ions have a positive charge, so they're attracted to the negative cathode.
7) The ions move towards the cathode and metal gets deposited on the object being electroplated.

Higher

You Need to Know What's Happening at the Electrodes

1) You might get asked to complete equations to show what's happening at the cathode or anode.
   - At the anode, metal atoms lose electrons and become positively charged metal ions.
   - At the cathode, metal ions gain electrons and become metal atoms (with no charge).
2) So, if the metal at the anode is silver, the equations would be:

ANODE: $Ag \rightarrow Ag^+ + e^-$
silver atom → silver ion + electron

CATHODE: $Ag^+ + e^- \rightarrow Ag$
silver ion + electron → silver atom

3) The number of electrons lost or gained is always the same as the charge on the metal ion. For example, if the metal at the anode is copper, the equations would be:

ANODE: $Cu \rightarrow Cu^{2+} + 2e^-$

CATHODE: $Cu^{2+} + 2e^- \rightarrow Cu$

Higher

I'd rather have a rain coat than a metal coat...

You really need to learn how electrolysis works — no excuses. This stuff might seem tricky, but it's really not too bad once you've got your head around it. Honest. Use the diagram to help you.

Uses and Risks of Electroplating

Here's why you'd want to electroplate something. And also, er, why you wouldn't.

Electroplating Has Lots of Different Uses

There are a few different reasons why metals are electroplated. The main ones are:

Decoration:

1) Jewellery and decorative items are often electroplated with metals like gold or silver.
2) These metals make the items look shiny and attractive.
3) Jewellery made out of nickel (a cheap metal) is electroplated for decoration and because it prevents allergies.

People are often allergic to nickel, but not gold or silver.

Prevention of Corrosion:

1) Some metals corrode, e.g. iron rusts.
2) Household objects like cutlery, cooking utensils and steel food cans are electroplated with metals to stop them corroding.
3) The metals used for protection are unreactive and don't corrode easily (for example, zinc and tin).

Electroplating Has Risks

1) Electrolysis involves electricity — so there's an obvious risk of electrocution.
2) The chemicals and materials used in electroplating can be quite hazardous too:

Take a look back at page 42 for more on how to deal with chemical hazards.

- The electrolyte can contain corrosive acids that can burn the skin.
- It can also contain toxic (poisonous) chemicals like cyanide.
- The chemicals used to clean the equipment can make you feel sick and dizzy.
- Some of the chemicals can cause explosions.

3) This means that employees working in the electroplating industry have to be really careful:

- They have to know how to use and handle chemicals safely.
- They must wear protective clothing and goggles.
- They must know what to do if something goes wrong, e.g. a chemical is spilt, or gets on the skin.

There's nothing funny about electroplating...

Make sure you know the risks faced by employees in the electroplating industry. Not only will it make you appreciate your electroplated cutlery all the more, it might actually come up in the exam. And those are both pretty good reasons for learning this page if you ask me. Turn over when you're done — the next page is a hoot.

New Products

Scientists are developing new materials all the time — this allows new and better products to be developed. Here are some examples of materials that scientists have developed — and you need to learn them, I'm afraid.

Some Paints Can Heal Themselves

1) Some paints are really clever — if they get scratched they can heal themselves.
2) They're called smart paints (or self-healing paints).
3) To heal themselves, they must be exposed to sunlight.
4) Smart paints can be used on pretty much anything that gets scratched, including electronic stuff (like mobile phones), cars and aircraft.
5) Smart paints mean you don't have to repaint your car every time it gets scratched — much better than traditional paint.
6) However, smart paints are more expensive than traditional paints.

Superconductors Reduce Energy Loss

1) Most materials that conduct electricity have some electrical resistance (they fight against the flow of electricity).
2) This means that when electricity flows through them, they heat up.
3) So some of the electrical energy is wasted as heat.
4) But at very low temperatures, materials called superconductors have almost zero resistance.
5) Without any resistance, none of the electrical energy is turned into heat, so none of it's wasted.
6) Superconductors can be used in powerful electromagnets (magnets that are powered by electricity). These electromagnets get used in:

Magnetic Levitation

This is basically 'floating' due to magnets. Superconductor electromagnets are used by some Maglev trains (very fast trains).

MRI scanners

These are used to scan your insides in hospitals.

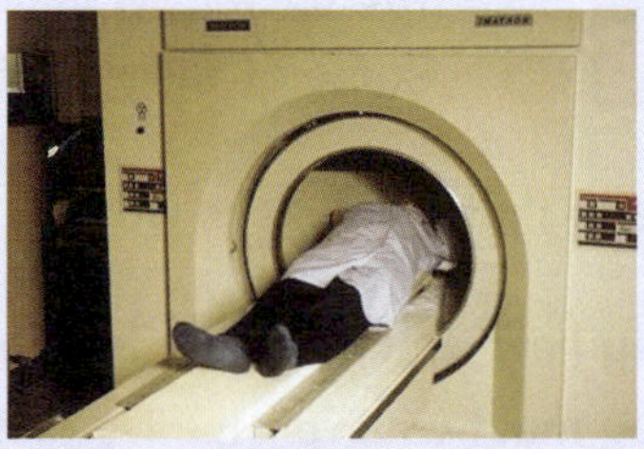

7) However, superconductors have to be kept very, very cold to work — and this is expensive.

I met a guy on the bus this morning — he was a super conductor...

Some of those scientists are really quite clever if you ask me. Paint that heals itself? They'll have invented wallpaper that carries out minor surgeries next. There's more on new materials like these on the next page.

More New Products

So many new products have been developed, I've had to write another page on them...

Smart Materials Respond to Their Environment

Smart materials change their properties in response to changes in their environment. Here are some examples:

Shape Memory Alloys

1) Some metals return to a 'remembered shape' if you heat them above a certain temperature.
2) So if you accidentally bend them, you can just heat them up a bit and they'll jump back into shape.
3) These materials are used in dental braces and glasses frames.
4) If they're bent repeatedly though, it does make them more likely to break — and they're expensive.

Shrink Wrap

1) Some plastics can return to a 'remembered shape' if you heat them up too.
2) They're used to make shrink wrap packaging, e.g. for food, CDs, etc.
3) The plastic is made, then stretched around the object you want to package.
4) When it's heated again, it shrinks — sealing the object up tightly.

Smart Dressings

1) Some smart materials are used as wound dressings.
2) They can change their structure in response to things like pH and salt concentration.
3) This allows them to control bleeding and the amount of moisture getting to the wound.

Chromic Materials are Smart Materials That Change Colour

Photochromic Materials

1) Photochromic materials change colour in response to changes in light intensity.
2) They're used in glasses' lenses that get darker in the sunshine.
   This stops your eyes being damaged by bright light on a sunny day.
3) They have lots of other uses too. For example, they're also used in:
   - windows and rear-view mirrors — to block very bright light.
   - light detectors and light intensity meters — to measure light intensity.
   - optical switches — light is used to transfer (switch) data from one circuit to another.

Thermochromic Materials

1) Thermochromic materials change colour in response to changes in temperature.
2) Intelligent packaging contains inks that change colour according to storage temperature.
3) This lets you check you're storing things (like food) at the right temperature.

Don't get smart with me...

You might be asked to talk about the advantages and disadvantages of modern materials like these, compared with traditional ones. One of the main disadvantages of the modern materials is the cost — they're often very expensive to produce. But then again, some of them are pretty darn useful.

Selective Breeding

Scientists don't just improve metals and things — they work on the living world too...

Selective Breeding is Very Simple

Selective breeding is where we select the plants or animals that breed based on their characteristics. This is what it involves:

1) You select the plants or animals with the best characteristics.
2) The 'best' characteristics will vary, but it usually means things like:
   - Maximum yield of meat, milk, grain etc.
   - Good health and disease resistance.
   - An animal's temperament (if it's calm or crazy), speed or fertility.
   - Whether a plant has pretty flowers or a nice smell.
3) Breed them with each other (this is sometimes called cross breeding).
4) Select the best of the offspring, and breed them together.
5) And continue doing this over lots of generations, to develop the desired characteristics.

The Main Drawback is a Reduction in the Gene Pool

1) The farmer keeps breeding from the same 'best' plants or animals — so all the plants or animals in a population are genetically very similar.
2) As there's not much genetic variation, there's more chance of the organisms suffering from genetic diseases.
3) There can also be problems if a new infectious disease appears. All the stock are closely related to each other, so if one of them is going to be killed by the new disease, the others are also likely to die.

Selective Breeding → Fewer different variations of a gene → Less chance that members of the population have resistance to disease → Many in population die or population could even be wiped out.

I use the same genes all the time too — they flatter my hips...

Selective breeding's not a new thing. People have been doing it for yonks. That's how we ended up with something like a poodle from a wolf. Somebody thought 'I really like this small, woolly, yappy wolf — I'll breed it with this other one'. And after thousands of generations, we got poodles. Hurrah.

Tissue Culture and Cloning

This page is all about how scientists make loads of copies of plants and animal cells.

Cloning is Making an Exact Copy of Another Organism or Cell

1) Clones are GENETICALLY IDENTICAL ORGANISMS or CELLS.
2) Scientists can clone both plants and animal cells using tissue culture.

Cloned Plants can be Made Using Tissue Culture

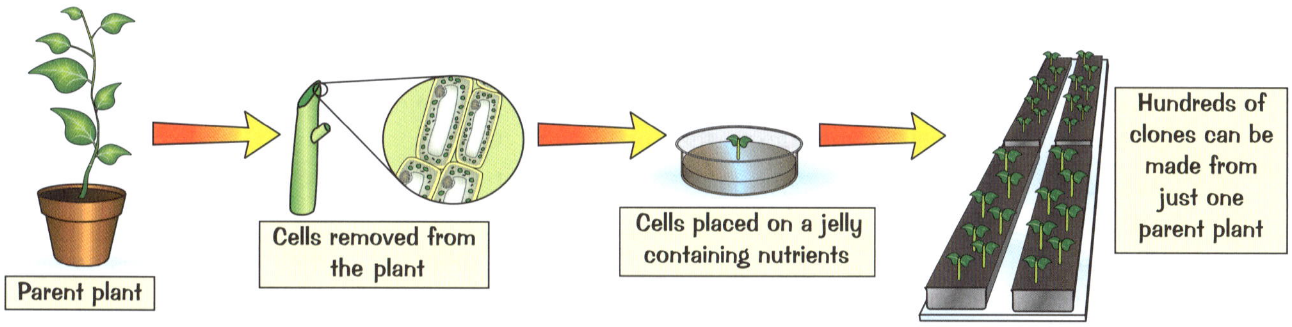

1) Cells or pieces of tissue are removed from a parent plant (sometimes called the donor).
2) The cells or tissue are grown (cultured) in a jelly containing nutrients.
3) After shoots and roots grow the plants are moved to soil to carry on growing.
4) The plants that are produced are clones of the parent plant — and of each other.
5) This means that they're genetically identical to the parent plant (and to each other).

Animal and Human Cells can Also be Cloned

1) Scientists can also clone animal and human cells using tissue culture.
2) The cells are removed from the donor and grown in a nutrient solution.
3) The nutrient solution contains everything the cells need to survive and function.
4) The cells divide to make more copies that are genetically identical to the original cells.
5) Scientists can also culture tissues and organs in a similar way.
6) The cultured cells, tissues and organs can be used in lots of ways. For example, they can be used to test drugs (see page 45) or they can be transplanted into patients with damaged organs.

Thank goodness they didn't do that with my little brother...

Plant cloning is used all the time — it's a really easy way to grow loads of plants with the characteristics you want. You just pick the perfect parent plant and, like magic, you end up with lots of perfect offspring.

Genetic Engineering

Genetic engineering is basically playing around with genes. Cool.

Genes Can be Transferred Into Different Organisms

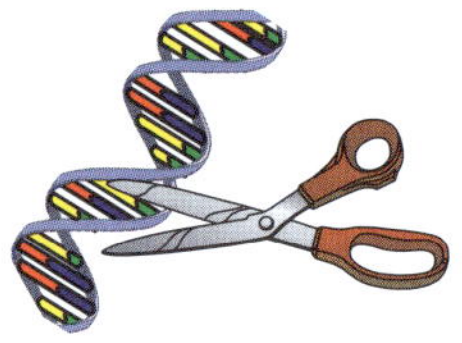

1) Scientists can move genes from one organism to another — this is called genetic engineering.
2) Bacteria, plants and animals can all be genetically engineered.
3) The genes that are transferred are sometimes called 'foreign' genes.
4) The transfer must be done in the very early stages of the plant or animal's development so that it develops with the desired characteristics.
5) The characteristics that the genetically modified (GM) organism has depends on the type of gene inserted.
6) The possibilities are endless, for example:
   - The gene for human insulin has been put into bacteria. These are grown in a lab and the human insulin is taken from the culture medium as they produce it. Great.
   - We can genetically modify crops to increase their yield, making more food. This means that farmers can make more money — so there are economic benefits.
   - People living in poorer countries can lack nutrients (e.g. vitamins) in their diets. Crops can be engineered to contain the extra nutrients that are needed.
   - People with genetic diseases could have the faulty genes replaced with working ones.
   - Babies could be 'designed' to have characteristics their parents want, e.g. blue rather than brown eyes.

Genetic Engineering is a Controversial Topic

You need to be able to weigh up the benefits and risks of genetic engineering, and consider the ethical issues:

1) One risk is that an inserted gene could have harmful effects that we can't predict.
2) Not everyone is convinced that GM foods are safe. People are worried they may develop allergies to the food — although there's probably no more risk of this than for eating normal foods.
3) A big concern is that transplanted genes may get out into the natural environment. For example, a herbicide-resistance gene may be picked up by weeds, creating a new 'superweed' variety.
4) Some people think it's wrong to genetically engineer other organisms for human benefit — especially if they are animals which suffer as a result.
5) Replacing the faulty genes in a person who has a genetic disease would help make them better. However, people worry that it won't stop at medicine. People who can afford it might start 'designing' their children — some characteristics such as height or hair colour might be seen as 'better' than others.

If only there was a gene to make revision easier...

At the end of the day it's up to the Government to weigh up all the evidence for the pros and cons before making a decision on how this scientific knowledge is used. All scientists can do is make sure the Government has all the information it needs to make the decision — but you still need to know about the ethical issues.

Revision Summary for Section 3.2

Well, here we are again, the end of another section — yay. By now you should know everything you need to know about the ways scientists improve things. There's only one way to find out if you really do though. Yep, you guessed it — a good old revision summary. If you can't answer the questions then you'd better go back and learn it again — or, er, I'll steal your shoes.

1) What is electroplating?
2) Do metal ions have a positive or negative charge?
3) In electrolysis, what are the names of:
   a) the positive electrode,
   b) the negative electrode,
   c) the solution of metal ions?
4) Complete the following equation: $Ni \rightarrow Ni^{2+} + \_e^-$
5) Give two reasons why metals are electroplated.
6) Name two risks to employees in the electroplating industry.
7) Give two uses for smart (self-healing) paints.
8) Describe what a superconductor is.
9) Give two ways superconductors are used.
10) Give one advantage and one disadvantage of using shape memory alloys in glasses frames.
11) What do photochromic materials do?
12) Give one use for thermochromic materials.
13) Describe the process of selective breeding.
14) What is the main drawback of selective breeding?
15) What are clones?
16) How would you make a plant clone using tissue culture?
17) Describe one advantage and one disadvantages of using cloning.
18) What is genetic engineering?
19) Describe two examples of useful applications of genetic engineering.
20) Give two ethical issues of genetic engineering.

Greenhouse Gases

You've already learnt a bit about greenhouse gases in Unit 1 (see page 14) — but there's more to know yet. Before you get started on this page, flick back to Unit 1 and make sure you know the greenhouse gas basics.

Human Activity Produces Lots of Greenhouse Gases

1) Greenhouse gases help to keep the Earth's atmosphere warm.
2) Carbon dioxide, methane and nitrous oxide are all natural greenhouse gases.
3) Emissions of greenhouse gases are increasing — so the levels in the atmosphere are increasing.
4) This is because of the products that human beings make and use, e.g. food, packaging, cars...

Emissions are things that have been released into the air.

Burning Fossil Fuels Produces Lots of Carbon Dioxide

1) Humans burn a lot of fossil fuels — these are things like coal, oil and natural gas (see page 57).
2) The combustion (burning) of fossil fuels produces a lot of carbon dioxide.

Fossil fuels are burnt in:

Vehicles — like cars and lorries.

Power stations

Methane is Also a Problem...

1) Methane is formed when organic matter decays, e.g. plants, kitchen waste.
2) Lots of it is produced in wet, boggy places, where there's not much air, e.g. swamps, wetlands.
3) Agriculture (farming) produces a lot of methane.
4) The main sources of methane in agriculture are:
   a) Rice growing — bacteria in watery rice fields release methane.
   b) Animals — bacteria in the stomachs of cows and sheep release methane.
5) Rubbish decomposing (breaking down) in landfill sites also produces methane.

...And so is Nitrous Oxide

1) Nitrous oxide is produced by vehicles and power stations.
2) It's also released by bacteria in soils in a process called denitrification.
   - More nitrous oxide is produced in this way when nitrogen-based fertilisers are applied to the soil.
   - More people are farming intensively — they try to get as much produce from the land as possible.
   - So the use of these fertilisers is increasing because they improve crop yield.
3) Using too much animal waste as a fertiliser can also produce lots of nitrous oxide from the soil.

A nitrogen-based fertiliser is one that contains nitrogen.

Methane is a stinky problem but an important one...

There are 1.5 billion cows in the world (apparently), which means a good supply of chocolate milk shakes and double cheeseburgers. But it also means a lot of methane gets released into the atmosphere every day.

Global Warming and the Kyoto Agreement

The phrase 'global warming' pops up in the news practically every other week. You've stumbled across it in Unit 2 (see page 58), but now you need to know even more about it. I know, life's cruel.

The Increase in Greenhouse Gases is Causing Global Warming

1) You should know from page 14 how greenhouse gases keep the Earth warm.
2) Greenhouse gas levels are increasing, so more long-wave radiation (heat energy) from the Earth is being absorbed.
3) This means that more heat gets trapped in the atmosphere.
4) This is causing the Earth to warm up — and that's what global warming is.
5) Global warming is an example of climate change.

The Kyoto Agreement Puts Limits on Greenhouse Gas Emissions

1) The Kyoto Agreement is an international (world-wide) agreement on what to do about climate change.
2) The main aim of the Kyoto Agreement is that:

> By 2012 greenhouse gas emissions from the countries who signed the agreement should be 5% lower overall than they were in 1990.

3) This is meant to help stabilise the amount of dangerous greenhouse gases in the atmosphere. This includes the levels of carbon dioxide, methane and nitrous oxide.
4) Hopefully, this will stop global warming getting much worse.

Stabilise means to keep something at a steady level.

Lots of Countries Have Signed the Kyoto Agreement...

1) 39 industrialised countries from all over the world have signed the agreement — including every country in Europe.
2) They have promised to meet targets to reduce the amount of greenhouse gases they produce.
3) The USA refused to sign the agreement though. Tut tut.
4) This means the USA doesn't have to cut down its emissions.
5) Australia refused to sign the agreement to begin with, but they've now signed it.

Industrialised countries are ones with lots of industry.

> 1) So, the Kyoto Agreement isn't perfect.
> 2) But it's seen as an important first step towards reducing greenhouse gas emissions.

Global warming — better than global freezing if you ask me...

Actually, global warming is really not that great. The Earth getting warmer means that polar ice caps are melting, sea levels are rising and flat areas close to coasts will be flooded more. It also changes weather patterns — this might make it harder to grow crops in some places, or to predict big storms in others. That's why it's so important that the Kyoto Agreement gets signed — to try to reduce global warming and the problems it causes.

Pollution

When human beings release harmful substances into the environment, it causes pollution.
Lots of nasty things can happen then...

Artificial Fertilisers, Herbicides and Pesticides All Cause Pollution

1) Many farmers use artificial fertilisers, herbicides and pesticides to help their crops grow.
2) These have different jobs:

'Artificial' means they're man-made.

FERTILISERS add nutrients to the soil to help crops grow.

HERBICIDES kill the weeds that compete with crops for water and space.

PESTICIDES kill the insects and other animals that feed on crops.

3) These chemicals can get washed into lakes and rivers by heavy rain — it's called leaching.
4) Once there, they can all cause pollution.

Too Much Fertiliser Causes Eutrophication

The process of eutrophication is explained in the diagram below.

1) Eutrophication can happen when too much fertiliser is applied to fields, especially if it rains afterwards.
2) It's caused by the fertiliser leaching into nearby lakes and rivers.
3) When it gets there it can cause serious damage to plants and fish.

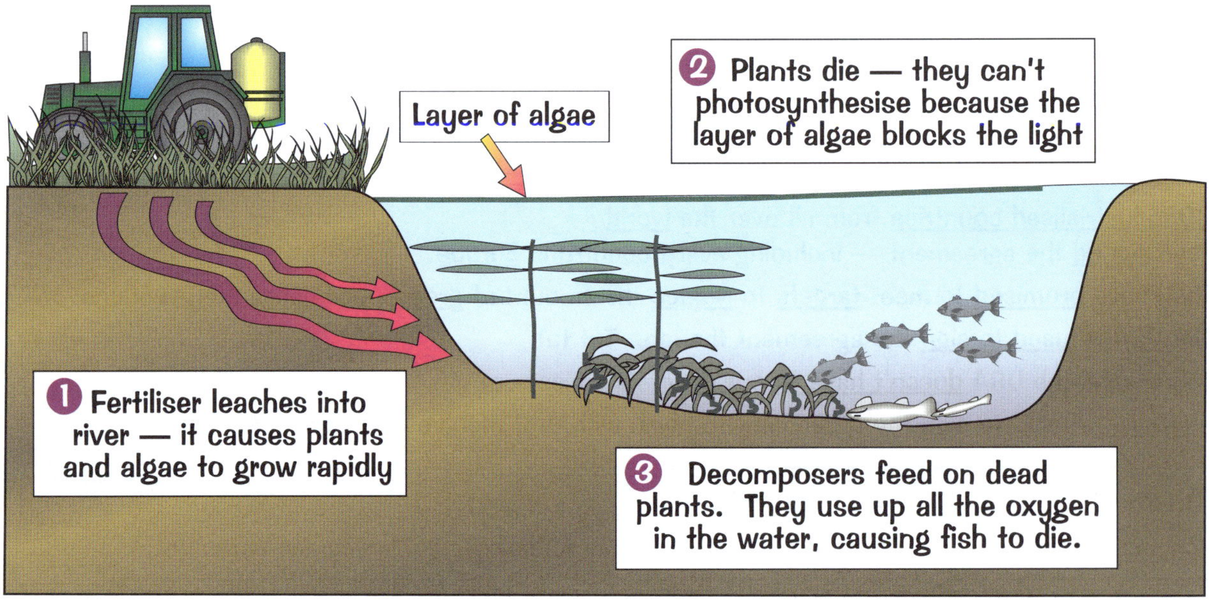

I'm sure this never happened on Old MacDonald's farm...

Make sure you learn that diagram — it's not just there to look pretty. Although I can see it being considered something of a work of art. The fish are particularly great. Especially the little dead ones... Anyway, keep the word 'leaching' in your head. You'll need to know what it means for the next page (more pollution, I'm afraid).

Pollution and Indicator Species

As promised, here's another page on pollution. Well, there's an awful lot of it about. So it stands to reason that there's quite a bit to learn on the topic...

Herbicides and Pesticides Can Poison Food Chains

1) If herbicides or pesticides get into rivers, they can build up in food chains to harmful levels.
2) The animal at the end stage of the food chain could be poisoned.
3) In the diagram below, the poor otter's probably had it...

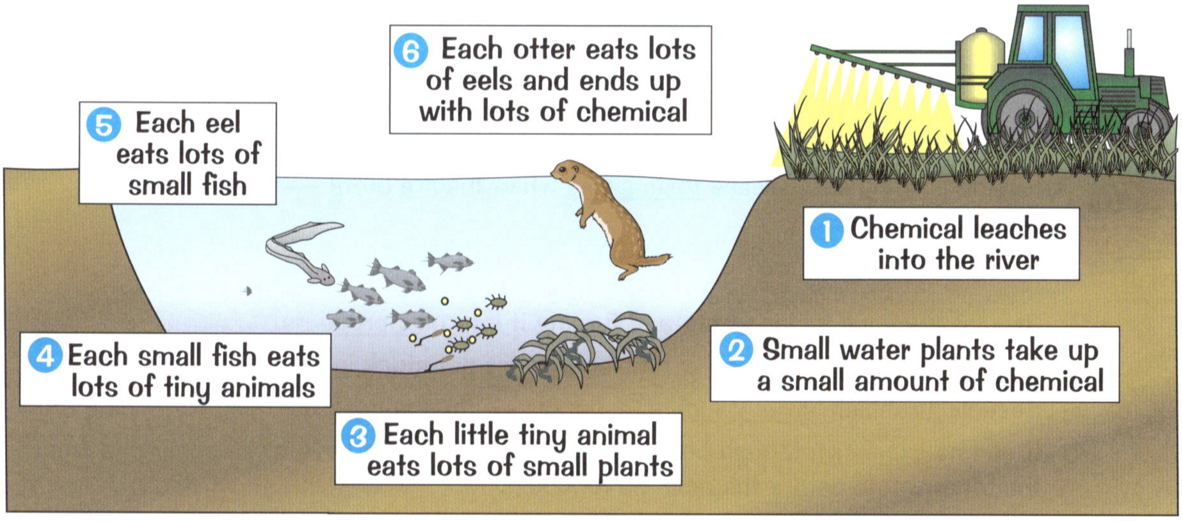

4) If pesticides are used too much, pests can become resistant to them. Also, the pesticides may harm useful insects in a food chain, as well as pests.

Pollution Levels can be Monitored Using Indicator Species

1) Some plants and animals are very sensitive to pollution in their environment.
2) You can study these plants and animals to monitor pollution levels (keep an eye on them).
3) They're called indicator species.

Lichens

4) Air pollution can be monitored by looking at lichens.
5) Lichens only grow in areas where there's clean air.
6) So if there are lots of lichens in an area, it means the air's pretty clean.
7) Water pollution can be monitored by looking at:

   Rat-tailed maggots, sludgeworms, bloodworms and water lice.

8) All these creatures actually quite like polluted water.
9) So if you find them in a river, you know there's a high level of pollution.
10) You can tell when pollution levels in an area change because the types of species that grow there change. Handy.

Teenagers are an indicator species — not found in clean rooms...

You might have to interpret data on indicator species in the exam, but don't panic. Everything you need to know is on this page. For example, you might get a table showing what species are in a river. If there are loads of sludgeworms and bloodworms, you can say something like: 'There's water pollution in this river'. Easy.

Waste Disposal and Plastics

Pollution and waste disposal — the fun just keeps on coming...

There are Different Methods of Waste Disposal

Landfill sites

1) Landfill sites are big holes in the ground where waste is buried.
2) They're smelly, ugly and take up a lot of useful land.

Incineration

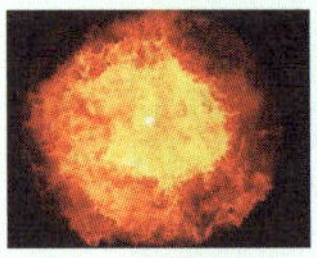

1) Waste can be burnt so it doesn't take up space in a landfill site. This is called incineration.
2) One problem with incineration is that it releases a lot of smoke — a big pollutant.
3) Some plastics also release toxic gases when they're burnt — not good.

Recycling

1) Recycling means taking waste and turning it into new products.
2) This is great because it means rubbish doesn't get stuck in landfill sites or burnt.
3) Recycling rubbish saves valuable resources — this reduces the need for mining etc.
4) It can be expensive though because recyclable materials have to be separated from the other waste before they can be recycled.

Higher

Biodegradable Plastics Help Solve the Problem of Plastic Disposal

1) Most plastics don't biodegrade (break down) very well.
2) They take up space in landfill sites and if they do start to break down they can release toxic chemicals.
3) Plastics made from plants are renewable. They're also biodegradable — they can be broken down by microbes (e.g. bacteria).
4) Sometimes their breakdown products are useful materials like compost.
5) They don't biodegrade well in landfill sites though — so they can't be thrown away with normal rubbish.
6) They're also more expensive to produce and areas may be deforested to make way for the plants grown to make the plastic.

Biodegradable Plastics Break Down in Different Ways

There are different types of biodegradable plastics — and they break down in different ways:

1) Photo-degradable plastics break down if they're left for a long time in sunlight.
2) Oxo-degradable plastics have an additive that helps microbes to break them down.
3) Water-soluble plastics dissolve in water.

- Water-soluble plastics include Polyvinyl Alcohol (PVOH) and Ethylene Vinyl Alcohol (EVOH).
- They're used to make shopping bags and plastic films used in packaging.

Higher

Here's another method of waste disposal — hide it under your bed...

The key thing to understand about this page is that there are advantages and disadvantages to all the waste disposal methods — as well as to the use of biodegradable plastics. Learn it, learn it, learn it, learn it.

Heat Loss in the Home

Your home loses heat left, right and centre. (I know mine does — it's blumming freezing in winter.) Heat loss happens when heat transfers through stuff. It's bad for the environment because it means you have to generate more heat, which usually involves burning more polluting fossil fuels.

You Need to Know About the Different Types of Heat Transfer

CONDUCTION

This is the transfer of heat energy through a substance, without the substance moving.

E.g. this is how heat gets transferred through the bottom of a metal pan or through walls in a house.

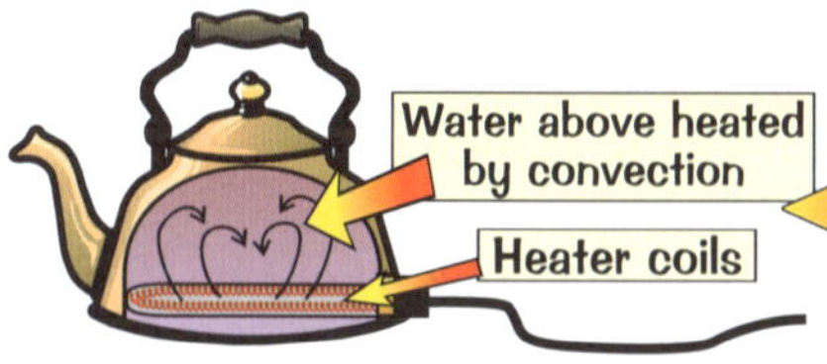

CONVECTION

This is the transfer of heat energy by liquids or gases moving.

E.g. this is how the water gets heated in a kettle, or how heat is transferred around a room.

RADIATION

Hot objects radiate (give off) energy to their surroundings.

E.g. a hot car engine radiates heat to the air around it.

You can reduce heat loss by reducing these three types of transfer — e.g. by reducing air or water movement or by using shiny materials to reflect back radiated heat.

U-Values Show the Rate of Heat Loss Through a Material

1) A material with a low U-value loses heat more slowly than a material with a higher U-value.
2) Here are typical U-values of some everyday materials:

Material	U-value
Glass	40
Snow	5.5
Thick cardboard	1.42
A duvet	0.75
Loft insulation material	0.15

3) As you can see from the table, heat is lost much more quickly through glass than loft insulation.
4) So you lose heat faster through your windows than your properly insulated loft.
5) If you have to pick a material to reduce heat loss in an exam, pick the one with the lowest U-value.

U-value me a lot I hope...

This page may be dull, but at least it's straightforward. Learn the main types of heat transfer and make sure you understand what a U-value is. Job done. You should have time to catch your favourite soap if you're quick.

Reducing Heat Loss in the Home

Reducing heat loss at home is good for your pocket and good for the environment.
You'll be as snug as a bug at home once you've read this page...

There are Lots of Ways to Minimise Heat Loss in Your Home

Reducing heat loss in your home saves money because you use less energy keeping warm.
There are a few ways to do it:

1) INSULATION — a thick layer of foam or material between walls, or laid out on floors.
2) DOUBLE GLAZING — windows made up of two panes of glass.
3) HOT WATER TANK JACKETS — thick foam or material wrapped around a hot water tank.
4) DRAUGHT EXCLUDERS — strips of foam or material to fill gaps around doors and windows.
5) THERMOSTATIC CONTROLS — controls that switch your heating on and off automatically.

Efficiency and Cost-effectiveness are Not the Same...

1) Efficiency is how well something works.
2) Cost-effectiveness is how well something works compared with how much money you've spent on it.
3) So something that's really efficient might not be very cost-effective if it's really expensive.
4) You can measure how cost-effective something is by its 'payback time'.
5) This is the length of time it takes you to make your money back on something.

...Especially When it Comes to Reducing Heat Loss in the Home

This diagram shows different ways of reducing heat loss in the home:

Loft or Roof Insulation
Initial Cost: £200
Annual Saving: £50
Payback time: 4 years

Hot Water Tank Jacket
Initial Cost: £15
Annual Saving: £30
Payback time: 6 months

$$\text{payback time} = \frac{\text{initial cost}}{\text{annual saving}}$$

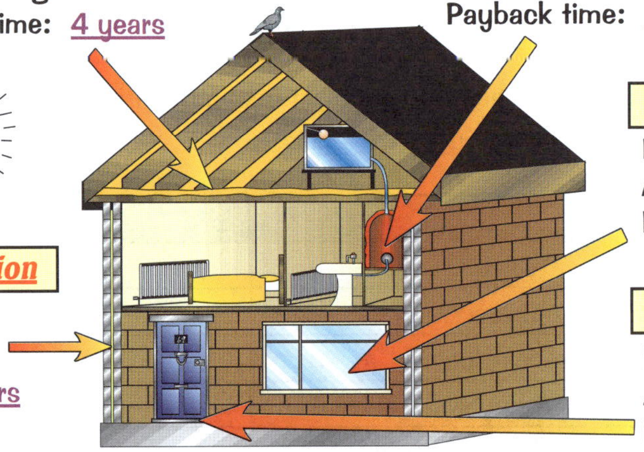

Cavity Wall Insulation
Initial Cost: £500
Annual Saving: £70
Payback time: 7 years

Double Glazing
Initial Cost: £3000
Annual Saving: £60
Payback time: 50 years

Draught Excluders
Initial Cost: £100
Annual Saving: £50
Payback time: 2 years

1) You can see that cavity wall insulation is efficient at reducing heat loss because it saves a lot of money each year.
2) It's not very cost-effective though because the payback time is so long.
3) The hot water tank jacket isn't as efficient, but it's more cost-effective because it's so cheap.

It's payback time...

And it's the same with, say, cars. Buying a more fuel-efficient car might sound like a great idea — but if it costs loads more than a clapped-out old fuel-guzzler, you might still end up out of pocket. And no one wants that.

Pollutants in the Home

You just can't escape pollution. Even indoors...

Pollutants in the Home can Affect Our Health

Pollutants in the home include:

Spores are small particles given off by mould.

Dust

Pollen

Smoke

Fumes from household products, e.g. cleaning products

Mould and spores

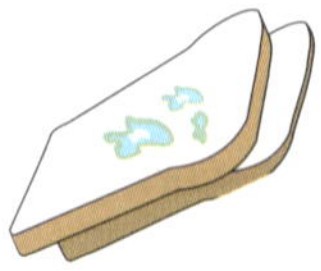

Large amounts of these pollutants can sometimes cause health problems, for example:

1) Pollen can cause an itchy nose or a sore throat.
2) Dust and mould can make asthma worse. Mould can also make you feel tired.
3) Fumes from household products can make you feel nauseous (sick) and dizzy — or give you a headache.

Look Out for Hazard Symbols on Household Products

1) You can find hazard symbols on the labels of lots of household products, e.g. bleach, floor polish.
2) They're there to tell you in what way the product is dangerous.
3) The symbols are exactly the same as the ones you learnt in Unit 2 (see page 42). If you can't draw them all and say what they mean, I'm afraid it's time to go back and learn them.
4) Understanding the hazard symbols will help you to reduce the risks of using the product, e.g.

Harmful

The product could make you ill if you get it on your skin, swallow it or breathe it in.

To reduce the risks of using it, you should:

- Wear gloves.
- Use it in a well-ventilated area.
- Keep it away from children.

A well-ventilated area is one that gets plenty of fresh air.

5) You can reduce pollution in the home by using less toxic products, e.g. vinegar is good for cleaning.

Some Pollutants in the Home are More Serious

1) Radon is a radioactive gas. At high levels, it can cause cancer.
2) Radon is produced when uranium and radium break down.
3) So it's a problem in areas where there's lots of uranium and radium in the rocks and soil.
4) The rocks and soil in these areas release radon gas. This gas can get trapped inside people's houses and become a pollutant.
5) In areas with a lot of radon, new houses have to be built with good ventilation systems.
6) Ventilation systems let fresh air into houses and old air out. This stops the radon building up.

That'll teach you to clean your room...

Well. Now you know just how important it is to do the housework. You can even do it safely. Excellent. Of course, vacuuming your hallway is still the most boring activity in the world. Possibly only a fraction less boring than revising this page in fact. You've still got to do it though. Sorry.

Domestic Boilers

Domestic boilers. They sound fun, don't they? No? Oh well, at least this is the last page of the section (almost) — and practically the last page of the entire book. There, I knew that'd cheer you up. OK, time to learn about burning and stuff...

Domestic Boilers Need Air To Work Efficiently

Domestic boilers are just boilers you have in your house.

1) Domestic boilers heat the water for your central heating system.
2) To do so, they have to burn fuel — this releases energy in the form of heat.
3) To burn properly and produce lots of energy, fuels need oxygen — this comes from the air.
4) So to work efficiently, a domestic boiler needs a good air supply.

This is the reaction that happens inside a domestic boiler that's working efficiently:

fuel + oxygen → carbon dioxide + water (+ energy)

These are the products of the reaction. They're not very dangerous.

Boilers Don't Work Properly if There's Not Enough Air

1) When you burn a fuel, it's known as combustion.
2) If there's not enough air about, something called incomplete combustion takes place.
3) This just means that combustion doesn't happen properly — because not enough air means not enough oxygen.
4) Incomplete combustion produces soot (black, powdery stuff) and less energy.
5) It also produces a toxic (poisonous) combustion product — carbon monoxide. Carbon monoxide can cause headaches, dizziness and tiredness.
6) So, when incomplete combustion happens inside a domestic boiler...
   - The boiler has a lower energy output (it produces less energy).
   - The boiler releases soot and carbon monoxide into the house.

This is the reaction for incomplete combustion:

fuel + oxygen → soot + carbon monoxide + carbon dioxide + water (+ energy)

There's still some oxygen around or the fuel wouldn't burn at all. (oxygen)

This is a toxic combustion product. (carbon monoxide)

Less energy is produced. (+ energy)

Low energy output? Have a chocolate biccie...

Carbon monoxide is a colourless gas with no smell. It's really dangerous. Every year, people are killed while they sleep due to faulty boilers filling the room with it and nobody noticing. That's why it's important to get boilers serviced regularly — to make sure that everything's working the way it should. Black sooty marks on the walls around a boiler are a clue that incomplete combustion is taking place.

Revision Summary for Section 3.3

You may or may not be pleased to know that this is the last revision summary for the entire book. Personally, I'd be pleased — but possibly not for the reason you think. Basically, being the last one, this revision summary is the bee's knees. It's the best of the best, the cream of the crop, the revision summary to end all revision summaries. It's so beautiful you might well fall to your knees and weep.
Don't believe me? Well the only way to find out is to get stuck in...

1) What greenhouse gas is produced when fossil fuels are burnt?
2) Name two sources of methane in agriculture.
3) What is the name of the process (involving bacteria) that releases nitrous oxide from soils?
4) Describe how the increase in greenhouse gases is causing global warming.
5) What is the Kyoto Agreement? What's its main aim?
6) What does a fertiliser do?
7) What is meant by the word 'leaching'?
8) Describe the process of eutrophication.
9) What happens if herbicides and pesticides get into a river?
10) What are indicator species?
11) What does it mean if you find:
    a) lots of lichens in an area,
    b) lots of bloodworms in a river?
12) a) Name three methods of waste disposal.
    b) Give one advantage and one disadvantage of each method.
13) What are biodegradable plastics?
14) Describe three ways that biodegradable plastics can break down.
15) What is conduction?
16) What is convection?
17) What is radiation?
18) Bricks have a U-value of 33. Straw bales have a U-value of 3.8.
    Which one will have the fastest heat loss?
19) Name five ways you could reduce heat loss in your home.
20) Describe the difference between efficiency and cost-effectiveness.
21) What is payback time?
22) a) Name five common pollutants in the home.
    b) What health problems can they cause?
23) What do hazard symbols on household products tell you?
24) Why is radon regarded as an indoor pollutant?
25) How do ventilation systems help in houses where there might be a lot of radon?
26) Why do domestic boilers need a good supply of air?
27) What is incomplete combustion? What toxic product does it produce?

Index

A

accuracy 6
acids 42-44
adaptations
  in animals 28
  in microorganisms 29
  in plants 29
air 23
alcohol 83, 84
alkalis 43
alleles 48
aluminium 21, 52
aluminium oxide 21
amps (A) 67
animals
  adaptations in 29
  cells 46
  testing on 45, 82
anomalous results 6
antacids 45
antibiotics 81, 82
antibodies 79, 80
antigens 79, 80
argon 23
atmosphere 14, 23
atomic numbers 16
atoms 15
auxins 31
averages 7

B

bacteria 78
balancing equations 19
bar charts 7
bases 42
biased data 3
Big Bang theory 12
biodegradable plastics 100
biomass
  for generating electricity 59, 61
  in food chains 32-34
biosphere 32
blood clots 79
blood sugar 41
body temperature 40

C

calcium carbonate 51
calibrating equipment 6
cancer 85
carbon cycle 35
carbon dioxide 14, 58, 96
carbon monoxide 58, 104
cell membranes 46
cells 46
cement 51
central nervous system (CNS) 37, 38
ceramics 54, 56
chemical equations 18, 19
cholera 78
chromic materials 91
chromosomes 46
classification of organisms 26
cloning 93
competition between organisms 27
composites 55, 56
compounds 18
conclusions 9
concrete 51, 55, 86
conduction (of heat) 101
constant internal environment 40
control groups 5
controlled assessment 10
control systems 40
control variables 4
convection 101
copper 52
correlations 8, 9
cost-effectiveness 102
crude oil 20, 53, 57, 58
current 67
cystic fibrosis 48
cytoplasm 46

D

dependent variables 4, 8
diabetes 41
diesel 57
directly proportional graphs 8
disease 78, 80
distribution of organisms 27
domestic boilers 104
Doppler effect 12
drugs
  addiction to 83
  personalisation of 81
  recreational 83, 84
  testing of 45, 82
  to treat disease 81

E

Earth
  atmosphere of 13, 14
  structure of 13
earthquakes 13
ecological relationships 30
economics of chemical production 24
ecosystems 32
effectors 37, 38, 40
efficiency
  of electrical appliances 69-71
  of energy transfer in ecosystems 33
electrical circuits 67
electricity
  bills 68
  generation of 64
  meters 68
  supply of 65
electrolysis 21, 88
electromagnetic radiation dangers 76
electromagnetic spectrum 72
electromagnetic waves 72, 74
electrons 15-17
electron shells 17
electroplating 88, 89
elements 15-17
energy
  consumption 70
  diagrams 71
  efficiency 69, 70
  transfer (in ecosystems) 33
  use and costs 68
Energy Labels (EU) 70
errors in data 6
eutrophication 98
evaluating data 10
evidence (to support a hypothesis) 1
evolution 30
evolutionary trees 30
extremophiles 29

F

fair tests 2, 4, 5
fibreglass 55, 56
fibreoptic cables 75
film badges 86
flammable chemicals 42
flu (influenza) 78
food chains 32, 33
formulas 18
fossil fuels 57-64
  alternatives to 59-63
fractional distillation
  of air 23
  of crude oil 20
frequency (of waves) 39, 72, 73
fuels 57

G

gamma cameras 85
gamma rays 72, 76, 85
  dangers of 76
genes 46, 47
gene therapy 49
genetic disorders 48
  screening for 49
  treatment of 49
genetic engineering 94
geothermal energy 59, 61
global warming 58, 97
glucose 41
gravitropism 31
greenhouse gases 14, 96, 97

H

haemophilia 48
harmful chemicals 42
hazards 5, 42, 103
hazard symbols 42, 103
hearing 39
heartburn 45
heat transfer 103
heating oil 57
helium 23
herd immunity 80
heroin 83
hertz (Hz) 39, 72
high blood pressure 81
homeostasis 40

Index

hormones 41
hydrocarbons 20, 57
hydroelectric power 59, 60
hydrogen ions 43
hydroxide ions 43
hypotheses 1, 4

I

immune system 79, 80
incomplete combustion 104
independent variables 4, 8
indicator species 99
indicators (pH) 43
indigestion tablets 45
influenza (flu) 78
infrared radiation 72, 75
  dangers of 76
insulin 41, 94
intervals in data 5
ions 15
iron 21, 52
iron oxide 21

J

joules (J) 68

K

kerosene 57
kilowatt-hours (kWh) 68
kilowatts (kW) 68
kingdoms 26
kitchen blenders 69
Kyoto Agreement 97

L

lab experiments 2
lead 21, 52, 86
lead aprons 76
lead oxide 21
lead screens 76
lichens 99
light waves 12
limestone 35, 51
line graphs 8
lines of best fit 8
liver disease 84
longitudinal waves 39
lung cancer 84
lymphocytes 79

M

marijuana 83
mass number 16
MDF (medium-density fibreboard) 55
mean 6, 7
measles 78, 80
metals 52, 56
metal carbonates 44
metal extraction 21, 22
metal hydroxides 44
metal ores 21
metal oxides 44
methane 14, 96
microorganisms 29, 32, 78
microwave ovens 74
microwaves 72, 74
  dangers of 76
Milky Way 11
Miller and Urey experiment 14
mining 20, 22
mixtures 18
mobile phones 74
molecules 15
monomers 53
mortar 51
motor neurones 37, 38
MRSA (methicillin-resistant *Staphylococcus aureus*) 82
mucus 79
mumps 78, 80

N

National Grid 64
natural gas 57
natural selection 30
negative feedback 40
nervous system 37
neurones 37, 38
neutralisation reactions 43-45
neutrons 15
nicotine 83, 84
nitrogen 23
nitrous oxide 96
non-renewable fuels 58, 62, 63
nuclear energy 62
nucleus 46
nutrient cycling 32

O

ores 21

P

painkillers 81
pathogens 78
payback times 102
penicillin 81
periodic table 16
personalisation of drugs 81
petrol 57
phagocytes 79
photochromic materials 91
photosynthesis 14, 32, 35
phototropism 31
pH scale 43
phytomining 22
plant adaptations 29
plant growth 31
plastics 100
platelets 79
plate tectonics 13
plutonium 62
polio 78, 80
pollution 58, 98, 99
pollution (indoor) 103
polydactyly 48
polyethene 53
polymers 53, 56
potential difference 67
power 67, 68
precise results 6
predictions 1, 4
protons 15
Punnett squares 48
pyramids of biomass 34
pyramids of number 34

Q

quarrying 20
quicklime 51

R

radiation (heat) 101
radiation (nuclear)
  medical uses of 85
  safety of 86
radioactivity
  hazards of 42
  waste 62
radiopharmaceuticals 85
radiotherapy 76, 85, 86
radio waves 11, 72, 74, 76
  dangers of 76
radon 103
range of data 5, 7
receptors 37, 40
recreational drugs 83, 84
red shift 12
reflex arcs 38
reflexes 38
reinforced concrete 55
relay neurones 38
reliability 2, 6
remote controls 75
renewable energy 59-61, 63
resolution 6
rice growing 96
rock salt 20
rubella 78, 80

S

salts 43, 44
sample size 2
Sankey diagrams 71
satellite TV 74
selective breeding 92
self-healing paints 90
sense organs 37
sense receptors 37
sensory neurones 37, 38
shape memory alloys 91
shrink wrap 91
sickle-cell anaemia 48
slaked lime 51
smart materials 91
smart paints 90
smoking 83, 84
solar energy 59, 60
Solar System 11

Index and Answers

sound waves 39
species 26
speed (drug) 83
sprouts 22
standard form 73
steel 52, 56
step-up / step-down transformers 65
stomach acid 45
studies 2
sulfur dioxide 58
superconductors 90
sustainable materials 56
symptoms 81
systematic errors 6

T

tectonic plates 13
telescopes 11
tetanus 80
theories 1
thermochromic materials 91
thermoregulatory centre 40
tidal barrages 59
tissue culture 93
tobacco 83, 84
toxins 78
tracers 85
trial runs 5
trophic levels 32, 33
tuberculosis 78, 80
TV signals 74
typhoid 78

U

ultraviolet light 72, 75
  dangers of 76
Universe 11, 12
uranium 62
U-values 101

V

vaccination 80
validity 2
variables 2, 4, 5
variation in plants and animals 47
viruses 78
visible light 11, 72, 75
  dangers of 76
volcanoes 13
volts (V) 67

W

waste disposal 24, 100
watts (W) 67
wave equation 73
wavelength 72, 73
wave power 59
waves 72
wave velocity 73
white blood cells 79
white goods 70
whooping cough 80
wind power 59, 60
withdrawal symptoms 83

X

X-rays 11, 72, 76, 85
  dangers of 76

Z

zero errors 6

Answers

Revision Summary for Section 1.1 (page 25)

13) a) 6   b) 5

18) $CaCO_3 + 2HCl \rightarrow CaCl_2 + H_2O + CO_2$

Revision Summary for Section 2.1 (page 50)

17) $2HCl + Na_2CO_3 \rightarrow 2NaCl + H_2O + CO_2$

27)

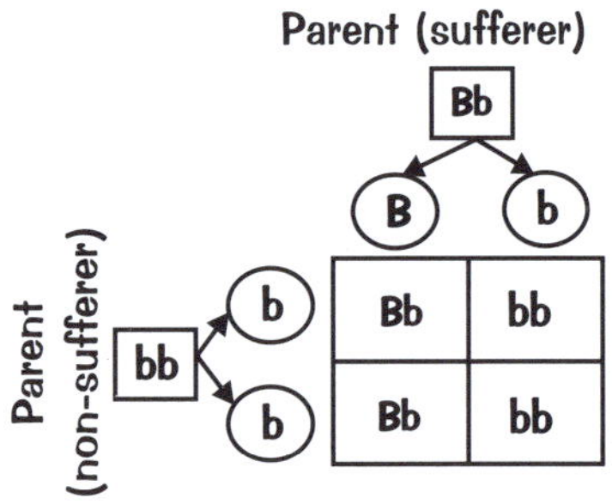

There is a 2 in 4 (50%) chance that their child will be a sufferer.

Revision Summary for Section 2.2 (page 66)

18) $C_7H_{16} + 11O_2 \rightarrow 7CO_2 + 8H_2O$

Revision Summary for Section 2.3 (page 77)

2) $12 \times 230 = 2760$ W

3) 45 kJ = 45 000 J,
1 minute = 60 s
so, 45 000 / 60 = 750 W

4) 45 minutes = 0.75 h
so, energy units = $3 \times 0.75 = 2.25$ kWh
cost = $2.25 \times 8 = 18$p

6) 4 J / 50 J = 0.08 (or $\times$ 100 = 8%)

7) 70 J / 100 J = 0.7 (or $\times$ 100 = 70%)

9) E.g.

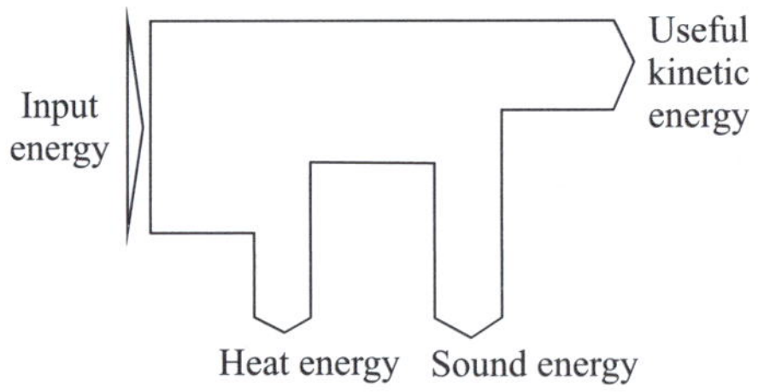

16) 50 kHz = 50 000 Hz
0.3 cm = 0.003 m
so, $50\,000 \times 0.003 = 150$ m/s

Photography in India

Photography in India

A Visual History from the 1850s to the Present

Nathaniel Gaskell
Diva Gujral

Prestel
Munich • London • New York

Introduction/7

1 Archaeology & Ethnography/18

2 Pictorialism & the Picturesque/58

3 Power & Posterity/80

4 Proof & Propaganda/106

5 The New Exotic/134

6 Modernism & Modernity/154

7 Society & the Street/184

8 Essay & Enquiry/210

9 Postmodernism & Play/242

10 The Book & the Biennale/268

Endnotes/300

Image Credits/302

Index/303

Introduction

The camera arrived in India within the first few months of its invention in Europe in the mid-nineteenth century. Its early use in visualising the country, agitated by complex political and cultural transitions, has resulted in an especially rich photographic archive.

FROM TOP TO BOTTOM

Henry Peach Robinson, *Fading Away*, 1858

Shapoor Bhedwar, detail from *Tyag No. 4. The Mystic Sign*, from the album *Art Studies*, c.1890

Maharaja Sawai Ram Singh II, hand-painted self portrait, c.1860

Roger Fenton, *The Valley of the Shadow of Death*, Crimea, 1855

Felice Beato, *Interior of Secunderabad after the Massacre*, 1858

Murray are both relevant here, with Bourne's work discussed in this book in the context of the picturesque, an aesthetic ideal introduced in the late eighteenth century by William Gilpin and Uvedale Price. The picturesque was used as a visual description of printed pictures, but also by extension as a conceptual framework with which to make sense of actual landscapes. Transplanted to the Himalayas and elsewhere in the Indian "countryside", the genre seems to enact a visual colonisation of the land – the Indian landscape is viewed, understood and therefore "owned" by the West rather than on its own terms. Art and empiricism, from different departure points, end in the same place.

In the last decade of the nineteenth century, the reign of the picturesque was making way for another photographic movement typically thought of as Western – pictorialism, which championed the "creation" rather than the "taking" of an image and, crucially, the photographer's self-labelling as an artist. A key figure in this genre was Bombay-based photographer Shapoor Bhedwar, who staged intentionally soft-focus studio portraits of subjects arranged in theatrical scenes in a style deeply reminiscent of British pictorialist Henry Peach Robinson, a pioneer of early photography in the West. Bhedwar was even a member of the exclusive yet somewhat elusive Linked Ring, a photographic society created in 1892 defending photography's dual art and science remit. From the mid-twentieth century, and well into the 1970s, pictorialism was no longer limited to professional Indian photographers, but embraced by amateurs too.

The turn of the century also saw a marked rise in portraiture on the Indian subcontinent, with new local clients anxious to have their likenesses taken as a token of their status. The genre was in fact one of the very first uses of photography, with studios clustering throughout the important port cities of Bombay, Madras and Calcutta as early as the 1840s. Within a century it would be democratised and the camera would be a familiar presence in the 9,000-odd small towns across the country.

While the identity of sitters in ethnographic photographs, such as the Andaman orphans we saw in Saché & Westfield's photographs, was thrust upon them, commissioned portraits allowed sitters from the burgeoning urban middle class to have more of a say in how they were portrayed, if not interpreted. Early portraits tended to service mercantile families, important colonial administrators and royalty – the latter forced to kowtow to the British establishment in real life but able to convey their ancestry, power and "rightful" identity as rulers through the codes of dress and countenance that could be emphasised in photographs.

As camera technology became more affordable and spread to smaller towns, middle-class subjects began to patronise studios and explore and perform their own complex identities. For example, at the small-town establishment Studio Suhag (established 1979) run by the photographer Suresh Punjabi, sitters received a range of aspirational props: a suit jacket, a telephone, a glass of wine. While ethnographic "portraiture" spoke only of those in power, studio portraits allowed sitters to momentarily reclaim their identities – albeit still defined elsewhere by "the elite". The result is a fascinating take on home-grown anthropology; as Christopher Pinney reports, Punjabi's images are a key record of the width of flairs and the length of collars sported by provincial Indian men in Western-style suits.

Photography's innate and usually successful capacity to sway its audience, deviating from reality to serve needs and biases, formed the basis for one of the most pervasive genres in the early to mid-twentieth century: photojournalism. Enabled by the arrival of more mobile medium and large-format cameras with faster film and portable flashes, and later propelled by smaller, more agile cameras and 35mm film, it offered up the conceit of capturing events in real time. In India the genre had deeper roots, seeming to begin with the images of Anglo-Italian Felice Beato (1832–1909), who documented the aftermath of the 1857 Rebellion. According to legend, for one photograph Beato himself rearranged the bones of the sepoy mutineers for dramatic effect, having arrived well after events unfolded. As with Roger Fenton's more famous image of the Crimean War, made only two years earlier, the "aftermath" came to be poetic proof of the event itself. It is interesting to note that Beato would have been well aware of Fenton's work, having taken over from him in Crimea in 1855.

This ability of photography to record staged events or amplify real ones would prove invaluable to the British in their mission to portray themselves as all-powerful – a point which the colonial state was understandably anxious to

FROM TOP TO BOTTOM

William H. Burke, detail from *George V and Queen Mary, Delhi Durbar, from Queen Mary's album, volume 15*, 1911

Narayan Virkar, *Survivors of the Jallianwala Bagh massacre, showing bullet holes as proof of the atrocity*, 1919

Suresh Kumar, *Le Corbusier and Pierre Jeanneret at Sukhna Lake in Chandigarh*, 1960

Marg, vol. 14, no. 1, December 1960

Exhibition catalogue for *The Family of Man*, 1955

emphasise (and reinforce countrywide through its control of the press). An example can be found in the image of King George V and Queen Mary at the 1911 Delhi Durbar – a pageant orchestrated to display the pomp of the Raj and the splendour of empire. In reality, India's vast population of over 252 million was being ruled by a presence of not more than 164,000 British (mostly soldiors and civil servants), so the impression of might mattered more than power in real numeric terms – a situation akin to the role of the durbars themselves, which can be seen as the Raj's take on Potemkin villages. But just as photography could exploit the capacity for illusion, it could also deliver hard-hitting truths; just eight years later, Indian photographer Narayan Virkar documented the aftermath of the Jallianwala Bagh massacre, depicting the families of those unlawfully murdered by Colonel Dyer's troops by pointing at the bullet holes in the walls of the public garden where they were shot. Torn between its capacity for fiction and truth-telling, photojournalism in India, as elsewhere, continued to unravel as a tense, irresolvable negotiation.

As India passed from the jewel in an imperial crown to a democratic nation with challenges and contradictions of its own, continued contact with outsiders fuelled heated debates – on identity, hegemony and cultural belonging. These debates equally play out in photographs, as cameras captured an eventful epoch climaxing in India finally gaining independence from the British Empire in 1947. Photography was then mobilised to chart the fallout as the newly born nation, caught between celebrating its hard-won autonomy and remaining open to the world, grappled with self-definition – including in the cultural realm. The country's first prime minister, Jawaharlal Nehru, urged Indians "not to go abroad in search of the past [but to] go to [the] foreign countries in search of the present. The search is necessary, for isolation from it means backwardness and decay."

Amongst many progressive cultural initiatives, Nehru's government invited Swiss-French modernist architect Le Corbusier to design the planned city of Chandigarh, and Americans Charles and Ray Eames to suggest a programme for Indian design pedagogy, resulting in the National Institute of Design (NID) in Ahmedabad (attended or engaged with by several of the photographers discussed in this book). At the same time, Nehru's non-aligned India was determined to resist Western cultural hegemony at all costs – this included Triennale-India, launched in the tumultuous year of 1968 (two years after Nehru's death), drawing artists from around the world and demonstrating the ability of modernism and internationalism to thrive outside the Euro-American monopoly. India wasn't seeking to divorce the old world, but rather to remake the new one in its own image, absorbing the best that the global marketplace had to offer to its own devices.

Indian artists were meanwhile entering an introspective phase – keen to shrug off the long shadow cast by British-established art schools. Many practitioners turned to the camera for the first time, finding in it a liberating tool to develop their own "modern" visual vocabulary. Yet running counter to this reawakening of the country's modernist art scene, the West continued to assert its cultural influence through headline exhibitions such as the Museum of Modern Art's *The Family of Man*, in 1955. Curated by Edward Steichen in New York, its official, and strikingly lofty, mission was to reveal how photography could be used to capture "the gamut of life from birth to death".

The Family of Man toured seven Indian cities between 1956 and 1957, becoming the most important and most popular photography exhibition ever seen in the country. Despite its mission to celebrate "universal aspects of the human experience", it was tremendously Western-centric in its vision: well over half of the 273 participating photographers were American, and a grand total of one was Indian. In response, the country staged its own version of the show, *Images of India*, in 1960, dedicated to Indian photographers. Its success swiftly encouraged the day's leading Indian cultural journal, *Marg*, to dedicate an entire issue to photography. Yet despite its promising title, "Photography as an Art Form", and its essays, including "Contemporary Trends in Indian Photography" by R. J. Chinwalla, for instance, it was dogged by largely derivative pictorialism and the predictable "humanism" of *The Family of Man* – a far cry from the free, progressive art form championed in the rhetoric of Nehru and the Triennale-India.

Around the same post-war era, well-known Western photographers including Norman Parkinson, Cecil Beaton and later Derry Moore arrived in India, and set about repainting the newly independent country not with the

FROM TOP TO BOTTOM

British Vogue, November, 1956

Nasreen Mohamedi, *Untitled*, 1967

Cindy Sherman, *Untitled Film Still #21*, 1978

Bernd and Hilla Becher, *Zwei Fördertürme*, 1967

Edward Ruscha, *Twentysix Gasoline Stations*, 1963; published 1967 brush of modernism, but with that of imperial nostalgia. Theirs was an India still stuck in the past – a feat achieved, in Moore's case, by casting out of the frame all signs of the fast-modernising times. Whether his photographs are a consciously distorted notion of a country on the verge of globalisation or a document of its long struggle to shake off anachronisms is an interesting question (the photographer himself likened his task to "fishing in an increasingly emptied sea", suggesting the former). Regardless, the results are sympathetic, exquisitely detailed and arguably less problematic than later photographers such as Steve McCurry, who would use careful staging (and later digital manipulation by his studio) to revive the exotic land of the Western imagination familiar from the "ethnographic" staged photographs of the nineteenth century, and that, too, well into the twenty-first.

In parallel to this period of what in this book we call the "New Exotic", Nehru's progressive attitude to the arts began to bear fruit, as Indian artists ventured abroad "in search of the present", to recall his speech in Bandung in 1955. Among them were Nasreen Mohamedi (born in 1937 in Karachi, in present-day Pakistan), who studied at Saint Martin's School of Art in London, and later in Paris, before going back to India to produce her work; and Raghubir Singh (born in Jaipur in 1942), who spent fifteen years in the French capital while regularly journeying back to India. Mohamedi's *Untitled* (1972) is the height of her modernist vision. Not only does the image's title shrug off any conventional sense of fidelity to place, it pushes to the periphery architectural clues as to the building's geographic and cultural whereabouts, becoming an exploration of the economy of line and geometry, and not a document of a country. Photography, it suggests, could exist for photography's sake, and not necessarily as a medium or instrument of external forces and motivations.

Mohamedi's photographs specifically, and Indian modernism in photography more generally, form a seminal moment in India's modern art history that continues to be underexplored academically. In the end, however, so-called Indian modernism (at least in the context of photography) would turn out to be a niche affair. Despite the promise of a pluralist and economically optimistic country, India was still very much a land of staggering social divides and contradictory politics, and photographers were therefore questioning how far modernist abstraction could go towards telling the stories that needed to be told, as well as reacting against a still prevalent form of Western exoticism in the genre that either glossed over, or romanticised, the complexities that it encountered. Amongst them were Pablo Bartholomew, who adopted a grainy, purposefully unmediated style to document the lives of morphine addicts in Delhi as well as the streets of Bombay in the 1970s; Mary Ellen Mark, creator of the hard-hitting social documentary series *Falkland Road*, a long-form photoessay looking at sex workers in Bombay; and Raghu Rai, who borrowed the vocabulary of street photography and Cartier-Bresson's intuition-led "decisive moment" to depict the "common man" while suggesting a spontaneous relationship to his subjects. Social issues ruled the era's photography, which regressed to an earlier form of image-making seemingly inspired by Steichen's humanistic *Family of Man*, creating fertile ground for those wishing to study the ethics of representation – in light of these stories typically being told by the elite – using the downtrodden as their protagonists.

Beginning in the early 1990s, when Manmohan Singh liberalised the economy in his role as finance minister, India was actively embracing globalisation. For artists, this meant exposure to a new flow of ideas from the West (in a more natural way than with Nehru's state-driven directives) – photography having morphed into a very different creature in the preceding two decades. In the 1960s and 1970s, conceptualism had uprooted the format from the dictates of time and fine art, turning it into a vehicle for ideas – be it Cindy Sherman's self-portraits re-appropriating female stereotypes or Edward Ruscha's consciously bland concertina photo-books. These were also the years of Bernd and Hilla Becher, heads of the photography department at the Kunstakademie Düsseldorf, whose large-format typologies of industrial buildings, allied to the New Topographics movement, in turn inspired a generation of influential German photographers, and in combination with conceptualism introduced a modish style of photography taught in art schools around the world. Photography had been reborn as contemporary art – featuring in biennales, blue-chip galleries and auction houses, and feeding an eager global art market.

Odeypour. Temple hindou moderne
en marbre blanc

1 Archaeology & Ethnography

The fact that the history of the camera and the history of colonialism came to be so entwined is hardly surprising: it was a tightly bound world, held together by networks of trade and mercantilist industry, power and empire, into which the photograph was born.

Saché & Westfield
British India, active 1865–70

Established in 1865 at 15 Waterloo Street in Calcutta, India's capital under the British Raj, the studio of John Edward Saché and W. F. Westfield produced some of the most fascinating ethnographic work of the early period in Indian photography, despite being in business for only five years. In its first year of operations it was commissioned by the Asiatic Society of Bengal to photograph a group of Andamanese subjects who had been brought to Calcutta by Jeremiah Nelson Homfray, superintendent of the Andamanese Orphanage, as part of an ethnographic study – the popular British colonial theory at the time was that a slave ship had been shipwrecked just off the coast of India and that the Andamanese were descendants of black slaves. The resultant photograph was then exhibited at the Paris International Exposition of 1867. The erroneous understanding of anthropology coupled with the deeply problematic way in which the subject is rendered, as well as the speed at which it was digested by Western audiences, sets the tone for much of the way early photographs made in India functioned.

This particular portrait shows seven Andamanese subjects with Homfray. A description of their session illustrates how quickly the impact of colonisation modified behaviour: "At the studio of Messrs. Saché and Westfield, where several gentlemen – strangers to the Andamanese, were present when the photographs were taken, – [*sic*] we encountered positive difficulty in inducing them to group themselves, stripped of their European clothes. That difficulty overcome, however, it was remarkable to observe how quickly they appreciated the fact that they were required to keep steady, and how willingly they did the best they could, when undergoing an ordeal, which is disagreeable even to those whose vanity it is pleasing."[1]

It's interesting to note that whilst Homfray is in the European portrait convention of the three-quarter profile, the Andamanese are shown frontally, drawing comparisons with the conventions of photography in forensics, ethnography and criminology. The very caption of this photograph, *Andamanese group with their keeper Mr Homfray*, is revealing of the infantilising nature of the colonial gaze: here the Andamanese subjects are posed with Mr Homfray and equated with orphaned children, while he assumes a patronising, parental role as the Englishman and imperial agent with the "white man's burden".

Although the studio of Saché & Westfield itself shut down by 1870, both photographers continued to work in India subsequent to this date.

Andamanese group with their keeper Mr Homfray, 1865
Albumen print, 14.1 × 19.7 cm

Linnaeus Tripe
b. England, 1822–1902

Linnaeus Tripe joined the East India Company army in 1838, was nominated as a cadet for the Madras Infantry, and eventually ended his career, after thirty-five years of service, as a colonel. Between 1850 and 1854, while on leave in England, he began to experiment with photography. Returning to Bangalore in 1854, Tripe made his first photographs of India, showing the temples of Halebid and Belur, on leave from his regiment. The following year he took part in the Madras Exhibition of Raw Products, Arts, and Manufactures of Southern India, displaying sixty-eight photographs of previously un-photographed temples from his trip. The jury noted: "The majority of these are clear, sharp, and well defined in the details ... The half tints and reflected lights are also well brought out ... As studies for the artist, the antiquary, or the engraver, these are invaluable."[1]

Tripe began work in Madras in 1857. He then set off on a tour travelling via Srirangam, Tiruchchirappalli, Madurai, then Pudukkottai and Tanjore, looking for subjects with architectural or antiquarian interest. Tripe wanted to ensure his images were practical, and before he set out he asked the chief engineer for guidance on what would be most useful from an engineering perspective, and incorporated this into his work. In 1858, he also photographed sculptures from the ruined Buddhist stupa at Amaravati, the "Elliot Marbles", named after Walter Elliot, the antiquarian, linguist and member of the Madras Council who recovered them.

Tripe entered fifty of his South India photographs in the 1859 annual exhibition of the Madras Photographic Society. Though he was ineligible to win the gold medal, since he could not be classed as an amateur, the jury dubbed his photographs "the best in the exhibition", stating that they "illustrate admirably the architecture of the Hindoo Temples and Places of Southern India, and in particular the Madura and Tanjore series comprise in this respect all that is most worthy of record in those cities."[2] Midway through 1859, however, the government – now under the British Crown following the 1857 Rebellion – ordered that Tripe undertake no new work, questioning not only the financial justification but also his ability to make photographs in line with the colonial agenda.[3]

The Pagoda jewels, 1858
Albumen print, 21.3 × 30.2 cm

143

Central Museum Madras: Group 27, 1858
Albumen print, 30.2 × 21.6 cm

Alexis de La Grange
b. France, 1825–1917

In 1849, after completing his studies in Paris and having served in the naval artillery from 1844 to 1847, Alexis de La Grange embarked upon a two-year trip to India, Sri Lanka, Java, Malaysia and Singapore – equipped with his camera and accompanied by his older cousin, Félix Lambrecht, who detailed the trip in his publication *Souvenirs* (1873). In spirit, their journey was not unlike that of the Grand Tours undertaken by rich aristocratic Europeans since the seventeenth century. Whilst the majority of such tours focused on Italy, Egypt and Jerusalem, de La Grange spent a significant amount of time in India and his work provides an interesting contribution to the period as a European, though not British, photographer.

Only sixty-three photographs survive from this two-year trip – all architectural views, including famous monuments such as the Taj Mahal and the Jama Masjid, as well as lesser-known tombs, temples and private residences, with the sole exception of a portrait of a "native" servant. Unlike most European photographers in India at the time and after, de La Grange's eclectic photographic choices are those of a tourist, indicative of little agenda, imperial or otherwise. Numbering among the earliest photographs taken in the subcontinent, they firmly establish him as a pioneer in the field of travel photography.

For his photographs in India, de La Grange employed the wet waxed paper negative process, a modification of the calotype process that had been introduced in the late 1840s, and used a pre-salted and silver-nitrate coated paper negative that did not require the addition of gallic acid until the development stage – making it more convenient for use in hotter climates. Upon his return to France in 1851, he produced two leather-bound albums, both titled *Photographies de l'Inde Anglais* [Photographs of British India], using the recently introduced albumen printing process. One of these albums was dedicated to the French statesman Adolphe Thiers and contained sixty-one photographs and is accompanied by de La Grange's extensive handwritten notations. The other, with forty-eight photographs – and all but two identical to those in the Thiers album – is captioned but is lacking a dedication and annotations.[1]

De La Grange's admiration for Indian architecture is clearly expressed in his commentary, and while he frequently notes the decaying conditions of his architectural subjects, his photographic frame avoids a display of these elements of disintegration. This can be seen in contrast to other colonial photographers of the time who often focused on the monuments of India as emblems of ruin.

Victory Tower (Vijay Stambh), Chittor, 1849
The Taj Mahal, Agra, 1849
Albumen prints, approx. 22.1 × 17.3 cm each

Asafi Imambara, Lucknow, 1849
Hawa Mahal, Jaipur, 1849
Albumen prints, approx. 18 x 21.8 cm each

Odeypour. Temple hindou moderne
en marbre blanc

Hindu temple, Udaipur, 1849
Albumen print, 21.8 × 18 cm

Francis Frith & Co.
England, active 1859–1971

Born in Chesterfield, England, Francis Frith (1822–1898) amassed a fortune as a businessman by the time he was thirty four, before going on to become one of the pre-eminent travel photographers of his day, journeying broadly across the Middle East and India. In John Hannavy's *Encyclopedia of Nineteenth-Century Photography*, Maxim Leonid Weintraub notes: "While not the only photographer of his era to publish scenic views of exotic places and monuments commercially, Frith was ... an integral figure in the popularisation of the travel photograph specifically, and commercial photography generally."[1] Francis Frith & Co. was indeed the largest producer of topographical photographs in the nineteenth century and the company sold individual prints as well as popular souvenir picture postcards of his scenic views.

From the late 1860s onwards the company began to publish series of Indian views in their catalogues – running up to over 800 images in total. Their 1875 catalogue cover listed views from "Bombay, Poonah, Calcutta, Madras, Benares, Cawnpore, Lucknow, Agra, Delhi, Cashmere, the Himalayas, Punjaub, etc.", and these images came endorsed with a Gold Medal from the Bengal Photographic Society. Although some of the Indian photographs in the Frith & Co. collection have been attributed to William Johnson (see p. 41), J. M. Drury and Oscar Mallitte, the majority of photographers employed by Frith in India remain unknown.

Whilst these images therefore do not speak about the vision of one particular author, they tell us much of the commercial appetite for photographs of India, and of how such imagery was communicated to the world, setting down very early on a global image of India designed to appeal especially to the European imagination. Photographs published by Francis Frith & Co. in India typically came in three formats – 20 × 25 cm, 40 × 50 cm and smaller stereoscopic pairs. Prints from these negatives reveal the company's interest with exposure times and vantage points in order to discern the most pleasing composition for each site.

Underscoring his comprehension of the artistic possibilities of photography were the many articles he wrote about the subject in which he argued for the ability of photographs to communicate divine truth and aesthetic awareness to the general population.[2] His use of language here shows how his rendition of the East was filtered through a religious ideology of Western superiority, despite many of his sites being the product of other religions. Francis Frith & Co. remained in business until 1968, long after its founder's death.

Annotated file prints from F. Frith & Co.'s *Universal Series*, c.1859–70
Albumen prints, approx. 25 × 20 cm each

Oodypour. Temple hindou moderne en marbre blanc

Hindu temple, Udaipur, 1849
Albumen print, 21.8 × 18 cm

Nicholas & Curths
British India, active *c.*1870s–1905

Little is known of John P. Nicholas's early life, but he is believed to have moved to Madras in 1857. His photographs were shown at an 1858 exhibition of the Madras Photography Society, where the jury noted: "Some portraits of religious mendicants, [*sic*] were also exhibited by Mr Nicholas. These were executed with the assistance of Mr Underwood. They are curious in their way, and the selection of subjects were [*sic*] excellent. One party had a wire passed through his cheeks. Two others had large square iron frames riveted to their necks. The pictures are well executed, and copies are for sale at Mr Nicholas' studio."[1]

In 1861, along with his brother James, he established Nicholas Brothers – which would grow to become one of the most important photographic firms of South India. The studio traded under various names over the years: Nicholas Bros. & Co. for a year between 1864 and 1865, and in partnership with Herman Ralph Curths as Nicholas & Curths for a few years around 1869–73. After the departure of Curths, the studio remained in business as Nicholas & Co. as late as 1905, although Nicholas himself probably left India sometime in the 1890s. There is also record of a briefly surviving London branch in 1866, while the Ootacamund branch set up in 1868 was eventually taken over by A. T. W. Penn (see p. 69).

Apart from their views of Madras and the surrounding region – architectural and picturesque – the firm was known for its portraiture and was patronised by royals and the upper classes. It was also interested in photographs of the "types of native Indians" or anthropological images and scenes of everyday life. Nicholas's poignant photographs of the Great Madras Famine of 1876–78 were also of particular note, as he believed that the visual record would have a larger impact than print journalism.

Studio group of domestic servants in Madras, *c.*1875
Albumen print, 10.1 × 13.5 cm

Francis Frith & Co.
England, active 1859–1971

Born in Chesterfield, England, Francis Frith (1822–1898) amassed a fortune as a businessman by the time he was thirty four, before going on to become one of the pre-eminent travel photographers of his day, journeying broadly across the Middle East and India. In John Hannavy's *Encyclopedia of Nineteenth-Century Photography*, Maxim Leonid Weintraub notes: "While not the only photographer of his era to publish scenic views of exotic places and monuments commercially, Frith was … an integral figure in the popularisation of the travel photograph specifically, and commercial photography generally."[1] Francis Frith & Co. was indeed the largest producer of topographical photographs in the nineteenth century and the company sold individual prints as well as popular souvenir picture postcards of his scenic views.

From the late 1860s onwards the company began to publish series of Indian views in their catalogues – running up to over 800 images in total. Their 1875 catalogue cover listed views from "Bombay, Poonah, Calcutta, Madras, Benares, Cawnpore, Lucknow, Agra, Delhi, Cashmere, the Himalayas, Punjaub, etc.", and these images came endorsed with a Gold Medal from the Bengal Photographic Society. Although some of the Indian photographs in the Frith & Co. collection have been attributed to William Johnson (see p. 41), J. M. Drury and Oscar Mallitte, the majority of photographers employed by Frith in India remain unknown.

Whilst these images therefore do not speak about the vision of one particular author, they tell us much of the commercial appetite for photographs of India, and of how such imagery was communicated to the world, setting down very early on a global image of India designed to appeal especially to the European imagination. Photographs published by Francis Frith & Co. in India typically came in three formats – 20 × 25 cm, 40 × 50 cm and smaller stereoscopic pairs. Prints from these negatives reveal the company's interest with exposure times and vantage points in order to discern the most pleasing composition for each site.

Underscoring his comprehension of the artistic possibilities of photography were the many articles he wrote about the subject in which he argued for the ability of photographs to communicate divine truth and aesthetic awareness to the general population.[2] His use of language here shows how his rendition of the East was filtered through a religious ideology of Western superiority, despite many of his sites being the product of other religions. Francis Frith & Co. remained in business until 1968, long after its founder's death.

Annotated file prints from F. Frith & Co.'s
***Universal Series*, c.1859–70**
Albumen prints, approx. 25 × 20 cm each

Dogras, Kashmir, c.1875
Nautch girls, Kashmir, c.1875
Albumen prints, approx. 16.3 × 20.8 cm each

Annotated file prints from Francis Frith & Co.'s *Universal Series*, c.1859–70
Albumen prints, approx. 20 × 25 cm each

1042. Mohairs.

1049. Surgurrah

1033. Meena.

1021. Dholeas

1013 Bheels

1029 Menas

Four bone objects found at Sirkap, Taxila (present-day Pakistan), 1913–33
Gelatin silver print, 14.6 × 10 cm

John Marshall
b. England, 1876–1956

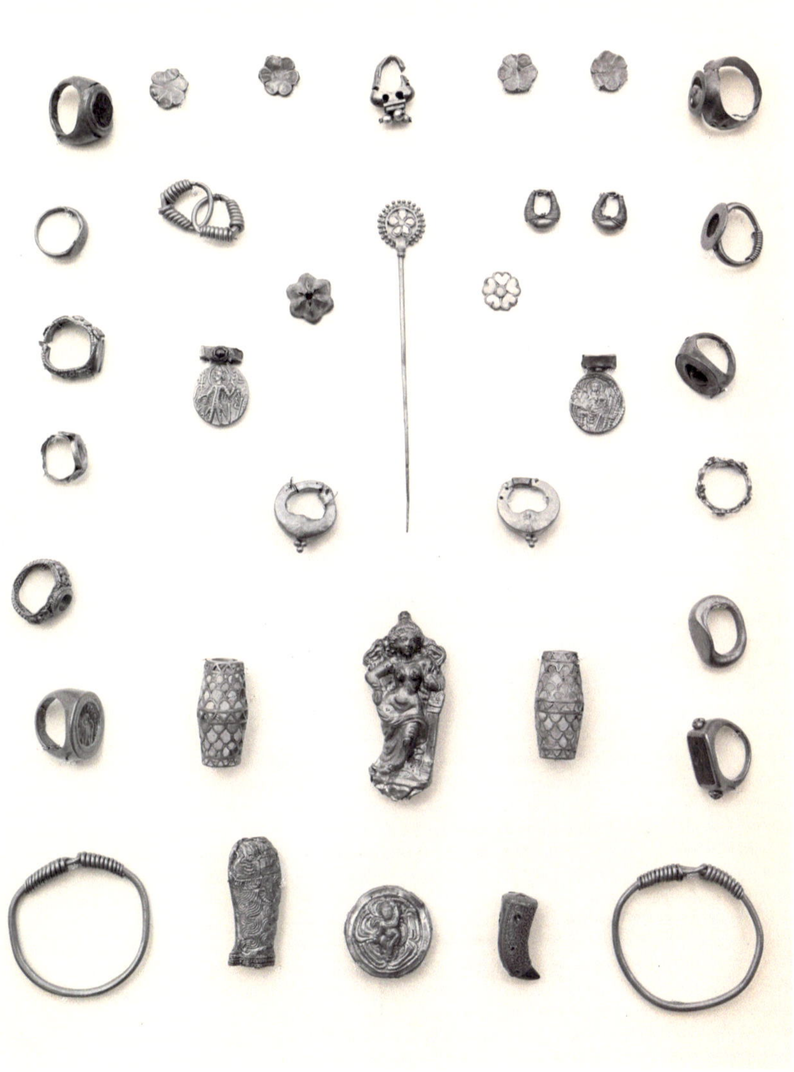

Sir John Hubert Marshall was one of the most reputed British archaeologists in India. He established many photographic practices that became essential to archaeology and collated hundreds of photographs documenting the early archaeological "findings" in British India. In 1902, Marshall, then a 26-year-old professor of classical studies at Cambridge, was appointed to the post of Director General of the Archaeological Survey of India (ASI) by Lord Curzon, who was then Viceroy of India. He reinvigorated the ASI's dwindling role, and under his tenure it was first professionalised. Marshall was one of the archaeologists responsible for the excavations of Harappa and Mohenjo-daro, two of the main cities of the Indus Valley Civilisation, which were discovered by Daya Ram Sahni. The photographs taken during these excavations, which allowed for international study, became the basis for much of the initial knowledge of the Indus Civilisation. However, Marshall did not allow Indian newspapers any access to the photographs and published them for the first time in the *Illustrated London News* in 1924, stoking nationalist outrage and leading to Marshall being questioned by the Council of States in 1925 – the first time that archaeological photos were subjected to a legislative enquiry.[1]

Marshall's magnum opus was a painstaking survey of the monuments of Sanchi (made with his collaborator Alfred Foucher). They were published in 1918 in the now iconic book *A Guide to Sanchi*. Marshall also carried out a major excavation at Taxila in present-day Pakistan, which further showed how photography could be employed in the place of archaeological drawings, allowing for a faster and more complete resource for further study, with each and every archaeological feature described photographically in great detail. Over two thousand of these painstakingly organised and often aesthetically very adept images are now in the collection of Durham University, and still used to this day as archaeological references to the site.

Miscellaneous gold objects from Sirkap, including pendants, brooches, rings and pins, Taxila (present-day Pakistan), 1913–33
Gelatin silver print, 27.5 × 20 cm

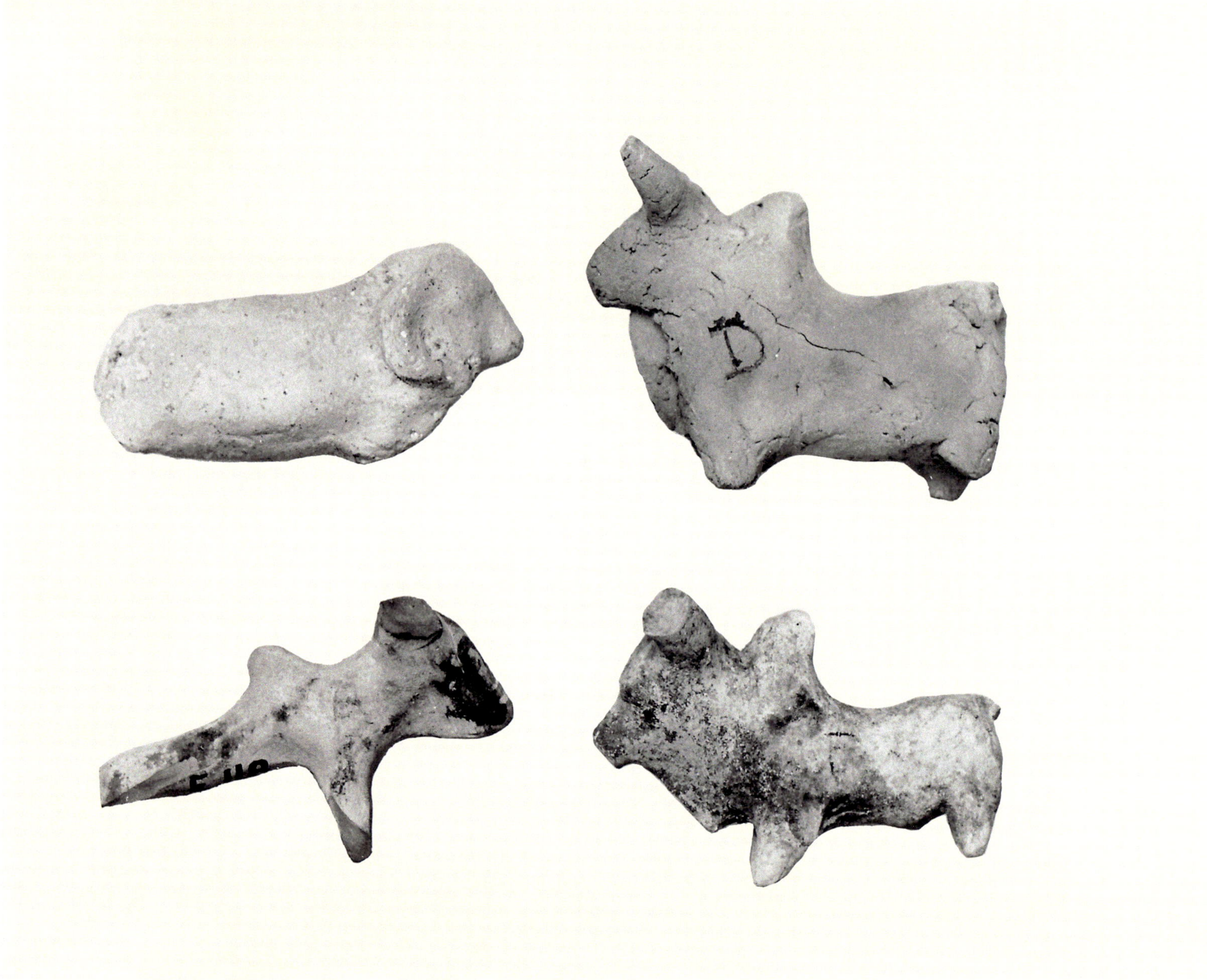

ABOVE AND OPPOSITE, CLOCKWISE FROM TOP LEFT

Four terracotta animal figurine fragments from Nal (present-day Pakistan), 1913–33
Gelatin silver print, 7.7 × 10 cm

Artefact numbers 1–33, Bent brass punch-marked coins from the Bhir mound, Taxila (present-day Pakistan), 1913–33
Gelatin silver print, 27.3 × 20.4 cm

Artefact numbers 34–133, Obverse side of punch-marked coins from the Bhir mound, Taxila (present-day Pakistan), 1913–33
Gelatin silver print, 27.3 × 20.4 cm

Artefact numbers 974–1029, Obverse side of punch-marked coins from the Bhir mound, Taxila (present-day Pakistan), 1913–33
Gelatin silver print, 27.3 × 20.4 cm

Artefact numbers 638–693, Obverse side of punch marked coins from the Bhir mound, Taxila, Punjab (present-day Pakistan), 1913–33
Gelatin silver print, 27.3 × 20.4 cm

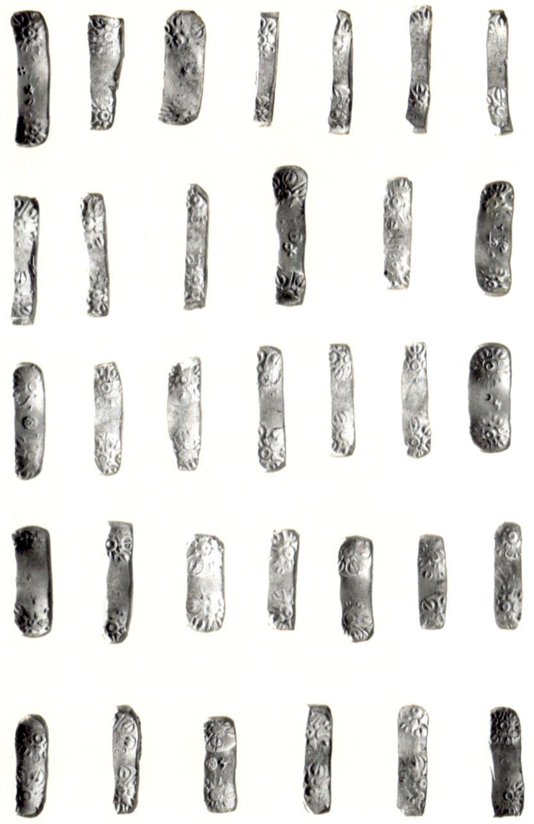

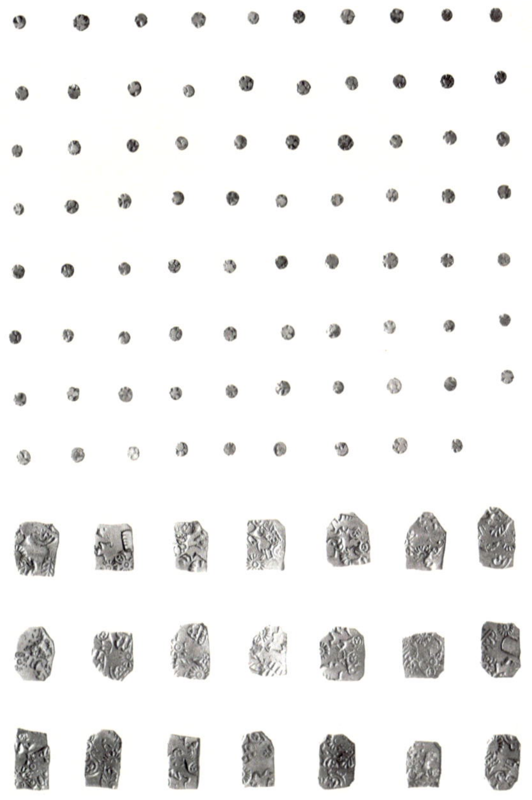

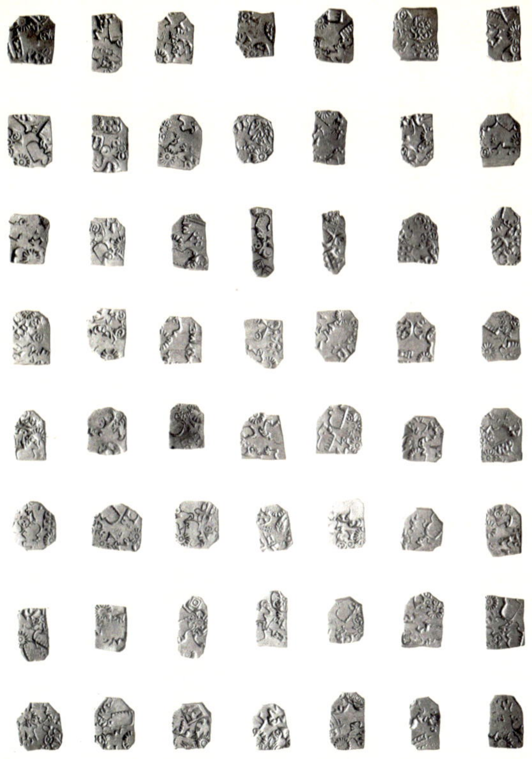

William Johnson
b. England, unknown–1886

Although information on William Johnson is scarce, historical records show that he worked as a clerk in the Uncovenanted Civil Service (recruited almost entirely from persons born in India, whether European, Eurasian or Asian) in Bombay from 1848 to 1851, before being promoted to the position of an assistant in the General Department in Girgaum, a post he occupied until 1860–61.[1] Apart from his duties as a civil servant, Johnson practised photography extensively, establishing a photography studio in Grant Road, Bombay, as early as 1852, and producing daguerreotypes and subsequently albumen prints made from wet plate collodion negatives.

Johnson was one of the founding members of the Bombay Photographic Society in 1854, and served as the society's joint secretary as well as co-editor of its journal.[2] From 1856 to 1858, the Bombay Photographic Society published the *Indian Amateur's Photographic Album*, of which Johnson would become one of the main contributors, partnering with William Henderson to create photographic studies of the inhabitants of Bombay and its surrounding districts. Some of these later re-appeared in *The Oriental Races and Tribes, Residents and Visitors of Bombay* (1863 and 1866), a two-volume work authored by Johnson, where he declared that the "photographic delineations of the numerous peoples and tribes frequenting ... Bombay ... have long been desired both among students of geography and ethnography, and the lovers of art." Containing a series of portraits of racial and caste groups, with montage techniques used to place them against appropriate backgrounds, this work is considered to be the first photographically illustrated ethnographical publication to appear in India.

As with architecture, photographs of Indians (as ethnography rather than portraiture) suggested a natural area for documentation and had by the 1860s become a photographic genre in its own right. As John Falconer writes: "Whether in the service of the rising science of ethnography, or as the creation of 'exotic' souvenirs of the East, the photography of racial types became, alongside architectural photography, the most important of the 'officially' sponsored uses of the medium."[3]

ABOVE AND FOLLOWING PAGES
Photographs from the album *The Oriental Races and Tribes, Residents and Visitors of Bombay*, photographed 1852–55, published 1863 and 1866
Albumen prints, approx. 24 × 19 cm each

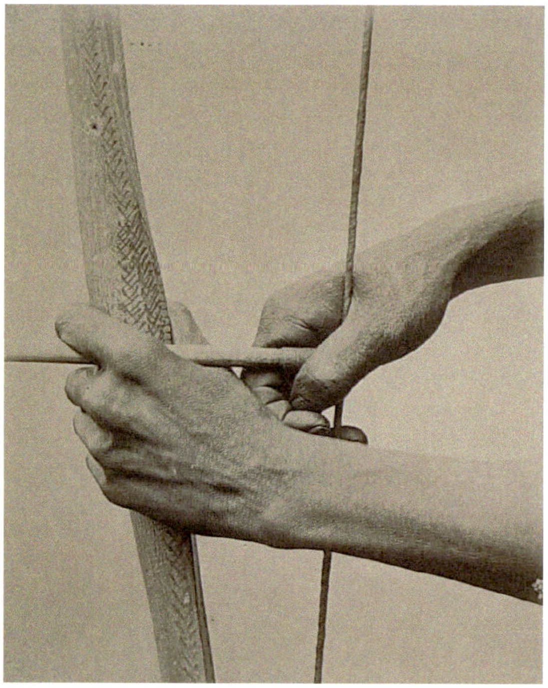

Studies from the Andaman Islands, c.1890
Albumen prints, 20.3 × 15.5 cm, 20.6 x 16 cm and 19.6 × 14.8 cm

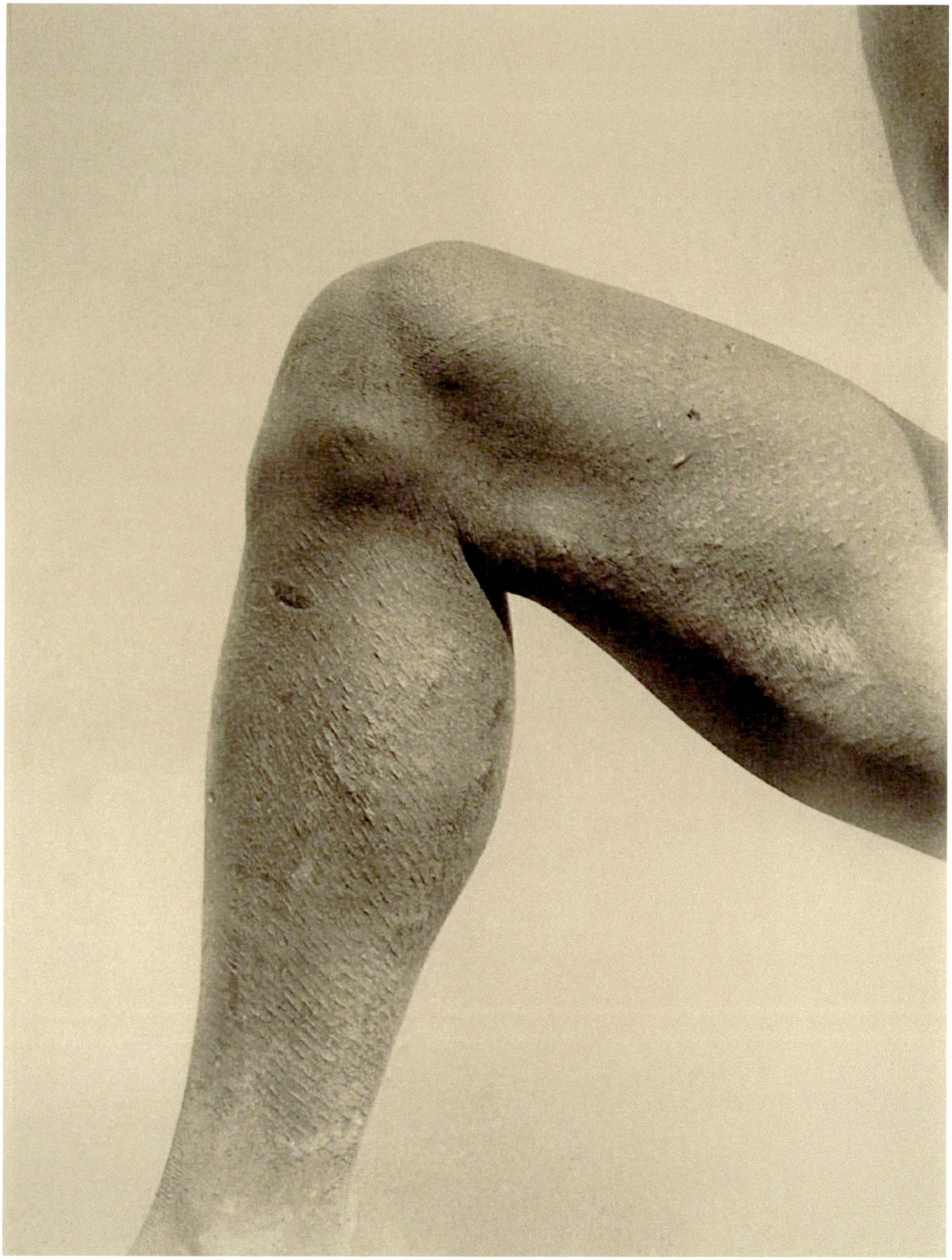

John Edward Saché
b. Prussia, 1824–1882

John Edward Saché, born Johann Edvart Zachert, first worked as a photographer in the United States for a brief period in the 1850s before arriving in Calcutta in late 1864, where he set up a partnership with W. F. Westfield, trading as Saché & Westfield (see p. 23), and became a member of the Bengal Photographic Society.

The various partnerships and highly itinerant career that John Saché pursued in India are poorly documented and very often confusingly overlap in their dates, but Saché & Westfield appear to have traded at least until early 1868. Saché also seems to have been briefly involved in other partnerships: trading as Saché & Hennah in Calcutta and, at some point, Saché & Murray in Bombay, where along with John Murray he produced some images of the Marble Rocks at Jabalpur. By 1867 he was established in a studio under his own name in Nainital where he worked during the summer season. He also had a winter studio in Lucknow, and continued business at these two premises until he left India for a while in 1872, after the death of his second wife. An advertisement in *The Pioneer* on 22 February 1872, recorded: "Saché's Photo Studio will re-open at Nynee Tal on 15th April 1872, for portraits & Groups at greatly reduced rates, as it is his last Season in India." However, we know that he returned to India sometime shortly afterwards, married again, and in 1873–74 made a series of views in Kashmir – the last topographical views he produced. Between 1874 and 1876, seasonally operating studios were opened in Meerut, Kanpur and Banaras. In 1876 he also opened a branch in Mussoorie that he continued to manage along with the studios at Nainital and Lucknow until his death in 1882.[1]

His photographs of insects are highly unusual subjects for the time (Saché was well known for architectural and topographical views emulating Samuel Bourne in both subject matter and style), yet they are no less illustrative of the nature of colonial photography and its motivations – clearly demonstrating the Victorian desire to document, categorise and order a world still unfamiliar to the West.

Insect studies from an untitled album, c.1870
Albumen prints, approx. 14 × 18 cm each

Joseph Beglar
b. British India, 1845–1907

Born in Dacca, present-day Bangladesh, Joseph Beglar was an Armenian-Indian who worked first as an executive engineer in the Public Works Department and then moved to work with the Archaeological Survey of India (ASI) in the 1860s. In his two decades with the ASI, he worked largely under the aegis of the British Army engineer Alexander Cunningham, and produced over 400 photographs including views of various architectural remains, temples and most famously the Bharhut stupa.

Between 1871 and 1874 Beglar formed part of multiple surveys under the stewardship of General Cunningham, covering Agra, Delhi, Bundelkhand and the greater and eastern half of the Central Provinces. His photographs from this period were published in his *Report of a Tour in Bundelkhand and Malwa, 1871–72; and the Central Provinces, 1873–74* (Calcutta 1878), in the preface to which Cunningham states: "One of the main objects in Bundelkhand was to obtain photographs of the magnificent temples of Khajuraho. This was successfully accomplished ... Mr Beglar also made a very rich collection of photographs of the curious old temples in these little known places."[1]

In a report in 1869 describing some of his early photographs taken in Bengal, particularly around Panchet Hill (today Panchakot Pahar), Beglar lyrically wrote: "The view of these ruins is very imposing and very humiliating; these massive structures meant to endure forever, have become ruins, to be gazed at and pitied, to stand desolate and shattered, by apparently the weakest agencies, mementos alike of human wisdom and of human folly, of power and of weakness, of man's aspirations, and of their disappointment."[2]

General view of the Panchanana Temple, Barakar, Burdwan District, 1872
Albumen print, 24 × 18 cm

Temple studies in Manbhum District, 1872
Albumen prints, approx. 24 × 16 cm each

Vallabhacharya Maharajas (photomontage from an original negative by Narayan Dajee), c.1860
Albumen print, 17.2 x 22.2 cm

Narayan Dajee
b. India, dates unknown

One of the earliest known Indian photographers working at the time, Narayan Dajee was the lesser-known brother of Bhow Dajee – both of whom were among the few non-European members of the Bombay Photographic Society as well as former students of Bombay's Grant Medical College. As part of the Photographic Society, Narayan served as a council member between 1857 and 1861 and was among the first to explore the entrepreneurial possibilities of photography, establishing and running a studio in Rampart Row in Bombay from 1858 to 1868.

He is known to have photographed with both waxed paper negatives and using the wet collodion process,[1] making prints of landscapes and monuments. What Dajee is most particularly remembered for, however, are his ethnographic photographs, thirty of which were shown at the Photographic Society of Bengal exhibition of March 1857. This body of work, which includes studies of fakirs, snake charmers, musicians, soldiers and other "types", trades and communities, set him apart from much of the other exhibited work – leading the organisers to observe that "the castes and costumes of the natives of the country have not yet received ... that attention which they deserve, and which they will no doubt in time obtain."[2]

As a wealthy, mercantile and educated individual, Dajee was, as with other men of his standing, very much aligned with the British, and was an accepted and important part of the burgeoning colonial photographic community at the time. As an example of this, William Johnson (see p. 41), the well-known European ethnographic photographer, used one of Dajee's photographs in his book *The Oriental Races and Tribes: Residents and Visitors of Bombay*, the first photographically illustrated ethnographic publication in the country.[3] Shown here we can see Dajee's original negative alongside its use in Johnson's montage for his publication, in an early example of photographic manipulation.

Many of Dajee's photographs are ethnographic in nature, and without captions one would not know they were taken by an Indian rather than a European photographer. One way to read his images is to presume that Dajee is not concerned with the sitters as people but rather positioning them as an ethnic "type", devoid of individualism and personality beyond their role in reinforcing the stereotype, and in creating a study for the camera in line with his colonial colleagues. Rather than revealing a contradiction, Dajee's work demonstrates how the relationships between the British and Indians at the higher end of society were often closely entwined, and this extended not only in terms of civic administration and sympathies but also in how they viewed – or encouraged – others to represent the country and its people.

Vallabhacharya Maharajas, *c.*1860
Albumen print, 17.2 x 22.2 cm

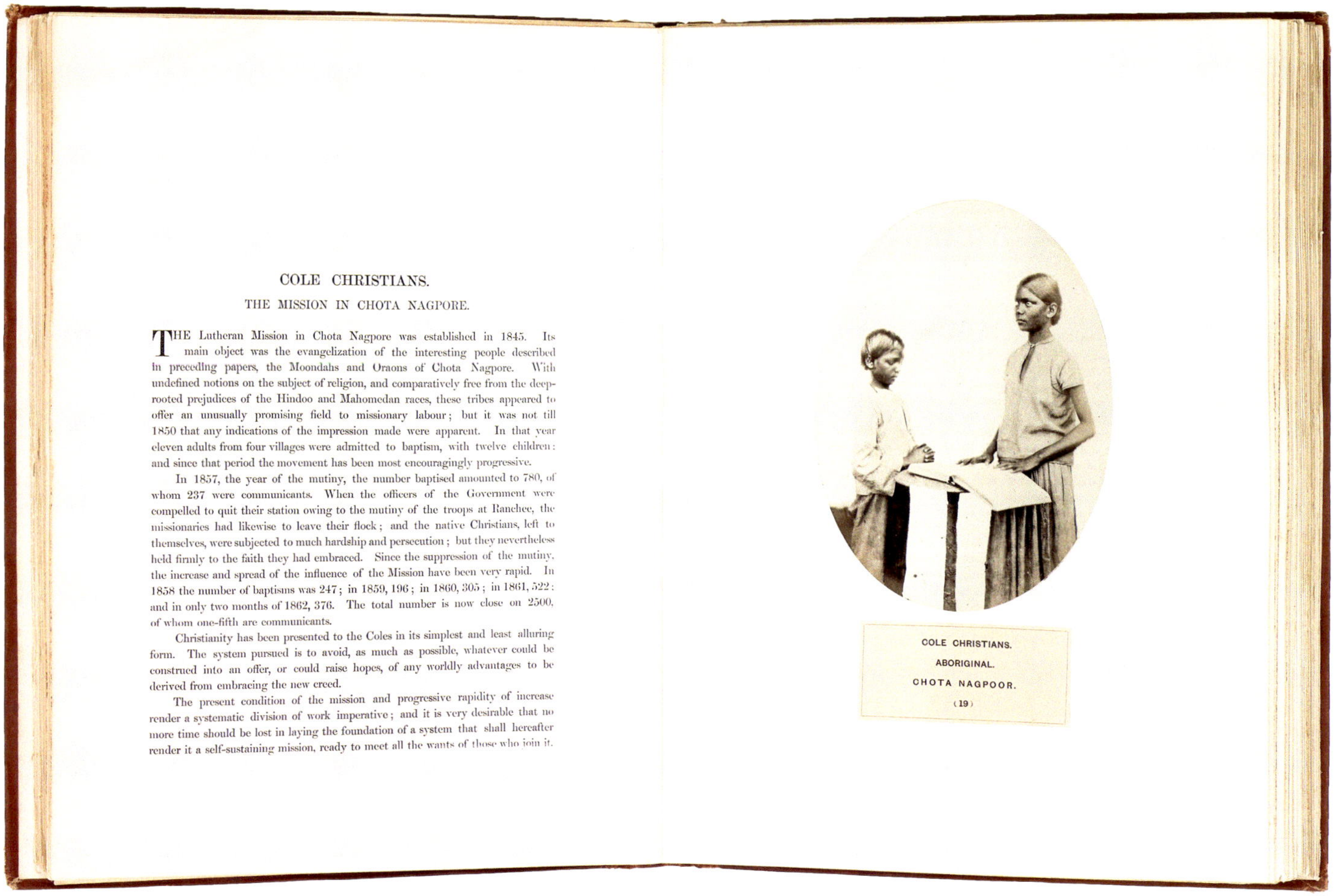

COLE CHRISTIANS.

THE MISSION IN CHOTA NAGPORE.

THE Lutheran Mission in Chota Nagpore was established in 1845. Its main object was the evangelization of the interesting people described in preceding papers, the Moondahs and Oraons of Chota Nagpore. With undefined notions on the subject of religion, and comparatively free from the deep-rooted prejudices of the Hindoo and Mahomedan races, these tribes appeared to offer an unusually promising field to missionary labour; but it was not till 1850 that any indications of the impression made were apparent. In that year eleven adults from four villages were admitted to baptism, with twelve children: and since that period the movement has been most encouragingly progressive.

In 1857, the year of the mutiny, the number baptised amounted to 780, of whom 237 were communicants. When the officers of the Government were compelled to quit their station owing to the mutiny of the troops at Ranchee, the missionaries had likewise to leave their flock; and the native Christians, left to themselves, were subjected to much hardship and persecution; but they nevertheless held firmly to the faith they had embraced. Since the suppression of the mutiny, the increase and spread of the influence of the Mission have been very rapid. In 1858 the number of baptisms was 247; in 1859, 196; in 1860, 305; in 1861, 522; and in only two months of 1862, 376. The total number is now close on 2500, of whom one-fifth are communicants.

Christianity has been presented to the Coles in its simplest and least alluring form. The system pursued is to avoid, as much as possible, whatever could be construed into an offer, or could raise hopes, of any worldly advantages to be derived from embracing the new creed.

The present condition of the mission and progressive rapidity of increase render a systematic division of work imperative; and it is very desirable that no more time should be lost in laying the foundation of a system that shall hereafter render it a self-sustaining mission, ready to meet all the wants of those who join it.

COLE CHRISTIANS.
ABORIGINAL.
CHOTA NAGPOOR.
(19)

Often described as one of the most important nineteenth-century attempts to harness photography to an ethnographic project, *The People of India* was published in eight volumes between 1868 and 1875 and contains over 486 pasted-in albumen prints depicting the "Races and Tribes of Hindustan". It was edited by Dr John Forbes Watson And John William Kaye. During his work for the India Office and the India Museum, he developed the idea of a "portable industrial museum", which led to the publication of the *Collections of the Textile Manufactures of India*.[1] He was a Scottish physician who was appointed assistant surgeon in the Bombay Army Medical Service in 1850, and John William Kaye was a British military historian who was an officer in the Bengal Artillery from 1832 to 1841; the work was produced under the instruction and patronage of Governor-General Lord Canning and his wife, Lady Canning. It is reported that the Cannings simply wanted a photo album to carry home with them to England "which might recall to their memories the peculiarities of Indian life".[2]

The known photographers who contributed images include: J. C. A. Dannenberg; Lieut. R. H. De Montmorency; Rev. E. Godfrey; Lieut. W. W. Hooper (see p. 112); Major Houghton; Capt. H. C. McDonald; J. Mulheran; Capt. Oakes; Rev. G. Richter; Shepherd and Robertson; Dr B. Simpson; Dr B. W. Switzer; Capt. H. C. B. Tanner; Capt. C. C. Taylor and Lieut. J. Waterhouse, but several other unnamed photographers, many of whom were officers of the British army, are also known to have submitted images.[3]

Throughout the volumes sitters are described in derogatory language. Among several examples we learn that the character of a "Kashmir Musulmani" is "not very respectable", but that by contrast the women grasscutters of Madras are "a very industrious and useful race."[4] The publication reveals some subjective interpretations of systemic racism found in ethnographic photography from this time.

In his book *The Coming of Photography in India*, Christopher Pinney cites a letter by Syed Ahmed Khan – "a prominent Muslim of the day" – to the Aligarh Scientific Society: "In the India Office is a book in which all the races of India are depicted both in picture and in letterpress, giving the manners and customs of each race. Their photographs show that the pictures of the different manners and customs were taken on the spot, and the sight of them shows how savage they are – the equal of animals. The young Englishman ... desirous of knowing something of the land to which they are going ... look over this work. What can they think, after pursuing this book and looking at its pictures of the power and honour of the natives of India?"[5] This early critical reading of *The People of India* shows us that the debate and realisation of how problematic this kind of project is, is not only a modern phenomena but had in fact existed contemporaneously with its production.

ABOVE, OPPOSITE AND FOLLOWING PAGES
The People of India, 1868–75
Albumen prints, approx. 17.5 × 12.5 cm each

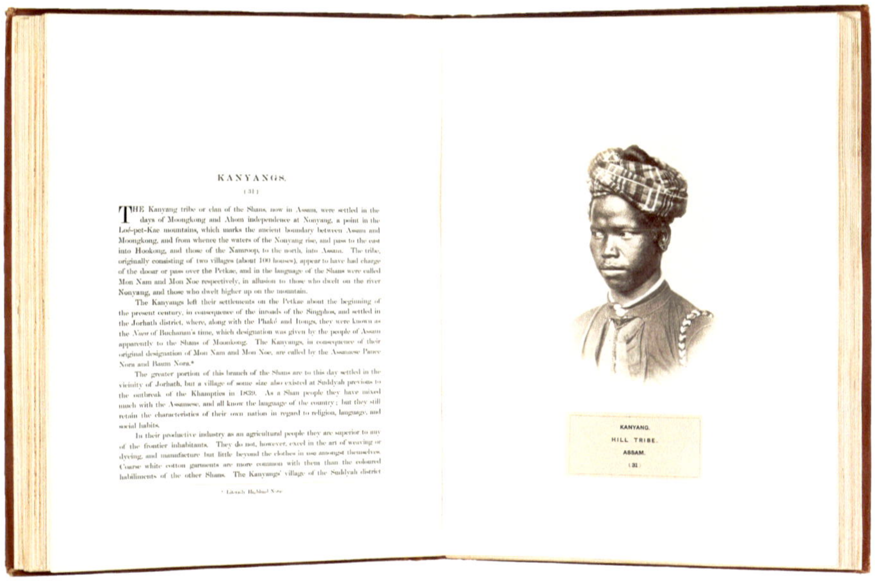
KANYANGS.
(31)
KANYANG.
HILL TRIBE.
ASSAM.
(31)

THE KOREWAHS.
ORAON COLE FEMALE.
ABORIGINAL.
CHOTA NAGPOOR.
(16)

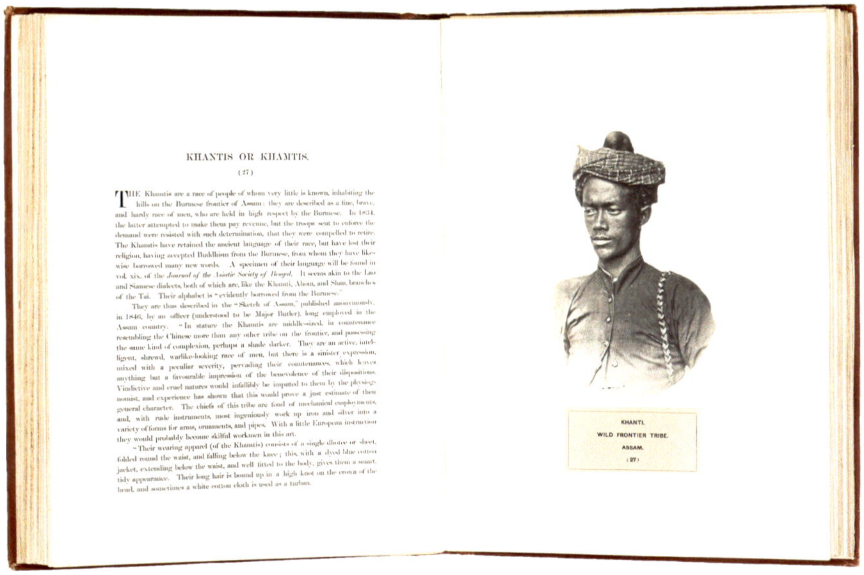
KHANTIS OR KHAMTIS.
(27)
KHANTI.
WILD FRONTIER TRIBE.
ASSAM.
(27)

THE KOOKIES.

(39)

THE Kookie tribes inhabit the hills east of the Chittagong district, and are separated from the plains by the Tipperah and Chuckma tribes. They are fair in complexion compared with the natives of the plains. Their houses are built of logs, on the top of the high ranges, in a much more substantial manner than those of the Tipperah Reangs and other neighbouring clans. They cultivate rice and vegetables, of which their diet of necessity chiefly consists; they are fond of animal food, which, however, can be obtained only by hunting, and are fond of hunting and marauding. They believe in a Supreme Being and a future state, also in hill gods or demons, to whom they sacrifice; but these gods hold a very inferior position when compared with the "Great Spirit." The Kookies are fierce and warlike, as compared with the other tribes, on whom they are in the habit of making raids for the purpose of procuring plunder and slaves. Their method of attack is surprise, and they seldom attempt to stand before regular troops, preferring a guerilla warfare, and hiding themselves and firing from behind rocks and trees. Their arms are flint muskets, spears, and daos. The habits and dress of the women are the same as those of the Tipperah tribes. The men in full dress wear a coarse sheet—in undress, nothing at all. The sheets of the men and women are often dyed blue with a kind of wild indigo found in the hills. Their habits are extremely dirty, even worse than the Tipperahs. In their manners they are frank and outspoken. They place small value on human life.—*(MS. Documents.)*

"The custom of tattooing, which so generally prevails among the Khyens and Karens, is wholly unknown to the Kookies. All the tribes north, west, and east of the Munnipoor valley, partake strongly of the characteristic features of the Tartar countenance; and, viewed in contrast with the tribes occupying the southern borders of the Munnipoor territory, are remarkable for superior height, fairer complexions, and more elevated foreheads; their dialects are harsh and guttural, and their voices particularly inharmonious and discordant. The Kookies, or southern tribes, are, on the contrary, remarkable for their extreme softness of voice, and the euphonic sweetness of their language, when not spoken under great excitement: in stature

KOOKIE.

ROBBER TRIBES.

CACHAR.

(39)

Bourne

2 Pictorialism & the Picturesque

In his discussion of photography in late nineteenth century India, Christopher Pinney opens up an alternative history of the photographic image, proposing that the lofty aspirations of its early practitioners can easily be placed within the study of "late painting".[1]

Although it is a notion that Pinney invokes in relation to photographic portraiture, the question of "late painting" offers much to our study of the inheritance of pictorialism and the picturesque in the late nineteenth and early twentieth centuries. Developing somewhat later than archaeological and ethnographic photography in India, two parallel strains emerge with these genres: pretty, soft photographs of cherubs, maidens, fakirs; and romantic images of the Indian countryside that could redeem it from the squalor with which its colonisers most associated the land.

One can argue that these two movements, spanning almost a century between them, mark the beginning of photographers' assertions that the medium could be a fine art and not simply a tool of science. While the picturesque borrowed from European painterly conventions of framing the landscape, the hazy, pleasing compositions by pictorialist photographers were drawn from parallel photographic movements in Europe and the United States, where photographers such as Constant Puyo, Henry Peach Robinson and Alfred Stieglitz had rejected the sole use of the camera as an instrument of truth or indexicality.

The artistic notion of the picturesque was first articulated by William Gilpin, whose texts in the 1760s and 1770s described the picture-like quality of the landscape observed on walks through the English countryside. In his 1768 text *An Essay upon Prints*, Gilpin wrote: "He is the true artist, who copies nature; but where he finds her mean, elevates her from his own ideas of beauty."[2] A working theory of the picturesque was subsequently achieved in the writings of Uvedale Price (who wrote, in 1794, *An Essay on the Picturesque, as compared with the Sublime and Beautiful*) and Richard Payne Knight (whose 1805 text *An Analytical Enquiry into the Principles of Taste* elaborated upon the aesthetics of the picturesque). In painting and then in photography, the aesthetic theory encouraged the creation of digestible, beautiful images of nature and of rural idyll, realism somewhat modified in favour of an imagined real.

There is no singular reason for the remarkable tendency towards the picturesque in the Indian subcontinent at this time, abundant as it is in the practices of Samuel Bourne, Felice Beato, the studio of Francis Frith and, indigenously, the likes of Lala Deen Dayal from the 1860s onwards. For one, it is likely that early photographers from Britain may have sought to consummate already existing scenes of India made by their painter predecessors – such as those of Thomas and William Daniell, whose paintings of Indian landscapes and monuments had already established a standard in Indian image-making. One can propose that these early photographers worked in stylistic allegiance to East India Company painters as a means of validating their own aesthetic experience of the unfamiliar lands in which they now found themselves. The camera too, then, could be utilised to formulate and construct a certain notional beauty, well furnished with motifs of architectural ruin, stone bridges over meandering rivers and charmingly wild foliage.

Further, the upsurge in the picturesque in photography corresponds closely with the burgeoning popularity of postcards and cartes de visite across the world, especially between the 1870s and 1920s with the improvement of photographic technologies. Photographs of exotic lands and peoples became sought after as souvenirs and collectible items; to this end, photographic studios in India responded by "undertaking their own architectural and ethnographic surveys in their quest to produce views that would appeal".[3] Many commercial studio owners such as Bourne, Frith and Deen Dayal found their adoption of ordered images of the views of Ooty, Simla and Kashmir most profitable, entering thus into a global economy of image exchange, circulation and collection. In contrast to the earlier photographic techniques and their reception, it was picturesque photography that facilitated the importance of individual authorship and the accolades that often came with it, such as photography society prizes and individual recognition. Bourne, for example, sought in his work to explore and photograph unchartered territory and his snowy, stark and explicitly sublime photograph of Manirung Pass in the Himalayas taken in 1866, earned him the recognition of having taken the highest-altitude photograph in the world. Photographs such as these were signed or initialled before they were circulated: a marked contrast to archaeological and ethnographic studies where the photographer was often unknown, uncredited or eclipsed by the publisher or patron.

Zahid R. Chaudhary suggests that the sustenance of the picturesque was also hinged on a sense of nostalgia for Britain among photographers and their clients.[4] By the 1850s, the kind of assimilation and social and cultural intermixing of the early administrators of the East India Company had come to an end, the 1857 Rebellion serving as the last nail in the coffin of the romance of cultural hybridity. It is possible to consider photographs such as those of A. T. W. Penn while keeping in mind the moment of stark cultural separation during which they raised their cameras: creating, for themselves and for their British customers, images of India that were not unlike England. To see Bourne's photograph of his wife, Mary, at Barrackpore Park is to witness the act of re-framing a foreign land for oneself and one's own. These images, although existing within a rigid British template of image-making, therefore serve as curious spaces of reconciliation and resistance, where the Indian countryside may not always adhere to the standards that are applied to it. This is not to say that this genre, so concerned as it was with uplifting images and artistic vigour, worked at all in isolation of the colonial economy. Bourne reportedly required thirty porters to accompany him on his photographic excursions in the Himalayas,[5] and his own account in the *British Journal of Photography* describes his multiple beatings of the porters who refused to carry his equipment through the mountains. The industry of picturesque image-making was indeed built upon the foundations of the race and labour relations forged in a time of colony, even if its practitioners chose to cloak the "poison" of colonial exploitation in vivid beauty.[6]

Decades later, it was pictorialism that was perhaps the first photographic style to be "imported" to India for adoption in a new cultural landscape, and it became the fixation of amateur photography clubs and studios until the 1940s. One of its earliest Indian practitioners, the Parsi photographer Shapoor Bhedwar, may perhaps have adopted its visual tenets during his studies in London at the Polytechnic School of Photography in the late 1880s. Bhedwar was the first Indian member of the Photographic Salon (the organisation established by pictorialist photographers when they seceded from the too-scientific Royal Photographic Society in 1892); he achieved international renown when *The Photographic Times*, an American publication, exhibited four pages worth of his photographs in a series featuring the distinguished photographers of the day.[7] A larger sweep across Bhedwar's practice reveals his ability to shift between two sets of visual worlds: in the photograph *The Mystic Sign*, for example, a group of nymph-like women, entirely pre-Raphaelite in their pose and drapery, are in fact dressed in Indian textiles, bearing Indian fans. In other images, more stereotypically Indian subjects such as holy men and sari-clad women are presented in the classic saccharine, stylised trappings of pictorialism, figures posing as though enacting a novelistic painting. Bhedwar was far from the only pictorialist of his time: J. N. Unwalla notes that amateur photographers flocked in their numbers to the Simla Fine Art Society (est. 1872), the Bombay Art Society (1888) and the Bombay Pictorialists of Bombay (1932), showing their painterly photographs in annual exhibitions and competitions.[8] It is uncertain why, despite such fervent support for the style, such a small selection of work remains in the public sphere. We have, for purposes of its at least token representation, chosen to include in our selection the works of Bhedwar, Umrao Singh Sher-Gil's photographs of his daughters bedecked in elaborate costumes, and A. L. Syed's accomplished work with light and shadow in his depictions of India in the 1920s, although he continued well into the 1980s.

Reviewing the relationship of this chapter – illustrative as it is of the appeal of particular aesthetic strategies in photography – to its predecessor, one is struck by the steady transition of photography from the realm of science, earlier on in its utilisation, towards the concerns of art practice.

1 Christopher Pinney, 'Stirred by Photography', in: *Allegory and Illusion: Early Portrait Photography from South Asia* (exhib. cat., New York, Rubin Museum of Art / Alkazi Collection of Photography), New Delhi and New York 2013, p. 12.
2 William Gilpin, *An Essay upon Prints*, 2nd edn., London 1768, p. 32, quoted in Zahid R. Chaudhary, *Afterimage of Empire: Photography in Nineteenth-Century India*, Minneapolis 2012, p. 111.
3 *Re-orientations: Photography from South Asia, 1845–1920* Collection of Photography), New York 1999, p. 11.
4 Zahid R. Chaudhary, *Afterimage of Empire: Photography in Nineteenth-Century India*, Minneapolis 2012, p. 141.
5 See Desmond, 'Photography in Victorian India', p. 51; Christopher Pinney, *The Coming of Photography in India*, New Delhi 2008, p. 29.
6 For an account of selective image-making in Bengal and the erasure of indigo plantations at the hands of Samuel Bourne, see Pinney, *The Coming of Photography*, pp. 57–61.
7 Malavika Karlekar, 'A Parsi Pictorialist – Complex images and stylized models', in: *The Telegraph*, 14 July 2013, https://www.telegraphindia.com/1130714/jsp/opinion/story_17028654.jsp.
8 J. N. Unwalla, 'Indian Photography – 50 Years', in: *MARG* 14, no. 1 (1960), p. 6.

Samuel Bourne
b. England, 1834–1912

Samuel Bourne travelled to India in 1863 and despite only spending seven years in the country, he was responsible for producing over two thousand negatives. Bourne defined the genre of landscape photography in India, bringing with him the aesthetic, cultural and philosophical notions of the Victorian tradition of the picturesque, as well as at times capturing the corresponding notion of the sublime. In addition to working independently, Bourne established commercial studios for portraits of the ruling classes and architectural surveys, demonstrating the commercial possibilities of the medium. Initially partnering with William Howard, Bourne set up the Howard & Bourne studio in Shimla. They were joined by Charles Shepherd, and after the departure of Howard, the studio dropped his name to become the iconic Bourne & Shepherd. In 1866 the Bourne & Shepherd establishment set up a branch in Calcutta, where it continued to trade until June 2016, making it one of the longest functioning photographic studios in the world.

Upon first arriving in Calcutta and holding various meetings with photographers and new organisations such as the Bengal Photographic Society, Bourne began a twelve-hundred-mile journey up to Shimla, summer capital of the British Empire in India. En route he visited Varanasi, Allahabad, Agra, Delhi, Ambala and Kalka, where many of his earliest photographs were made. He then proceeded on the first of his three photographic surveys of the Indian Himalayas. One of the earliest photographers to capture its majesty, he wrote extensively about his travels in the mountains in a long series of letters appearing in the *British Journal of Photography* between 1863 and 1870. In these letters he writes of his initial fascination "[t]o see what elements of beauty and grandeur lay concealed in some of the higher and little known regions of the Himalayas."[1] It is worth noting that to take such photographs in the 1860s involved tremendous effort and skill. To complete such tasks, Bourne had a "mobile" darkroom which consisted of a horse-drawn carriage containing all the chemicals and equipment for coating, loading and processing a negative. When high up in the Himalayas, this equipment was then carried by an army of over forty porters.

Always of superb technical quality, several of Bourne's photographs stand firmly alongside the finest travel photography produced anywhere in the nineteenth century.[2] In addition to his landscape work, Bourne also made many exemplary topographical views, ethnographic studies and portraits of the period. The best preserved of these are in a set of albums originally compiled for Maharaja Ram Singh II (see p. 92), now in the private collection Rajeev Rawat in Jaipur.

Gothic ruin with creepers in Barrackpore Park, Calcutta, 1865
Albumen print, 24 × 29.5 cm

Bridge over the Rungnoo, Darjeeling, 1863–70
Albumen print, 22.5 × 28 cm

Up the Jhelum, from below the island, Srinagar, 1863–70
Albumen print, 28.7 × 24.2 cm

The Manirung Pass, Western Himalayas, border of Tibet, 1866
Albumen print, 22 × 27.5 cm

Near the Zoji-la Pass, Western Himalayas, border of Tibet, 1865–70
Albumen print, 28.7 × 24.2 cm

A. T. W. Penn
b. England, 1849–1924

Albert Thomas Watson Penn left home before the age of 12, became proficient in photography, and found his way to Ootacamund, where he had a studio at Cranley Cottage from 1880 under the name of Ootacamund Photo Establishment.[1] Whilst there he began working as a commercial photographer with the Nicholas Brothers in 1865, the year he turned 16. A decade later, in 1875, he was to buy this very studio and run it under his own name for the next twenty-four years. Portraiture formed the primary source of his income, including private individual portraits on cartes de visite, family groups and other group portraits, such as those of the Ooty hunt or of entertainments and fancy dress balls, though these were less regular and only happened during "the season", from April to September. Scenic views were Penn's second source of business and, like Samuel Bourne (see p. 63), these photographs demonstrate an affinity towards the institutionalised picturesque landscape traditions of Europe, where one could be forgiven for assuming the photographs were made. Penn's photographs therefore represent a very different kind of image-making in India, at a time when it was common to present India as a place of exotic curiosity. The third significant section of his work was also linked to the production of portraits, many of which were ethnographic studies of the type described in the preceding chapter.

Following the development of photogravure printing (a form of intaglio printing that reproduced the tones and details of photographs) at the end of the nineteenth century, a new market opened up for photographic publications. Penn contributed several photographs to Edgar Thurston's seven-volume ethnographic study *Castes and Tribes of Southern India* (1909). He also supplied illustrations for Sir Frederick Price's *Ootacamund, a History* (1908), and photographs for the young missionary Amy Wilson Carmichael's book *Overweighs of Joy* (1907) which she described as "the work of an expert in capturing the spirit of the wild".[2]

The Lake, Ootacamund, 1903
Albumen print, 21.5 × 26.4 cm

John Murray

b. Scotland, 1809–1898

John Murray was a Scottish army doctor employed by the East India Company. He came to India in 1833, after receiving his MD in Edinburgh in 1831. By 1848 he was a surgeon in Agra, rose to the rank of Deputy Inspector General by 1858, and in 1865 he was promoted to Inspector General.

Having settled into his post in Agra by the mid-1850s, Murray had already taken up photography, the value of which for documentary purposes was widely recognised by the colonial government. In 1856, for instance, Murray's fellow surgeon John McCosh made the statement: "I would strongly recommend to every assistant-surgeon to make himself a master of photography in all its branches."[1] Following this advice Murray spent close to a decade on his photographic pursuits, creating hundreds of views of Delhi, Agra, Fatehpur Sikri, Kanpur and Benares. He focused his attentions on architectural scenes of Mughal India and its environs, producing a formidable collection of paper negatives and corresponding salted paper and albumen prints.[2] Murray also adopted the waxed negative process, a method introduced by French photographer Gustave Le Grey in 1853, that required waxing paper negatives prior to sensitisation in order to make the paper receptive to more detail. These waxed negatives still exist today, and allow us to see how much care Murray took to enhance certain areas of the image, controlling light and dark to enrich texture.

A member of the Bengal Photographic Society, Murray participated in its first exhibition in March 1857 where twenty-seven of his prints were shown, including landscapes of Nainital and architectural views of Agra. In November of that year, John Hogarth exhibited thirty of Murray's paper prints in London. Murray's work was also published by Hogarth in two books: *Photographic Views in Agra, and Its Vicinity*, with descriptions by J. Middleton, principal of the East India Company's College at Agra (1858), and *Picturesque Views in the North-Western Provinces of India* (1859). The latter was accompanied by a text by Major-General J. T. Boileau.[3] Murray continued to photograph for a few more years, but by the mid-1860s he seems to have stopped exhibiting and the last known dated photographs attributable to him are from January 1864.[4]

The Taj Mahal from the East with John Murray seated in the foreground, 1858–62
Albumen print, 37.1 × 43.6 cm

Colin Murray
b. Scotland, 1840–1884

Colin Murray is most well known for his work with Bourne & Shepherd. Subsequent to the departure of Bourne in 1870, Murray quickly became one of the firm's leading photographers, particularly in regards to architectural and topographical subjects. In 1872–73, Murray made a photographic tour through western India, and work from this trip was later published in James Burgess's *Photographs of Architecture and Scenery in Gujarat and Rajputana*. Murray died of cholera in 1884 and is buried in the Scotch Burial Ground, Calcutta.[1]

Although relatively little is known about Murray's activities in India in comparison to some of his contemporaries, the image he made of the Jagmandir Island Palace in Udaipur has become one of the most iconic and widely produced images of the country from the nineteenth century. Unlike the purely topographical or ethnographic work discussed in the previous chapter, this image paints India firmly in the guise of "the orient", whilst also using the vocabulary of the picturesque as explored elsewhere in this chapter. Architecture becomes not an objective study nor a crumbling ruin in need of being saved by the Archaeological Survey of India under the British, but rather something rich with narrative possibility and romance. The figures are shown not as ethnographic types, but as props in the compositional structure and an opportunity to expand the tonal range and contrast within the image. Taken together, these strategies demonstrate Murray's knowledge, interest and competence in Western devices of image-making and the very height of picturesque promise in photography.

Jagmandir Island Palace, Udaipur, 1873
Albumen print, 34.9 × 22.7 cm

Shapoor Bhedwar
b. British India, 1858–unknown

Shapoor Nusserwanjee Bhedwar was born to a wealthy Parsi family in Bombay, where he developed an early affinity with art and literature. He is known to have had a keen interest in the theatre and to have also composed short plays himself (none of which are known to have been performed professionally), and he also wrote poems. In 1888 Bhedwar took up photography to illustrate one of his own texts, and soon became more closely interested in the capacity of the medium in its own right as an art form. He travelled to England to study at the Polytechnic School of Photography in London in 1889, and was soon winning medals in the Photographic Salon (later the Royal Photographic Society). Bhedwar went on to become a well-known practitioner in the art photography circuits of Europe and America. In 1894, *The Photographic Times* carried a four-page spread on him with a selection of his work as part of a series, "Distinguished photographers of to-day". He also won awards back home in India, notably a gold medal at the Photographic Society of India's 1892 exhibition held in Calcutta.

Unlike his Indian contemporaries who emulated European studio photography, Bhedwar was experimental and subscribed to the Western ideals of pictorialism – questioning the idea of the photograph as a simple record of transpired reality. His portraits were, therefore, dramatically lit, elaborately posed and highly stylised. In the manner of staged performances, his tableaux often revealed a narrative thread and were carefully staged to present a mood, and also referenced his interest in the theatre and literature. Bhedwar was the only Indian member of the Brotherhood of the Linked Ring, established in London in 1892 to promote pictorialist aesthetics, and even after moving back to Bombay he played an active role in the General Committee, often serving on the exhibition selection committee until the group's dissolution in 1910. Despite individual differences, the members of the Linked Ring were united in their belief that the significance of photography as art lay in the portrayal of mood, character and sentiment. Through this aesthetic, Bhedwar in his own work transcended imperial conventions of photography, as well as the colonial assumptions of artisanal skill associated with non-Western artists.[1]

Tyag No. 4. The Mystic Sign, from the album *Art Studies*, c.1890
Carbon print, 26 × 34 cm

Umrao Singh Sher-Gil

b. British India, 1870–1954

Umrao Singh Sher-Gil, father of the famed modernist painter Amrita Sher-Gil, was born to a landed aristocratic family of Majitha, near Amritsar, in Punjab. He was a scholar of Sanskrit and Persian as well as having interests in philosophy, astronomy, yoga and photography, which he took up in the early 1890s at a time when the camera was becoming more portable and easily available, and thus a more popular hobby for the leisured classes. Sher-Gil began to develop his photographic practice in the 1880s; the earliest self-portrait (which would become a consistent exploration in his practice) dates to 1889, although no photographs of his first marriage and four sons remain. After his second marriage to the Hungarian opera singer Marie Antoinette, the couple left for Budapest in 1912, where their two daughters, Amrita and Indira, were born. With the outbreak of the First World War, the family was forced to stay on in Hungary until 1921.

Sher-Gil's interest in artistic and intellectual concerns influenced his image-making and provide an important early promise of the artistic practice of photography in India. Rather than emulating the British stylistic concern with topography or ethnography, Sher-Gil's work was a purely personal documentation of family approached with an artistic mind, and the photographs he produced conform more to the ideals of pictorialism as practiced in Europe than they do to the history of Indian art, or colonial-era photography. Sher-Gil's photographic archive provides an astounding and rich record of his wife and daughters, as well as his prolific body of self-portraits. The images provide a point of entry into the luxury and cosmopolitanism of their world – in Hungary, France as well as India.[1] In addition to the soft, intimate atmosphere in which he would photograph his family, his subjects would also appear in stylised, performative and carefully considered dress – conjuring up an image of a cultured, privileged and artistically diverse family. His photographs also provide an example of the complexities of transculturalism which would later become so central to the history of photography as practiced in the country.

Amrita and Indira, Simla, c.1923
Autochrome prints, 8.8 × 6.3 cm each

Julia Margaret Cameron
b. British India, 1815–1879

Julia Margaret Pattle was born in Calcutta as the fourth of seven sisters. Her father was an East India Company official and her mother descended from French aristocracy.

Considered one of the foremost pioneers of photography, Cameron's work is globally synonymous with the pictorialist movement and its potential and acceptance as a fine art. She is famous for her allegorical and illustrative studio photographs, posing and costuming family members and servants in imitation of the popular Romantic and Pre-Raphaelite paintings of the day.[1] Educated mainly in France, Cameron returned to India in 1834. In 1836, while recovering from an illness in the Cape of Good Hope, South Africa, she met the British astronomer Sir John Herschel (1792–1871). In 1842 Herschel introduced her to photography, sending her examples of the then new invention. He remained a lifelong friend and teacher on technical photographic matters. During the same stay in South Africa, Julia Margaret met Charles Hay Cameron (1795–1880), twenty years her senior, a reformer of Indian law and education who would later invest in coffee plantations in Sri Lanka. They married in Calcutta in 1838 and she became a prominent hostess in colonial society. A decade later, the Camerons moved to England. Staying first in Tunbridge Wells, Kent, then moving to East Sheen and then to London, and then in 1860 settling in Freshwater, on the Isle of Wight, where Julia Margaret later made many photographs. They lived there until 1875, when they moved to Sri Lanka to be near four of their sons and the family's coffee plantations.[2]

Although Cameron, as far as we know, did not make any photographs in India, her early life (as a child of colonial India) and her legacy amongst the intellectuals and artists of the country, as well as her global influence in the development of pictorialism, are significant to the history of the medium in the country.

John Herschel, 1867
Albumen print, 31.8 × 24.9 cm

Ceylonese Girl, 1878
Albumen print, 31 × 22 cm

Jantar Mantar Observatory, Jaipur, c.1938
Gelatin silver print, 20 × 16 cm

A. L. Syed
b. British India, 1904–1991

Abidmain Lalmain Syed is a significant, though often overlooked, twentieth-century Indian photographer who was influenced by both pictorialism and humanism in his work. He represents a group of photographers from the era with shared concerns, occupying a space between the amateur and the artist, who produced a prolific record of India from the 1920s onwards. Born to the physician of the royal family of Palanpur in Gujarat, he first made a name for himself in the early 1920s when a photograph he took on a school trip to Bombay won the first prize in the *Illustrated Weekly of India*'s photography competition. In the following years his photographs would come to be published in a number of reputed magazines at all levels of diffusion, from the Gujarati-language publication *Kumar* to *Illustrated Weekly of India* and US-based *Popular Photography*. He is also said to have taken the stills for the film *Mughal-e-Azam* (1960). Syed died in 1991 at the age of 87, leaving behind a body of work that had become ubiquitous at the time because of its reproduction in popular publications, though much forgotten about today.

Syed's photographic practice broadly prescribes to the style of pictorialism, with which he produced some of the most compelling images of rural India in the 1930s in sharp swathes of light and shadow. He often photographed his subjects from a point below them, as seen in both photographs here, allowing the sky to dominate in these compositions. The images hover between a kind of rural idyll and a careful constructivist modernity, and in doing so they reveal Syed's particular interest in exploring the aesthetic range that photography could provide.

Farmer Girl, Rajasthan, c.1938
Gelatin silver print, 20 × 18 cm

3 Power & Posterity

From the late nineteenth century onwards, there was a decided shift in the concerns of photography in the Indian subcontinent, most notably in that it developed a range of new Indian clients who were anxious to have their images fixed as a mark of their status and social mobility.

The earliest photographic portraits, although they were created among the local elite (such as Maharaja Ram Singh II of Jaipur, who set up a *tasveer khaana*, or picture gallery, in his palace), began, from the 1870s, to filter into the bazaar and, with it, into the home. A growing demand for photographic portraiture had, of course, been facilitated by developments in the instruments of the medium itself. The shift from wet collodion plates and the burden of tripods towards dry plates and portable camera equipment from the 1870s onwards did much for the proliferation of camera practices in India, lending a convenience and ease to the act of photography. One can presume that the technology became considerably cheaper on both sides of the lens: for the photographer, previously dependent on a host of costly materials, chemicals and assistants, as well as for the photographed subject, no longer confined to an exclusive circle of Indian kings and wealthy landowners. Advertisements for American cameras in the 1890s list prices ranging from 215 to 365 rupees,[1] and whereas the first commercial photographic studios were concentrated in Calcutta, Bombay and Madras (all bastions of British administrative power), they had spread into a number of other prominent towns by the 1890s, such as Lucknow, Lahore, Poona as well as seats of royal power in Hyderabad, Baroda and Jaipur. The emergence of hundreds of photographic studios across the country, and the professional rivalries that ensued, often led to the creation of lengthy posters listing the photographers and their patrons: ranging from Del Tufo & Co. of Madras's grand announcement of their establishment being "By Special Appointment to His Majesty the King of Italy", to studios in the frenzied anti-colonial movements in the 1930s listing popular freedom fighters among their certifiers. The rich archives that remain, marked by their portraits of reasonably affluent Indians, speak to the vast appeal of the photographic studio as a site of prestige, of social arrival and – as we see in this chapter – of hybridity, swinging between traditional attire and status and the camera's promise of European modernity, between Indian painting and photography.

The photographic portraits that have endured from the 1870s onwards reveal the enthusiastic adoption of European portraiture conventions by the colonised middle class, featuring the opulent painted backgrounds, Graeco-Roman props and velveteen curtains within which the Indian subject could be situated. In a photograph dated to 1867 from the Bombay-based studio of Hurrichund Chintamon, two Rajputs, one of them replete with his sword, have been made to sit at a little table complete with a vase of flowers that are echoed in the large printed roses on the carpet of the studio floor. In this and other such photographs we witness a marriage of two iconographies of status, where the trappings of caste or nobility are inserted into the those of Victorian affluence and refinement, often functioning, as Pinney has argued, within the visual vocabulary of the Grand Tours conducted by British aristocrats in Italy and France.[2]

The references of these studio photographs to the visual modes of European portraiture are not the camera's only relationship to painting at this time. Although hand-coloured photographs existed elsewhere in the world, the portraits produced in Indian studios developed a distinct vernacular direction in their frequent skilled turn to painting traditions, fusing the visual vocabulary of court painting with that of the camera.[3] Painted photographs were of roughly two types, engaging in two simultaneous aesthetic inheritances from painting: on the one hand, the indisputable borrowing from the poses and compositions of European oil painting (complete with the aforementioned Roman columns, plush Victorian furniture and a particular approach to stance and posturing of the subject); and on the other, a continuation of Mughal and Rajasthani miniature painting by means of the flat, uniform blocks of paint that compressed the composition into a single visual plane. The intertwining of the two aesthetics is vividly presented in the photograph of Bhadariji Devarajaji by Ghasiram Hardev Sharma (p. 98), where the flat turquoise background that is introduced in paint is juxtaposed with a Victorian carpet, richly floral, on the floor under the male subject's feet.

As Judith Mara Gutman's research on Indian painted photographs has shown, Indian photography of this period began to radically depart from Euro-America; whereas in Europe to paint over a photograph would suggest an impurity, an invasion, a trespassing, in India paint becomes an intimate part of the image, a way to define, enhance and complete it. In order to appeal to the tastes of their new Indian clients, many studio photographers hired painters to make interventions on the photographic plate, ranging from the subtle use of painted lines to bestow a level of definition to enlarged photographs, to completely painting over the photograph – effectively confining the photograph to a first draft, or first stage, on which subsequent stages must be practised. In many cases paint was used to bestow the photograph with colour, often leaving only the hands and faces of the subjects untouched.

The relationship of photography to painting is a challenging one to assess. It is tempting, especially in relation to older photographic images of the ethnographic and archaeological genre, to suggest that these images were a radical departure from other photographic styles. But do these images not also connote, as Pinney argues, the democratisation of pre-existing painterly aesthetic forms to a new group of Indian clients, this time in the guise of the (significantly cheaper) photograph?[4] In extension, is it possible to suggest that these composite images represent a combination of continuity (with painting traditions) and radical change (from previous photographic modes)? Whereas Gutman's indiscriminate description of the "'peculiar' Indian way of making photographs derived from an Indian way of seeing life"[5] is not without its problems, it does point to the possibility that this subcontinental iteration of photography was driven by more local solutions to capturing "reality" in the studio space, ranging from the painted-on embellishments on women's saris to the creation of devotional images in which photographs of devotees at Nathdwara were made to flank painted inserts of the temple shrine. In our reading of these images, they are illustrative of a claiming of the medium, of wrenching it away from its colonial context and into local production, consumption and ownership.

Studio photographs, as well as the sense of curiosity and amusement that surrounds them, continue into the present day. Their particularities have been revisited by several contemporary artists and photographers, mostly in their collaborations with painters who are trained in the meticulous art of hand-coloured photographs and miniature painting. Thus Gauri Gill's series *Fields of Sight* (p. 296) was completed alongside the Warli painter Rajesh Vangad. The very nature of such collaborations harks back to a much earlier moment in Indian photography, from practically a century before, when "artists' and photographers' studios" employed dozens of painters as co-authors in the production of inter-media images.

Finally, the aesthetic of studio photography in general has also carried over the decades, moving from the grandeur of courtly photographs through the mercantile class and – more universally – to local studios across the country, where they remain an immensely popular means of portrayal and self-performance.

Our chapter ends with the work of Suresh Punjabi, the proprietor of a small-town photo studio in Nagda in Madhya Pradesh, whose photographs from the 1970s reveal the careful lengths taken, by studio and subject alike, to create images of a certain sociocultural "arrival" – here (p. 103), a young man, taking great pains to display his sartorial excellence, poses nonchalantly with a parrot on his finger, reminiscent of portraits of Mughal emperors with their prized birds in tow. Although Punjabi is only one of the thousands of such photographers who continue, in large parts of India, to bring their subjects' aspirations to life in the image, we include him here as an example of the persistence of self-image in the studio portrait, and the particular aspirations of grandeur that continue to be attached to it.

1 G. Thomas, *History of Photography in India, 1840–1890*, Hyderabad 1981, p. 29.
2 Christopher Pinney, *Camera Indica: The Social Life of Indian Photographs*, London 1997, p. 74.
3 Deepali Dewan, 'The Painted Photograph in India', in: *Embellished Reality: Indian Painted Photographs; Towards a Transcultural History of Photography* (exhib. cat., Toronto, Royal Ontario Museum), Toronto 2011, p. 16.
4 Pinney, *Coming of Photography in India*, p. 135.
5 Judith Mara Gutman, 'Through Indian Eyes', in: *Illuminations: Women Writing on Photography from the 1850s to the Present* ed. Liz Heron and Val Williams, Durham, NC and London 1996, p. 433.

Robert Christopher Tytler
b. British India, 1818–1872

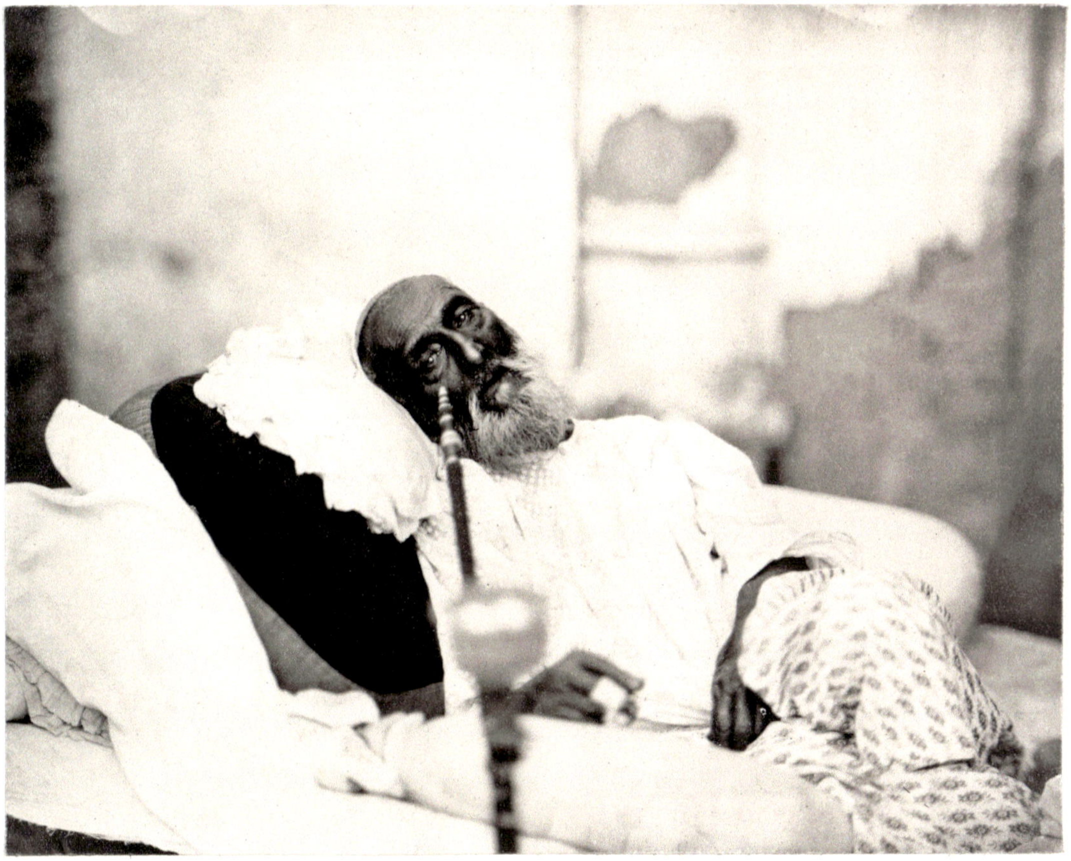

The Ex-King of Dehli.

Although of Irish ancestry, Tytler was born in India as his father, a surgeon, was stationed in the city of Cawnpore. After returning to Britain for a classical education from Leith High School in Edinburgh, he became a cadet in the East Indian Army in 1834 and saw many active years of military service there. He later became interpreter and quartermaster and took part in the actions of the First Anglo-Afghan War (1839–42). In the first Anglo-Sikh War (1845–46), a few years later, Tytler was put in charge of the campaign funds, and subsequently moved all over northern India with his regiment. Later, as Major Tytler, he was present in Delhi during the Rebellion of 1857 and was assigned duties in the siege to retake the city. Although not known precisely when, it appears Tytler had received instruction in photography from two important photographers active in India at the time, Felice Beato (see p. 111) and John Murray (see p. 70), seeming to have learned the waxed paper process from them.

In many ways, Tytler can be considered a precursor to the era of photojournalism. In addition to architectural and picturesque subjects common to his time, he is also credited with (and best known for) producing at least five hundred negatives of the siege of Lucknow and its aftermath. As the report of an 1859 meeting of the Photographic Society of Bengal, where some of these negatives were exhibited, notes: "Major Tytler exhibited a most interesting and valuable collection of Calotype negatives, forming perhaps the finest series that has ever been exhibited to the Society. Major Tytler took occasion to observe that he is quite a novice in Photography, having only been working at it about six months altogether ... He wished it to be understood that the full merit of his photographs did not lie with himself; that Mrs Tytler, who is a most successful photographer, not only selected most of the subjects, but even developed the pictures herself."[1]

Amongst his series of photographs showing the aftermath of the Indian Rebellion, Tytler is credited with the iconic image, shown here, of Bahadur Shah Zafar, the last Mughal emperor of India. The photograph represents a brief moment when the Mughals and such modern technology as the camera existed in the same temporal landscape, a fact that is often taken for granted in the writing around this image.

Bahadur Shah Zafar, the last Mughal Emperor, in exile in Burma, 1859
Albumen print, 10.5 × 14.5 cm

J. W. Newland

b. England, unknown–1857

John William Newland was a prolific travelling photographer, retailer and showman. He was active in New Zealand, Australia, North America, South America and India, particularly from 1845 until his death in 1857, and he is known for his formal portraits of Europeans in these various territories at the time. Among the earliest professional daguerreotypists in Australia, Newland opened a studio in Sydney in 1848. His first advertisement, appearing in the *Sydney Morning Herald* of 7 March 1848, offered "a perfect likeness, coloured or in shade" and boasted that "from the use of the best instruments and long practice, Mr N. is enabled to insure a picture in an incredibly short space of time ... Taken in any weather." A week later, the newspaper corroborated in their review "that perfection in the art which the Messrs. Newland now present to us. The Australian public should pay a visit to this gallery."[1] After closing his studio and gallery in Sydney, Newland moved to Tasmania where he set up a new studio, and then repeated the process, moving to Maitland, New South Wales. In around 1850, Newland arrived in India, where he ran what is thought to have been the first professional daguerreotype studio and photographic business in Calcutta[2] – producing and selling plates, cases, chemicals and paper – in Loudon's Buildings.

Although advertisements in the press at the time would suggest that there were several studios offering the daguerreotype process in India in the 1840s to the 1860s, due to their fragile nature (made of highly polished silver-plated copper) and low production number, very few have survived. Those that did, such as Newland's, demonstrate not only the earliest portraits made in the country but also some of the finest, most detailed and, when seen in reproduction, most tonally rich of this period of photography. Newland died in 1857, an early victim of the violence of the Rebellion though the studio continued to be run by his brother and survived until 1860.[3]

Portrait of a British officer (possibly Thomas Waugh Esq.) stationed in Calcutta, c.1850
Quarter-plate daguerreotype, with metal surround, 10.8 × 8.3 cm

Hurrichund Chintamon

b. British India, *c.*1830–unknown

Hurrichund Chintamon was one of the more prominent and successful Indian photographers of his time, who, after learning the medium under the guidance of W. H. S. Crawford at the Elphinstone Institution in 1855, went on to exhibit photographs at the Bombay Photographic Society as early as 1856. He then set up one of the first photographic firms in Bombay, active from 1858 to 1881,[1] where he made portraits of many of the mercantile families of the city. In the example shown here, we see tropes typical of portraiture of the time: the illusionistic backdrop does not extend across the whole frame, leaving the audience in full awareness of the real studio setting; the "prop" of the flowers on the table encourages an incongruous narrative between the two sitters, held rigid by the need to keep still for the camera, in discord with the casualness proposed by the setting and composition. In addition to his formal portraits such as these, Chintamon produced hundreds of ethnographic studies of tribes and castes. Several of these found their way to the Archaeological Survey of India's collection as well as being frequently featured in John Forbes Watson and John William Kaye's eight-volume album *The People of India* (see p. 54), published between 1868 and 1875.

Despite his obvious success as a photographer, there is relatively little information about Chintamon's photographic career. Other aspects of his life, however, are more closely documented, in light of his active role in various religious groups. He was a prominent disciple of Swami Dayanand (an important Hindu religious leader of his time) and president of the Arya Samaj (a reform movement in Hinduism) of Bombay in 1878, when the Theosophical Society formed an alliance with the organisation. Soon after the founders of the Theosophical Society arrived in the city, they discovered Chintamon had apparently mishandled the funds sent by them from the United States, and he was disgraced and expelled.

Studio portrait of two Rajputs, Bombay, *c.*1867
Albumen print, 16.7 × 21.2 cm

Wajid Ali Shah, King of Oudh, c.1850
Salt print on illustrated mount, 12.2 x 9.8 cm

Ahmad Ali Khan
b. British India, active 1850s

Ahmad Ali Khan was an architect from Lucknow and thought to be one of the first Indian photographers and daguerreotypists. Although little is known of his life other than him being closely connected to the Awadhi royal family, his photographic legacy is fairly well documented. Two significant albums are attributed to him, dating from between 1856 and 1857, the more famous of which is the *Lucknow Album*, consisting of salt prints of Lucknow's prominent residents, particularly British couples, army officers and their wives, as well as group portraits including civil servants and children. Khan's reputation as a skilled photographer led to him being sought out by British families and visitors, who travelled to the Husainabad Imambara (a large congregation hall for Shia Muslims in Lucknow), where he served as steward and trustee, to be photographed by him – often so that they could send images of themselves back home. These photographs provide the most extensive visual record of the British in Lucknow before the 1857 Rebellion, and became inscribed with a sense of poignancy, loss and memorialisation, since several of these subjects lost their lives during the siege of the Lucknow Residency.[1]

In addition to photographing British subjects, many of his photographs show members of the Lucknow court. In 1855, Khan was commissioned by Wajid Ali Shah, the last ruler of the province of Awadh, to photograph him and his family. Particularly notable is the presence of women in these photographs, including Shah's wives and daughters – a rarity in an Islamic court. In contrast to other photographs from this era, it shows not the embellishment of the photograph but a highly illustrated border in which the photograph is contained, representing a kind of early form of collage and coming together of book-making, photography, illustration and text at a time before the formal conventions of photographic portraits were fully established.

Mumtaz Alam Nauwab Qaisar Mahall Sahibah, 1855
Nawab Raj Begum Sahibah, 1855
Salt prints on illustrated mounts, 12.2 x 9.8 cm each

Lala Deen Dayal

b. British India, 1844–1905

In 1866 Lala Deen Dayal graduated as an engineer after completing a five-year course at the Thomason College of Civil Engineering in Roorkee, Uttarakhand. Remarkably, photography had been introduced as a subject in the college in 1854, and it is therefore likely to have been where Deen Dayal first developed an interest in the medium. Following his studies he entered government service as the head estimator and draughtsman in the Public Works Department of the princely state of Indore. Meanwhile, he also began to experiment with photography, catching the eye of Tukoji Rao II, Maharaja of Indore, as well as Sir Henry Dale, agent to the Governor General for Central India, who became early patrons, and by 1874 he opened his first commercial studio in the city of Indore. Around this time, Deen Dayal also came into contact with Sir Lepel Griffin of the Bengal Civil Service, who commissioned him to join a mission documenting monuments showcasing the architectural heritage of Central India. Eighty-six plates from this trip were published along with Sir Griffin's monograph in the album *Famous Monuments of Central India*. This built his reputation further and the Archaeological Survey of India became a regular client. In the following years Deen Dayal worked as official photographer to several viceroys, including Lord Dufferin and Earl Elgin. Towards the end of the nineteenth century, he received the Royal Warrant of Appointment as photographer to Her Majesty Queen Victoria.

In 1885, Deen Dayal was offered the position of court photographer to the sixth Nizam of Hyderabad, Asif Jah VI – a position he occupied until his death in 1905. In 1886 he opened his studio, Deen Dayal & Sons, in Secunderabad; in 1892 he also opened a *zenana* studio in Hyderabad where the photographer Mrs Kenny-Levick photographed "native ladies only" protecting them "from the gaze of the profane and the stern". During these years Deen Dayal produced an extensive visual archive of the life and territories of the Nizam. In appreciation of his work, the Nizam bestowed upon him the title "Musawwir Jung Raja Bahadur" (the Bold Warrior of Photography), in the 1890s. During that same period, Deen Dayal closed his Indore studio and opened a studio in Bombay under the name Raja Deen Dayal & Sons: Art Photographic Salon.

Deen Dayal's photographs prove to be fascinating for their presentation of tradition and modernity (the perceived bastions of the Indians and the English respectively) jostling against one another in their subject matter, and he is unique in his simultaneous and sustained patronage by both princely India and the British Empire.[1]

Devadasis from a south Indian temple, c.1880
Albumen print, 22 × 17 cm

Sir Auckland Colvin and family, Simla, c.1885–87
The Maharaja of Ajaigarh with his three sons, c.1882
Albumen prints, 20 × 14.8 cm each

Maharaja Sawai Ram Singh II

b. British India, 1833–1880

Maharaja Sawai Ram Singh II of Jaipur, well known as a reformist and progressive ruler, was also known as the "Photographer Prince". At his court he had eighteen administrative divisions, including the *tasveer khanna*. His subjects covered a wide range: self-portraits as well as portraits of local nobility and distinguished visitors; views of the city; landscapes; and, most intriguing of all, a record of the women of the royal household. Yaduendra Sahai notes in the first publication dedicated to his work that "Maharaja Sawai Ram Singh II was a very keen experimenter and used all sorts of background[s], sometimes painted with strange scenes. In some photographs, he exposed the faces and superimposed them on different bodies. One of the female's face [*sic*] he exposed on a painted lady's body which sat in the pose of Goddess Laxmi seated on [a] lotus."[1]

Scarce information exists of exactly when and how the Maharaja first took up photography, but it is most likely to have been in the 1860s, when the photographer T. Murray came to Jaipur. For eight months in 1870 he maintained a journal in which he noted, in bullet-point style, his main activities of the day. The diary, which begins in Calcutta and ends in Jaipur, includes several mentions of his photographic pursuits: "Saturday, 1 January. At 11 o'clock photographed the Duke of Edinburgh [and] then returned home ... Wednesday, 16 February. Went into the photography room. Printed photographs ... Tuesday, 29 March: Jaipur; took photographs from the corner of the palace ... Friday, 3 June: Jaipur; Took some pictures in the aatish (stables) some of which did not turn out; then in the photography department, took 3 photos of the zenana out of which one was spoilt."[2]

As well as being a highly experiemental, pioneering and creative photographer and book-maker, Ram Singh II was also an early collector of the work of other photographers active at the time, often collecting albums in which he would include his own work alongside that of his contemporaries.

Self portrait as a Sadhu, c.1858
Glass-plate negative

The guards of Maharajah Ram Singh II,
in the Royal Palace of Jaipur, c.1858
Glass-plate negative

Untitled portraits from Ram Singh II's court, Jaipur, c.1860–80
Albumen prints, approx. 16 × 10 cm each

Darogah Abbas Ali
b. British India, active late 1860s–c.1880

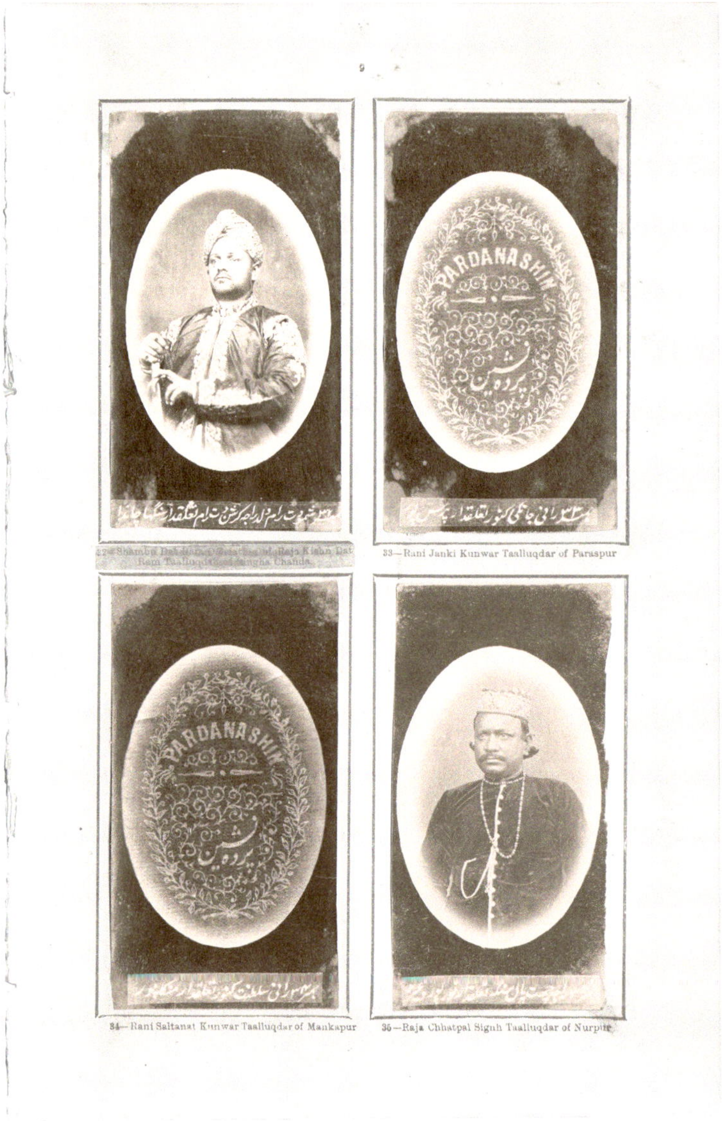

Darogah Abbas Ali was a nineteenth-century municipal engineer in Lucknow who took to photographing the city and its surroundings in the 1870s. In 1874 he published fifty of these photographs in a guide to the city, known today as *The Lucknow Album*. In keeping with a growing trend for photographic albums that presented Indian culture and traditions, Ali also produced two further albums, particularly geared for an Indian clientele. *The Beauties of Lucknow*, containing twenty-four portraits of women with descriptive text and produced in two editions (English and Urdu) states in its preface that its patrons are "the nobility and gentry of Oudh" – who also form the subject of Ali's 1880 album, *An Illustrated Historical Album of Rajas and Taaluqdars of Oudh*. Containing roughly 344 carte de visite-sized photographs with ruled borders and text in both English and Urdu, this second album was also designed to cater to two sets of audiences. Both albums borrow heavily from the Mughal *muraqqa* in terms of technique, style and aesthetic appeal, while the photographs within each album follow a similar compositional format. In *The Beauties of Lucknow*, the women are not only dressed uniformly with heavy jewellery and layered garments but are also seen with the same prop, striking a similar pose. In the album detailing the local rajas and wealthy landowners around Lucknow, each portrait is of half length and posed similarly, with changes only in headgear, attire and props at each turn. Both albums are therefore interesting when viewed through the lens of gender, illustrating two ends of a spectrum. Even as the women of *The Beauties of Lucknow* stare directly and comfortably into the camera lens, *An Illustrated Historical Album of Rajas and Taaluqdars of Oudh* features unique examples of the complete visual erasure of women in the form of cartouches that simply have "Pardanashin" (in purdah) written in them in place of their portraits.[1]

Plates 32 – 35 from *An illustrated historical album of the Rajas and Taaluqdars of Oudh*, 1880
Albumen prints, 8.9 × 5.4 cm each

Portraits from the album *The Beauties of Lucknow*, 1874
Albumen prints, approx. 15 × 10.5 cm each

Ghasiram Hardev Sharma
b. British India, 1868–1930

Ghasiram Hardev Sharma was one of the chief painters and photographers associated with the Shrinathji Temple at Nathdwara (a pilgrimage town situated in Mewar, Rajasthan). Sharma, like many others of his time, was fascinated by the photographic medium and its possibilities. His embrace of photography led to the establishment of the Ghasiram studio which offered devotees a chance to have their portraits taken, prints of which they could take back with them as souvenirs from their pilgrimage. These portraits were also likely used as references to produce *manorath* paintings for patrons that depicted them worshipping at the shrine of Shrinathji (see Khubiram Gopilal, p. 100). It also allowed several of the Nathdwara artists a chance to sit for studio portraits, surviving examples of which seem to indicate a preference to being "portrayed seated on a chair with a European palette in hand, putting the finishing touches on an easel portrait."[1]

In her book *Gods in the Bazaar*, Kajri Jain describes the work of Sharma as being "characterised by his photographic treatment of figures, and in particular of faces: photographic not in the sense of hyperrealism but in the literal replication of the monochrome tonalities of black and white photography."[2] This form of photo-realism also worked the other way around. Sharma would begin with a photograph and then paint over the top of it – not in a thin veil of colour, but blocking out entire regions of the gelatin silver photographic surface below with opaque pigments, which might then additionally be heightened with gold. Whether in his painting or in his painted photographs, Sharma presents a clear example of the fusion between painting and photography in India at the time.

Bhadariji Devarajaji, c.1890
Hand-coloured gelatin silver print, 24 × 20 cm

Johnston & Hoffmann
India, active 1870s–1950s

Johnston & Hoffmann was a successful commercial photography firm established by Theodore Julius Hoffmann and P. A. Johnston in Calcutta in 1882. They expanded to open a branch in Burma (only briefly in business between 1889 and 1890) and another in Darjeeling in 1890. When Johnston passed away in 1891, Hoffman took over the business, which continued to trade in both their names, and photograph mounts from the mid-1890s also advertise a Johnston & Hoffman branch in Shimla. Ranking perhaps only behind the studios of Bourne & Shepherd, Johnston & Hoffmann is recognised for having built a large catalogue of views of north and north-eastern India, Sikkim and Nepal. In the early twentieth century the firm expanded its catalogue to include views of Sri Lanka.[1]

Photographs such as this (shown in both its original and overpainted forms), of Maharaja Sir Bhagwati Prasad Singh, introduce one of the main lines of business for the studio. Portraits of maharajas would have been made and circulated within the extended royal families, and due to their now having become collectors' items in the West are well represented and, importantly, preserved in many Western private collections, ensuring that their condition is much finer than the landscapes or ethnographic studies.

Whilst the original negative and black-and-white print would have been made by the studio, the overpainting would have been applied by a commissioned Indian artist trained in the fine brushwork of Indian miniature painting. At times this embellishment would have been limited to a thin application of watercolour to give natural tone to the image, as was typical with "hand-tinted" photographs of the period. In other examples, portraits would have been heightened with metallic paints which sat in relief on the surface of the image, creating incredibly rich and intricately unique portraits, and a genre unto itself in the history of photography in the region.

Maharaja Sir Bhagwati Prasad Singh, c.1900
Hand-coloured and original platinum print, 50.2 × 34.9 cm each

Khubiram Gopilal
b. British India, 1891–1970

The painter and photographer Khubiram Gopilal came from Nathdwara, a small pilgrimage town in Rajasthan, where he had a studio and worked alongside several other artists from the region. Art and devotion are deeply intertwined in this town where paintings play an important role in temple worship: large paintings on cloth are hung behind the deity in the temples, and simpler works (such as these *manorath* collages) were often sold to pilgrims during their visit to take home for domestic worship.

In his early work Gopilal would produce straightforward paintings of pilgrims to mark their visit to Nathdwara, and although the faces of the sitters may have been based on photographs, they were still simply single-media paintings. He then began experimenting with pasting the photographed heads of the subjects directly onto the painting, as if further proof of the pilgrims' visit. In doing so, Gopilal can be seen as a pioneer of a unique and new confluence of photography and painting that evolved in this period, and a different version of the more well known hand-tinted or completely overpainted portraits, typically of more illustrious sitters, such as royals and merchants from larger cities.

In her book *The Artists of Nathadwara: The Practice of Painting in Rajasthan*, Tryna Lyons suggests a different reading of the motivations for inserting photographs into these paintings which complicates our understanding of these collages simply being the hand of a known artist and of his style being the result of creativity alone. Referring to his collaborations with the artist Gopilal Govardhanji, she states: "The two artist/merchants served as middlemen for a large number of painters, generally signing their own names to whatever works passed through their hands. They specialised in *pichhavais*, Krishna *lila* scenes set in European-influenced landscapes ... and, especially, various peculiar genres involving photography. For example, they hand-coloured black and white photographs, painted generic pictures of Vaishnav devotees worshipping Shrinathji onto which they pasted faces and hands cut from photos of the people who ordered the image, and even made *trompe l'oeil* paintings meant to resemble photographs. Elderly Hiralal and Kanhaiyalal, who formerly worked for the Khubiram-Gopilal shop, characterised all of this activity as *thagi* (duping or cheating), and say that a lot of innocent devotees were fooled by Nathadwara's sly businessmen."[1]

Familes worshipping the deity Shrinathji in Nathdwara, c.1940
Opaque natural pigments and photograph cut-outs on paper, 43 × 55 cm each

ચિત્રકાર ખુબીરામ ગોપાલલાલ
શ્રીનાથદ્વારા (મેવાડ.)

Suresh Punjabi
b. India, 1957

Suresh Punjabi established Studio Suhag along with his brother Mahesh in 1979 in the small industrial town of Nagda in Central India. In many ways, this was a completely typical studio of its time and place, of the type one would expect to find in the thousands of similar towns across India. What caused the practice of Studio Suhag to come to light is the writings of British anthropologist and photography historian Christopher Pinney, who on a visit to Nagda saw its archive of an estimated 50,000 35mm and medium-format negatives being cast upon the streets by a monsoon storm. Pinney subsequently saved a considerable collection of these, which he documented in his 2014 publication *Artisan Camera*. In this volume Pinney writes of the two main kinds of portraits Studio Suhag produced: "Suresh was keen to make a distinction between what he referred to as 'bhejna' (prospective marriage) and 'istyle' images. Bhejna derives from the Hindi verb to send and denotes images made of unmarried men or women which are commissioned with the intent of then being sent out to the families of prospective partners. Istyle derives from the English word 'Style' and refers to a genre of portraiture made for the theatrical pleasure of the customer and in which the sitter often holds their hands against their face in certain stylised poses. Bhejna and istyle point (in Suresh's usage) to two modes of photography with different aesthetics and different audiences but they are both equally future-oriented, both equally prophetic."[1] We can in fact view much of the studio portraiture as seen elsewhere in this chapter in a similar way: as functional portraits with a clear, non-artistic purpose; or as a creative exercise and a piece of theatre between the photographer, the sitter and the viewer. Studio Suhag is still in operation as a portrait studio, with much of the operations taken over and digitised by Suresh's son, Pratik Punjabi.

ABOVE, OPPOSITE AND FOLLOWING PAGES
Untitled portraits from Studio Suhag, c.1978
Reproduced from the negatives

HONEST

4 Proof & Propaganda

In thinking about the genre of photojournalism, it is important to consider the relationship of a photograph to the historical event it is intended to capture. Which of the two, event or image, is responsible for immortalising the other?

Do we carry these images with us, decades later, because of the particular skill with which they are captured, or because they are the living remnants of a history, now lost? As we compiled this small selection of Indian photojournalism (either photojournalism made in India, or by Indian photographers elsewhere, as is the case of Kishor Parekh in Bangladesh), it became apparent that a number of the photographs we have included do much to complicate our understanding of the photographic afterlife of an event, as well as the veracity of photojournalism itself. David Douglas Duncan's iconic photograph for *Life* magazine, of a librarian of the Imperial Secretariat dividing books between India and Pakistan, has been proven to have been a staged event: indeed the library collections under imperial control were never partitioned.[1] A similar circumstance unfolded some ninety years before Duncan, when Felice Beato, a few months late to the scene of the 1857 revolt, seems to have had the skulls of slaughtered rebels dug up and restored to the foreground of his frame in order to heighten his authenticity as witness to the scene. As mentioned in the introduction, Beato's photographs came at the heels of Roger Fenton's 1855 photographs of the Crimean War, which had been equally constrained by slow camera exposures, and were therefore largely limited to empty landscapes with cannonballs added into the foreground for added effect.[2] These slight surrenders of photographic authenticity can be explained variously across the medium's history. Well into the 1890s, photojournalism, or its stylistic precursor, bore similar expectations to those of war painting: the slow exposures of Beato's and Fenton's cameras curtailed the ability to photograph an event in action, resultant of which photographic reportage was either confined to the production of "aftermath images" or to the reconstruction of elaborate scenes for the viewers' benefit. Newspapers, caught in the ever-pressing constraint of space, didn't want to waste pages on a series of images, resultantly creating a new regard for the single, symbolic image.[3] Even in the twentieth-century, publications such as *Life* were the distributors of representative images such as Duncan's: photographs that, although themselves constructed or fictitious, were intended to encapsulate an entire news story in one frame.

Photographers of this time congregated not simply in times of war or revolt but for moments of imperial splendour. Elaborate bodies of work were created around the Delhi Durbars, especially the Durbar of 1903, where Lord Curzon was adamant that the event be documented photographically. In these iterations of British ceremonial power in India, the camera was used to capture the sheer scale of British might, ranging from panoramic views of the scale of the Durbar proceedings, to the smaller ceremonies and balls that were held in Delhi, the Mughal seat of power, as a symbolic statement of the British position in India's imperial lineage. Here, in the photographs of William H. Burke (from the 1911 Durbar), the camera is an active component of a larger apparatus of power, positioning Queen Victoria, King Edward VII and King George V as the legitimate inheritors of the Delhi throne.

In his considered and thorough text *The Coming of Photography in India*, Christopher Pinney refers to a dichotomous distinction in camera practices of the late nineteenth century: photography as cure and as poison. Whereas cure denotes the jubilant adoption of the camera in various bureaucratic capacities as a means of solving "existing representational problems" in the imaging of India (such as the countless photographs by Maurice Vidal Portman, Linnaeus Tripe and the Archaeological Survey of India), the camera turns poisonous when the images it generates begin to favour the cause of the colonised. Willoughby Wallace Hooper's haunting photographs from the Madras famine of 1876–78, for instance, although not unlike previous efforts to depict India as a place in need of radical colonial intervention, do much to undo any viewers' faith in the colonial project. Pinney notes that the publication of Hooper's photographs in England activated a great sense of disillusionment among the British public in their government's ability to improve India, as they began to wonder whether British colonialism had generated any reform at all.[4] Similarly poisonous for colonialism was the utilisation of the camera by local photographers to present a counter-narrative of colonial rule: where some of the earliest British images of the Jallianwala Bagh massacre in 1919 sought to "offset Dyer's massacre against the silent ... counter-evidence of earlier events",[5] (with titles such as *Scene of first assault on Miss Sherwood* and *Alliance Bank. Room where Mr Thompson was murdered*), they are challenged by Narayan Vinayak Virkar's photographs of the bullet-specked walls of the park where Colonel Reginald Dyer's atrocity was committed. Virkar's photographs of survivors indicating towards the cavities left by the bullets that were intended to kill them are powerful in their starkness, implicating the viewer in the scene of a heinous imperial crime. Virkar's photographs do not trifle with artistic technique or skill; they derive their power from the sheer horror of the scene. These are photographs that speak of the growing disenchantment with British rule – a sentiment that would only amplify in the decades building up to the liberation of India in 1947.

The invention of easy portable cameras such as the Leica in the early decades of the twentieth century changed the pace and course of photojournalism across the world, allowing the photographer to "seize content and composition from fluid events,"[6] thereby replacing heavily staged studio photographs that had been the cornerstone of camerawork from the previous century. The camera was ubiquitous in the freedom movement, with scores of (mostly uncredited) photographs dating from the earliest national independence movements organised by Mahatma Gandhi. Kulwant Roy (the head of Associated Press Photographs during the 1940s) and Sunil Janah (photographer for Communist Party of India journals *The People's War* and *The People's Age*) were prolific contributors to the nationalist Indian press, respectively immortalised by their images of political deliberations between Congress leadership and the British and views of the Bengali subaltern during the famine of 1943. One must, of course, remember the huge curtailment of press freedom during the struggle for Indian independence. Even Jawaharlal Nehru, in his tour de force *The Discovery of India*, noted the spectacular surveillance and censorship of any press coverage of India both within the country and abroad, as the British struggled to underplay the scale of devastation of the Bengal famine by controlling the number of images of the suffering masses that were published.[7]

Foreign reporters also found India to be a profitable place to produce "newsworthy" images: it is reputed that upon the formation of Magnum Photo Agency in 1947, Henri Cartier-Bresson specifically asked for Asia to be the region he would report on, in order to capture the rapid decolonisation movements that were taking place across the continent.[8] Cartier-Bresson's iconic images of the days following Gandhi's assassination were reportedly divided between *Life*, *Harper's Bazaar*, *Reader's Digest* and *The Saturday Evening Post*, indicating the immense competition in 1940s print media to procure the most iconic picture of an event. Margaret Bourke-White, then a more established photographer than Cartier-Bresson, had a much more stable arrangement with *Life* magazine.

In this chapter we restrict ourselves to the study of news images in the course of the century from 1857 to the 1960s, in an attempt to show India under the lens from pre-independence through the freedom struggle and onwards to post-partition. The selection of photographs may betray a bias towards images from the mid-twentieth century – this is because of our particular interest in the decades in which photojournalists possessed a particular celebrity, often travelling the world of their own accord. Because of our interest in the authorship of these photographs, we have not been able to draw upon the vast archive of (often equally compelling) photographs taken by uncredited press photographers. We have, where possible, included iconic images from important episodes of India's vast history, ranging from Felice Beato's photographs of the aftermath of the 1857 Rebellion, to the glamorous photographs from the Kennedys' state visit to India in 1962. Although by no means a conclusive or complete set of defining India images, these are photographs that have persisted into the present day for a variety of reasons: be it the celebrity of the author, or the monumentality of the event itself.

1 See Anhad Hundal, 'Getting the Picture: The mystery of an iconic Partition photograph', in: *The Caravan Magazine*, 1 September 2016, http://www.caravanmagazine.in/lede/getting-the-picture-iconic-partition-photograph.
2 Noting the particular emptiness of nineteenth-century photo-reportage, Zahid R. Chaudhary asks the question: "What does it mean to capture absence indexically?... We certainly are being asked to imagine the event ... rather than invited to see the event itself." Chaudhary, *Afterimage of Empire*, p. 39.
3 Claude Cookman, 'Margaret Bourke-White and Henri Cartier-Bresson: Gandhi's Funeral', in: *History of Photography* 22, no. 2 (1998), p. 202.
4 Pinney, *Coming of Photography in India*, pp. 98–99.
5 Ibid., p. 88.
6 Cookman, 'Bourke-White and Cartier-Bresson', p. 200.
7 Jawaharlal Nehru, *The Discovery of India*, Calcutta. 1946; repr. 1964, pp. 522–27.
8 Cookman, 'Bourke-White and Cartier-Bresson', p. 199.

Felice Beato
b. Italy, 1832–1909

In a career that spanned five decades, Italian-British photographer Felice Beato covered a wide swathe of colonised Asia and was among the first photographers to create images of India, China, Japan, Korea and Burma. Beato's earliest registered studio was in Constantinople in the 1850s, where he worked alongside his brother-in-law, photographer James Robertson, at their studio, Robertson & Beato (1853–54). His early photographic expeditions took him to Malta, Greece and in 1857 to Jerusalem, as well as to Crimea in the mid-1850s to document the Crimean War following Roger Fenton's departure from the region. This is arguably where Beato acquired his first experiences of photographing conflicts and, more specifically, the aftermath of conflicts.

In his later travels, Beato sought to cater to a Western audience, producing an exceptionally diverse body of work that ranged from topographical and architectural views and panoramas to portraits and costume studies of the countries he visited or in which he resided. He arrived in Calcutta in 1858 to capture the end of the Rebellion of 1857 and its impact on north India, before proceeding into reportage of the Second Opium War in 1860 and the American expedition to Korea in 1871. His photographs of battlefields, believed to be among the first to show images of war casualties, are considered to have provided a new direction to the genre of aftermath photography.

During his time in India, Beato made a prolific record of the primary sites of the Rebellion, tracing the course of its events in Delhi, Cawnpore and Lucknow in order to recreate them and give a sense of urgency to the images. In some views, he famously staged elements in the frame, adding rebel corpses or arranging disinterred bones, in order to heighten the dramatic effect of his images. This photograph of the hanging of rebels captures a broader moment of the British return to order, when power over India had passed from the East India Company to the Crown. Photographing months after the events of the revolt had passed, the hangings and damaged buildings were in a way the only incidents related to the revolt that Beato could in fact capture.

The execution of mutineers, 1858
Albumen print, 23.5 × 29.8 cm

Willoughby Wallace Hooper
b. England, 1837–1912

Child born of Famine-Stricken Mother - Age 3 mo: Weight 3 lbs

Colonel Willoughby Wallace Hooper began his career at East India House in London in the Secretary's Department and then left for India in 1858 to join the 7th Madras Cavalry, where he would serve for the next forty years. As a young lieutenant, Hooper came to be known for his photography skills – leading to him being released from his military duties and transferred to the 4th Cavalry, Saugor and Secunderabad, in order to produce a series of ethnographic portraits of the peoples of the central provinces of India, as per the directives issued by Lord Canning, Governor-General (later Viceroy) of India. Perhaps encouraged by the official support for his photography, Hooper entered into a commercial partnership with photographer George Western, trading under the name Hooper & Western. A veterinary surgeon with the Madras Army from 1857 to 1883, Western is primarily known for his collaborative photographs with Hooper during the 1860s and 1870s, particularly a series of ethnographic "native types" from southern India, scenes of Anglo-Indian life, and pictures of hunts.

Between 1876 and 1878 Hooper also photographed the victims of the Madras famine, such as those shown here. These photographs were first published in Britain, following which Hooper was caricatured in *Punch* when reports circulated that he had offered no assistance to the starving subjects he was photographing, an interesting precursor to the debates around the ethics of intervention which have frequently occurred in the history of twentieth and twenty-first-century reportage. In 1886, Hooper's photographs landed him in controversy again, and he was brought before a court of enquiry to answer charges of extorting evidence and the cruel and inhumane treatment of a group of Dacoit prisoners that had been sentenced to be executed in Burma.

In 1885 Hooper took part in the Third Burmese War as Provost Marshall of the Burma Expeditionary Force, making an extensive photographic record of the expedition as well as the surrounding country, native life and industries. Many of these photographs were later published in his last known book, *Burmah* [*sic*]*: A Series of One Hundred Photographs* (1887).[1]

ABOVE, OPPOSITE AND FOLLOWING PAGES
Scenes of the Madras Famine, 1876–78
Albumen prints, approx. 10.4 × 15.5 cm each

Forsaken

Deserving objects of gratuitous relief

David Douglas Duncan
b. United States, 1916–2018

David Douglas Duncan was one of America's foremost twentieth-century war photographers, especially known for his coverage of the Second World War and the Korean War. Amongst his best-known publications is *This Is War!* (1951). Duncan also produced two more books on the Vietnam War – *Protest!* (1968) and *War Without Heroes* (1970) – critical of the government's handling of the conflict.

His career as a photojournalist began when he took photographs of a hotel fire in Tucson while he was studying archaeology at the nearby University of Arizona. His images included one of a hotel guest who made repeated attempts to go back into the burning building for his suitcase. That photo proved to be newsworthy when the guest turned out to have been notorious bank robber John Dillinger, and the suitcase to have contained the rewards from a bank robbery in which he had shot a police officer. After college Duncan began as a freelance photographer, selling his work to local journals, before joining the Marine Corps, earning an officer's commission, and becoming a combat photographer. After the Second World War, Duncan was hired by *Life* to join its staff at the recommendation of J. R. Eyerman, *Life's* chief photographer. During his time with the magazine, Duncan covered many events, including conflicts in Turkey, Eastern Europe, Africa and the Middle East, and the end of the British Raj in India. Of his work in India, his most iconic photograph is of B. S. Kesavan, then a junior librarian for the Imperial Secretariat Library, burying his head in his hands whilst at the task of dividing books between India and the new nation of Pakistan. This image, although heavily staged (this was not how books came to be divided between the two countries), became one of the most iconic photographs of the Partition, revealing an interest in contemporary photojournalism for powerful representative images with little visual reference to actual events. It was later referenced in the 2017 film *Viceroy's House*, in a way revealing the persistence of the photograph in the popular imagination of independence and Partition.

B. S. Kesavan ostensibly dividing books in the Imperial Secretariat Library, New Delhi, 1947
Gelatin silver print, 23.7 × 18.5 cm

Homai Vyarawalla
b. British India, 1913–2012

Homai Vyarawalla, India's first woman photojournalist, was a key visual chronicler of the last days of the British Empire and the new nation-state following independence. Her archive of over three decades of Indian history received less attention and importance than the Indian work of her international contemporaries such as Henri Cartier-Bresson (see p. 144) and Margaret Bourke-White (see p. 121), and it is perhaps in more recent times that she is now being discussed more fairly amongst them. Vyarawalla first learned photography from Maneckshaw Vyarawalla, a photographer and accountant with the *Times of India* whom she eventually married. Her early images of urban life and modern young women in Bombay show a pictorial perspective influenced by her training at the Sir J. J. School of Art and the photographs she was exposed to through issues of *Life* magazine. Belonging to a time when this was a male profession, these early portraits were initially published in the *Illustrated Weekly* and the *Bombay Chronicle* in her husband's name. With the Second World War and Singapore overrun by the Japanese, the British Information Services (BIS) relocated to India. They were looking for photographers, and Stanley Jepson at the *Illustrated Weekly* recommended the Vyarawallas. In 1942 the couple moved to Delhi – while her husband was "lent" to them for a year by the *Times*, Vyarawalla became a full-time employee at BIS and was also allowed to take up freelance projects.

Apart from photographing a significant meeting when Congress members voted for the partition of India as well as Gandhi's funeral, Vyarawalla documented the rituals of independence: the building of dams and steel plants, and the state visits of many famous figures in twentieth-century history, including Mohammad Reza Shah Pahlavi, Martin Luther King, Jr., Ho Chi Minh, Marshall Tito, the Russian leaders Nikita Khruschev and Leonid Berzhnev, Queen Elizabeth II and the Kennedys. She is perhaps best known for her many photographs of India's first prime minister, Jawaharlal Nehru, such as the one shown here, taken during his 62nd birthday celebration, where he is seen releasing a dove into the air as a symbol of the hope he embodied as leader. In 1970, disheartened by the Emergency in India that was leading to a growing lack of freedom in the press as well as a changing atmosphere that heralded a newer generation of photojournalists with whom she could not see eye to eye, Vyarawalla decided to cease her photographic practice.

Jawaharlal Nehru releasing a dove at the National Stadium, New Delhi, 1951
Gelatin silver print, 22.8 × 17.7 cm

Margaret Bourke-White
b. United States, 1904–1971

Known for her extensive contributions to photojournalism, particularly for *Life* magazine, Margaret Bourke-White is recognised as having been the first woman documentary photographer to be accredited by and to work with the US Armed Forces, a considerable achievement considering the almost complete male dominance of the field. Her interest in photography began as a hobby supported by her father's own enthusiasm for cameras. Despite this interest, in 1922 she began studying herpetology at Columbia University but left after one semester following her father's death. After transferring colleges multiple times, Bourke-White eventually graduated from Cornell University with a bachelor's degree in 1927. A year later, Bourke-White moved to New York where she took up freelance photography. In 1929 the publisher Henry Luce hired her as associate editor and staff photographer at *Fortune*, a position she held until 1935. In 1930 *Fortune* sent her to photograph the Krupp Iron Works in Germany, and she continued on her own to photograph the First Five-Year Plan in the Soviet Union. In 1936 she left *Fortune* to become one of the first four staff photographers for *Life* magazine when it began publication. At *Life* her photographs of the construction of the Fort Peck Dam in Montana were featured on the cover and used in the feature story of the first issue in 1936.

Through the 1930s Bourke-White photographed Germany, Austria, Czechoslovakia and the Soviet Union – refining the dramatic style she had used in industrial and architectural subjects, and developing a compassionate, humanitarian approach to people and social issues. After the war she travelled to India and came to be known both for her portraits of important Indian figures of the time, B. R. Ambedkar and Muhammad Ali Jinnah in particular, and of her now iconic photograph of Gandhi at the spinning wheel, as well as her documentation of Partition and the famine in Bengal. In India she was best known for her abrasive manner and frequent use of flash, due to which she was evicted from the scene of Gandhi's prayer ceremony after his assassination in 1948. In the 1950s, despite developing Parkinson's disease, she continued to photograph the Korean War, and wrote her autobiography *Portrait of Myself*, until officially retiring from *Life* in 1969. She died in 1971.

Gandhi at his spinning wheel, 1946
Gelatin silver print, 30.4 × 40 cm

Sun-warmed beaches like Montego Bay, Jamaica, are waiting for you in the West Indies . . . No snow, no cold rain, just the trade wind blowing every day—and fun—and *rest!*

Plan now to ESCAPE FROM WINTER to these SUNLIT ISLES

By Flying Clipper, the West Indies are now less than a day away from any point in the U.S. . . . New York to San Juan is only 8 hours.

M-m-m! New hat, West Indies style? No, just the way the natives in Haiti carry bananas, baskets and many other wares to market. Wouldn't you like (left) to taste the milk, right out of a fresh coconut, at St. Thomas, Virgin Islands? . . . At San Juan (see map) you're only 45 minutes by Clipper from St. Thomas.

NEW YORK
BERMUDA
8 hours
NASSAU
MIAMI
HAVANA
CAMAGUEY
PORT AU PRINCE
SAN JUAN
JAMAICA
C. TRUJILLO
ST. THOMAS
TO ALL SOUTH AMERICA

Tropical luxury. The Dominican Republic's Hotel *Jaragua*, at Ciudad Trujillo, is one of the most modern winter resorts in the West Indies. Every room has a radio, telephone and bath . . . and besides the ocean-water swimming pool (above), there are tennis courts, and an excellent golf course nearby.

SEE YOUR TRAVEL AGENT or the nearest Pan American office for rates and reservations to the West Indies not only from the points shown above but also from New Orleans, Houston and Los Angeles . . . Clippers also fly on regular schedule to Europe, the Near East, India, Africa, Alaska, Hawaii, New Zealand, Australia and the Orient.

AMONG THE MILLIONS OF PASSENGERS WHO HAVE FLOWN ABROAD BY CLIPPER

Norman Corwin
Miriam Hopkins
Roy Howard
General George C. Marshall
General Carlos P. Romulo
Mrs. Franklin D. Roosevelt
Harold E. Stassen
Myron C. Taylor
Harold Tittmann, Jr.
John G. Winant

Four centuries will look down on you at San Juan, P. R. In the background (above) is Puerto Rico's "White House"—oldest governor's mansion under the U. S. flag! Built for the family of Ponce de Leon in 1523, it is one of the finest architectural gems in the whole Caribbean area . . . Sir Francis Drake tried to take the surrounding *Fortaleza* in 1595, but failed.

Today you'll be fascinated by these remnants of Spain's ancient glory, and by Puerto Rican embroidery and handicrafts.

PAN AMERICAN WORLD AIRWAYS
WORLD'S MOST EXPERIENCED AIRLINE
The System of the Flying Clippers

SPINDLY BUT DETERMINED OLD SIKH, CARRYING AILING WIFE, SETS OUT ON THE DANGEROUS JOURNEY TO INDIA'S BORDER

The Great Migration

Five million Indians flee for their lives

PHOTOGRAPHS FOR LIFE BY MARGARET BOURKE-WHITE

Last week the Indian earth trembled with the tread of millions of shuffling feet, and the Indian air, heavy with the smell of death, still echoed the screams of the dying. In nine weeks of freedom the new nations of India and Pakistan had gone through a bloody slaughter that took 100,000 lives and from which 5,000,000 fled in history's greatest mass migration.

The ultimate terror began Aug. 15, when the subcontinent was divided into Moslem Pakistan and predominantly Hindu India. It centered in the Punjab, which was split by the new boundary (*map, p. 119*). The warlike, anti-Moslem Sikhs of Lahore found themselves a minority in Pakistan. The impoverished Moslems of Amritsar, the holy Sikh city, suddenly were residents of a Hindu India they feared. Spurred by religious fanaticism, fright and economic frustration, Sikhs, Moslems and Hindus fell upon each other with knives, swords, clubs and the torch.

For the millions there was only one solution: flight. Like the Children of Israel, but in nearly 10 times the numbers, they began their exodus over the footpaths and bullock-cart roads (*above*). Sometimes in small and sometimes in great caravans, 2,750,000 Moslems plodded into West Punjab and 2,700,000 Sikhs and Hindus crossed the new frontier to the east. On this and the following pages are Margaret Bourke-White's photographs of the terrible odyssey.

CONTINUED ON NEXT PAGE 117

"The Great Migration", *Life*, 3 November 1947

MISERY OF THE DISPOSSESSED is reflected in the face of this Moslem boy, perched on the wall of the Purana Qila fortress in New Delhi. Below him thousands of his unhappy fellows, who have fled their homes in terror, are trying to survive until they can organize a convoy for the long march to Pakistan. In their squalid city of tents and lean-tos they have almost no room to sleep and little to eat. They are surrounded by filth and many will die without ever leaving camp.

MIGRATIONS CROSS IN THE BLOODY PUNJAB

The Camps

They are unspeakably dirty, crowded and sorrow-ridden

To escape the slaughter in unfriendly cities and at the same time gather the strength of numbers for the long migration, Moslems in India and Sikhs and Hindus in Pakistan have moved into ancient fortresses like New Delhi's Purana Qila (*opposite*). These primitive camps are squalid concentrations of disease and sorrow. Yet they are distinguished by a color and vitality that cut through the stench and the wailing of the bereaved.

In the Purana Qila fort more than 60,000 Moslems sleep on dirt ledges, under crazy lean-tos made of a bit of canvas or a dirty blanket. There are no toilets or sewers. For many the only food is a daily ration of four *chappatis* (disks of unleavened bread). Day and night there is movement—new refugees come in carrying some of their possessions on their heads in burlap bags, and old refugees search again and again for missing relatives or frantically scurry for food and water.

Almost all have lost parents, husbands, wives or children. Some have been wounded before they reached the camp. Behind them lie abandoned homes and their shattered families. Ahead, if they survive the camp's rigors, lies only the fearful prospect of a long journey beset by danger and greater hardships, and a future whose shape they cannot even guess at.

MOSQUE WITHIN FORT also is packed with homeless Moslems. The great dome provides a measure of shelter against the elements for some of the refugees.

CONTINUED ON NEXT PAGE

Great Migration CONTINUED

THE EMIGRANT TRAINS of crude wooden carts drawn by bullocks creak across the barren land of the Punjab all day long. In this convoy, starkly silhouetted against the vivid Indian sky, are 45,000 uprooted Sikhs on their way to the Ferozepore and Ludhiana districts of the eastern Punjab. Unlike the U.S. wagon-train pioneers, hopefully en route to a new land, these migrants have little to look forward to and are losing everything that they cannot carry with them. Despite the presence of an escort of Gurkha soldiers, thousands of stinking bodies along the road constantly remind the travelers that they may never reach safety.

CONTINUED ON NEXT PAGE

Grain bags as bed, Calcutta, 1951
Unloading corn sent by foreign countries
for India's famine-stricken areas, Calcutta, 1951
Gelatin silver prints, approx. 21 × 21 cm each

Werner Bischof
b. 1916–1954, Switzerland

Bischof studied at the Zurich School of Arts and Crafts (Kunstgewerbeschule) under abstract photographer Hans Finsler, following which he established his own photographic studio in the late 1930s. His attempt to pursue abstract photography in Paris in 1939 was cut short with the announcement of the Second World War, whereupon Bischof returned to Switzerland and was conscripted by the army as a soldier at the Swiss border. He was appointed a member of Magnum in 1949 for his founding photographic projects that documented the devastation of Europe after the war.

Bischof's first project in India was in 1951, when he was commissioned by *Life* magazine to report on famines in present-day Bihar. These photographs follow his attempt to reconcile his aesthetic interest in the medium with the expectations of mid-century photojournalism as demanded by contemporary publications. This is prominent in his images of India: although many of his photographs of elderly women begging for food bring to mind the humanist documentary work of Henri Cartier-Bresson from a few years before, the photographs presented here, such as the man gathering corn in a basket, are unabashedly modernist in their mobilisation of light and shadow in sharp divisions across the composition. His photograph of Jamshedpur similarly betrays Bischof's use of industrial lines and geometries to produce a linear composition in which the labouring woman is at the absolute centre. Bischof subsequently travelled to Vietnam to work as a war reporter for *Paris Match*. He died in a road accident in Peru in 1954.

An employee of the Tata Iron and Steel Company from the town of Jamshedpur, 1951
Gelatin silver print, approx. 21 × 21 cm

Kishor Parekh
b. British India, 1930–1982

Kishor Parekh studied film-making and documentary photography at the University of Southern California, and in the early 1960s he returned to India, where he became the chief photographer of the *Hindustan Times*. He set about introducing to Indian photojournalism multi-column pictures and the use of 35mm. Prior to this, newspaper photojournalism in India was largely concerned with manufactured photo-ops and ribbon-cutting ceremonies shot with the more restrictive twin-lens reflex cameras,[1] but Parekh's aggressive sense for storytelling drove him to use the more modern 35mm format and seek out images that captured larger social and political narratives. While at the *Hindustan Times* he covered the Sino-Indian War of 1962, the 1965 conflict between India and Pakistan, the 1966–67 famine in Bihar, and realised extensive essays on prime ministers Nehru and Lal Bahadur Shastri. Parekh's images typically combine the factual with a potent artistic rendition, much in the tradition of the photographers he admired, such as W. Eugene Smith, Margaret Bourke-White (see p. 121) and Henri Cartier-Bresson (see p. 144), the work of whom he had analysed in his university thesis.

After six years at the *Hindustan Times*, where Parekh continued to have a radical impact on photojournalistic news culture in India, such as his introducing full-page photo essays and ensuring that photographers were given credit lines, in 1967 he joined *Asia Magazine* in Hong Kong. Despite having moved away from news stories and photojournalism work by the late 1960s, when he heard the news of Bangladesh in 1971, Parekh took the first flight out, forced his way through a restricted cordon and apparently jumped onto an army helicopter carrying an official press corps to Dhaka, coercing them to carry him as well. His book on the subject, *Bangladesh: A Brutal Birth*, came to be the most iconic representation of the Bangladesh Liberation War and its human losses, with the Indian government commissioning 20,000 copies of the book to raise awareness of the conflict.

ABOVE, OPPOSITE AND FOLLOWING PAGES
Bangladesh Liberation War, 1971
Gelatin silver prints, 33.8 × 50.8 cm each

Marilyn Silverstone
b. England, 1929–1999

After graduating from Wellesley College in Massachusetts, Marilyn Silverstone became an associate editor for *Art News*, *Industrial Design* and *Interiors* during the 1950s. In 1955 she began to photograph professionally as a freelancer with the Nancy Palmer Agency, New York, working in Asia, Africa, Europe, Central America and the Soviet Union.

In 1959 Silverstone was sent on a three-month assignment to India to photograph the musician and composer Ravi Shankar. On the same trip she was also to photograph the Dalai Lama, who was escaping from the Chinese invasion of Tibet (a body of work that was a lead story in *Life*). That year she met and fell in love with Frank Moraes, then editor of *The Indian Express* newspaper, and moved with him to New Delhi. She was to live with him for the next fourteen years and the couple existed in a social world of the diplomatic corps, Indian officials, politicians, journalists and intellectuals. Whilst living in India she produced the books *Bala: Child of India* (1962) and *Gurkhas and Ghosts* (1964), and, after she moved back to London, *The Black Hat Dances* (1987) and *Ocean of Life* (1985). As her reputation grew, she became an associate member of Magnum in 1964, a full member in 1967.

In India, Silverstone photographed her own socio-economic class, fearful of falling into the same trap as many of her Western photographer predecessors, and attempted to provide an intimate insightful glimpse into the elite India and her subjects' lives and work. Her photograph of First Lady Jackie Kennedy on her official visit to India is a classic example of this, and an interesting counter to the more traditional subject matter of this time. Here, seen with the Maharani of Mewar, Silverstone seems to point to international "royalty" meeting their Indian counterparts, in a way describing a shift in notions of celebrity in the twentieth century.

Mrs Kennedy, the Maharani of Mewar and Princess Lee Radziwill returning from their visit to the Lake Palace Hotel in Udaipur, 1962
Gelatin silver print, 30.4 × 40 cm

Sati Sahni
b. British India, 1922–2010

In a career spanning six decades, Sati Sahni is best known as a war correspondent and documenter of political events in his home state of Kashmir. After completing his schooling from Mission School, Sheikh Bagh and Sri Pratap High School, Srinagar, Sahni graduated from Sri Pratap College, Srinagar. At the time, he also was associated with the All India Students Federation and served as the general secretary of its Jammu and Kashmir branch for two terms, from 1939 to 1943. He later joined the Central Information Office and subsequently served as private secretary to Bakshi Ghulam Mohammad when the latter was prime minister. Although he was a participant in the nationalist politics of the time, Sahni did not actively join any party. His first job was with the *Indian News Chronicle*, which hired him as a Kashmir correspondent. Before this, he had filed dispatches during the Second World War for the BBC, Reuters and *Time*. Closely associated with various senior political leaders of Kashmir and having worked with some of them, including Bakshi Ghulam Mohammad, G. M. Sadiq and D. P. Dhar, Sahni was also involved in sports and other cultural activities, and was a member of the first cultural delegation which toured different parts of the country in the 1950s. He was also to later serve as the bureau chief of the United News of India (UNI) in Srinagar, the Kashmir correspondent for *The Times of India*, and as director general of information in Farooq Abdullah's regime. His access to elite political and social circles allowed Sahni to build a rare collection of photographs of leading figures of the time, including Mahatma Gandhi, Jawaharlal Nehru and other national and international dignitaries who visited Kashmir. His photographic archive also included picturesque landscapes as well as sites of cultural, religious and historical significance spread across Kashmir, Ladakh and Jammu.

Sahni authored four books about Kashmir, including *Kashmir Underground* and *My Dismissal*. Posthumously, in 2011, a selection of his previously unpublished work was produced as the book *Nehru's Kashmir*, which provided a more intimate perspective into Nehru's world in later years, including the photograph shown here.

Jawaharlal Nehru at Dal Lake, Kashmir, 1951
Gelatin silver print, 24 × 24 cm

5 The New Exotic

This chapter attempts to delineate a concrete turn, or perhaps return, towards a mode of imaging India that had been the norm in cartes de visite and other such collectibles over a century before. Like their predecessors, the makers of the Indian picturesque, these photographers appear to have attempted to picture the subcontinent as a land of timeless exoticism, seemingly untouched by the effects of mid-twentieth-century industry and modernity.

In their imaging of India as a distant, mystical "other" site, the photographs presented here form a collection in which India is irreconcilably exotic, marked by palaces and poverty, bright colours and sensuous draperies – the classic tropes of what Edward Said referred to as "Orientalism" in his book of the same name from 1978. Said, primarily drawing upon studies of the Middle East in French literature and painting, described the act of intellectual formulation and representation of the East by the West as a site of inherent difference and irrationality, plagued by sexual and spiritual excess. Although Said's text itself made no mention of the politics of orientalist photography,[1] and despite the fact that orientalism's iteration in the twentieth century has been little addressed in the context of Indian visual culture, we have chosen to assess a number of post-war photographic practices through the lens of the oriental, having noted the particular proclivity of (largely) foreign commercial photographers – commissioned by and published in fashion and lifestyle magazines – to produce these staid images of exotic and inexplicable India. As this chapter will address, the aesthetic of an "other" India has been lasting and persists not simply in photography but in popular culture at large.

Ali Behdad refers to the orientalist photograph as a site within which two parallel processes occur: it is simultaneously a site of repetition, where pre-established visual tropes of Eastern exoticism are reproduced, and a site of invention, where new means of depicting the non-European subject are formulated and activated. In the case of Indian photography, one could argue that the visual vocabulary of South Asian orientalism had crystallised well before the influx of foreign photographers into the country in the mid-twentieth century. This new, oddly postcolonial exotic, drawing as it did upon the colonial gaze of earlier ethnographers and painters (such as Edwin Lord Weeks) in the subcontinent, was itself a site of deep anachronism as it fixated upon a slice of the country that was all but lost, such as Cecil Beaton's photograph of traditionally dressed young boys climbing a coconut tree and Derry Moore's portraits cast in the splendour of ruin. Moore's interest in the majesty of the interiors and architecture of the Indian elite resuscitates an older idea of the aesthetic atmosphere of India, one that was doubtless maintained by the cross-pollination between the British and Indian aristocracy during the British Raj.

Financially, from the 1940s onwards the commission of these projects depended upon the bigger budgets of Western magazines such as *Life*, *Vogue* and *National Geographic*, as photographers and photojournalists could be sent around the world at the cost of their publishers, allowing for big-budget projects, long-term assignments and elaborate sets. The desire for such exotic destinations as India, Japan and Sri Lanka to be seen by readers speaks to how the genre was reliant on the imagery and imagination of South Asia and the "Far East" as an exotic destination, an appealing site of the past, a delight of vivid scenes and unfamiliar colours in which the Euro-American viewer could lose themselves as they perused the pages of the magazine. It is possible that these opulent images of Eastern luxury provided a means of escaping the gloom and confusion brought upon by the economic fragility and political uncertainty in the years following the Second World War. An example of this commercial escapism was the 1956 *Vogue* magazine spread by British photographer Norman Parkinson, who decided to use the allure of Indian sites as far-ranging as Mahabalipuram and Kashmir's Dal Lake as scenes against which to photograph European couture. In Parkinson's indulgent shoot, the monuments and characters (for instance, the royal servants at the gate of Udaipur City Palace) that are presented seem to fade into the background in order for the clean silhouettes and light colours of his European models' clothing to be better emphasised. Indeed, to survey these photographs is to observe India as a backdrop, a site of oriental excess against which the white subject would stand out in stark contrast.[2] Images such as those of Parkinson were not considered to be particularly intellectual or political, instead forming a new, easily digestible and catchy visual language that was tied first and foremost to commercial interest: the immense sexiness and marketability of an exotic land.

The popularity of this particular vision of India was aided by the rise and establishment of Magnum Photos, a conglomeration of photographers and photojournalists who would establish and encourage a new kind of photographic storytelling dependent on reportage from various parts of the world. In a new era of image production in foreign lands, it is not surprising that a rich collection of India images develops at the hands of Magnum. Member photographers such as Marc Riboud and Don McCullin, who were both on assignment in Vietnam, and more than familiar with conflict photography and the present-ness and immediacy it bestowed upon the photographic subject, appear to abandon time in their photographs of India. The former turns to dark figures cast against their white draperies on the riverbank, while the latter was concerned with a sort of figurative photography whose stillness and shadows harked back to the Kashmir portraits of Samuel Bourne. Similarly, Henri Cartier-Bresson's photograph of refugees exercising in a camp reiterates the country's association with impenetrable chaos. The underlying notion apparent in these photographs is that India can't be captured in real time; its photographers can't resist in indulging in its exoticisation and temporal distancing. They enact what Johannes Fabian referred to as the "denial of coevalness": the photographs fix India in a designated past, a "there and then", out of which its inhabitants cannot escape.[3] What these disparate practices, ranging from Beaton to McCullin, have in common is this enacted role of the photographer as a sort of time traveller who, in photographing India, appears to reach into the past in order to bring an "authentic" India to light.

The position that India is perhaps inherently photogenic is one that tends to be taken in defence of these practices, that the light, the landscape and the visual culture resurrect of their own accord a kind of meaty visual scene. We wonder whether this argument can be easily countered by noting the centrality of the Euro-American narrator to the means by which the wider world is imaged and understood. After all, in a world in which the formula for photographic and photogenic vision continues to be commanded by the camera's inventors, a country such as India comes to be reviled for its inherent difference. This difference is also reiterated by Indian photographers and the diaspora whose work also speaks to the immense potency of this encapsulation of India as a site of mystery, fantasy and a past wisdom. One cannot deny the remarkable influence that the work of Norman Parkinson and Henri Cartier-Bresson, among others, have had on the popular genre of somewhat anachronistic photo-reportage in India today. That the institutional support of Magnum, *National Geographic* and even *Vogue* created a validated way of envisioning India photographically made this aesthetic a valuable one, one that amateur Indian photographers have strived towards as a consummation of their own skill and success. Steve McCurry, for example, who edited his India photographs into a kind of acceptable palette of Indian-ness, has met with a tide of Indian followers who in turn also saturate the nation into being. The denial of coevalness remains a consistent caveat to photographing India today. The Indian iteration of *Vogue* magazine echoes the work of Norman Parkinson in its continued evocation of luxurious palaces, most notably in a May 2017 editorial spread of model Kendall Jenner shot by famed photographer Mario Testino. Be it in film (such as *Slumdog Millionaire*, 2008), popular culture (Coldplay's controversial music video for their song "Hymn for the Weekend"), or on the many popular pages on Instagram that are dedicated to India, the country is posed as a site existent in the past, with the camera as the sole marker of present-ness in the photographic scene.

1 See Edward W. Said, *Orientalism*, New York 1978. The lacunae in Said's text have since been addressed by Malek Alloula (1986), Ali Behdad (2013, 2016) and, in the particular case of India, by Malavika Karlekar (2005, 2013) and Zahid R. Chaudhary (2012), among many others.

2 Race and image-making are perhaps more widely studied in the context of African American/ African diaspora art practice. In relation to the authors' invocation of the racial relations of foreground and background in Parkinson's images, perhaps the now-famous declaration of Harlem Renaissance writer, Zora Neale Hurston, that "I feel most colored when I am thrown against a white background" ('How It Feels to Be Colored Me', in: *The World Tomorrow*, May 1928), is here a useful tool to assess the politics of Parkinson's European models cast against an idealised India.

3 See Johannes Fabian, *Time and the Other: How Anthropology Makes its Object*, New York 1983.

Young village boys beside a river in Bengal, c.1944
Gelatin silver print, 22.8 × 22.8 cm

Cecil Beaton
b. England, 1904–1980

Born into an affluent family in London, Beaton's interest in photography developed at a young age and he reportedly spent his childhood taking photographs of his sisters dressed in a variety of costumes. He went on to become one of the best-known portrait, fashion and society photographers of twentieth-century Europe, equally famous for his public persona as an aesthete and dandy as for his photographs of iconic figures including Marilyn Monroe, Audrey Hepburn, Pablo Picasso, Winston Churchill, Jackie Kennedy and Coco Chanel, as well as the British royal family and other members of the European aristocracy. His ability to chronicle society and celebrity with such success relied on his devotion to the social scenes he inhabited. However, this was only one part of his career, and during the Second World War another side of Beaton emerged.

In 1943 the reviewer Henry Saville declared: "As far as any one man typifies any one thing, Cecil Beaton can be considered today to symbolise the revolution the war has brought to Britain."[1] He was referring to the shift in Beaton's focus from chronicling the worlds of theatre, fashion, high society and royalty, or the "pleasure class", as Beaton termed them, to his work on the Second World War. Aside from portraits of prominent politicians, military leaders and the destruction of the London Blitz, Beaton was commissioned by the Ministry of Information to photograph the British Army in the Middle East, Burma, India and China. The resultant 7,000 photographs, taken between 1940 and the end of the war, form a unique and important body of work, framing the sombre realities of death and violence.

In India, Beaton captured many portraits of Indian royalty and the official British circles in their final days. He was fascinated by the aesthetic potential of the country at large, observing that "everywhere one found unexpected sequences of colour – no gorgeous oriental riot but an extraordinary jumble of apparently inharmonious colours, harmonised nevertheless by some unknown law."[2] As is evident here, despite having been on government commission Beaton couldn't resist his search for the splendid orientalist scene in his photographs, which he seemingly retrieves most clearly in his self-portrait, reflected in an opulent *pietra dura* mirror – symbolically enveloping himself in what is framed as the excess of Eastern opulence.

The photographer and his Rolleiflex reflected in a mirror of a Jain temple, Calcutta, c.1944
Full-length portrait of the dancer, Ram Gopal, c.1944
Gelatin silver prints, 22.8 × 22.8 cm each

Norman Parkinson
b. England, 1913–1990

Norman Parkinson was one of the twentieth century's best-known fashion photographers and his images provide a comprehensive and unique record of the development of the changing face of fashion, high society and celebrity from the 1940s to 1990. Throughout these five decades, he had long associations with *Vogue*, *Harper's Bazaar*, *Town and Country* and a host of other international magazines, famously citing that a "photographer without a magazine behind him is like a farmer without fields". Far from merely documenting the styles of the day, Parkinson was hugely influential in changing the way that fashion photographs were made. His key contribution to the development of the genre was in bringing photography out of the studio and *en plein air*. Prior to the 1950s, shoots were typically carried out in studios, in black and white, and were much more static and formal than today. Parkinson challenged this, first bringing models out into the streets of London, and then later to foreign and "exotic" destinations such as Africa and South Asia. This shift occurred in tandem with fashion magazines increasing their budgets in the post-war years and readers developing a thirst for seeing colour images from around the world. The result was an era of fashion photography that was brighter, more spontaneous and more exciting than ever before.

The photographs shown here, made in India on assignment for British *Vogue* in 1956, are fitting examples of this. On this ambitious shoot, Parkinson travelled with models Barbara Mullen and Anne Gunning from Mahabalipuram in the southern state of Tamil Nadu to nearly 2,000 miles north, to Dal Lake in Kashmir, stopping in Delhi, Agra, Jaipur and Aurangabad along the way. Upon seeing this work, the then editor of *Vogue*, Diana Vreeland, made the famous comment: "How clever of you Mr. Parkinson, to note that pink is the navy blue of India" – and the shoot has since gone down in fashion history. By the end of his life Parkinson had become a household name, the recipient of a CBE, a photographer to the royal family and an Honorary Fellow of the Royal Photographic Society. He died whilst on location in Singapore shooting for *Town and Country* in 1990.

Anne Gunning, Honeycomb Marble, Red Fort, Delhi, for "Winter Sunshine in India", British *Vogue*, 1956
Gelatin silver print, 33 × 33 cm

INDIA

BY PENELOPE GILLIATT

For the first week in India one's urgent wish is to be a photographer. The eye is stormed a million times a day: not only by colour of a full-throated kind that makes our own seem constricted, and by strangeness—a peacock pacing along a trunk road—but still more by the Indian instinct for beauty. It shows everywhere, as much in a baked mud village as in rich ceremony. One sees a Maharashtrian fisherwoman wearing an orange head-covering with her fuchsia cotton sari. A twig-thin palmist asleep on the pavement in the noon heat, with his knees up to his chin and his head drooping, has a quiescent grace that to him is quite simply the most natural way to sit. Half a dozen men in white *dhotis* squat on the steps of a public building with their incongruously clerkly umbrellas hung in the gate, and one is intricately carving the handle of his with a penknife as he gossips. The South Indian child we photographed on the cover of this issue carried in her pocket, where our own children keep meaningful stones and toffee papers, a deep pink flower clearly picked for the pleasure of its colour with her clothes. Even cattle have feast-days when they are decorated, their flanks stippled with paint and their horns stuck with mosaic fragments of coloured and silver paper. Here and there a hen is drawn into the act and turns a Chagall pink.

And when the onslaught of the visual becomes less pressing, it is not that the beauty passes as it becomes more familiar, but that one begins to be overwhelmed by another sort of richness. Where Europeans and Americans are deliberately isolated individualists, in India it seems as though each lifetime is borne like a leaf by a great communal tide of history and belief and custom, submissive to the gathered strength. After a while in India one can feel that there is a weight and force beyond the intrinsic in most things one sees, even though ignorance cuts one off from understanding what it is. In this richly annotated country everything carries a cross-reference of meaning, from the movement of a dancer's eyebrow or the use of a coloured handkerchief instead of a white, to the presence or no of a gap between the feet of the reclining Buddha.

But India is now more than ever before a two-headed Janus, looking to the future as well as the past. The English visitor will inevitably be more aware of the past, which is so marvellously crystallized in the Caves of Ellora and Ajanta, in Moghul tombs, South Indian temples, Rajasthani paintings. The head that looks forward will not be so apparent. You could, conceivably, if you read no newspapers and talked to no Indians but the guardians of ancient monuments, miss it altogether; or mistake Westernization for it, and so be disappointed. Anglicized cities like Bombay and Calcutta have a "progressive" look that is not necessarily to be taken as the look of the Indian future. As yet most of this lies underground, in schools where a whole new proportion of the people is learning to write, in technical colleges, in design centres that succour dying village crafts, in the new Le Corbusier-designed capital of the Punjab—Chandigarh—which could originate a whole new pattern of city living in India. You can see the first shoots in the community projects: the pilot villages, gigantically significant, of the development programme now four years old that puts the onus of initiative on the villagers themselves. The Government provides each village with technicians and advisers to help in education, public health, sericulture, and so on, but the village council is drawn from the inhabitants and every anna of public money used is doubled by an anna from the village, contributed in cash or in voluntary labour. The people are *involved:* that is the wisdom of it. Send a spruce Government visitor to a village with propaganda about drainage and tractors, and any unlettered villager will become more and more deeply embedded in affection for his familiar mud and hand plough. This way, with the people themselves making the pace, the new look of fertile soil and clean wells and paved roads is in no sense imposed, but has fine roots.

When the Government of India invited four of us to spend a month there none of us had been there before. We went with foreknowledge of the beauty and antiquity

(*continued on page 146*)

FULLY CAPARISONED ELEPHANT, with his half-ton gold and silver *howdah*, his make-up that takes four hours to do, is the illustration of India's ancient and celebrative love of colour; this one is at Jaipur, city of pink sandstone, in the City Palace.

The pink mohair coat costs 28½ gns. at Jaeger, Regent St., Edinburgh and Manchester. The magnificent jewellery was lent by the Gem Palace, Jaipur: silk headscarf, from the local bazaar. Make-up: Elizabeth Arden's Nymph Eye, Rose Aurora lipstick

For other shops at which to buy the coat: see page 210

NORMAN PARKINSON

THE PILLARS OF QUWWAT-UL-ISLAM MOSQUE at dusk seem gilded, and even the air full of gold dust. This mosque near Delhi, now derelict, was built in 1193 by a Muslim conqueror: but the heavily carved pillars were taken from Hindu buildings.

Echoing the golden gleam—a ball dress in gold lamé organza, by Christian Dior-London, to order at Galeries Lafayette. At the same store, the Dior-designed necklace, £21 12s., earrings, 5 gns.; by Mitchel Maer. Lipstick (also above): Coty's Magnet Red

THE SHORE TEMPLE AT MAHABALIPURAM in the falling light casts a long shadow into the sea, back to the Pallava rulers who built this town of temples near Madras over a milennium ago. Erosion has muffled its detail; its beauty has a strange cadence.

The dress is white organza, silver-embroidered; the coat, moonstone-blue organza. By Horrockses, 38 gns. at Chanelle, Knightsbridge; County Clothes, Bristol, Cheltenham. Pearl and rhinestone necklet, 10½ gns., the rhinestone bangles, 3½ gns. each; Paris House

For other shops at which to buy the clothes: see page 210

"Winter Sunshine in India", British *Vogue*, November 1956

THE PALE COOL OF KASHMIR is only a few flying hours from India's burning colour. Planes go daily from Delhi to what seems another existence. The landscape has a silken, languorous quality that consists partly in the gleaming light and partly in the stillness: sound seems to travel farther than in the rest of the world, so that the bubbling of a hookah can be heard miles away. Here, on Dal Lake, not a willow-leaf stirred: even the two little figures on the bridge stood as obligingly still for the camera as though they were really drawn in a willow pattern. The boat—used for spear-fishing and for ferrying flowers to be sold to visitors on holiday in the house-boats—rides no higher than a lotus in this windless lake-water.

The dress is as lovely and gentle as the scene: cotton mousseline printed with a feathery jade green design on white. It falls loosely from a high waistline, banded by a green rouleau long enough to circle the waist and tie in front. By Atrima, 17½ gns. at Woollands; McDonalds, Glasgow; and Kendal Milne, Manchester

94 NORMAN PARKINSON

"Winter Sunshine in India", British *Vogue*, November 1956

Floating with Flowers, Dal Lake, Kashmir, for "Winter Sunshine in India", British *Vogue*, 1956
C-type print, 33 x 33 cm

Henri Cartier-Bresson
b. France, 1908–2004

Born in Chanteloup-en-Brie in 1908, Cartier-Bresson came from a wealthy French family who encouraged him towards a career in the arts from an early age. In 1926 he began his education studying painting under the guidance of the Cubist painter André Lhote. In 1931 he came across the work of the Hungarian humanist photographer Martin Munkácsi, who facilitated his turn towards photography. Throughout the 1930s and early 1940s Cartier-Bresson began publishing his work in magazines, and holding exhibitions, all whilst immersed in circles of the French cultural elite of intellectuals, writers and artists.

During the Second World War, Cartier-Bresson was conscripted to the French Army as a corporal in the Film and Photo Unit. He was captured during the Battle of France in 1940 but managed to escape in 1943. He went on to photograph the liberation of Paris with a group of professional journalists in 1945, following which he filmed the documentary *Le Retour* [The Return]. In 1947, with fellow photographers Robert Capa, George Rodger, David Seymour and William Vandivert, he co-founded Magnum Photos, one of the first independent photo agencies which enabled photojournalists to reach a broad audience through magazines while retaining control and copyright over their work, thus changing the model by which photojournalism was created and disseminated. The defining vision of Magnum, in allowing more creative freedom to the photographer in his or her commissions, is in part responsible for a photographic style in the 1950s – a style that blended intense subjectivity and personal vision with the more factual, clinical demands of photojournalism.

A resultant preoccupation in Cartier-Bresson's photography is an interest in what he referred to as the "decisive moment" – photographing only when all the variables of time, subject and composition came together before the camera. In the decade following the war, Cartier-Bresson produced major bodies of photographic work in India and Indonesia at their moments of independence, China during the revolution, the Soviet Union after Stalin's death, the United States during the post-war boom, and Europe as its old cultures confronted modern realities. In India, Cartier-Bresson produced two kinds of images: those which documented the post-war political realities of Gandhi's funeral and the shaping of independent India; and images which satisfied his artist and creative bent. His India photographs very much set the tone for Magnum, overlaying often serious political reportage with Cartier-Bresson's own aesthetic idealism. In his search for visual poetry his photographs occasionally wandered towards self-indulgence and away from the urgency of a decolonialising political climate.

Women on the slopes of Hari Parbal Hill, praying toward the sun rising behind the Himalayas, 1948
Gelatin silver print, 18 × 24 cm

Refugees exercising in a camp to drive away lethargy and despair, Kurukshetra, Punjab, 1947
Gelatin silver print, 18 × 24 cm

After bathing in the Ganges, Benares, 1956
Gelatin silver print, 40.6 × 50.1 cm

Marc Riboud
b. France, 1923–2016

Marc Riboud became interested in photography in 1937, when he took his first photographs with his father's Vest Pocket Kodak camera. It was not until 1953, however, that he became a full-time photographer. During the intervening years, Riboud studied engineering and participated in the French Resistance during the Second World War. After meeting Henri Cartier-Bresson (see p. 144) – and through him Robert Capa and David Seymour – in Paris in 1951, Riboud quit his engineering job to pursue photography professionally and in 1953 he was invited to join Magnum. In the same year, his now-famous photograph *Zazou painting the Eiffel Tower* earned him his first spread in *Life* magazine. In 1955, he travelled through the Middle East and Afghanistan and eventually landed in India, where he remained for one year. He then became one of the first European photographers to travel to China. After three months in the Soviet Union in 1960, he followed the independence movements in Algeria and West Africa. Between 1968 and 1969 he was one of the few photographers allowed to travel in both South and North Vietnam, and he captured both sides of the Vietnam War by also taking images of anti-war protest in America. He continued to photograph over the years, including Barack Obama's presidential campaign in the United States in 2008.

Although the theme of political conflict has informed much of his work, Riboud claimed: "I am not either a war photographer or a news photographer ... I have always been more sensitive to the beauty of the world than to its violence and monsters. My obsession has been with photographing life at its most intense, as intensely as possible."[1] This is evidenced in both the photographs reproduced here, where unlike his powerful and topical images of the Vietnam War, he bestows upon his Indian imagery a sort of return to the imagination, rich with white draperies and romantic scenes.

Riboud's prolific output includes over thirty books, including *The Three Banners of China* (1966), *The Face of North Vietnam* (1972), *Visions of China* (1980), *Capital of Heaven* (1990), *Marc Riboud In China: Forty Years of Photography* (1996), *Marc Riboud: 50 Years of Photography* (2004) and *A Lasting Moment: Marc Riboud Photographs Leeds, 1954 and 2004* (2009).

Darjeeling, India, 1956
Gelatin silver print, 40.6 × 50.1 cm

Derry Moore
b. England, 1937

Derry Moore, 12th Earl of Drogheda, studied painting at Oskar Kokoschka's School of Seeing in Salzburg, Austria, before taking photography lessons from the iconic British photographer Bill Brandt, whose influence is subtly evident throughout much of his photography. He began his photography career in 1973 with a commission from *Architectural Digest*, and he then defined his practice with photographs and books of portraits, architectural interiors and gardens, focusing particularly on the European aristocracy as well as British literary and cultural figures. His photographs are now in the collections of the Metropolitan Museum of Art in New York, the National Portrait Gallery in London, the Bibliothèque Nationale in Paris and the Museum of Art & Photography in Bangalore, among others.

Moore began photographing in India during a series of visits in early 1976. In his essay on the project, *A Photographer in India*, he wrote: "My initial idea had been to photograph some of the places whose days, I knew, were numbered. In the event what fascinated me was not simply the places themselves but also the hybrid quality of many of the lesser buildings that had been constructed since the first arrival of the British in India ... a grandeur and a sense of space, such as are rarely seen in Britain, were frequently the outcome: rooms were higher, windows larger, corridors wider, detail more lavish; the porticoes of relatively humble houses might have been snatched from the front of the British Museum. The appearance of their inhabitants too surprised me. I had been expecting folkloric looks, whereas what I found was far more interesting – the look and atmosphere of another century."[1]

In his work on India, Moore consciously selects scenes which speak of a romanticised aspect of the country's past. As a result of this, his photographs have done much to reinforce the idea of India itself as belonging to a former age, presenting a version of the country that in reality has all but disappeared. All and any signs of postcolonial modernity are carefully eliminated from frame, instead focusing on the splendour of ruin and portraits which capture a countenance of a bygone era, and whilst they can be read as a longing for the aesthetics of a colonial past, they also preserve a record of a heritage that is, with each year, more and more irretrievable.

Chowkidar, Lucknow, 1977
Amrita Patel, New Delhi, 1976
Gelatin silver prints, 30.5 × 30.5 cm each

Owners of the Marble Palace, descendants of Raja Rajendra Mullick, Calcutta, 1977
Gelatin silver print, 30.5 × 30.5 cm

Don McCullin
b. England, 1935

McCullin is one of the most celebrated photojournalists of the twentieth century. Born in 1935, and following an impoverished childhood in north London, he studied at the Hammersmith School of Arts and Crafts from 1948 to 1950. He then worked for British Railways and as a colour mixer in an animation studio, before being called up for National Service with the RAF. After postings to Egypt, Kenya and Cyprus, he returned to London and began photographing friends from a local gang named The Guv'nors. Persuaded to show them to the picture editor at the *Observer* in 1959, he earned his first commission and started his photographic career more by accident than design at the age of 23. For the next two decades, conflict became the focus of McCullin's photography, initially for the *Observer* and, from 1966, for the *Sunday Times*. He travelled the world, photographing in Congo, Biafra, Uganda, Chad, Vietnam, Cambodia, Israel, Jordan, Lebanon, Iran, Afghanistan and Northern Ireland. Aside from capturing the terror of war, McCullin's photographs often focused on the suffering of the poor and disenfranchised, resulting in moving studies of the homeless in London's East End and the working classes of Britain's industrialised cities. He joined Magnum in 1967.

From the early 1980s, McCullin moved away from only documenting the subject of conflict, instead travelling extensively through Indonesia, India and Africa and returning with powerful essays on the places and people he encountered. In his own words: "I had long been uncomfortable with my label of war photographer, which suggested an almost exclusive interest in the suffering of other people. I knew I was capable of another voice."[1] McCullin's black-and-white photographs are viscous, textured and evocative, reflecting his own brooding approach to the medium. In his conscious desire to escape the aesthetic of conflict and suffering, his work on India was instead imbued with a sense of mystery and distance. The eerie stillness of his photographs on the river Gandak, reproduced here, were produced for the book *India* (1999). What is evident here is McCullin's constant play with light to produce photographs that are powerful in their enigmatic quality, and we can read the images' particular intensity as perhaps being informed by earlier influences in McCullin's practice.

The River Gandak, 1987
Platinum prints, 34.3 × 50 cm each

Flower seller at Dal Lake, Srinagar, 1999
C-type print, 61 × 50.8 cm

Steve McCurry
b. United States, 1950

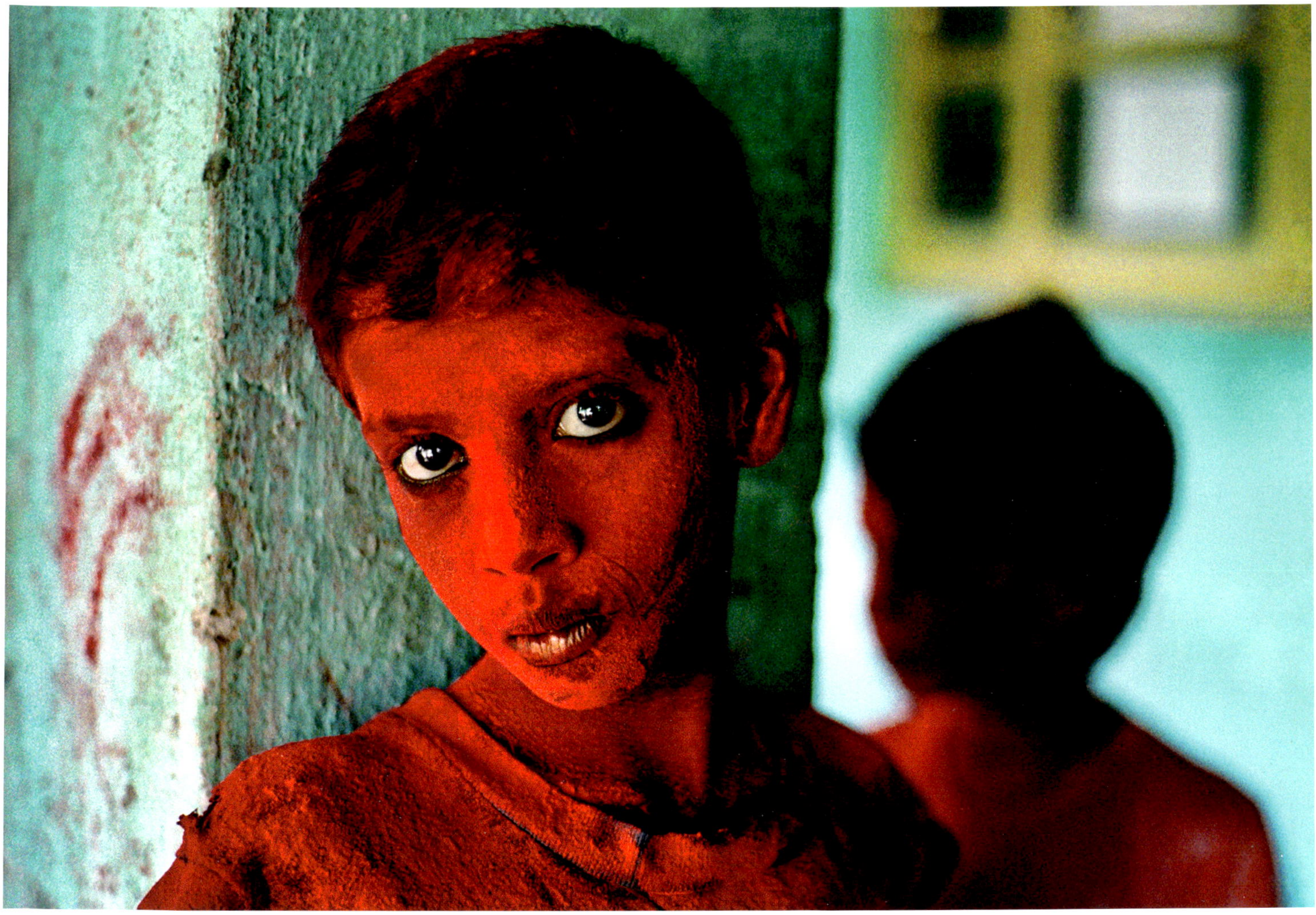

Steve McCurry graduated from Penn State University in 1974. He became interested in photography when he started taking pictures for the university newspaper *The Daily Collegian*, and after working at *Today's Post* for two years, he went to India, selling his photographs to small magazines to support himself. In 1979 he travelled to Pakistan where he saw the effects of the post-Soviet coup manifesting at the Pakistan-Afghanistan border. Here he met a group of insurgents who invited him to document the war, and dressed him as an Afghan, enabling him to cross the border in disguise. McCurry reportedly had to sneak his exposed film out by having the rolls sewn into his clothes, and these images – subsequently published by the *New York Times*, *Time* and other prominent news outlets – established his reputation and earned him the Robert Capa Gold Medal for Best Photographic Reporting from Abroad in 1980. His best-known photograph from the time is his iconic photograph of a young Afghan girl with green eyes, which became the cover of *National Geographic* in June 1985 and was acknowledged as the most recognised photograph in the history of the magazine. McCurry continued to cover armed conflicts, including the Iran-Iraq War, civil wars in Lebanon, Cambodia and Afghanistan, the Islamic insurgency in the Philippines, and the Gulf War. He also continued to build a fairly large archive of images across the world from his many travels, including multiple visits to India. Perhaps McCurry's greatest legacy is his informing of the Western imagination's idea of India as a place of saturated splendour, working in Kodachrome film and deftly manipulating his images to create the vibrant bursts of colour for which he is best known. What has resulted is the creation of a vast industry of photography around India concerned with presenting the country in McCurry's own palette, often at the expense of faithful depiction.

Red boy during Holi festival, Bombay, 1996
C-type print, 50.8 × 61 cm

Subhas Chandra Bose Statue, Calcutta, West Bengal, 1986
C-type print, 25.4 × 37.8 cm

6 Modernism & Modernity

It is difficult to ignore a moment in post-independence India in which the photographs take a decided turn towards starker and flatter compositions. Whereas the subcontinent had been photographed with characteristic opulence and excess – of luxury, of disaster, of coloniality – here the camera begins to be pared down, reduced to the inherent networks of lines, light and uniform colour.

With this chapter we aim to suggest that there was a period of decidedly modernist photography in India, during which the focus on form supplanted a preoccupation with content or theme.

In India, modernist photography, if one can transplant the term to the subcontinent, appears to have been an unlikely offshoot of Prime Minister Nehru's cosmopolitan vision for South Asian art and culture.[1] It emerged out of the feverish movement of artists, architects and photographers in and out of the country's borders – just as it was in this moment that India became the site for a number of sustained creative projects such as those of Le Corbusier in Chandigarh and Charles and Ray Eames in Ahmedabad, and of visits by the likes of Clement Greenberg and John Cage, Indian artists and intellectuals such as F. N. Souza, Jyoti Bhatt and S. H. Raza went abroad in search of artist residencies and (with them) new forms of visualising an independent India and its art practice. For Indian photographers, the arrival of visiting photographers including Henri Cartier-Bresson, Lucien Hervé and later Harry Gruyaert appears to have aroused a decidedly new turn away from the pictorialism of the 1930s and 1940s, surveyable in the countless amateur photography clubs of the time.

Instead, modernist photographers began streamlining their practices towards a style of photographic abstraction that benefitted from this extended moment of cultural and intellectual transnationalism. Their sources were of course varied, ranging from foreign travel to the barrage of international photography magazines available in India, such as *Popular Photography* and *Amateur Photographer*, that entered their homes and places of work.[2] It was also enriched and informed by a range of other visual media; many practitioners such as Nasreen Mohamedi, Krishen Khanna and Dashrath Patel were in fact painters, printmakers and designers who seem to have adopted the camera as an aside to their primary artistic production, using it both as an additional medium as well as (in the case of Mohamedi) as a tool with which to consider their artistic practice. Observing a broader sweep of these images reveals a shared commitment to the formal qualities that the camera could offer: to light, to line, to light spectrum, and to evading or eluding realistic representation.

The question of how to describe these practices is a difficult one. Indeed the term "modernism" is itself not without its problems – on the one hand, as it presumes that the Indian photographers were derivative of their Western counterparts (therein undoing the originality of their own practices); on the other, as pedagogical debate from the 1960s and 1970s revealed an anxiety about losing the regional specificity of Indian art in a wave of internationalism.[3] That the abstraction in Indian photography is most notable some decades after the modernist movements of the United States and the Soviet Union, and already behind parallel developments in Indian cinema, makes it particularly vulnerable to the allegations of copy or belatedness. Rather than frame these photographs within the rubric of vernacular modernism,[4] demeaning for its implication that India provides but a derivative dialect of the Euro-American "mother language", we make the argument that what is on show here is a sort of hybridised photographic Creole, at once involved in a number of multimedia and multi-geographical conversations. It is one that is unruly and layered, formed in a weave of global and local, colonial and postcolonial.

We acknowledge that modernist photography at this time can encompass two broad areas: on the one hand, photographs that themselves display a certain level of abstraction, an attention towards shape and line; on the other, practices that were preoccupied with capturing sites of modernity in the new nation on camera. New architectural sites across cities such as New Delhi, Bombay, and Chandigarh became the favourite playgrounds of photographers both of India and elsewhere. One notes a number of repetitions across the archives of various mid-twentieth-century photographers: monuments such as Jaipur's Jantar Mantar and the newly built city of Chandigarh appear in the oeuvres of foreign photographers Marc Riboud, Lucien Hervé and Isamu Noguchi as well as Indian photographers including Dashrath Patel and Jeet Malhotra. The archive of Delhi-based photographer Madan Mahatta, largely unexplored until a few years ago, and the architect Habib Rahman, who photographed many of the buildings of his own creation, make the relationship of photography to modernist architecture unambiguous: to photograph the modern building in new India indeed demanded a modernist lens.

Nevertheless, we have been careful in our selection to address and highlight these multiple forms of the "modern". Colour, although not strictly part of the modernist toolkit in Europe or the United States, is resolved and mobilised by Dashrath Patel, Harry Gruyaert and Raghubir Singh in their photographs – the careful uniformity with which they deliver colour in their balanced, remarkably toned renderings of India can be argued for as a geographically specific response to the clinical, greyscale modernism produced elsewhere. In the case of Raghubir Singh, he argued for vast swathes of bright, flat colour in his photographic compositions as a means of reconciling the modernist photograph with Rajasthani miniature paintings, creating a hybrid style that was specific to his geographical context.

In this chapter we have sought to question the rigid timeline with which Indian photographic modernism tends to be associated and our selection transcends the time period of the 1950s to the 1970s to include much earlier and much later practices. We present Bombay-based photographer Mitter Bedi's remarkably composed images of Indian industry from the 1950s to introduce the relationship of photographic abstraction to the project of nation-building in a manner not unlike early industrial photographs from the Soviet Union. We then also include the practices in which Indian modernism is at its most apparent, such as Jyoti Bhatt's careful, flattened diptychs and young Nasreen Mohamedi's stripped down, stark photographs of the deserts of Rajasthan and Bahrain. This chapter ends with the work of photographer Andreas Volwahsen as a means of proposing the horizontal spread of modernism as a visual mode unto itself. Even as his work circulated in entirely different contexts from the other photographers presented here – Volwahsen was a scholar of architecture whose photographs served as illustrations for his books – we argue that these photographs display a continued concern with the pared-down, geometric frame, to the almost scientific concentration on form itself, reconciling the splendour of subcontinental palaces, tombs and other historic buildings with the pared down visual language that this chapter is concerned with.

1 See Rebecca M. Brown, *Art for a Modern India, 1947–1980*, Durham, NC and London 2009; Saloni Mathur and Kavita Singh (eds.), *No Touching, No Spitting, No Praying: The Museum in South Asia*, New Delhi 2014.

2 Jyoti Bhatt (painter, printmaker), in conversation with the author, 24 January 2017.

3 See Hermann Goetz, 'The Great Crisis: From Medieval to Modern Art', in: *Lalit Kala Contemporary*, no. 1 (1963), pp. 9–16; Geeta Kapur, 'Art and Internationalism', in: *Economic and Political Weekly* 13, no. 19 (1978): pp. 802–3.

4 See Geeta Kapur, 'The Uncommon Universe of Bhupen Khakhar', in: *Pop and Vernacular Cultures*, ed. Kobena Mercer, London and Cambridge, MA 2007, pp. 110–35.

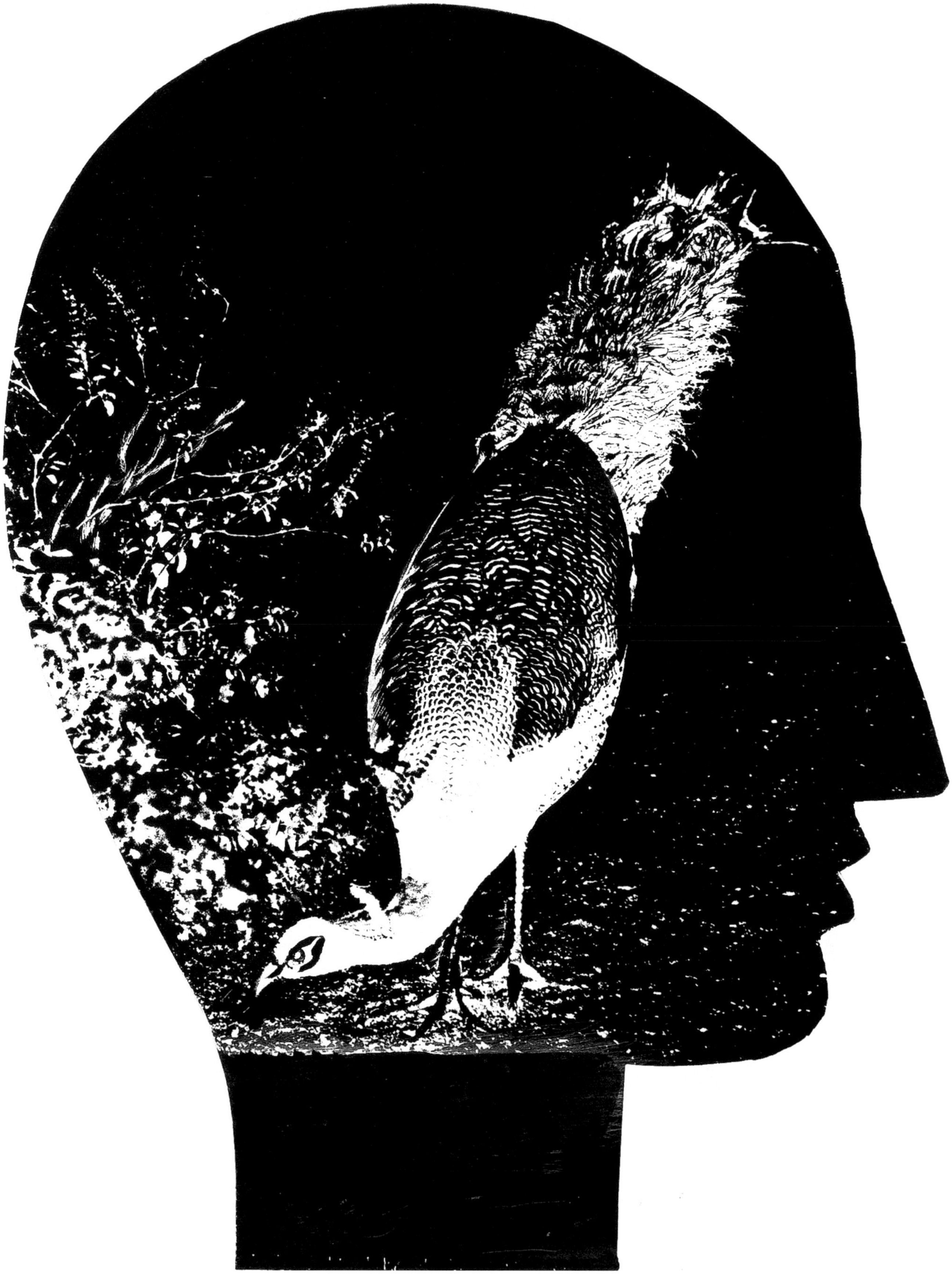

Untitled, 1969
Gelatin silver print, 17.5 × 16 cm

Jyoti Bhatt
b. British India, 1934

Jyotindra Manshankar Bhatt, popularly known as Jyoti Bhatt, has worked during the course of a long career primarily with printmaking, painting and photography. Growing up in a stimulating environment in Bhavnagar, Gujarat, with his father managing an institute that trained and guided young art students, Bhatt took to the arts at an early age. He was among the first retinue of students at the Faculty of Fine Arts in Baroda, India's first postcolonial arts institution, and he also studied fresco painting at Banasthali Vidyapith in Rajasthan. In 1961, Bhatt won a scholarship to study at the Accademia di Belle Arti in Naples for two years. From Italy, he went to the Pratt institute in New York where he trained in the graphic arts. Bhatt then returned to Baroda in 1966 and continued to teach painting at the Faculty of Fine Arts. It was around this time that his interests began to deviate away from painting and move towards printmaking and photography. Bhatt's first camera, acquired in 1957, very quickly replaced his sketchbook.[1] His initial use of photography was as a means to document the folk arts that he felt were on the cusp of change. In doing so, he created an extensive archive of photographs of wall and floor paintings as well as scenes from everyday life among the communities of rural Saurashtra, Rajasthan, Haryana, Madhya Pradesh and, in later years, the north-east. Despite the documentary content of his photographs, these images display Bhatt's instinctive turn to emphasising the flatness of the photographic plane and exploration of an economy of form, which ultimately resulted in the more modernist concerns of photography we see here.

Bhatt spent much of the 1960s and 1970s appealing for the institutional recognition of photography as an art form, collaborating with six other Baroda artists in 1968 to put on the exhibition *Painters with a Camera*. His disinclination to be labelled, whether as photographer, painter or printmaker, stems from a fluid understanding of media. His experimental photographs, with his frequent turn to vehicles of the collage/montage and meticulous darkroom post-production, reflect his sensibility as a graphic artist, just as his prints reflect a photographer's perspective.

Self-portrait, 1969
Gelatin silver print, 10 × 15 cm

Venice, 1966
Gelatin silver print, 28.2 × 22 cm

Monument (diptych), 1984
Gelatin silver print, 28 × 21.6 cm

Raghubir Singh
b. British India, 1942–1999

Raghubir Singh was a pioneer of colour photography and its use as an artform. Born to an aristocratic Rajput family, Singh's early exposure to Rajput miniature painting and aligned traditions are often said to have significantly informed his interest in the photographic potential of colour. After dropping out of college, Singh moved to Calcutta to try and make a career in the tea industry. He started during this time to dedicate himself to photography. In Calcutta, Singh was introduced to the city's artistic circle. He met the historian R. P. Gupta, who wrote the text for his first book *Ganges* (1974), and the filmmaker Satyajit Ray, who designed the cover of *Ganges* and wrote the preface for Singh's *Rajasthan* (1981) – setting a precedent for literary input in Singh's future publications. In later years, the writer V. S. Naipaul conducted a dialogue with him for the preface to the book *Bombay: Gateway of India* (1994), while R. K. Narayan wrote the introduction to *Tamil Nadu* (1997).

Singh made a breakthrough when *Life* magazine published an eight-page spread of his photographs of student unrest. This eventually led to him moving to Hong Kong and subsequent commissions for publications such as *National Geographic* and the *New York Times*. Although he continued to travel, living in Paris, London and New York, Singh's subject clearly and unequivocally remained India: "The pulse of my being beats to the music of India,"[1] as he wrote in the introduction to the last book he published during his lifetime, *River of Colour* (1998).

When writing on colour photography, Singh said: "If photography had been an Indian invention, I believe that seeing in colour would never have posed the theoretical or artistic problems perceived by Western photographers. In condemning colour photography, Henri Cartier-Bresson [see p. 144] has privately used unprintable French-army language and publicly called it the province of painting ... André Kertész, in his books and exhibitions, never showed his colour photographs ... [preferring] the distancing quality inherent in black and white ... Unlike those in the West, Indians have always intuitively seen and controlled colour. Our theories, from early in antiquity, became a flowing and rhythmic entity of India's river of life – its river of colour."[2]

On Vivekananda Rock, Kanya Kumari, Tamil Nadu, 1994
C-type print, 40.4 × 59.7 cm

Monsoon Rains, Monghyr, Bihar, 1967
C-type print, 36.2 × 24.2 cm

Subhas Chandra Bose Statue, Calcutta, West Bengal, 1986
C-type print, 25.4 × 37.8 cm

Victoria Terminus, Bombay, Maharashtra, 1991
C-type print, 40.3 × 59.4 cm

Mitter Bedi
b. British India, 1926–1985

In an extended moment when newly independent India was fashioning an identity of postcolonial modernity for itself, Bedi documented and chronicled the rapidly developing forms of industry in the country – textiles, pharmaceuticals, steel, fertiliser, paper and sugar – from the late 1950s well into the 1980s. Born in Lahore, he made his way to Bombay in 1940 and found a job in a printing press. In 1947 he joined a film production house as a publicity officer. After leaving the motion picture industry, he was appointed the official photographer to Air India International, for whom he would take pictures of arrivals and departures at the airport.

In 1959 Bedi received a commission from Standard Vacuum Oil Company, which engaged him to take pictures of the company executives for their annual report. It was here that he encountered Arthur d'Arazien, the famous American industrial photographer. D'Arazien greatly influenced his practice and shaped the rest of his subsequent oeuvre. From 1960 to 1985, Bedi traversed the industrial regions of India and his assignments covered both public sector corporations and private enterprises. His photographs, unlike other photographic documentation of the same period, depicted a nation in which the factory, reactor and machine towered over the human figure and social life.

In spite of the limiting aspects of photographs taken primarily for advertising, he managed to introduce a modern aesthetic to his work, using shapes and geometric planes to create artistic rather than simply functional images. Bedi's legacy has become these images of industrialisation in the early years of India's independence which connote a kind of optimism of technology. Whilst Bedi's industrial photographs were his most creative, his fashion photography was equally well regarded and he came to produce familiar images in popular visual culture through his advertising work, such as for Farex Baby Formula, and the Kwality Ice Cream mascot child.

Commissioned photograph for Bharat Electronics Limited, Bangalore, 1978
Commissioned photograph for Fiberglass Pilkington, 1961
Reproduced from the negatives

Commissioned photograph for Hindustan Lever, 1961
Commissioned photograph for Larsen and Toubro, 1962
Reproduced from the negatives

Habib Rahman
b. British India, 1915–1995

Habib Rahman was an engineer, musician and photographer. As a pivotal architect in the early years of independence, Rahman laid the foundation of a modernist architectural vocabulary for an entire generation. He trained at the Massachusetts Institute of Technology in the 1940s under Lawrence Anderson, William Wurster and Walter Gropius. When he returned to India in 1946, he brought the design approach of architecture's new International Style with him, drawing on clean and simple structures formed with modern materials like steel and glass. Beginning with his design for Rabindra Bhavan in 1961, however, Rahman began to develop a distinct design style that fused a Bauhaus approach with a contemporary Indian idiom.

Over the years Rahman created a regional modernist approach, visible in his designs for a number of buildings built under Nehru's leadership, including the Lalit Kala Akademi building, the University Grants Commission office and several low-cost housing blocks under the Public Works Department. His concern with aesthetics, as much as utility, elevated his photographs of buildings (usually his own) from mere historical documents into fine-art architectural photography. His photographs of the modern buildings he designed are infused with his own extensive knowledge of the style of photographic modernism. As evidenced by this photograph of Delhi's Curzon Road Hostel, Rahman often photographed from unexpected angles in order to produce a sort of disorienting mesh of lines reminiscent of the avant-garde photographers of the Soviet Union and the Bauhaus. Rahman's photographs, both in their visual mode and the buildings they capture, have come to represent the glories of Indian postcolonial modernism at the moment at which it was being produced and defined. Married to Indrani Rahman, a classical dancer of international fame, he was also close at hand during an extended moment of the revival of Indian classical music and dance, going on to photograph many of the major dancers of the period. Habib and Indrani's son, Ram Rahman (see p. 200), also became a distinguished photographer, documenting Delhi's society, its streets and its architecture.

The façade of Delhi's Curzon Road hostel, 1967
Reproduced from the negative

Lucien Hervé
b. Hungary, 1910–2007

Born as László Elkán, Lucien Hervé studied fine art in Vienna and moved to Paris in the early 1930s to work in fashion. He later joined the French Communist Party and in 1939 was drafted as a military photographer, during which time he was captured by the Nazis and sent to prison, where he became very active in the Resistance. After the war Hervé left politics behind to write for art journals. He began experimenting with photography, overexposing or underexposing images or severely cropping them to attain unusual compositions – following the work of avant-garde artists such as Piet Mondrian, László Moholy-Nagy and Alexander Rodchenko, appreciative of their stark geometry and abstracted forms. In 1949, upon the recommendation of one of his editors, Hervé travelled from Paris to Marseille to see the Unité d'Habitation, a housing complex by the architect Le Corbusier. Awed by its modern design, Hervé took 650 photographs of the complex in a single day. When he returned, he mailed them to Le Corbusier. "You have the soul of an architect," Le Corbusier is believed to have replied.

The Unité d'Habitation collection marked the start of a collaboration between Hervé and Le Corbusier that would last the next sixteen years until the architect's death in 1965. It was also the beginning of a transformation in the status quo of architectural photography in Europe, repudiating the conviction that wide-angle pictures and head-on angles were the best (or only) way to communicate the style and character of buildings. Hervé took thousands of photographs of Le Corbusier's projects in France and India, as well as portraits of the architect at work and visual studies of objects such as tree trunks or concrete. Once he developed the photographs as contact sheets, he edited them down and pasted them into an album, which he and Le Corbusier used when selecting images for publications, lectures and books.

When Le Corbusier was commissioned to build a new capital city, Chandigarh, for the state of Punjab, Hervé travelled to India to photograph the new city. His resultant series played with Chandigarh as a site not simply of modernist architecture but also of modernist image-making. As a result, his images are not merely documents of specific buildings but also exist as artworks in their own right, forged out of careful observation of the shapes of light and shadow created in Chandigarh's new buildings.

High Court of Justice, Chandigarh, 1955
Gelatin silver print, 15 × 15 cm

Dashrath Patel
b. British India, 1927–2010

Dashrath Patel, a prominent industrial designer, was born in Sojitra, Gujarat. He studied at the Government College of Fine Arts, Madras (1949–53), where Debi Prasad Roy Choudhury was his mentor, and thereafter at the École des Beaux-Arts, Paris (1953–55). Patel was subsequently the founder secretary of the National Institute of Design in Ahmedabad, working closely with Charles and Ray Eames in the establishment of the institution. Aside from his founding work on design pedagogy, Patel was a diverse artist who experimented with painting, photography, ceramics and collage as well as graphic, industrial and exhibition design. Following an apparent encounter with Henri Cartier-Bresson (see p. 144) at Patel's first exhibition in Paris in 1952, he reports the following anecdote about how he got into photography: "When I exhibited at the Galerie Barbizon, Cartier-Bresson had come to see. Afterwards he put his camera in my hand and said, 'Can you shoot a frame for me?' At that time I hated the camera. All I wanted was to draw at the time. I said, 'I don't do photography. Why should I?' He said, 'You are clear in your drawing, but I also want to know what you see with another tool.' So I clicked a shot and forgot about it. A couple of weeks later he invited me home for a meal and to meet his wife. He showed me many prints. He held up one and said, 'You like it?' By then I had already forgotten that I had shot a picture with his camera – I had done it with so much resistance and prejudice. I said, 'Yes, it's very well seen!' He said 'It's you and it's important you buy a camera and work with it!' That's how I got my first camera."[1]

Patel's lifelong commitment to design registers across all the media in which he operated. His fundamental interest in quotidian form and function is visible in objects ranging from the carpets and ceramics he designed to collages made of industrially produced raw material. In his photographs Patel conceives of composition in terms of blocks of uniform colour, a lyrical visual mode that finds comparison in his mixed-media collages.

Pushkar, 1959
Reproduced from the negative

The Crows Around My Studio, c.1975
Gelatin silver prints, approx. 76 × 81 cm each

Krishen Khanna
b. British India, 1925

Krishen Khanna, one of India's representative modernist painters, grew up in Lahore and began to study art after he graduated from college through evening classes held at the Mayo School of Art. In 1947 Khanna's family moved to Shimla as a result of the Partition of India, and Khanna was deeply affected by not only the change in his personal life but also the socio-political chaos that reigned around him. Partition was to remain a recurring theme in his oeuvre. After his family's relocation to India, Khanna went to Bombay for a job with Grindlays Bank, where he remained for over a decade. In his spare time, however, he kept up his artistic practice – reportedly working on paintings late into the night. As a result of this output, he was invited to join the now famous Progressive Artists' Group, and he finally resigned from his bank job in 1961. In the late 1960s he became interested in the potency of photography when he accidentally projected a slide of a Japanese artwork all over his studio and subsequently photographed the fragmented, multilayered effects of his error. He went on to explore the interface of the real and the projected more vividly, creating a number of photographs by projecting his collection of slides onto jagged and imperfect surfaces. The resultant body of work, *The Crows Around My Studio*, is disorienting in its play with projection as it flickers between light, dark, shadow and illusion.

Harry Gruyaert
b. Belgium, 1941

Harry Gruyaert studied at the Institut National de Radioélectricité et Cinématographie in Brussels in the late 1950s and early 1960s, later relocating to Paris to work as an assistant to William Klein. After a short-lived fascination with fashion photography, Gruyaert's journey through colour began with a visit to Morocco in 1969. In the early 1970s, while he was living in London, Gruyaert worked on a series of colour television screen images to make *TV Shots*, which explored the increasing influence of television on society. Around the same time he also photographed his homeland, resulting in two bodies of work: *Made in Belgium* and *Roots*. By the end of the 1970s he had travelled to the United States, India, Egypt, Japan and Morocco. Of his interest in travel and exploration, he explained: "I move around a lot, I like to be excited and discover things. It's about freedom. If you stay in the same place for too long you'll start to think it's normal, but nothing is normal. One shouldn't get used to things; it's really important to me to see things with fresh eyes."[1] Along with photographers such as Joel Meyerowitz, Stephen Shore, Saul Leiter and Mitch Epstein (see p. 214), Gruyaert was one of the first photographers to artistically exploit the creative power of colour film, a tool until then relegated largely to the field of advertising. His saturated non-narrative images forged new ground at the time and reflect a broader trend in photography away from the confines of black-and-white humanism. Of his approach he noted: "There is no story. It's just a question of shapes and light."

Gruyaert's photographs of India, as elsewhere, highlight the beauty of everyday banality. His invocation of dramatic, flat, uniform, often unfamiliar sweeps of colour traverses and brings to mind the subcontinent's own rich tradition of painting, with its shared concern for the mobilisation of colour as space.

Jewish town in Cochin, 1989
Dye transfer print, 45.1 × 67.9 cm

Pushkar, 1976
Dye transfer print, 67.9 × 45.1 cm

Madan Mahatta
b. British India, 1932–2014

Madan Mehta, known professionally as Madan Mahatta (an anglicised version of his last name) started taking photographs with a box camera at a young age. The Mehta family, synonymous with the development of Indian studio photography, had opened their first studio in Sialkot in 1915. They moved it to Jammu and then to Srinagar in 1930. There were also branches of the studio in Rawalpindi and Murree which were closed down after Partition. The family then moved to Delhi, where the studio Mahatta & Co. continues to be run by Madan Mahatta's sons. In 1950, Mahatta travelled to England; initially an apprentice at the Ilford Lab in Cricklewood, London, he went on to study at the Guildford School of Arts and Crafts in Surrey (1951–53) where he was formally trained in photography. Although it was a two-year course, Mahatta stayed back at the recommendation of the head of the institute, since the college was introducing colour photography, a relatively new development, into the curriculum. He returned to work at the family studio in Delhi in 1954, and Mahatta & Co. became the first studio in the country to introduce colour printing. Despite the studio growing to become a famed and iconic destination, particularly for emerging photographers, little of Mahatta's work was seen outside of their commissioned spaces or his immediate circle. He rarely displayed his work during his lifetime – and was only brought to public attention in 2012, through an exhibition of his architectural photographs curated by the architectural photographer Ram Rahman (see p. 200).

Shooting on medium-format monochromatic film for more than three decades, from the 1950s to the 1980s, Mahatta documented the development of New Delhi. He worked closely with a generation of architects in India – including J. K. Choudhury, Charles Correa, Achyut Kanvinde, Habib Rahman (see p. 168) and Kuldip Singh – photographing such landmark modernist constructions as the Asian Games Village, the Shri Ram Centre as it stood isolated on Safdar Hashmi Marg, and the Hall of Nations. Mahatta experimented in a range of subject matter beyond his architectural images, such as studio portraits and industrial photography as well as dance, theatre, product photography and feature magazine work. Social and political documentary images also appear in his vast archive, including photographs of Nehru's funeral procession.

British Council Building, New Delhi, designed by Charles Correa, 1995
Pigment print, 25.4 × 25.4 cm

Hindustan Times Building, New Delhi,
designed by Habib Rahman, 1975
Pigment print, 38.1 × 25.4 cm

Andreas Volwahsen
b. 1941, East Germany

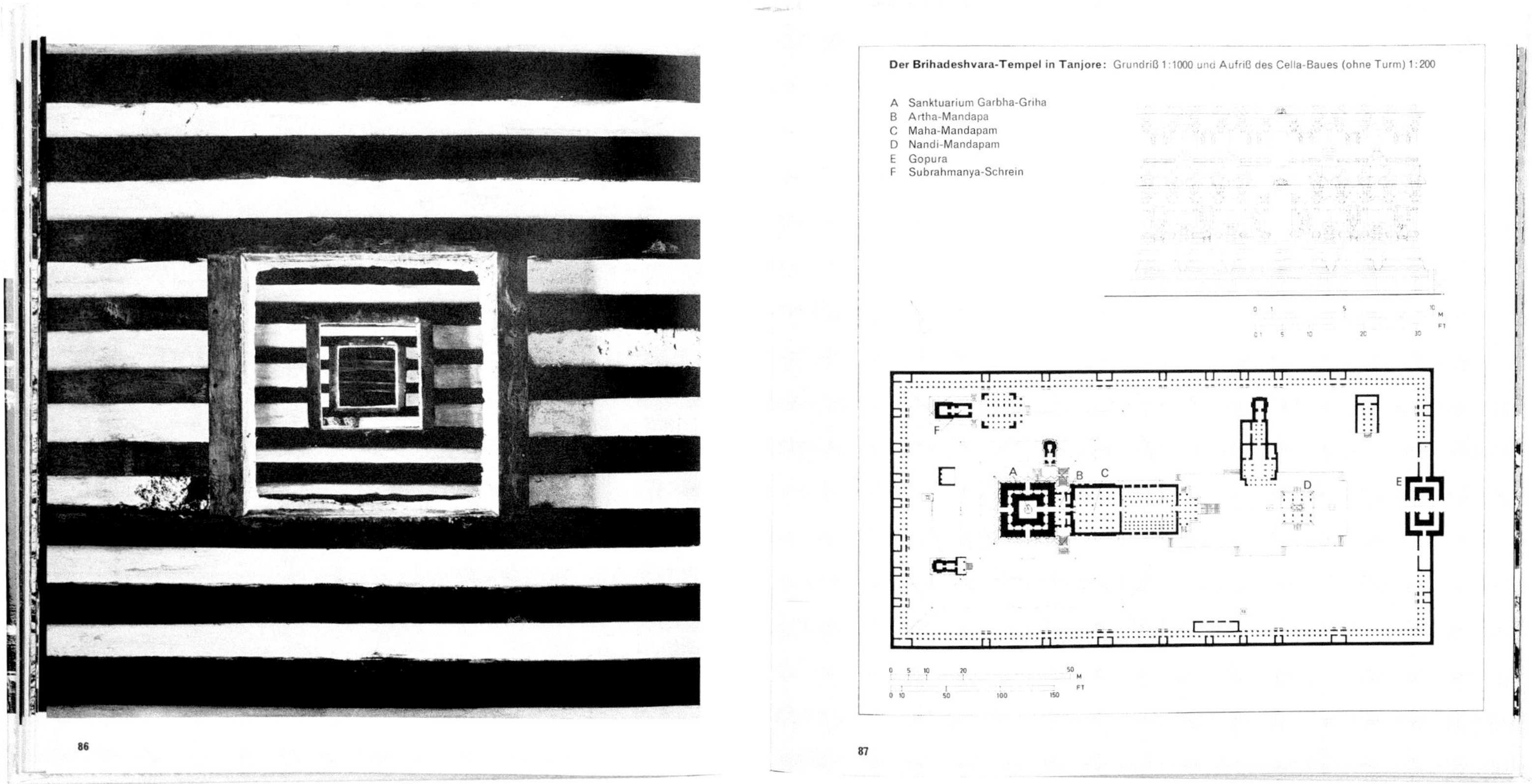

Volwahsen is a noted architectural historian whose engagement with the Indian subcontinent began while studying at the Technical University of Munich in the 1960s, during which time he published one of his first books, *Indien: Bauten der Hindus, Buddhisten und Jains*. In 1972 he obtained his PhD, titled *Architecture of the Observatory of Maharaja Jai Singh of Jaipur*. This investigation became the basis of the book *Cosmic Architecture of India: The Astronomical Monuments of Maharaja Jai Singh II*, published in 2001. Following his PhD, Volwahsen went to Harvard University, where he obtained a master's degree in city planning and urban design.

Notable amongst all his books, especially his publications in the late 60s and early 70s, are the photographs Volwahsen made to accompany his texts and diagrams. He approaches his subject with the objective rationalism which mirrors the intellectual debates of modernism now well versed in Germany. By transplanting this aesthetic and methodology to a field of art history and the geographical site of India that has been traditionally photographed as a space of excess, irrationality and exoticism, he not only allows for a clinical, academic study of the architecture and monuments themselves, but also reveals a different, underlying clarity in the structures, lending his photographs utmost function. This is most clearly demonstrated in his photographs of the Jantar Mantar. Here we see Volwahsen indulging in his technical, almost clinical search for perfection in his frame, almost always adopting the square format and seeming to shoot when the sun is at its zenith so as to offer clean, exact shadows and high contrast. Volwahsen's camera comes into dialogue with the Jantar Mantar itself, allowing for the camera's own temporal nature to play with the clean lines and architectural precision of the sundial complex, which also measures time but on a more monumental scale.

ABOVE, OPPOSITE AND NEXT PAGE
Indien: Bauten der Hindus, Buddhisten und Jains, 1968

168
169

164
165

160

161

7 Society & the Street

Public space at large, and its most quintessential Euro-American iteration, the street, is rich with photographic possibility, teeming with contrasting people, communities, signals and circumstances that make for thoughtful and interesting image-making.

In India, although public space is not strictly defined by the street as it is elsewhere, photographers have turned their lenses towards the rich chaos of Indian urban and semi-urban spaces. Much as the street was the subject in the practices of Garry Winogrand, Imogen Cunningham and Lee Friedlander, among others, it is Indian public space in general – the vast tracts of beach along Chennai and Mumbai's shores, the maidan in former colonial cities, the neighbourhood park and the situations that emerge in and are generated by these spaces – that is the subject of much photography. Indian streets merit being photographed for their own sake, as thronging sites where diverse communities, their professions and their aspirations converge, as sites of informally organised commerce, chaotic commute, and dwelling. Bruce Gilden has noted of the New York City streetscape – once the centre of street photography's sustenance as a genre – that it has lost the very sense of potency and diversity that made it appealing. In contrast, we wonder if it is the ever-lively nature of the Indian street, and the plurality it continues to embody, that makes it an attractive subject for the camera. India's street, a difficult, fluid and unresolved space, a site in which varied communities and classes jostle against one another, lend it a friction and a humorousness that has sustained the genre. This is not lost on Ram Rahman or Raghu Rai, whose photographs of hoardings of Mahatma Gandhi and the Gandhi family respectively as they are carried through the streets, show another side to the cultish worship of Indian celebrity by capturing these images in a state of undress, stripped of their grandeur and gravitas. For others there is a sense of bewilderment, as is perhaps the case with Bhupendra Karia's series *Population Crisis*, in which, shooting carefully cropped views of the busy street from a balcony above, he manages to convey the sense that his subjects are interchangeable with one another and infinite in their numbers, posing a threat to the structural integrity of the city of Mumbai. In both cases the ultimate subject is the street and its tension, photographed precisely for its unpredictability.

Street photography is founded on fast-paced and inconspicuous shooting, quick thinking and improvisation, often requiring the photographer to succumb to the pulse of the public space to create images. It is unsurprising, then, that the development of the genre is inextricably linked to the shortened exposure times in camera technology, as well as to the reduction of the camera's size, weight and conspicuousness. Whereas the earliest photographs of the street (including Louis Daguerre's own *Boulevard du Temple*) either appeared to be eerily empty or were specked with hazy outlines of people disfigured by long exposure, the development of such instruments as Kodak's box camera in the late 1880s and the proliferation of the simple, portable point-and-shoot allowed for the amateur to photograph easily and instantaneously, often without their subjects becoming aware of the camera's presence. It was out of the culmination of technology and thematic interest in the street that Henri Cartier-Bresson's notion of the "decisive moment" – in which subject, light, angle and movement all converge for the photographer to "seize upon [the] moment and hold immobile the equilibrium of it"[1] – emerges. It is precisely this temporal alignment that Raghu Rai also searches for in his photography of the Indian public, painstakingly composing images to realise an aesthetic of spontaneity. That their photographs are as much composed out of conversation with time is unmistakable – in turn producing bodies of work that may not be about a preconceived, cohesive project, but rather about instinctive, reactive, instantaneous shooting, producing a series of chance moments strung together. The photographer, armed with this set of concerns, is a curious figure: simultaneously at work and at leisure as they wander the streets, they must prise images out of the very unpredictability of the city.

As was the case with social documentary, the problem of photographic consensuality makes street photography a morally and ethically difficult genre. A. D. Coleman writes in his significant text "Private Lives in Public Spaces: Street Photography Ethics", "What rights do we have as citizens over the control of representation of ourselves, and what rights do photographers have in regard to making images in public situations?"[2] To shoot complete strangers in a public space, most often without their knowledge, invariably entails a loss of agency on the part of the photographic subject, as they have no say in their staging for the street photograph, nor in where and how it is circulated. In this way autonomous people can be reduced to types, not unlike the dangers of the continuing exoticisation of rural India by foreign photographers.[3] In India, the politics of the urban, Anglophone photographer capturing and fixing the less affluent inhabitant of the street speaks to an inequality that is near inescapable and always slippery. Vicky Roy, once a ragpicker in New Delhi who has returned to the street as a photographer of street children, is an interesting anomaly to the usual narrative of exploitation that critics have been known to raise against street photographers. Sooni Taraporevala's photographs of fellow Bombay dwellers in the 1980s reveals the centrality of collaboration in her pictures, as her subjects are comfortable with her photographing them in a light-hearted moment.

Our selection of photographers for this section was not an easy one to make, partially because it is a genre that so many photographers presented in this book have explored; partially because the texture of street photography often makes it difficult to disentangle from the concerns of social documentary and photojournalism. Our selection concentrates on the period most known for its street photography, the 1960s to 1980s, through the practices of T. S. Satyan, Bhupendra Karia and Raghu Rai in the late 1960s and early 1970s, and their immediate successors, Sudharak Olwe, Ram Rahman and Prashant Panjiar. We have, however, included Clyde Waddell's 1945 coverage of Calcutta and Vicky Roy's series from this past decade in order to argue that the medium's appeal has persisted over the decades.

1 Henri Cartier-Bresson, *The Decisive Moment*, New York 1952, p. 47.
2 A. D. Coleman, 'Private Lives in Public Spaces: Street Photography Ethics', in: *Journal of Mass Media Ethics* 2, no. 2 (1987), p. 62.
3 There is, furthermore, a considerable unease with public photography for the means by which it skims the surface of the spaces it captures without necessarily engaging with the social complexities of the individuals that inhabit the space.

Street in Old Delhi, 1973
Gelatin silver print, 18 × 27 cm

Raghu Rai

b. British India, 1942

Despite initially training as a civil engineer, Raghu Rai went on to become arguably the most successful, and certainly the most well known, photographer in the country. He was encouraged by his brother, the photographer S. Paul, who is said to have entered one of Rai's photographs into a weekly photography competition run by *The Times*, London, in 1965, which he won. By the following year Rai was employed as the chief photographer of *The Statesman* newspaper in New Delhi, a position he held for a decade. In 1971 Henri Cartier-Bresson (see p. 144) saw an exhibition of Rai's work at the Galerie Delpire in Paris. Reportedly impressed by the work (which reflected many of the idiosyncrasies and ideals of Cartier-Bresson himself, such as a dynamic spontaneity and richness of narrative), Cartier-Bresson encouraged and mentored Rai, nominating him to join Magnum Photos (where he became a member in 1977), making him the first Indian to be part of the then almost exclusively American and European photo agency. Over the last five decades, often on assignment for Magnum, Rai has photographed a range of subjects, but is particularly known for his street photography, social and political documentation, and his portraiture, most notably of Indira Gandhi and Mother Teresa.

Like Cartier-Bresson and others from Magnum who were documenting India at a slightly earlier point, Rai believed in the importance of the telling detail and the captured moment: the crucial accent that gives greater meaning to the whole. "Either you capture the mystery of things or you reveal the mystery," he explains, "Everything else is just information."[1] Alongside his work for Magnum, from 1982 to 1992 Rai served as the director of photography for the magazine *India Today*, before returning his focus on his personally motivated social documentary work, building up a remarkable body of photography documenting daily life, primarily in public spaces and on the streets. Remarking on his discomfort with posed and staged subjects, Rai underlines his preference for "spur-of-the-moment" photographs, in the style of Henri Cartier-Bresson. Indeed, it is his deftness at teasing out, revealing and capturing these moments that elevate the ordinary to something more exciting for his audience. This has become his signature style and one he has adopted without deviation for over fifty years.

Portrait of the Gandhi family, 1977
Gelatin silver print, 24 × 30.5 cm

Children in traffic, Brabourne Road, Calcutta, 1991
Diving into Ugrasen Baoli, Delhi, 1971
Gelatin silver prints, 18 × 27 cm each

The Day Before, Ayodhya, 1992
Gelatin silver print, 24 × 30.5 cm

Untitled, from the series *In Search of Dignity and Justice*, Mumbai, 1999
Pigment prints, 14.5 cm × 21.5 cm each

Sudharak Olwe
b. India, 1966

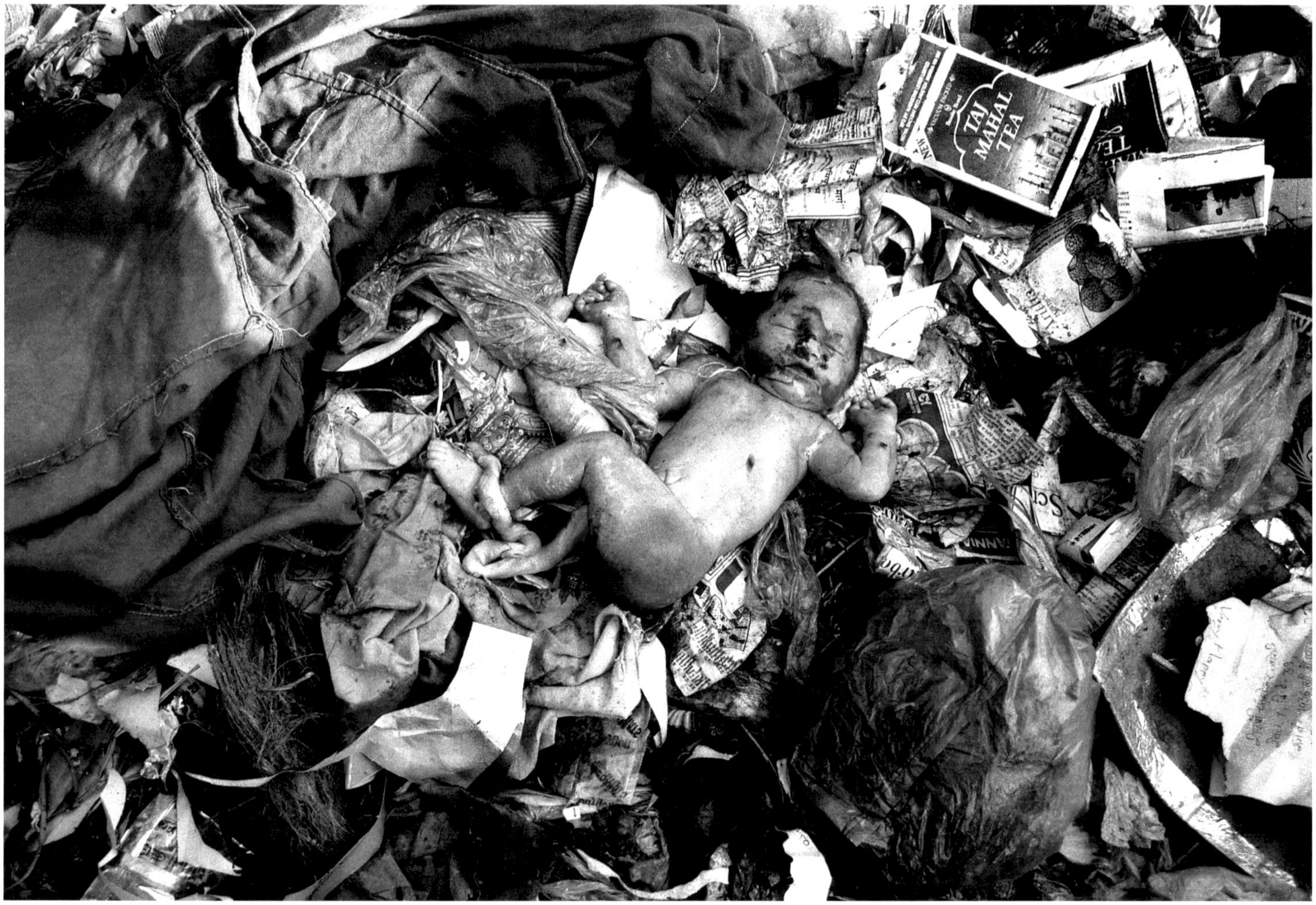

Sudharak Olwe has been a photojournalist in India since 1988, and is currently photo editor of *Lokmat*, the country's most widely-read Marathi newspaper. Olwe's extensive practice has been mostly concerned with capturing photographs of the disenfranchised – *Justice Delayed is Justice Denied* (2017) documented the lives of members of the Dalit community in Maharashtra and the atrocities and hate crimes to which they are subjected; *11th Lane: Kamathipura* (2003) is a photoessay that documents the lives of sex workers. He was awarded the prestigious Padma Shri award by the President of India in 2016, for his dedication to bringing these issues to public attention through his photography.

In the series *In Search of Dignity and Justice* (1999) Olwe provides a visceral look into the working conditions of conservancy workers employed in the Brihanmumbai Municipal Corporation. In photographing a profession that is still ridden with caste-based injustices, Olwe sheds light on the horrific nature of the work – sanitation workers are given no protective gear or professional equipment, leaving them constantly exposed to disease or death. The unapologetic nature of Olwe's images, showing animal corpses, human waste, even the body of an abandoned infant that the sweepers are supposed to clear away, educate the viewer about the persistence of caste-based atrocities now disguised as government employment. Although the series doesn't strictly fall into the category of street photography as defined in Euro-American practices, it throws light on how the street in public space in India is a complicated zone, and for many, a source of sustenance, work, and suffering.

Bhupendra Karia

b. India, 1936–1994

Following his graduation from the Sir J. J. Institute of Applied Arts in Bombay, Bhupendra Karia left India for Japan in 1956. He continued his studies in 1957 at the Tokyo University of Fine Arts where he became an assistant to the renowned artist Nobuya Abe, a member of the Japanese avant-garde. It was in Japan that he first began working with photography, and as a result of his interdisciplinary approach to the visual arts he was one of a small number of Indian photographers who began to explore the medium's capacity beyond the prevailing documentary genre. Accordingly, his style quickly diverged from photojournalism, instead creating images structured around the principle of composition. In 1964 he became a professor at the Department of Graphic Arts. He later studied interior architecture and design at the New York School of Interior Design before moving back to India in 1963 to work as the chief consultant for the National Cooperative Union of India, and the following year as professor at the Department of Graphic Arts at the Faculty of Fine Arts in Baroda.[1]

Karia's career continued to be spent working and photographing between the United States and India, where, despite using the modernist vocabulary of photography, he explored his interest in documenting societies with humanist intent. He photographed both rural communities (at times alongside his contemporary Jyoti Bhatt; see p. 158) and also urban India, such as his studies on the streets of Bombay. In both subjects he blended a flatness of composition more typical of a modernist persuasion, sometimes shooting series from above in a disorienting style reminiscent of the Hungarian photographer László Moholy-Nagy. Many of his photographs of crowded street scenes formed part of the project *Population Crisis*, a commissioned series for Cornell University's International Population Program and fellow photographer Cornell Capa's International Fund for Concerned Photography. Capa went on to enlist Karia's collaboration in establishing the International Center of Photography in New York in 1974 and Karia held many positions at ICP, including as curator, director of special projects and as associate director.[2]

Untitled, from the series *Population Crisis*, 1970s
Gelatin silver print, 22.2 × 32.3 cm

Prashant Panjiar
b. India, 1957

Whilst a student of political science at Pune University, Panjiar began pursuing photographic projects focusing on peasant movements and crime in the Chambal region, setting the tone for a career defined by an engagement with social issues and the social dynamics of modern India. In 1984 he joined mainstream journalism with the *Patriot* newspaper and in 1986 moved on to *India Today* magazine as a senior photographer. During this time he was engaged in covering international stories and areas of conflict, including in Iraq, Kuwait, Israel, Saudi Arabia and Pakistan, as well as major national events such as the demolition of the Babri Masjid at Ayodhya, the elections of 1989 and 1991, and the Bihar earthquake. In 1995 Panjiar joined the Outlook Group of Publications as associate editor in charge of photography, and was part of the core team that launched *Outlook* magazine. In 2001 Panjiar left *Outlook* to return to his earlier interest in socially concerned documentary projects, resulting in his extended project *King, Commoner, Citizen* (published as a book in 2007). In this project, Panjiar sought out many of his subjects on the street, but turned the expectations of the genre on its head by focusing on the commonality of dignity and humour that transcends social class. Of his work he notes:

"All through my career, I have had no secrets, no tricks, but let me share with you the core philosophy that has driven my work. One of the most important attributes that make a picture is respect towards the person being portrayed ... So when you see the picture of a farmer, you do not necessarily see that he is poor, but instead notice a certain pride, grace and dignity. We are able to empathise with him more. The image is no longer distant. It is ... just a question of ethics. The king can be a commoner, the commoner can be a king ... by ensuring that your approach and the final image have a sense of respect, you are dissolving the differences, even momentarily."[1]

Delhi, 1984
Reproduced from the negative

Beawar, 1986
Reproduced from the negative

Ram Rahman
b. India, 1955

The son of architect and photographer Habib Rahman (see p. 168) and celebrated classical dancer Indrani Rahman, Ram Rahman grew up in Delhi during the early years of a newly independent India, surrounded by the city's artistic and intellectual elite who were shaping the ideas and ideals of a new form of modernism in the country. Rahman first studied at the Massachusetts Institute of Technology before completing a degree in graphic design at Yale University School of Art in 1979. On his return to India he began working in photography and documented the artists, thinkers and politicians of the day, often in privileged environments. At around the same time, he began photographing extensively on the streets of Delhi. In these street photographs, Rahman focuses not on chaos but on the street as a site in which the socio-political complexities of India are on display. Working before the days of mechanically printed signage, hand-painted hoardings and advertisements are a common motif in his work. He uses these to explore a play of image and text, and in particular how language and the mix of religious, commercial and political iconography interact within the public space of the city. By often eliminating people from the frame in many of his photographs, we are encouraged to view the street as a set, a stage and as a blank canvas for Rahman's witty and thoughtful observations to unfold. In this way his photographs offer a counterpoint to the more predictable vocabulary of street photography in India, sharing more in common with the intellectual ideas of India's community of modernist artists than with his fellow photojournalists.

Rahman's work in photography has been complimented by a series of curatorial projects, lecture series and his work as a social activist, particularly through his position as co-founder of Sahmat, a New Delhi-based collective of artists and scholars dedicated to promoting cultural pluralism and secularism in India.

Gandhi March, Delhi, 1995
Gents Urinal, Delhi, 1991
Gelatin silver prints, approx. 25 × 20 cm each

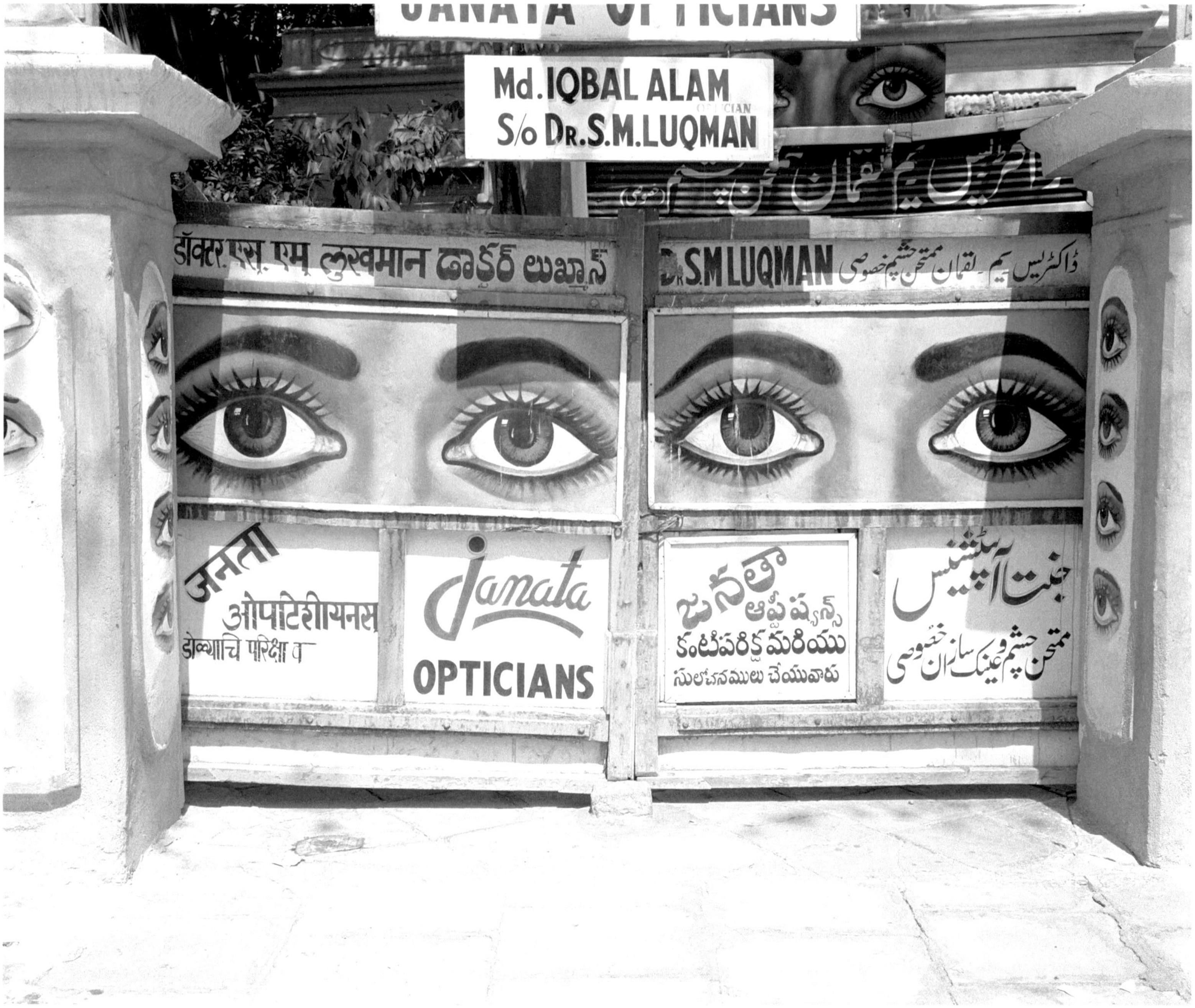

Gate, Hyderabad, 1983
Gelatin silver print, approx. 20 × 25 cm

William Gedney
b. United States, 1932–1989

William Gedney grew up in upstate New York and moved to Manhattan at the age of 19 to attend the Pratt Institute, where he discovered his interest in photography. In 1955 he graduated and worked at Condé Nast for two years before leaving to pursue his own work. In 1961, he was hired by *Time*, where he focused on photo layouts for the publication, and was later offered positions teaching photography at both Pratt and Cooper Union, remaining a member of the faculty at both schools.

Gedney died in 1989, aged 56, in New York City, and did not earn the recognition he deserved during his lifetime, in spite of his now-seminal *Kentucky* series being exhibited at the Museum of Modern Art in New York in 1968. He left his photographs and writings to his lifelong friend, the photographer Lee Friedlander. In time, Friedlander chartered a posthumous revival of Gedney's work, gifting a significant collection – including large photographic prints, work prints, contact sheets, notebooks, and diaries, as well as correspondence – to the Rubenstein Library of Duke University, North Carolina, including the two prints shown here. This has allowed for the recent rediscovery of Gedney's work, resulting in exhibitions and publications in both the United States and India, and he is now considered an important part of the history of documentary and street photography in the two countries.

As Samanth Subramanian wrote in a 2017 article in *The New Yorker*, whereas other Western photographers such as Henri Cartier-Bresson (see p. 144) and Margaret Bourke-White (see p. 121) who visited India focused on iconic figures such as Mahatma Gandhi, or of the violence of Partition, radiating political import, Gedney seemed to exist almost outside his time – with no obvious signifiers of the political condition of the country.[1] His street photography in India did not exploit the notion of timelessness to suggest Western nostalgia, nor did it attempt to try and explain or bring home a vision of India for a curious Western audience. Instead, its power is perhaps a continuation of the themes one sees throughout his career – his simple exploration of people, often creating melancholic images which speak of a universal sense of stillness, quiet and perhaps loneliness – a theme compounded in the most recent posthumous publication of his work, *William Gedney: Only the Lonely, 1955–1984* (2017).

Benares, 1969–71
Gelatin silver prints, 14 × 20.8 cm each

Vicky Roy
b. India, 1987

Born in West Bengal to a family too poor to raise him, Vicky Roy was sent to live with his grandparents when he was two years old. This traumatic and troubled early life resulted in Roy running away from home in 1999 at the age of 11. He took a train to Delhi and began working as a ragpicker at the New Delhi Railway Station, before he was taken in by the NGO Salaam Baalak Trust.[1] Here he was encouraged to engage with photography and completed a photography workshop, where he was inspired by his tutor to explore the potential of the lens: "From the beginning, I saw photography as a means to travel. I was overjoyed to take up something that would give me the opportunity to be on the move."[2]

Roy went on to study photography at Triveni Kala Sangam and then apprenticed under the commercial photographer Anay Mann. In 2007 he held his first solo exhibition, *Street Dreams*, at India Habitat Centre, supported by the British High Commission. He was chosen for a six-month residency at the International Center for Photography in 2009; his first monograph, *Home Street Home*, was published by the Nazar Foundation and released at the second edition of the Delhi Photo Festival (2013); and he was awarded the MIT Media Fellowship in 2014.

Whereas criticism of social documentary and street photography in India has been directed at its practice by either Indian photographers of a different socio-economic class or by foreign photographers, Vicky Roy's first-hand experience living in poverty as a child, and working amongst the street children of the New Delhi Railway Station, provides a rare counterpoint and suggests a personal engagement with the image. The ethics and politics not only of representation but also of the mechanisms of the industry, quick to realise the cinematic appeal of Roy's uplifting story, add a further context from which we can view and try to understand what has become a significant and refreshing body of work in the history of photography in the country.

Lachi, 12, Balloon Seller, Connaught Place, New Delhi, from the series *Street Dreams*, 2005–08
Pigment print, 40 × 50 cm

Sonu, 10, Ragpicker, GRP Police Station, New Delhi Railway Station, from the series *Street Dreams*, 2005–08
Pigment print, 40 × 50 cm

Sooni Taraporevala

b. India, 1957

Sooni Taraporevala is a screenwriter best known for her screenplays of films including *Salaam Bombay* (1988), *Mississippi Masala* (1991) and *The Namesake* (2006). She graduated from Harvard College, studying English and American literature, and went on to complete her MA from New York University in film theory and criticism. Taraporevala's interest in photography began in the United States, but her subjects were typically back in India. In 1982 she met the photographer Raghubir Singh (see p. 162), who suggested she make work focusing on her own community of Parsis – a religious and ethnic minority in South Asia who follow the religion of Zoroastrianism – in Bombay. Singh's suggestion, based on his recognition of Taraporevala's talent and the dearth of photoessays produced on the subject beyond its colonial attention in the early twentieth century, led to the publication in 2000 of the book *Parsis: The Zoroastrians of India – A Photographic Journey*. Photographed mainly in colour, this became amongst the first photographic works published on the community. In 2015 Taraporevala produced a further book of photographs, *Home in the City*, published by HarperCollins India, which expanded her interest beyond her local community to look at a broader portrait of the city of Mumbai, but still with an interest in the variety of communities who inhabit the city and the complex layerings of society. A case in point is her triptych of a dance party in the 1990s. Rather than turning her lens to the thronging street, Taraporevala captures members of the public at a ball, possibly in a Bombay club, in a moment of unguarded enjoyment of Bombay's cosmopolitanism.

Rocking and rolling at the New Year's Eve Ball, Bombay, 1985
Gelatin silver prints, 83 × 55 cm each

N. B. MODERN AGENCIES
APRIL
1 2 3 4 5 6 7
8 9 10 11 12 13 14
15 16 17 18 19 20 21
22 23 24 25 26 27 28
29 30

8 Essay & Enquiry

If the chapters on photojournalism and "exotic" images commissioned by magazines intended to take a critical look at the conflation of photography and profit, this chapter surveys bodies of work that are motivated by a sense of concern, of drawing the eye towards neglected subjects and spaces.

As a genre, social documentary photography was born in the late nineteenth-century projects of Jacob Riis and Henry Mayhew, who turned their cameras respectively towards the urban poor of New York and London: these were pioneering efforts to urge policy shifts in the treatment of the destitute, utilising the veracity of the camera to create empathy of the shameful squalor in which their photographic subjects lived. The years of American social documentary in the 1930s culminated in the formation of the International Center of Photography in New York in 1966, a school and centre for documentary photography that had a canonising effect on its practice all over the world, including India.[1] As a visual mode that is most alike in its objectives and detail to the long-form article, social documentary tends to operate as a series of multiple images that generate meaning in their numbers. To peruse the photoessay, as it is called, is to negotiate with a series of simultaneous relationships: between image and title (if presented), between image and accompanying text (as is often the case), and most importantly between the images themselves, and the sequences and patterns that are formed across them.

A rich collection of social documentary projects have emerged in India over the decades, both in the practices of foreign photographers (who had already worked in this genre abroad), such as Sebastião Salgado, Mary Ellen Mark and Julia Knop, as well as at the hands of Indian photographers who adopted the photoessay as a visual mode, such as Sunil Gupta, Ketaki Sheth and Amit Madheshiya. Following the organising logic of the genre, these photographic series derive from or speak to socio-economic or sociocultural phenomena rather than the immediacy of a political "event", often drawing concern towards the plight of the downtrodden, such as in the case of Mark's photographs of prostitution in Bombay, or Salgado's images of miners' families in rural Bihar. Far removed from the immediacy of change that is the concern of the news image, these are photographs that stand testament to what *doesn't* change, to the exploitation that has persisted over the decades and that will continue.

Indeed time moves far slower in the documentary image. Series such as Ketaki Sheth's photographs of Gujarati twins (both in India and amongst the Gujarati diaspora abroad) who share the last name "Patel" unfold almost languorously, at the pace of intergenerational inheritance. Others, such as Julia Knop, allow their work to be hinged upon temporal narratives – not historical shifts themselves, but what historical shifts produce – turning her gaze to an IT park in Bangalore in the early optimistic years after the liberalisation of the Indian economy in 1991.

The photographers we have selected for this chapter have done much to ground their subjects in their authentic contexts, purposefully avoiding the visual tropes of colonial photography. To shoot in the genre of social documentary is to bear the difficult burden of representation, one that must escape the simultaneous risks of exoticism and of confining the photographic subject of the image to an inescapable identity. The fact that the subjects of these photographs often circulate in different geographical and linguistic spaces than the images that are taken of them speaks to an incurable malaise that is at the very heart of social documentary: photographic subjects seldom have the ability to frame themselves as they would themselves like to be represented, and can therefore be left vulnerable to the lens. The very vocabulary of social documentary does little to reverse this murky, exploitative dimension of the medium. Similar to Susan Sontag's comparison of the vocabulary of encountering both the camera and the gun (both of which are loaded, pointed and shot),[2] there is much to be said about how documentary photography enters the visual and verbal terrain of the anthropological field experiment, making subjects of the people before the lens, dependent on the total immersion of the photographer into a scene for the purpose of discreet capturing, and the paramount importance of *authenticity* and *objectivity*. Immersion, then, is not bereft of conflict, insofar as it still belongs to a genre that transmits "information about a group of powerless people to ... the socially powerful."[3] In Martha Rosler's and Allan Sekula's respective encapsulations of documentary, photography performs as a sort of middleman for a formal and perpetual social hierarchy. Despite their own best intentions, photographs are never fully unblemished by the politics of viewing and the demographic discrepancy between the photographed subject and the viewer. Thus, a series reproduced here, although created from the photographer's formidable attempt to shed light on human rights abuse in the sex industry of Bombay, has not escaped the accusation that the work fixes the images of its subjects as sex workers caught in an indeterminate, brutal past to be contrasted with a Euro-American present. Even more worrying is the realisation that the photographer, as bystander to scenes of underage sex in the Bombay brothel, is complicit in its horrors as she refuses to interfere on behalf of her photographic subjects. Unsurprisingly, the series continues to divide ethical opinion today.

The trap of documentary can, however, be redeemed by the methods utilised by its authors; in Gauri Gill's series *Balika Mela* (not shown in this volume), the young girls pictured were asked to pose for her as they wanted, therein introducing the possibility of collaboration and equal participation rather than coercion. In the case of Amit Madheshiya, an interest in photographic consensuality led him to enter the intimate space of the cinema-goers he captures, shooting his subjects at close range as an insider to their world. His photographs are infused with the sense of the subjects' familiarity with the photographer, unselfconscious in the camera's gaze. Soham Gupta turns the concerns of documentary condescension on their head in his intentionally disturbing depictions of the marginalised inhabitants of Kolkata. Although reaffirming the appearance of his subjects as "freakish" or "other", Gupta creates a collaborative series in which the individuals are complicit in their own dramatic staging.

In this chapter we also include the documentary work of London-based photographer Sunil Gupta. Gupta, one of the earliest Indian photographers to adopt methods of photo-documentation from the United States, created a series, entitled *Exiles*, surveying the lives of gay men in New Delhi in the 1980s. Using a combination of text and image, Gupta weaves together a series of stories that present his subjects intimately and at close range, using the tools of documentary to bestow a sense of intimacy into his photographs. What we hope our selection will offer is a glance into questions of intimacy and belonging, inside and outside, that shape the genre.

1 Svati P. Shah, 'Brothels and Big Screen Rescues: Producing the idea of "Prostitution in India" Through Documentary Film', in: *Interventions: International Journal of Postcolonial Studies* 15, no. 4 (2013), p. 560.
2 Susan Sontag, *On Photography*, New York 1977; repr. 2014, p. 14.
3 Martha Rosler, 'In, Around, and Afterthoughts (on Documentary Photography)' (1981), in: *Decoys and Disruptions: Selected Writings, 1975–2001*, Cambridge, MA et al. 2004, p. 179.

Mitch Epstein
b. United States, 1952

Mitch Epstein studied at Union College, New York; Rhode Island School of Design; and the Cooper Union, New York City. A student of photographer Garry Winogrand, Epstein was influenced by both Winogrand's and William Eggleston's work. Beginning in the 1970s, Epstein helped pioneer colour photography as an art form and was one of the early practitioners of this new genre.

In his books, which include *In Pursuit of India* (1987), *Vietnam: A Book of Changes* (1996), *Recreation: American Photographs 1973–1988* (2005), *Family Business* (2003), *American Power* (2009), and *Berlin* (2011), Epstein's colour sensibility emerges, revealing the importance not only of colour but also of sequencing, narrative structure and a sustained interest in his subjects.

In 1978, Epstein began to work in India as a film producer, production designer and cinematographer on several films by the director Mira Nair. His book *In Pursuit of India*, published by Aperture in 1987, is a compilation of his photographs from this period set across a range of places in the country, from the temple towns of the south, to the cities of Mumbai and Delhi, and the Mughal gardens of Kashmir. These photographs reject the prevailing Euro-American tendency for the exotic and instead echo Epstein's photographic approach in America during the same period of time.

His Indian photographs are layered and thought-provoking. They encourage us to reflect on the tensions and relationships between the people in the frame – not only to each other but also to their society and the landscapes in which they are photographed. To emphasise these relationships and create the cohesive sense of stillness that pervades each image, Epstein sometimes made small interventions. On this, he comments, "I draw my pictures from the real world, I find facts far stranger than fiction, so I haven't felt the impulse to invent from scratch. But I will move or add or subtract an object or ask someone to be still or turn if I think it helps the picture. These are very small shifts, but they violate the classical notion of street photography."[1] In the genres of landscape, social documentary and street photography, Epstein's slower method of image-making and complex compositions were new in India at the time, contrasting with the more spur-of-the-moment style of some of his contemporaries, as seen elsewhere in this book.

Lodi Gardens, New Delhi, 1983
C-type print, 41 × 60 cm

Shravanabelagola, Karnataka, 1981
C-type print, 41 × 60 cm

Rosy, Meghraj Cabaret #2, Bombay, 1984
C-type print, 41 × 60 cm

Kutch, Gujarat, 1984
C-type print, 41 × 60 cm

Sebastião Salgado
b. Brazil, 1944

Sebastião Salgado initially trained as an economist, studying at the Universidade de São Paulo in Brazil before going on to work for the International Coffee Organization, often traveling to Africa on missions for the World Bank. He began making photographs in the 1970s, embarking on grand global projects which combine a cinematic ability to convey drama and emotion whilst keeping his subject matter rooted in the real-life issues facing some of the most marginalised and threatened communities in the world today. Influenced by his grounding in economics, Salgado's work therefore typically explores the people, communities and landscapes that are both exploited by, and under threat from, the industrialised world. As he explains: "Each of my stories is about globalization and economic liberalization: a sample of the human condition on the planet today."[1] In his book *Workers: An Archaeology of the Industrial Age*, first published by Aperture in 1992, Salgado explored activities that have defined labour from the Stone Age through to the present across twenty-one countries. His work in India from this publication forms its own photoessay on the coal-mining districts of Jharkhand in Bihar, oscillating between portraits and documents of subjects engaged in their back-breaking work, which is then contextualised within a larger global narrative. By leaving markers of industrial modernity outside the frame, the viewer is encouraged to engage on the timelessness of manual labour. Salgado's work is often lauded as the pinnacle of photographic humanism, using his highly stylised, textured monochrome images as a comment of the power of the human spirit. As one of the most widely recognised documentary photographers in the world, Salgado's photographs have set the aesthetic guidelines for a whole generation of practitioners.

Coal Mining, Dhanbad, Bihar, 1989
Gelatin silver print, 50.8 × 61 cm

Cage girls of Bombay

The squalid brothel district of Bombay is hardly the place to look for tenderness and beauty. Yet the distinguished American photographer Mary Ellen Mark, famous for her reportage of Indian life, went on such a search. After three months living among the prostitutes she produced some haunting images, to be published next week in a remarkable book

Left: Photographer Mary Ellen Mark, on assignment in India

A Bombay madam with her girls in one of Falkland Road's more elite establishments.

'They worship and fear the madam,'' says Mary Ellen Mark. ''They have a master-slave, mother-daughter relationship.'' Top left: a Falkland Road exterior

A young prostitute gets made up. Sometimes they will dress as little girls, sometimes as 'English ladies'

Potential customer, potential goods. The first stages in a deal that will probably cost five rupees (about 25p)

Later stages in a similar deal. Girls rely on their colleagues and madams for protection. Pimps are rare

Cage girl. ''All of them, even the most seemingly aggressive, are vulnerable,'' says Mary Ellen Mark

Companionship. A prostitute sits with an elderly friend now retired from the game. They are both transvestites

Cage girl at home. Girls eat, sleep, rear their children and work – all within the confines of the brothel

Indian prostitutes solicit their clients from cages. Many of them are children, kidnapped or bought from Indian villages. Others are *hijras*, transvestites or eunuchs castrated shortly after birth.

Prices are cheap – the average in rupees is the equivalent of 20 pence – but few Europeans who have come to scoff remain to pay, and trade is mainly plied with Indians of the lower middle-class. For the European, therefore, the common Bombay prostitute has remained merely a tourist curiosity, a beckoning unfortunate imprisoned in a cage. Such is not the case with Mary Ellen Mark, who first saw Falkland Road and its girls as a young American photographer in 1968. She tried to photograph it then and failed. "The hostility and aggression were just too much," she says. But the faces she had seen haunted her for the next ten years. She went back a dozen times to India, where her reportage of all aspects of life won her international acclaim. On each visit she returned to Falkland Road, and each time it continued to elude her. Then, in 1978, she came to Bombay prepared to spend three months living with its prostitutes, in a final, determined effort to get beneath the bizarre and inhuman surface of their lives.

At first Mary Ellen Mark found the going tough. Hostile men would gather round. Women would hurl insults and garbage. But eventually she made friends and after a few weeks she was popping in and out of brothels like a French bishop. What she is most concerned to show is that the cage girls are thinking people rather than trained animals. "They were just great people. Those months were really joyous."

She also uncovered a few hitherto hidden layers of sociology and, perhaps less unexpectedly, some sisterhood. The prostitutes of Falkland Road can be divided into four groups. There are the street girls, who hire rooms from madams by day and sleep among beggars on the pavement by night. There are the transvestites, who have heterosexual as well as homosexual clients. There are the posher girls with rooms on the upper floors of Falkland Road houses (Ms Mark once had to hide under a bed there during a police raid). And then there are Falkland Road's most famous inhabitants, the cage girls, ridiculed and abused by the rest. No-one seems to know where the idea comes from, but the cages are used to protect and display their contents not imprison them.

The girls defend one another. They form close friendships, share food and jokes. They asked few questions of their visitor. She writes: "They wanted to know only my age, why I didn't wear a brassiere and why I wasn't married. I think the reason I was finally accepted was that I was single – alone in the world like they were."

Mary Ellen Mark describes Falkland Road as "the most gentle and interesting street I've ever visited. Prostitution is a way for these girls to survive, and the one thing they have going for them is that they're not involved with drugs or pimps."

During the 1890s American missionaries came to Bombay and patrolled the streets from 7p.m. to 3a.m., knocking on brothel doors and windows and quoting scripture ("Be sure your sin will find you out."). Sometimes – in ill-lit streets – their female helpers were mistaken for prostitutes by the British soldiery. Fighting ensued. One courageous Christian, Malcolm Moss, would sing hymns outside brothel windows and follow clients home – by tricycle – to note their addresses, thence to bombard them with tracts through the post. According to records recently unearthed by Professor Kenneth Ballhatchet of London University, Moss was frequently assaulted for his pains – once by a major and once by a lance-corporal of the Lancashire Regiment; presumably buttoning up their flies first.

Beside this Ms Mark's own intrepidity pales somewhat. But then great fortitude is often a product of great moral certainty. **Ian Jack**

'Falkland Road' is published by Thames & Hudson. Hardback, £12, paperback, £5·95. Most of the photographs in this article appear in the book. An exhibition is now at the Olympus Cameras Centre, 151 Piccadilly, London W1 and is on until June 19. Opening times are Monday to Friday, from 10a.m. until 5.30p.m. Admission is free.

"Cage Girls of Bombay", *The Sunday Times Magazine*, 24 May 1981

Mary Ellen Mark
b. United States, 1940–2015

A graduate of the University of Pennsylvania with a BA in painting and art history (1962) and an MA in photojournalism (1964), Mary Ellen Mark went on to become one of the most critically acclaimed American documentary photographers of her generation. She published several long-form photoessays and portraits in publications such as *Life*, *New York Times Magazine*, *The New Yorker*, *Rolling Stone* and *Vanity Fair*, and for over five decades she explored marginalised groups and communities in the United States as well as abroad.

Taken over a four-month period during the winter of 1978–79 and originally intended for publication in the American *GEO* magazine, Mark's first photo-essay in India concentrated on the sex workers of Mumbai's infamous red-light district around Falkland Road. The photographs were originally considered too graphic for that audience and were instead published in *GEO*'s partner publication, the German newsmagazine *Stern*, in 1979. Two years later, in 1981, Mark published the full-length book *Falkland Road: Prostitutes of Bombay* (an extract of which was published in *The Sunday Times Magazine* in the same year). She was the first photographer to produce a book on the subject that would reach a wide Western audience, and has been commended with bringing the reality of India's red-light districts to global attention.[1] The series, however, continues to generate debates in the world of documentary photography surrounding the idea of interventionism – the moral and legal notion of whether or not the photographer ought to intervene in a situation that is damaging to their subject. As a comment on the changing attitudes in the genre she herself helped to define, a 2005 reprint of *Falkland Road*, Mark noted: "I often wonder how the women of Falkland Road would react to me if I approached them now. Would they be afraid to be labeled or sensationalized? Would they ask me for money? They never did before." Mark produced other projects over the years in India, including an essay on Mother Teresa and her home in Calcutta in 1985, and an essay on Indian circuses begun in 1989 (later parodied as a typical example of Western exoticism by Pushpamala N. and Clare Arni (see p. 253). Her influence in the world of concerned documentary photography is extensive in both the United States and – as a result of *Falkland Road*'s fame – in India as well. During her time in the country, she was on occasion assisted by Dayanita Singh (see p. 293), who cites her as an important early mentor in her career.

Lata lying in bed. Falkland Road, Mumbai, India, 1978
C-type print, 50.8 × 61 cm

Ketaki Sheth
b. India, 1957

Ketaki Sheth is known for her long-term black-and-white photographic projects that enquire into notions of identity, community and belonging which she explores in books and long-form photoessays. Whilst in the UK, Sheth encountered a London directory listing only Patels (a community from the state of Gujarat), with twenty-five Patel twins in Greater London alone. This set her on a four-year quest of seeking out twins with the last name Patel, both across the United Kingdom and in Gujarat. The search, which she likened to that of an anthropologist of her own community, resulted in her finding 125 pairs of Patel twins, consequently producing the photobook *Twinspotting* in 2000. Sheth's picturings of the twins themselves, existing as imperfect reproductions of one another, seems almost to depart from Diane Arbus's iconic 1967 photograph of identical twin girls, although it is more concerned with an intimate telling of the lives of Gujaratis and Gujarati diaspora – all united by a shared last name. Simultaneously rigid in its criteria and open-ended in its outcomes, Sheth's photobook presents a test of the photographic project itself without necessarily resolving it.

Similarly, her encounter in 2005 with a settlement of Siddis (Indians of African origin who have been present in the subcontinent for centuries but have been left in relative isolation) led Sheth to photograph the community, learning of their language and customs, documenting their religious and social practices, and capturing the fluidity between their African heritage and the means by which they negotiate with their Indianness. This extensive documentation, the first of its kind, of the daily rhythms and lives of the Siddis, led to the publication of *A Certain Grace* (2013). Sheth states of her practice: "There are two things that help me interact with my subjects and photograph them in the best way possible – simplicity of approach and a certain freshness. This is what inspires me to narrate the subject's story in its true essence."[1]

Riddhi and Siddhi, London, from the series *Twinspotting*, 1997
Gelatin silver print, 50.9 × 60.8 cm

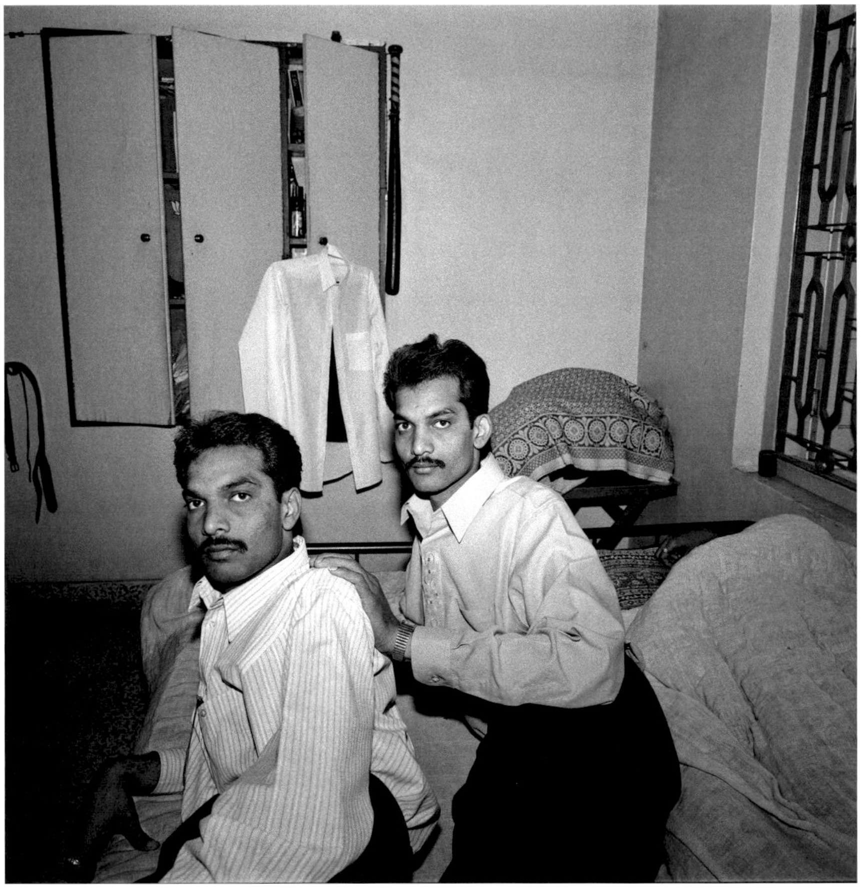

Milan and Mayur, Gujarat, from the series *Twinspotting*, 1998
Ramesh and Suresh, Middlesex, from the series *Twinspotting*, 1997
Gelatin silver prints, 50.9 × 50.9 cm each

Yesha and Niddhi, Gujarat, from the series *Twinspotting*, 1998
Gelatin silver print, 50.9 × 50.9 cm

Manoj Kumar Jain
b. India, 1970

Manoj Kumar Jain studied at the Delhi College of Art from 1992, and although working primarily as a commercial photographer, he published a significant photoessay in the book *The Forgotten Frames* (2014), a documentation of the tribal communities of Bastar. In his choice of subject matter, Jain refers to an earlier history of photographic representation of the tribal body, and from this series individual photographs bear a likeness in sentement to the works of Johnson and Henderson's *The Oriental Races and Tribes, Residents and Visitors of Bombay* (see p. 41), and the twentieth-century practices of Sunil Janah and Sri Lankan photographer Lionel Wendt. Although contentious territory given the legacy of ethnographic photoessays in the country, and in particular the frequent photographic interest in the tribes of Bastar by photojournalists, Jain's work has been praised for overcoming a burden of what has been traditionally considered a condescending or orientalist representation. The apparent success of *The Forgotten Frames* perhaps lies in encouraging questions on behalf of the viewer on how far it is possible to escape such connotations. It can be argued that Jain's invocation of a largely blissful existence of the community among animals bends towards the popular imagination of a rural idyll, and that the work is therefore problematic in its presentation of an untouched community. However, seen in parallel with the book's accompanying essay, by anthropologist Nandini Sundar, professor of sociology at the Delhi School of Economics, the contemporary existence of the Bastar and the problems they face in light of increased urbanisation in the region provide the necessary context for these images to elevate themselves beyond romanticism. They instead show the use of the extended photoessay to both communicate and document some of the social shifts at work in India today.

Deer horn dancer, village Bahigaon, Bastar, 2008
Gelatin silver print, approx. 25 × 20.3 cm

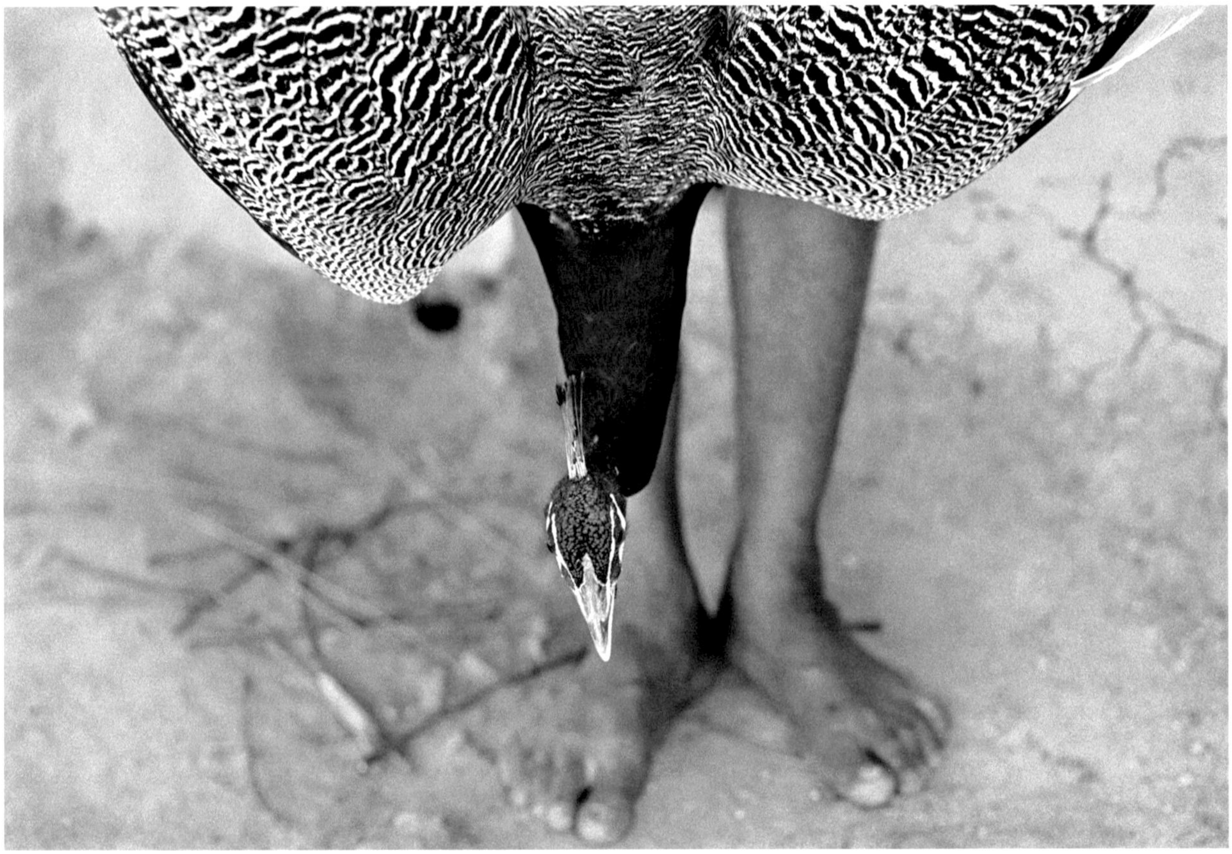

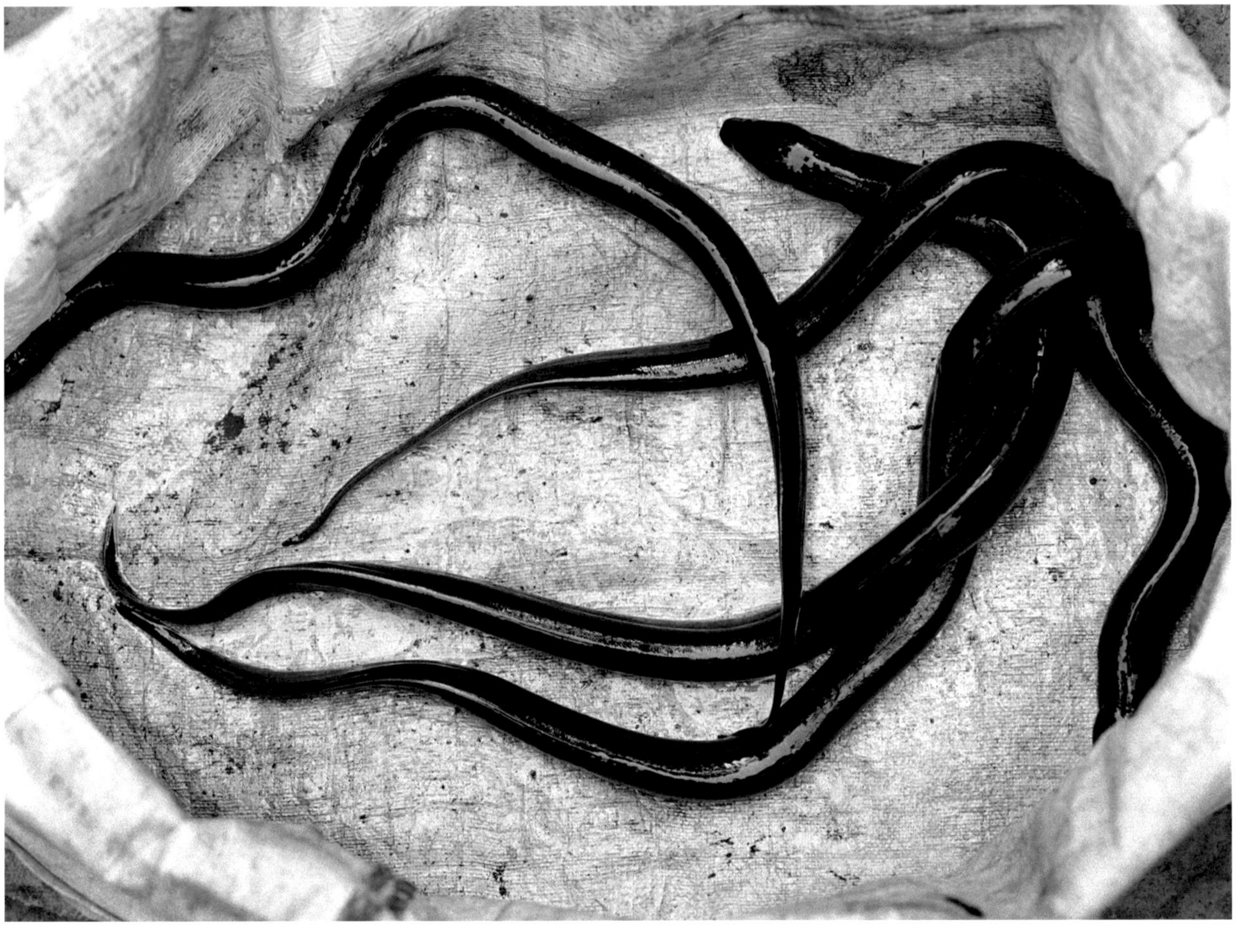

Man with domesticated peacock, village Pulcha, Bastar, 2002
Eels for sale at the Pamela Market, Bastar, 2008
Gelatin silver prints, approx. 20.3 × 25 cm each

Sunil Gupta
b. India, 1953

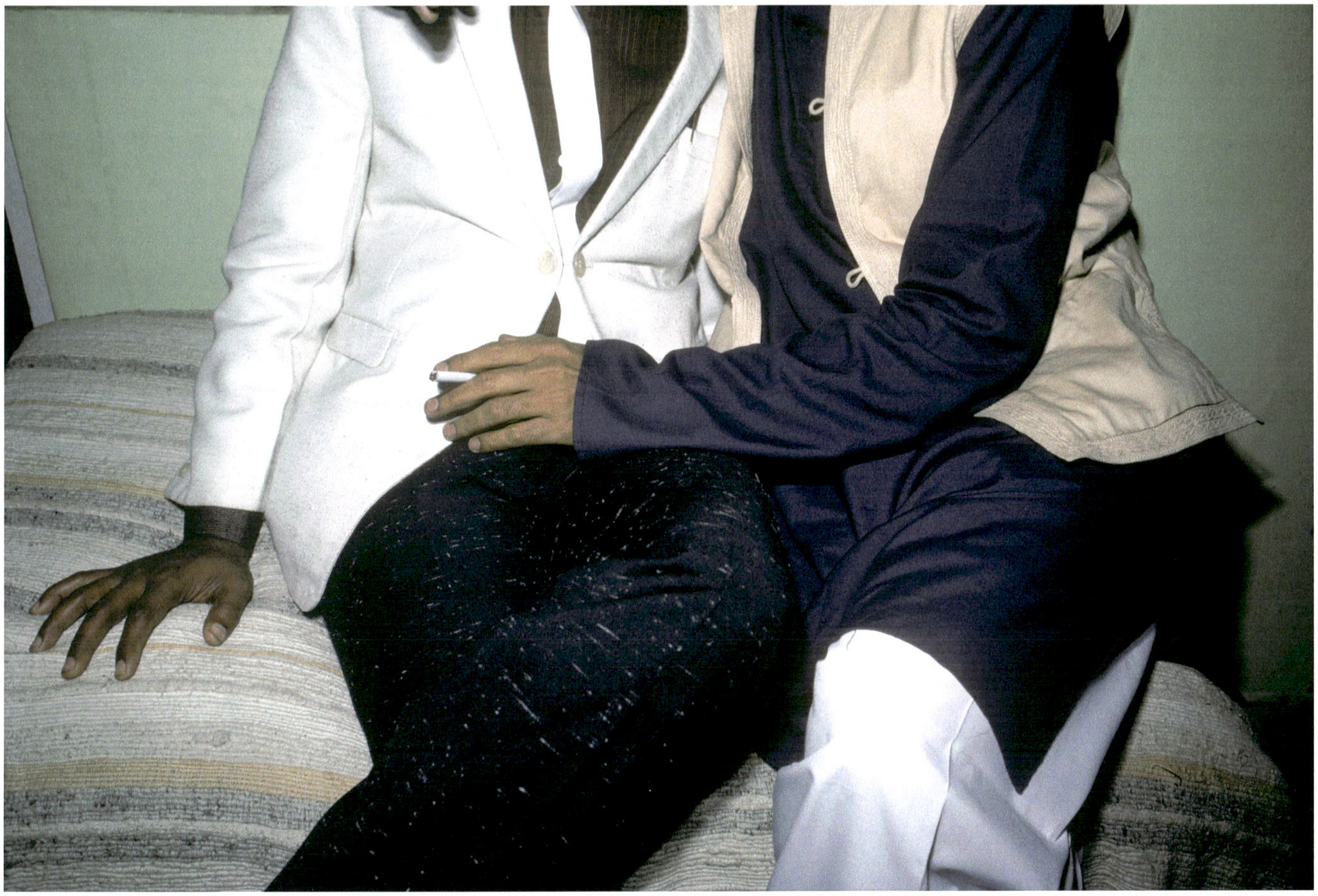

The Party.

We tried to organise a group but
it turned into a social event and
eventually broke up because
of petty jealousies.

In the late 1960s Sunil Gupta and his family emigrated to Canada, where his interest in photography began to develop alongside his work as an activist, writer and, later, curator. From the mid-1970s he lived in New York, where he studied photography at the New School for Social Research under Lisette Model. At the end of the 1970s he moved to London to continue his studies at the West Surrey College of Art and Design, Farnham, and the Royal College of Art, where he was actively involved in the founding of Autograph (the Association of Black Photographers) with Stuart Hall, a prominent activist for non-white artists in the United Kingdom. He also set up the Organization for Visual Arts in London to promote a greater understanding of cultural differences and their manifestation in the arts.

Across his work, Gupta has consistently explored questions of gay identity, politics, diaspora and belonging, at many times adopting a straightforward documentary style, accompanied by text, to produce visual essays. In *Ten Years On* (1984–85), he photographed a number of gay couples from his extended social circle in London, often in their homes, creating intimate and sincere portraits in spaces where his sitters were free of the scorn or abuse of the public sphere. What started as a simple study and piece of photographic social documentary gradually grew in meaning in light of the project being made during the AIDS crisis of the 1980s.

In *Exiles* (1987), Gupta returned to New Delhi to photograph the double lives and often concealed identities of the city's gay men. In this project, Gupta took an intentional turn away from photographing the faces of his subjects in order to explore the anxiety around their being unwillingly "outed" to the viewers of his images, using captions based on his subjects' conversations with him in an early invocation of combined text and image in "art documentary" photography. In particular, a photograph captioned "It must be marvellous in the West with your bars, clubs, Gay Liberation and all that" points to the vast chasm that existed between Gupta's own life abroad and those of his friends living in India.

The Party, from the series *Exiles*, 1986/87
Pigment print, 50.8 × 137 cm

Martin Parr
b. England, 1952

Martin Parr studied photography at Manchester Polytechnic from 1970 to 1972 before moving to West Yorkshire where he produced his first significant body of work, *Rural Communities*, an investigation into rural life in northern England. He has since become best known for photographic projects that take a more satirical look at aspects of modern life in the UK, in particular documenting the social classes of England with a typically sardonic tone.

Most famously in his book *The Last Resort* (1982–85), Parr focused on holidaying working-class families during Margaret Thatcher's time as prime minister. Shot in colour during a time when traditional black-and-white imagery was the exclusive medium of "proper" photography, a trend first dismantled by Americans like Stephen Shore, William Eggleston and Mitch Epstein (see p. 214), *The Last Resort* ushered in the turn towards colour photography in the UK, fundamentally changing the way it was received and displayed. This body of work faced criticism when shown in London, accused of condescension with regard to one social class photographing another, but Parr's skill perhaps lies in his ability to escape such condescension. He explained: "At the time, when I first showed it in Liverpool, no one batted an eyelid because everyone knew what New Brighton was like." It was this more contemporary brand of social realism, which used humour but never at the expense of truth, that would become the signature style of Parr's work.

Although going on to produce many series mainly in colour to represent British culture at home, Parr also made various trips to India, where, before his exploration of British holidaymakers at leisure in his 1993 series *Goa*, he also made a lesser-known series entitled *Darjeeling* in the mid-1980s. Here Parr produced a photoessay based in a boarding school and its surrounding shops and restaurants in the peaceful and picturesque hills of West Bengal, returning to the monochrome style of *Rural Communities*. What results is a traditionally composed study of a school that was a doubtless offshoot of British colonialism in India. In line with Parr's interest in British class and its fallouts, he observes an institution that seems to have retained some of the more anachronistic facets of its colonial counterparts, such as the schoolmaster's robes and the earnestness of the boys themselves, in their sombre school uniforms.

A cricket match, St Paul's School, Darjeeling, 1984
Gelatin silver print, 30.4 × 40.6 cm

The Gymkhana Club, Darjeeling, 1984
Glenary's Tearoom, Darjeeling, 1984
Gelatin silver prints, 30.4 × 40.6 cm each

Julia Knop
b. (West) Germany, 1971

Julia Knop is a German photographer working at the intersection of editorial and social documentary. Her work in India, *Electronics City*, a project she began in the late 1990s, marks a sophisticated and nuanced turn in social realism that sets it apart from other contemporary documentary projects in the country at this time. In the series Knop uses the office spaces of one of Bangalore's earliest IT parks, and those who inhabit them, to comment on a shift in India's economy and the social fallout of its liberalisation. She presents both a document of one of the key drivers of India's booming economy – the opening up of its markets and the focus on IT as part of this – and a subtle critique on the vacuous nature of long hours spent in drab environments between the water cooler and computer. The project is reminiscent of British photographer Anna Fox's series *Workstations*, published a decade before, which examined office life during the Thatcher years in Britain (a similar time of upward social mobility with all its aesthetic quirks). Taken as they were at the beginning of this economic shift, they occupy a middle ground between the early establishment of Bangalore as an IT hub and the present-day result of this: a highly developed, wealthy and cosmopolitan city with the reputation of being India's Silicon Valley. Along with Bangalore's upward mobility began the homogenising effect on the visual landscape and vocabulary of the city, where cultural signifiers are pushed to the periphery. Seen now in the light of a more complete form of transculturalism and globalisation, Knop's photographs could almost have been taken in any corporate office in world. Therein lies the strength of the project, as it captures the tipping point of the globalised landscape and the dislocation of national identities within it.

School for computer science, Bangalore, 1997
C-type print, 50 × 70 cm

Electronics City, Bangalore, 1997
C-type print, 50 × 70 cm

Engineer at Novell, Electronics City, Bangalore, 1977
C-type print, 70 × 50 cm

Soham Gupta
b. India, 1988

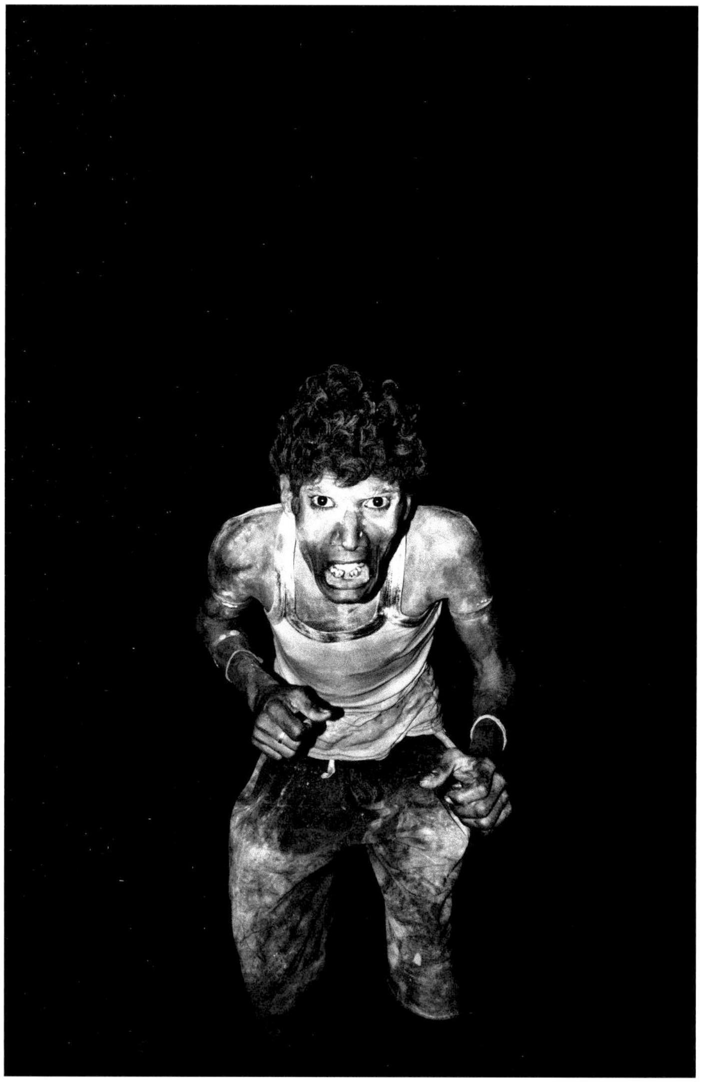

Soham Gupta studied photography at the Ateneo de Manila University in the Philippines. Despite much of his work being made in his home city of Kolkata, it consciously dislocates any sense of time or place by casting all but the subjects in shadow, using them not as portraits but as devices to explore internal and psychological themes of vulnerability and anxiety. Gupta's photographs gained attention when they were exhibited as part of the Delhi Photo Festival in 2015, where he presented images from the photobook *Angst*. The project speaks directly to Gupta's broader interest in capturing life on the margins, featuring a series of black-and-white, high-contrast photographs in violent flash, that show inhabitants of Kolkata – poor, ill, visibly disturbed and socially outcast – in what can only be thought of as anti-portraits.

According to Gupta's own writing on the subject, these figures are intended to converse with the inner figurings of his own mind, creating images that are nightmarish in their being simultaneously real and too strange to be real. Their intensity make it clear that they are intended to repulse, producing a sort of self-consciousness in the viewer as they question what it is they are repulsed by: the subject him- or herself, or the situation of the subject, as they have been cast out of society and are forced to live hidden in plain sight, only brought back in the momentary flash of Gupta's camera.

Angst adds a pertinent dimension to the representation of the marginalised in India – a common theme in the history of photography in the country – but handles its subjects in a way that clearly departs from earlier, more staid photographic depictions. Not unlike South African photographer Roger Ballen, Gupta turns the concerns of social documentary on their head, almost revelling in the unabashed ugliness of poverty. In this way *Angst* seeks to be an unambiguous exposé of the unforgiving social realities in much of the country, where any kind of abnormality, however arbitrary, is often punished by exile and ostracism.

From the series *Angst*, 2013–17
Pigment prints, 48 x 33 cm each

***The Cinema Travellers*, 2008–**
Pigment prints, 25.4 × 38 cm each

Amit Madheshiya
b. India, 1982

Amit Madheshiya graduated from the University of Delhi, where he studied English Literature, and then completed his Masters in Mass Communication at Jamia Millia Islamia in New Delhi. There he and his fellow student Shirley Abraham began to explore the history of cinema from the point of view of its experience and reception, journeying around the country to document travelling cinemas that still weave their way through rural India. Their collaboration resulted in the film *The Cinema Travellers* (2016), an award-winning investigation into the industry of mobile cinemas in rural areas that hundreds of local people frequent and enjoy as their main source of cinematic entertainment.

Over the course of many years of research and documentation for the film, Madheshiya also created a photo series of the same name. Whereas the film presented a look into the entire ecosystem of mobile cinemas – turning the viewer's attention to the hand-cranked projectors and the billowing tents that form the theatre – the photographic series instead provides a closer look at the cinema-goers themselves, offering an intimate and yet cinematic view of their emotions and reactions as they watch the films.

Madheshiya's images are testament to the sheer range of human emotion and reflective of how this is produced by cinema both on-screen as well as off. The visible emotions of Madheshiya's subjects make their experience of the films (that are never revealed in the compositions) palpable and identifiable for the viewer. Photographs from the series have won the World Photography Award (2009, 2011), the World Press Photo Award (2011) and the Grand Award at the Humanity Photo Awards (2009).

9 Postmodernism & Play

With this chapter we touch upon a few thematic routes that photographers between the 1980s and early 2000s appear to have been preoccupied with. Kobena Mercer's distinction between "modern" art and "post-modern" art is one that may allow us to unpack some of the thematic considerations of late twentieth- and early twenty-first-century photography in India.

Annu Palakunnathu Matthew
b. England, 1964

Photographer Unknown

FEATHER INDIAN

Photograph by White & Matthew

DOT INDIAN

Annu Palakunnathu Matthew is a professor of art at the Department of Art and Art History, University of Rhode Island. She describes herself as transcultural and her work addresses the political, social and transformative issues that stemmed from the unwieldy experience of oscillating between three cultures and spaces (Britain, the United States and India). From her early work to later projects that included the use of video, Matthew also explores the connection between past and present. Her photographs therefore function as document and fiction, as re-enactment and projection, and locate her simultaneously as a global citizen and outsider, both at home and in transit.

In *An Indian from India*, Matthew addresses the historical slippage due to which indigenous Americans were mistaken for Indians, and – centuries later – South Asians in the United States are referred to as 'Indians from India'. The series of images consists of diptychs pairing nineteenth-century photographs of indigenous Americans with the artist's own tableaux interpreting the same scene. In repeating the image centuries apart, and with the visual iconographies of "Indianness", Matthew addresses the questions of identity and assimilation with which any non-white experience of the United States are constantly imbued. Her use of South Asian jewellery and dress in the series (at one point even adopting the American flag as a sari) also references the specificity of the British ethnographic project in India, equating the South Asian and indigenous American experiences of colonisation and "civilisation".

Feather Indian, Dot Indian, from the series *An Indian From India*, 2001
Pigment print, 30.5 × 53 cm

9 Postmodernism & Play

With this chapter we touch upon a few thematic routes that photographers between the 1980s and early 2000s appear to have been preoccupied with. Kobena Mercer's distinction between "modern" art and "post-modern" art is one that may allow us to unpack some of the thematic considerations of late twentieth- and early twenty-first-century photography in India.

Whereas modernism considered authenticity and originality central values to the consideration of an artwork, postmodernism "deconstructed the high/low hierarchy between the original and the copy and thus added a critique of the social relations of representation in a world of mass reproduction".[1] This perhaps explains the appreciation for reappropriating and remixing traditional forms of representation in artistic practices on a global level, such as in the photographic practice of Yinka Shonibare, who adopted self-portraiture-oriented styles to disrupt and de-centre narratives of literature and art-world convention by inserting his own body into elaborate Victorian settings. These pastiche practices have their parallels in Indian and Indian diaspora photographers such as Pushpamala N. and Annu Palakunnathu Matthew. Just as Pushpamala, in her *Ethnographic Series* with Clare Arni, recasts herself as the ethnographic subject in many diverse attires of many Indian women, each thrown against the chequered Lamprey's grid, as used in earnest in the work of Maurice Vidal Portman from over a century before (see p. 44), Annu Palakunnathu Matthew restages photographic portraits of Native Americans in order to bring to light the multiple invocations of the word "Indian" in the United States. Jitish Kallat equally references colonial uses of the grid and the Becherian typologies of the Düsseldorf School in his mammoth photographic installation of men's breast pockets. Yasumasa Morimura, well known for his playful enactments of famous photographs and paintings, is also included here for his restaging of an iconic portrait of Mahatma Gandhi by Margaret Bourke-White.

Pastiche photography proves to be rich in its potential for subversive humour. Invoking the camera's history in America as well as exploring the particularity of her own identity as an Indian in the United States, as opposed to the Native Americans who were once mistakenly called Indians, Annu Palakunnathu Matthew parodies the racial relations of nineteenth-century photographs of indigenous Americans in her series *An Indian from India*. In French photographer Olivier Culmann's not-uncontroversial series *The Others*, he photographs himself dressed as a variety of Indian men – the old-fashioned bureaucrat, the portly policeman, prime minister Manmohan Singh – and merges these images using Photoshop into actually existing backdrops in Indian photographic studios.

One could argue that these practices, however diverse, converge around a shared concern: they are photographs about photographs, reckoning with the camera's (often violent) colonial past and subverting old forms of depicting the native, "other" body with tongue-in-cheek humour.[2] Using strategies of remixing, reworking, reappropriating and revising, techniques that are, as Kobena Mercer and Hal Foster have each addressed,[3] already important theoretical tools for postcolonial artists across the world, these photographers still bring their work back to the iconography, archives and colonial legacies that are unique to South Asia.

Even apart from these new "colonial" photographs, a large part of the selection of work in this chapter displays the political preoccupations of its photographers in a broader thinking-through of time. In *Retake of Amrita*, Vivan Sundaram uses paintings by, as well as photographs of, his aunt, the painter Amrita Sher-Gil, taken by his grandfather Umrao Singh Sher-Gil (see p. 75), to create elaborate digital montages which allow his renowned ancestors, both famed makers of portraits and self-portraits, to interact and merge at various points of their own staged narratives. By surrendering Umrao's and Amrita's own artistic autonomy to his own, Sundaram reveals the fickle, ever-changing nature of the photograph as document.

Appropriation, pastiche and photography about photography that are used to comment on the history of colonialism and its influence on representation are the clearest manifestations of what can be called post-modernist photography in India. This new way of thinking about the potential of photography opened up new, largely political opportunities for photographers in India, which expanded into gender studies, an examination of the body and also sexuality. Sheba Chhachhi's extended photographic commitment to the female body is here reproduced with the grid-like composition of *Silver Sap*. In response to the more traditional gender division of photography – man frames woman – Chhachhi's photo series was a project of collaborative image-making in which the artist rescues excerpts of the female form from dominant market-driven depictions of the naked body. Pamela Singh, in her photographs of rural and semi-rural India, similarly challenges the fixedness of the Indian woman as subject.

Her photographs (often containing a cropped or out-of-focus view of the photographer) capture the precarious, often all-male nature of the Indian public sphere that is in a sense disturbed by her presence. This is similarly at work in her photograph *Tantric Self-Portrait A*, where the photographer engages the viewer in witnessing the homosocial act of spectatorship that is immediately behind her.

Raqs Media Collective's lens-based installation *An Afternoon Unregistered on the Richter Scale* also plays with the past in Indian art practice. The work is a silent looped video projection, using a recast version of a 1911 photograph by James Waterhouse entitled *Examining Room of the Duffin Section of the Photographic Department of the Survey of India*, taken in Calcutta. That Waterhouse's original image captured the very beginnings of institutional image-making and documentation puts the history of Indian photography at the heart of this installation. While some of the other projects shown in this chapter have bestowed a sort of present-ness to archival or historical images, in Raqs's disentangling of the image into a three-minute, thirty-second video – in which the ceiling fan steadily whirs along, the surveyors' shirts are steadily tinged with indigo, and a man seems to walk up a hill outside the window – linear time and the presumption of present-ness is denied. The viewer is invited to exist outside of time, with the subjects of the image-turned-video, at an extended point where 1911 meets the moment of viewing and merges with all other times in between the two.

1 Kobena Mercer, 'The Cross-Cultural and the Contemporary', in: *Travel & See: Black Diaspora Art Practices since the 1980s*, Durham, NC 2016, p. 268.
2 Jodi Throckmorton invokes the term "postdate" as a useful term to think through the interplay of postcolonial contemporary art and the colonial ghosts by which it chooses to be haunted. See Jodi Throckmorton, 'Introduction', in: *Postdate: Photography and Inherited History in India*, San Jose, CA 2015.
3 Hal Foster, 'An Archival Impulse' in: *October* 110 (Fall 2004), pp. 3–22.

Annu Palakunnathu Matthew
b. England, 1964

Annu Palakunnathu Matthew is a professor of art at the Department of Art and Art History, University of Rhode Island. She describes herself as transcultural and her work addresses the political, social and transformative issues that stemmed from the unwieldy experience of oscillating between three cultures and spaces (Britain, the United States and India). From her early work to later projects that included the use of video, Matthew also explores the connection between past and present. Her photographs therefore function as document and fiction, as re-enactment and projection, and locate her simultaneously as a global citizen and outsider, both at home and in transit.

In *An Indian from India*, Matthew addresses the historical slippage due to which indigenous Americans were mistaken for Indians, and – centuries later – South Asians in the United States are referred to as 'Indians from India'. The series of images consists of diptychs pairing nineteenth-century photographs of indigenous Americans with the artist's own tableaux interpreting the same scene. In repeating the image centuries apart, and with the visual iconographies of "Indianness", Matthew addresses the questions of identity and assimilation with which any non-white experience of the United States are constantly imbued. Her use of South Asian jewellery and dress in the series (at one point even adopting the American flag as a sari) also references the specificity of the British ethnographic project in India, equating the South Asian and indigenous American experiences of colonisation and "civilisation".

Feather Indian, Dot Indian, from the series *An Indian From India*, 2001
Pigment print, 30.5 × 53 cm

AMERICAN INDIAN WITH DOT ON FACE

INDIAN AMERICAN WITH DOT ON FACE

American Indian with Dot on Face, Indian American with Dot on Face, from the series *An Indian from India*, 2001
Pigment print, 30.5 × 53 cm

Sheba Chhachhi
b. Ethiopia, 1958

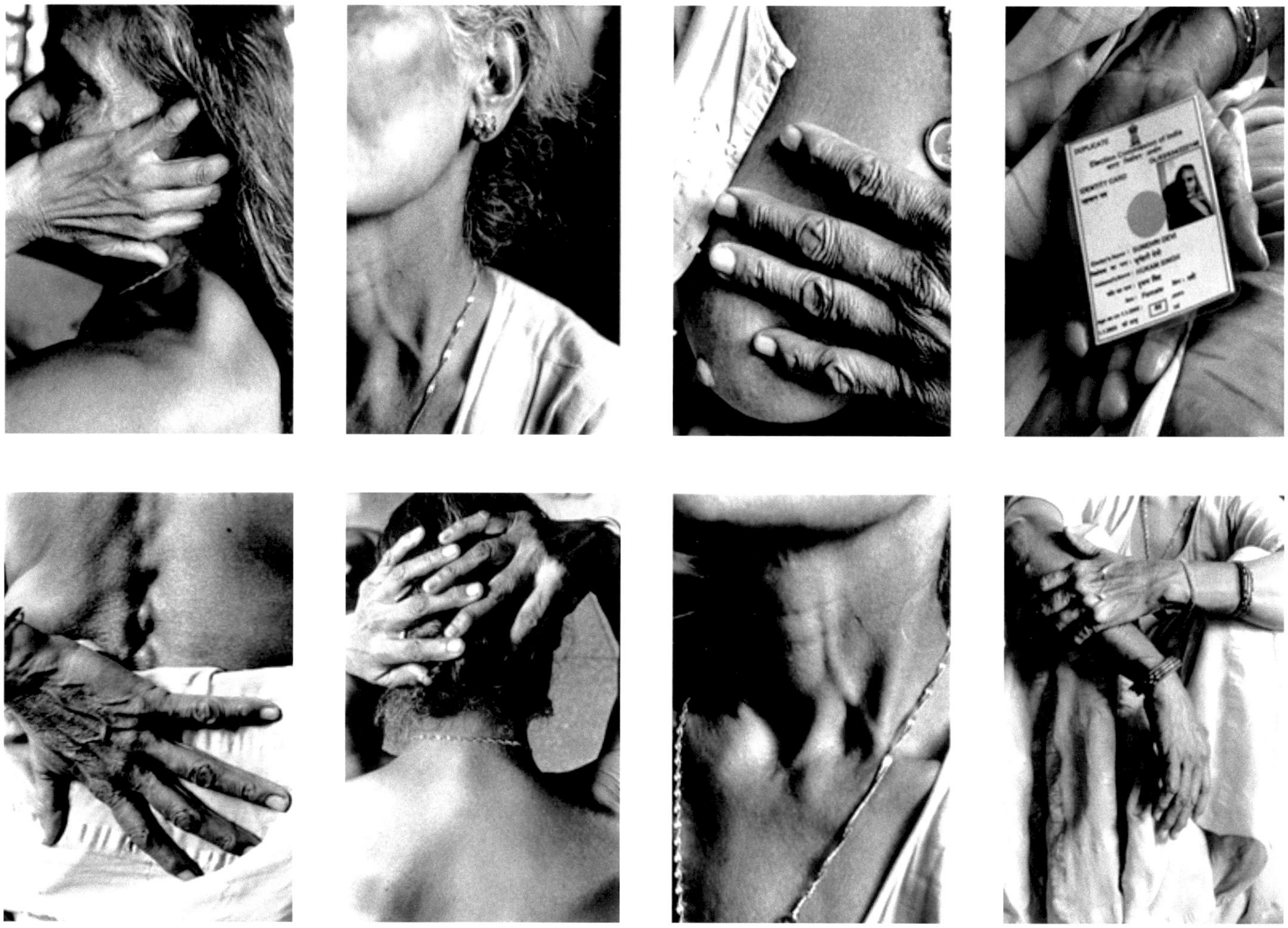

Chhachhi is well known for her photography, multimedia installations and writing, as well as for her activism in the sphere of women's rights. She studied at the University of Delhi, Chitrabani in Kolkata, as well as at the National Institute of Design in Ahmedabad. Her earliest photographic series documents the women's movement in India across more than a decade, from 1980 onwards. Both as activist and photographer, "pointing the camera one moment, shouting slogans the next," she recorded protests against dowry deaths, domestic violence, rape and sexual violence, as well as consciousness-raising workshops, street theatre and solidarity gatherings.

Chhachhi's photographic practice reveals her consistent interest in gender politics and its photographic manifestations. This is a theme that runs through series such as *Seven Lives and a Dream* (1998), a set of collaborative portraits of seven women activists; here, documentary images of struggle were juxtaposed with staged portraits for which subjects co-created their own representation by choosing the *mise en scène*, postures and objects. Similarly, in *When the Gun is Raised, Dialogue Stops* (2000), Chhachhi, in collaboration with Sonia Jabbar, presented testimonies and photographs of Kashmiri women in a large multimedia installation to consider the intersections of gender and violence in the state; and *Ganga's Daughters: Meetings with Women Ascetics* (1992–2004) observes the simultaneously traditional and often transgressive lives of woman monks in northern and eastern India. Her more recent work shows her concern with the intersections of feminism and ecological activism for their shared rejection of the economic and cultural hegemonies of corporations and market forces. In *Silver Sap* (2000), shown here, a grid of eight black-and-white photographs forms a tremendously defiant collection in which Chhachhi upturns traditional (commercial) expectations of youth and beauty, instead celebrating the ageing, labouring body.

Silver Sap, 1998–2001
Gelatin silver prints, 76 × 50 cm each

Raqs Media Collective
Founded 1992, India

Raqs Media Collective was founded in Delhi in 1992 by three artists, Jeebesh Bagchi (b. India, 1965), Monica Narula (b. India, 1969), and Shuddhabrata Sengupta (b. India, 1968). They chose the word "Raqs" for its double meaning, on the one hand for its Urdu/Persian invocation of the transcendental state into which dervish dancers enter whilst in motion; the other as an acronym for "rarely-asked questions".

The collective is known for a multidisciplinary and intertextual approach to dissecting identities that have been produced out of colonisation and globalisation, using material from the past to comment on the contemporary condition. Other artists in this chapter have used the strategy of appropriation in an often singular sense of recasting themselves in or as older art forms; Raqs, however, cleverly remixes a variety of past influences, styles and media, beginning with fractured points of departure which often include photographs. Photography is a recurring medium in their work because of how it contains the legacy of past structures of power, and especially colonialism, as explored in the earlier chapters of this book. In *Untold Intimacy of Digits* (2011), for example, the collective created a video installation out of a handprint of a nineteenth century Bengali peasant that found its way into the collection of Francis Galton, the father of modern eugenics who was interested in the capacity for photography to police and monitor the deviant human body. Similarly, *An Afternoon Unregistered on the Richter Scale* (2011) is forged from a related act of archival remix as, over the course of three and a half minutes, the still image from Waterhouse's collection meets with a series of gradual manipulations, such as a steady infusion of the colour indigo (itself borne from a colonial crop) to create a humorous and subversive reflection on the ecosystem of colony.

Raqs' work has been exhibited widely across the world, such as at the biennales of Venice, Istanbul, Kochi-Muziris, São Paulo and Shanghai, as well as at the Isabella Stewart Gardner Museum in Boston, Tate Modern in London, and at Documenta, among many others.

An Afternoon Unregistered on the Richter Scale, after an archival photograph by James Waterhouse, 2011
Film still, 3:30 min.

Pushpamala N. and Clare Arni
b. India, 1956 / b. Scotland, 1962

The photographic work of writer, curator and sculptor Pushpamala N. is arguably the most prominent example of performance photography in the Indian subcontinent. She has been exploring the genre from the mid-1990s, although initially in the form of "photo-romances" such as *Phantom Lady* or *Kismet* (1997). Clare Arni's photographic work, on the other hand, has traditionally been more concerned with architecture and collaborative performances. Pushpamala N. and Clare Arni came together from 2000 to 2004 to produce the series *Native Women of South India: Manners and Customs* as part of an Arts Collaboration Grant from the India Foundation for the Arts. This project investigates lasting images of South Indian women, recreating, re-envisioning and deconstructing them through the genre of photo performance. Through its reproduction of "types" of South Indian women from familiar and/or historical sources – ranging from newspaper photographs, calendar art and film stills to sixteenth-century miniature painting. The project comments on and raises questions about female representation, the hierarchies of art practice, the legacies of ethnography, and ideas of race and caste in subcontinental photographic practice. Playing with the constructed binaries of original and reproduction, black and white, subject and object, real and fake, *Native Women of South India: Manners and Customs* consists of four series of images and was originally exhibited in its entirety as an installation, with more than 250 photographs and several of the painted backdrops, props and costumes, based on the concept of a film or theatre museum. The four series into which the work is divided are *The Native Types*, *The Ethnographic Series*, *The Popular Series* and *The Process Series*, each examining and commenting on different aspects of imaging and representation, while also playfully indulging in cross-citation.

Toda H-26, from *The Ethnographic Series*, 2000–14
Gelatin silver print, approx. 50 × 60 cm

Velankani E-14A, from *The Ethnographic Series*, 2000–14
Returning from the Tank G-1, from *The Ethnographic Series*, 2000–14
Gelatin silver prints, approx. 60 × 50 cm each

Returning from the Tank (after an oil painting by Raja Ravi Varma),
from the series *The Native Types*, 2000–14
Lady in the Moonlight (after an oil painting by Raja Ravi Varma),
from the series *The Native Types*, 2000–14
C-type prints, approx. 60 × 50 cm each

Yogini (after a sixteenth-century Bijapur miniature painting), from the series *The Native Types*, 2000–14
Circus (after a photograph by Mary Ellen Mark), from the series *The Native Types*, 2000–14
C-type prints, approx. 50 × 60 cm each

Pamela Singh
b. India, 1961

Pamela Singh began her photographic career in the early 1990s. After studying at Parsons School of Design in New York, she attended the American College in Paris and later the International Center of Photography in New York. Although once a pageant queen who was crowned Miss India 1982, Singh's photographic practice rejects the aesthetic of glamour photography, instead exploring the relationship between her own body and the social landscape as both an insider and an outsider of contemporary Indian society. Singh typically inserts herself into the frame in curious self-portraits in order to make apparent the intersections of class, gender and language of which the photographic scene in India is almost invariably constructed. Her work explores the balance and tussle between tradition and modernity, the material and the spiritual. Although at times veering towards the trappings of ethnographic enquiry, Singh's photographs are playful and performative. Such is the case in *The Lorry Driver* (1994–95), in which Singh mimics a young man reclining on a charpoy in what appears to be a roadside shack for long-distance drivers. Other works present an active use of hand-painting over photographs, referring to a much older legacy of overpainted photography on the Indian subcontinent (see pp. 98–101). These range from the subdued colours of the series *Tantric Self-Portraits*, which mobilises hand-painted motifs to create playful textures outside of the confines of the photographed image, to the lurid, commercial colours in the painted photographs *Treasure Maps* (2014) that invoke the rich miniature painting tradition of the Rajputs.

Tantric Self Portrait A, 2003
Gelatin silver print overpainted with oil, acrylic, gold, mud and vermillion powder, 94 × 94 cm

Yasumasa Morimura
b. Japan, 1951

Yasumasa's first appropriationist photographs, in which he began to recreate easily identifiable, ubiquitous paintings from the Western artistic canon using himself as a model, began in the 1980s with his *Self-Portrait as Van Gogh with Bandaged Ear* (1985). Yasumasa's subsequent practice disrupts the viewer's expectations of iconic paintings and photographs through the process of almost perfect mimicry. It is in the slippages of imperfect reproduction, however, that the exactitudes of Yasumasa reveal themselves. The photographer's best-known images include *Vermeer Study: Looking Back (Mirror)* (2008), *Daughter of Art History* (1990) in which he inserts himself into the scene of Éduoard Manet's *A Bar at the Folies-Bergère*, as well as a number of renditions of Frida Kahlo's self-portraits. Equally, Yasumasa shows an interest in ubiquitous images of photojournalism and political portraits, exploring how particular photographs themselves become immortalised in a relentless stream of images. Among these, his most successful works are *Self-Portrait: After Ingrid Bergman* (1996) and his self-portraits as Che Guevara and Mao Zedong produced for the exhibition *Requiem for the XX Century: Twilight of the Turbulent Gods* (2007). It was in a similar political vein that he produced *Spinning a thread between the light and the earth/1946, India* (2010), an appropriation of Margaret Bourke-White's photograph of Mahatma Gandhi sitting by his *charkha* (see p. 121). Yasumasa successfully recreates the sobriety and meditative quality of Bourke-White's photograph, and the similarity of his own slight bodily frame to Gandhi's makes the photograph eerily similar to its iconic original.

Spinning a thread between the light and the earth/1946, India, from the series *A Requiem*, 2010
Gelatin silver print, 90 × 120 cm

Cafe Window, Ladysmith, Wisconsin, 1989
7th Up, Soda Advertisement, Udaipur, Rajasthan, 1996
Gelatin silver prints, 24.2 × 31.8 cm each

Lewis Koch
b. United States, 1949

Working around traces of text in unlikely places, Lewis Koch has developed his own powerful yet playful archive of images that document text in its many iterations: as language, as shape, as form, but also as unhinged from any context or referent. In his lifelong consideration of text in relation to the ephemeral, the ubiquitous and the democratic qualities it possesses, Koch also displays his work in unlikely sites, such as garages, or pasted onto billboards and kiosks, as well as in galleries and museums worldwide. Signage for Koch therefore becomes a vehicle of viewing outside of contextual or predetermined expectations. In his images, words such as "Dream" or "Yes" float in unlikely worlds, transplanted from typical contexts in his images to form something much more confounding. In his work in India, Koch provides a humorous glance at the country's particular culture of text and sign. In *7th Up* – a slippage between names of two popular soda drinks – he captures the specificity of the English sign in India, where the painters of public notices are often non-English speakers and therefore address text purely in the realm of the visual, as a set of inexplicable symbols. Unlike other international photographers who sought to capture the regional specificity of India in their respective practices, Koch's work reveals a decided turn away from the local, instead demonstrating a universalising tendency in his picturing of the country. Koch's work features in permanent collections throughout the world, including the Metropolitan Museum of Art in New York, the Maison Européenne de la Photographie in Paris, the Museum for Fotokunst/Brandts in Odense, the Staatsgalerie Stuttgart, the Whitney Museum of American Art in New York, the San Francisco Museum of Modern Art, and the Museum of Contemporary Art in Chicago.

Young Monk's Math Practice,
Upper Dharamsala, Himachal Pradesh, 1995
Gelatin silver print, 24.2 × 31.8 cm

Jitish Kallat

b. India, 1974

Jitish Kallat's work, both as artist and curator, traverses a range of media, including painting, photography, collage, sculpture and installation. Themes of time, death, life cycles, familial ancestry and celestial movements can frequently be found. In curator Ranjit Hoskote's words: "Jitish's work is about different scales of time, and this notion of scale is very important. His work is about cosmic time, geological time, the time it takes for galaxies to rise and fade."[1]

As Kallat's practice reconciles broader timescapes, such as celestial and civilisational time, with the time of the body, photography has proven to be a suitably mechanical vehicle for many of his more playful temporal investigations. Kallat is interested in the artistic potential of the quotidian – for instance, while curating the second edition of the Kochi-Muziris Biennale (2014), his attention to the apples that were served for his breakfast everyday led to *Sightings*, an almost microbiological investigation into fruit. Kallat noted: "When I came back, I started photographing all sorts of fruit, arranged side by side – apples, blueberries, and more. I was not just looking at the fruit, but the inversion of colour and the colours that it absorbs. If you peel off that colour, you might peel off the illusion. So, each time a viewer moves, he can go between the image of the world as we see it or the image we want it to be."[2] In a similar exploration of the archive and its grid-like clinical potential, Kallat's *Epilogue* (2010–11), a photographic collage made of thousands of partially eaten rotis in succession, captures each of the moons in his father's 62-year lifespan. An earlier work, *The Cry of the Gland* (2009), presents an overwhelming grid of men's breast pockets, each laden with the marks and weight of white-collar labour. The actual scale of the work is overwhelming, towering over the viewer. Its reproduction of a multitude of breast pockets becomes an almost synaesthetic phenomenon, invoking the weight of the pocket, the smell of the body and the surrounding noise of the city.

Detail from *Epilogue*, 2010–11
C-type print, 28 × 35.5 cm

The Cry of the Gland, 2009
C-type prints, 61 × 45.7 cm each, installation 358 × 820 cm

V GHNAHARTA
M.S. ALLoys
CAR DRIVER
E.S.S.

Vivan Sundaram
b. British India, 1943

Over a long career, artist Vivan Sundaram has produced work in many different media, including painting, photography, installation and video art. He studied painting at the Faculty of Fine Arts, Baroda, and the Slade School, London, where he was heavily engaged in a turbulent moment of student politics and anti-Vietnam War protest. In the early 1970s, after his return to India, Sundaram continued to be involved in the student movement and politics in New Delhi. There he was also among a group of then-emerging artists who advocated local and indigenous modernist techniques through the visual language of figurative narration.

Experimentation with alternative media led Sundaram to shift away from painting in 1991, and with the project *Collaboration/Combines*, displayed at Gallery Chemould in 1992, Sundaram became one of the first artists in India to work with installation art. Over the years his practice has remained concerned with social issues and ideas of perception, memory and history. In 2001–02 Sundaram began the photomontage and video project *Re-take of Amrita* – manipulating photographs of his aunt, the iconic painter Amrita Sher-Gil, taken by Umrao Singh (see p. 75), Sher-Gil's father and Sundaram's grandfather. The consequent series, which produces a sense of intended chaos and time in its reproduction of several renditions of Sundaram's family members in a single frame, explores issues of pre-existing artistic agency, familial relationships and the nuances of authorial vision as they are passed down from grandfather to aunt to the artist himself. Drawing from the Sher-Gil Archive, which Sundaram created in 1995–96, the series also engages with the afterlife of photography in its rich hetero-temporality.

Lovers, from the series *Re-take of Amrita*, 2001
Pigment print, 38 × 53 cm

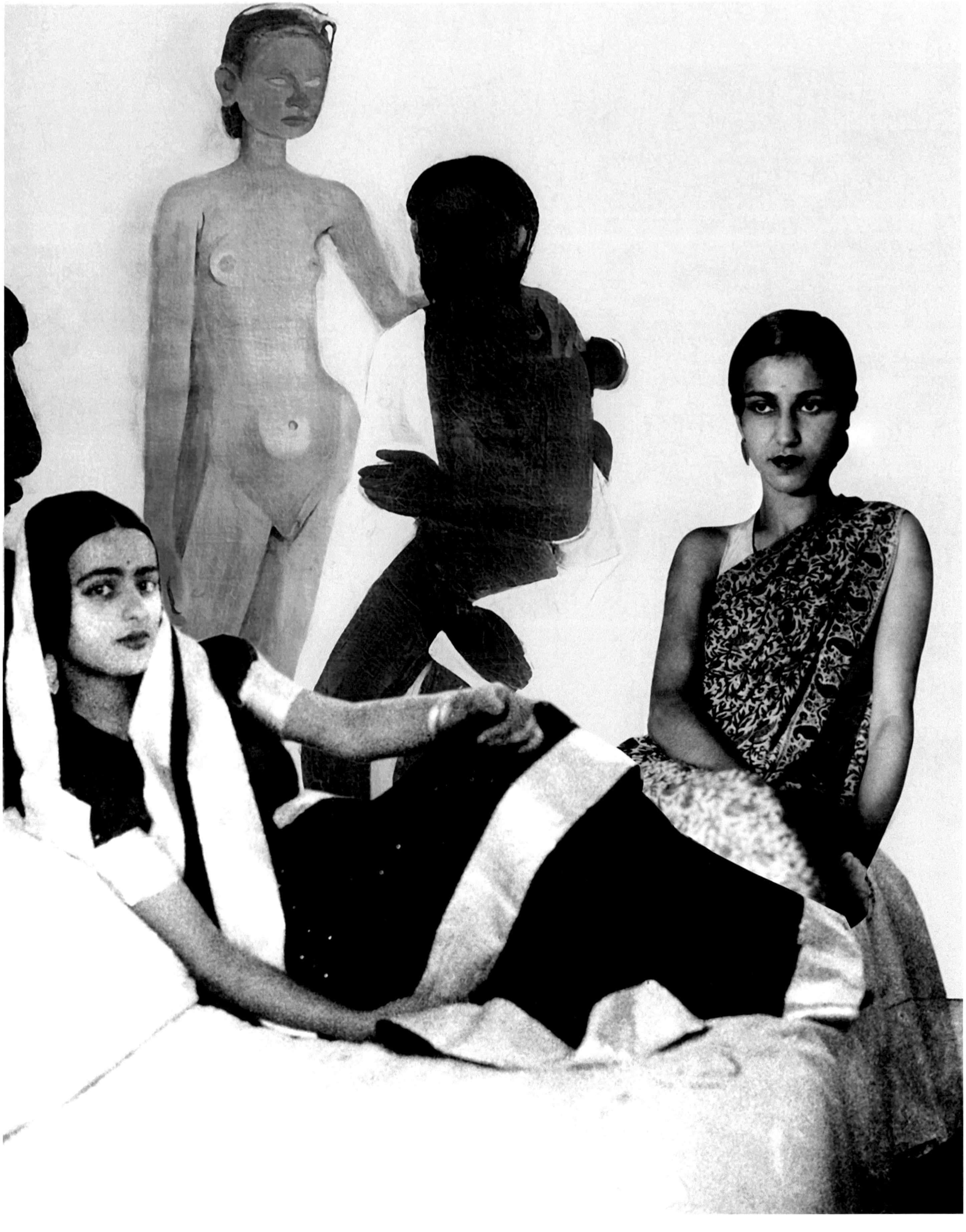

Sisters with "Two Girls", from the series *Re-take of Amrita*, 2001
Pigment print, 56 × 38 cm

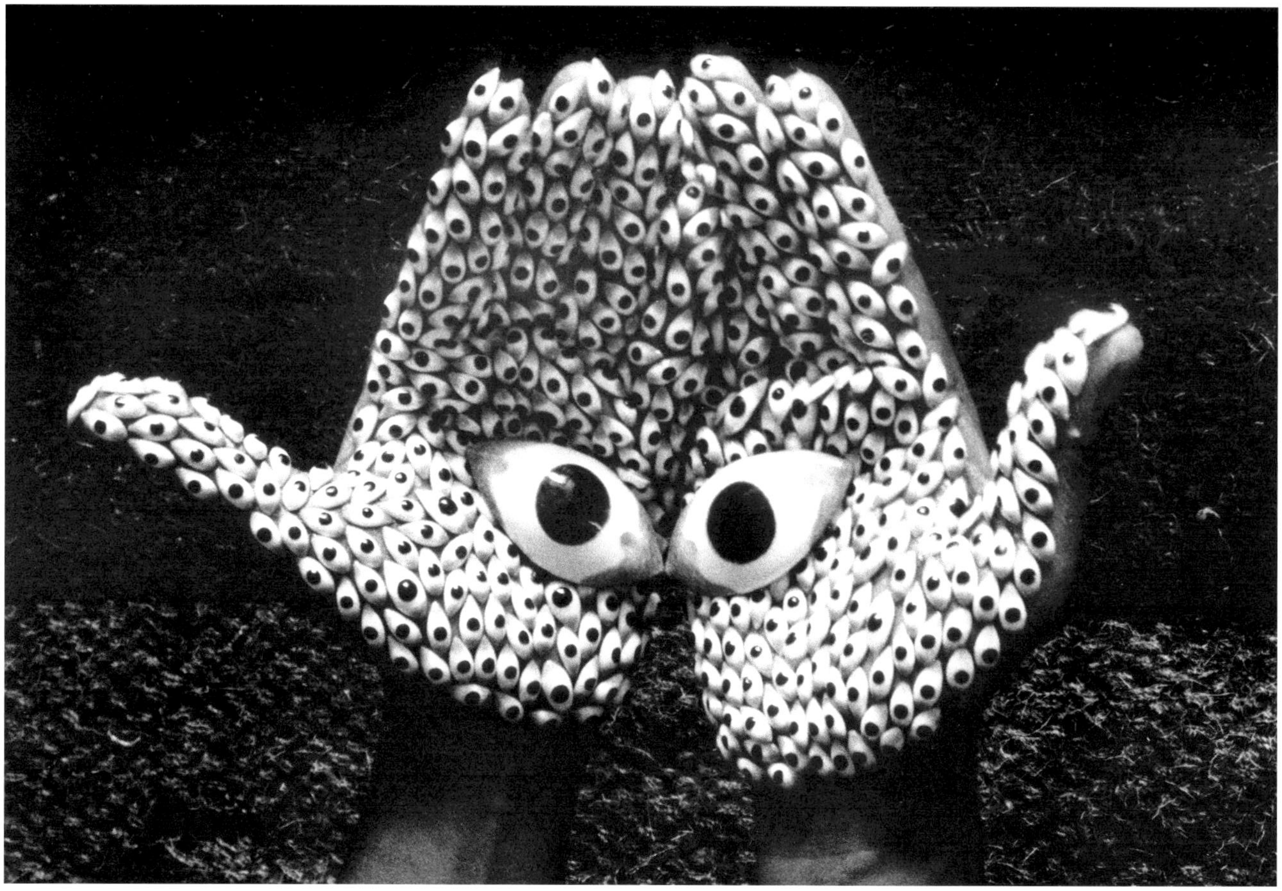

Offering, 2002–07
Gelatin silver prints, 40 × 62 cm each

Anita Dube
b. India, 1958

Anita Dube, whose work ranges from video to installation to performance art, is known for the political nature of her artistic practice, engaging with issues of territory, state control and the confrontation of the Indian state with queer erotics and desire. She graduated from the University of Delhi in 1979 before completing an MFA in Art Criticism at the renowned Faculty of Fine Arts, Maharaja Sayajirao University of Baroda, which she completed in 1982. Her participation in the Radical Painters and Sculptors Association in Baroda led her to produce a manifesto that denounced the commodification of Indian art and what the group saw to be the political impotence of Baroda's previous generation of figurative painters. Her engagement with the association left its mark on her artistic practice, leading her to use industrial materials, found objects and "readymades" in her work – these range from Styrofoam and beads to the many ceramic eyes (usually affixed to devotional imagery). Dube's work has been exhibited widely, including at the KHOJ International Artists' Association, Kiran Nadar Museum of Art in New Delhi, the Walker Art Center in Minneapolis, Centre Georges Pompidou in Paris, Museo Rufino Tamayo in Mexico CIty, and at the Havana Biennial.

For the photographs in the series *Offering* (2000–07), Dube created intricate images out of ceramic eyes – here planted onto human hands in the hundreds – allowing them to morph with the movement of the hands into forms that are both monstrous and devotional, capable equally of affixing their gaze on the viewer and of flowing in river-like forms. Dube describes her work with eyes as being like people, and therefore representative of the ebb and flow of human migration.

Sea Creature, 2002–07
Pigment print, 151.1 × 113.3 cm

Olivier Culmann
b. France, 1970

Olivier Culmann studied photography at the Ecole Supérieure de Réalisation Audiovisuelle (ESRA) in Paris and in 1992 began working as a photographer. In 1996 he joined Tendance Floue, a photographers' collective whose objective is to explore the world and diversify the modes of representation in contemporary photography. Culmann's photographic practice works towards undoing the assumptions of indexicality and authenticity with which the photographic medium is constantly constrained: "I appreciate the photographic medium for its subjective aspect. Photography never gives a real image of the world – it is always a proposition of a particular vision on reality. And that's what I appreciate every time I discover a new photographic work: the singular subjective vision of someone."[1] Discussing his project in India, *The Others*, he notes: "As most photographers, I used to go to some other countries with my own photographic style and skills, and bring back home pictures of the people living in those countries. For this project, I decided to reverse the process: I came to live in India, I adopted a practice that was not mine and I came back home without any pictures of Indian people. By reproducing on myself the appearance of the people, I have brought back only what I could see and catch of Indian society. But, in a way, isn't it what photographers always do?"[2] The photographic series has not shied away from controversy in its premise – in which Culmann adorns himself in the garb of popularly identifiable figures in India (the civil servant, the Punjabi athlete, the sage, even erstwhile Prime Minister Manmohan Singh) in local photo studios, taking advantage of the lurid backdrops that these spaces provided to his performance. In other stages of the project, Culmann gives photographs of himself to digital photo studios that paste his head onto the templates of bodies and backdrops that exist ever ready in their collections; presents damaged or torn photographs of himself for the studios to fix, creating bizarre results; and approaches local painters to create portraits of him based on his photographs. The resultant project is a light-hearted testament to the ingenuities and inventiveness of the Indian photographic studios with whom Culmann collaborates.

Untitled, Phase 1, 2009–13
Pigment print, 100 × 100 cm

Untitled, Phase 1, 2009–13
Pigment print, 100 × 100 cm

10 The Book & the Biennale

To write about photography in its present moment denies that most useful lens of hindsight on which much of this book has been dependent. Unlike the photographic practices of Pushpamala N. and Annu Palakunnathu Matthew, the photographers we address here seem to have been freed from the legacy of colonialism in representation, instead focusing on the possibilities of a new, diffused, international aesthetic.

Bodies of work such as Michael Bühler-Rose's series *Constructing the Exotic* (2006–2010), *Camphor Flames on a Pedestal* (2010), and *Removing the Evil Eye* (2010–2013), although rich in their visual references to the rituals of Hinduism, find new visual modes in which to situate their subjects. In doing so his work locates itself in a larger, more global aesthetic in contemporary photography than the regional specificities of subcontinental practice. As Meenakshi Thirukode has argued, to view Bühler-Rose's images in the series *Constructing the Exotic* purely from the lens of "a white male artist continuing the Orientalist fixation of the 'other'" would paint an all-too-simple picture of what is in fact a product of sustained transcultural exchange.[1] Bühler-Rose, as is the case with his photographic subjects, joined the Hare Krishna movement, proceeding to work at many Hindu temples in the United States during young adulthood. He chose to photograph the women of the same faith who were, like him, situated between two spaces – the West, to which they belonged, and India and Hinduism, to which they had pledged spiritual allegiance. He makes apparent the state of in-betweenness that is at work in the series, as young white women are perfectly adorned in South Indian silk saris and jewellery, pictured in the suburban terrain of Alachua, Florida. Reading across his practice reveals a plural endeavour that ranges between images of these young Indophiles, and other, more clinical photographs – shot with blank clarity – of the objects and instruments that are indispensable to Hindu rituals, such as turmeric, a coconut, and of a knot of holy grass. The photographer creates a vocabulary in his engagement with *Camphor Flame on a Pedestal* that is entirely his own, at once reckoning with documentarian and diaristic visual modes. The uniform nature of the work, the manner in which its variations unfold in part due to the uncontrollable, unpredictable nature of flame, derives its references elsewhere, more from the straight, flat portraits of the Düsseldorf School of photography than any previous engagement with Hinduism in photographic practice.

Other practices mobilise staged photographs in order to make apparent the camera's presence in the photographic scene. In his series *The Fourth Wall*, Belgian photographer Max Pinckers draws on the aesthetic of 1970s Bollywood films to create highly dramatised, brightly lit depictions of Mumbai's residents as they enact scenes inspired by film billboards and advertisements. Drawing his viewers' attention to how everyday life in India so often is derived from cinema itself, and vice versa, the series steadily grew into Pinckers' own fictional narrative in his deliberate departure from the visual tropes of social documentary. The series is rich with scenes of male bravado, conspiring gangs, and determined policemen; these photographs are in turn interspersed with newspaper articles capturing the outrageous and dramatic nature of Mumbai (such as a Goya painting mysteriously turning up in the house of a property broker, or a young girl running away from home to meet the celebrity Salman Khan). The photographs, oscillating between the imaginary and the hyperreal, pose the notion that in a city such as Mumbai the "fourth wall" (separating a theatrical scene from reality) is constantly on the verge of breaking. In these many bodies of work the photographers appear to reconcile the possibilities of photography with fiction, either a fiction that is the photographer's own (as in the case of Pinckers) or in a conversation with literature or folklore (as with photographers such as Karen Knorr and Gauri Gill). Pinckers shows a steady engagement with the question of photography's relation to reality as he plays upon the hyperreal in his compositional constructions. And younger practitioners like him find the reinforcement of a division between the viewer and the scene to be a productive means of image-making. This is similarly the case in Gauri Gill's series *Acts of Appearance*, where the use of papier mâché masks reinforces elements of theatricality and performance before the lens, as well as in Cristina de Middel's *The Perfect Man*, which mobilises one Indian town's adoration of Charlie Chaplin in order to create a series that comments on labour and the achievement of the self at work and at play.

This dance around documentary that appears in newer elements of photographic practice in and around India is evidenced throughout the series shown in this chapter. What seems to be at work in a number of practices is documentary that stretches the possibility of document, expanding out of the sociocultural concerns of the news magazine image and into the gallery space; a documentary form that expands to the real and imagined visual concerns of the photographer. Sohrab Hura's series *The Coast* also speaks to the boundaries between the real and the imaginary, beginning with a short story, titled "The Lost Head and the Bird", that sets the tone for his photographic project. Unfolding as a multi-platform video work, the series is sinister and dreamlike, with views of religious extremism and social deviance that appear on the edge of frenzy. In all these cases we witness a liberation from what previously anchored photography in its own specificity: time, fact, geographies all collapse into each other, while photographers search out new props in their visual modes, such as text, found objects and installations.

Finally, a number of these threads and patterns of contemporary Indian image-making – the role of the narratorial voice, the use of text, and the fact that photography now occupies a middle space between reality and the artist's own deliberate construction of reality – are precisely what have dissolved the distinctions between its own regional specificity and the artistic concerns of photography in the world at large. In a globalised art world, to speak of the specifically Indian is now passé; this is certainly the case with such photographers as Taryn Simon, whose photographic series *A Living Man Declared Dead and Other Chapters I–XVIII* turns to Indian subject matter incidentally as part of a larger concern with the bureaucracy of death and its manifestations the world over.

In a now decade-old essay reviewing photographic exhibitions in Delhi, Alexander Keefe wrote of a particular challenge to Indian photography in the early twenty-first century: "At a time when young Indian painters and installation artists are increasingly dependent upon digital media and software ... photographers are struggling to carve out a separate space for their chosen medium, even as its once secure boundaries dissolve."[2] Keefe's assessment of photography's envelopment by other art practices is equally true today. When photography has moved so far away from itself, and further and further into the realm of contemporary art practice, one wonders whether the medium is moving rapidly towards its own dissolution.

In battling this translation of the medium into contemporary art practice, there has been a return to older forms of photographic affiliation, where a resurgence of the photobook embraces and highlights the idiosyncrasies of the photographic medium. Some of Dayanita Singh's more recent projects, such as *Sent a Letter*, *File Room* and *Museum Bhavan*, for example, collapse the museum and the displayable photograph into the pages of a book whilst equally rendering the photobook displayable. In purchasing *Museum Bhavan*, for example, the viewer is invited to become curator of Singh's photographs, forming their own arrangements and combinations of display out of the nine volumes of photographs that the larger "museum" contains. A number of these works are taken from across a larger breadth of Singh's oeuvre, but it is the photograph's return to the printed page, to the album or book, that sustains and revives it in a new avatar. That India is now less the source of identity than it is of subject matter is also witnessed in the work of Dayanita Singh, who states that she is not an Indian photographer, nor, in that case, a photographer at all.

1 Meenakshi Thirukode, 'Construction of the Exotic', in: *Whitewall*, October 1, 2009.
2 Alexander Keefe, 'Someone Clicked the Shutter: Indian photography on display in Delhi, 2007–2008', in: *Camerawork Delhi* 1, no. 4 (June 2008), p. 1.

Chandra and Kalyani, from the series *Constructing the Exotic*, 2007
C-type print, 137.2 × 111.8 cm

Michael Bühler-Rose
b. United States, 1980

A member of the Hare Krishna movement since the age of 14, Michael Bühler-Rose studied Sanskrit and philosophy in India over a number of years and is today an ordained Hindu priest. He graduated with a BFA from Tufts University and an MFA from the University of Florida in 2008. He has taught at the Rhode Island School of Design as well as the Cooper Union in New York. These are the diversities (or contradictions) of Bühler-Rose's identity that come together in his photographic practice. In the series *Constructing the Exotic*, he engages with elements of Hinduism and its American followers as a means of addressing issues of cross-cultural inflection, identity, and belonging. Young women who are second-generation followers of the Hare Krishna movement are shown in traditional Indian attire in compositions that make conscious reference to the paintings of Raja Ravi Varma, although here captured in Florida. The photographer creates what are at first glance incongruous images, in order for the viewer to reconsider the very terms of that incongruity. In *Evil Eye Removal* and *Camphor Flame on a Pedestal*, the pared-down compositions recast the splendour of Hindu religious ceremonies in almost clinical form, shedding the context that makes the objects meaningful by presenting them in wonderfully disorienting ways.

Untitled, from the series *Camphor Flames on Pedestal*, 2010
Untitled, from the series *Removing the Evil Eye*, 2010
C-type prints, 50.8 × 40.6 cm each

Karen Knorr
b. (West) Germany, 1954

Whilst a student at the University of Westminster in the mid-1970s, Karen Knorr began producing work that addressed emerging debates in cultural studies and film theory concerning the politics of representation. Her work typically investigates and questions normative political, economic and gendered representations in a number of global contexts. Over the course of her career Knorr has developed a critical and playful dialogue with documentary photography in series such as *Belgravia* (1979–81), *Country Life* (1983–85) and *Academies* (1994–2005), using a range of different visual and textual strategies. Through these series, Knorr has examined issues of power that underlie cultural heritage, looking at the privileged rather than the disenfranchised. This is a principal theme of later series such as *Fables* (2003–08), *India Song* (2008–) or *Monogatari* (2012–) in which Knorr uses manipulated image-making processes in order to question the assumption of indexicality, puncturing spaces and meanings through unexpected and unnatural juxtapositions.

Knorr began the *India Song* series in 2008. The work takes inspiration from predominantly Hindu mythology, exploring cultural heritage, Western appreciation and/or appropriation of Eastern culture and form, and the Indian tradition of representing and personifying animals in literature and art. Examining the past and its relationship to India's contemporary heritage sites, these photographs particularly explore Rajput and Mughal visual cultures and their relationship to questions of feminine subjectivity and animality.

In her work with animals which makes up the broader *Transmigrations* series, Knorr combines two or more different photographs in the same frame – the animals and the architectural interiors – which produces an uncanny tension, disrupting reality towards a magical realism favoured by storytellers and folk tales. In doing so, her photographs present a blended universe of fiction and reality, which she examines in European and Indian cultural contexts, typically underlined by power structures, imperialism and transculturalism.

The Passage, Villa Savoye, 2003–08
Pigment print, 122 × 152.4 cm

Light of the World, Zenana Room, Nawalgarh, 2008
Pigment print, 121.9 × 152.4 cm

Max Pinckers
b. Belgium, 1988

Max Pinckers's work challenges the confines and concerns of documentary photography, using highly staged photographs in an attempt to explore the popular mythologies and narratives which dominate our contemporary experience of the world. In 2011, Pinckers produced *Lotus* during the course of which he was to establish a working method and aesthetic that would lead the way for future series made in India, including his critically acclaimed books *The Fourth Wall* (2012) and *Will They Sing Like Raindrops or Leave Me Thirsty* (2014). A proponent of the photobook form, Pinckers also founded the independent publishing house Lyre Press in 2015.

Pinckers is particularly interested in visual language and the intersections between documentary, fine art and popular image vocabularies. His aesthetic resists photographic conventions, instead creating a distinctive voice with its precise nature and its interlinking of rhythms, lines and colours. Fusing fictional narratives with a documentary structure, his photographs may be read as situated between conceptual and documentary photography, while upending the expectations of both.[1] In *Will They Sing Like Raindrops or Leave Me Thirsty*, for instance, Pinckers simultaneously employs newspaper cuttings, classified ads and studio portraits alongside his own highly staged photographs and abstract images in order to create a series that heightens and makes apparent a representation of love and romance that is informed by Bollywood and popular literature.

Of the work *She Will Use the Birds*, from *The Fourth Wall* (2012), Pinckers explains that it is "a visual interpretation of a passage from Suketu Mehta's book *Maximum City: Bombay Lost and Found*. The passage describes an encounter between a dancing girl and her client, who go on their first date. The dancer invites the man into a taxi, buys a flock of songbirds from a near by street vendor, and lets them flutter around in the car. She then asks him to play a game with her: catch the birds. This quickly turns into a flirtatious exercise of touching, gasps, laughter and giggles. When reading stories like this one, it is in the instant imagination of a visual narrative that I find my satisfaction – where my subjects also play out their own fantasies, which are then left open for the viewer to form their own interpretation of the scene."

She Will Use the Birds, 2012
Pigment print, 71.1 × 81.3 cm

Dreams, 2012
Paradise Lost and Regained, 2012
Pigment prints, 81.3 × 71.1 cm each

Sohrab Hura
b. India, 1981

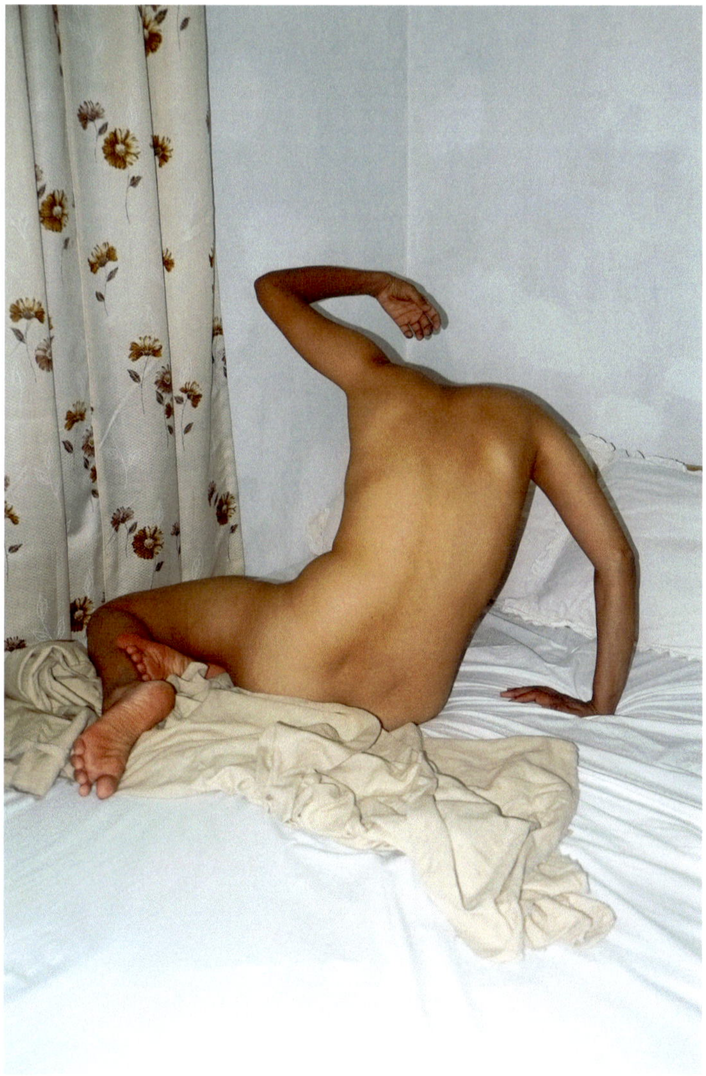

Following on from his early work, which explored rural strife and access to food in India (such as in the series *The Land of a Thousand Struggles*, 2005), Hura became increasingly interested in his own internal psychological unease. It was in part this return to the personal that drove Hura to photograph his mother, who had been diagnosed with schizophrenia, in the photobook *Life is Elsewhere* (2005). As Hura commented in an interview: "I think it's always easier to photograph someone else's misery and not one's own, and I didn't want to feel like a hypocrite. It was important for me to photograph someone close to me I could be accountable to."[1] *Life is Elsewhere* unfolds as a series of seemingly unrelated snapshots, all in a hazy monotone, that in their seeming randomness appear to mirror the sensation of instability and disorientation in the viewer. Hura's subsequent projects form an enquiry into how photography can explore and project a space of discomfort in contemporary society.

Hura's objectives are further explored in the ongoing series *The Coast* (2017–). The project unfolds as a synesthetic cacophony of abrasive images in a set of constantly changing diptychs. Each image is a snapshot, taken and added to the ever-changing slide show seemingly at random, mostly presenting views from the margins of society. Cast together, the photographs are simultaneously euphoric and disturbing, possessing a distinctively uneasy quality. Hura's use of violent flash brings to mind the work of Roger Ballen, and in its use of glaring colour is reminiscent of Mary Ellen Mark's *Falkland Road* series (see p. 222). The images are intended to disturb even as they delight, implicating the viewer simultaneously as witness and voyeur. It speaks to a wider moment in Indian photography that, departing from the more literal genre of social documentary, reflects a turn into one's own internal mind.

ABOVE AND FOLLOWING PAGES
Untitled, from the series *The Coast*, 2014
Various media and dimensions

Nishant Shukla
b. England, 1982

Born in Liverpool, Nishant Shukla studied photography at Thames Valley University in London. In 2016 he won the Alkazi Photobook Grant, through which he produced the photobook Seeking Moksha. It captures Shukla's own path to the source of the river Ganga, where he collected holy water for the funeral rites of his grandfather. Reading across Shukla's images reveals a documentation project that includes images of the holy men who inhabit sacred parts of the Himalayas, and photographs – shot with an almost microscopic clarity – of stained, crinkled pieces of paper with talismanic writing, of fossil rocks, of a branch of a young sycamore tree. Shukla creates a vocabulary in the Himalayas that is entirely his own, at once reckoning with documentarian and diaristic visual modes. The uniform nature of the work, the manner in which its variations unfold in part due to the particularities and postures of the men in each photograph, derives its visual references more from the straight, flat portraits of the Düsseldorf School of Photography than the (much earlier) preoccupations of Samuel Bourne (see p. 63) in similar Indian terrain, and in turn infusing the starkness of his photography with a clear narrative that unfolds through the work. In doing so his work locates itself in a larger, more global aesthetic in contemporary photography than the regional specificities of subcontinental practice. Alongside his photographic practice, Shukla is one of the founding members of BIND, a platform based in Mumbai that hosts projects and exhibitions of photography, as well as a permanent library of photobooks.

Sundaranand, Gangotri, 2011
Lambda C-print, 61 × 50.8 cm

Kissing Mountains, Gangotri, 2015
Lambda C-print, 61 × 50.8 cm
Unidentified Stem, Gangotri, 2016
Lambda C-print, 30.5 × 25.4 cm
Himalayan Stone #3, Gomukh, 2015
Lambda C-print, 30.5 × 25.4 cm
Nomi Giri, Gangotri, 2013
Lambda C-print, 61 × 50.8 cm

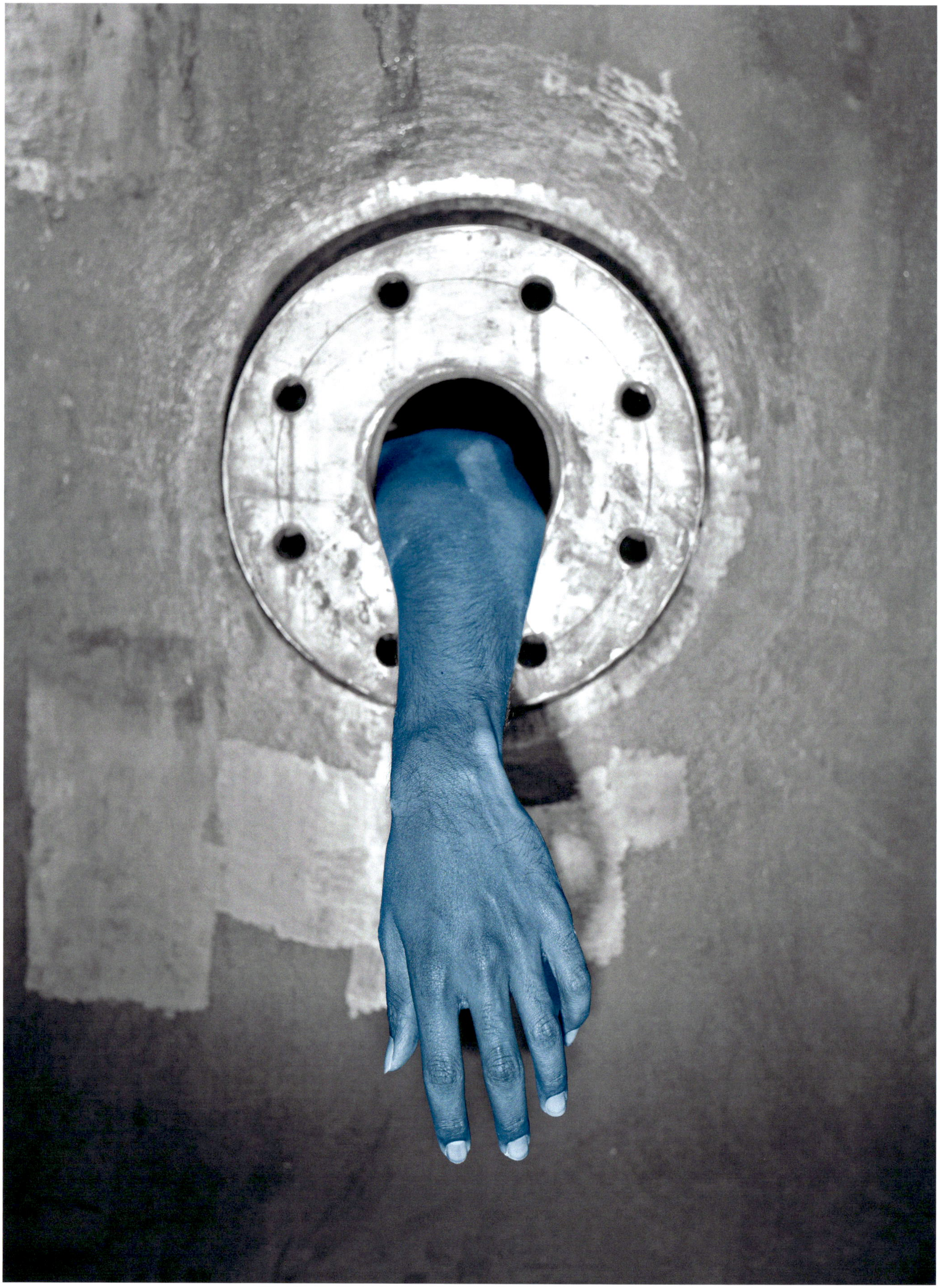

Kidake, from the series *The Perfect Man*, 2016
C-type print (overpainted), 90 × 66 cm

Cristina de Middel
b. Spain, 1975

Despite training as a war correspondent, which led to a ten-year career in photojournalism, Cristina de Middel's more recent work has shown a consistent interest in the photograph's difficult status as an instrument of truth-telling. Her 2012 project *The Afronauts* explored the instance of a failed space program in Zambia, using highly staged re-enactments that harked back to a fleeting moment of techno-optimism in decolonising Africa.

In *The Perfect Man* (2017), de Middel turned her attention to a small town in India where, due to the efforts of Dr Ashok Ashwani, there is now an annual festival of Charlie Chaplin impersonators. Departing from this unlikely resurrection of a long-dead British comedian in India, de Middel photographs the impersonators at work, using the industrial backdrops of the factory as a space within which to situate them in often humorous juxtapositions. The series is completed in monotone except for the use of a commercial blue paint over the subjects' skin, heightening a sense of cold mechanisation in the images but also furthering the photographs' own surreal, theatrical rigging. The series' highly staged and conversational tone comments on photography as a broader exploration of performance and self-fashioning. That Charlie Chaplin was both a figure of comedy and of capitalist critique is the central conceit that informs the series, as de Middel reconciles the cold, bleak spaces of industry with subversive humour. The title of the series, aside from invoking the tone of Chaplin's own film titles, also refers to Ashok Ashwani who, in turning to impersonation, rejected the expectations of the perfect labouring man.

Samani, from the series *The Perfect Man*, 2016
C-type print (overpainted), 90 × 66 cm

From the artist's book *Early Times*, 2016
from the series *A Myth of Two Souls*

Vasantha Yogananthan
b. France, 1985

Born in France to a Sri Lankan family, Vasantha Yogananthan has spent several years working in the field of book-making and editing. He considers the photobook to be his primary medium for research into original narrative approaches, first producing his critically acclaimed photobook *Piémanson* (2014), which documented the camping families who flock to France's last wild beach for their summer holidays, and now working on his ambitious seven-volume book project, *A Myth of Two Souls* (ongoing since 2013), which is mostly set it India.

A Myth of Two Souls is an exploration and reconceptualisation of the Hindu epic, the *Ramayana*, that brings together many different histories, timelines, spaces and aesthetic styles. When Yogananthan first visited India in 2013, he began to comprehend the pervasiveness of the epic and the complicated layering of history, religious mythology, local folklore and everyday life that collapse into each other in the tale's many tellings and retellings. In an interview with the *British Journal of Photography*, he noted: "I realised the distinction between truth and falsehood wasn't important. This was an important discovery for me, that this is where my photographs should lie – in this in-between world between physical reality and the imagined."[1]

The project blends landscape images and street scenes with staged portraits, combining monochromatic "found" photographs, subdued colour photographs, as well as hand-painted photographs, and uses illustrations and local material, such as excerpts from the adaptation of the *Ramayana* for the Indian comic book series *Amar Chitra Katha*. He explains further: "I have this question that I ask the people I photograph: "Is the *Ramayana* a true story?' People say very different things. The story occurs in real places – Ayodhya, Hampi, Adam's Bridge – and I was interested in the way the physical world interacts with the fictional." [2]

In *Longing for Love*, shown here, Yogananthan succeeds in invoking various possible motifs in the *Ramayana* simultaneously. On the one hand, the negotiation between the young girl and the water as she draws in the fishing nets brings to mind the initial struggle by Lord Ram and his monkey army to conquer the ocean in order to cross to Lanka. On the other, the photograph is also strangely prophetic or prescient – the tightly bound nets seemingly referring to the muscular tail of the monkey-god Hanuman, which he uses to set the island of Lanka alight after he finds the abducted princess Sita.

Longing for Love, Danushkodi, Tamil Nadu, from the series *A Myth of Two Souls*, 2018
Pigment print, 81 × 65.5 cm

11. Yadav, Rajendra (यादव, राजेंद्र), ~41 (birth date unknown)
Mechanic, Jalandhar, Punjab, India

12. Yadav, Dabloo (यादव, डबलू), ~11 (birth date unknown)
Student, Jalandhar, Punjab, India
[Emergency/70 homes destroyed in village fire, including grandmother's]

22. Yadav, Amit (यादव, अमित), ~4 (birth date unknown)
Student, Masuriapur, Uttar Pradesh, India
[Participation not permitted for religious and social reasons]

23. Yadav, Santra (यादव, संतरा), ~21 (birth date unknown)
Homemaker, Nahroompur, Uttar Pradesh, India
[Participation not permitted for religious and social reasons]

I

While visiting the local land registry office, Shivdutt Yadav (1) discovered that official records listed him as dead. His land was no longer registered in his name. Yadav's two brothers, Chandrabhan (18) and Phoolchand (19), and their first cousin, Ram Surat (a), were also listed as dead. Land registry records documented the transfer of Yadav's property to his father's other living heirs, allowing them to inherit his share of the family's ancestral farmland. These relatives reportedly threatened to destroy the family home on the property unless it was vacated immediately.

In Uttar Pradesh, India, land provides the primary source of income for most residents. Exponential population growth, property shortages, and repeated subdivision have heightened competition for land. Records officials are frequently bribed to have living people declared dead in order to redirect the hereditary transfer of land to new owners. These bribes commonly range from 45 to 2,250 INR (1 to 50 USD).

Yadav, his brothers, and his first cousin have been trying to reverse land registry records and regain legal status as living owners and heirs. Several official letters, including some signed by village residents, were sent to local police and records officials supporting their claims. According to the Yadav family, the local court has been scheduling dates for a case review since 2001, but a judge has never appeared. Judicial delay is common in Uttar Pradesh due to corruption, backlogs, and a shortage of judges. In several instances, people have died before their cases were reviewed.

Yadav and his family vacated their home but still farm the contested land. The house is currently unoccupied.

Dayanita Singh
b. India, 1961

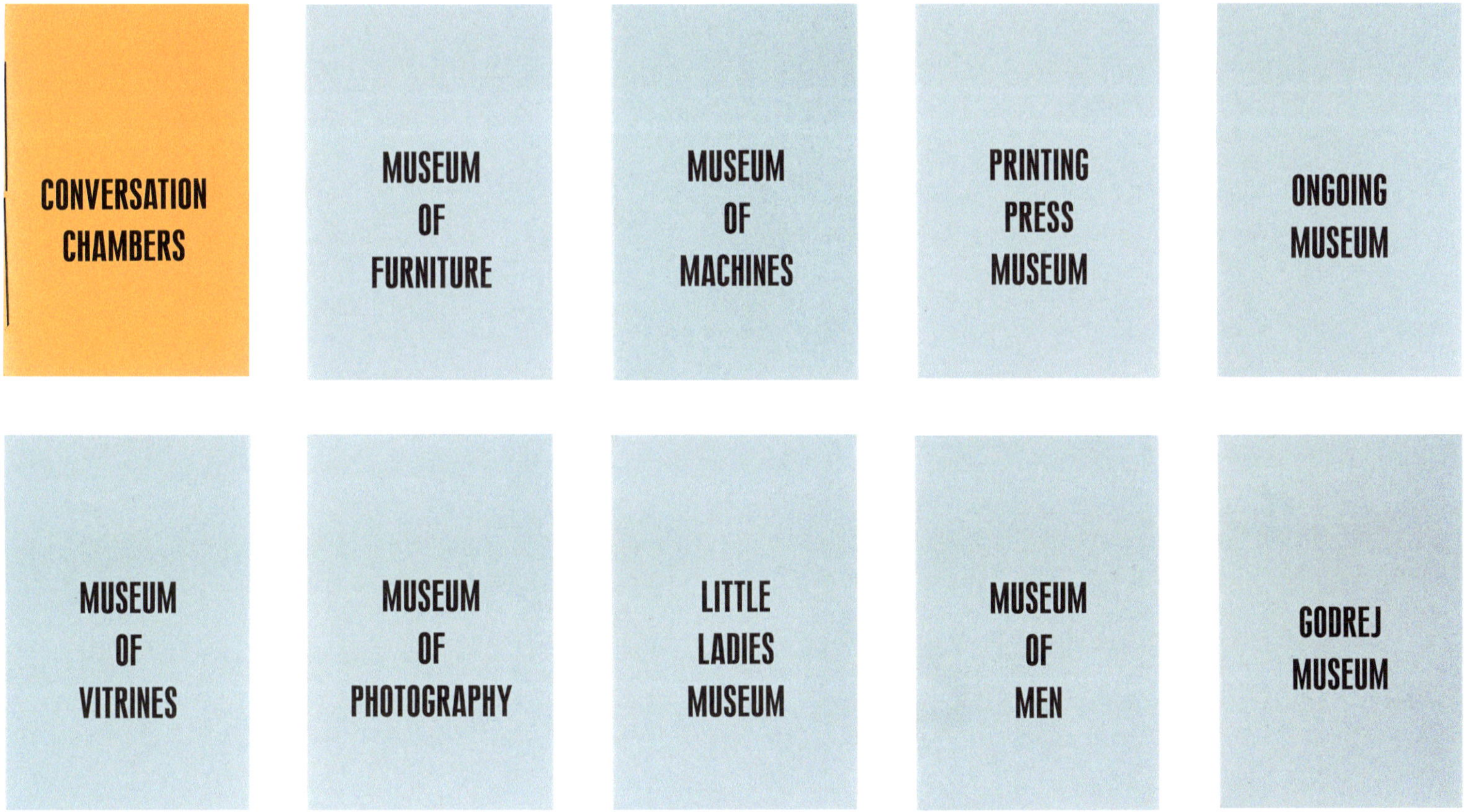

Dayanita Singh studied visual communication at the National Institute of Design, Ahmedabad, where her final project was the photobook *Zakir Hussain* (first published in 1986) in which she documented her time with the tabla maestro. After further studying the medium at the International Center of Photography in New York, Singh began working on the project *Myself Mona Ahmed* (2001), a book that follows the life, networks of community and family of Mona Ahmed, a transgender person who became a lifelong friend. Whilst originating from a photojournalistic tradition in this work, Singh resists relegating Ahmed to documentary condescension, instead producing a book that, in its combination of photographs and letters from Ahmed to the publisher, is deeply moving and reveals an interest in the medium of the book that Singh has revisited through her career. She subsequently moved away from photojournalism, instead focusing on members of her own social milieu. Her resulting practice has been a constant exercise in disrupting the borders by which photography is constantly constrained, testing the permeability of the photobook and the exhibition, and the tyranny of labels and categorisation, whilst inventing new modes of display and dissemination for the photograph.

Museum Bhavan (2017) is a further exploration of the photobook as an exhibition space, following from earlier projects *Sent a Letter* (2008), *File Room* (2010) and *Museum of Chance* (2015). By collapsing together the two modes in which photography is most traditionally received, Singh creates books that can produce the dual instinct to read and to behold. *Museum Bhavan* consists of nine volumes and a text, each its own museum, that unfold to reveal photographs from across Singh's career arranged in curious themes: the "Museum of Vitrines", for example, or the "Museum of Machines", each rich with time as decades-old images converse with those among Singh's newest. Returning the photograph to the book page, Singh reminds us, inevitably entails a return to the rich tactility, and often fragility, of the page. It restores the photograph's ability to be held, to be read and to be arranged ad infinitum, as Singh encourages the viewers to curate their own portable museum from the pages of the artwork.

***Museum Bhavan*, 2017**
Book objects, 13.6 × 9.2 cm each

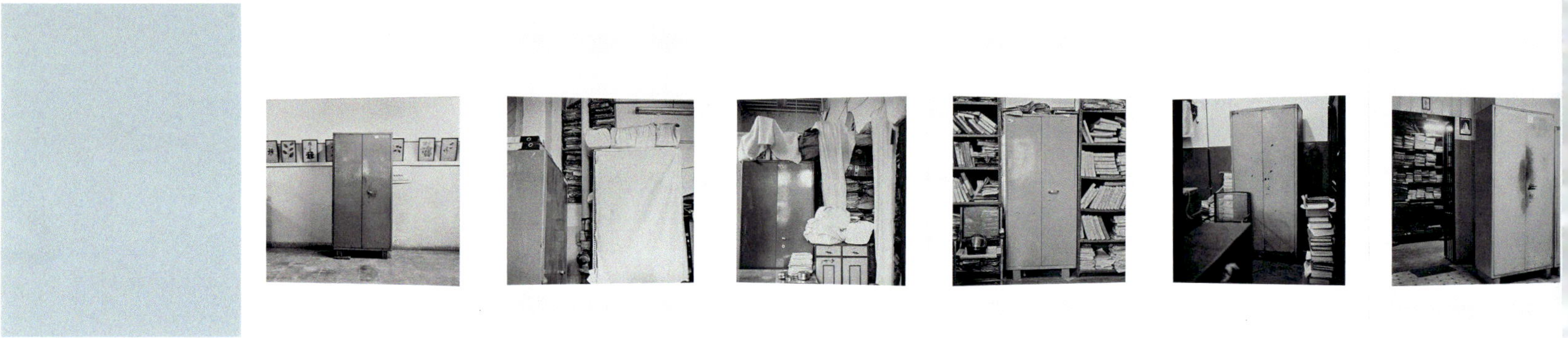

FROM TOP TO BOTTOM
Godrej Museum, 2017
Printing Press Museum, 2017
Museum of Photography, 2017
Book objects, 13.6 × 9.2 cm each (closed),
13.6 × 280.5 cm each (extended)

A Forest of Trees, 2015, from the series *Fields of Sight*, 2013–
Ink on pigment print, 61 × 40.6 cm

Gauri Gill
b. India, 1970

Born in Chandigarh in 1970, Gauri Gill studied painting and applied art at the College of Art, New Delhi, before she continued into a BFA in Photography at Parsons School of Design/The New School in New York and an MFA in Art Practice at Stanford University. Over the years, Gill's pursuit of photography has come to transcend the limitations of genre or geography. Whereas *Traces* (1999–) was conceived as a monochrome monument to the unmarked or bricolage graves she encountered in the Rajasthani desert, *The Americans* (2000–07) is captured in vivid colour on Gill's travels through vast parts of the American East and West Coasts, the Midwest and a number of southern states. Extending outward from her family and friends to complete strangers, it captures informal glances into the lives of the South Asian diaspora, while invoking Robert Frank's pivotal work of the same name which questioned national ideals half a century before. A survey of her work shows a sustained interest in the rural communities of Rajasthan that she has been visiting since 1999. The overarching title of the archive is *Notes from the Desert*, containing various sub-series within it. Her standpoint here varies between photographer, social activist and anthropologist. This is made most vivid in *Balika Mela* (2003 and 2010), one of the series for which Gill is best known, which was formed of a series of playful and often moving photographic collaborations between Gill and the girls and young women who visited her makeshift photo studio at a fair for rural girls held in western Rajasthan.

From 2013 onwards, whilst visiting the predominantly Adivasi district of Dahanu in Maharashtra, Gill began to collaborate with Warli painter Rajesh Vangad to create a monumental series of composite images that combine Gill's broad landscapes and Vangad's deftly drawn interpretations. What emerges from their collaboration is *Fields of Sight*, a series in which Gill's photographs of the land and rural life are continuously infused and resuscitated by local Vangad's overdrawings of the area's rich myths and his own personal history, creating works that oscillate between different times, media and visual languages. Gill's collaboration with local Adivasi artists from Maharashtra continues in *Acts of Appearance* (2015–). Here, she commissioned the brothers Subhas and Bhagvan Dharma Kadu, along with their extended families and several others belonging to a community of paper mâché artists, to create masks responding to contemporary realities in the village, across "dreaming and waking states". Created over three years, and after extensive dialogue, the masks ranged from animals and human figures to familiar objects, while incorporating particular emotions and moods. These masks were subsequently worn by a series of volunteer actors from the same community who would perform before the camera in fictional scenarios inspired by mundane reality. *In Acts of Appearance*, Gill poses the mask as possessing the potential to simultaneously conceal and reveal; now able to withhold their identity, her photographic subjects can perhaps be more candid about their everyday experiences and tribulations.

Building the City, 2016, from the series *Fields of Sight*, 2013–
Ink on pigment print, 40.6 × 61 cm

Untitled, from the series *Acts of Appearance*, 2015–
Untitled, from the series *Acts of Appearance*, 2015–
Pigment prints, 106.5 x 71.1 cm each

Untitled, from the series *Acts of Appearance*, 2015–
Pigment print, 153 × 101 cm

Endnotes

Archaeology & Ethnography

Saché & Westfield

1 Proceedings of the Asiatic Society of Bengal [November 1865], Calcutta 1886, p. 186. William Johnson.

Linnaeus Tripe

1 Roger Taylor and Larry J. Schaaf, Impressed by Light: British Photographs from Paper Negatives, 1840–1860, New York 2007, p. 384.
2 Ibid.
3 'Linnaeus Tripe: life and work', Victoria and Albert Museum, http://www.vam.ac.uk/content/articles/l/linnaeus-tripe-biography/.

Alexis de La Grange

1 See John Hannavy, ed., Encyclopedia of Nineteenth-Century Photography, New York and Oxon 2008, p. 47.

Nicholas & Curths

1 'Proceedings', in: Madras Journal of Literature and Science [April – September 1858], n.s. 4 (1858–59), p. 173.

Francis Frith & Co.

1 Maxim Leonid Weintraub, 'Francis Frith & C', in: Encyclopedia of Nineteenth-Century Photography, ed. John Hannavy, New York 2008, p. 560.
2 Lisa Hostetler, 'Francis Frith', International Center of Photography, https://www.icp.org/browse/archive/constituents/francis-frith?all/all/all/all/0.

John Marshall

1 Ambarin Afsar, 'Excavating the Past', in: Better Photography, 24 May 2011, http://betterphotography.in/perspectives/great-masters/excavating/1827/; and Sudeshna Guha, The Marshal Albums: Photography and Archaeology, The Alkazi Collection of Photography, New Delhi 2010.

William Johnson

1 'Johnson and Henderson', RCS Photographers Index, Cambridge University Library, http://www.lib.cam.ac.uk/rcs_photographers/entry.php?id=266.
2 'Photographs of Western India', Texas Archival Resources Online, https://legacy.lib.utexas.edu/taro/smu/00237/smu-00237.html.
3 Stuart Macmillan, 'Colonial Representations of British India: A Description and Analysis of the First Twenty-Four Issues of The Indian Amateur's Photographic Album', MA diss., Ryerson University, Toronto 2011.

Maurice Vidal Portman

1 Maurice Vidal Portman, in: Report on the administration of the Andaman and Nicobar Islands and the penal settlement of Port Blair for the year 1893–94, Calcutta.
2 'On things in general, regarding Port Blair, and photography', in: Journal of the Photographic Society of India 5, no. 11 (November 1892).
3 Quoted in: Report on the administration of the Andaman and Nicobar Islands and the penal settlement of Port Blair for the year 1892–93, Calcutta.

John Edward Saché

1 Hugh Ashley Rayner, John Saché: A Photographer in British India, 1864–1882, Somerset 2012.

Joseph Beglar

1 A. Cunningham, Preface to J. D. Beglar, Report of a Tour in Bundelkhand and Malwa, 1871–72; and the Central Provinces, 1873–74, Calcutta 1878, p. v.
2 Letter from J.D. Beglar, Officiating Executive Engineer, Burhee Division, to the Superintending Engineer, Western Circle, dated Bogodhur, 24 April 1869, enclosed with a memorandum sending the photographs on to the General Department of the Bengal Government. Bengal General Proceedings, no. 93 of May 1869.

Narayan Dajee

1 Journal of the Bombay Photographic Society, February – June 1856.
2 John Falconer, India: Pioneering Photographers 1850–1900. London 2001.
3 Journal of the Photographic Society of Bengal, no. 3, 20 May 1857, p. 68.

John Forbes Watson & John William Kaye

1 'Forbes Watson, John (1827–1892)', TCR Needles, 9 September 2017, https://trc-leiden.nl/trc-needles/people-and-functions/authors-scholars-and-activists/forbes-watson-john-1827-1892.
2 Quoted in Max Houghton, 'Book Spotlight: The People of India', in: Foto8, no. 26 (26 October 2009), p. 132.
3 See 'Lot 2093: Watson, John Forbes, and John William Kaye', Bonhams, https://www.bonhams.com/auctions/20048/lot/2093/.
4 Quoted in Houghton, 'The People of India', p. 132.
5 Christopher Pinney, The Coming of Photography in India, New Delhi 2008, pp. 41–49.

Pictorialism & the Picturesque

Samuel Bourne

1 Samuel Bourne, British Journal of Photography, 1863, cited in Ciaran Thaper, 'Early British Colonial Travellers Show Earliest Images of India', in: British Journal of Photography, 5 May 2016, http://www.bjp- online.com/about-british-journal-of-photography/.
2 John Falconer, India: Pioneering Photographers 1850–1900. London 2001. and Bourne & Shepherd: Figures in Time, Bangalore 2015.

A. T. W. Penn

1 'Penn, Albert Thomas Watson, 1849–1924, photographer', RCS Photographers Index, http://www.lib.cam.ac.uk/rcs_photographers/entry.php?id=373.
2 Amy Wilson Carmichael, cited in Christopher Penn, 'Rebuilding the Catalogue of Albert Thomas Watson Penn, the Leading Commercial Photographer in Ootacamund, 1875–1900', in: SAALG Newsletter, no. 3 (2008), p. 17.

John Murray

1 Ray Desmond, '19th century Indian photographers in India', in: History of Photography 1, no. 4 (1977), p. 314.
2 John Hannavy, Encyclopedia of Nineteenth-Century Photography, New York and London 2008, p. 529.
3 Roger Taylor and Larry John Schaaf, Impressed by Light: British Photographs from Paper Negatives, 1840–1860, New York et al. 2007; and John Falconer, India: Pioneering Photographers 1850–1900. London 2001.
4 Sophie Gordon, 'Monumental visions: architectural photography in India, 1840–1901', PhD diss., School of Oriental and African Studies, London, pp. 310.

Colin Murray

1 John Falconer, India: Pioneering Photographers 1850–1900. London 2001.

Frederick Fiebig

1 John Falconer, A Biographical Dictionary of 19th Century Photographers in South and South-East Asia.
2 Illustrated Indian Journal of Arts (Madras), 1852, p. 32.

Shapoor Bhedwar

1 Malavika Karlekar, 'A Parsi Pictorialist: Complex images and stylized models', in: The Telegraph, July 14, 2013, https://www.telegraphindia.com/1130714/jsp/opinion/story_17028654.jsp.

Umrao Singh Sher-Gil

1 Umrao Singh Sher-Gil: His Misery and His Manuscript, New Delhi 2008.

Julia Margaret Cameron

1 'Julia Margaret Cameron', Encyclopaedia Britannica, https://www.britannica.com/biography/Julia-Margaret-Cameron.
2 Marta Weiss, Julia Margaret Cameron: Photographs to electrify you with delight and startle the world, London 2015.

Power & Posterity

Robert Christopher Tytler

1 Roger Taylor and Larry J. Schaaf, Impressed by Light: British Photographs from Paper Negatives, 1840–1860, New York 2007.

J. W. Newland

1 Sydney Morning Herald, 14 March 1848.
2 'J. W. Newland: Artist (Photographer)', Design and Art Australia Online, 1992 (updated 2011), https://www.daao.org.au/bio/j-w-newland/biography/.
3 John Falconer, British Library. A Biographical Dictionary of 19th Century Photographers in South and South-East Asia.

Hurrichund Chintamon

1 'Persian group, Bombay. Photographer: Chintamon, Hurrichund, 1867', The British Library, Online Gallery, http://www.bl.uk/onlinegallery/onlineex/apac/photocoll/p/019pho001000s42u04338000.html.

Ahmad Ali Khan

1 John Falconer, India: Pioneering Photographers 1850–1900. London 2001.

Lala Deen Dayal

1 Deepali Dewan and Deborah Hutton, Raja Deen Dayal: Artist-Photographer in 19th-Century India, New Delhi and Ahmedabad 2013; Jyotindra Jain et al., Raja Deen Dayal: The Studio Archives from the IGNCA Collection (exhib. cat., New Delhi, Indira Gandhi National Centre for the Arts), New Delhi 2010.

Maharaja Sawai Ram Singh II

1 Yaduendra Sahai. The Photographer Prince: Maharaja Sawai Ram Singh II of Jaipur, Jaipur 1996.
2 Quoted in B. N. Goswamy, 'A photographer prince', in: The Tribune (India), 12 March 2017, http://www.tribuneindia.com/news/spectrum/arts/a-photographer-prince/376061.html.

Darogah Abbas Ali

1 The Indian Portrait, vol. 6: A Photographic evolution from documentation to posterity: From the Collection of Anil Relia, Ahmedabad 2015.

Ghasiram Hardev Sharma

1 Tryna Lyons, The Artists of Nathadwara: The Practice of Painting Rajasthan, Ahmedabad and Bloomington 2004, p. 174.
2 Kajri Jain, Gods in the Bazaar, Durham, NC 2007, p. 136.

Johnston & Hoffmann

1 John Falconer, India: Pioneering Photographers 1850–1900. London 2001.

Khubiram Gopilal

1 Tryna Lyons, The Artists of Nathadwara: The Practice of Painting Rajasthan, Ahmedabad and Bloomington 2004, p. 295.

Suresh Punjabi

1 Christopher Pinney, Artisan Camera: Studio Photography from Central India, Chennai 2014, p. 9.

Proof & Propaganda

Willoughby Wallace Hooper

1 Sujaan Mukherjee, 'Who was the photographer who took these dehumanising images of the Madras famine?', in: Scroll.in, 20 November 2017, https://scroll.in/magazine/855532/who-was-the-photographer-who-took-these-dehumanising-images-of-the-madras-famine.

Sunil Janah

1 Quoted in Malavika Vyawahare, 'The Photography of Sunil Janah', in: India Ink (blog), New York Times, 11 July 2012, https://india.blogs.nytimes.com/2012/07/11/the-photography-of-sunil-janah/.

Kishor Parekh

1 http://www.betterphotography.in/perspectives/great-masters/kishor-parekh/43904/.

The New Exotic

Cecil Beaton

1 Henry Saville, quoted in: Philippe Garner and David Mellor, Cecil Beaton, London 1994, p. 45.

2 Cecil Beaton, Indian Diary & Album, Oxford 1991, p. 13.

Mark Riboud

1 Marc Riboud, 'Pleasures of the Eye', 2000.

Derry Moore

1 In the Shadow of the Raj: Derry Moore in India, ed. Nathaniel Gaskell, Munich et al. 2017.

Don McCullin

1 https://donmccullin.com/don-mccullin/.

Modernism & Modernity

Jyoti Bhatt

1 Jyoti Bhatt:, Photographs from Rural India, Tasveer, Bangalore 2014.

Raghubir Singh

1 Raghubir Singh, River of Colour: An Indian View, London 1998, p. 13.

2 Ibid, p. 8.

Dashrath Patel

1 Dashrath Patel, quoted in: Suneet Chopra, 'Understanding Dashrath Patel', in: Frontline 16, no. 15 (17–30 July 1999), http://www.frontline.in/static/html/fl1615/16150820.htm.

Harry Gruyaert

1 Harry Gruyaert, quoted in: Giulia Mutti, 'Harry Gruyaert: A Career in Technicolour', in: AnOther, 15 September 2015, http://www.anothermag.com/art-photography/7782/harry-gruyaert-a-career-in-technicolour.

Society & the Street

Raghu Rai

1 Elizabeth Day, 'Interview with Raghu Rai', in: The Guardian, 17 January 2010, https://www.theguardian.com/artanddesign/2010/jan/17/raghu-rai-photography-exhibitions-london.

Bhupendra Karia

1 See Jonas Cuénin, 'Bhupendra Karia, a Savvy Observer', International Center of Photography, https://www.icp.org/perspective/bhupendra-karia-a-savvy-observer.

Prashant Panjiar

1 Prashant Panjiar in conversation with Raj Lalwani, 'Prashant Panjiar: Respect is Sacrosanct', in: Better Photography, 5 October 2014, http://betterphotography.in/perspectives/15-photographers-secrets-secret-6-respect-sacrosanct/14059/.

2 See 'Bhupendra Karia / 1968–1974',exhibition announcement, sepiaEYE (gallery), https://www.sepiaeye.com/copy-of-copy-of-copy-of-template/.

William Gedney

1 Samanth Subramanian, 'William Gedney's Travels in India', in: The New Yorker, 28 March 2017, https://www.newyorker.com/culture/photo-booth/william-gedneys-travels-in-india.

T. S. Satyan

1 T. S. Satyan, interview with V. R. Devika, 'A witness to his times', in: The Hindu, Sunday, 30 January 2000, http://www.thehindu.com/2000/01/30/stories/1330078b.htm.

2 Ibid.

3 T. S. Satyan, In Love with Life: A Journey Through Life In Photographs, Bangalore 2002.

4 T. S. Satyan, interview with V. R. Devika, 'A witness to his times', in: The Hindu, Sunday, 30 January 2000, http://www.thehindu.com/2000/01/30/stories/1330078b.htm.

Vicky Roy

1 A non-governmental initiative that manages homes for children who have no place else to go, formed from the proceeds of the Mira Nair movie *Salaam Bombay.*

2 Vicky Roy, interviewed by Bhumika Popli, 'Street Dreams', in: LensCulture, n.d. [2018], https://www.lensculture.com/articles/vicky-roy-street-dreams.

Essay & Enquiry

Mitch Epstein

1 'Mitch Epstein by Richard B. Woodward', in: BOMB Magazine, https://bombmagazine.org/articles/mitch-epstein/.

Sebastião Salgado

1 'Sebastião Salgado', biography on Artsy, https://www.artsy.net/artist/sebastiao-salgado.

Mary Ellen Mark

1 Elizabeth A. Lance, 'Standing on Falkland Road, Sitting in America: Mary Ellen Mark's Representation of the Indian Other', MA diss., University of Missouri-Columbia, 2011.

Ketaki Sheth

1 Ketaki Sheth, quoted in Raj Lalwani, 'Ketaki Sheth: Freshness Helps', in: Better Photography, 2 September 2012, http://betterphotography.in/perspectives/15-photographers-secrets-secret-12-freshness-helps/14335/.

Postmodernity & Play

Jitish Kallat

1 Avantika Bhuyan, 'Jitish Kallat: Anthologist of everyday life', in: LiveMint, 13 January 2017, http://www.livemint.com/Leisure/jGW0OSurdNEOwZA8LE P4vl/ Jitish-Kallat-Anthologist-of-everyday-life.html.

2 Ibid.

Olivier Culmann

1 Olivier Culmann, interviewed by FotoRoom, 'The Others – Olivier Culmann Shows Us the Many Ways the Indians Go About Self-Portraits', in: FotoRoom, n.d., http://fotoroom.co/the-others-olivier-culmann.

2 Ibid.

The Book & the Biennale

Max Pinckers

1 Sean O'Hagan, 'India's Love Commandos – and the runaway couples they protect', in: The Guardian, 24 October 2014 (https://www.theguardian.com/art and design/2014/oct/24/bollywood-runaway-couples -love-commandos-max-pinckers-photobook).

Sohrab Hura

1 Kevin Wy Lee, 'Getting Personal with Sohrab Hura – An interview with Magnum's new nominee', in: Invisible Photographer Asia, 1 August 2014. http://invisiblephotographer.asia/2014/08/01/interview-sohrabhura/.

Vasantha Yogananthan

1 Vasantha Yogananthan, quoted in Diane Smyth, Arles 2017: The Promise by Vasantha Yogananthan shortlisted for the Author Book Award, in: The British Journal of Photography, 3 July 2017, http://www.bjp-online.com/2017/07/arles-author-book-award-nominee-the-promise-by-vasantha-yogananthan/

2 Ibid.

Image Credits

Every reasonable effort has been made to trace the copyright holders, but if any have been inadvertently overlooked, the necessary arrangements will be made at the first opportunity.

8 Dayanita Singh and Ai Weiwei. Courtesy the Biennale Foundation, Venice
10 Henry Peach Robinson. Courtesy George Eastman Collection, Rochester
Maharaja Sawai Ram Singh II. Courtesy the Rajeev Rawat Collection, Jaipur
Roger Fenton. Courtesy the Hugh Huxley Collection, London
Felice Beato. Courtesy the Wellcome Collection, London
12 Marg Magazine. © Marg Foundation, Mumbai / courtesy the publisher
14 Norman Parkinson, Vogue. © Condé Nast / Courtesy the Museum of Art & Photography, Bangalore
Cindy Sherman. © Cindy Sherman / courtesy the Museum of Modern Art, New York
Bernd and Hilla Becher. © Hilla Becher / courtesy the Theo Politowicz Collection, London
Edward Ruscha. © Edward Ruscha / courtesy the Theo Politowicz Collection, London
18 Courtesy the J. Paul Getty Museum, Los Angeles
23 Courtesy the British Library, London
24 Courtesy the Victoria & Albert Museum, London
25 Courtesy the Metropolitan Museum of Art, New York
27–29 Courtesy the J. Paul Getty Museum, Los Angeles
31 Courtesy the British Library, London
32 Courtesy the Victoria & Albert Museum, London
33 Courtesy the Rajeev Rawat Collection, Jaipur
34–35 Courtesy the Victoria & Albert Museum, London
36–39 Courtesy Oriental Museum, Durham University, Sir John Marshall Collection given by Dr & Mrs Spalding
41–43 Courtesy the Hugh Huxley Collection, London
44–47 Courtesy the British Library, London
48–49 Courtesy the J. Paul Getty Museum, Los Angeles
50–51 Courtesy the Hugh Huxley Collection, London
52 Courtesy the Rajeev Rawat Collection, Jaipur
53 Courtesy the Hugh Huxley Collection, London
54–57 Courtesy the Museum of Art & Photography, Bangalore
58 Courtesy the Hugh Ashley Rayner Collection, Bath
63 Courtesy the British Library, London
64–66 Courtesy the Rajeev Rawat Collection, Jaipur
67 Courtesy the Hugh Ashley Rayner Collection, Bath
69 Courtesy Christopher Penn
70 Courtesy the Victoria & Albert Museum, London
71 Courtesy the Hugh Huxley Collection, London
72–73 Courtesy the British Library, London
74 Courtesy the Alkazi Collection of Photography, New Delhi
75 Courtesy Photoink, New Delhi
76 Courtesy the Metropolitan Museum of Art, New York
77 Courtesy the J. Paul Getty Museum, Los Angeles
78–79 Courtesy the Hugh Huxley Collection, London
80 Courtesy the Museum of Art & Photography, Bangalore
85 Courtesy the British Library, London
86 Courtesy the Collection of Catherine Benkaim and Barbara Timmer
87 Courtesy the British Library, London
88–89 Courtesy the British Library, London
90 Courtesy the Rajeev Rawat Collection, Jaipur
91 Courtesy the Hugh Huxley Collection, London
92–93 Courtesy the Fratelli Alinari Museum Collections, Florence
94–95 Courtesy the Museum of Art & Photography, Bangalore
96 Courtesy the Museum of Art & Photography, Bangalore
97 Courtesy the Rajeev Rawat Collection, Jaipur
98 Courtesy the Royal Ontario Museum, Toronto
99 Left: Courtesy the Museum of Art & Photography, Bangalore
Right: © Christie's Images Ltd. / courtesy Christie's Images Ltd.
100–101 Courtesy the Museum of Art & Photography, Bangalore
102–105 © Suresh Punjabi / courtesy the family of Suresh Punjabi and Christopher Pinney
106 Courtesy the Hugh Huxley Collection, London
111 Courtesy the Hugh Huxley Collection, London
112–115 Courtesy the J. Paul Getty Museum, Los Angeles
116 © Her Majesty the Queen / courtesy the Royal Collection Trust, London
117 Courtesy the Nehru Memorial Library, New Delhi
118 Courtesy the Harry Ransom Center, The University of Texas, Austin
119 Courtesy the Hugh Huxley Collection, London
121 © Getty Images
122–123 © Time Life / Courtesy the Museum of Art & Photography, Bangalore
124–125 Courtesy the Swaraj Art Archive, New Delhi
126–127 © Werner Bischof / Courtesy Magnum Photos
128–131 Courtesy the Kishor Parekh Estate, Mumbai
132 Courtesy Magnum Photos
133 Courtesy Wisdom Tree Press, New Delhi
134 © Norman Parkinson Ltd. / Courtesy the Museum of Art & Photography, Bangalore and Iconic Images, London
138–139 Courtesy the Hugh Huxley Collection, London
140–143 © Norman Parkinson Ltd. / Condé Nast / Courtesy the Museum of Art & Photography, Bangalore
144–145 © Magnum Photos / courtesy the Museum of Art & Photography, Bangalore
146–147 © Magnum Photos / Courtesy the Museum of Art & Photography, Bangalore and Catherine Riboud
148–149 © Derry Moore / courtesy the Museum of Art & Photography, Bangalore
150–151 © Don McCullin / courtesy Magnum Photos
152–153 © Steve McCurry / courtesy Magnum Photos
154 Courtesy Navjot and Sasha Altaf
158–163 © Jyoti Bhatt / courtesy the Museum of Art & Photography, Bangalore
162–165 © Succession Raghubir Singh, Paris / courtesy Succession Raghubir Singh, Paris
166–167 Courtesy the Museum of Art & Photography, Bangalore / Preeti Bedi
168 Courtesy Ram Rahman
169 Courtesy the Lucien Hervé Foundation, Paris
171 © Dashrath Patel Foundation / Courtesy the Dashrath Patel Museum, Alibag
172–173 Courtesy Karan Khanna
174–175 © Harry Gruyaert / courtesy Agentur Focus, Hamburg
176–177 Courtesy Navjot and Sasha Altaf
178–179 Courtesy Photoink, New Delhi
180–183 © Andreas Volwahsen / the Museum of Art & Photography, Bangalore
188–191 © Raghu Rai / courtesy the artist / the Museum of Art & Photography, Bangalore
193 Courtesy the Museum of Art & Photography, Bangalore
194–195 © Sudharak Olwe / courtesy the artist
197 Courtesy SepiaEYE, New York
198–199 © Prashant Panjiar / courtesy the artist
200–201 © Ram Rahman / courtesy the artist
202–203 Courtesy Duke University Libraries, North Carolina
205 Courtesy the Museum of Art & Photography, Bangalore
206–207 © Vicky Roy / courtesy the artist
209 © Sooni Taraporevala / courtesy HarperCollins India, Noida and Sunaparanta, Goa
210 © Martin Parr / courtesy Agentur Focus, Hamburg
214–217 © Mitch Epstein / courtesy the artist
219–221 © Sebastião Salgado / courtesy Agentur Focus, Hamburg
222 © Times Newspaper Ltd. and Mary Ellen Mark / Courtesy Times Newspapers Ltd. and the Museum of Art & Photography, Bangalore
223 © Mary Ellen Mark / courtesy Mary Ellen Mark Library, New York
225–227 © Ketaki Sheth / courtesy Photoink, New Delhi
228–229 © Manoj Kumar Jain / courtesy the artist
231 © Sunil Gupta / courtesy SepiaEYE, New York
232–233 © Martin Parr / courtesy Agentur Focus, Hamburg
235–237 © Julia Knop / courtesy the artist
238–239 © Soham Gupta / courtesy the artist
240–241 © Amit Madheshiya / courtesy the artist
242 © Pushpamala N. and Clare Arni / courtesy Pushpamala N.
246–247 © Annu Palakunnathu Matthew / courtesy SepiaEYE, New York
248 © Sheba Chhachhi / courtesy the artist
249 © RAQS Media Collective / courtesy Frith Street Gallery, London
250–253 © Pushpamala N. and Clare Arni / courtesy Pushpamala N.
254 Courtesy SepiaEYE, New York
255 © Yasumasa Morimura / courtesy Luhring Augustine, New York
256–257 © Lewis Koch / courtesy the artist
259–261 © Jitish Kallat / courtesy the artist
262–263 © Vivan Sundaram / courtesy SepiaEYE, New York
264–265 © Anita Dube / courtesy Nature Morte, New Delhi
266–267 © Olivier Culmann / courtesy the artist
268 © Sohrab Hura / courtesy the artist
272–273 © Michael Bühler-Rose / courtesy the artist
274–275 © Karen Knorr / courtesy the artist
276–277 © Max Pinckers / courtesy the artist
279–281 © Sohrab Hura / Magnum Photos
282–283 © Nishant Shukla / courtesy the artist
284–285 © Cristina de Middel / courtesy Agentur Focus, Hamburg
286–287 © Vasantha Yogananthan / courtesy the artist
288–289 © Taryn Simon / courtesy the artist
293–295 © Dayanita Singh / courtesy the artist
296–299 © Gauri Gill / courtesy the artist

Index

Abbas Ali, Darogah 96
Beato, Felice 111
Beaton, Cecil 138
Bedi, Mitter 166
Beglar, Joseph 50
Bhatt, Jyoti 158
Bhedwar, Shapoor 74
Bischof, Werner 126
Bourke-White, Margaret 121
Bourne, Samuel 63
Bühler-Rose, Michael 272
Burke, William H. 116
Cameron, Julia Margaret 76
Cartier-Bresson, Henri 144
Chhachhi, Sheba 248
Chintamon, Hurrichund 87
Culmann, Olivier 266
Dajee, Narayan 52
Deen Dayal, Lala 90
Dube, Anita 264
Duncan, David Douglas 118
Epstein, Mitch 214
Fiebig, Frederick 72
Francis Frith & Co. 32
Gedney, William 202
Gill, Gauri 296
Gopilal, Khubiram 100
Grange, Alexis de La 27
Gruyaert, Harry 174
Gupta, Soham 238
Gupta, Sunil 231
Hervé, Lucien 169
Hooper, Willoughby Wallace 112
Hura, Sohrab 279
Janah, Sunil 124
Johnson, William 41
Johnston & Hoffmann 99
Kallat, Jitish 259
Karia, Bhupendra 197
Khan, Ahmad Ali 88
Khanna, Krishen 172
Knop, Julia 235
Knorr, Karen 274
Koch, Lewis 256
Kumar Jain, Manoj 228
Madheshiya, Amit 240
Mahatta, Madan 178
Mark, Mary Ellen 222
Marshall, John 36
Matthew, Annu Palakunnathu 246
McCullin, Don 150
McCurry, Steve 152
Middel, Cristina de 284
Mohamedi, Nasreen 176
Moore, Derry 148
Murray, Colin 71
Murray, John 70
Newland, J. W. 86
Nicholas & Curths 31
Olwe, Sudharak 194
Panjiar, Prashant 198
Parekh, Kishor 128
Parkinson, Norman 140
Parr, Martin 232
Patel, Dashrath 171
Penn, A. T. W. 69
Pinckers, Max 276
Portman, Maurice Vidal 44
Punjabi, Suresh 102
Pushpamala N. and Clare Arni 250
Rahman, Habib 168
Rahman, Ram 200
Rai, Raghu 188
Raqs Media Collective 249
Riboud, Marc 146
Roy, Vicky 206
Saché & Westfield 23
Saché, John Edward 48
Sahni, Sati 133
Salgado, Sebastião 219
Satyan, T. S. 205
Sharma, Ghasiram Hardev 98
Sher-Gil, Umrao Singh 75
Sheth, Ketaki 225
Shukla, Nishant 282
Silverstone, Marilyn 132
Singh, Dayanita 293
Singh, Maharaja Sawai Ram II 92
Singh, Pamela 254
Singh, Raghubir 162
Sundaram, Vivan 262
Syed, A. L. 78
Taraporevala, Sooni 209
Tripe, Linnaeus 24
Tytler, Robert Christopher 85
Virkar, Narayan 117
Volwahsen, Andreas 180
Vyarawalla, Homai 119
Waddell, Clyde 193
Watson, John Forbes &
Kaye, John William 54
Yasumasa, Morimura 255
Yoganathan, Vasantha 286

Acknowledgements

When I first moved to India nearly a decade ago, I was warmly welcomed by Abhishek Poddar and his family. It is to Abhishek and Radhika that I owe the highest debt of gratitude for their kindness as they laid the foundation, in life and work, for making this book possible.

Although this project first began as my own, in 2016 I met the scholar Diva Gujral and, over the course of several conversations, we became aware of a shared approach and commonality of thought on the subject of photography in India. Diva subsequently became the book's co-author and has been integral in shaping and articulating many of the arguments contained herein.

In the course of our research, Diva and I sought guidance from various individuals whose opinions and advice have been important in shaping this book. Significant among them are Amrita Jhaveri, Pramod Kumar KG, Prashant Panjiar, and Ram Rahman.

Special thanks are also due to Rajeev Rawat, whose generosity in opening up what is one of the finest collections of 19th century Indian photography, is central to the early chapters of this book.

A project of this scale is naturally indebted to those who have dedicated years to organising photographic archives and oeuvres relating to India. We would like to acknowledge the contributions of the Alkazi Foundation; Sabih Ahmed and Asia Art Archive; Devika Daulet-Singh of PHOTOINK; Deepali Dewan of the Royal Ontario Museum; Esa Epstein of SepiaEYE, John Falconer and Malini Roy of the British Library; Peter Nagy at Nature Morte; the Nehru Memorial Museum and Library; and the staff of the Museum of Art & Photography, Bengaluru. A list of all those who kindly contributed images can be found on the credits page; but we would like to additionally thank some individuals for going out of their way in helping to provide images: these include Sasha Altaf, Preeti Bedi, Roland Belgrave, Catherine Benkaim, Karan Khanna, Pinakin Patel, Christopher Penn, the family of Suresh Punjabi, Deepak Puri, Hugh Ashley Rayner, Catherine Riboud, Lorène Durret, Navneet Sahni and Devika Singh.

We would also like to thank Andrew Hansen and Curt Holtz from Prestel; Jonathan Fox for his careful copy-editing; Shilpa Vijayakrishnan for some of the early biographical research, Sneha Kapote for her fact-checking, Clifford Jeffrey for preparing the images for print and photographing much of the nineteenth century images and albums; Gemma Gerhard for all her help and patience, and Stuart Smith for designing and sequencing the book.

Note

Throughout the period of history that this book covers, places and spellings have changed, and borders have been constantly redrawn – the most prominent example of this, of course, is India itself, which changes from undivided British India to the independent nation. We have wherever possible used the spelling or name most consistent with the period in which the photograph was made: for instance, while 19th century photographs were taken in Bombay, those made in the same city but in this century refer to Mumbai.

Cover image: Vasantha Yogananthan, Rama Combing His Hair, Ayodhya, Uttar Pradesh, 2015
Back cover image: John Murray, The Taj Mahal from the East (detail), 1858–62, Courtesy the The Alkazi Collection of Photography
Page 2: Raghubir Singh, Monsoon Rains, Monghyr, Bihar, 1967
Page 4: Lewis Koch, Upper Dharamsala, Himachal Pradesh, 1995
Page 6: Taryn Simon, Chapter I, from the series: *A Living Man Declared Dead and Other Chapters I–XVIII*, 2008–11

Prestel Publishing Ltd.
14-17 Wells Street
London W1T 3PD

Prestel Publishing
900 Broadway, Suite 603
New York, NY 10003

Library of Congress Control Number is available; British Library Cataloguing-in-Publication Data: a catalogue record for this book is available from the British Library.

Editorial direction: Curt Holtz
Picture research: Kira Uthoff
Design and layout: SMITH, London
Production management: Corinna Pickart
Separations: Reproline Mediateam GmbH, Munich
Printing and binding: Grafisches Centrum Cuno, Calbe
Paper: Condat matt Périgord

FSC www.fsc.org
MIX
Paper from responsible sources
FSC® C043106

Verlagsgruppe Random House FSC® N001967

Printed in Germany

ISBN 978-3-7913-8421-4

www.prestel.com

BAKING COURSE

pastry, cakes and bread

Edited by Isabel Moore

ROYDON

CONTENTS

PASTRY 5

Making Pastry 7
Types of Pastry 8
Techniques of Using Pastry 16

RECIPES

Beef Steak and Kidney Pudding 19
Veal and Ham Pie 19
Cheese Straws 19
Portuguese Shrimp Rissoles 20
Vol-au-Vent 20
Asparagus Quiche 21
Rhubarb Flan 21
Spotted Dick 21
Cheesecake 22
Normandy Pear Tart 23
American Apple Pie 24

CAKES

Preparation 28
Methods of Cake-Making 29
Fillings and Toppings 32
Piping 36

RECIPES

Dundee Cake 39
Orange Cake Fingers 39
Almond Cake 39
Chocolate Roulade 40
Madeira Cake 40
Viennese Fingers 41
Chocolate Refrigerator Biscuits 41
Shortbread 42
Ginger and Cream Wafers 42
Cherry-Filled Cakes 42
Mocha Gateau 43
Madeleines 44
Scones with Dried Fruit 44
Scones with Sour Cream 45
Drop Scones 45
Nougatine Cakes 46
Praline Cream Filling 47
Jamaican Spice Loaf 47

BAKING WITH YEAST 49

Using Yeast 50
Techniques 50
Types of Bread 52

RECIPES

Brioche 57
Savarin 57
Gugelhopf 58
Orange Yeast Buns 59
Danish Pastries 60
Croissant Dough 60

Distributed by
Roydon Publishing Company Limited
81 Goswell Road
London EC1V 7ER

Published by Marshall Cavendish Books Limited
58 Old Compton Street
London W1V 5PA

Printed and bound by L.E.G.O., Vicenza, Italy

ISBN 0 946674 01 9

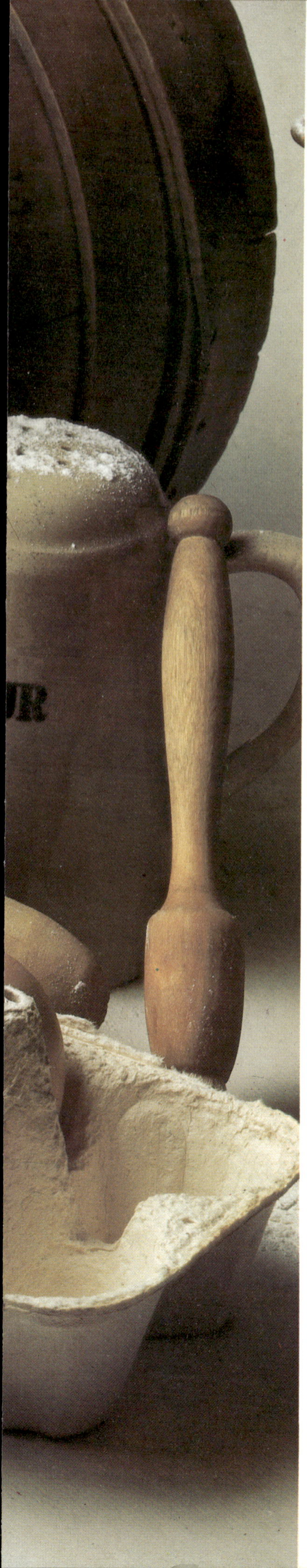

PASTRY

Pastry is an unleavened dough made from shortening (fat), flour and liquid. It is used either to provide a lining for a filling or to encase or envelope a filling completely. Such fillings can be sweet or savoury. There are several different types of pastry, ranging from the simple everyday shortcrust used in flans and quiches, to the more exotic choux pastry (paste), which provides the basis for some of the most glorious cakes of classic French haute cuisine.

Quantity

It is useful to note that when a recipe calls for, for instance, 225g/8oz (2 cups) pastry, it means pastry made from that quantity of flour.

Ingredients

Flour
Usually plain (all-purpose) white wheat flour. Self-raising (self-rising) flour is only used when a heavy ingredient such as suet is included.

Salt
Most dough has salt added—between $\frac{1}{8}$ teaspoon and 1 teaspoon.

Sugar
Sugar is added to sweet pastry doughs.

Shortening
The more shortening in relation to flour, the richer the dough. Butter is usually used, but margarine, suet, lard, vegetable fat (shortening) or oil, or goose or duck fat can be used. If using margarine, make sure it is hard, not soft 'whipped' margarine.

Liquid
A small amount of liquid is added to the flour and shortening mixture to bind it. Water is usually used, but eggs, milk, cream, sour cream and buttermilk may be used.

Flavourings
Cheese, herbs, spices and essences (extracts) may be added.

Yeast
Yeast is added to some pastry doughs such as that used for Danish pastries.

Making pastry

There are many different kinds of pastry, but several techniques apply to all pastry-making. The basic points to remember are:

1. Unless the dough is made with yeast or already cooked, keep the ingredients and implements cool. Your hands should be freshly washed in cold water. For some pastries, such as puff, the ingredients should be chilled.

2. Again, with the exception of yeast and cooked doughs, handle as little as possible. If you can, use a table knife or electric mixer to rub the fat into the flour. When doing this with your fingers, use the fingertips and

Sift flour and salt together then add fat. Use a sharp knife to cut the fat into the flour until the pieces are small and well coated.

Rub the fat into the flour until the mixture resembles fine breadcrumbs. To do this rub the ingredients between your fingers.

Sprinkle about 2 tsp of cold water over the surface of the mixture and carefully stir this into the ingredients with the knife.

Add more water, in small quantities, until the mixture clings together in small lumps. Continue cutting with a knife until it makes large lumps.

Add the remaining water and stir in. Use your fingers to test if the mixture is moist enough to stick together, it should leave the sides of the bowl clean.

Draw the lumps together to make a dough and place on an unfloured surface. Knead lightly until it is smooth. Chill before using.

work quickly. The more you handle the dough, the stickier and less manageable it becomes. If using a mixer, switch off the minute the ingredients are like breadcrumbs.

3. When rolling out dough, place it on a lightly floured working surface and use a lightly floured rolling pin. Roll the dough lightly, away from you. Do not turn it over, or it will absorb too much flour from the working surface. If it is sticky or contains a lot of shortening or needs a lot of rolling, chill it, first folding it like puff pastry, to make rolling easier.

4. Usually pastry should be baked, or at least start its baking time, at a high oven temperature. Long, slow baking produces hard, tasteless pastry.

If you have a freezer, it is well worth making a large quantity of pastry at one time, as it freezes perfectly. Divide it into easy to use portions before freezing. Remove from the freezer at least 30 minutes before cooking. Pie and flan cases can also be frozen—it is best to freeze them uncooked.

Types of pastry

The basic pastry types are shortcrust, rich shortcrust, puff, rough puff, flaky, suetcrust, hot water crust, choux and strudel. The difference between them is mainly determined by the method used to incorporate the shortening into the flour. In puff, rough puff and flaky pastry, the shortening—generally butter—is added either in one large or several smaller pieces and rolled and folded into the flour and liquid. The result is light and flaky. In closer textured pastries such as shortcrust, the shortening is cut into small pieces and rubbed into the flour until the mixture resembles fine or coarse breadcrumbs. For even closer-textured pastry, such as choux or hot water crust, the shortening is

melted with the liquid and stirred or beaten into the flour. The eggs in choux pastry open out the texture; strudel pastry also contains eggs but they are added in a different way. It requires a lot of kneading and has to be rolled out very thinly.

All types of pastry doughs are suitable for covering pies and enveloping sweet or savoury fillings. Close textured pastry, such as shortcrust and rich shortcrust, are more suitable for lining flans and pie dishes and baking blind.

1. Shortcrust Pastry

Basic shortcrust pastry can be used for making sweet or savoury pies or tarts.

	Metric/UK	US
Flour	175g/6oz	1½ cups
Salt	¼ tsp	¼ tsp
Butter	40g/1½oz	3 Tbsp
Vegetable fat (shortening)	40g/1½oz	3 Tbsp
Iced water	2–3 Tbsp	2–3 Tbsp

Sift the flour into a medium-sized mixing bowl. Add the butter and vegetable fat (shortening) and cut them into small pieces with a table knife. With the finger tips, rub the fat into the flour until the mixture resembles fine breadcrumbs. Add 1 tablespoon of the iced water and mix it into the flour using the knife. With your hands, mix and knead the dough until it is smooth. Add a little more iced water if necessary. The dough should be smooth, soft, pliable and silky, leaving the sides of the bowl clean. Chill for 30 minutes. The pastry is now ready to be used.

2. Rich Shortcrust Pastry

Use for rich or sweet fillings. Rich desserts taste delicious in it.

	Metric/UK	US
Flour	175g/6oz	1½ cups
Salt	⅛ tsp	⅛ tsp
Butter, chilled	75g/3oz	6 Tbsp
Sugar	1 Tbsp	1 Tbsp
Small egg, lightly beaten	1	1
Iced water	1–2 Tbsp	1–2 Tbsp

Proceed as for the Basic Shortcrust method until the mixture resembles fine breadcrumbs. Stir in the sugar. Mix the egg with 1 tablespoon of iced water and use this to make the dough, adding more water if necessary. Chill for 30 minutes before use.

Cheese Pastry is based on rich shortcrust pastry, with the addition of grated cheese in the proportion, 4 tablespoons of grated cheese per 100g/4oz (1 cup) of flour. Cheese pastry can be substituted in savoury flans and tartlets, where a cheese flavour is complementary to the filling. It can also be made into cheese straws or biscuits (crackers).

Sift the flour and salt into a bowl, then chill. Put about half the water into a bowl with ice.

Make a well in the flour and add half the chilled water. Beat with your fingers until it is creamy.

Add the rest of the water and flour and form into a ball. Knead lightly and chill for 30 minutes.

Work the fat until it is spreadable. Spread out carefully on greaseproof or waxed paper to make a large rectangle.

Unwrap the chilled dough and roll out on a floured surface to a large circle. Peel off paper from the fat and put in the centre of the dough circle.

Lift the short edges over and press the same way. You will now have a rectangle of dough. Push it into shape with a knife, if necessary.

Turn the rectangle so that the long sides face you. Rolling in one direction, lightly roll out until the dough is twice its size. Rest.

Fold again, then rest for 15 minutes. Unwrap the dough–the fold should be on your left, the longest sealed edge on the right. Roll, fold and rest.

Repeat this operation until the dough has been rolled and rested six times. Wrap and chill for about 2 hours before using.

3. *Puff Pastry*

This is considered to be the queen of all pastries. It is the best in flavour and texture and generally only the finest ingredients should be used. Use best quality flour and unsalted butter. Add a squeeze of lemon juice to the iced water, to help counteract the greasiness of the butter. Uncooked pastry dough can be stored in the refrigerator for 3 days or deep frozen for up to 3 months. The object is to produce thin layers of dough interspersed with thin layers of butter. Puff pastry is used for sweet or savoury bouchées (mouthfuls), vol-au-vents (pastry cases shaped into an oval, square or round and filled with a savoury mixture in a creamy sauce), and little savouries such as Portuguese Shrimp Rissoles which are deep fried.

	Metric/UK	US
Flour	**450g/1lb**	**4 cups**
Salt	**½ tsp**	**½ tsp**
Butter	**450g/1lb**	**2 cups**
Iced water with lemon juice added	**250ml/8floz**	**1 cup**

Sift the flour and salt into a large mixing bowl. With a table knife cut 100g/4oz (½ cup) of the butter into the flour. Quickly rub it into the flour with your fingertips and add enough of the iced water to make a firm dough. Form the dough into a ball and chill for 15 minutes. Form the remaining butter into a flat oblong slab about 2cm/¾in thick. The easiest way is to put it between two sheets of greaseproof or waxed paper and beat it with the back of a wooden spoon or a wooden mallet. The consistency of the butter and the dough should be as nearly the same as possible—that is, they should be pliable but not sticky.

Roll out the dough into a rectangle about 5mm/¼in thick. Place the slab of butter in the centre and fold the dough over to make a neat parcel. Keep the corners pulled out and squared. Chill for 10 minutes. Place the dough, folds down, on a floured board and roll out gently into a rectangle. Pull the corners square and fold into three. Chill again. Roll out and fold. Chill for 15 minutes. Repeat this twice more. Chill for a final 15 minutes.

The dough is now ready for use.

A classic example of a raised pie is Melton Mowbray Pie. The dough is hot water crust, one of the easier pastries to make.

4. *Rough Puff Pastry*

This rich pastry is easy to make, but does not rise so well as puff pastry. It is mainly used for pie crusts and turnovers. It is particularly good for meat pies.

	Metric/UK	US
Flour	**225g/8oz**	**2 cups**
Salt	**½ tsp**	**½ tsp**
Butter or half butter/half other fat	**175g/6oz**	**¾ cup**
Iced water	**4–6 Tbsp**	**4–6 Tbsp**

Sift the flour and salt into a medium-sized mixing bowl. Add the butter, cut into walnut-sized pieces. Pour in 4 tablespoons of the iced water and quickly mix to a dough with a knife. It will be lumpy at this point. Add a little more water if the dough looks too dry.

Shape into a ball and place on a lightly floured board. Roll out into an oblong. Pull the corners square. Fold the dough in three, turning it so that the open end faces you.

Roll out again to an oblong shape, pull the corners and fold again in three. Repeat this once more, then chill for 30 minutes. If the dough looks streaky, repeat the rolling and folding once more. The dough is now ready to use.

5. *Flaky Pastry*

A light, butter pastry used for mincemeat or fruit pies.

	Metric/UK	US
Flour	**175g/6oz**	**1½ cups**
Salt	**¼ tsp**	**¼ tsp**
Butter	**50g/2oz**	**¼ cup**
Cold water	**3–4 Tbsp**	**3–4 Tbsp**
Lard	**50g/2oz**	**¼ cup**

Sift the flour and salt into a mixing bowl. Divide the butter into two equal pieces and add one piece to the flour. Rub it into the flour until it resembles fine

Step-by-Step to Hot Water Crust Pie

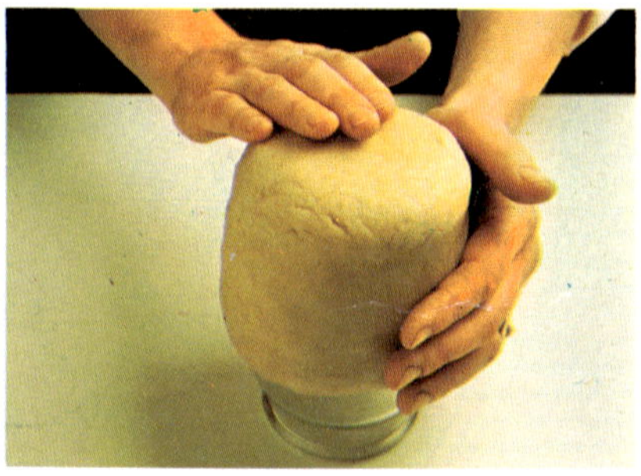

To make the case for a raised pie, warm hot water crust pastry is moulded around the outside of a greased storage jar until 1cm/½in thick.

Now support the dough case with greaseproof or waxed paper and place on a baking sheet. The filling should be added now.

Finally, dampen the edges of the case, put the dough lid on top and very carefully crimp the edges to seal in the filling.

breadcrumbs. With a spatula, mix in the water to form a firm dough.

Put the dough on a floured board and shape it into a square. Roll it out into an oblong and dot two thirds of it with small pieces of half the lard. Fold over one third of the dough, then the other third, to make a neat parcel. Press the edges gently with a rolling pin to seal them.

Turn the dough round so the sealed ends face you, and roll out again into an oblong. Dot with pieces of the remaining lard, fold in three, seal the edges, turn the dough and roll out as before.

Repeat this process with the remaining butter. Chill for 10 minutes before using.

6. Suetcrust Pastry

This is simple to make and can be used for sweet or savoury dishes, baked or steamed. It can also be made into balls and cooked in stock to make dumplings.

Suet is the fat found around the kidneys of sheep and bullocks. If you buy fresh suet, discard the membranes and fibres, then chop or mince (grind) very finely. Commercially prepared suet, which is ready shredded, can be easily bought.

	Metric/UK	US
Flour	**225g/8oz**	**2 cups**
Salt	**½ tsp**	**½ tsp**
Shredded suet	**100g/4oz**	**½ cup**
Cold water	**150ml/5floz**	**⅔ cup**

Sift the flour and salt into a mixing bowl. Use a table knife to stir in the suet and water, mixing to form a firm dough. Chill for 10 minutes. The dough is now ready to use.

7. Hot Water Crust Pastry

This is the traditional pastry used for raised pies such as pork, veal, ham, and game.

	Metric/UK	US
Flour	**350g/12oz**	**3 cups**
Salt	**1 tsp**	**1 tsp**
Water	**150ml/5floz**	**⅔ cup**
Vegetable fat (shortening) or lard	**100g/4oz**	**½ cup**
Egg yolk, lightly beaten	**1**	**1**

Sift the flour and salt into a large mixing bowl. Bring the water and fat to the boil over a high heat, stirring until the fat has melted. Remove the pan from the heat. The pastry must be made quickly before the fat can solidify. Pour in the egg yolk and the water and fat mixture. Gradually draw the flour into the liquids with a wooden spoon to form a dough. Knead well on a lightly floured board until smooth and shiny. Roll to shape and use at once.

8. Choux Pastry

This is a delicious light pastry which is used in cream puffs, éclairs, profiteroles and savoury cheese recipes. It can also be used for more elaborate dishes such as Gâteau St. Honoré. It is named 'choux'—the French for cabbage—because it puffs up during baking into a cabbage shape.

	Metric/UK	US
Water	**300ml/ ½ pint**	**1¼ cups**
Butter, cut into small pieces	**75g/3oz**	**6 Tbsp**
Salt	**1 tsp**	**1 tsp**
Flour	**275g/10oz**	**2½ cups**
Large eggs	**5**	**5**

In a large heavy saucepan, bring the water to the boil. Add the butter and salt. Sift the flour on to a sheet of greaseproof or waxed paper or foil. When the butter has melted, remove the pan from the heat and shoot in the flour at once. Beat until the paste is smooth and pulls away from the sides of the pan. Add the eggs, one by one, beating after each addition until the mixture is thick and glossy. Do not overbeat. Use while still warm.

Choux Puffs are easy to make once you have mastered the techniques of making choux pastry. Serve as a dessert or snack.

9. *Strudel Pastry*

This dough requires careful handling and should be rolled and pulled until it is transparently thin. The dough does not keep well, so make it up just before you use it. Strudel pastry can be filled with sweet fillings such as mincemeat, apple, dried fruit or chocolate, or with savoury fillings such as minced (ground) beef or liver pâté. You can make one large strudel to cut up into small pieces, pull it into horseshoe shape or make up small individual shapes for snacks or desserts.

	Metric/UK	US
Flour	**275g/10oz**	**$2\frac{1}{2}$ cups**
Salt	**$\frac{1}{2}$ tsp**	**$\frac{1}{2}$ tsp**
Egg, lightly beaten	**1**	**1**
Tepid water	**200ml/7floz**	**Scant 1 cup**
Unsalted butter, melted	**25g/1oz**	**2 Tbsp**

Sift the flour and salt into a large mixing bowl. Mix the egg, water and butter in a small mixing bowl. With a wooden spoon, stir the egg mixture into the flour and mix well. Knead well until a firm dough is formed and continue kneading for about 10 minutes, or until smooth and elastic. Place in a large, warm mixing bowl. Cover the bowl and set aside to rest for about 30 minutes.

Spread out a large clean cloth on a table or work surface. Sprinkle with a little flour. Place the dough on the cloth and roll out as thinly as possible. With the back of your hands, lift and stretch the dough, trying not to tear it. Trim the outer edges with scissors to neaten them. Fill as required.

French Pastry (Pâte)

The French use similar ingredients in their pastry but it is mixed by a different method. The flour is sifted on to a flat floured surface and the butter (in rough cubes), egg yolks and sugar, if used, are placed in a well in the centre. The sugar can be icing (confectioner's), which gives a very soft dough, or castor (superfine). Use the fingertips of one hand to mix the egg, butter and sugar. Gradually incorporate the flour. As soon as the flour has all been worked in, clean your fingers, then knead the dough lightly with the heel of your hand. Do not overmix or the dough will become sticky. Form the mixture into a ball and chill in the refrigerator for about 1 hour before rolling out and using.

Step-by-Step to Strudel Pastry

To make Apfelstrudel, roll out strudel dough as thinly as possible on a cloth sprinkled with flour.

Using the backs of your hands, pull the dough until it stretches over the table and is wafer thin.

Brush the stretched dough with melted butter and cover generously with dry breadcrumbs.

Place the sliced apples on the edge nearest to you, about 7.5cm/3in from the edge.

Lift the cloth and use it to roll the dough over the filling. Continue rolling until all dough is rolled.

Brush the top of the roll with melted butter and sprinkle with breadcrumbs before cutting and cooking.

The best known pâtes are:

1. Pâte sucrée

A rich, sweet pastry. Use in place of Shortcrust Pastry with sweet fillings, for a melting pastry dessert.

	Metric/UK	US
Flour	**175g/6oz**	**$1\frac{1}{2}$ cups**
Butter, at room temperature	**75g/3oz**	**6 Tbsp**
Icing (confectioner's) sugar, sifted	**75g/3oz**	**$\frac{3}{4}$ cup**
Egg yolks	**3**	**3**

Mix as for Basic Pâte.

2. Pâte brisée

Similar to shortcrust pastry. The proportions of fat to flour are the same, but the method of mixing, with the addition of an egg, is as for Basic Pâte.

3. Pâte à pâté

An excellent rich crust for Pâté en Croûte, such as veal and pork in pastry.

	Metric/UK	US
Flour	**350g/12oz**	**3 cups**
Salt	**$\frac{1}{2}$ tsp**	**$\frac{1}{2}$ tsp**
Egg yolks, lightly beaten	**2**	**2**
Water	**4–5 Tbsp**	**4–5 Tbsp**

Mix as for Basic Pâte.

Preparing a Flan Dish

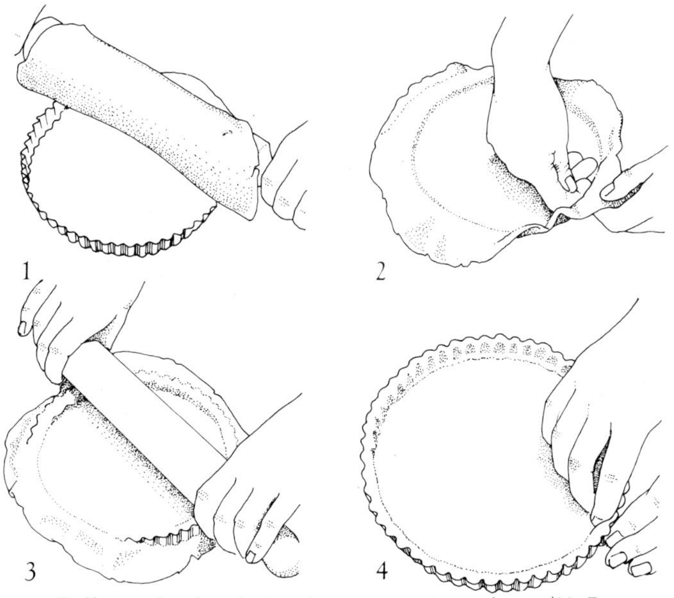

Roll out the dough 4cm/$1\frac{1}{2}$in larger than the ring. Put the ring on a baking sheet. (1) Lift the dough and centre over the ring. Unroll into the ring and ease into place. (2) Press gently into shape, making sure it fits round the bottom edge. (3) Bend surplus over rim and remove with the rolling pin. (4)

Biscuit (Crumb) Crust

A popular and delicious alternative to a shortcrust pastry case is one made from biscuit (cookie or graham cracker) crumbs. This is used for sweet dishes only, such as cheesecake and chiffon desserts, and it provides an interesting flavour and crunchy contrast to creamy fillings. Use digestive (graham crackers) or shortbread biscuits (cookies) which have a coarse crumbly texture. Crush them between two sheets of greaseproof or waxed paper or in a polythene (plastic) bag, using a rolling pin.

	Metric/UK	US
Digestive biscuits (cookies or graham crackers), crushed	**175g/6oz**	**$2\frac{1}{4}$ cups**
Sugar	**2 Tbsp**	**2 Tbsp**
Butter, melted	**75g/3oz**	**6 Tbsp**

Preheat the oven to moderate (180°C/350°F, Gas Mark 4). Sift the crushed biscuits (cookies or crackers) through a coarse strainer into a mixing bowl. Add the sugar and melted butter and stir until well mixed. Scatter over the bottom of a greased 23cm/9in flan tin or cake pan with a removable bottom and press down with the back of a spoon. Coat the sides with crumbs and press flat and smooth. Bake for 10 minutes, then allow to cool. Remove from the tin or pan and place on a flat serving dish. Fill.

TECHNIQUES OF USING PASTRY

Lining a pie plate for an open pie

Roll out the dough to 5mm/$\frac{1}{4}$in thick, and 10cm/4in wider than the plate (pan). Lift the dough on the rolling pin and cover the bottom and sides of the plate (pan). Trim with a knife to 1cm/$\frac{1}{2}$in from the plate (pan) edge and fold the dough under the rim. Decorate the edge by pressing down along the rim with your thumb.

Covering a (deep) pie dish

Roll out the dough evenly to about 5mm/$\frac{1}{4}$in thick, and 10cm/4in wider than the dish. Cut a 2.5cm/1in wide strip from the outer edge of the dough, place it on the moistened rim of the dish and seal the ends together with a little water. Fill the pie dish to just below the rim, place a funnel in the centre, and lift the dough over the dish with the rolling pin, taking care not to stretch it. Press the lid to the rim and cut off any excess dough.

Preparing a double crust pie

Divide the dough into two portions, one slightly larger than the other. Roll out the larger portion to a little less than 5mm/$\frac{1}{4}$in thick, and about 2.5cm/1in wider than the top of the pie dish (pan). Lift the dough over the pie dish (pan) with the rolling pin and press it into the dish (pan) without stretching the dough. Trim off excess with a knife. Put the prepared filling into the dish (pan), making a slight mound in the centre.

Roll out the smaller portion of dough to about 1cm/½in larger than the top of the pie dish (pan). Brush the rim of the lining with water, place the dough lid over the filling, trim the edges and knock up (flute). Another method is to trim the top crust to within 5mm/¼in of the dish (pan) and tuck the overhang under the edge of the bottom crust. Make a slit in the centre of the dough to allow steam to escape during cooking.

Knocking up (Fluting)

This prevents the edges of the double crust pies from coming apart during cooking. Make a series of shallow parallel cuts, at right angles to the edge, with the back of a knife in the dough edges or press with the prongs of a fork; or crimp the pastry with the thumb and forefinger. You can also decorate the edges of a pastry cover for an unlined pie, with cuts, indentations or crimping.

Making a raised pie

A hinged pie mould can be used, but you can manage without. To make a raised pie to contain pork, veal, ham or game, mould the freshly-made dough over the outside of a lightly greased glass storage jar turned upside down. This makes the pie case. Turn over, tie a band of greaseproof or waxed paper or foil round the dough to support it, remove the jar, and put the case on a baking sheet. Spoon in the prepared filling, dampen the edges of the case, fit a round dough lid on top to cover completely, and crimp to seal the edges.

Baking blind

Cooking dough before it is filled is known as baking blind. Flan cases and tartlets are often cooked in this way.

Preheat the oven to fairly hot (200°C/400°F, Gas Mark 6). Roll out the dough to a circle about 5mm/¼in thick. Carefully lift the dough on the rolling pin and lay over a 23cm/9in flan ring or flan tin on a baking sheet or a pie pan. Ease the dough down and press against the edges of the tin, ring or pan. Trim any overhanging edges with a knife. Prick the pastry base with a fork. Line with foil or greaseproof or waxed paper and weigh this down with dried beans or rice. Place in the oven and bake for 10 minutes. Remove the foil or paper and beans and continue baking for 5 minutes until the pastry is golden brown. Remove from the oven and allow to cool. It can now be filled.

Glazing

A glaze is brushed on dough before baking to give it a good finish. Beaten egg yolk, lightly beaten egg white, egg white and sugar, whole beaten egg, milk, milk and sugar, or cream can be used. Egg yolk gives the shiniest glaze. Sweet pastry can be brushed with water and then sprinkled with sugar for a pretty sparkling finish.

Asparagus Quiche (see recipe on page 21) is made from shortcrust pastry. It can be served either hot or cold.

Sift the flour, salt and cayenne into a mixing bowl. Rub in the fat. Stir in the grated cheese. Mix to a smooth dough with the beaten egg and water. Chill for 1 hour.

Preheat the oven to fairly hot (200°C/400°F, Gas Mark 6). Roll out the dough to a rectangle about 5mm/ ¼in thick. Cut into strips 5cm x 5mm/2 x ¼in. Arrange on an ungreased baking sheet and bake in the centre of the oven for about 15 minutes or until golden brown. Cool.

About 30 straws

Portuguese Shrimp Rissoles

	Metric/UK	US
Puff pastry dough (half original quantity), chilled	225g/8oz	2 cups
FILLING		
Shrimps, shelled and chopped	½kg/1lb	1lb
Hard-boiled (hard-cooked) egg, finely chopped	1	1
Béchamel Sauce	175ml/6floz	¾ cup
Cayenne pepper	⅛ tsp	⅛ tsp
Paprika	1 Tbsp	1 Tbsp
Salt	¼ tsp	¼ tsp
Chopped parsley	1 Tbsp	1 Tbsp
Oil for deep frying		

Roll out the dough to an oblong about 5mm/¼in thick. Using a sharp knife cut it into 7.5cm/3in squares. Combine the filling ingredients thoroughly in a large bowl. Place a teaspoon of the filling on each square. Moisten the edges with a little water and fold over to make a triangle. Press the edges firmly together to seal.

Heat the oil to 180°C/350°F on a deep fat thermometer. With a slotted spoon, lower 4 or 5 rissoles into the hot oil. Fry for 2 minutes or until puffed up and golden brown. Remove with a slotted spoon. Drain on kitchen paper towels. Serve hot.

About 30 rissoles

Vol-au-vent d'Ete (Puff Pastry Case with Lettuce and Egg)

This basic vol-au-vent case can be used for many other varieties of filling.

	Metric/UK	US
Puff Pastry dough, chilled	450g/1lb	4 cups

Vol-au-vent d'Eté is a puff pastry case filled with eggs, walnuts and cream, bound with béchamel.

Egg, beaten	1	1
Butter	25g/1oz	2 Tbsp
Lettuces, shredded	2	2
Salt	½ tsp	½ tsp
Black pepper	½ tsp	½ tsp
Sugar	1 tsp	1 tsp
Fresh white breadcrumbs	3 Tbsp	3 Tbsp
Béchamel Sauce	250ml/8floz	1 cup
Hard-boiled (hard-cooked) eggs, sliced	6	6
Walnuts, coarsely chopped	175g/6oz	1½ cups
Double (heavy) cream	125ml/4floz	½ cup
Grated nutmeg	½ tsp	½ tsp

To make the vol-au-vent case: divide the dough in half and roll out two equal-sized ovals. Place one on a baking sheet. Cut a smaller oval from the second oval, this forms the lid. Dampen the bottom of the oval ring with water. Place it on top of the large base oval on the baking sheet to form the case. Press together. Flake up the sides of the case with a knife to help the pastry rise. With a sharp knife, make a criss-cross pattern across the tops of both the case and the lid. Place them in the refrigerator to chill for 30 minutes.

Preheat the oven to very hot (240°C/475°F, Gas Mark 9). Paint the tops of the case and lid with lightly beaten egg, avoiding sealing the cut sides, as they will not rise.

Bake both case and lid for 20 minutes. Remove the lid from the oven and transfer to a wire rack to cool.

Reduce the oven to moderate (180°C/350°F, Gas Mark 4). Discard any soft dough from the centre of the case. Return to the oven and continue baking for about 30 minutes or until crisp and golden brown. Allow to cool on a wire rack.

In a medium-sized saucepan, melt the butter over a moderate heat. Add the lettuces, cover and simmer for 10 minutes. Add the salt, pepper and sugar. Remove from the heat and strain. Discard the liquid. Return the lettuce to the pan. Add the breadcrumbs and stir well. Add the Béchamel Sauce, eggs, walnuts, cream and nutmeg. Stir gently. Pile into the vol-au-vent shell. Bake in the preheated moderate oven for 5–7 minutes or until heated through. Serve hot.

4–6 servings

Asparagus Quiche

	Metric/UK	US
1 x 23cm/9in uncooked flan case (pastry shell) made with Shortcrust Pastry		
FILLING		
Lean cooked ham, chopped	175g/6oz	1 cup
Single (light) cream	125ml/4floz	½ cup
Milk	75ml/3floz	⅓ cup
Eggs	3	3
Cheddar cheese, grated	25g/1oz	¼ cup
Salt	¼ tsp	¼ tsp
White pepper	½ tsp	½ tsp
Asparagus tips, cooked and drained	12	12

Preheat the oven to fairly hot (200°C/400°F, Gas Mark 6). Cover the bottom of the flan case (pastry shell) with ham. Set aside. In a mixing bowl, combine the cream, milk, eggs, grated cheese, salt and pepper. Beat well. Pour the mixture over the ham. Arrange the asparagus tips on top like the spokes of a wheel, tips to the centre. Bake in the centre of the oven for 35–40 minutes or until set and golden brown. Serve hot or cold.

4–6 servings

Rhubarb Flan

	Metric/UK	US
Sugar	100g/4oz	½ cup
Water	250ml/8floz	1 cup
Fresh rhubarb, cut into 5cm/2in lengths	½kg/1lb	1lb
Ground cinnamon	½ tsp	½ tsp
Rich Shortcrust Pastry dough	225g/8oz	2 cups
Egg, lightly beaten, to glaze	1	1

In a medium-sized saucepan, dissolve the sugar in the water over a low heat. Bring to a boil. Add the rhubarb and cinnamon and bring back to the boil. Reduce the heat to moderate and simmer for 20–25 minutes until the rhubarb is tender. Remove from the heat and allow to cool. Preheat the oven to moderate (180°C/350°F, Gas Mark 4).

Roll out two-thirds of the dough into a round 5mm/¼in thick. Ease it into a 23cm/9in flan ring or pie pan and trim with a sharp knife. Fill the case with the rhubarb mixture and smooth flat with a spatula. Roll out the remaining dough into a rectangle 5mm/¼in thick. Cut it into 8 strips 1cm/½in wide. Lay over the filling to form a lattice. Glaze the dough with the beaten egg. Bake for 40 minutes or until golden brown.

6 servings

Spotted Dick

	Metric/UK	US
Flour	225g/8oz	2 cups
Salt	1 tsp	1 tsp
Sugar	2 Tbsp	2 Tbsp
Baking powder	2 tsp	2 tsp
Ground cloves	⅛ tsp	⅛ tsp
Shredded suet	75g/3oz	⅓ cup
Currants	100g/4oz	⅔ cup

Sultanas or raisins	50g/2oz	$\frac{1}{3}$ cup
Water	6 Tbsp	6 Tbsp
Strawberry jam	6 Tbsp	6 Tbsp
Milk	3 Tbsp	3 Tbsp

Sift the flour, salt, sugar, baking powder and cloves into a large mixing bowl. Stir in the suet, currants, sultanas or raisins, and water, mixing to a smooth, pliable dough. Add more water if the dough is too stiff.

Roll out the dough to a rectangle 5mm/$\frac{1}{4}$in thick. Spread the jam over the surface, leaving a margin around the edge. Brush the edges with the milk. Roll up the dough, Swiss (jelly)-roll style, pressing the edges together to seal. Wrap the roll loosely in foil or cheesecloth, making a pleat to allow for expansion.

Half fill a large saucepan or steamer with water. Place over a high heat and bring to the boil. Put the pudding on a trivet or the top of the steamer, cover and place over the water. Reduce the heat to moderate. Steam for $2\frac{1}{2}$ hours, adding more water if necessary.

Unwrap the pudding and transfer to a warmed serving dish. Serve hot.

6–8 servings

Cheesecake

	Metric/UK	US
1 basic quantity of Biscuit (Crumb) Crust		
FILLING		
Full fat cream cheese	700g/$1\frac{1}{2}$lb	3 cups
Castor (superfine) sugar	75g/3oz plus 2 tsp	$\frac{1}{3}$ cup plus 2 tsp
Eggs, separated	3	3
Cornflour (cornstarch)	1 Tbsp	1 Tbsp
Lemon juice	2 Tbsp	2 Tbsp
Grated lemon rind	1 tsp	1 tsp
Currants	50g/2oz	$\frac{1}{3}$ cup
Glacé (candied) cherries, chopped	40g/$1\frac{1}{2}$oz	$\frac{1}{4}$ cup

Below: A Cheesecake, with cream cheese filling. Right: Normandy Pear Tart.

Sour cream	**150ml/5floz**	**⅔ cup**
Vanilla essence (extract)	**½ tsp**	**½ tsp**

Preheat the oven to moderate (180°C/350°F, Gas Mark 4). Press the crumb mixture into the bottom only of a 23cm/9in loose-bottomed cake pan. Set aside.

In a large mixing bowl, combine the cream cheese and the 75g/3oz (⅓ cup) of sugar with a wooden spoon. Add the egg yolks and beat until smooth. Mix together the cornflour (cornstarch) and lemon juice. Stir the lemon rind, currants, glacé (candied) cherries and cornflour (cornstarch) mixture into the cream cheese mixture.

In another bowl, beat the egg whites until stiff. With a metal spoon, fold the egg whites into the cheese mixture. Spoon into the prepared pan and bake for 30 minutes or until the centre is firm when pressed.

Combine the sour cream, remaining sugar and the vanilla and beat well. Remove the pan from the oven and spread the sour cream mixture over the top. Return to the oven and bake for 5 minutes. Cool, then remove from the pan and chill before serving.

6 servings

Normandy Pear Tart

	Metric/UK	US
Rich Shortcrust Pastry dough	**225g/8oz**	**2 cups**
Walnuts, finely chopped	**40g/1½oz**	**⅓ cup**
FILLING		
Sugar	**50g/2oz**	**¼ cup**
Water	**150ml/5floz**	**⅔ cup**
Large pears, peeled, halved and cored	**4**	**4**
GLAZE		
Egg white, beaten	**1**	**1**
Sugar	**2 Tbsp**	**2 Tbsp**
TO DECORATE		
Double (heavy) cream, stiffly whipped	**150ml/5floz**	**⅔ cup**
Chopped walnuts	**2 Tbsp**	**2 Tbsp**

Prepare the dough, adding the walnuts with the dry ingredients, and chill. In a medium-sized saucepan dissolve the sugar in the water. Add the pears and cook for 15 minutes or until tender. Set aside to cool. Preheat the oven to fairly hot (190°C/375°F, Gas Mark 5).

Roll out two thirds of the dough into a round and use to line a 23cm/9in flan ring or loose-bottomed pie pan. Remove the pears from the syrup with a slotted spoon and arrange them, pointed ends to the centre and cut sides down, in the pastry case. Dampen the edges of the

dough. Roll out the remainder of the dough to a round large enough to make a lid for the tart. Use a pastry cutter 7.5cm/3in in diameter to cut out a hole in the centre. Lay the lid on top of the pears and gently press the edges together. Trim off any excess. Brush the top with the egg white and dust with the sugar. Bake for 30–35 minutes or until golden and firm. Remove from the flan ring or pan. Spoon the whipped cream into the centre of the tart and sprinkle over the chopped walnuts. Serve at once.
6 servings

American Apple Pie

	Metric/UK	US
PASTRY		
Flour	**275g/10oz**	**2½ cups**
Salt	**¼ tsp**	**¼ tsp**
Vegetable fat (shortening) or lard	**100g/4oz**	**½ cup**
Margarine or butter	**50g/2oz**	**¼ cup**
Iced water	**6 Tbsp**	**6 Tbsp**
Single (light) cream, to glaze	**1 Tbsp**	**1 Tbsp**
FILLING		
Sugar	**175g/6oz**	**¾ cup**
Ground cinnamon	**1 tsp**	**1 tsp**
Ground allspice	**¼ tsp**	**¼ tsp**
Grated nutmeg	**¼ tsp**	**¼ tsp**
Cornflour (cornstarch)	**1 Tbsp**	**1 Tbsp**
Cooking apples, peeled, cored and thickly sliced	**1kg/2lb**	**2lb**
Lemon juice	**1 Tbsp**	**1 Tbsp**
Butter, cut into small pieces	**25g/1oz**	**2 Tbsp**

This is a shortcrust pastry with a greater proportion of fat. The method of preparation is the same as for Basic Shortcrust Pastry. Prepare the dough and chill for 30 minutes.

Grease the bottom and sides of a deep 23cm/9in pie dish (pan). Divide the dough into two portions, one slightly larger than the other. Roll out the larger portion of dough into a round big enough to line the pie dish (pan). Lift it carefully into position and trim off the excess dough with a knife. Preheat the oven to fairly hot (190°C/375°F, Gas Mark 5).

Mix together the sugar, spices and cornflour (cornstarch) in a large bowl. Add the apple slices and lemon juice and toss thoroughly until well coated. Fill the pie with the apple mixture, doming it in the centre. Dot with the butter. Roll out the remaining dough to about 30cm/12in in diameter and lift it on top of the pie. Trim the edges and knock up (flute). Brush with the cream. Make two small cuts in the centre to allow steam to escape, then bake in the oven for 40 minutes or until golden brown. Dust with sugar, and serve hot.
6 servings

American Apple Pie, with a shortcrust pastry with cream added. Serve hot and crisp with vanilla ice-cream for a truly superb dessert.

CAKES

Cake-making is one of the traditional cooking arts still lovingly practised today. It is an art which can give endless satisfaction—both to those who make the cakes and those who eat them! Cakes also freeze well, so the old 'bake-in' makes sense in a modern context too, when you can bake one for the pot, and two or three for the freezer at the same time. Cakes are versatile, too, ranging from simple plain sponge cakes to exotic gâteaux, from small individual cakes and pastries to elaborately iced and filled offerings.

Preheat the oven to moderate (180°C/350°F, gas mark 4). Sift icing (confectioners') sugar over two sandwich tins (tart pans).

Sift 175g/6oz (1½ cups) of self-raising flour into a bowl. Cream 175g/6oz (¾ cup) of softened butter in a second bowl until light.

Add 175g/6oz (¾ cup) of castor (superfine) sugar to the fat in the bowl and beat vigorously until the mixture is light and fluffy.

Whisk 3 eggs lightly, then beat them into the mixture, a little at a time with a wooden spoon, beating after each addition.

Using a rubber spatula scrape the mixture down the sides of the bowl and off the spoon. Beat again, then fold in the flour.

Add milk to make a dropping consistency if necessary and divide between the prepared pans (tins). Bake for 25–30 minutes or until cooked.

fruit is added before the flour is folded in. They require long, slow cooking to produce a well risen, firm cake. Cakes made by the creaming method have a firm consistency, so they are ideal for cutting and shaping, as for instance in Battenburg Cake.

3. *Melting method*

This method makes moist cakes which keep well. Plain (all-purpose) flour is usually used with the addition of bicarbonate of soda (baking soda) or baking powder as the raising (leavening) agent. When bicarbonate of soda (baking soda) is used, often treacle (molasses) or syrup is included in the recipe as it acts as the acid which produces carbon dioxide to raise the cake. Moist brown sugar is preferable to white sugar as it increases the keeping quality and makes the colour richer. Sift the dry ingredients into a large mixing bowl and make a well in the centre. Gently melt the fat with the sugar, syrup and other liquid ingredients. Then stir the liquid into the dry ingredients to make a soft dough.

4. *Whisking method*

This is the true sponge cake method, depending for lightness on the air beaten in with the eggs, rather than on a raising (leavening) agent. Cakes made by this method need not contain fat. Eggs and castor (superfine) sugar are whisked together, entrapping air in the mixture until they are light, thick and mousse-like. Use a wire whisk or electric mixer to do this. The flour is then lightly folded in with a metal spoon, to prevent the air escaping from the mixture. These cakes have a drier texture and do not keep at all well. However, fat in the form of melted butter or oil can be folded in after preparation to produce a moister, richer sponge known as Genoese Sponge Cake. This is often used as a basis for rich gâteaux.

Basic sponge mixture can be placed in spoonsful on a baking sheet to bake, making delicious little sponge drops to accompany fruit and ice-cream desserts.

Swiss (jelly) rolls are made with a whisked sponge mixture. The baked sponge is spread with filling, then rolled up tightly.

Small cakes

Small cakes can be made in paper cases using the creaming method sponge. They should be neatly and carefully iced and decorated. Genoese Sponge can be made into small rich cakes for icing, by making the sponge in a square or rectangular baking tin or pan and cutting into squares once it has cooled.

Scones (biscuits)

These are a type of small, plain cake made by the rubbing-in method, using flour, a raising (leavening) agent, a very small proportion of fat, and liquid to bind the mixture. They do not keep well, except in a freezer, and are best eaten freshly baked and still warm.

Drop-scones (griddle scones or pancakes) are made from batter, cooked in small rounds on a hot greased griddle or heavy frying-pan, and eaten hot with butter and maple syrup or jam.

Biscuits (cookies)

Biscuits (cookies) are simple to make, very economical and absolutely delicious. If made from a soft dough, they can be shaped by dropping the mixture in spoonsful on to a baking sheet; these are Dropped Biscuits (Cookies). A stiffer dough can be chilled in the refrigerator and cut into shapes before baking—these are Shaped Biscuits (Cookies). A simple example is Shortbread, which can be cut into fingers with a sharp knife or pressed into a traditional wooden shortbread mould. The dough can also be cut out with a pastry (cookie) cutter into round or any fancy shapes. Piped Biscuits (Cookies) are shaped by squeezing the dough through a large forcing (pastry) bag fitted with a star nozzle. Refrigerator Biscuits (Cookies) are made from a special stiff dough which is shaped into rolls and

The Whisking Method

Preheat the oven and prepare the tins (pans). Sift the flour, baking powder and dry flavourings. Beat eggs.

Add sugar to the eggs and set over a saucepan of hot water. The bowl must not touch the water.

Whisk the eggs and sugar together with a rotary beater or whisk until it leaves a trail.

Remove from the heat and continue whisking briskly until the mixture cools slightly.

Carefully and quickly fold in the flour, about a quarter at a time until it has been incorporated.

Pour the mixture into the prepared tins (pans) and bake until the cakes are cooked.

stored in the refrigerator for up to 3 weeks; slice off thin wafers of dough as required and bake until crisp.

FILLINGS AND TOPPINGS

Many cakes and biscuits (cookies) benefit from a creamy filling or icing to enhance their appearance and to make them richer and less dry to eat. Use a broad, flat bladed palette knife or spatula to spread the creams and icings, giving a smooth finish. Invest in a nylon forcing (pastry) bag with several nozzles to vary your decoration. Your skills will soon improve with a little practice.

Buttercream and Crème au Beurre Mousseline freeze extremely well. Make a large batch at one time in a basic flavour, then use with the addition of chosen flavours as required. You can freeze cakes which have been filled, iced and decorated, although you do lose a little of the shine on the icing when defrosted. Crème Pâtissière, having a custard base, does not freeze, but Fondant Icing will store in a cupboard for weeks. Cakes filled or decorated with whipped cream freeze extremely well also.

FILLINGS

Buttercream

A quick and easy filling for sponge sandwich (layer) cakes and sweet biscuits (cookies).

	Metric/UK	US
Unsalted butter	**100g/4oz**	**½ cup**
Icing (confectioner's) sugar, sifted	**225g/8oz**	**2 cups**
Flavouring		

Beat the butter until soft, white and shiny. Gradually beat in the sugar until smooth and creamy. Add a few drops of milk if the mixture is too stiff to spread easily. Flavour and colour to complement the cake: for orange or lemon, beat in a little finely grated rind and add a few drops of the juice to give a smooth, creamy texture; for coffee, beat in a little coffee essence (extract) to taste; for chocolate, dissolve 4 level teaspoons of cocoa powder in a little boiling water, and beat in gradually.
To fill one 23cm/9in cake

Crème au Beurre

There are three types of Crème au Beurre, which are used for filling and decorating cakes and pastries. These are a little more complicated to prepare than Buttercream, but absolutely delicious.

1. SIMPLE CREME AU BEURRE

	Metric/UK	US
Milk	**150ml/5floz**	**⅔ cup**
Castor (superfine) sugar	**50g/2oz**	**¼ cup**
Egg yolks	**2**	**2**
Unsalted butter	**175g/6oz**	**¾ cup**

Make the milk, sugar and egg yolks into custard as in Basic Custard Sauce. Pour the custard through a strainer into a bowl and allow it to cool. Cream the butter until white and smooth. Gradually beat in the cooled custard and continue beating until smooth and creamy. Flavour as required.
To fill one 20cm/8in cake

2. CREME AU BEURRE MOUSSELINE

	Metric/UK	US
Sugar	**75g/3oz**	**6 Tbsp**
Water	**5 Tbsp**	**5 Tbsp**
Egg yolks	**2**	**2**
Unsalted butter	**100g/4oz**	**½ cup**

Dissolve the sugar in the water over a low heat. Cover and bring to a boil. Boil rapidly, without stirring, until it reaches 105°C/215°F or makes a short thread when a little of the cooled syrup is stretched gently between the thumb and forefinger. Remove from the heat immediately. Lightly beat the egg yolks in a small bowl and add the sugar syrup in a steady stream, beating until thick and mousse-like. Cream the butter until soft and white. Gradually beat in the egg mousse until smooth. Flavour as required. If the mixture begins to curdle, simply place over a pan of hot water and beat until smooth.
To fill one 20cm/8in cake

3. CREME AU BEURRE MERINGUEE

This is light and useful for sandwiching meringue layers together. A cooked meringue is added to the butter and can be flavoured as required.

	Metric/UK	US
Icing (confectioner's) sugar	**100g/4oz**	**1 cup**
Egg whites	**2**	**2**
Unsalted butter	**100g/4oz**	**½ cup**

Sift the sugar into a heatproof bowl and add the egg whites. Place the bowl over a pan of simmering water and beat until the meringue is very thick and will hold its shape. Remove from the heat and continue beating for a few minutes. Cream the butter as before and gradually beat in the meringue. Curdling can be remedied as in Crème au Beurre Mousseline.
To fill one 20cm/8in cake

Crème Pâtissière

This is also known as pastry custard or confectioner's custard. It has a wide variety of uses from filling choux puffs and éclairs to spreading on cakes and in pastry cases to be topped with fresh fruit. It does not keep for more than a few days in the refrigerator.

	Metric/UK	US
Egg yolks	**2**	**2**
Sugar	**50g/2oz**	**¼ cup**

Decorating with Icing Sugar

To decorate a cake with icing (confectioners') sugar, place a doily on top and sift over the sugar.

Gently lift the doily from the top of the cake with your fingertips, so that the pattern remains.

Cornflour (cornstarch)	**1 Tbsp**	**1 Tbsp**
Flour	**1 Tbsp**	**1 Tbsp**
Vanilla essence (extract)	**½ tsp**	**½ tsp**
Milk	**300ml/ ½ pint**	**1¼ cups**
Egg white (optional)	**1**	**1**

Beat the egg yolks and sugar until creamy. Sift in the cornflour (cornstarch) and flour and add the vanilla. Gradually mix in about one quarter of the milk. Heat the remainder of the milk without boiling and then add it to the egg mixture, beating well. Pour into the saucepan and heat gently, stirring, until the mixture just reaches the boil. Remove from the heat and beat until smooth. Allow to cool.

If you want to lighten the custard cream, beat the egg white until stiff. Fold the egg white into a quarter of the cream mixture, then fold that into the remaining cream. Cook over a low heat for 1–2 minutes, stirring occasionally. Allow to cool before using.
About 350ml/12floz (1½ cups)

Crème Chantilly

This is simply a flavoured, sweetened whipped cream.

	Metric/UK	US
Double (heavy) cream, chilled	**300ml/ ½ pint**	**1¼ cups**
Vanilla essence (extract)	**1 tsp**	**1 tsp**
Castor (superfine) sugar	**1 tsp**	**1 tsp**

In a mixing bowl, beat the cream until it begins to thicken. Add the vanilla and sugar and continue beating until the mixture is stiff and forms soft peaks.
About 350ml/12floz (1½ cups)

TOPPINGS

Glacé Icing

This is a simple water icing which can be coloured and flavoured and used to ice the tops of cakes.

	Metric/UK	US
Icing (confectioner's) sugar, sifted	**225g/8oz**	**2 cups**
Warm water or strained fruit juice	**1½ Tbsp**	**1½ Tbsp**
Flavouring or colouring		

Mix the sugar with most of the warm water or juice. Beat hard until it is smooth, shiny and will coat the

Glacé Icing

Beat warm water or juice into sifted icing (confectioners') sugar until the ingredients are mixed.

Beat the mixture vigorously for about 3 minutes, or until it is shiny, thick and smooth.

Pour the icing on to the cake and spread it evenly over the top and sides with a palette knife.

back of the spoon thickly. Thin a little if required. It is easy to make it too soft. Flavour and colour as required, keeping the colouring very discreet. Pour over the cake at once, spread smoothly to the edges and add any decoration while the icing is still soft. Allow to set.
To ice one 20cm/8in cake

Marbling

This is an effective but simple decoration for cakes covered with white glacé icing. Add a few drops of food colouring to 1 tablespoon of prepared glacé icing. The colour should be sufficiently bold to contrast with the white icing. Use a small forcing (pastry) bag, or make a small greaseproof or waxed paper forcing (pastry) bag. Draw parallel lines over the surface of the cake with the coloured icing, about 1cm/½in apart. Use a skewer to draw aside the icing in lines at right angles to the coloured lines. First draw the skewer from left to right, then from right to left. Leave to set.

Cooked Frostings

Frostings are a type of soft icing which can fill or ice a cake. Chopped nuts are often added with the flavouring.

BASIC FROSTING

	Metric/UK	US
Sugar	225g/8oz	1 cup
Water	5 Tbsp	5 Tbsp
Egg white	1	1
Cream of tartar	⅛ tsp	⅛ tsp
Vanilla essence (extract)	½ tsp	½ tsp

Dissolve the sugar in the water over a low heat. Bring to the boil and boil rapidly until the temperature reaches 115°C/240°F on a sugar thermometer. In a medium-sized mixing bowl, beat the egg white with the cream of tartar until it forms stiff peaks. Pour the sugar syrup in a steady stream on to the beaten egg white, beating continuously until the frosting is thick enough to spread. Stir in the vanilla.
To ice one 20cm/8in cake

Marbling

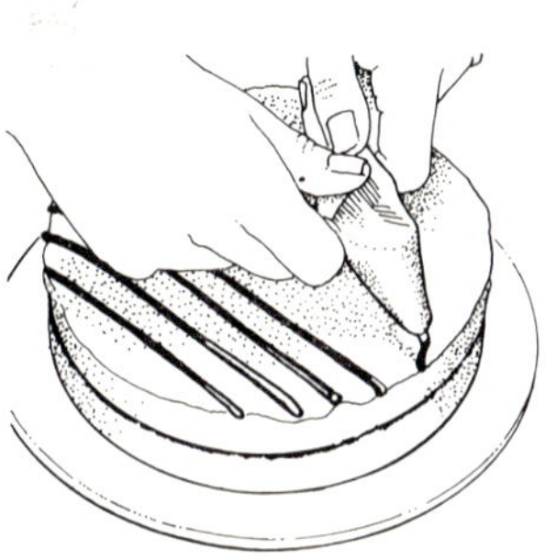

Pipe a contrasting colour of icing in lines over the white icing.

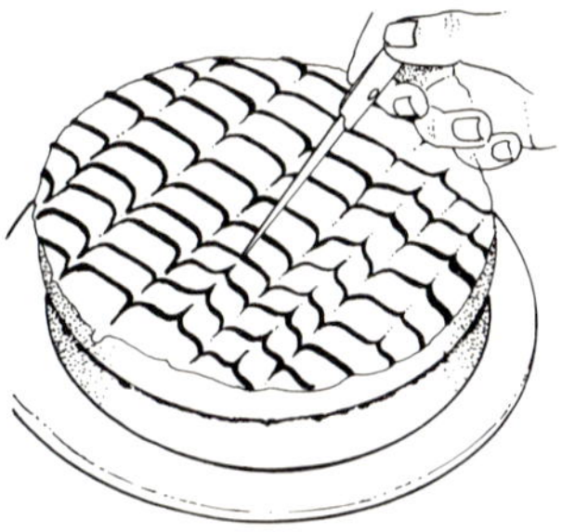

Make a leafy pattern by altering the lines with a knife, as shown.

Fondant Icing

This is a sweet, smooth icing used for cakes and gâteaux. It can be stored in an airtight jar in the refrigerator for 2–3 weeks.

	Metric/UK	US
Sugar	450g/1lb	2 cups
Water	200ml/7floz	1 cup less 2 Tbsp
Cream of tartar	$\frac{1}{8}$ tsp	$\frac{1}{8}$ tsp

Use a spotlessly clean, heavy-based saucepan. Dissolve the sugar in the water slowly, then bring to the boil. Add the cream of tartar (dissolved in a few drops of water) and boil rapidly until the syrup reaches 115°C/240°F on a sugar thermometer. Remove from the heat and pour on to a flat surface to cool. Do not stir or scrape the pan or the mixture will become gritty and uneven. When it is cool enough to handle, work the fondant with a palette knife or spatula until it turns opaque and white. Knead hard with your hands until smooth and pliable. Roll into balls and place in polythene (plastic) bags to mature for several hours before using.

Use Fondant Icing in its finished state to mould and shape sweets (candies). To use the icing as a frosting or coating, combine it with 3 or 4 tablespoons of sugar syrup until it is thick and creamy but pours and spreads easily.

To make the sugar syrup, take 250ml/8floz (1 cup) water and proceed as before, but remove from the heat when the temperature reaches 110°C/220°F and the mixture looks syrupy. Allow to cool completely before using.

To ice a cake, gently warm the prepared fondant in a heatproof bowl over hot water. Gradually add enough of the sugar syrup and flavouring to make a smooth, thick pouring consistency. Place the cake on a wire rack over a tray to catch drips. Carefully pour the warm fondant over the top of the cake so that it eventually covers the top and sides completely. Avoid spreading and moving with a knife — it should spread fairly evenly by itself. Leave to cool before cutting the cake. It gives a shiny, beautiful finish to a special cake and is worth the effort.

About 450g/1lb (4 cups)

Seven Minute Frosting

	Metric/UK	US
Sugar	350g/12oz	$1\frac{1}{2}$ cups
Water	4 Tbsp	4 Tbsp
Cream of tartar	$\frac{1}{4}$ tsp	$\frac{1}{4}$ tsp
Salt	$\frac{1}{8}$ tsp	$\frac{1}{8}$ tsp
Egg whites	2	2

Put all the ingredients into a medium-sized heatproof bowl. Beat for 1 minute. Place the bowl over a saucepan of simmering water and continue beating for 7 minutes. Remove from the heat and continue beating until the frosting is thick enough to spread.

To ice one 23cm/9in cake

Rough Icing

Put a blob of icing on the centre of your cake board and set the cake on top.

Put all the icing on the cake. Work back and forth to remove bubbles, then spread over the sides.

Using the blade of a knife or the handle of a teaspoon, rough the icing up in peaks.

Almond Paste

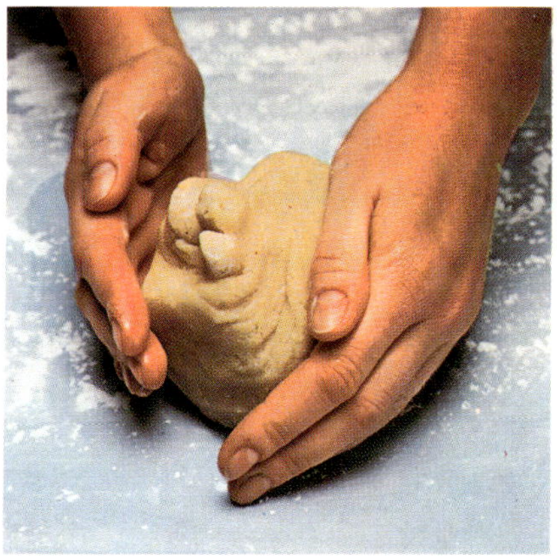

To make marzipan (almond paste), sift the icing (confectioners') and castor (superfine) sugars into a bowl with the ground almonds.

Add the lemon juice, almond essence (extract) and some of the egg and beat well. Add more egg if you need more liquid.

Mix to a smooth paste. Turn out on to a board sprinkled with icing (confectioners') sugar. Knead for 3 minutes until smooth and oily.

Royal Icing

This is a pure white icing which is traditionally used for icing Christmas, wedding and rich fruit cakes. It produces a smooth, hard finish which can be decorated as elaborately as you wish.

	Metric/UK	US
Icing (confectioner's) sugar sifted	450g/1lb	4 cups
Egg whites, lightly beaten	2	2

Place the sugar in a large mixing bowl. Add the egg whites and stir gently with a wooden spoon until smooth. Beat gently for 2 minutes, then vigorously for 10 minutes until the icing is fairly thick and holds stiff peaks.

To ice two 23cm/9in cakes

To Ice a Rich Fruit Cake

Place the fruit cake on a board and brush all over lightly with Apricot Glaze. Roll out Almond Paste to about 1cm/$\frac{1}{2}$in and cut in a strip as wide as the side of the cake. Press the strip gently against the sides of the cake and trim neatly to fit. Roll out the remainder of the almond paste to a round slightly larger than the top of the cake. Gently place on top of the cake. Press into position and trim any excess to make a neat, smooth finish all over.

Spread the prepared Royal Icing over the top and sides of the cake, smoothing it carefully with the blade of a knife over the top and sides. Leave to harden for 4–5 days before decorating.

To give a 'snow effect', gently pull the icing upwards in soft peaks with a rounded palette knife or spatula and leave to harden for 1–2 days.

Apricot Glaze

Useful for glazing fruit flans (pies) and tartlets, brushing over cakes before icing, holding almond paste on to cakes and glazing Danish pastries. These quantities are for making in bulk.

	Metric/UK	US
Sugar syrup	150ml/5floz	$\frac{2}{3}$ cup
Apricot jam	450g/1lb	1lb ($1\frac{1}{3}$ cups)
Juice of $\frac{1}{2}$ lemon		

Make the sugar syrup as in Fondant Icing. Put the jam, syrup and lemon juice into a pan and heat almost to boiling. Rub through a wire strainer into a clean pan. Boil gently for a few minutes until the glaze hangs in drops from a wooden spoon. Store in a covered bowl in the refrigerator.

Almond Paste

	Metric/UK	US
Icing (confectioner's) sugar	100g/4oz	1 cup
Castor (superfine) sugar	100g/4oz	$\frac{1}{2}$ cup
Ground almonds	225g/8oz	2 cups
Lemon juice	1 tsp	1 tsp
Almond essence (extract)	3 drops	3 drops
Egg, lightly beaten	1	1

Work the ingredients into a smooth ball. Do not over-knead.

About 225g/8oz (2 cups)

PIPING

This is the most effective method of decorating cakes with Royal Icing or Buttercream. Use a small grease-proof or waxed paper bag for small quanitities and a large forcing (pastry) bag for large quantities. The consistency is very important; it must be smooth to be

Decorating with Almond Paste

To colour almond paste, work edible food colouring into it. Deep colours, such as the green used here, look better than light tones.

For holly leaves, draw a leaf shape on to a card. Use the card as a template to cut shapes. Mark the veins with a knife.

Another way to do it is to cut out small rounds using a plain cutter. Then simply cut away the edges of the circle with a smaller cutter.

piped evenly and easily, but stiff enough to hold the piped shape. There are many different shaped nozzles available which can produce many interesting swirls and flowers.

Buttercream piping

Cover the cake with prepared buttercream and coat the sides with chopped nuts or other decorations. Use a large, plain nozzle fitted in a piping (pastry) bag and pipe lines across the cake. Pipe a border with an up and down movement or a border of 'rosettes' with a star nozzle. The patterns are essentially bolder with this type of soft icing.

Piping with Royal Icing

Attractive borders can be made using small shaped nozzles, in shells, spirals or zig-zag patterns. Thin lines. can be drawn and messages piped with thin, plain nozzles. Make flowers in advance, piped on a piece of greaseproof or waxed paper and set aside to dry. Place them in position on the iced cake with a small dot of icing.

The icing pattern can be as simple or as elaborate as you choose. The golden rule is always to practice first on greaseproof or waxed paper if you are a little unsure of yourself, before proceeding with the finished cake.

Making a Piping Bag

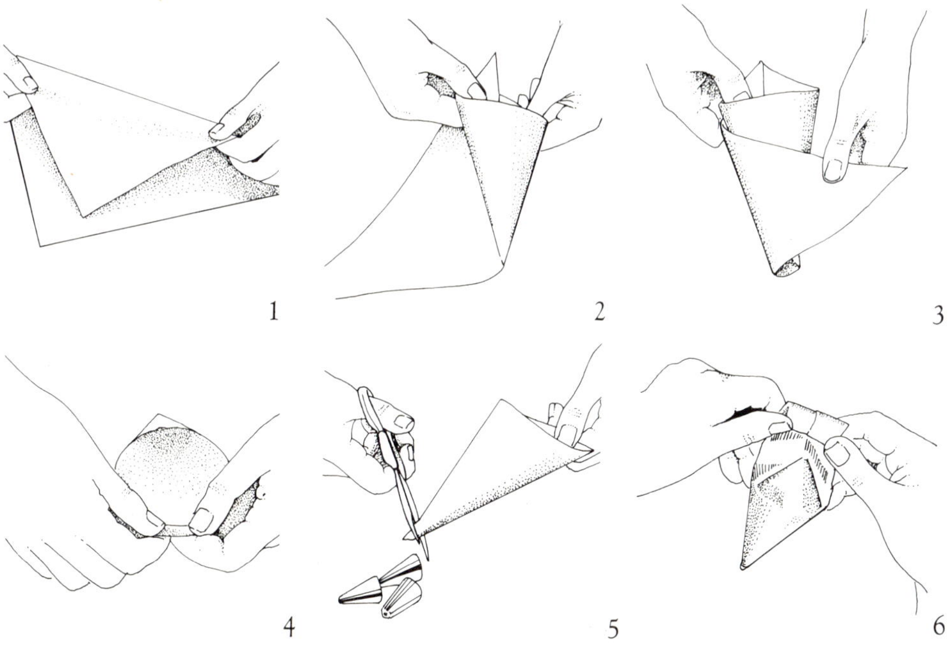

Cut a 25cm/10in square from greaseproof or waxed paper. Fold diagonally to make two triangles. (1) With the base facing away, bring up the lefthand corner of the base to meet the top of the triangle. (2) Holding the two points together, bring up the righthand corner and wrap around the back. (3) Fold the three corners towards the inside of the cone. (4) Cut off the point of the bag to fit the chosen nozzle. Slip on the nozzle. (5). Fill the bag at an angle, no more than half full. Fold down to secure. (6)

RECIPES

Dundee Cake

	Metric/UK	US
Butter	225g/8oz	1 cup
Castor (superfine) sugar	225g/8oz	1 cup
Flour	275g/10oz	2½ cups
Baking powder	½ tsp	½ tsp
Eggs	5	5
Raisins	100g/4oz	⅔ cup
Currants	100g/4oz	⅔ cup
Sultanas (seedless raisins)	100g/4oz	⅔ cup
Mixed candied fruit	50g/2oz	⅓ cup
Glacé (candied) cherries	50g/2oz	⅓ cup
Grated rind of 1 orange		
Grated rind of 1 lemon		
Mixed spice (apple pie spice)	½ tsp	½ tsp
Ground cinnamon	½ tsp	½ tsp
Blanched almonds, halved (to decorate)	50g/2oz	½ cup

Line a 20cm/8in diameter, deep cake tin (pan) with greaseproof or waxed paper or foil then grease. Preheat the oven to warm (170°C/325°F, Gas Mark 3).

Prepare the batter by the creaming method. Add the spices at the same time as the flour. Turn the mixture into the tin (pan) and smooth it flat. Arrange the halved almonds on top of the cake. Bake in the lower part of the oven for about 2 hours. Test with a skewer. Turn off the heat and leave the cake in the oven for about 10 minutes. Remove and allow to cool in the tin (pan) until you can turn it out on to a rack to become completely cold. Peel off the paper or foil.

Orange Cake Fingers

	Metric/UK	US
Castor (superfine) sugar	75g/3oz	⅓ cup
Eggs	2	2
Flour	75g/3oz	¾ cup
Ground almonds	2 Tbsp	2 Tbsp
Grated rind of 2 oranges		
Orange-flavoured liqueur	1 tsp	1 tsp

Preheat the oven to moderate (180°C/350°F, Gas Mark 4). Grease and flour an 18×23cm/7×9in Swiss (jelly) roll tin.

Place the sugar and eggs in a heatproof bowl over a pan of hot water. Beat until the mixture is thick and pale and will make a trail on itself when the whisk is lifted. (If using an electric beater, no heat is needed). Remove from the heat. Use a metal spoon to fold in the flour and almonds. Fold in the orange rind and liqueur. Pour into the tin and bake for 30 minutes or until the cake springs back when lightly pressed. Cool for 5 minutes, then turn out on to a wire rack. Cool. Cut into fingers before serving.

About 20 fingers

Dundee Cake, a rich fruit cake made by the creaming method.

Almond Cake

This cake uses ground almonds instead of flour.

	Metric/UK	US
Egg yolks	6	6
Castor (superfine) sugar	100g/4oz	½ cup
Ground almonds	175g/6oz	1½ cups
Milk	2 Tbsp	2 Tbsp
Egg whites	6	6
ICING		
Icing (confectioner's) sugar	450g/1lb	4 cups
Hot water	2 Tbsp	2 Tbsp
Egg white	1	1
Almond essence (extract)	¼ tsp	¼ tsp
Slivered (shredded) almonds (to decorate)	50g/2oz	½ cup

Preheat the oven to moderate (180°C/350°F, Gas Mark 4). Line a Swiss (jelly) roll tin with greaseproof or waxed paper or foil. Grease and set aside.

Beat together the egg yolks and sugar. Fold in the ground almonds and milk. Beat the egg whites until they are stiff and gently fold into the batter. Place in the tin and bake for 15–20 minutes or until golden and cooked through. Cool for 5 minutes, then turn out on to a clean sheet of greaseproof or waxed paper or foil dusted with cornflour (cornstarch). Discard the lining. Leave to cool. For the icing, put the sugar, water and egg white in a heatproof bowl over a pan of hot water. Beat until the icing is glossy and will coat the back of the spoon. Stir in the almond essence (extract). Set aside to cool.

Use a sharp knife to cut the cake into 4 rectangles the same size. Place one rectangle on a serving dish. Spread with a little of the icing and continue to make layers with the cake and icing. Spread the remaining icing evenly over the top and sides of the cake. Sprinkle the top with the slivered (shredded) almonds.

Classic Madeira Cake, made with self-raising flour.

Chocolate Roulade

	Metric/UK	US
Eggs, separated	**5**	**5**
Castor (superfine) sugar	**175g/6oz**	**¾ cup**
Dark (semi-sweet) cooking chocolate	**175g/6oz**	**6 squares**
Cold water	**3 Tbsp**	**3 Tbsp**
TO FILL		
Double (heavy) cream	**250ml/8floz**	**1 cup**
Vanilla essence (extract)	**½ tsp**	**½ tsp**

Preheat the oven to hot (220°C/425°F, Gas Mark 7). Grease a Swiss (jelly) roll tin. Line with greaseproof or waxed paper or foil and grease. Set aside.

Beat the egg yolks and sugar together until the mixture is pale, thick and fluffy. Melt the chocolate and water in a small pan over a low heat, stirring continuously. Remove from the heat. When cool, beat into the egg yolk mixture. Beat the egg whites until they are stiff. Fold into the chocolate mixture carefully with a metal spoon. Spoon into the tin and bake for 10 minutes.

Reduce the heat to warm (170°C/325°F, Gas Mark 3). Bake for a further 10 minutes or until a skewer inserted into the cake comes out clean. Remove from the tin and cover with a damp cloth. Leave for 15 minutes.

Turn the cake out on to a fresh piece of sugared greaseproof or waxed paper or foil. Chill for 30 minutes. With a sharp knife, make a shallow cut across the cake at one end to make rolling easier. Using the paper or foil to lift, roll the cake carefully, rolling the paper or foil inside so it can be unrolled again. Keep it rolled until it is completely cold. Then, unroll the cake carefully and remove the paper or foil. Whip the cream with the vanilla until thick and spread over the cake. Roll up the cake again, and sprinkle with icing (confectioner's) sugar before serving.

Madeira Cake

	Metric/UK	US
Butter	**225g/8oz**	**1 cup**
Castor (superfine) sugar	**225g/8oz**	**1 cup**
Self-raising (self-rising) flour	**225g/8oz**	**2 cups**
Eggs	**5**	**5**
Grated rind of 1 lemon		
Juice of ½ lemon		
Candied citron peel	**3 strips**	**3 strips**

Preheat the oven to moderate (180°C/350°F, Gas Mark 4.) Grease and flour a 15cm/6in round, deep tin (pan). Make the cake batter by the creaming method, adding a tablespoonful of the flour with each egg to avoid curdling. Stir in the lemon rind and juice. Spoon into the prepared tin (pan) and sprinkle with 1 tablespoon

Viennese Fingers–delicious biscuits (cookies) sandwiched together with buttercream and decorated with melted chocolate.

of sugar. Bake for 30 minutes. Place the candied citron peel on top, return to the oven and continue baking for 45–50 minutes or until cooked through. Turn on to a wire rack to cool.

Viennese Fingers

	Metric/UK	US
Butter, softened	**225g/8oz**	**1 cup**
Icing (confectioner's) sugar	**50g/2oz**	**½ cup**
Flour	**225g/8oz**	**2 cups**
Grated orange rind	**2 tsp**	**2 tsp**
Orange juice	**1 Tbsp**	**1 Tbsp**
Dark plain chocolate (to decorate)	**175g/6oz**	**6 squares**
BUTTERCREAM		
Unsalted butter, softened	**50g/2oz**	**¼ cup**
Icing (confectioner's) sugar sifted	**100g/4oz**	**1 cup**
Vanilla essence (extract)	**⅛ tsp**	**⅛ tsp**

Grease two baking sheets. Preheat the oven to moderate (180°C/350°F, Gas Mark 4). Prepare the dough using the creaming method. Fill a large forcing (pastry) bag, fitted with a star-shaped nozzle, with the mixture and pipe out 24 fingers, each about 7.5cm/3in long on to the baking sheets. Bake for 10–15 minutes or until golden and firm. Leave the biscuits (cookies) to cool for 5 minutes, then transfer to a wire rack to cool completely. Make the Buttercream as in the basic recipe and use to sandwich together pairs of biscuits (cookies).

Melt the chocolate in a small heatproof bowl over a pan of hot water. Dip each end of each biscuit (cookie) into the melted chocolate and place on greaseproof or waxed paper to harden and dry.

This type of biscuit (cookie) dough can be shaped to an S-shape, a star shape or whatever shape you choose, using a forcing (pastry) bag and a large star nozzle.

About 24 fingers

Chocolate Refrigerator Biscuits (Cookies)

	Metric/UK	US
Flour	**175g/6oz**	**1½ cups**
Baking powder	**1 tsp**	**1 tsp**
Salt	**¼ tsp**	**¼ tsp**
Butter	**100g/4oz**	**½ cup**
Sugar	**100g/4oz**	**½ cup**
Vanilla essence (extract)	**½ tsp**	**½ tsp**
Egg, beaten	**1**	**1**
Plain (semi-sweet) chocolate, melted	**40g/1½oz**	**1½ squares**

Make the basic dough using the creaming method. Divide the dough in half. Add the melted chocolate to one half. Chill well.

Madeleines

tins (layer cake pans). Dust lightly with flour.

Make the batter by the whisking method, gently folding in the melted butter until absorbed. Take care not to overmix or the cake will not rise well. Pour into the prepared tins (pans) and bake for 15–20 minutes or until golden brown and springy to the touch. Turn out on to a wire rack to cool.

Sandwich the cakes together with one third of the icing. Use the remainder to cover the top and sides of the cake. Sprinkle toasted chopped nuts over the top and sides of the cake.

Madeleines

These little sponge cakes are baked in a traditional shell-shaped mould.

	Metric/UK	US
Butter, melted	**100g/4oz**	**½ cup**
Flour	**100g/4oz**	**1 cup**
Castor (superfine) sugar	**100g/4oz**	**½ cup**
Eggs	**4**	**4**
Vanilla essence (extract)	**½ tsp**	**½ tsp**

Preheat the oven to fairly hot (200°C/400°F, Gas Mark 6). Grease 36 madeleine moulds and dust lightly with flour. Set aside. Make the batter using the whisking method, and lightly fold in the butter.

Fill each mould no more than three-quarters full. Bake for 7–10 minutes or until golden brown and cooked through. Leave to cool for 5 minutes, then turn out of the moulds and cool on a wire rack.

36 cakes

Scones (Biscuits) with Dried Fruit

These traditional British scones (biscuits) are served warm, split and spread with butter.

	Metric/UK	US
Flour	**225g/8oz**	**2 cups**
Baking powder	**2 tsp**	**2 tsp**
Bicarbonate of soda (baking soda)	**1 tsp**	**1 tsp**
Salt	**¼ tsp**	**¼ tsp**
Vegetable fat (shortening) or margarine	**40g/1½oz**	**3 Tbsp**
Castor (superfine) sugar	**50g/2oz**	**¼ cup**
Raisins	**50g/2oz**	**⅓ cup**
Currants	**2 Tbsp**	**2 Tbsp**
Large egg	**1**	**1**
Milk	**75ml/3floz**	**⅓ cup**

Preheat the oven to very hot (230°C/450°F, Gas Mark 8). Grease a large baking sheet. Sift the dry ingredients into a large bowl. Rub in the fat as in the rubbing-in method. Stir in the sugar and fruit and make a soft dough with the egg and milk. Knead very lightly until just mixed and smooth.

Turn on to a floured board. Flatten out with the hands (a rolling pin knocks out the lightness) to about 1cm/½in thick. Use a 5cm/2in pastry (cookie) cutter to cut the dough into rounds. Re-knead and use up the scraps. Place the rounds on the baking sheet. Bake for 10–12 minutes or until well risen and golden brown. Cool on a rack.

About 12 Scones (biscuits)

Scones (Biscuits) with Sour Cream

	Metric/UK	US
Flour	**350g/12oz**	**3 cups**
Bicarbonate of soda (baking soda)	**2 tsp**	**2 tsp**
Salt	**½ tsp**	**½ tsp**
Vegetable fat (shortening)	**50g/2oz**	**¼ cup**
Sour cream	**175ml/6floz**	**¾ cup**
TO GLAZE		
Egg yolk	**1**	**1**
Milk	**2 Tbsp**	**2 Tbsp**

Preheat the oven to very hot (230°C/450°F, Gas Mark 8). Grease two baking sheets and set aside. Make the scones (biscuits) by the basic rubbing-in method, adding the sour cream as the liquid. Divide the dough into 2 rounds, about 20cm/8in in diameter and place on the baking sheets. Cut each dough round with a sharp knife into 8 triangular shapes. Do not separate. Brush with the beaten egg and milk mixture. Bake for 10–15 minutes or until risen and golden brown. Pull apart and cool on a wire rack.

16 scones (biscuits)

Drop Scones (Pancakes)

Use a flat, iron griddle or heavy frying-pan to make these batter scones (biscuits).

	Metric/UK	US
Self-raising (self-rising) flour	**225g/8oz**	**2 cups**
Golden (light corn) syrup	**2 Tbsp**	**2 Tbsp**
Eggs	**2**	**2**
Vegetable oil	**2 Tbsp**	**2 Tbsp**
Milk		

Lightly grease the griddle with a little oil. Sift the flour into a bowl. Make a well in the centre and add the syrup, eggs and oil. Beat well together, gradually drawing in the flour. Beat in enough milk to make a batter which is the consistency of thick cream. Drop

Scones (Biscuits) with Dried Fruit.

Nougatines are luscious little sponge cakes.

spoonsful of the batter on to the heated griddle and cook for 3 minutes or until bubbling. Turn over with a spatula and cook the other side until golden. Remove the cooked scones (biscuits) and cover with a clean cloth. Use the remainder of the batter in the same way.
28 scones (pancakes)

Nougatine Cakes

	Metric/UK	US
8 small rectangular cakes, cut from basic Genoese sponge		
Apricot Glaze		
Blanched almonds	8	8

Jamaican Spice Loaf is a sort of gingerbread with treacle or molasses. Serve warm with lots of butter.

PRALINE CREAM FILLING

Castor (superfine) sugar	100g/4oz	½ cup
Almonds	100g/4oz	1 cup
Butter, softened	100g/4oz	½ cup
Icing (confectioner's) sugar	100g/4oz	1 cup
Double (heavy) cream, whipped	50ml/2floz	¼ cup

ICING

Dark (semi-sweet) chocolate, in small pieces	100g/4oz	4 squares
Fondant Icing	350g/12oz	1½ cups
Sugar syrup (optional)	up to 6 Tbsp	up to 6 Tbsp

To make the filling, in a small saucepan, melt the castor (superfine) sugar over a low heat. When it has melted, increase the heat to high and boil, without stirring, for 1–2 minutes or until a rich golden brown. Add the almonds and stir to coat them evenly. Remove from the heat. Pour on to a cold surface and leave to harden completely. Crush with a rolling pin or put in an electric blender and blend to a fine powder.

Beat the softened butter with the icing (confectioner's) sugar and whipped cream until smooth. Beat in the crushed praline powder and set aside.

To make the icing, melt the chocolate in a heatproof bowl over hot water. Beat in the Fondant Icing, a little at a time until smooth. Dilute with sugar syrup if necessary. Keep hot. With a sharp knife, slice each cake across into three layers. Spread a little Praline Cream over the first two layers and reassemble. Brush the top and sides of each cake with a little Apricot Glaze to stop crumbs from spoiling the icing. Smoothly coat each layered cake with the hot chocolate Fondant Icing, to cover the top and sides completely. Press a blanched almond on to each cake. Allow to cool completely for 30 minutes before serving.

About 8 cakes

Jamaican Spice Loaf

	Metric/UK	US
Butter	50g/2oz	4 Tbsp
Flour	350g/12oz	3 cups
Bicarbonate of soda (baking soda)	1½ tsp	1½ tsp
Salt	¼ tsp	¼ tsp
Mixed spice (apple pie spice)	½ tsp	½ tsp
Ground cinnamon	½ tsp	½ tsp
Grated nutmeg	½ tsp	½ tsp
Ground ginger	1 tsp	1 tsp
Raisins	75g/3oz	½ cup
Black treacle (molasses)	4 Tbsp	4 Tbsp
Eggs	3	3
Milk	50ml/2floz	¼ cup

Preheat the oven to warm (170°C/325°F, Gas Mark 3). Grease a 1kg/2lb loaf tin (pan) and set aside. Sift the dry ingredients into a large bowl. Add the raisins. Heat the treacle (molasses) and butter and pour into the flour, stirring continuously. Stir in the eggs and milk to make a soft dough. Turn into the tin (pan) and bake in the centre of the oven for about 1½ hours, or until cooked through. Turn out on to a wire rack to cool.

USING YEAST

Using yeast is not difficult providing you remember a few basic facts about it and keep these in mind as you work with it. Above all, remember that yeast is a living organism and needs warmth, food and moisture if it is to work properly. Yeast is the raising agent in dough, and the more efficiently it works, then the better will be the rise.

You can buy fresh yeast in cakes or dried yeast in granules and both are extremely effective. The advantage of dried yeast is that it has good storing properties, while fresh yeast will only last for 4–5 days in the refrigerator. However, it will freeze for a few weeks, which is very convenient. Fresh yeast should smell slightly of mushrooms, be creamy-grey in colour, break cleanly and crumble well. Do not buy fresh yeast that is dark, hard and strong-smelling. Dried yeast looks like small hard granules and is more concentrated than fresh yeast, so use only half the quantity of dried yeast in a recipe giving quantities for fresh yeast.

Yeast is activated by moisture, which is provided by the liquid added; food, which is supplied by added sugar or the sugar in the flour; and by warmth. The yeast is killed off in the process of baking at 43°C/110°F, but requires a temperature of between 24°C/75°F and 29°C/85°F to produce a good rise. It gives off bubbles of carbon dioxide gas which cause the gluten in the flour to stretch and expand, giving the light open texture which we associate with yeast products.

Note: *All the quantities in this chapter are for fresh yeast, so halve them for dried yeast.*

OTHER INGREDIENTS

Liquid

This can be water or a mixture of milk and water. It is usually heated to lukewarm (about 24°C/75°F to 29°C/85°F) before adding to the flour.

Salt

Always add a little salt to the dough, or the flavour will be rather flat. However, avoid adding too much as this inhibits the action of the yeast.

Flour

Have the flour at room temperature before using it. Almost all flours are soft, household blends which do not produce a well-risen loaf. Aim to buy strong flour, made from hard wheat. This has a high gluten content, which produces a more springy, elastic dough. Choose from white strong flour, wholemeal flour or wholewheat flour. These are available from health-food shops and big supermarkets. You can mix the white and brown flours to produce varying colours and flavours of brown bread.

Eggs, butter or oil can be added to produce a richer mixture. The finished product is yellower in colour, a little lighter in texture and has better keeping qualities.

TECHNIQUES

1. *Dissolving the yeast*

Crumble fresh yeast into a small bowl, add the sugar (if called for in the recipe) and a small quantity of the warmed milk, or milk and water. Mix to a smooth cream and set aside in a warm place for about 20 minutes until puffed up and frothy.

If you are using dried yeast, dissolve a little sugar in a little warm liquid and sprinkle on the dried yeast. Leave for 10 minutes in a warm place to separate and swell.

The yeast is now active and ready to use.

2. *Mixing the dough*

Put the dry ingredients (usually flour, salt and sugar) into a large warm mixing bowl. Make a well in the centre and add the liquid ingredients (milk, water, egg, butter, oil, etc.). Use your fingers or a spatula to draw down the flour and mix into the liquids until the flour has all been incorporated. If the dough is too soft and wet, then add a little more flour.

3. *Kneading*

This can be done successfully in an electric mixer fitted with a dough hook, but hand kneading is a satisfying process. To knead by hand, turn the dough on to a lightly floured board or marble slab. Fold the dough over towards you from the opposite side, then push it away firmly using the heel of your hand. Turn the dough slightly and repeat. Continue doing this for at least 10 minutes until the dough is soft, smooth and elastic. Successful rising depends on this kneading and if you can continue for about 10–15 minutes, so much the better.

4. *Rising*

Shape the dough into a ball and place in a large bowl. Cover the bowl with a damp cloth or lightly oiled polythene (plastic) sheet to prevent the dough from drying out. The yeast is now evenly dispersed throughout the dough and activated by warmth, liquid and food. Place the bowl in a draught-free place and leave it to rise. If the kitchen is cold, place the bowl over warm water, but without touching it, to speed up the rise. *Do not* put the dough over heat, in a slow oven or over a pilot-light or hot-plate. This will produce a coarse dough and a grey-looking crumb tasting too strongly of yeast.

The length of time the dough takes almost to double its bulk will vary enormously. But between half an hour and $1\frac{1}{2}$ hours is usually adequate. A high proportion of sugar and fats retards the rising process. Do not let the dough rise too far; it will break the gluten pockets and collapse when cooked.

You can give the dough a 'slow-rise' in the refrigerator overnight, producing a lighter, springier loaf, which keeps well. If you do this, the dough needs longer knocking back and longer proving time.

5. *Knocking back*

Take the swollen dough and place on a board. Knuckle it down with your fist to expel surplus carbon dioxide and bring the yeast back into contact with its food supply. Knead for 2 minutes.

Use a sharp knife to cut into loaves or rolls and check the size by weighing the pieces. Shape into loaves or rolls, paying attention to the uniformity of the shapes.

6. *Proving*

This is to ensure that the yeast is still active. Put the dough in the greased tins (pans) and push it out to roughly the shape of the tins (pans), cover with a damp cloth again and place in a warm, slightly moist position for 45–60 minutes. The dough will rise up again and fill the tins (pans).

For a plain finish, dust with a little flour. For a shiny finish brush with a little beaten egg and milk. Cracked wheat can be sprinkled on brown loaves and poppy-seeds on rolls and sweet breads.

7. *Baking*

Preheat the oven to very hot (240°C/475°F, Gas Mark 9) while the bread is proving. Always place the dough in a very hot oven. Initially, the bread will rise; this is called 'oven spring'. The high temperature kills the action of the yeast and the gluten cells will continue to set while baking. After 15 minutes reduce the oven temperature to the temperature given in the recipe (usually between 190°C/375°F, Gas Mark 5 and 220°C/425°F, Gas Mark 7). Bake for about 25–30 minutes or until the bread sounds hollow when rapped on the underside with your knuckles. Cool on a wire rack before attempting to cut it. Bread freezes well, so it is well worth making a large batch at one time.

Types of Bread

Household White Bread

Bake the bread in a simple loaf tin (pan), braid it or shape it into round loaves.

	Metric/UK	US
Butter	**2 tsp**	**2 tsp**
Yeast	**25g/1oz**	**½ cake or 1½ envelopes**
Sugar	**1 Tbsp plus 1 tsp**	**1 Tbsp plus 1 tsp**
Warm water	**900ml/1½ pints**	**3¾ cups**
Flour	**1.35kg/3lb**	**12 cups**
Salt	**1 Tbsp**	**1 Tbsp**

Grease four loaf tins (pans) with the butter. Prepare and cream the yeast with 1 teaspoon of the sugar and 4 teaspoons of the warm water. Proceed following the basic method. Put the 4 loaves to prove. Preheat the oven to very hot (240°C/475°F, Gas Mark 9). When

the loaves have risen up to fill the tins (pans) after about 30–40 minutes, place in the centre of the oven. After 15 minutes, reduce the temperature to hot (220°C/425°F, Gas Mark 7) and put the bread on a lower shelf. Bake for another 25–30 minutes. Tip the loaves out of the tins (pans), test that they are cooked through and put to cool. If not quite ready, return to the oven, upside down, at fairly hot (190°C/375°F, Gas Mark 5) until cooked.

Four 450g/1lb loaves

Wholewheat Bread

	Metric/UK	US
Butter	1½ tsp	1½ tsp
Yeast	25g/1oz	½ cake or 1½ envelopes
Brown sugar	1 tsp	1 tsp
Warm water	900ml/1½ pints	3¾ cups
Stone-ground, wholewheat flour	1.35kg/3lb	12 cups
Salt	1 Tbsp	1 Tbsp
Clear honey	2 Tbsp	2 Tbsp
Vegetable oil	1 Tbsp	1 Tbsp

Prepare and cream the yeast with the brown sugar and about 4 teaspoons of the warm water. Proceed as for the basic method, adding the honey and oil with the remaining warm water. Bake in well-greased tins (pans), or flower pots for an attractive, unusual shape. Sprinkle with a little cracked wheat before baking.

Oven temperature and cooking time as for Household White Bread.

Four 450g/1lb loaves

Danish Pastries

Danish Pastries are made with Croissant dough, rolled like puff pastry. Many mouth-watering flavourings are added as fillings, and they have distinctive shapes.

CROISSANT DOUGH AND GLAZE

CROISSANT DOUGH

	Metric/UK	US
Yeast	**28g/1oz**	**½ cake or 1½ envelopes**
Sugar	**1 tsp**	**1 tsp**
Sugar	**2 Tbsp**	**2 Tbsp**
Warm milk	**250ml/8floz**	**1 cup**
Flour	**525g/1¼lb**	**5 cups**
Salt	**1 tsp**	**1 tsp**
Chilled butter	**275g/10oz**	**1¼ cups**
Eggs, lightly beaten	**2**	**2**

Prepare and cream the yeast with the teaspoon of sugar and 2–3 tablespoons of the warm milk.

Sift 450g/1lb (4 cups) of the flour, the remaining 2 tablespoons of sugar and the salt into a mixing bowl. Add 50g/2oz (¼ cup) of butter and cut into small pieces. Rub the butter into the flour until the mixture is like breadcrumbs. Make a well in the centre, add the remaining milk, the yeast mixture and eggs. Draw the flour down until you have a sticky dough. Cover and put to chill in the refrigerator for 1 hour. Shape the remaining butter into an oblong block using a rolling pin. Place in the refrigerator to chill.

Sift the remaining flour on to a clean board. Turn out the dough and knead for 10 minutes until all the flour has been incorporated. Roll out the dough into an oblong 30×20cm/12×8in. Place the chilled butter in the centre. Fold it over to enclose the butter and roll out to a strip about 37cm/15in long. Fold in three and chill for 10 minutes. Roll out and fold three times more, as for Puff Pastry. Chill the dough in the refrigerator for 1 hour.

	Metric/UK	US
Croissant dough	**525g/1¼lb**	**5 cups**
GLAZE		
Egg, lightly beaten	**1**	**1**
Icing (confectioner's) sugar	**4 Tbsp**	**4 Tbsp**
Hot water	**2 Tbsp**	**2 Tbsp**

Preheat the oven to hot (220°C/425°F, Gas Mark 7), When the pastries have been shaped, prove and glaze with beaten egg, before putting in the oven for 15 minutes. Mix the sugar and water glaze and paint it on after they are cooked, while still warm.

Step-by-Step to Danish Pastries

1. *Making slits in combs.*

2. *Roll pinwheels and slice.*

3. *A filled pastry star.*

4. *Pastry filled triangle.*

1. APPLE FILLING

Crisp eating apples	**2**	**2**
Lemon juice	**1 tsp**	**1 tsp**
Apricot jam	**4 Tbsp**	**4 Tbsp**

Peel, core and thinly slice the apples. Sprinkle over the lemon juice. Stir in the apricot jam. Use in triangles or combs.

2. ALMOND FILLING

Butter	**1 Tbsp**	**1 Tbsp**
Castor (superfine) sugar	**75g/3oz**	**⅓ cup**
Ground almonds	**75g/3oz**	**¾ cup**
Egg, lightly beaten	**½**	**½**
Almond essence (extract)	**3 drops**	**3 drops**

Cream the butter with the sugar. Add the other ingredients and stir to make a firm paste. Use in stars.

3. CINNAMON SUGAR FILLING

Butter	**50g/2oz**	**4 Tbsp**
Sugar	**50g/2oz**	**¼ cup**
Ground cinnamon	**2 tsp**	**2 tsp**
Raisins	**2 Tbsp**	**2 Tbsp**

Cream the butter with the sugar and stir in the cinnamon and raisins. Use in pinwheels.

£5.50

FOO BALL
26

Contents

7 WELCOME...
8 RANGERS IN 1995-96 – PART ONE
18 CAPTAIN MARVEL
20 RANGERS FACT FILE
21 RANGERS GALLERY
22 GAZZA THE GREAT!
26 MR SMITH
28 ROBBO
29 'ANDY ANDERSEN
30 ALLY McCOIST- SUPERSTRIKER
32 IBROX - A WORLD CLASS STADIUM
34 MR VERSATILITY
35 RANGERS GALLERY
36 ANDY GORAM - KING OF THE KEEPERS
38 MR DURABLE!
40 THE WRIGHT MAN FOR THE JOB!
41 RANGERS GALLERY
42 STUART McCALL - THE YORKSHIRE TERRIER!
43 RANGERS IN EURO ACTION
46 LORD LAUDRUP!
48 RANGERS IN 1995-96 - PART TWO
58 CELEBRATION TIME FOR RANGERS
60 1995-96 FACTS & FIGURES
61 RANGERS ROLL OF HONOUR

Written by Ray Laurence
Designed by David Saunders
All facts believed correct at time of going to press

Published by Grandreams Ltd,
Jadwin House,
205-211 Kentish Town Road,
London NW5 2JU

Printed in Belgium

Welco

WELCOME TO THE SECOND OFFICIAL RANGERS FC ANNUAL FROM GRANDREAMS.

THIS YEAR THERE ARE EVEN MORE PAGES PACKED WITH FEATURES ABOUT YOUR FAVOURITE TEAM.

THE SEASON REVIEW TELLS THE STORY OF RANGERS' DRAMATIC ATTEMPT TO WIN A FORTY-SIXTH SCOTTISH CHAMPIONSHIP IN 1995-96 - THE CLUB'S EIGHTH IN SUCCESSION - AS WELL AS OTHER SILVERWARE.

me...

THE BOOK ALSO TELLS OF THE DISAPPOINTMENTS OF RANGERS EURO ADVENTURE IN 1995.

ALL OF THIS IS ILLUSTRATED WITH SOME GREAT PHOTOGRAPHS.

WE HOPE YOU ENJOY THIS BOOK AS MUCH AS WE'VE ENJOYED PUTTING IT TOGETHER!

RANGERS FOR EVER!

Rangers in 1995-96 - Part One

AUGUST 1995

Last year's *Official Rangers FC* Annual from Grandreams ended with the club poised to sign one of Europe's biggest talents, Paul Gascoigne, from Italian club Lazio. Well, as everyone now knows, it happened!

Gazza arrived at Ibrox on 11 July 1995, complete with a brand-new blond hairdo, to sign for the club in a Scottish record £4.3 million transfer deal and to greet the fans.

Some 2,000 supporters turned out to witness his arrival - Ibrox had never seen anything quite like it and now every Rangers supporter was anxious to see how Paul would fit into the team.

Gazza on the ball

His first official game for the club - after the pre-season warm-up programme - came right at the beginning of Rangers' European Champions' Cup adventure in a Preliminary Round first leg match against ANORTHOSIS FAMAGUSTA, champions of Cyprus, at Ibrox.

In truth it should have been an easy job for Rangers, a formality. Yet, the game proved a difficult one for the home side, and it took all of 68 minutes before the deadlock was broken. Gordon Durie was the scorer, after collecting a Stuart McCall pass and beating a defender. In the end this single goal proved enough for the victory.

Ten days later Rangers were in cup action once more, this time in a Coca-Cola Cup Second Round tie against MORTON, at Ibrox. Gazza was involved in the build-up to the first goal, supplying the pass from which Ally McCoist notched the 300th goal of his remarkable career.

Seventeen minutes later Mark Hateley made it 2-0 with a hard hit penalty. Then in the 63rd minute Paul Gascoigne turned on his famous style to beat three defenders before slotting home Rangers' third goal (his first for the club) past goalkeeper Wylie. The Gers were safely through to the next stage.

On 23 August Rangers were in Cyprus for the away leg of the European Champions Cup encounter with ANORTHOSIS FAMAGUSTA. And, after an incredibly tense 90 minutes a place in The Champions' League was assured with a 0-0 draw (and a 1-0 aggregate).

After the tie Rangers boss Walter Smith was among those who condemned the Preliminary Round, claiming that it puts too much pressure on teams attempting to qualify for the Champions' League stage and rightly saying that defeat in the Preliminary Round would effectively ruin the season before its gets properly underway. However, the other teams in Group C - Steaua Bucharest, Borussia Dortmund and Juventus - ensured that there would be some interesting games ahead.

Rangers' Premier League campaign got underway three days later with the visit to Ibrox of KILMARNOCK, and in front of a 44,000+ crowd. The only goal of the game came in the 79th minute when Stuart McCall fired home from close range to give the Gers their first points of the season. Other impressive performances came from skipper Richard Gough and 'keeper Andy Goram, chalking-up his fourth consecutive clean sheet of the season.

Rangers last match in August was the Coca-Cola Cup Third Round meeting with Second Division STIRLING ALBION - managed by ex-Ranger Kevin Drinkell - at Ibrox. Mark Hateley opened the Gers' account on 15 minutes, heading home from a Charlie Miller corner-kick.

Richard Gough has just missed against Celtic

Rangers' second came on the hour when Stuart McCall's shot found its way through the Albion defence and ended up in the net. In the 71st minute Charlie Miller took a corner which found Stuart McCall on the edge of the box. McCall fired the ball goalwards, it was intercepted by Ally McCoist who tuned it home for a 3-0 scoreline.

Rangers now appeared to be cruising into the next round. But then came a remarkable comeback by the boys from Stirling. They scored twice - through Craig Taggart and Steve McCormick - in the space of four minutes. And when Joe McLeod suddenly found himself free in front of goal it looked as though a replay was on the cards. Luckily, Joe shot straight at Andy Goram and the result was secured in Rangers favour - but only just!

RANGERS MATCH-FAX – AUGUST 1995

EUROPEAN CUP PRELIMINARY ROUND FIRST LEG 9.8.1995
Rangers 1
Anorthosis Famagusta 0
Att 43,519

COCA-COLA CUP SECOND ROUND 19.8.1995
Rangers 3 Morton 0
Att 42,941

EUROPEAN CHAMPIONS' CUP PRELIMINARY ROUND SECOND LEG 23.8.1995
Anorthosis Famagusta 0
Rangers 0
Att 9,500

PREMIER LEAGUE 26.8.1995
Rangers 1 Kilmarnock 0
Att 44,686

COCA-COLA CUP THIRD ROUND 30.8.1995
Rangers 3 Stirling Albion 2
Att 36,685

SEPTEMBER 1995

Rangers' first match in September saw the team in devastating form at Ibrox. The victims on this occasion were newly promoted RAITH ROVERS who found themselves on the zero end of a 4-0 scoreline.

The stars of the show were Paul Gascoigne and Brian Laudrup, lining up together for only the second time in Rangers' blue. Together they dominated the match, producing some truly magical touches and passes.

It was Ally McCoist who scored first - on 16 minutes. The goal came courtesy of Laudrup who drew three defenders out of position before providing Ally with the pass from which he headed home from eight yards out.

Rangers' second was netted seven minutes later by Charlie Miller who put the finishing touch to a chance set-up Oleg Salenko and Paul Gascoigne. Goal Number Three was deftly netted by David Robertson in the 29th minute, after he had been set-up by a superb chip from Brian Laudrup.

An 'own goal' by a Raith defender was disallowed early in the second half following an offside decision. But there was more to come - from Ally McCoist who nudged home Rangers' fourth goal with an outstretched leg to score from a neat pass from Paul Gascoigne.

Three Celtic men take on Gazza!

Rangers' European adventure continued on 13 September with the trip to Bucharest to take on Romanian champions STEAUA BUCHAREST in the opening Group C match. Despite a fine defensive performance, particularly by Superkeeper Andy Goram and Superskipper Richard Gough, the Gers went down 1-0. The goal came from Daniel Prodan with five minutes remaining - just as it had begun to look as if the two teams would get an equal share of the points. It was a superb strike, volleyed home by Prodan after a corner-kick.

'Come on you, Gers!'

It was back to Premier League action three days later, with Rangers' first visit of the season to Brockville Park, FALKIRK. In the 33rd minute Russian international Oleg Salenko scored his first goal for the Light Blues - a wonderful drive from twelve yards. Rangers second came after 75 minutes when David Robertson converted an Alexei Mikhailichenko square pass by sliding the ball beneath Bairns' 'keeper Tony Parks.

The newly redeveloped Parkhead looked in pristine condition for the season's first Old Firm derby on 19 September, when Rangers took on CELTIC in the Coca-Cola Cup quarter-finals. It was great to see the blue-and-white of Rangers and the green-and-white of Celtic in action once again at one of the spiritual homes of Scotland's top domestic fixture.

It proved a tight, tough match in which both sides had gone close on numerous occasions, when Ally McCoist broke the deadlock on 75 minutes with a brilliant header from a Gazza cross. No reply came from Celtic and Rangers went through to the semis.

Rangers suffered their first Premier League defeat of the campaign on 23 September when HIBERNIAN came to Ibrox and won 1-0 through a penalty converted by Darren Jackson in the 63rd minute. It was the first Premier League goal scored against the Gers all season, and it was Hibs' first victory at Ibrox in more than five years.

The 1-0 result meant that Rangers slipped to second place in the table, a point behind city rivals Celtic.

September drew to a close with two more Big Games for Rangers. The first, against BORUSSIA DORTMUND in the European Champions' League, was played at Ibrox. German champs Dortmund were a classy side boasting such star names as Kohler, Sammer, Reuter and Moller - and they were one-nil up after 18 minutes through a Heiko Herrlich header.

But Rangers were in fine form - in truth they were on

Paul Gascoigne in action against Aberdeen

top for most of the match and went close several times. The equaliser eventually came on 64 minutes when Richard Gough drifted forward for a Paul Gascoigne free kick and headed home from a virtually unmarked position.

Four minutes later a Dortmund corner was converted by Martin Kree to restore the visitors' lead. But Rangers were determined not to allow all the points to slip away, and in the 72nd minute a Stuart McCall corner was struck goalwards by Paul Gascoigne. The ball struck 'keeper Klos and rebounded to Ian Ferguson who headed into the net. The points were shared and Rangers' hopes of Euro glory were still very much alive.

Rangers' wonderful supporters

The second of those 'Big Games' was the Premier League clash with CELTIC at Parkhead. And it was a dominant Rangers who came out on top, going ahead just before half time through Alex Cleland who put the finishing touch to a fine move involving Oleg Salenko.

Twelve minutes after the break the Gers struck again with another brilliant move, this time Oleg Salenko fed the ball to Ally McCoist out wide on the right. Ally then delivered a fine cross to Paul Gascoigne who then scored with the most clinical of finishes.

Celtic had no reply and the 2-0 scoreline meant that Rangers ended September with a two point lead over Aberdeen and Celtic at the top of the Premier League.

OCTOBER

Rangers kicked-off October with another Premier League victory, this time at home to MOTHERWELL. Paul Gascoigne was in devastating form, controlling events from midfield and showing his sheer class time and again. On 10 minutes Gazza collected a pass from Alexei Mikhailichenko and with two deft touches had the ball in the back of the net for the Gers' first goal.

Unfortunately, Gazza was not to stay the course. Midway through the second period he suddenly pulled-up with a muscle strain and had to be carried off for treatment.

Rangers' second goal came in the 68th minute from Ally McCoist who headed home an Ian Durrant free-kick from some nine yards out. Shortly afterwards, though, Ally joined Gazza in the treatment room when he too suffered a muscle strain.

Although the result was all sewn-up by then, at 2-1 in Rangers' favour, the two injuries did not bode well for the forthcoming trip to Turin to take on mighty Juventus in the Champions' League.

Neither Gazza or Ally played in the next Premier League match, against title challengers ABERDEEN at Pittodrie. It was Rangers' very own Australian, Craig Moore, who was the hero of the day when he grabbed the only goal of the game, in the 78th minute.

The match had been dominated by the home side for much of the time, but they failed to break through the Gers' defence. Then, just as it looked as though the points were to be shared, up jumped Moore to head home from a Stuart McCall free-kick and give the Light Blues victory

RANGERS MATCH-FAX – SEPTEMBER 1995

PREMIER LEAGUE 9.9.1995
Rangers 4 Raith Rovers 0
Att 43,535

EUROPEAN CHAMPIONS' CUP GROUP C 13.9.1995
Steaua Bucharest 1
Rangers 0
Att 26,000

PREMIER LEAGUE 16.9.1995
Falkirk 0 Rangers 2
Att 11,445

COCA-COLA CUP QUARTER-FINAL 19.9.1995
Rangers 1 Celtic 0
Att 32,798

PREMIER LEAGUE 23.9.1995
Rangers 0 Hibernian 1
Att 44,364

EUROPEAN CHAMPIONS' CUP GROUP C 27.9.1995
Rangers 2
Borussia Dortmund 2
Att 33,209

PREMIER LEAGUE 30.9.1995
Celtic 0 Rangers 2
Att 34,500

Another goal for Ally McCoist!

over their closest rivals in the title race.

Paul Gascoigne was still out for the next Premier League encounter, against PARTICK THISTLE, but Ally McCoist was back on the subs' bench and he entered the fray on 84 minutes as a replacement for Gordon Durie. By then the result was well and truly wrapped up at 4-0 in Rangers' favour - and 'Juke Box' Durie had bagged himself a brilliant hat-trick.

The scoring began in the 25th minute with a long range header from Richard Gough who connected with David Robertson's brilliant cross. Five minutes before half time, Gordon Durie notched his first strike of the afternoon, a simple tap-in from an Alex Cleland drag-back. Early in the second half Gordon was on target once again with a 12-yard drive, again after a fine pass from David Robertson, Gordon's third and Rangers' fourth, came in the 82nd minute - this time a powerful header from a Stuart McCall cross.

Rangers' Dazzling Dane, Brian Laudrup

After that four-goal spree, Rangers were to find themselves on the wrong end of a hefty scoreline, in the European Champions' League match against JUVENTUS in Turin.

Paul Gascoigne was still on the injury list and unavailable for selection by Walter Smith. But it is debatable that even the great Gazza would have been able to do much about the devastation wreaked by 'Juve'.

Within twenty-two minutes of the kick-off the men in the black-and-white stripes were 3-0 ahead, with goals from Ravanelli, Conte and Del Piero. Rangers simply could not get back into the match after such a blow, and the cause was definitely lost when Ravanelli made it 4-0 in the 73rd minute. Another blight on the evening came with Alex Cleland's dismissal for a late tackle on Del Piero.

A small measure of Scottish pride was restored five minutes later when Oleg Salenko made a great run down the left flank before crossing to Richard Gough, whose shot beat Peruzzi in the Juventus goal.

Unfortunately, the result left Rangers firmly at the foot of the Group C table, with only a single point from three games. There was, as they say, a mountain to climb.

Three days later Rangers were back in Premier League action when HEARTS came to Ibrox. The 45,000+ crowd had hardly had time to settle when fit-again Paul Gascoigne played a delicate one-two with Gordan Petric before setting off on a magnificent solo run which cut through the Hearts defence and resulted in the first goal of the game. All of this happened before a minute had passed - and the disappointment of the thrashing in Italy was suddenly lifted.

And, taking their example from Juve in that match, Rangers were three-up by half time. Oleg Salenko grabbed the second in the 25th minute after wrong-footing the defence before firing home from 12-yards. The third came on 36 minutes when Gordon Durie put the finishing touch to a brilliant flowing move involving Paul Gascoigne, Alexei Mikhailichenko, Richard Gough and Alex Cleland.

John Millar pulled one back for Hearts with a fine curling shot on 79 minutes. But five minutes later Oleg Salenko made it 4-1 with a great shot from 16-yards. The result stretched Rangers lead at the top of the Premier League table to six points.

Brian Laudrup chases Celtic's John Hughes

Next came the Gers' first real disappointment of the season - dismissal from the Coca-Cola Cup in the semi-final at Hampden. ABERDEEN were the opponents and Billy Dodds was their star player, scoring twice in the second half. Oleg Salenko replied with a late goal for the Gers, five minutes from time. But it was too little, too late and the Dons marched into the final.

It was off to Stark's Park for Rangers' last match in October, the second Premier League meeting of the season with RAITH ROVERS. This time things did not go all Rangers' way as they had in September. After a tension-filled first half in which no goals were forthcoming, the second half exploded in a frenzy of action. Raith finally broke the deadlock, beating the offside trap and then scoring through Lennon.

Six minutes went by, and then a Paul Gascoigne free kick was headed home by Richard Gough for the equaliser.

Then, on 65 minutes, Gordan Petric stuck his first goal for Rangers, a brilliant header from a Gazza corner-kick. It now looked as though three more points were on their way to Ibrox. But, within a minute of taking the lead, the Gers found themselves pinned back again when Colin Cameron fired home Rovers' equaliser. That was the last goal of the match and the points were shared.

NOVEMBER

November began with a crunch match - the European Champions' League Group C return with JUVENTUS at Ibrox. This was Rangers big chance to salvage the situation if they were to progress in the tournament. Unfortunately things did not go to plan. The Gers found themselves completely outclassed by the Italian Champions who achieved an even better winning scoreline than they had done in the first game in Turin.

The first goal came on 16 minutes from a side-footed shot by Del Piero. After that the Gers knuckled down in an attempt to at least secure a draw. But by half time 'keeper Andy Goram was ruled out of the action due to a hip injury and Stephen Wright had been earlier carried off following a collision with Vialli - both players were substituted.

Rangers went close a couple of times after the restart, but then in the 64th minute Torricelli took advantage of a brilliant pass from Vialli to shoot Juve into a two-goal lead. In the last four minutes of the match the Italian giants increased their lead - first though Ravanelli and then Marrochi, and a feeling of Euro gloom descended on Ibrox.

To stand any chance of progression Rangers would have to win their last two Group C games, against Steaua Bucharest and Borussia Dortmund, and then hope that the results of other Group games went in their favour. It was a long shot, to say the least.

Tommy Boyd (Celtic), Brain Laudrup (Rangers)

RANGERS MATCH-FAX – OCTOBER 1995

PREMIER LEAGUE
3.10.1995
Rangers 2 Motherwell 1
Att 37,348

7.10.1995
Aberdeen 0 Rangers 1
Att 22,500

14.7.1995
Partick Thistle 0 Rangers 4
Att 16,346

EUROPEAN CHAMPIONS' CUP
GROUP C 18.10.1995
Juventus 4 Rangers 1
Att 50,000

PREMIER LEAGUE
21.10.1995 Rangers 4
Hearts 1
Att 45,155

COCA-COLA CUP SEMI-FINAL
(at Hampden Park)
24.10.1995
Rangers 1 Aberdeen 2
Att 26,131

PREMIER LEAGUE
28.10.1995
Raith Rovers 2 Rangers 2
Att 9,200

Ally makes a point

Three days after the Euro disappointment Rangers took on FALKIRK at Ibrox in the Premier League. Ally McCoist was the star of the show, providing both of Rangers' goals. The first came on 33 minutes - a close-range header from a cross by Alex Cleland. Four minutes before half time, Super Ally struck again, this time capitalising on a fine pass from Ian Durrant before firing home from some 16-yards out. Three more points were in the bag.

Next came the visit to Rugby Park for the Premier League clash with KILMARNOCK. The highlight of this match was Alan McClaren's first goal for Rangers. And it came in the nick of time - the 87 minute to be precise. Up until that moment it looked as though the points would be shared as the Killies had successfully shut out all Gers' efforts to breach their defence.

It's all smiles as Brain Laudrup is flagged down

Then up popped Alan Mac to fire home Oleg Salenko's cross from the right, after the Russian star had beaten three defenders. Oleg was also on target two minutes later with Rangers' second after he had been set-up by Paul Gascoigne. Another three points were safely gathered.

But there was only one point for Rangers from the next Premier encounter - with ABERDEEN at Ibrox. Eion Jess opened the Dons' account in the 27th minute, after making a powerful run from the centre circle and then blasting the ball home from all of 25-yards.

Oleg Salenko evened things up five minutes before half-time. The goal came from a Paul Gascoigne corner-kick which found Alexei Mikhailichenko who chipped the ball to Stuart McCall who then crossed for Oleg to head home. Result: 1-1.

The Old Firm clash with CELTIC at Ibrox on 19 November was a truly dramatic affair and a great game. The visitors opened the scoring after just six minutes with an Andreas Thom 20-yarder. Shortly afterwards a questionable offside decision denied Rangers a David Robertson equaliser. But then, on 39 minutes, Brian Laudrup - back in the team for the first time since injury had ruled him out in September - evened up the scoreline when he collected a Gazza through ball and then blasted a great shot which went in off the post.

The second half began in dramatic fashion when Richard Gough upended John Hughes in the box. John Collins stepped up to convert from the penalty spot to put Celtic back in the lead.

In the 60th minute Rangers had another refereeing decision go against them, after Celtic defender Jackie McNamara had appeared to handle the ball in his own area. Three minutes later, however, substitute Ally McCoist popped-up to head Rangers' second equaliser of the game, from a Paul Gascoigne free kick.

The action quickly switched to the other end, where Andy Goram made the save-of-the-season from a point-blank shot from Pierre

Alexei Mikhailichenko moves down the wing

RANGERS MATCH-FAX – NOVEMBER 1995

EUROPEAN CHAMPIONS' CUP GROUP C 1.11.1995
Rangers 0 Juventus 4
Att 42,523

PREMIER LEAGUE 4.11.1995
Rangers 2 Falkirk 0
Att 42,059

8.11.1995
Kilmarnock 0 Rangers 2
Att 14,823

11.11.1995
Rangers 1 Aberdeen 1
Att 45,427

19.11.1995
Rangers 3 Celtic 3
Att 46,640

EUROPEAN CHAMPIONS' CUP GROUP C 22.11.1995
Rangers 1
Steaua Bucharest 1
Att 30,800

PREMIER LEAGUE
25.11.1995
Hibernian 1 Rangers 4
Att 13,558

Van Hooijdonk. In the 70th minute Rangers went ahead when an Oleg Salenko cross was deflected into the net by Celtic's Tosh McKinlay.

The lead was short-lived as Van Hooijdonk headed the last goal of the game in the 73rd minute. It had been a pulsating encounter, full of end to end action - and a great advertisement for Old Firm football!

On 22 November, at Ibrox, Rangers European Championship dreams disintegrated when they failed to record a victory over STEAUA BUCHAREST. The Gers went ahead in the 32nd minute when Gazza topped a fine individual run from half way by delivering a side foot shot into the corner of the Steaua goal. The lead lasted until ten minutes into the second half. Then Ilie equalised for the visitors after a neat one-two with Militaru. No more goals were forthcoming and the points were shared.

Meanwhile Borussia Dortmund were producing an unexpected victory over Juventus which took them through to the semi-finals along with the Italian champions. Rangers now had to concentrate their efforts on the domestic tournaments, particularly the Premier League in which success would, of course, ensure another European Championship entry in the following season.

Ally McCoist gets in a shot against Celtic

That process resumed three days later with the visit to HIBERNIAN. Putting those Euro Blues behind them, the Gers performed brilliantly to emerge as 4-1 winners. The goals came from Ally McCoist, Charlie Miller, Gordon Durie and an own goal by Darren Dods. But the emphatic manner of Rangers victory served notice of intent on all other nine Premier League clubs.

November closed with the Ibrox men four points ahead of Celtic at the top of the table.

DECEMBER

It took more than an hour for Rangers to get on top of things in the Premier League match against HEARTS at Tynecastle Park on 2 December. The breakthrough, in what had been a close encounter, came when Steve Fulton tripped Brian Laudrup in the penalty area. Ally McCoist took the spot kick - Rangers' first of the season - and put the Gers ahead with a masterful shot. The goal was Ally's 250th in the Scottish League.

Ouch!

Shortly afterwards Paul Gascoigne had the ball in the net, but the 'goal' was disallowed after an offside ruling. Then, in the 68th minute, Gazza did get his name on the scoresheet after executing a clever one-two with Gordon Durie and then firing home from six-yards out.

Gazza takes care of it

Pride was the name of the game when the Gers travelled to Germany for the formality of their final Champions' League Group C fixture, against BORUSSIA DORTMUND.

Rangers went ahead after just ten minutes when Brian Laudrup filled an empty net after collecting a pass from Charlie Miller. Dortmund came back strongly after that and scored twice through Moller and Reidle. With five minute left Gordon Durie equalised from 10-yards to earn a well-deserved draw. Unfortunately Paul Gascoigne had been sent off late in the game.

On the following Saturday, the Premier League campaign resumed with the visit of PARTICK THISTLE to Ibrox. The match was decided by a single goal, scored by Gordon Durie in the 48th minute. It came from a Craig Moore cross, headed home at the back post by the Juke Box man.

In truth Rangers, who were dominant throughout, should have had a whole hatful of goals. As it was, just one had to suffice. The result kept the Gers four points ahead of Celtic in the title race. Now it had become a two horse race, as third placed Hibernian were ten points adrift of Celtic.

By the time Rangers had played their next match, against MOTHERWELL at Fir Park, the gap at the top was down to just two points. The Gers could have wrapped it all up several times, but failed to capitalise on their opportunities. Result: 0-0.

Things got back to normal with the visit to Ibrox of KILMARNOCK who found themselves on the wrong end of a 3-0 scoreline. The goals came from Oleg Salenko (24 mins), Gordon Durie (a 44th minute penalty) and Paul Gascoigne (in the last minute of the match).

1995 closed on a real high note when third placed HIBERNIAN came to Ibrox and received a right royal roasting from rampant Rangers!

The Light Blues' scoring spree started in the 30th minute when Charlie Miller ran on to a Gordon Durie through ball and then chipped Jim Leighton in the Hibs' goal. Gordon scored himself, ten minutes later - with a marvellous diving header from a Brian Laudrup cross.

'Juke Box' grabbed his second on 52 minutes when he spotted Leighton off his line and proceeded to chip the ball over him and into the net. Paul Gascoigne got in on the act in the 76th minute with a marvellous solo goal, cutting through the Hibs' defence like the proverbial knife through butter, before firing home from twelve yards.

A minute passed, then Gordon Durie made it 5-0, courtesy of a great through ball from Brian Laudrup. Laudrup was also involved in the build-up to the sixth goal. He passed to Oleg Salenko who drove into the box to force the ball into the net on 82 minutes.

Gordon Durie completed a marvellous afternoon for himself and for Rangers by hitting his fourth goal of the afternoon after a Brian Laudrup shot rebounded to him. The 7-0 scoreline was Rangers' best in the league since beating Greenock Morton in September 1987.

And it was a great way to end the year!

RANGERS MATCH-FAX – DECEMBER 1995

PREMIER LEAGUE
2.12.1995
Hearts 0 Rangers 2
Att 15,105

EUROPEAN CHAMPIONS' CUP GROUP C
6.12.1995
Borussia Dortmund 2
Rangers 2
Att 35,800

PREMIER LEAGUE
9.12.1995
Rangers 1 Partick Thistle 0
Att 43,173

19.12.1995
Motherwell 0 Rangers 0
Att 10,179

26.12.1995
Rangers 3 Kilmarnock 0
Att 45,173

30.12.1995
Rangers 7 Hibernian 0
Att 44,692

RANGERS IN 1995-96 CONTINUES ON PAGE 48

Richard Gough...

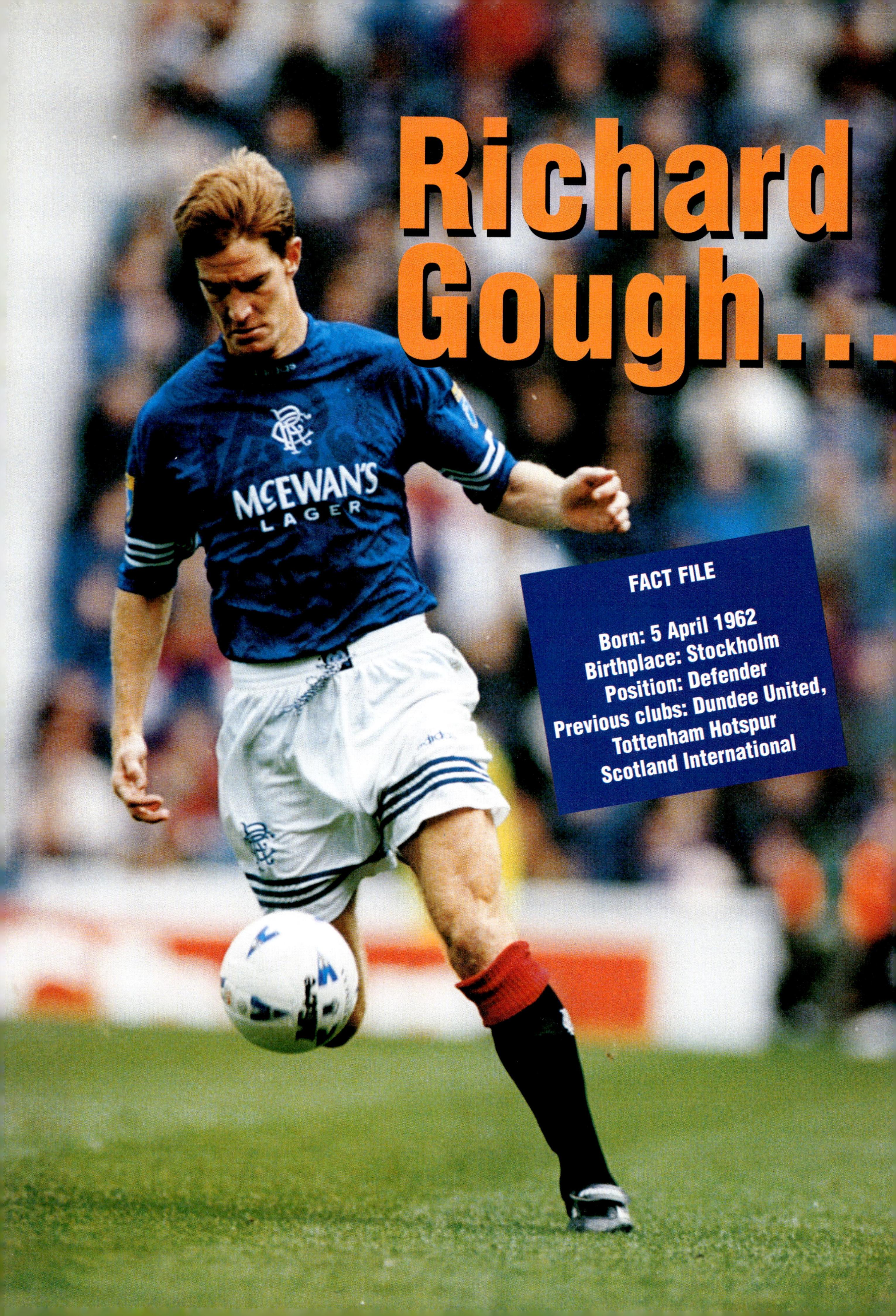

FACT FILE

Born: 5 April 1962
Birthplace: Stockholm
Position: Defender
Previous clubs: Dundee United, Tottenham Hotspur
Scotland International

Captain Marvel

Richard Gough had another exceptional season in 1995-96, playing superbly at the heart of Rangers' five-man defence and leading the side by example – proving himself to be one of the finest captains in modern football.

Richard began his professional career at Dundee United but arrived at Tannadice by a roundabout route, being born in Stockholm to Scottish parents who then emigrated to South Africa.

He made his debut as a 19-year-old in 1981 and two seasons later won a League Championship medal as United won the title for the only time in their history.

In 1983 he made the first of more than 60 international appearances, and has scored six times for Scotland. The sweetest goal came in 1985 at Hampden Park when he scored the only goal of the game to defeat 'Auld Enemy' England.

In the summer of 1986 Richard moved south of the border in a £1 million transfer which took him to Tottenham Hotspur. Although he was playing as well as ever, his stay at Spurs was brief due to a touch of homesickness. After just 49 League matches Rangers' boss Graeme Souness broke the transfer record between English and Scottish clubs by paying £1.5 million for his signature.

This has proven to be one of the greatest bargains of all time as apart from his first season at Ibrox Richard has won eight consecutive League Championship medals, three Scottish FA Cup winner's medals, five League Cup winner's medals and he was elected Player of the Year in 1989.

Richard Gough - the skipper who leads by example

A vastly experienced defender, he was a member of Scotland's 1986 and 1990 World Cup and 1992 European Championship squads but has not played for Scotland since 1993, following a dispute with Andy Roxburgh. This has been a body blow to Scotland as Gough is now one of Europe's best defenders.

His consistency is remarkable and during the 1995-96 season he missed just one of the first 37 matches. He moved up from the back to score a vital goal against Borussia Dortmund in a European Cup match at Ibrox Park to snatch a 2-2 draw. He was also on target in Turin as he gallantly tried to get Rangers back in the match against eventual European Cup winners Juventus.

Rangers factfile

ADDRESS:
Ibrox Stadium, Edmiston Drive, Glasgow G51 2XD

TELEPHONES:
0141-427 8500
TICKETS: 0141-427 8800
FAX: 0141-427 2676

HOW TO GET THERE
By Underground
Ibrox GGPTE underground station is two minutes walk from the stadium.

By Bus
A number of buses which pass within 300 yards of the stadium can be boarded at Glasgow City Centre. They are numbers 4, 9a, 23, 23a, 52, 53, 53a, 54a, 54b 65, 89 & 91

By Car
From Motorway M8 take the B768 turning for GOVAN. This will take you to the stadium. Parking facilities are available at the Albion car park.

BEHIND THE SCENES AT IBROX
Chairman
David Murray

Vice Chairman
Donald R. Findlay QC, LL.B.

Director/Secretary
Campbell Ogilvie

Directors
Jack Gillespie, Ian B. Skelly, Hugh Adam

Associate Directors
Ian Russell, Bill Thornton
Commercial Manager
Bob Reilly

Team Manager
Walter Smith

Assistant Manager
Archie Knox

Club Doctor
Dr Donald Cruickshank

Physio
Bill Collins

Coach
Davie Dodds

Reserve Coaches
John McGregor, Billy Kirkwood

Youth Coach
John Chalmers

SFA Community Officer
Ewan Chester

PR Executive
John Greig MBE

STADIUM FACTS
Capacity 46,836 (all seated)
Pitch size 115x78 yards

TEAM COLOURS
Shirts
Royal blue with red/ white trim
Shorts White
Socks Red

CLUB SHOPS
The Rangers Shop
150 Copland Road
Glasgow G51
Opening hours 10.00am-5.00pm Monday-Saturday

Also at:
103 St. Vincent Street
Glasgow G2
Opening hours
10.00am-5.30pm Monday-Saturday

OFFICIAL SUPPORTERS' CLUB
Rangers FC Supporters Association
250 Edmiston Drive
Glasgow G51 1YU

Rangers Gallery

IAN FERGUSON

IAN DURRANT

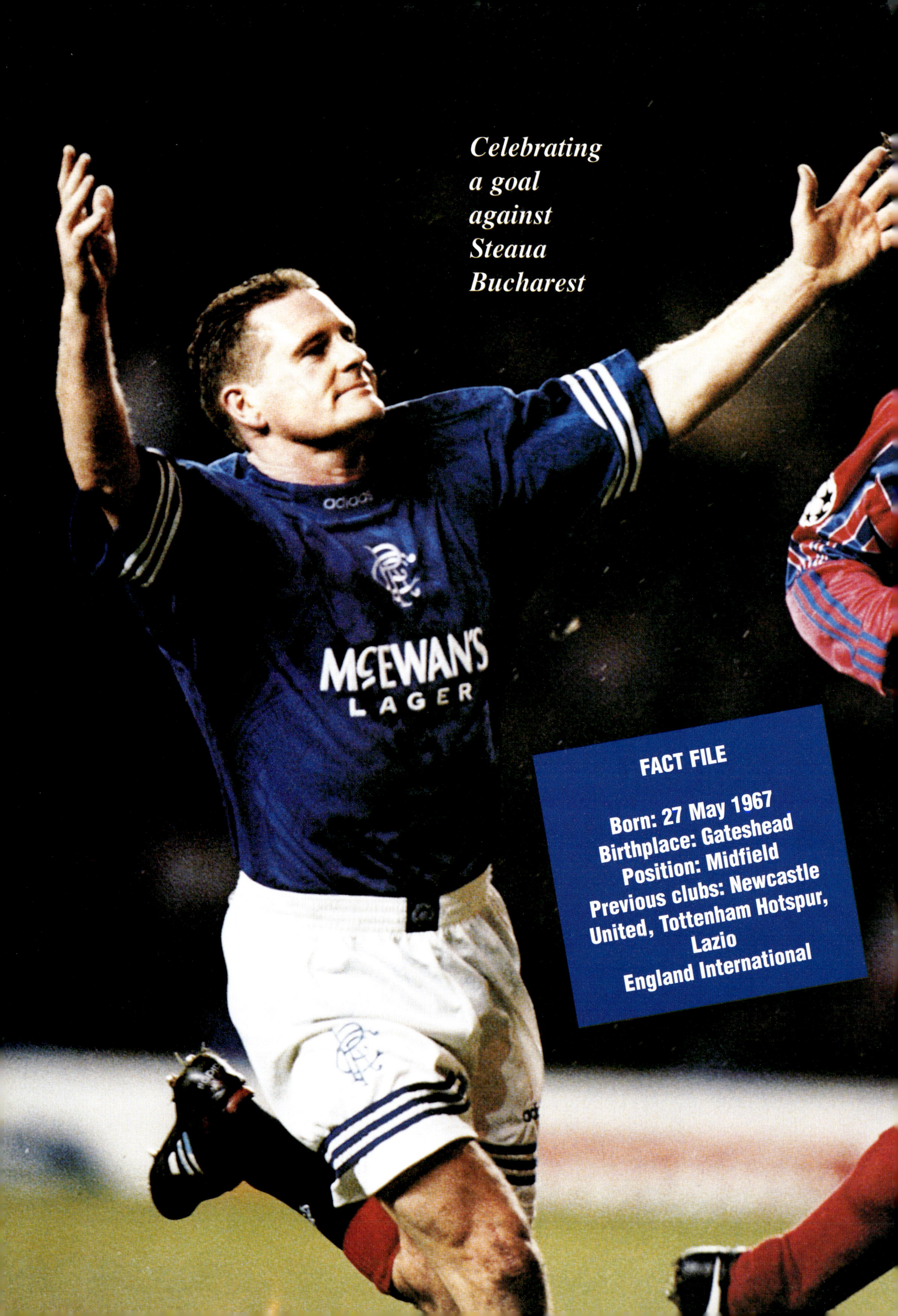

Celebrating a goal against Steaua Bucharest

FACT FILE

Born: 27 May 1967
Birthplace: Gateshead
Position: Midfield
Previous clubs: Newcastle United, Tottenham Hotspur, Lazio
England International

GAZZA the GREAT!

From a very early age Paul Gascoigne was earmarked for greatness and his form during the 1995-96 season when he deservedly won Scotland's Player of the Year trophy fully justified those predictions from his teenage years.

Gazza's career reads like a thriller with desperately low periods mixed with exhilarating highs and has received fierce criticism and extravagant praise in equal measure.

A Geordie by birth, he began with his local club Newcastle United where his displays as a teenager brought him instant stardom. In 1988 it was obvious that Newcastle couldn't hold on to their most valuable asset and a transfer scramble among the giants of English football started for Gazza's signature and Terry Venables' Tottenham Hotspur broke the British transfer record to snap him up.

The Spurs' faithful took the extrovert Geordie to their hearts and his all-action midfield style, long range shooting and dead ball skills made it impossible for England to ignore him for the 1990 World Cup finals in Italy. It was during this tournament that Gazza established himself as a world-class player, showing astonishing maturity for a 23-year-old as he played a major part in England's run to the semi-finals. It was during this titanic match against West Germany that he became an English hero when, after a harsh booking in extra-time which would have ruled him out of the final, he wept openly and tugged the nation's heartstrings.

Gazza the blond, in his early days with Rangers

He continued his outstanding form over the next season, playing a big part in Tottenham's progress to the 1991 FA Cup Final against Nottingham Forest and securing a £5.5 million transfer to Italian club Lazio. It was during this match that Gazza had his worst moment in football. He stretched to make a reckless tackle on Forest full-back Gary Charles and tore a cruciate ligament in his knee and it was feared that he would never play again.

Gazza always lets you know how he feels!

Lazio stood by the injured Gascoigne and after a long rehabilitation he reappeared to become a cult figure to the Lazio fans and one of the top players in Serie A.

Gazza moved to Ibrox in July 1995 for £4.3 million in preference to tempting offers from England's Premiership and made his debut against Anorthosis Famagusta in a European Cup qualifier on 9 August.

Paul Gascoigne had an outstanding first season in Scottish football, showing that he still retained his mercurial skills and impish sense of humour!

Against Hibernian the referee Mr Smith dropped his yellow card. Gazza picked it up and gave the referee a joke booking. Unfortunately Mr Smith didn't see the funny side of the incident and gave the England star a proper caution!

Sunday 28 April 1996 was a special day for Gazza as his brilliant hat-trick at Ibrox against Aberdeen wrapped up the 'Gers eighth consecutive title and after the match he was elected Scotland's Player of the Year in succession to team-mate Brian Laudrup.

He went on to star for England in the European Championship finals - and he scored one of the best goal in the tournament, England's second against Scotland of all teams!

Celebrating another goal

'Hello, Glasgow!'

The un'mask'ing of a Rangers star

Mr Smith

Rangers' supremo Walter Smith moved into the manager's office in 1991 as successor to Graeme Souness - and that was quite a tough act to follow.

Walter with the Premier League trophy

Souness had really shaken things up around Ibrox since his arrival as player/manager in April 1986. Among his revolutionary idea was the introduction of a number of English stars into the Rangers squad - a policy which paid off with several trophy successes.

Then, in April 1991, it was announced that Souness was to take over from Kenny Dalglish at his old club, Liverpool. That shock to the Ibrox faithful was followed by the news that Souness' former assistant Walter Smith would take his place in the Rangers hot-seat.

As a player Glasgow-born Walter Smith had been a tough-tackling defender with Dundee United where he later became assistant manager to Jim McClean. Now, he had the top job in Scottish club management.

His first job was to oversee the remaining three games of the 1990-91 season, in which Rangers completed their 41st Championship-winning success.

Since then he has presided over a further five title winning campaigns.

Long may he continue to do so!

An anxious moment

Would you look at that!'

'Robbo'

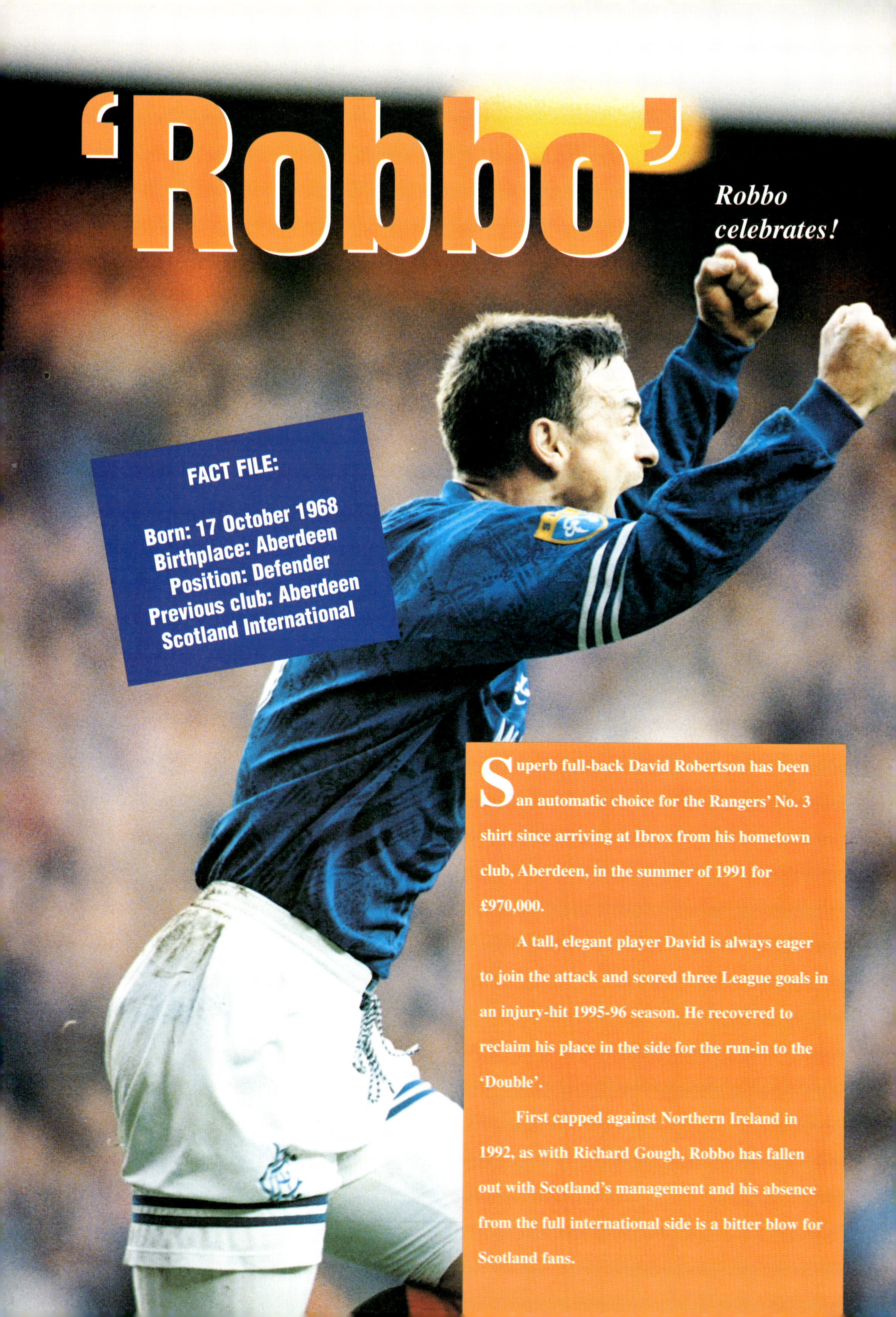

Robbo celebrates!

FACT FILE:

Born: 17 October 1968
Birthplace: Aberdeen
Position: Defender
Previous club: Aberdeen
Scotland International

Superb full-back David Robertson has been an automatic choice for the Rangers' No. 3 shirt since arriving at Ibrox from his hometown club, Aberdeen, in the summer of 1991 for £970,000.

A tall, elegant player David is always eager to join the attack and scored three League goals in an injury-hit 1995-96 season. He recovered to reclaim his place in the side for the run-in to the 'Double'.

First capped against Northern Ireland in 1992, as with Richard Gough, Robbo has fallen out with Scotland's management and his absence from the full international side is a bitter blow for Scotland fans.

FACT FILE

Born: 14 November 1970
Birthplace: Denmark
Position: Forward
Previous club: Aalborg
Denmark International

Erik in goalmouth action against Aberdeen

'Andy Andersen!

Rangers paid Danish club Aalborg £1.5 million for Erik Bo Andersen in February 1996 to link-up with his international team-mate Brian Laudrup.

The tall striker top-scored with 24 goals for Aalborg in the 1994-95 season as the club won the Danish title for the first time in their 114-year history. He settled in particularly quickly at Ibrox scoring twice against Falkirk in his second match and a hat-trick against Partick Thistle in his fourth.

Erik will obviously be hoping to build upon his understanding with Laudrup and is an invaluable addition to Rangers' already formidable firepower.

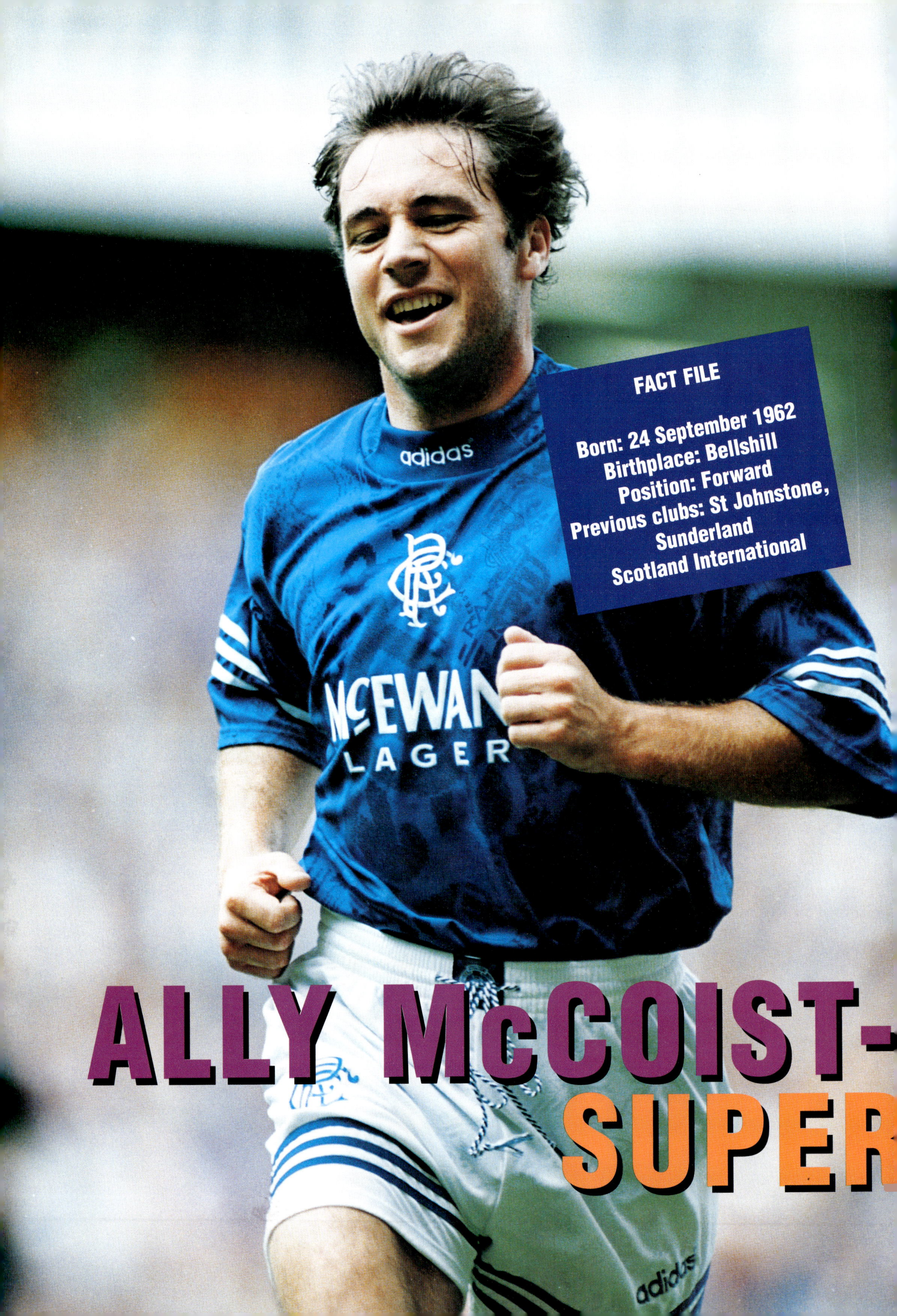

FACT FILE

Born: 24 September 1962
Birthplace: Bellshill
Position: Forward
Previous clubs: St Johnstone, Sunderland
Scotland International

ALLY McCOIST-
SUPER

On 13 January 1996 Rangers crushed Raith Rovers 4-0 in a League match at Ibrox Park and in the process Ally McCoist wrote his name in the history books.

In the 21st minute he crashed home a drive from the edge of the penalty area to score his 231st League goal and break the club scoring record held for 57 years by Bob McPhail.

The ever-popular 'Coisty' began his professional career with St Johnstone, making his debut as a 16-year-old. In his first full season at McDiarmid Park he scored 22 goals in 38 League matches and alerted the attention of big clubs on both sides of the border. Sunderland won the race for his signature but his spell at Roker Park was a bitter disappointment, over two seasons he managed just eight goals from 56 League matches.

Rangers stepped in to end Ally's English nightmare during the summer of 1983 and the bubbly striker hasn't looked back since. He won the first of his fifty caps in 1986 and has been a key figure in Rangers' modern success story, snatching many vital match-winning goals. His best season came in 1991-92 when he was top-scorer in Scottish football with 34 League goals and voted Player of the Year by both the Scottish PFA and the Football Writers' Association. Two years later, in June 1994, his outstanding contribution to Rangers and Scottish football was recognised by the award of the MBE in the Queen's Birthday Honours List.

Despite the fierce competition for forward places at Ibrox Park the club have offered the charismatic Ally McCoist a contract that will allow him to finish his career with his beloved Rangers.

The pin-up boy of Scottish football gives a special signal from the bench

STRIKER!

IBROX - A WORLD

IBROX STATS

Capacity 46,836 (all seated)
Pitch size 115x78 yards

CLASS STADIUM

The idea for a 'Glasgow Rangers Football Club' was conceived in 1872, by a group of young men from Gareloch who happened to be taking a stroll in West End Park at the time. From this small beginning would grow the most successful soccer club in Scotland, and the holder of the world record for domestic championship successes.

The club's first matches were played at Flesher's Haugh on Glasgow Green. From there Rangers moved, in turn, to Burnbank, Kinning Park, 'First' Ibrox and finally Ibrox Stadium itself, now regarded as one of the finest footballing venues in the world, as these pictures show.

Mr Versatility

FACT FILE:

Born: 10 December 1970
Birthplace: Glasgow
Position: Defender
Previous club: Dundee United
Scotland Under-21
International

Alex keeps his eyes on the ball

Glasgow-born Alex Cleland returned to Glasgow in January 1995 when Rangers paid Dundee United £400,000 for the talented utility full-back.

He moved from Tannadice to Ibrox on the same day as Gary Bollan and has settled into the side impressively. Equally at home in either full-back position, he proved to be a capable deputy when left-back David Robertson dropped out through injury. When Robbo returned in time for the Scottish Cup Final Alex switched across to right-back and played well in the 5-1 victory over Hearts.

Alex also popped up to score some valuable goals for The Gers – a great header against title rivals Celtic at Parkhead and a hat-trick against Highland League side Keith in the 10-1 Scottish Cup Third Round victory at Pittodrie.

Rangers Gallery

TREVOR STEVEN

ALEXEI MIKHAILICHENKO

ANDY GORAM - KING

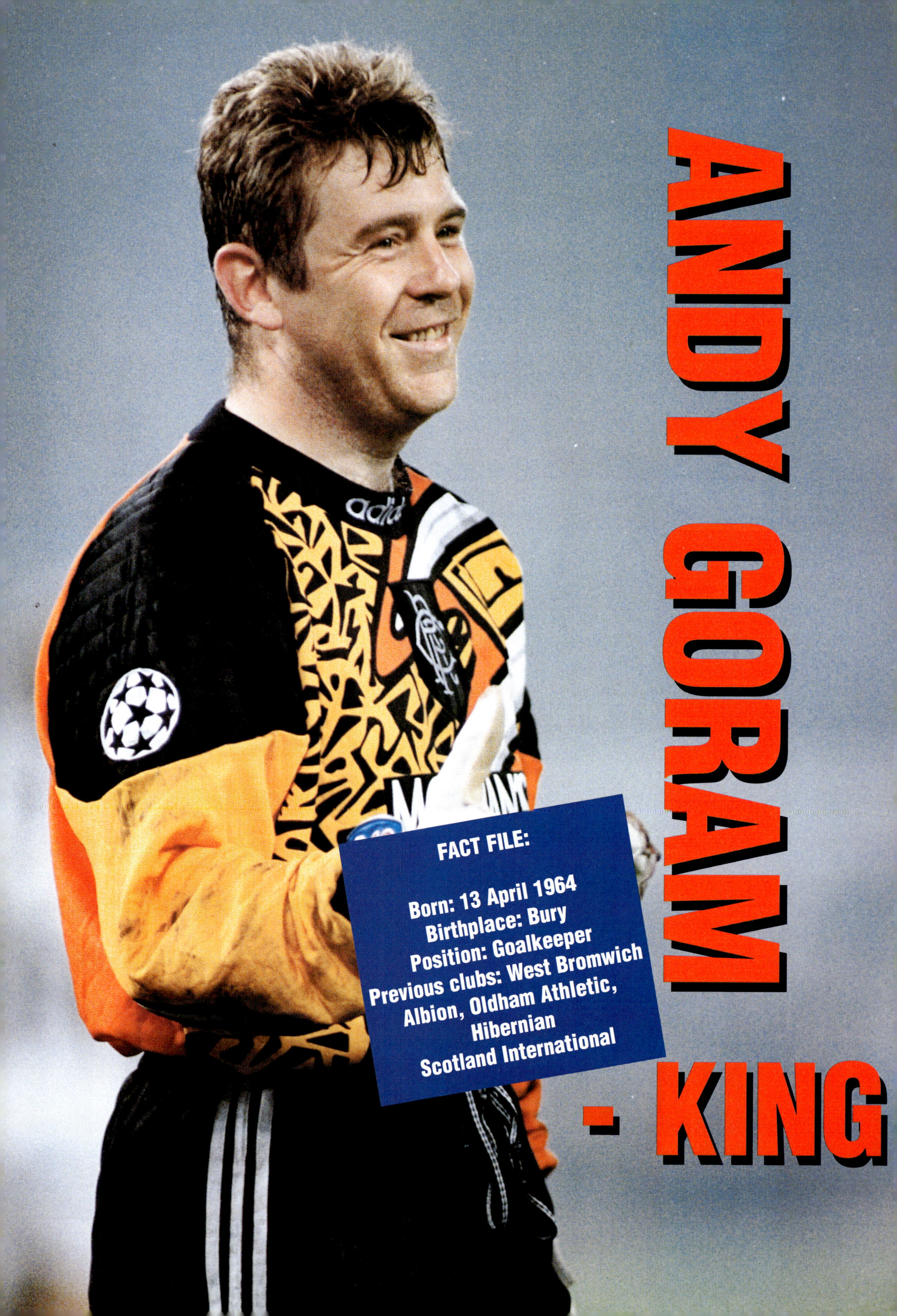

FACT FILE:

Born: 13 April 1964
Birthplace: Bury
Position: Goalkeeper
Previous clubs: West Bromwich Albion, Oldham Athletic, Hibernian
Scotland International

Andy Goram has proven to be a bargain since joining Rangers for £1 million from Hibernian in July 1991 to replace England international 'keeper Chris Woods.

Andy Goram - Scotland's Keeper supreme

Lancashire-born Andy qualifies through Scottish parentage to represent Scotland and has been first-choice goalkeeper since 1990, solving a problem position into the bargain. He made his international debut in 1986 against East Germany while still at Oldham Athletic in England's old Second Division.

A top-class cricketer, Andy joined West Bromwich Albion from school and moved to Oldham as an 18-year-old without playing a first-team match for West Brom. He stayed at Boundary Park for six seasons, becoming an automatic choice and a great favourite with the crowd as Oldham battled their way back to top-flight football after 56 years in the wilderness.

Hibernian paid their then-record fee of £325,000 to take Andy to Easter Road to replace ex-international Alan Rough in October 1987. He quickly established himself at Hibs and even managed to score against Morton with a long clearance in his first season!

After four excellent seasons he moved to Ibrox and has become one of the best goalkeepers in the British game. In 1992-93 he was outstanding in goal as Rangers won the coveted 'Treble' and was voted Player of the Year by both the Scottish PFA and the Football Writers' Association. Andy missed just four League matches in 1995-96 and was an important figure in Scotland's Euro '96 challenge.

of the KEEPERS

Mr Dura

After a series of injuries Gordon Durie had a sensational second half of the 1995-96 season scoring a four-times against his old club Hibernian in Rangers 7-0 drubbing and hat-tricks against Partick Thistle and Hearts in the 5-1 Scottish Cup Final victory. Restored to his favourite position of playing through the middle, Gordon forced his way into Craig Brown's squad for Euro '96.

He began his career at lowly East Fife where his outstanding form earned him a transfer to Premier League club Hibernian while still a teenager. He had two successful seasons at Easter Road before catching the eye of English giants Chelsea who paid £380,000 for the 20-year-old striker in 1986.

'Juke Box' – as he is known – was brought to replace popular Scotland international striker David Speedie and his fast, aggressive style soon won the fans over. He formed a prolific striking partnership with England striker Kerry Dixon over six seasons, scoring 51 League goals in 123 matches before a £2.2 million transfer to North London rivals Tottenham Hotspur in July 1991.

His stay at White Hart Lane was brief, playing just 58 games in two seasons with his goalscoring touch seemingly lost. His flagging career was revived when the call came from his footballing first love – Rangers – the lure of Ibrox proved irresistible and Gordon moved to Glasgow for a £1.2 million fee in November 1993.

Despite a catalogue of niggling injuries, being a part of Walter Smith's star-studded squad has brought the best out of this dynamic striker whose season, apart from his hat-tricks and four-timer also included long-range efforts against Raith and Hibernian.

Gordon Durie - The 'Juke Box' Striker

ble!

FACT FILE:

Born: 6 December 1965
Birthplace: Paisley
Position: Forward
Previous clubs: East Fife, Hibernian, Chelsea, Tottenham Hotspur
Scotland International

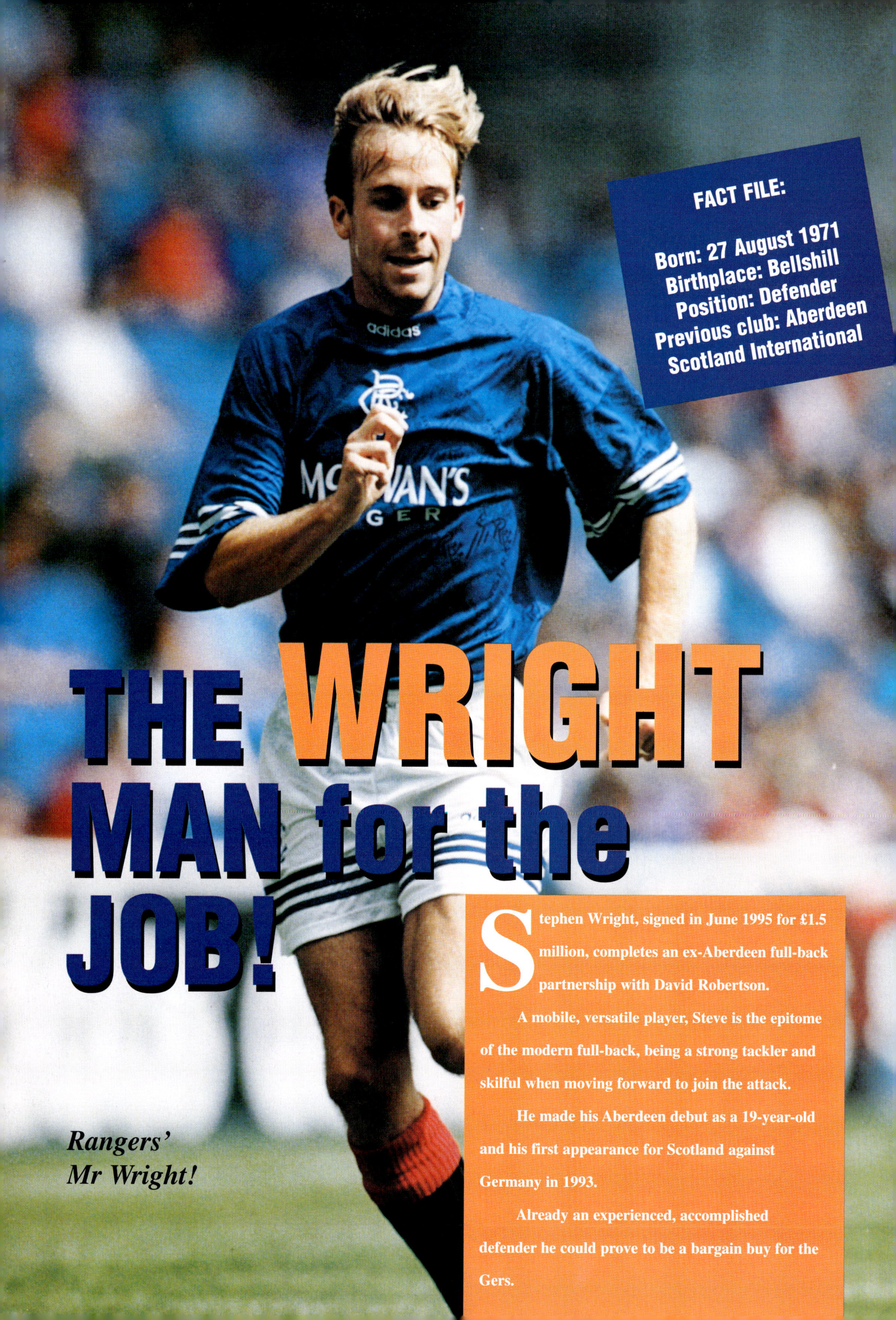

FACT FILE:

Born: 27 August 1971
Birthplace: Bellshill
Position: Defender
Previous club: Aberdeen
Scotland International

THE WRIGHT MAN for the JOB!

Stephen Wright, signed in June 1995 for £1.5 million, completes an ex-Aberdeen full-back partnership with David Robertson.

A mobile, versatile player, Steve is the epitome of the modern full-back, being a strong tackler and skilful when moving forward to join the attack.

He made his Aberdeen debut as a 19-year-old and his first appearance for Scotland against Germany in 1993.

Already an experienced, accomplished defender he could prove to be a bargain buy for the Gers.

Rangers' Mr Wright!

Rangers Gallery

CHARLIE MILLER

OLEG SALENKO

Stuart McCall - Yorkshire Terrier

FACT FILE:

Born: 10 June 1964
Birthplace: Leeds
Position: Midfield
Previous clubs: Bradford City, Everton
Scotland International

McCall on the move!

Stuart McCall, Rangers' midfield dynamo, is a never-say-die competitor who always gives 100 per cent in the club cause.

Flame-hared Stuart was born in Yorkshire and qualifies for Scotland through parentage. He joined Bradford City straight from school and had six successful seasons at Valley Parade, being a member of the Bantams' side that nearly gained promotion to the First Division – just missing out in the play-offs. Immediately after this disappointment Everton gave Stuart a chance to play First Division football when they bought him for £850,000 in June 1988.

He soon became a big favourite with the Goodison Park faithful and in his first season was a member of the Everton squad to reach the all-Merseyside FA Cup Final. Stuart wrote his name into the record books when he became the first player to score twice in an FA Cup Final after coming on as a substitute. But he still had to settle for a loser's medal as Liverpool triumphed 3-2.

Stuart had another two successful seasons at Everton, establishing himself as a Scotland regular before joining Rangers for £1.2 million in August 1991. He was a member of the Scotland squad at the 1990 World Cup and the 1992 and 1996 European Championships, being an automatic choice for Andy Roxburgh and Craig Brown.

Stuart had an injury-hit 1995-96 season, undergoing a hernia operation and suffering a torn calf muscle but returned to play in Rangers Cup Final triumph over Hearts.

Rangers in Euro *Action*

Gary Bollan challenges Moreno Torricelli of Juventus

Gazza is about to score against Steaua Bucharest

Gazza gets the attention against Borussia Dortmund

Rangers in Euro *Action*

Brian Laudrup in action against Borussia Dortmund

Gazza shoots!

Fabrizio Ravanelli gets in a cross for Juventus

Craig Moore tackles Didier Deschamps of Juventus

Oleg Salenko breaks away from the Juventus defence

Close contact between Moreno Torricelli and Alex Cleland

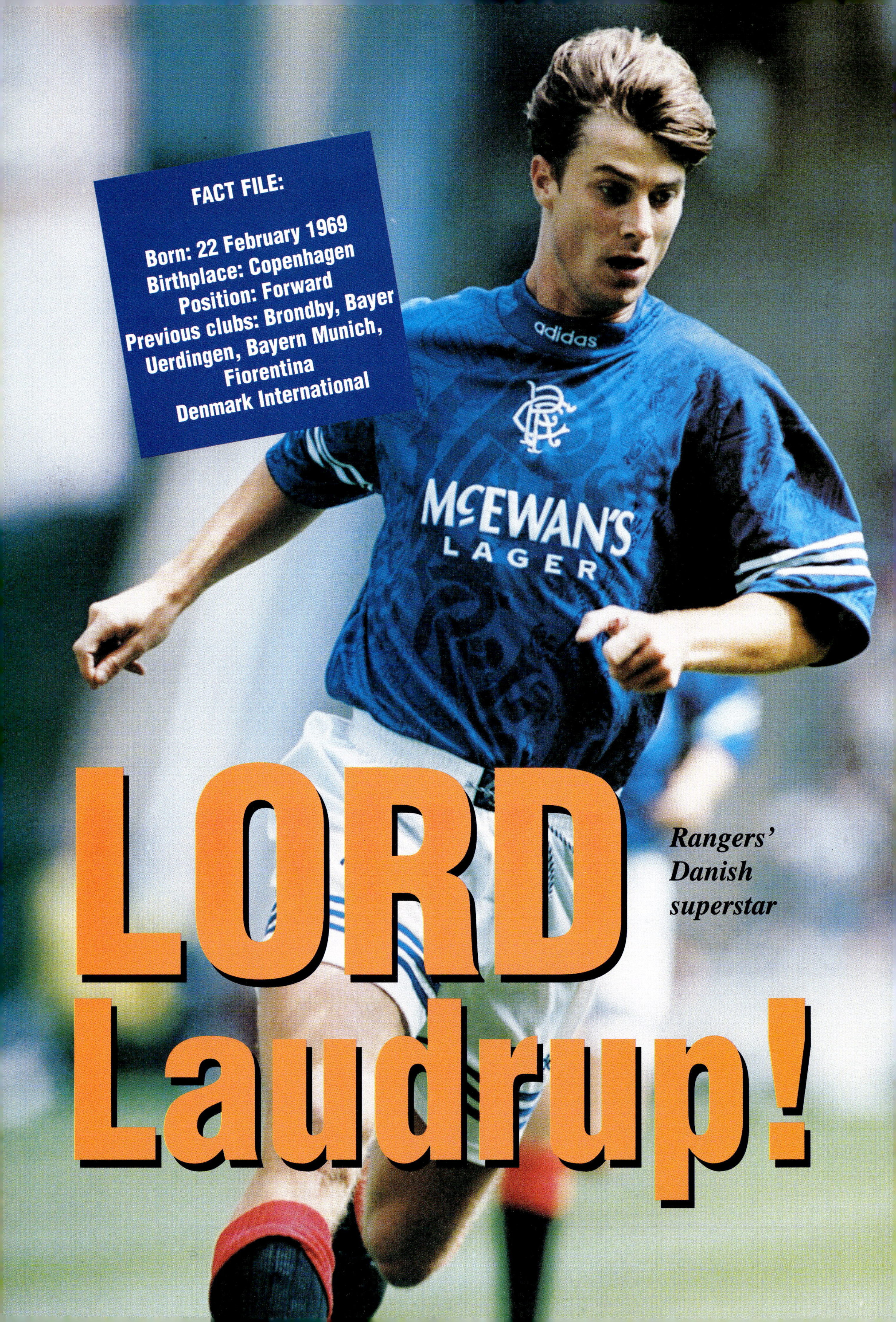

LORD Laudrup!

Rangers' Danish superstar

FACT FILE:

Born: 22 February 1969
Birthplace: Copenhagen
Position: Forward
Previous clubs: Brondby, Bayer Uerdingen, Bayern Munich, Fiorentina
Denmark International

Brian Laudrup, Rangers' wing wizard, comes from a football family of outstanding pedigree – his father, Finn, was a Danish international of the 1960s and elder brother Michael is one the finest Danish players of the modern era.

Brian started his career with Danish part-timers Brondby and was an instant success, being voted Danish Footballer of the Year three times. Europe's big clubs were soon taking an interest and he moved to West German club Bayer Uerdingen. Bundesliga giants Bayern Munich then paid a West German record fee of £2 million to secure his services but his spell at Bayern was brief and he moved on to Serie A club Fiorentina. This was also an unhappy move as Fiorentina were battling to avoid their first relegation in nearly 60 years.

Brian moved to Rangers in the summer of 1994 for £2.5 million and immediately settled at Ibrox Park. He had an outstanding season in 1994-95, being voted Scotland's Player of the Year and was a key figure in the Gers' seventh consecutive title success.

Brian had another brilliant season in 1995-96 as Rangers clinched the 'Double'. He gave a memorable performance in the Cup Final against Hearts being involved in all five goals, scoring two himself and creating Gordon Durie's hat-trick.

His most memorable moment on the international scene was as a member of Denmark's victorious 1992 European Championship team.

Brian has shown that he is really happy with life at Rangers by signing an extension to his contract that will keep him at Ibrox until 1998. And that's great news for all Light Blues' fans!

Brian celebrates a Rangers goal!

Rangers in 1995-96 - Part Two

JANUARY 1996

1996 began in traditional fashion with the Old Firm derby with CELTIC at a packed Parkhead on 3 January. Before the kick-off a minute's silence was observed in memory of the dreadful disaster which occurred at Ibrox 25 years earlier - on 2 January 1971 - when 66 fans lost their lives and 145 were injured after crush barriers collapsed on Stairway 13.

The match was action-packed and full of dramatic, end-to-end stuff - but it produced no goals. Rangers almost went ahead with four minutes to go, but Paul Gascoigne's free-kick rebounded off Celtic's crossbar - and the points were shared.

Next it was off to Brockville Park for the second away fixture of the season against FALKIRK who were now well down in the relegation zone. Rangers simply increased the Bairns' gloom with another devastating performance which produced four goals without reply.

The first came from Gordon Durie after just three minutes, from a Derek McInnes through ball. Ally McCoist supplied the second, on 26 minutes, when he hit a rebounding ball into the Falkirk net.

Twelve minutes later David Robertson made it 3-0 by putting the finishing touch to a brilliant move involving McInnes, Gascoigne and Durie who supplied the left-side cross from which Robbo headed home.

In the 74th minute David Robertson was pulled down in the Falkirk penalty area. Ally McCoist stepped up to take the spot kick, which he then blasted into the back of the net. This was Ally's 230th league goal for Rangers, and equalled the club record previously held, for nearly

Laudrup breaks away

Laudrup shoots

57 years, by Bob McPhail.

RAITH ROVERS came to Ibrox on 13 January and, just like Falkirk a week earlier, they found themselves on the wrong end of a 4-0 scoreline. Ally McCoist opened the scoring on 21 minutes to set a new Rangers record of 231 league goals.

Gordon Durie struck twice before half time with a header from a Brian Laudrup cross on 39 minutes and a spectacular overhead kick five minutes later. Late in the second period Ian Ferguson made it four to Rangers when he made a 30-yard run before firing into the Raith net.

Richard Gough shadows Hibernian's Keith Wright

Rangers' title challenge took a big blow on 20 January when HEARTS came to Ibrox and went away with all three points in the bag. The damage was done by a sensational hat-trick scored by Allan Johnston. Al's first came after just four minutes after which the Gers were always playing catch-up - something they clearly failed to do. It was Rangers second league defeat of the campaign.

The last match in January saw Rangers at Pittodrie for the Scottish Cup Third Round tie against KEITH. The Highland League side hardly stood a chance against Glasgow's giants. The rout started in the 2nd minute with an Ian Ferguson goal. Nine others followed - two more from Ferguson, a hat-trick for Alex Cleland, and one apiece for Gordon Durie (a penalty), David Robertson, Charlie Miller and Alexei Mikhailichenko.

Keith never gave up, and pulled one back in the 89th minute through Mark Garden who planted the ball in Andy Goram's goal after a free kick.

All in all Rangers had given a thoroughly professional performance to ensure a place the Fourth Round.

Ian Ferguson in action against Celtic

RANGERS MATCH-FAX – JANUARY 1996

PREMIER LEAGUE
3.1.1996
Celtic 0 Rangers 0
Att 37,000

6.1.1996
Falkirk 0 Rangers 4
Att 10,581

13.1.1996
Rangers 4 Raith Rovers 0
Att 42,498

20.1.1996
Rangers 0 Hearts 3
Att 45,096

SCOTTISH CUP THIRD ROUND
(at Pittodrie) 27.1.1996
Keith 1 Rangers 10
Att 14,000

FEBRUARY 1996

On 3 February Rangers were at Firhill Park for the third Premier League encounter of the season with PARTICK THISTLE. The Gers made it three-out-of-three with a 2-1 victory.

Back from suspension Paul Gascoigne was the star of the show in a hard fought game. He opened the scoring on 27 minutes after collecting a Charlie Miller pass then scything through the Thistle defence to fire past Nicky Walker. The Jags got back into the match eight minutes later when Rod McDonald equalised after a corner-kick.

But Gazza wasn't to be outdone, in the 37th minute he struck his second goal of the game, a brilliant, unstoppable shot from all of 30-yards.

Next came the Premier League clash with MOTHERWELL at Ibrox. The fireworks started almost immediately, when Ian Ferguson took advantage of a magical run and pass from Gazza to score the opening goal.

On 53 minutes Brian Martin pulled one back for the 'Well with a brilliant 20-yarder. This was cancelled out twelve minutes later when Alan McClaren put Rangers back into the lead with a close range shot.

But Motherwell, desperate for points, came back yet again an equalised once more, this time through Willie Falconer.

The decider came from substitute Ally McCoist who came on for Peter van Vossen in the 72nd minute. Five minutes later Paul Gascoigne was brought down in the box. Ally stepped up and fired the penalty home. It was

Celtic's Jackie McNamara challenges Paul Gascoigne

Trevor Steven

virtually his first kick of the match and it proved the most valuable. Rangers had won 3-2 and now stood three points ahead of Celtic in the title race.

Scottish Cup action followed with Rangers Fourth Round visit to Second Division CLYDE on 15 February. The Gers dominated most of the first half, but the opening goal did not come until the 53rd minute - from Clyde, the result of a fine passing move which began in their own penalty area and involved four players. The finishing touch was provided by Ian Angus.

This scare urged Rangers to step up a gear and the almost inevitable equaliser arrived on 66 minutes when Charlie Miller crashed an angled shot into the roof of the net, from a Craig Moore pass. Six minutes later Charlie was on target again, after Peter van Vossen had beaten three defenders before supplying a great cross.

In the 80th minute van Vossen scored his first goal for Rangers by putting the finishing touch to a great move involving Brian Laudrup and Paul Gascoigne. The mini rout was completed two minutes later when Gazza chipped 'keeper Hillcoat. Rangers marched into the quarter-finals.

Next, it was back to Premier League action with the visit to ABERDEEN on Sunday 25 February. Shortly after the half-hour mark, Brian Laudrup was making one of his trademark runs into the Dons' penalty area when he was tripped by Brian Irvine on the edge of the six-yard box.

The ref blew for a penalty-kick which was taken by Paul Gascoigne who sent 'keeper Michael Watt the wrong way. It was the only goal of the game and it kept the Gers ahead in the title race.

As February closed Rangers were on 65 points from 27 games, followed by Celtic with 62 from 27. Third placed Aberdeen were a massive 22 points adrift.

RANGERS MATCH-FAX – FEBRUARY 1996

PREMIER LEAGUE
3.2.1996
Partick Thistle 1 Rangers 2
Att 16,523

10.2.1996
Rangers 3 Motherwell 2
Att 45,566

SCOTTISH CUP FOURTH ROUND
15.2.1996
Clyde 1 Rangers 4
Att 5,722

PREMIER LEAGUE
25.2.1996
Aberdeen 0 Rangers 1
Att 21,000

MARCH 1996

Rangers needed to maintain their momentum in the final phase of the Premier League campaign. And that's precisely what happened on the visit to Easter Road for the last meeting of the season with HIBERNIAN.

Dazzling Dane Brian Laudrup was the main instigator of Rangers' pressure in the match - he was quite magnificent. In the 30th minute he was off on another of his mazy runs in which he bypassed no less than five Hibs men before crossing the ball. Defender Graham

Ally heads home!

Mitchell attempted to clear the danger, but succeeded only in putting the ball past Jim Leighton.

In the 70th minute the Danish star was tripped in the penalty area, after working a neat one-two with Paul Gascoigne. Brian stepped up to take the spot kick and he beat Jim Leighton for Rangers' second goal of the afternoon.Things were looking good at the top of the table.

Scottish Cup action followed with a trip to Tannadice to take on CALEDONIAN THISTLE in the quarter-finals. Things began to go wrong for Caley in the 15th minute when Brian Thomson steered Peter van Vossen's cross past his own 'keeper.

After that Paul Gascoigne took over, scoring two goals and ensuring the Gers progress to the semis. His first goal began with Brian Laudrup's 50-yard surge out of defence. He fed the ball to Gazza, who then floated a wonderful left-foot shot into the top of the net. Paul's second, in the 52nd minute, was a fine far post header from a Brian Laudrup cross. Result: 3-0.

Next came the last Premier League Old Firm derby of the season, when CELTIC came to Ibrox on 17 March. This was an important match for both sides. If Celtic won they would make a giant stride in the title race. If Rangers won, the gap at the top would widened in their favour. In the event the game ended in a 1-1 draw.

Alan McLaren opened the scoring for the Gers four minutes before half time, when he headed home a Paul Gascoigne free kick.

The home side hung on to their lead until the 86th minute. By then Celtic were down to ten-men, having had Jackie McNamara sent off following a second bookable offence. But the visitors did not cave in. Instead, they equalised through Hughes who headed home from a John Collins free-kick. Points shared, honours even.

March 23rd 1996 is a date which Rangers' reserve goalkeeper Colin Scott will always remember. Shortly before kick-off of the Premier League match against FALKIRK, he learned that he was to take the place of out of sorts Andy Goram in the first team line-up. The youngster, making only his third appearance of the campaign, performed heroically in the white-hot atmosphere generated by the 46,000+ crowd.

Rangers strode to a two-nil half time lead with goals from Paul Gascoigne on 8 minutes and Erik Bo Andersen on 27 minutes. It looked to be a surefire thing that the points would all stay at Ibrox.

In the second half, the complexion of the game changed somewhat when ex-Ranger Mo Johnston pulled one back for the Bairns on 55 minutes. It was then a question of knuckling down and getting the old act together again and in the 79th minute while several Rangers players were appealing for an handball decision, Erik Bo Andersen did not join in the protests but instead fired the ball into the Falkirk goal to put his side 3-1 ahead.

The Bairns were not prepared to lie down, however, and in the 82nd minute Kevin James scored after a corner kick. After that Rangers did all they could to keep the Bairns at bay and in the end were relieved to run out as 3-2 winners.

Rangers players and fans alike were also relieved to learn that closest rivals Celtic had been held to a draw by Motherwell at Fir Park. This meant that the Gers now edged a little further ahead of their city rivals and a little closer to that magical title.

That dream drew even closer after the last game of March, against RAITH ROVERS at Stark's Park, although Rangers started poorly as Rovers went into the lead on 29 minutes through a Pete Duffied volley from a Thomson cross. The balance was restored ten minutes later when Ally McCoist netted from the penalty spot after a foul on Erik Bo Andersen.

The scoreline remained even until the 68th minute when David Kirkwood restored Raith's lead from with a well-struck penalty following a foul on Duffield.

Now came the time for Rangers to dig deep and show just why they were Championship favourites. The breakthrough came on 83 minutes when Ally McCoist got his second of the game, heading home a loose ball in a penalty-mouth scramble. Six minutes later Super Al completed his hat-trick by shooting from close in after a Gazza corner had been flicked on by Gordon Durie. It was the Juke Box man who completed the scoring from the penalty spot after he had been fouled.

That Championship trophy was getting ever closer to the Ibrox Trophy Room!

RANGERS MATCH-FAX – MARCH 1996

PREMIER LEAGUE
3.3.1996
Hibernian 0 Rangers 2
Att 11,954

SCOTTISH CUP FIFTH ROUND
(at Tannadice Park)
9.3.1996
Caledonian Thistle 0
Rangers 3
Att 12,000

PREMIER LEAGUE

17.3.1996
Rangers 1 Celtic 1
Att 47,312

23.3.1996
Rangers 3 Falkirk 2
Att 46,014

30.3.1996
Raith Rovers 2 Rangers 4
Att 9,300

Perfect balance from Brian Laudrup

Ian Durrant

Gazza action against Aberdeen

APRIL - MAY 1996

April's programme began with Rangers' sixth meeting of the season with CELTIC - this time in the Scottish Cup semi-final at Hampden Park. This was a tough, defence-dominated game in which the Gers finally made the breakthrough on 43 minutes when Ally McCoist pounced on a loose ball to fire home from an acute angle. Brian Laudrup made it two-nil in the 67th minute, chesting the ball down before shooting past Celtic 'keeper Gordon Marshall.

Celtic got back into the match when Pierre van Hooijdonk headed home a Jackie McNamara cross. From then on it was a case of clinging on to that lead for Rangers. And that's what they did, to progress to the final against Hearts.

And it was the Edinburgh club who provided heartbreak for Rangers in their next Premier League match at Tynecastle. The HEARTS defence was in defiant mood, their attack in rampant form.

They went ahead on 34 minutes through Neil Pointon who expertly chipped Andy Goram in the Gers goalmouth. The next came on 83 minutes from Allan Johnston, whose hat-trick had helped destroy Rangers back in January.

There was no way back for the Gers - it was their first away defeat of the 1995-96 Premier League campaign.

Things got back on track in the next match, at home to PARTICK THISTLE. Erik Bo Andersen was the star of the show, scoring a superb hat-trick, his first for the Gers. The tall Danish striker struck twice before half time.

In the second period Rangers produced a virtual exhibition of fine football, with Bo heading home his third goal and two others coming courtesy of Stuart McCall and Richard Gough.

Rangers now need just six more points to put the Championship issue beyond doubt.

Stephen Wright

Brian Laudrup

Three of those points came in the next match at MOTHERWELL, in which Rangers powered to a 3-1 victory.

The opening goal came after just five minutes, when Stuart McCall put the finishing touch to a neat passing move. The second came from a Bo Andersen header from close in, four minutes before half time. Paul Gascoigne added the third after a brilliant 40-yard run by Brian Laudrup who fed a simple pass to Gazza in the 59th minute.

Motherwell pulled one back in the 70th minute through Dougie Arnott.

Rangers produced a Sunday-best performance against ABERDEEN at Ibrox on 28 April to clinch that eighth consecutive championship and a place in the 1996-97 European Cup competition.

Paul Gascoigne was the star of the show, scoring a wonderful hat-trick, including a penalty, and generally running the show with his own special brand of brilliance.

But, of course, it wasn't as simple as all that. The Dons had gone ahead in the 19th minute, through Brian Irvine who scored during a goalmouth scramble.

Then Gazza began to turn it on. His first goal came three minutes later, after beating two defenders. His second arrived in the 80th minute - another great solo effort and a rocket shot.

The penalty on 86 minutes was driven hard into the bottom right corner of the Aberdeen net. And it put the seal on a super Sunday for the boys in blue.

This left just one more Premier League match to play, against KILMARNOCK at Rugby Park. Two goals from Gordon Durie and one from Ally McCoist gave Rangers a 3-0 victory. And so the league programme was wrapped up in true blue style.

Now Rangers had the chance to wrap up a League and Cup 'double' in the Tennants Scottish Cup final, against HEARTS at Hampden Park on 18 May.

Hearts, who had twice beaten the Gers earlier in the season, were simply outclassed in the national stadium. Rangers were once again in rampant form. This time Brian Laudrup stole the show.

The dazzling Dane scored twice in the match (on 37 and 49 minutes) and his overall performance even upstaged hat-trick hero Gordon Durie (66, 79 and 85 minutes) as the Gers celebrated with a 5-1 victory, their biggest in the final for 24 years.

John Colqhoun replied for Hearts on 76 minutes, but by then their hearts were broken and Rangers had done the 'double'.

Ally McCoist

RANGERS MATCH-FAX – APRIL - MAY 1996

SCOTTISH CUP SEMI-FINAL
(at Hampden Park)
7.4.1996
Celtic 1 Rangers 2
Att 36,333

PREMIER LEAGUE
10.4.1996
Hearts 2 Rangers 0
Att 15,350

13.4.1996
Rangers 5 Partick Thistle 0
Att 46,438

20.4.1996
Motherwell 1 Rangers 3
Att 13,128

28.4.1996
Rangers 3 Aberdeen 1
Att 47,247

4.5.1996
Kilmarnock 0 Rangers 3
Att 17,056

SCOTTISH CUP FINAL
(at Hampden Park)
18.5.1996
Rangers 5 Hearts 1
Att 37,730

Celebration Time for Rangers

The captain and the Championship trophy

Champions again!

Walter, Gazza and Trevor salute the crowd

Gazza's happy!

facts & figures
1995-96

EUROPEAN CHAMPIONS' CUP - GROUP C TABLE

	P	W	D	L	F	A	Pts
Juventus*	6	4	1	1	15	4	13
B Dortmund	6	2	3	1	8	8	9
S Bucharest	6	1	3	2	2	5	6
Rangers	6	0	3	3	6	14	3

*Juventus went on to win the European Champions' Cup

GOALSCORERS IN ALL CUP COMPETITIONS

Gordon Durie	6
Paul Gascoigne	5
Ally McCoist	4
Brian Laudrup	4
Ian Ferguson	4
Alex Cleland	3
Charlie Miller	3
Richard Gough	2
Mark Hateley	2
Alexei Mikhailichenko	1
Peter Van Vossen	1
David Robertson	1
Oleg Salenko	1
Stuart McCall	1
Own goals	1

LEAGUE GOALSCORERS

Gordon Durie	17
Ally McCoist	16
Paul Gascoigne	14
Oleg Salenko	7
Erik Bo Andersen	6
Charlie Miller	3
Richard Gough	3
Stuart McCall	3
David Robertson	3
Alan McClaren	3
Ian Ferguson	2
Brian Laudrup	2
Alex Cleland	1
Craig Moore	1
Gordan Petric	1
Own goals	3

BELLS PREMIER DIVISION 1995-96 – FINAL TABLE

	P	W	D	L	F	A	Pts
RANGERS	36	27	6	3	85	25	87
Celtic	36	24	11	1	74	25	83
Aberdeen	36	16	7	13	52	45	55
Hearts	36	16	7	13	55	53	55
Hibernian	36	11	10	15	43	57	43
Raith Rovers	36	12	7	17	41	57	43
Kilmarnock	36	11	8	17	39	54	41
Motherwell	36	9	12	15	28	39	39
Partick Thistle	36	8	6	22	29	62	30
Falkirk	36	6	6	24	31	60	24

PLAYER OF THE YEAR
Paul Gascoigne

SCOTTISH CUP
Winners, beating Hearts 5-1 in the final at Hampden Park

COCA-COLA CUP
Semi-finalists

BIGGEST ATTENDANCE
47,312 v Celtic

AVERAGE ATTENDANCE
44,579

roll of honour

CLUB FORMED: 1873

LEAGUE CHAMPIONS: DIVISION ONE 35 times
1890-91 (shared), 1898-99, 1899-1900, 1900-01, 1901-02, 1910-11, 1911-12, 1912-13, 1917-18, 1919-20, 1920-21, 1922-23, 1923-24, 1924-25, 1926-27, 1927-28, 1928-29, 1929-30, 1930-31, 1932-33, 1933-34, 1934-35, 1936-37, 1938-39, 1946-47, 1948-49, 1949-50, 1952-53, 1955-56, 1956-57, 1958-59, 1960-61, 1962-63, 1963-64, 1974-75

PREMIER LEAGUE CHAMPIONS 11 times
1975-76, 1977-78, 1986-87, 1988-89, 1980-90, 1990-91, 1991-92, 1992-93, 1993-94, 1994-95, 1995-96

LEAGUE RUNNERS-UP
23 times

SCOTTISH CUP WINNERS
27 times
1894, 1897, 1898, 1903, 1928, 1930, 1932, 1934, 1935, 1936, 1948, 1949, 1950, 1953, 1960, 1962, 1963, 1964, 1966, 1973, 1976, 1978, 1979, 1981, 1992, 1993, 1996

SCOTTISH CUP RUNNERS-UP 16 times

LEAGUE CUP WINNERS
19 times
1946-47, 1948-49, 1960-61, 1961-62, 1963-64, 1964-65, 1970-71, 1975-76, 1977-78, 1978-79, 1981-82, 1983-84, 1984-85, 1986-87, 1987-88, 1988-89, 1990-91, 1992-93, 1993-94

LEAGUE CUP RUNNERS-UP 7 times

EUROPEAN CUP-WINNERS' CUP WINNERS
Once
1972

EUROPEAN CUP-WINNERS' CUP RUNNERS-UP Twice

RECORD ATTENDANCE
118,567 v Celtic, Division One 2 Jan 1934

BIGGEST VICTORY
14-2 v Blairgowrie, Scottish Cup 1st Round 1934

BIGGEST DEFEAT
2-10 by Airdrionians 1886

MOST LEAGUE APPEARANCES 496 by John Grieg – 1962-1978

MOST INDIVIDUAL LEAGUE GOALS IN A SEASON 44 by Sam English 1931-32

MOST INDIVIDUAL GOALS OVERALL 235 by Ally McCoist 1983-1996

MOST CAPPED PLAYER
George Young – 53 caps for Scotland

Already thinking about next season!

RÅN

Closer Look At

Orchids, Palms,

Toadstools and Other Plants

Jen Green

Franklin Watts
LONDON ● SYDNEY

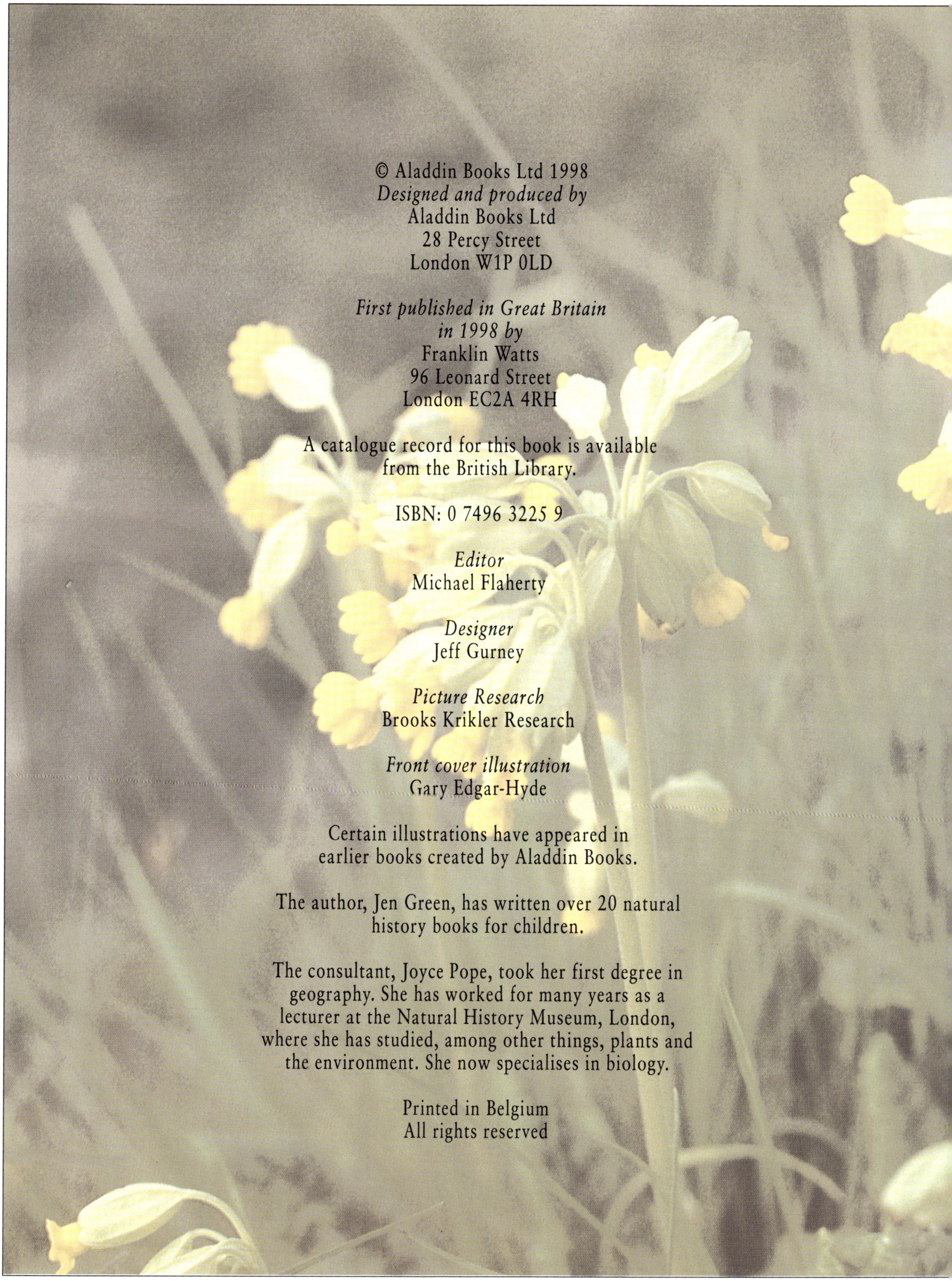

Designed and produced by
Aladdin Books Ltd
28 Percy Street
London W1P 0LD

First published in Great Britain
in 1998 by
Franklin Watts
96 Leonard Street
London EC2A 4RH

A catalogue record for this book is available
from the British Library.

ISBN: 0 7496 3225 9

Editor
Michael Flaherty

Designer
Jeff Gurney

Picture Research
Brooks Krikler Research

Front cover illustration
Gary Edgar-Hyde

Certain illustrations have appeared in
earlier books created by Aladdin Books.

The author, Jen Green, has written over 20 natural
history books for children.

The consultant, Joyce Pope, took her first degree in
geography. She has worked for many years as a
lecturer at the Natural History Museum, London,
where she has studied, among other things, plants and
the environment. She now specialises in biology.

Printed in Belgium

CONTENTS

4. Introduction
6. What are plants?
8. How plants work
10. Algae
12. Plants with spores
14. Mushrooms and toadstools
16. Cone-bearing plants
18. Flowering plants
20. Broadleaves and palms
22. Spreading seeds
24. Against the odds
26. Defence and attack
28. Plants and humans
30. Plant records
31. Glossary
32. Index

INTRODUCTION

Plants are vital to the survival of all living things on Earth. They produce the oxygen humans and animals breathe, and most of the food we eat. Plants and animals make up almost all life on Earth, but these two major groups of living things are very different from each other. Almost all animals stop growing when they become mature, whereas plants carry on growing until they die. Animals move around to find their food and have to feed on things that are or once were alive. Plants make their own food from inert (nonliving) substances, and higher plants are rooted in one place.

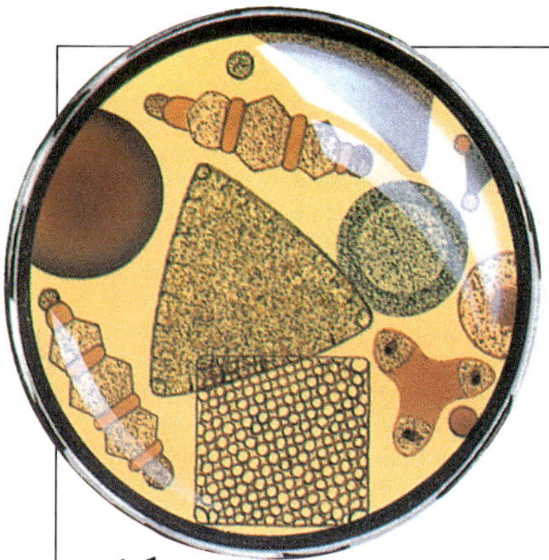

Algae
The simplest plants of all are algae (above), found in sea water or ponds and rivers. Microscopic water algae called diatoms consist of just one cell.

Plants vary greatly in size and shape. The smallest are tiny algae that can only be seen with a microscope. The largest are tall trees that tower over a hundred metres high. Plants grow in many different places, from tropical rainforests to Arctic wastes. Over millions of years, plants have adapted (changed) to help them survive in their particular habitat, or home.

WHAT ARE

Epiphytes
Epiphytes are plants that grow not in the ground but on the trunks or branches of trees (above left). All plants need light to grow. In dark forests, epiphytes perch high in the tree canopy, using tall trees as a means of reaching the light.

THE PLANT KINGDOM

The study of plants is called botany. Botanists, scientists who study plants, have identified over 275,000 species of plants so far. Over half of these are found in the tropical rainforests.

Botanists divide plants into two main groups: flowering and non-flowering plants. Non-flowering plants include the simplest plants, algae, and so-called "primitive" plants such as mosses, liverworts and ferns. Cone-bearing trees such as conifers are also non-flowering plants. Flowering plants make up over three-quarters of the plant kingdom. Broadleaved trees and palms, shrubs and grasses are all kinds of flowering plants.

On Closer Inspection – *Giant leaves*

Giant water lilies (right) from the Amazon region in South America have huge leaves that can measure almost 2 m across. Strong "ribs" beneath the leaves help keep them rigid as they float on the surface of the water. They can even support the weight of a small child.

PLANTS?

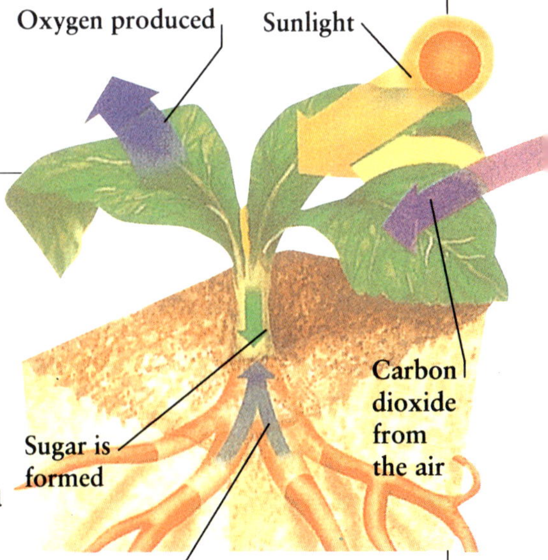

The cells in a plant's leaves work like miniature solar panels, converting sunlight into energy. Not all plants are green, but all contain chlorophyll, so they can make food from sunlight.

Photosynthesis

Most plants cannot move around to find their food, as animals do. Instead, they make it themselves, through photosynthesis. Chlorophyll, the green pigment in a plant's leaves, uses the energy in sunlight to perform a chemical reaction. Carbon dioxide from the air is combined with water and mineral salts to make glucose, which the plant needs to grow. The plant stores this food as starch, sugar or oil. The by-product of photosynthesis is oxygen, which is given off through the leaves.
Animals need oxygen to live and plants are constantly refreshing the oxygen in the air. Animals, in turn, produce carbon dioxide, which plants need, as a waste product.

The biggest plants are tall trees such as giant redwood conifers.

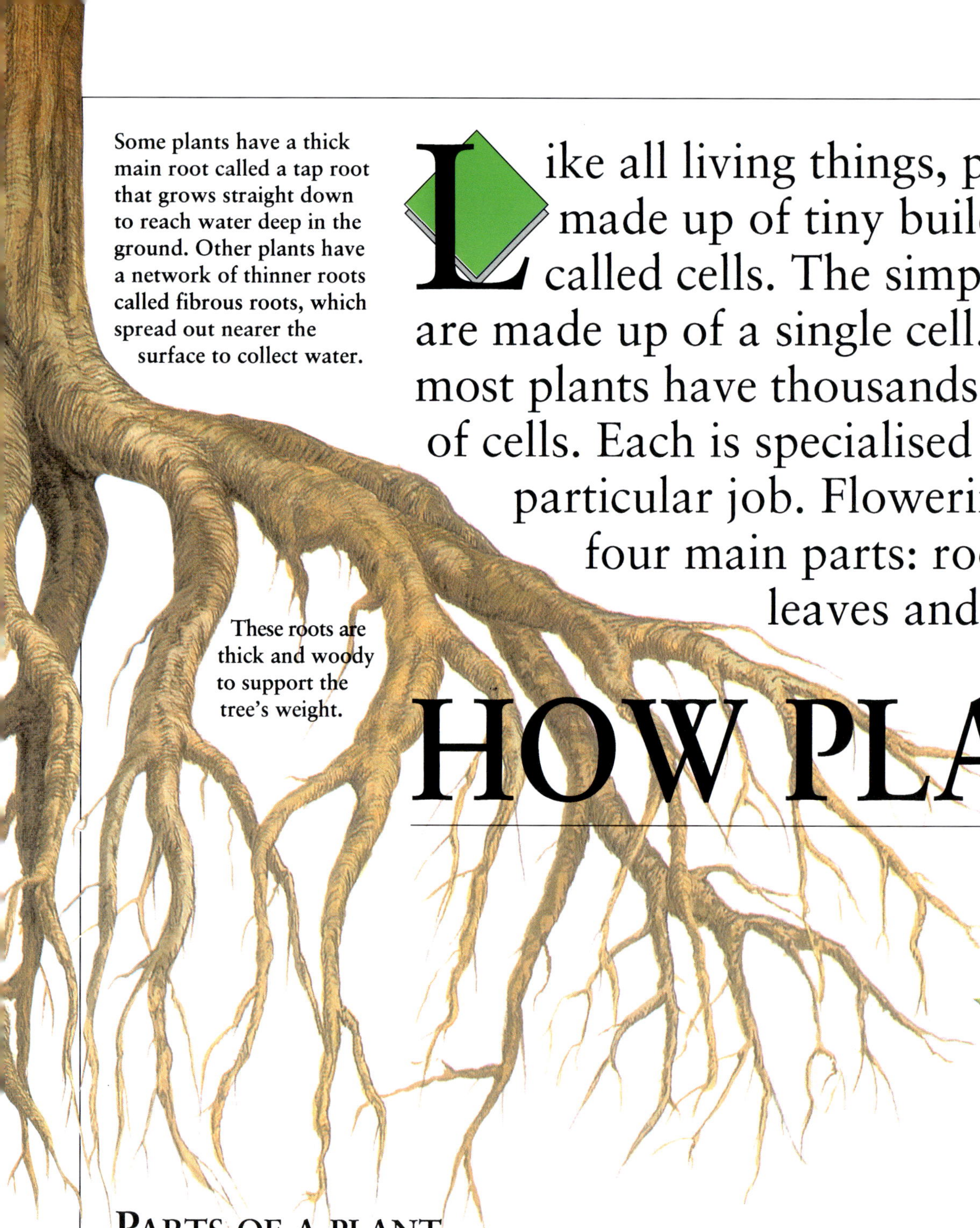

Some plants have a thick main root called a tap root that grows straight down to reach water deep in the ground. Other plants have a network of thinner roots called fibrous roots, which spread out nearer the surface to collect water.

These roots are thick and woody to support the tree's weight.

Like all living things, plants are made up of tiny building blocks called cells. The simplest plants are made up of a single cell. However, most plants have thousands, even millions of cells. Each is specialised to do a particular job. Flowering plants have four main parts: roots, stem, leaves and flowers.

HOW PLANTS

PARTS OF A PLANT

The roots of a land plant anchor it in the ground, and collect water from the soil. The water contains vital nutrients the plant needs to grow. The job of the plant's stem is to turn the leaves towards the light. The leaves are used to convert the energy from sunlight into food, through photosynthesis. Inside the roots, stem and leaves, special clusters of cells act as tubes, transporting food and water all around the plant to the parts that need it. Groups of cells called xylem cells carry water and minerals upwards from the roots. Phloem cells distribute food made through photosynthesis all around the plant.

On Closer Inspection – *Mangrove swamps*

Mangrove trees grow in swamps in coastal areas in the tropics. They root in salty sea water. Sea water is low in oxygen, which the mangroves need to breathe. So their main roots send up thin aerial roots above the water (right), to gather oxygen from the air.

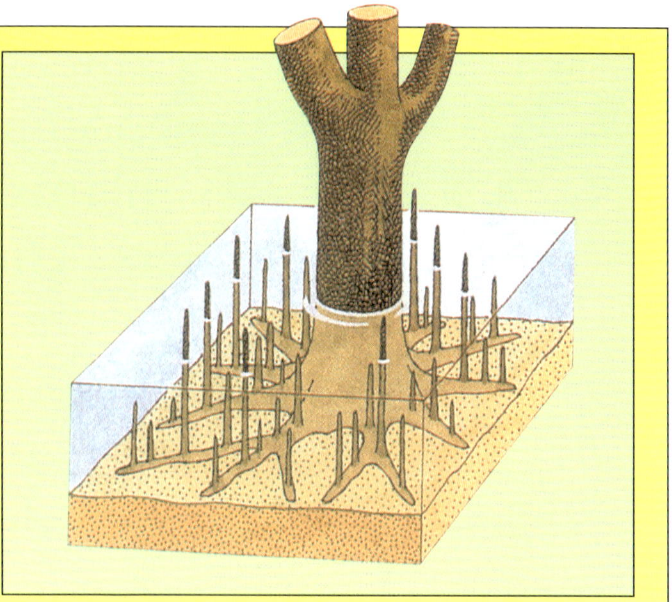

WORK

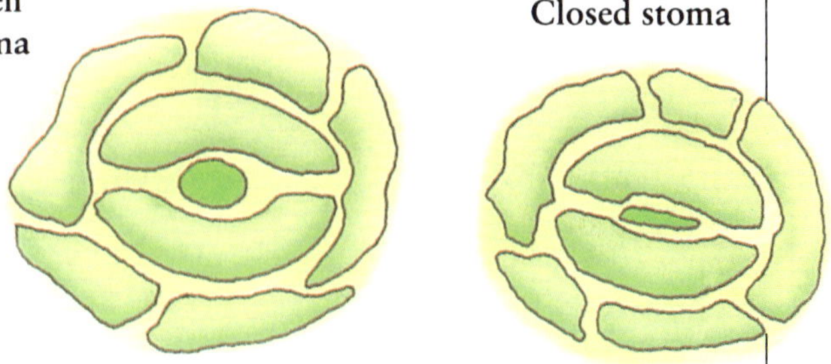

Stomata (singular: stoma)

During the day, the pores, or stomata, on a plant's leaves open to take in carbon dioxide, release oxygen, and allow water to evaporate. At night and in dry weather, they close up, so the plant does not lose too much water and dry out.

In flowering plants, the flowers (above) are used for reproduction.

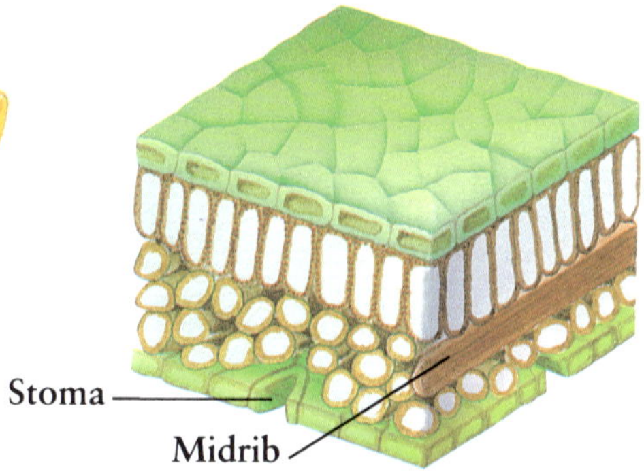

The leaf's midrib supports the leaf blades and contains phloem and xylem cells.

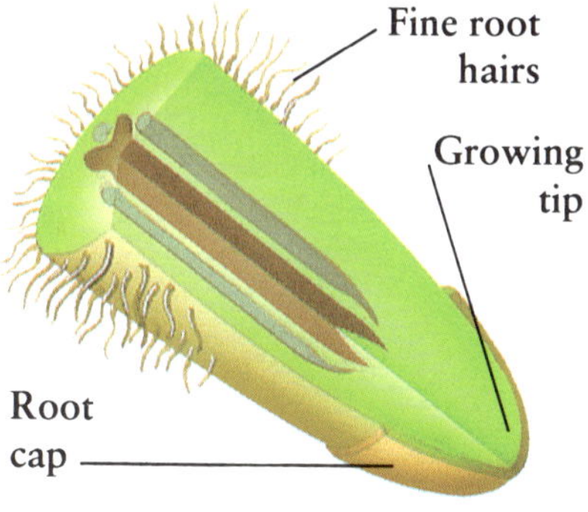

The fine root hairs take in water from the soil. The growing tip is protected by a tough root cap.

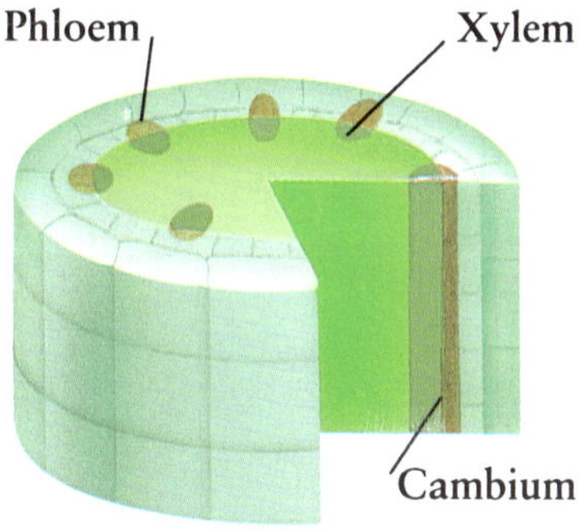

In the stem, the growing layer, called the cambium, produces new cells such as xylem and phloem.

Transpiration

The water drawn up by a plant's roots travels to the leaves, where it is used for photosynthesis. Extra water not needed by the plant is given off from the leaves, in the form of water vapour, a gas. This process is called transpiration. Tiny pores called stomata on the underside of the leaves release the water, and also let gases in and out, allowing the plant to breathe.

ALGAE

Plants first appeared on Earth about 550 million years ago. The first plants were small, simple water-dwellers. They developed in prehistoric oceans rich in minerals, and were probably much like modern algae, today's simplest plants. Today 25,000 different species of algae flourish. They range from microscopic weeds and slimes to giant seaweeds.

WATER LOVERS

Algae have no flowers and no true roots, stems or leaves. But they do contain chlorophyll, which they use to make their food. Algae grow only where there is water. They thrive in sea water, in freshwater ponds and streams, and in damp places. Some specialised algae even grow in snowfields and boiling springs, and in the fur of sloths.

Fronds

Seaweeds have no proper leaves or roots. Many kinds have long, strap-shaped fronds that wave about in ocean currents.

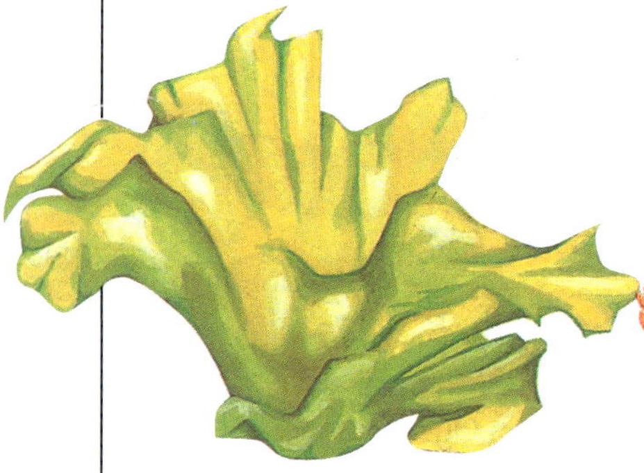

Sea lettuce – green seaweed

Holdfast

A root-like structure called a holdfast helps many seaweeds to anchor onto rocks on the seabed.

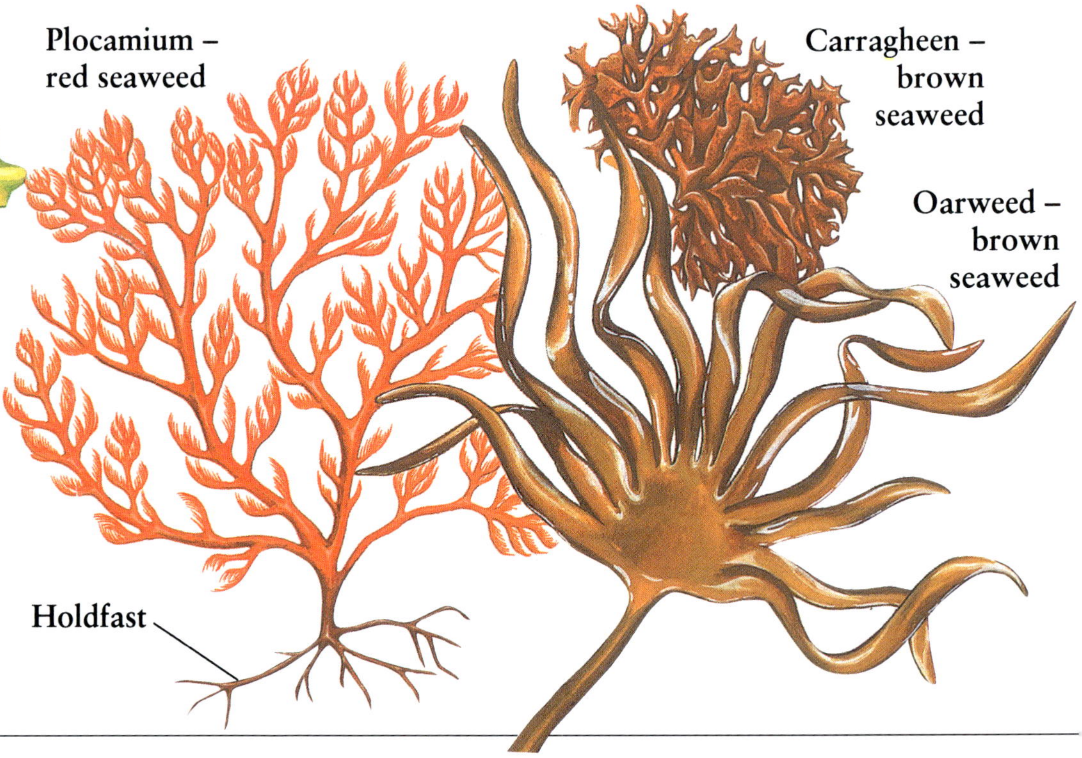

On Closer Inspection – *Seaweed food*

Seaweeds are rich in vitamins and minerals, but supply little else that is digestable. Different kinds are used in foods around the world. In Japanese cooking, seaweeds are eaten as vegetables and used in dishes such as sushi (right).

Simple plants

Some algae are very simple plants, consisting of a single cell. Diatoms are microscopic, one-celled algae that live in lakes, rivers and seas. Many thousands can be found in a single glass of pond water. A pond alga called spirogyra grows in long, thin chains of identical cells. Algae do not reproduce by making seeds. Instead, algae such as volvox (below) reproduce either asexually, by dividing, or sexually, by releasing male cells into the water which fuse with female cells to form a new plant.

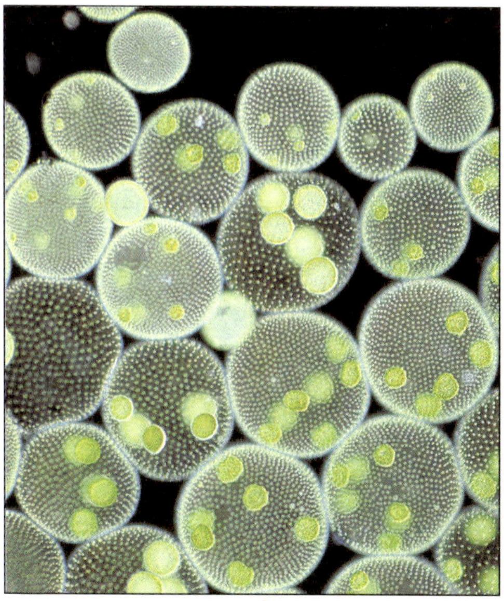

Seaweeds

Seaweeds are large algae that live in seawater on rocky coasts or seabeds. There are three main groups – green, red and brown. Red and brown seaweeds contain green chlorophyll like other plants, so they can photosynthesise. The green colour is masked by brown and red pigments which help the plants absorb sunlight in seawater. Giant kelp (above) is a brown seaweed whose fronds can measure up to 60 m long and grow up to 45 cm in a single day.

Plants first appeared on land 400 million years ago. Mosses, liverworts and ferns were among the earliest land-dwellers. These primitive plants have neither seeds nor flowers. Instead, they reproduce by making spores – specialised cells able to develop into new plants.

PLANTS WITH

Reproduction

Mosses and liverworts reproduce in two stages. They produce male and female organs; the umbrella-like growths on this liverwort (below) are female. After fertilisation in most species, a stalk bearing a spore capsule grows from the female organ (above). When the spores are ripe they are scattered to sprout into new plants

Mosses and liverworts

Mosses, liverworts and hornworts have no true roots or stems, so they cannot reach upwards towards the light. Instead they form low, dense mats of vegetation (above). These simple land plants thrive in damp, shady places such as bogs and riverbanks. Sphagnum moss, which grows as soggy carpets in swamp land, decays to form peat which can be burned as a fuel when dried out. Most kinds of liverworts have a flattish green body called a thallus.

On Closer Inspection – *Plant fossils*

Fossils are the remains or imprints in rocks of plants and animals that lived thousands or millions of years ago. They provide evidence of plants such as giant club mosses and horsetails that thrived in prehistoric forests.

SPORES

Ferns and their relatives

Ferns, horsetails and club mosses have stems and roots, so they can grow tall, and reach towards the light. The ancestors of horsetails and club mosses once dominated the plant kingdom. Now they form only a tiny part of it. Ferns are another early group of plants, but they are still widespread today. Bracken is a hardy fern that colonises fields and meadows.

Horsetails reproduce by growing cones that contain spores on a separate stem.

Life cycle

Ferns have a complicated life cycle that takes two generations to complete. If you lift up a fern leaf, or frond, you may find rows of brown or yellow spots growing underneath (1). These are tiny sacs called sporangia, which contain the spores. On a dry day the sacs burst open, and the spores are flung into the air. A spore may land to grow into a tiny plant shaped differently to its parent, called a prothallus (2). The prothallus contains both male and female cells. When it rains, the male cells swim to another prothallus, where they fertilise the female cells (3). Once fertilised, a new fern can grow from the prothallus (4). Eventually it will mature to produce its own spores.

Bracken

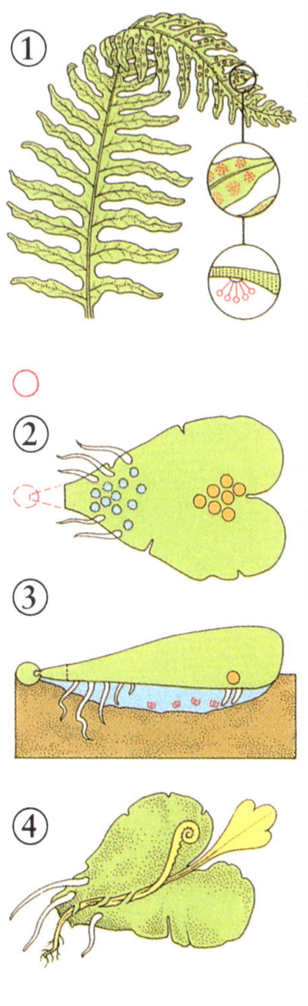

Mushrooms, toadstools, yeasts, moulds and mildews are all types of fungi. This large group of living things, with more than 70,000 species, are not true plants. They are among the most widespread living things in the world. Most fungi grow in damp, dark places. They reproduce by making spores.

MUSHROOMS

Gills
Under the mushroom's cap (above) are the gills, which produce the spores. Many mushrooms are edible, but some are poisonous. The poisonous ones are often called toadstools. Many toadstools are brightly coloured. *NEVER EAT FUNGI YOU FIND IN THE WILD UNLESS THEY HAVE BEEN IDENTIFIED BY AN EXPERT!*

Spores
Like mushrooms and toadstools, yeasts and moulds have a network of branching hyphae and spore-bearing structures called sporangia.

FEEDING

Without green chlorophyll, fungi cannot photosynthesise to make their food. Instead, they feed mainly on dead plants or animals, helping to return their goodness to the soil. Fungi, such as mushrooms and toadstools, are made up of hundreds of branching threads of cells called hyphae. The network of hyphae runs through the soil. The hyphae release chemicals called enzymes, which break down and dissolve plant and animal matter so the fungi can absorb the nutrients.

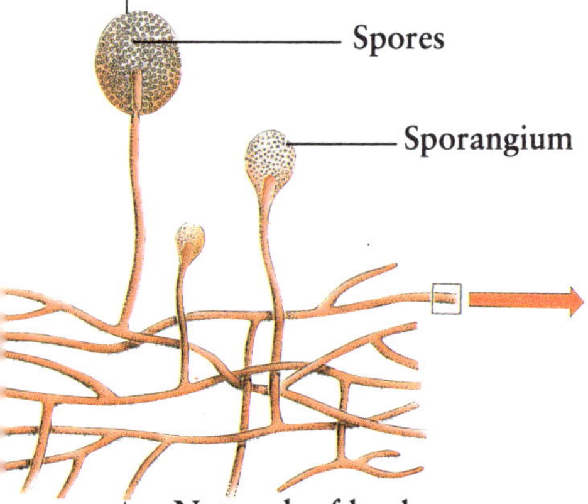

Network of hyphae

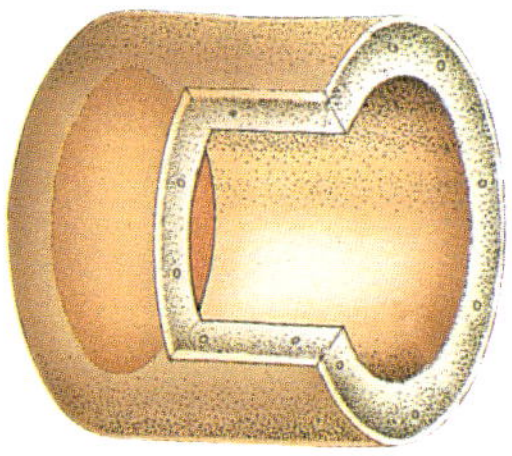

Close-up section through a hypha

Do not touch
The fly agaric (above) is an attractive but very poisonous toadstool. This cutaway section shows the gills under the cap, and a network of hyphae underground.

On Closer Inspection – *Lichen*

A lichen is an unusual organism, consisting of a plant (an alga) and a fungus together. The fungus shelters the alga and provides it with minerals. In return, the alga photosynthesises to feed the fungus. Lichens grow on stones, rocks and tree trunks.

& TOADSTOOLS

Reproduction

To reproduce, fungi form fruiting bodies above ground. This is the part of edible mushrooms we eat. The fruiting body is made up of a thick column of hyphae threads, topped by a cap. Under the cap, the gills produce millions of tiny spores. When the spores are ripe, they drop from the gills to the ground and grow into new fungi. The fruiting bodies of fungi such as puffballs (left) become hard and rigid when they are ripe. If they are knocked by a passing animal or rocked by the wind, they puff out millions of spores, which are dispersed by the wind.

Mould

Moulds and yeasts are types of smaller fungi. Mould will grow on moist, stale bread (above) or rotting fruit after a few days. Moulds are useful because they break down dead animal and plant matter. Yeast is used to make bread rise and beer and wine ferment.

Cycads

Cycads are a group of plants with leaves like spiky fronds (above). They bear the largest cones of any plant. The cycad's cone can measure up to 60 cm long and weigh 25 kg.

The plants that dominate the plant kingdom today reproduce by making seeds, not spores. Seed-bearing plants appeared about 300 million years ago. Botanists divide seed-producing plants into two groups: those that grow their seeds inside cones, and those whose seeds develop inside fruits. The cone-bearing plants developed first.

CONE-BEARING

Oldest known trees

Conifers are fast-growing trees with a single, tall, straight trunk. They are prized for their timber, which is known as softwood. The group also includes the oldest trees, bristlecone pines (below). Some of these knarled, hardy pine trees are more than 4,000 years old.

Conifers

Conifers are the largest group of cone-bearing plants, with more than 500 species. The group includes pines, spruce, fir, yew and cedar. Conifers are trees with narrow, waxy, tough-skinned leaves. The leaves hold moisture well. Most conifers do not shed all their leaves at one time, so they are called evergreens. They grow mainly in cool, temperate climates, and can survive in cold, windy or dry areas better than other trees. A great belt of conifer forests, called the taiga, stretches across northern Europe, Siberia and North America.

Douglas fir

ON CLOSER INSPECTION – *Cone breakers*

Crossbills are birds that live in the pine forests of the north, in Canada and Scandinavia. They eat only one food: pine-cone seeds. The crossbill's unusual, overlapping beak is designed to break open the cones to get at the seeds.

PLANTS

REPRODUCTION

Unlike spore-bearing plants, seed-bearers do not rely on water to reproduce. This has allowed them to spread widely. Conifers produce both male and female cones (below). In spring the small male cones release pollen, which lands on the sticky female cones to fertilise them. The winged seeds develop in the female cones.

Ginkgo

The ginkgo is very ancient and first grew 200 million years ago. It has unusual, fan-shaped leaves (below) and fleshy cones. Ginkgos originally came from China, but now are found all over the world.

Yew

Yew trees have narrow, dark-green leaves. The seeds are red and fleshy, and look like berries, but they are poisonous (above).

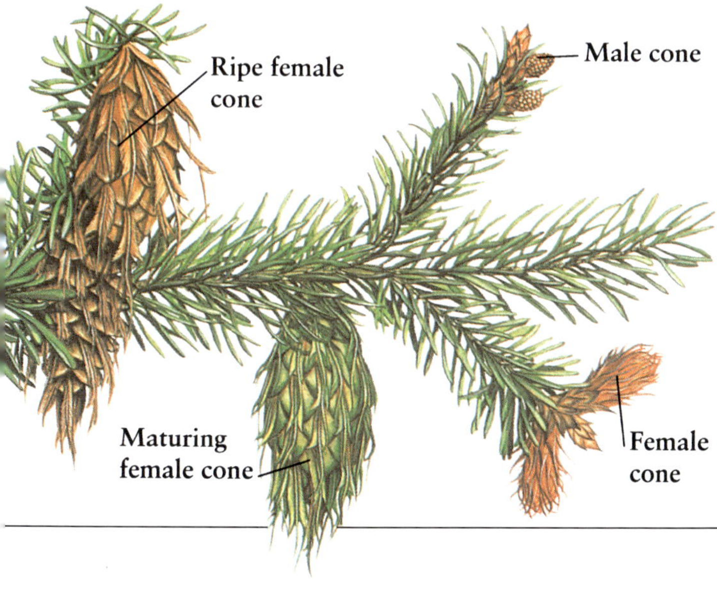

The colour, shape and scent of flowers like this orchid (above) are designed to attract insects, which are vital to the reproduction of many flowering plants.

Flowering plants are the late developers of the plant kingdom. They appeared on Earth about 150 million years ago, but now form about 80 per cent of all plant species. Wild flowers, vegetables, cacti, orchids and broadleaved trees are all flowering plants. Their seeds are protected by a fleshy coating called a fruit.

FLOWERING

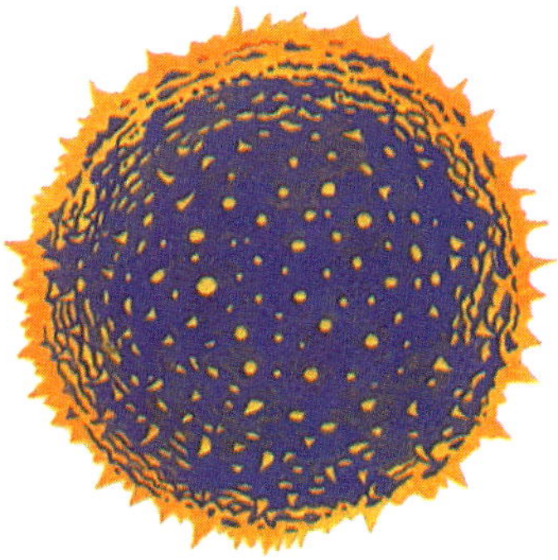

Pollen is a living substance made by the male parts of the flower. This is the pollen grain of a hollyhock, magnified 1,000 times (above).

The pollen of some plants is spread by the wind. The fine pollen of the hazel is released from hanging catkin flowers (below).

THE FLOWER

A plant's flower contains all the parts needed for reproduction. Most flowers contain both male and female parts, but some are either male or female. The male parts, the stamens, produce pollen. The female parts, the carpels, contain ovules which become the seeds. Most flowering plants reproduce sexually – male and female cells combine to create a new plant. Pollen grains from the stamens must be transferred to the stigma, on top of the ovules, for fertilisation to take place. This process is called pollination.

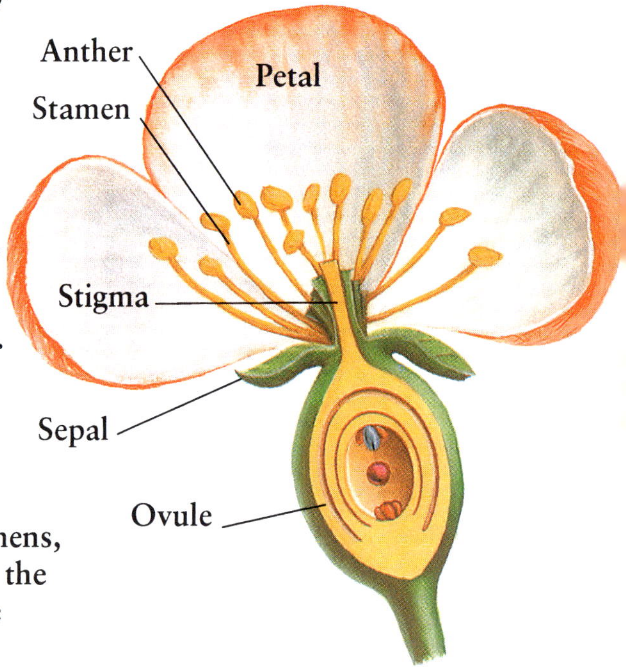

The plant's male parts, the stamens, consist of tiny stalks topped by the anthers. Pollen forms inside the anthers. The sepals protect the flower while it is a bud.

On Closer Inspection – *Orchids*

Many plants are pollinated by a range of different insects. Some orchids rely on only one insect species for pollination. The flowers of the fly orchid (right) look just like flies. They attract male flies that pollinate the plant.

PLANTS

Pollination

The pollen of some plants is carried by wind or water. But most plants are pollinated by insects such as bees and butterflies. The insects are attracted to the sugary nectar produced by the flower. While the insect feeds, pollen grains rub off onto its hairy body. It carries the pollen to the next flower it feeds from.

Most of the plants that are pollinated by animals are pollinated by insects. But some are pollinated by other animals, including birds (above) and even bats.

Grass

Grasses are a very successful family of flowering plants. They cover large areas of land in temperate and tropical regions around the world. Grasses, like timothy (right), produce clusters of tiny flowers called florets. The pollen grains are very light and are carried by the wind.

Palms
There are more than 2,700 species of palm (above). Their stalk-like trunks grow upwards but not outwards – they cannot make wood to widen the trunk, as broadleaved trees do. The trunks of palm trees have no bark. Instead, the trunk is protected by an outer layer of tough fibres. Palm trees grow in warm countries, and provide a range of foods, including dates and coconuts.

Some flowering plants are large trees, with woody stems called trunks. Like conifers, flowering trees grow for many years, and reproduce by making seeds. Unlike conifers, their seeds grow inside fruits, not cones. Flowering trees are also known as broadleaved trees because their leaves are wide and flat. Palms are a separate family of large trees.

BROADLEAVES

DECIDUOUS TREES

In temperate regions around the world, broadleaved trees shed their leaves in autumn. They do so to survive the cold, and to prevent too much water loss. Trees that lose their leaves are known as deciduous trees. The appearance of deciduous trees changes dramatically with the seasons. In winter they are bare of leaves. Only the tree's buds show that it is alive. In spring and summer the buds burst open and new leaves and flowers appear. In autumn, the leaves change colour and drop from the tree, in preparation for another winter.

On Closer Inspection – *Coconut palms*

The seeds of palm trees are protected by a dry fruit with a tough outer case, called a nut. Many coconut palms grow by the sea. When the nuts are ripe, they may drop into the sea. They drift along until they wash ashore on a different beach, to root and grow.

AND PALMS

Tropical rainforests

In tropical regions close to the equator, it is hot and wet all year round. Broadleaved trees there do not need to shed their leaves in autumn. Instead, they stay green throughout the year. Biologists divide up the plant life in a rainforest into vertical tiers called storeys. The crowns of the forest trees form a dense, leafy layer called the canopy. A few tall trees called emergents rise above it. Below the canopy is a layer called the understorey, and below that, the forest floor.

Tree trunks

The trunk is the strong, woody stem that supports a large plant. It is covered by a tough outer layer called the bark. In flowering trees and conifers, the trunk grows a little wider each year, as new cells are added to a layer called the cambium, near the bark. This growth produces the rings you can see in a trunk when a tree is felled.

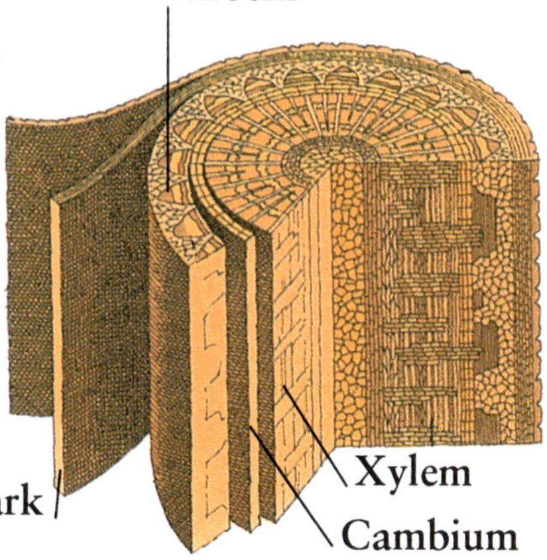

Inside a tree trunk, only the outer xylem near the cambium carries water. The inner xylem, or heartwood, is dead and only acts as support for the tree.

Once a plant has been fertilised, its seeds develop. In flowering plants the seeds are protected by a fleshy ovary – the fruit. Young plants need to grow as far as possible from their parents, so that they do not compete for light and moisture. So the ripened seeds need to be dispersed (spread) as far away as possible.

SPREADING

Scattering seed
The flowers of some plants develop into seed pods which split open to release their seeds. They are known as dehiscent plants. The poppy develops a hard seed case, filled with small, light seeds (above). When the wind blows, the seeds are scattered from the top.

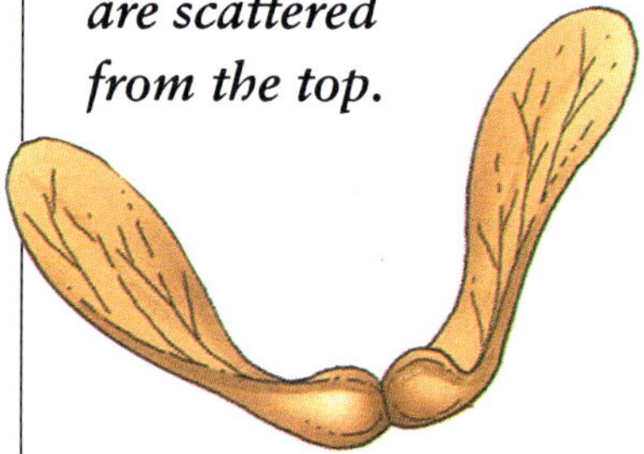

The sycamore seed (above) has a double wing which makes it spin through the air. It may be carried some distance before it lands.

Dandelions seeds (below) travel far on the wind and have crossed from Eurasia to North America.

Air and water

Some plants scatter their seeds themselves, by splitting open and spilling out their seeds. Others rely on wind, water or animals to do the job for them. The seeds of many plants that live in or near water will float. If the seeds of the lotus (above right) fall into the water, they drift along with the current to take root downstream. The seeds of many more plants are carried by the wind. Some have "wings" or hairs which help them to drift in the breeze. Dandelion and thistle seeds are light, with a tiny "parachute" of feathery hairs which help them float in the wind. Other seeds such as ash and sycamore seeds have a single or double wing to help them glide through the air.

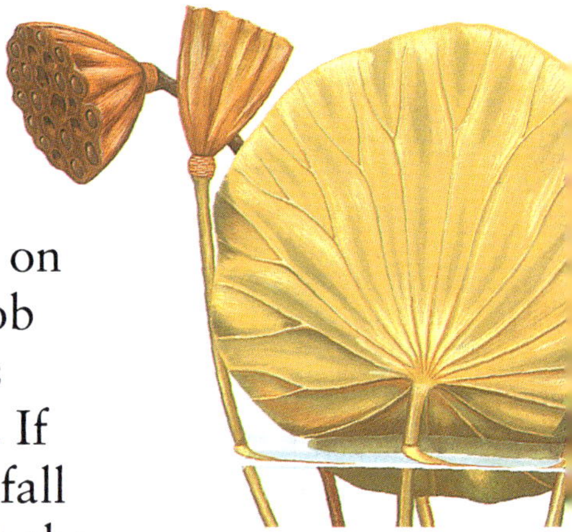

After fertilisation, the ovary at the base of the flower swells to form a fruit, like an apple (below). The fruit protects the seeds inside.

On Closer Inspection – *Germination*

A plant's seeds germinate, or sprout, in the soil if enough light and moisture are available, and if the temperature is not too hot or cold. The seed case splits open and first the root, and then the shoot of the new plant appear.

SEEDS

Birds spread seeds through their droppings after eating fruits.

Animal helpers

Many plants rely on animals to spread their seeds. The seeds may develop inside juicy fruits and berries which provide nutritious food for birds and mammals. When an animal eats the fruit, the seeds pass through its body unharmed, and fall to the ground with the droppings. Apple and cherry trees and blackberry bushes all spread their seeds in this way. Trees and shrubs such as oak and hazel produce hard-cased nuts and acorns, which are a favourite food of squirrels and other rodents. These animals often hoard their food for winter by burying it in the soil. Nuts that are not dug up and eaten may germinate and grow.

Burrs

After walking in long grass, you may find seeds called burrs sticking to your clothes. These seeds have tiny hooks designed to catch in animals' fur (left). They may be carried a long way before they drop off and fall to the ground.

DEFENCE

Cacti
In barren deserts, plants provide animals with a welcome snack. To avoid being eaten, cacti have developed sharp spines on their stems or fleshy leaves. Some kinds of cacti have short leaves growing from their stems, interspersed with long spines that keep browsing animals at bay.

Roses
Roses have sharp thorns on their stems which can give animals, including human gardeners, a painful prick (below). In some rose species the thorns point in different directions, so they snag and tear at flesh.

Being rooted in one place, plants cannot escape from danger, as animals can, by moving away. Instead, different plants have developed a range of defences against animals. Some plants have sharp spines or barbs that can give animals a nasty prick. Other plants are poisonous, or can deliver painful stings. A few plants turn the tables on animals, trapping and consuming them for food.

DEFENSIVE WEAPONS

Animals of all sizes feed on plants, from tiny insects to larger herbivores such as elephants. In their defence, various plants have developed an impressive armoury of weapons. The leaves of many plants are covered with fine hairs that repel small invaders such as insects. To deter larger creatures, plants such as nettles (right) are armed with stings on their leaves or stems. The nettle sting breaks the animal's skin and injects chemicals which cause a painful irritation. Other kinds of plants have unpleasant-tasting leaves, stems or flowers. An animal that has tasted the plant once is likely to remember the experience and avoid the plant in future.

On Closer Inspection – *Poisonous plants*

Ragwort is a common weed throughout Europe. It is very poisonous when eaten. But the caterpillars of cinnabar moths (right) can feed on ragwort without being harmed. The caterpillars become poisonous too and are avoided by birds and other caterpillar-eaters.

AND ATTACK

Insect traps

A few plants that grow in poor soil snare and eat insects to get extra minerals. Venus fly traps have paired lobes edged with sharp spines on their leaves (above). When an insect lands on the leaf, the hinged lobes snap shut to hold it fast. The plant then slowly dissolves and digests the insect's body.

Pitcher plants

Pitcher plants have modified leaves shaped like pitchers (below). Each jug has a tiny lid to keep rain out. Insects are attracted to the nectar found on the rim of the leaf. But when they land, they slip down inside the pitcher and drown in the liquid at the bottom. The plant gradually digests the insect and absorbs the minerals from its body.

Fruit and veg

Familiar fruits and vegetables are actually different parts of flowering plants. Strawberries, grapes and tomatoes are all fruits. Onions are bulbs, used to store sugary food. Potatoes are swollen stems called tubers. Carrots and turnips are roots, cabbage is the leaves, broccoli the flowers. Peas are sweet seeds.

Perfumes

Perfumes and scented oils are made from crushed flowers such as roses and lavender.

Besides providing us with oxygen to breathe, plants are also useful in a hundred other ways. They provide us with many different kind of foods and medicines. Plant fibres are used to make our clothing, and we depend on plants for other essentials such as paper, cork and rubber. Wood from trees is used for building and also provides us with fuel.

PLANTS AND

Cereals and other crops

Grains are a highly nutritious food source. Grains such as rice, wheat, oats and barley are used to make flour for bread and pasta. Maize (corn) provides us with flour and cooking oil. Wheat, maize and rice are all different types of grasses. They have been cultivated for thousands of years, and sown selectively to produce bigger plants than their wild cousins. The seeds of many food-producing plants have been introduced into other countries and now grow far from their original homes.

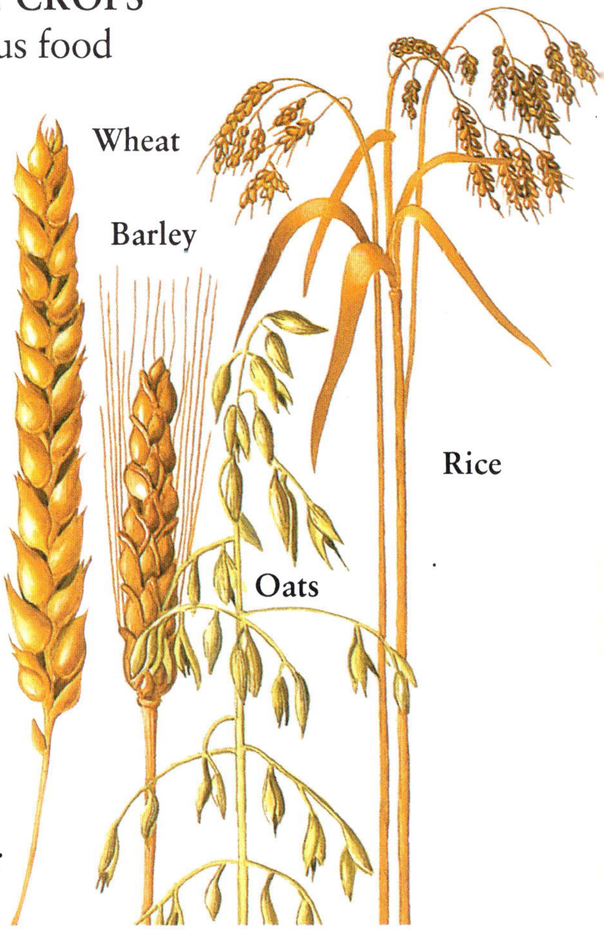

On Closer Inspection – *Medicines from plants*

Hundreds of different plants are used to make medicines. One of the most familiar drugs, aspirin, was originally made from willow bark. The leaves of the rosy periwinkle from Madagascar (right) is used to treat leukaemia, a kind of cancer.

HUMANS

Rainforest products

The vast rainforests of the tropics help to maintain a healthy level of oxygen in the air all around the world. But humans also have many other uses for the forest. Trees are cut down for their precious timber, or burned for fuel. Forest land is cleared for crops or ranches, or to make way for roads or towns. Rainforest plants and animals are endangered by all these developments. Experts fear that many plant and animal species will disappear before they have even been discovered.

Seeds and beans

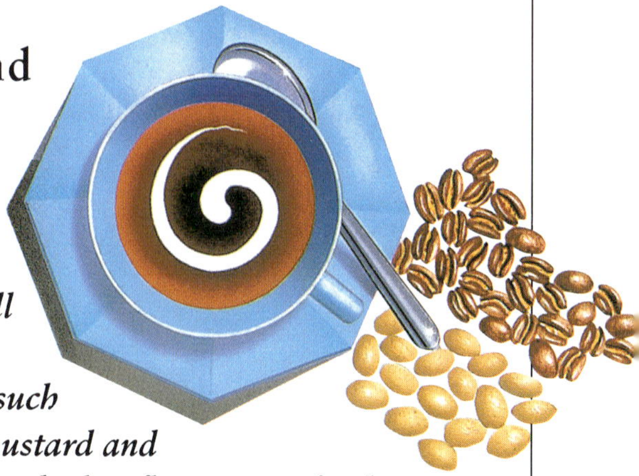

Plant seeds provide us with many foods as well as cereals. Spice seeds such as cumin, mustard and fennel are crushed to flavour our food. Coffee beans – the dried seeds of the coffee plant – are crushed to make coffee (above), and beans from the pods of the cacao tree are used to make chocolate.

Cotton

The white woolly fibres which surround the seeds of cotton plants are spun to make cotton thread for clothing. Linen is another plant fibre, made from the stems of flax plants.

PLANT RECORDS

SKYSCRAPING TREES
The tallest living tree is a Californian redwood growing in the western United States. When last measured, the tree stood over 112 metres high, but it is still growing. In Australia, eucalyptus trees also grow very tall.

A RARE BLOOM
One of the rarest flowers in Britain is a kind of Lady's slipper orchid . It is found at only one site in England. When the flower is about to bloom, it is guarded day and night. Lady's slipper orchids are also becoming rare in other countries

The tallest specimens of saguaro (left) are found in Arizona, USA. The tallest saguaro ever measured was 24 m tall.

A SLOW BLOOMER
The slowest-flowering plant is *Puya raimondii*, a rare giant bromeliad from the Andes Mountains in Peru. The plant blooms after about 100 years and then dies.

THE LONGEST LIVED
The oldest living tree is a redwood in California, USA, called "Eternal God". The 72-m high tree is estimated to be 12,000 years old.

Giant redwood trees (below) and their cousins the giant sequoias are among the tallest, widest and heaviest trees.

POWERFUL ODOUR
One of the world's smelliest trees is the ylang-ylang tree of Southeast Asia, which produces very strongly scented flowers. The flowers are used to make hair oil.

TOWERING CACTI
The tallest cactus is the saguaro cactus, found in the deserts of Mexico and western USA. The saguaro can reach over 17 metres tall, but grows only about 10 cm each year.

THE LARGEST SEED
The largest seed is the coconut of the coco de mer palm tree. The nut can weigh up to 20 kg.

THE SMALLEST FLOWER
Pond duckweed of Australia produces the world's smallest flowers and fruits.

THE LARGEST FLOWER
The world's largest flower is rafflesia (below), a parasitic plant found in the jungles of Southeast Asia. The flower measures up to 90 cm across and produces a smell like rotting meat, which attracts flies, which pollinate it.

GLOSSARY

Botanist Scientist who studies plants.

Cambium Layer of growing cells inside a plant stem or tree trunk.

Carpel Female part of a flower, which includes the ovary, where the seed develops.

Chlorophyll Green pigment (colouring) in a plant's leaves or stem which traps sunlight and converts it into sugary food through photosynthesis.

Deciduous Trees that shed their leaves in autumn.

Dehiscent plant A plant whose seeds develop inside a pod that splits open to release them.

Diatoms Microscopic algae which live in fresh or salt water.

Epiphyte A plant that grows not in the ground but high in the air, rooted on a tree trunk or the stem of a large plant.

Evergreen A tree that keeps enough of its leaves to remain green throughout the year.

Fibrous roots Network of fine roots that spread out underground near the surface to gather water.

Floret Tiny flower within a cluster of flowers.

Germination Growth of a plant from a seed or spore.

Herbivore An animal that feeds on plants.

Holdfast Root-like structure that anchors seaweed to the seabed.

Hyphae Long, thin strands of cells that make up many fungi.

Photosynthesis The process by which plants make their own sugary food, using the energy in sunlight.

Phloem Cell clusters in the roots, leaves and stems of plants that form tubes to carry food around the plant.

Pollination The transfer of pollen from the male part of a flower to the female part, so that fertilisation can take place and seeds can develop.

Sporangium Hollow capsule in which spores are made.

Spore A specialised cell that can develop without fertilisation into a new plant.

Stamen The male part of a flower, which produces pollen.

Stomata Tiny holes or pores on the underside of plant leaves, which allow water to evaporate, and let gases in and out.

Succulents Plants, often of dry places, that store water in their fleshy stems, leaves or roots.

Tap root Thick main root which grows downwards to reach moisture deep underground.

Transpiration Process by which plants shed excess water through tiny holes in their leaves.

Xylem Tissue in a plant's roots, stems and leaves which transports water and minerals from the soil up to the leaves.

INDEX

aerial roots 9
algae 6, 10, 11, 14, 25, 31
animals 4, 7, 13, 14, 15, 19, 22, 23, 26, 29, 31
anthers 18

bark 20, 21, 29
bats 19
birds 19, 23, 27
botanists 6, 16, 21, 31
bracken 13
breathing 4, 9, 28
bristlecone pines 16
buds 18, 20
burrs 23

cacti 18, 24, 26, 30
cambium 9, 21, 31
carbon dioxide 7, 9
carpels 18, 31
catkins 18
cells 6, 7, 8, 11, 12, 13, 14, 21, 31
chlorophyll 7, 10, 11, 14, 31
climates 16, 24
coconuts 20, 21
cones 16, 17, 20
conifers 6, 7, 16, 17, 20, 21
cycads 16

deciduous 20, 31
dehiscent plant 22, 31
deserts 24, 30
diatoms 6, 11, 31

epiphytes 6, 31
evergreens 16, 31

fermentation 15
ferns 6, 12, 13
fertilisation 18, 22, 31
fibrous roots 8, 31
florets 19, 31
flowers 6, 8, 9, 12, 18, 19, 20, 22, 24, 25, 26, 28, 30, 31
foods 4, 7, 8, 10, 11, 14, 17, 19, 21, 26, 28, 29, 31
forests 6, 13, 29
fossils 13
fronds 10, 11, 16
fruits 15, 16, 18, 20, 21, 22, 23, 28, 30
fuels 28, 29
fungi 14–15, 31

germination 22, 23, 24, 31
gills 14, 15
ginkgos 17
grasses 19, 23, 25, 28
growing tip 9
growth 4, 8

herbivore 31
holdfast 10, 31
hornworts 12
horsetails 13
hyphae 14, 15, 31

insects 18, 19, 26, 27, 30

kelp 11

leaves 7, 8, 9, 10, 16, 17, 20, 21, 24, 25, 26, 27, 28, 29, 31
lichens 15, 25
light 6, 8, 13, 14, 22
liverworts 6, 12

mangroves 9
medicines 29
midrib 9
mildews 14
minerals 7, 8, 10, 15, 27, 31
mosses 6, 12, 13, 25
moths 27
moulds 14, 15

nectar 19, 27
nuts 21, 23

oarweed 10
oils 7, 28, 30
orchids 18, 19, 30
ovaries 22, 31
ovules 18
oxygen 4, 7, 9, 28, 29

palms 20, 21
petals 18
photosynthesis 7, 8, 9, 14, 15, 31
phloem 8, 9, 21, 31
pigments 11, 31
poisons 14, 17, 26, 27
pollen 17, 18, 19, 31
pollination 17, 18, 19, 30, 31
prothallus 13

rainforests 6, 21, 29
redwoods 7, 30
reproduction 9, 11, 12, 15, 17, 18
roots 8, 9, 10, 12, 13, 21, 23, 24, 25, 26, 28

salts 7, 9, 25, 31
seawater 9, 10, 11
seaweeds 10, 11, 31
seeds 11, 12, 16, 17, 18, 20, 21, 22, 23, 24, 28, 30
sepals 18
soil 7, 8, 9, 14, 22, 23, 25, 27, 31
spices 29
sphagnum moss 12
spirogyra 11
sporangia 13, 14, 31
spores 11, 12, 13, 14, 15, 16, 17, 31
stamens 18, 31
stems 8, 10, 12, 13, 20, 21, 24, 26, 29, 31
stigmas 18
stomata 9, 31
succulents 24, 31
sugars 7, 21, 31
sunlight 7, 8, 11, 31
swamps 9, 12

taiga 16
tap roots 8, 31
thallus 12
transpiration 9, 31
trees 6, 7, 8, 9, 15, 16, 17, 20, 21, 23, 25, 29, 30, 31
trunks 16, 20, 21, 31

vegetables 11, 18, 28
volvox 11

water 7, 8, 9, 10, 11, 17, 19, 20, 21, 22, 24, 31

xylem 8, 9, 21, 31

yeasts 14, 15

Photo Credits

Abbreviations: t-top, m-middle, b-bottom, r-right, l-left

Pages 1, 11t, 16 & 29b – Frank Spooner Pictures; 7, 11m & b, 15b, 17, 18, 19 both, 24, 25, 26 both, 27 all & 29br – Bruce Coleman Collection; 2-3, 5, 12, 15t & 30 – Roger Vlitos.

THE NATURAL GARDEN

THE NATURAL GARDEN

Ellis Stones: His Life and Work

ANNE LATREILLE

VIKING O'NEIL

Viking O'Neil
Penguin Books Australia Ltd
487 Maroondah Highway, PO Box 257
Ringwood, Victoria 3134, Australia
Penguin Books Ltd
Harmondsworth, Middlesex, England
Viking Penguin, A Division of Penguin Books USA Inc.
375 Hudson Street, New York, New York 10014, USA
Penguin Books Canada Limited
10 Alcorn Avenue, Toronto, Canada M4V 11
Penguin Books (N.Z.) Ltd
182–190 Wairau Road, Auckland 10, New Zealand

First published by Penguin Books Australia Ltd 1990

1 3 5 7 9 10 8 6 4 2

Produced by Viking O'Neil
56 Claremont Street, South Yarra, Victoria 3141, Australia
A Division of Penguin Books Australia Ltd

Designed by Leonie Stott
Typeset in Perpetua by Midland Typesetters, Maryborough
Printed and bound through Bookbuilders Limited, Hong Kong

National Library of Australia
Cataloguing-in-Publication data

Latreille, Anne.
The natural garden: Ellis Stones, his life and work.

Bibliography.
Includes index.
ISBN 0 670 90235 7.

1. Stones, Ellis, 1895–1975. 2. Landscape architects—Australia—Biography. I. Title.

712.092

Foreword

This book had its beginnings late in 1976, when I attended a talk by David Yencken, then chairman of the Australian Heritage Commission, on the topic of Edna Walling and Ellis Stones. It was the last in a series of lectures on landscape history organised by the National Trust of Australia (Victoria). All had been well attended, but for the Walling/Stones lecture there was standing room only in the ballroom at the Trust property 'Illawarra', in Toorak. The audience was not quite swinging from the rafters, but people were even packed onto the small elevated balcony at the rear of the room, which creaked so horrendously that those standing beneath it – myself included – wondered whether its nineteenth-century construction would see out the night.

David Yencken spoke with affection and insight about Ellis Stones, whom I knew by repute but had never met. What a marvellous topic for a book, I thought. And then: 'Well, it should be easy. He hasn't been dead long and his office records will be there. I'll see what his family thinks of the idea.'

His family liked it, but once committed I was to find to my dismay that material with which to document Ellis Stones's long life was sparse, to say the least. There were tea chests of drawings, in the main from the years 1968–75, and office diaries intermittently filled in for the years

1959, 1961, 1963, 1965, 1967–73 and 1975. There were account books for 1960–61, 1965–67, 1972–74; and from 1972–75 a card file of jobs and some letters. Since Ellis had started building walls and outcrops for Edna Walling around 1935, beginning to design gardens in his own right around 1938, this left plenty of territory to cover. Papers lodged after his death in the National Library, Canberra, comprised mainly conservation-oriented newspaper clippings from the 1950s on, and Ellis's notes for lectures and the like. His two books on garden design (published in 1971 and 1976) were useful in conveying his ideas and philosophy, but contained little 'hard' information for research. The same was true of his unpublished manuscript on the importance of landscape.

This is one reason why preparation of this book has taken so long. The other is that there were long periods when it was put aside, because the task seemed so immense, and because other concerns intruded. Often, I would think I'd never get started on it again, but always the conviction that here was a tale worth telling lured me back. I felt a real commitment to Ellis Stones's memory – his own tenacity was an inspiration – and to his late wife, Olive, whose clear memories of the years between 1914 and 1959 are the bricks and mortar of the book.

Other major sources have been Ellis's employees between 1938 and 1975, his clients and business associates, and people he met; all have been generous with their time and unstinting in their memories and critical appraisal. I have made copious use of Ellis's philosophy of landscape design as expressed in his own books, since these are out of print, and have re-used extracts in my text. For written references I refer readers to the bibliography.

Illustrations of gardens have come in the main from Ellis's own photographs and, for 1970–75, from the files of *Australian Home Beautiful*. Many people have kindly lent photographs. Ellis photographed his own work extensively, but this important collection appears to have been lost. Most of his photographs reproduced in the book were excavated from a suitcase full of tiny negatives, thought to date from the 1930s; those showing gardens or open space – perhaps one for every forty shots of home, family and holidays! – were taken out, printed and eventually (in most cases) identified. There were also two boxes of glass-plate negatives. The 1915 photographs of army life in Egypt, some still in the tissue wrappings of the Cairo studio that had processed them, had lain undisturbed for almost three-quarters of a century. The family did not know of their existence.

In all my years of research I came across only a handful of people who had anything really negative to say about Ellis Stones, or who remembered him with anything much less than fondness or admiration. Time and again, seeking information, I would telephone someone who initially could spare only a minute to talk. Perhaps half an hour later the reminiscences about Ellis's enthusiasm, his gentleness, his talent, his sense of humour, his modesty, would tail off and I would hang up the phone with a smile on my face, thinking: 'He must have been a wonderful man'. Perhaps halfway through my research I became sceptical, questioning that anyone could have been so 'good'. Then as I prepared to assemble the book I decided to bow to the weight of evidence and accept that

Ellis Stones had a positive and uplifting effect on almost everyone he met. 'One of nature's gentlemen' is a hackneyed phrase, but it was used time and again to sum him up. The epitaph on the cards sent out by his family after his death – 'We are all the richer for knowing him' – is particularly apt.

I have been interested for many years in conservation and the broad landscape, but my fascination with gardens is much more recent, and this book is partly responsible. Chasing the early gardens was absorbing and fun; sadly, I never saw the garden that was generally regarded as his finest, which is now destroyed. I did not seek out a great many of those designed in the last few years of his life because, although to the very end he was punctilious about personally presenting his designs to each client, and explaining them, the gardens he designed from around 1968 were installed by others. Because Ellis was such an instinctive and natural worker, it seemed to me that from an historical point of view his most important gardens were those he both designed and built.

Few major pieces of Ellis Stones's work exist today, almost none is as he left it. This serves to emphasise how ephemeral a craft is garden-making. But much of his rockwork remains. Even when obscured by overgrown shrubs and creepers, or left virtually naked through lack of care and attention to the surrounding planting, it retains a spirit all its own. Even if it comprises only a corner of a garden it has a positive and reinforcing effect on the whole. He was a master of rockwork, and his understanding of the forms, shapes and flavour of nature was without peer. He was not particularly religious but when people would compliment him on a garden or an effect he had achieved he would simply say: 'Take a walk down any bush track and you'll see that God does it a whole lot easier and a whole lot better'. His acknowledgement of this fundamental truth – that nature is the greatest teacher – coloured everything he did in the fields of landscape, garden design and conservation.

Anne Latreille
Melbourne, March 1990

For my mother, Molly Dalrymple

Contents

Foreword v
Colour Plates x
Introduction xi
ONE Beginnings 1
TWO A huge, hazardous experiment 6
THREE 'Wounded leg Bill gone' 16
FOUR 'You're a natural' 22
FIVE 'It is a rare thing this gift for placing stones . . .' 29
SIX Walling: teacher, employer, colleague 52
SEVEN Building a career 64
EIGHT Towards an 'Australian' garden 78
NINE Of paving and planting 90
TEN Conservation begins at home 105
ELEVEN Living with landscape 120
TWELVE Birth of a profession 131
THIRTEEN 'Gardens are for people' 139
FOURTEEN A master in small spaces 153
FIFTEEN Success in town and country 168
SIXTEEN Of street trees, pools and pollution 182
SEVENTEEN Of publishing and playgrounds 190
EIGHTEEN Elliston – the importance of landscaping 213
NINETEEN 'I can't slow up – they won't let me' 227
TWENTY Achievement, acceptance, fame 238
Bibliography 250
Acknowledgements 253
Index 255

Colour Plates

Former George garden, Balwyn 38, 39
Ledger garden, Benalla 39
Ellis Stones's first signboard 39
Schubert nursery, Noble Park 42
Seaside steps 42, 46
Thornthwaite garden, Ocean Grove 43
Walters garden, Narre Warren 46, 47
Stone garden, Ivanhoe 50, 51
'Glenara', Bulla 51
Dickie garden, Hawthorn 150
Country garden, Berwick 150
Riverside garden, Templestowe 150, 151
Hawthorne garden, Hawthorn 154, 155, 158, 209
Jepp garden, Warrandyte 158
Baitz garden, Canterbury 162,163
Osborne garden, Warrandyte 159
Royal Botanic Gardens, Melbourne 197
Rockwork, University of Melbourne 197
Driveway for town houses, Malvern 200
Winter Park 200, 201, 204
Rosanna Parklands 201
Elliston 201
McLennan garden, Narre Warren 205
Swimming pool, Toorak 208
McCubbin garden, Sunbury 208
Downing/Le Gallienne garden, Eltham 209
Morgan garden 208, 209
Yarra River, Ivanhoe 212
Salt Creek, Rosanna 212

Introduction

Ellis Stones is remembered for his gentle, unassuming nature, his warmth and enthusiasm, his tenacity, and most of all his talent in his chosen field of landscape design.

He was a simple man with a simple approach. Halfway through his long life he found that he had a gift for creating beauty, and he spent the rest of that life sharing it with others. His touch in his finest gardens was so simple that there was a kind of inevitability about them . . . they looked as if they had just 'happened'. He used natural materials – stone, timber and where possible, native plants – to try to remind people of nature; in gardens, parks, or any space used by the public, he eliminated visual boundaries by softening hard edges, making paths curve out of sight, extending horizons and 'borrowing' nearby trees. At the same time he did his best to take into account his clients' likes and needs. Gardens, he said, were for people.

He created a restrained, subtle style of landscaping that today is often badly imitated or taken for granted. He thought it out for himself and could apply its principles unhesitatingly to any situation. He was not interested so much in flowers as in shape and form, and a plant's overall contribution to the landscape. Few of his important gardens have survived, but his books perpetuate his ideas.

Uncomplaining, he overcame ill-health and continual pain from a wartime injury. Many people he met did not notice his dreadful limp because they were so taken by his clear blue eyes, his smiling face, his happy disposition. A typical First World War soldier, he was philosophical, taking each day as it came. Money meant nothing to him. Screwed-up notes rained from his pockets, he gave financial help to anyone who asked for it. His volume of work grew, but he and his family always lived modestly.

Ellis loved his work, and over a forty-year period he was an inspiration to the people he employed. Some have gone on to considerable achievement in their profession, others have found the level they prefer; all are happy with it. They recall their work experience with him as a special time in their lives, in terms of learning and of personal development. He inspired his clients as well, teaching them a way of looking at gardens and the landscape that, once learned, is not easily forgotten.

During his lifetime the overall impact of his landscape design philosophy was diminished. In company he did not have the self-confidence to push himself, to present his ideas in the most favourable light. He was neither a 'systems person', a committee man nor a self-publicist, although towards the end of his life he did realise that publicity could be useful in putting across ideas. He had his denigrators – he still has. But claims have been put forward on his behalf that one could not imagine Ellis making himself. He never said he was 'the creator of the bush garden'; he would have been bemused to hear himself described as a great Australian landscape architect. However he did label himself – proudly and correctly – as one of our early conservationists.

He was Australia's first *popular* landscape architect. He gave the profession a public profile. His association in the mid-1960s with a leading project housing firm brought his name to a wide audience; his talent and personality did the rest. He really wanted to help people improve their environment and in so doing, to make cities and towns appear more natural. He maintained that he must always be available to anyone who wanted his services, at a cost they could afford. No job was too small.

Landscape architecture in Australia does not have many heroes. Perhaps it is a contradiction in terms to call such a modest man a 'hero'. But in Ellis Stones, the profession has a personality whose contribution will take some equalling.

ONE

Beginnings

*E*llis Stones, whose artistic ability with stone in the landscape was without peer – odd that his name should be so appropriate, Edna Walling once commented – came from an average background. His father, Thomas Stones, worked for H. M. Customs as an excise officer. His mother, Hannah, earned a living as a dressmaker before her marriage but as her four children arrived she settled down to life as a housewife.

Ellis was born on 1 October 1895 in Wodonga, Victoria, where his father manned the bridge that spanned the Murray River and separated the states of Victoria and New South Wales. He was Thomas and Hannah's second child and only son. He inherited his unusual name from his paternal grandfather, a plasterer. So different was it for the era that throughout his life he was known to family, friends and acquaintances not as Ellis, but by a variety of nicknames, among them 'Teena', 'Sam', 'Andy', and the best-known, 'Rocky'.

In 1892 his parents had been the first couple married in the new St James's Church, Moonee Ponds, so when they moved back to Melbourne in 1897 it was not surprising that they gravitated to the adjoining northern suburb of Essendon. Thomas Stones worked at the Port of Melbourne on the customs launch, checking ships for illicit cargo. His family stayed in the Essendon–Moonee Ponds area for the next twenty-three years. They made several moves during this time, but not for the purpose of acquiring bigger and better dwelling-places – they lived always in average suburban houses. Around 1904 Ellis started at the Moonee Ponds West State School where his elder sister, Selena, was already a student. The large red-brick school was handy to several racecourses. Flemington was nearby, Moonee Valley not far away, as were the Maribyrnong track and the Ascot pony track, part of the old John Wren empire. Ellis soon developed a special interest in a neighbour's racehorse. It was called Teena, and for a time he preferred helping exercise and groom it to playing with his mates. This earned him the nickname of 'Teena', which stuck so fast that even seventy years later some of his oldest acquaintances had no idea of his Christian name.

At Moonee Ponds West State School. Ellis is third from left, front row.

As a schoolboy Ellis was neatly turned out by his mother. One friend remembered him as tidier than the average small boy, an impression borne out by his neat collar and suit in an early school photograph. (This tidiness of appearance was to characterise him all his life.) But he was certainly one of the gang, involved in the usual fights around the back after school, most of them centred on misuse of his 'fancy' name.

Ellis never forgot his carefree early days, when unhampered play was every child's right. There was open space wherever a boy looked, to play cricket or kick a football, paddocks for mushrooming, river valleys for rabbitting. This rich experience coloured his reactions throughout his life and gave him great empathy with children who, in their turn, instinctively gravitated to him. He believed passionately that children should be able to run free, that they should enjoy enough space so that they could express themselves and dictate their own amusement. In later life, as open space in Melbourne was annexed for development and its creek valleys buried under concrete, he despaired for the children. In 1961, pausing while building a garden at Fairfield by the Yarra River, suddenly he hugged the clients' toddlers – who had been his devoted satellites throughout the project – to him while exclaiming ruefully: 'What's going to be left for *you*?' Children's playgrounds were among his favourite commissions. Always he would make sure that clients thought about creating playing space for their children – a corner for a swing, an open spot for cricket or football – as an integral part of their garden. 'It must be dreadful to forget that you were young once', he was heard to comment to a woman criticising noisy teenagers in the park.

Towards the end of his life Ellis Stones recalled his own boyhood in an unpublished manuscript, *Priority Landscaping*:

> *On looking back, I think I lived the life of the average boy . . . at that period. I was not brilliant at school, but very fond of football, cricket, in fact most sports, including boxing. Our pleasures then were simple and the height of our ambition was to own a bicycle.*
>
> *Apart from sport, excursions to the country, which was not far away, were one of my greatest pleasures. Whenever we had enough money my mates and I would travel a few miles into the country on a Saturday afternoon, rabbit shooting. A favourite spot . . . was a place called Donnybrook, which was only a short distance from my home and easily reached by train . . .*
>
> *We kids were friendly with the guard on this train, who was a great sport, and often used to give us hints on boxing. Sometimes on these trips Mick, the guard, would whisper in the engine driver's ear, and just as the train was opposite our favourite hunting spot, the driver would stop the train and get down with his oil can and do something to the engine. We would all tumble out with our dogs and guns thus saving ourselves about two miles' walk. We were very fond of Mick. We would sell the rabbits we shot to get our fares for the next trip.*

Another rabbitting haunt was the hills behind Euroa, where Ellis stayed with his cousins, the O'Neills, a family of builders. Often in country towns at that time the local builder, being the coffin maker, was also the undertaker. More than once Ellis and the O'Neill boys were caught in driving rain while out shooting and had to be rescued and driven home in the hearse, lying flat on the floor to avoid an unduly frivolous image. The beauty of the natural rock outcrops in the ranges near Euroa is legendary, and it proved a major influence on the landscapes Ellis designed in later life.

For most fourteen-year-olds, leaving school was a question of economics. Ellis left in 1910, and his father found him a job in a warehouse as a junior clerk. After a week he was told to wear long trousers to work. He didn't want to, so left. His father would not have been pleased. He was a stern man and he applied to his family the discipline born of many years in the civilian military forces. His wife, a quiet sweet woman, kept the peace. Ellis was charged with maintaining the home garden with its clipped lawns, annual borders and regularly shaped flower beds. It was a job he detested. (The garden exemplified the dictum of *Cole's Australasian Gardener*, the popular text of the day, that a garden should differ in all material qualities from anything existing in a natural condition.)

He then became an apprentice in the Newport railway yards, building wooden train carriages, while doing a part-time course in building at the Working Men's College. He didn't like the railway work much but he had always been good with his hands, and the techniques learnt there were useful later on, when he was earning a living as a builder and enjoying fine cabinet-making as a hobby. Luckily he was used to discipline because the tuition was exacting. One instructor had a habit of bringing his hammer down hard across the fingers of any apprentice who made a mistake.

The Stones family was close-knit and moral standards were high. It was no good Ellis telling his parents he was in trouble for misdemeanours at work. 'What did you do wrong, then?' was the usual reply. Family life was home-oriented and the front door of the two-storey terrace house in St James's Street, Moonee Ponds, where the family now lived, stood open to a stream of friends. Ellis's closest friend, Bill Elliott, boarded with the Stones after the death of his mother, as did his young brother, Harry. Another good mate, Ken Walker, dropped in constantly and the three – Ellis, Bill and Ken – became known around Essendon as the 'three musketeers'. Ellis found time to paint in watercolours, a hobby for which he showed great talent. He and his friends constantly used his gymnasium equipment in the back yard. And he was a promising footballer.

Even his military training included football. He played as a rover in the football club of the 58th Battalion – Essendon and North East, stretching from Essendon to Euroa. Ellis was always in the thick of things, in matches and at weekly training, and his father issued an ultimatum. If there were any more injuries, he said, football would have to stop.

The very next Saturday Ellis's jaw was fractured. Club officials took him to hospital where the jaw was set and bandaged, but before arriving home Ellis removed the bandages, threatened the Elliott boys with extinction if they breathed a word about his injury, made a short appearance at dinner, then went to bed pleading a tough match and tiredness. The next morning came a knock at the front door. Outside stood a captain from his battalion. 'Good morning, Mrs Stones. I've come to see how Teena is.' 'Still in bed – he's all right', said a surprised Hannah Stones. 'All right? We had him at the hospital yesterday with a broken jaw . . .!' This ability to conceal pain behind a matter-of-fact facade was typical of Ellis.

War broke out on 4 August 1914 and he enlisted at Broadmeadows on 3 September, just short of his nineteenth birthday. His mother hadn't

*E*llis and his good friend Bill Elliott enlisted in September 1914.

wanted him to volunteer but capitulated when she saw his misery as, one by one, his friends took the trip to Broadmeadows. He was given the regimental number of 437, Seventh Battalion, Australian Imperial Forces, being assigned to D Company and lodged in No. 4 tent with his friends. Bill Elliott wrote to Mrs Stones from Broadmeadows military camp on 3 September:

> *He was very lucky to get in here because today we were informed that D Company have a full complement of men, so Teena must have been the 120th man . . . If anyone comes up here on Sunday will you please send a toothbrush and paste for Teena . . .*

At enlistment he stood five feet five inches tall and weighed nine stone ten pounds. His occupation was described as carriage builder, his complexion as 'fresh', and a friend remembers him as 'a very strong type of boy, well-built'. A studio portrait taken with Bill Elliott shows, indeed, a fresh-faced boy. The uniform is spanking new, the hair is neatly parted in the centre, and the thumb casually hooked into the thick webbing belt does not mask the air of suppressed excitement and enthusiasm that characterised Ellis Stones throughout his life.

TWO

A huge, hazardous experiment

'Pretty good this turnout for the Essendon lads, isn't it? They are all looking forward to it', Bill Elliott wrote to Mrs Stones from the Broadmeadows camp in September 1914.

The camp was on an elevated, windswept plain. Tents stood near rows of pine trees and an old homestead. The weather was not kind and after rain the mud adhered to everything – some soldiers even complained after they had arrived in Egypt about the Broadmeadows mudstains on their clothes. The troops were put through intensive training, physical and squad drill, rifle exercises and lectures. Rations did not equal the

Sunday afternoon cakes at Broadmeadows. Pastrycook Olive Doyle is third from left, seated next to Ellis.

Ellis, October 1914.

quality or quantity of home cooking, so the 'three musketeers' were pleased to receive Sunday visits from Thomas and Hannah Stones with their daughters and Bill's good friend, Olive Doyle. Olive was a superlative pastrycook and her cakes brought queues of hungry hopefuls to No. 4 tent. Ellis had settled into military routine although his absent-mindedness – typified by the forgotten toothbrush and toothpaste – was already legendary. The last man dressed in the mornings, if missing a sock or any other component of his uniform, immediately knew who would be wearing it, because 'Teena' never had a full kit. His mates laughed, and looked after him.

None of the troops knew the destination but everyone was eager to be gone. The experience was new and exhilarating after the relative monotony of suburban life, where, in Essendon, church socials were red-letter nights, and street lights extinguished by 10 p.m. (these weren't even lit when the moon was full). Pushbike travel had been the norm for most of the Essendon 'lads', but now it was rumoured that they were off to England. On 18 October the 1100 men of the Seventh Battalion caught the train to Port Melbourne and filed onto the troopship *Hororata*.

Arriving eleven days later in the natural harbour of King George Sound near Albany in Western Australia, with thirty-seven troop ships from Australia and New Zealand they marked time for two days while the fledgling Australian navy cleared the waters nearby of German warships. There was plenty of time to write letters, and cheery postcards found their way to the Stones's house, like this one from Ken Walker: 'We are having a very good time aboard. We have all been innoculated and are suffering the effects. Ellis is getting on 'tip-top' and he is as happy as Larry.'

En route to Europe, war historian C. E. W. Bean wrote, it was decided to land in Egypt rather than pushing on to England, to take advantage of a climate the men were used to, and 'to save at least three weeks of sea voyage and give at least two hours more of daylight every day for training'. Ellis, Bill and Ken found themselves with the Seventh Battalion at Mena, a site on the fringe of the Sahara Desert just below the ridge on which stand the Sphinx and the pyramids – they were about 300 metres

'Ellis is getting on tip-top, and he is as happy as Larry.'

from Cheops pyramid. A neatly marshalled tent city arose. Early privations – excessive drill to the point of exhaustion, inadequate food and time off – gave way to a more settled routine, and letters home told of excursions and high jinks in Cairo as well as good fun in camp. One read:

> *Teena is well and as lively as usual. He has just stopped making a nuisance of himself. Will you just mention the fact to Mrs Stones and the girls that we miss the provisions which we used to receive of a Sunday. Nothing like that ever happens over here, worse luck!*

Each day the men marched about five miles into the desert. The Seventh Battalion drilled under its colonel, the much-loved Boer War veteran, H. E. 'Pompey' Elliott. A battalion history records how each man stepped into the footmark of his predecessor, and over all was a cloud of dust. 'The men were hard driven and became lean and hard.'

Bill Elliott wrote to Mrs Stones:

> *Please don't for one moment think that I am going to forget you so easily . . . But of late there hasn't been much time for letter writing. Pompey has been working us like the very deuce every night and only giving us enough time for sleep of a day then out for more work. He must have something up his sleeve because no other batt. is worked like us. We are recognised now as the best batt. so ought to get plenty of the spicy work.*

Photography was a favourite recreation – 'there are six cameras in our tent', wrote Ken Walker – and a large collection of Ellis's negatives has survived to illustrate the high and low moments of the months in camp, recording with rare sensitivity the minutiae of camp life, its inmates, its serried ranks of tents, its cooks, even the soldiers on latrine duty, mess queues and the boxing stadium.

Bill Elliott's lament is explained in a fine shot of two uniformed diggers stretched out on the sand (scanning the *Essendon Gazette*!) while behind them are stacks of guns and exhausted soldiers flat on their backs, with endless sand dunes in the distance.

Photography was a favourite recreation.

Desert drill.

Some photographs catch the very spirit of the moment. A human pyramid of nine sturdy men strains to stay in shape in a well-loved team game known as 'bok-bok', then collapses, participants and onlookers in gales of laughter. Another man is tossed aloft in a blanket. A group of half-dressed soldiers clowns for the camera, waving shirts and sleeping bags.

The battalion off duty: tossing the blanket near the boxing stadium; and at early morning call.

Others are more thoughtful. Two good-looking young men nurse their pipes as they sit beside their tent, surrounded by their kit. Another is lost in a letter from home (Ellis's inscription on the back of the original reads 'Griffiths when he received his last letter'). A lone soldier stands in the desert, dwarfed by the immensity of the pyramid behind him. What became of these boys? For Griffiths at least, we can guess.

A quiet pipe for two diggers.

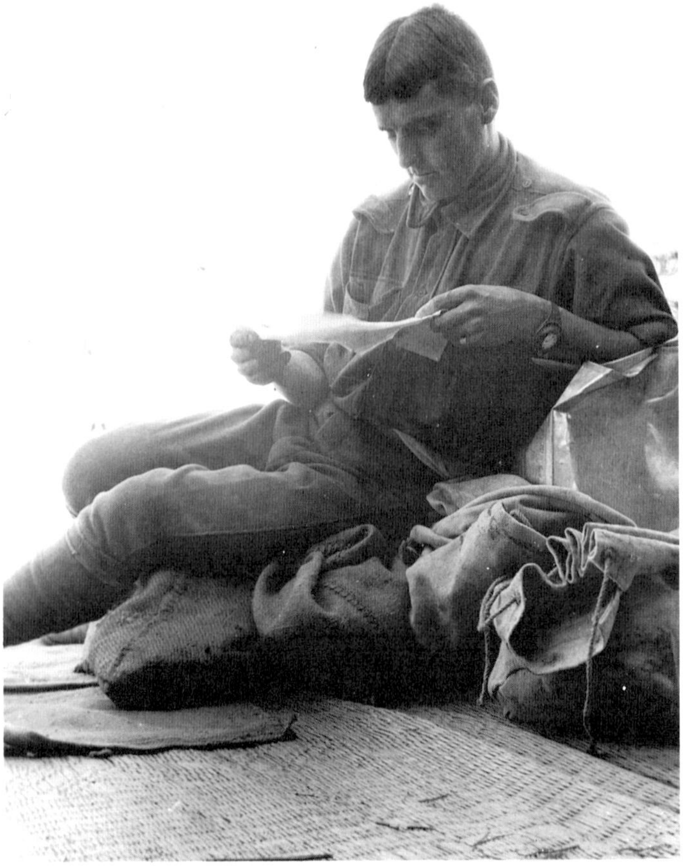

Letters from home: 'Griffiths when he received his last letter'.

Ellis, behind the camera, massed people, and 'hard' elements like tents or lifeboats, to unwittingly build up an atmosphere of grim foreboding even as he recorded the daily routines of camp life. There is a monumental quality to the photographs, which show the instinctive sureness of touch of his landscape work with rocks and stones, the first of which was not carried out until some twenty years later. Perspective is used to telling effect. Groups are perfectly positioned, each element is made to play its part. He is to be seen in some of the group shots but one can imagine him arranging his friends, positioning the camera, checking through the viewfinder and then, having asked a passer-by to make the exposure, rushing to his appointed spot. Even his standard 'tourist' shots of Cairo streets and natives ploughing in the fields handle space and perspective to create an evocative quality that puts them far above the average.

Soldiers in camp . . . and at sea.

This hobby must have been a diversion for him (and others) in camp, but as the weeks wore on rumours about departure dates flew back and forth, and the soldiers grew more eager. They sailed for the Dardanelles on 10 April for what war historian Bean called the 'huge, hazardous experiment' of Gallipoli. 75,000 Allied troops were to be landed; in the afternoon of 24 April the transports began to steam out of the bay. That evening, Brigadier-General W. Ramsay McNicoll recalled in the *Argus* one year later, there was excitement 'of a subdued and serious kind'. Each man, he said, checked his rifle and ammunition, his rations, water bottle and pack, went to bed and 'wonderful to tell, slept'. Some wrote farewell notes home, including Ken Walker to Mr Stones. Datelined Lemnos Island, 24.4.15 and written on both sides of a monogrammed envelope from the officers' mess of the Sixth Battalion, this read:

Teena asked me to send this note for him, as he has gone to bed and had no paper or envelopes to do so himself. We are to land on the Galiopoli [sic] *Peninsula at daybreak in the morning. We are now fifty miles from there we will have a big task before us but will come through alright. Teena and myself are as fit as possible and mean to do our best to get back to tell you all about our thrilling experiences . . . Ken.*

The Seventh Battalion, with its drilled-to-the-minute soldiers, was very unlucky. Its men were among the first to reach the shore and so suffered cruelly from the strong currents and from a mistake in directions that took the first 'tows' of rowing boats a mile further north than had been planned, landing them not on a gentle, sandy beach but at the foot of steep cliffs from which the Turkish snipers fired at will. 'Nearly all my tent mates have gone under', wrote Ken Walker, who got three miles inland before he 'stopped a bullet in the head'.

Perhaps the Stones family kept only the letters they received from their 'boys' who did not live through Gallipoli. However, one letter home has survived, which Ellis wrote from hospital on 16 May 1915 to a group of friends. In simple, dispassionate prose and firm, clear handwriting it relates an experience that must have been quite horrific for this ebullient, easy-going boy who had become used to having his friends look after him.

Dear Cobbers

I don't know what you will think of me for not writing to you before. But you know, I stopped it fairly solid, and it used to knock me up when I would write, but I am now on solid food and I feel much stronger so I can write all round. Well lads, I will try and give you an account of the scrap as I saw it.

We left the island of Lemnos, where the transports and warships mobilised, sometime after 8 p.m., when lights were put out and we lay down on the deck to have a couple of hours sleep . . . We were up at 2.30 a.m. and had our breakfast of biscuits and Bully Beef and a cup of tea. Then we fell in about four and just before daylight we dropped anchor and our platoon was the first to leave so we got into the boat. I might mention that while we were at Lemnos they asked for a volunteer crew to row the boat and Bill and I both passed the test, so we were on the rowing stakes . . . Well we were getting close to the shore when a destroyer told us we were too far to our left so we turned to the right just as we did the beggars on the beach opened fire with machine guns and rifles, and the bullets were flying all round us like rain, and hitting the boat, someone said 'They are a poor lot of shots' and I think he must have been the Joner [sic] *for just then the first two of our chaps went down, they were both rowers, as the rest of the chaps were told to get in the bottom of the boat one after another the rowers went down to it until there were only three of us left a chap named Hopkins, Bill and myself, then I stopped one, I tried to keep rowing but it was no good, so I fell into the bottom of the boat and someone took my place.*

When we ran aground those that were whole jumped out and charged the beggars . . . Bill got ashore safely and was shot shortly afterwards.

I will never forget the time that followed in that boat she was half full of water and here we were all mixed up, I had a chap who was nearly dead lying across my leg and couldn't get out as it was impossible to get him to move, or else I could have got to some of the worst and put something round to stop the bleeding.

We stayed like that for what they reckoned about an hour and a half, then a few of the AMC came along and sorted us out a bit and put us on the beach where we stayed a few hours, when Major Jackson who was wounded in three places came along and saw us there. He went and got stretcher bearers to take us along to the point where the troops were landing there we stayed until evening with only shrapnel bursting to pass the time away. This came from an armoured train a couple of miles inland . . . A chap who was on a stretcher next to me got hit with a piece while we were lying there.

Late in the afternoon they put us on pontoons and towed us over to the hospital ship which was full, then they took us over to another and that was full. Then the officer in charge of the launch took us over to his ship . . . and asked the skipper what he was to do with us, and he told him a certain transport (Siang Choon) *which had the 14th Batt. on board, and he said if we couldn't get on there to bring us back and they would take us on the warship. We moved off with a cheer from the boys, which we answered very weasy* [sic]. *We got to the* Siang Choon *and were put in slings and taken aboard. There I met the boy Jones I forget his name (not Ray the other) he gave me a good cup of cocoa and a couple of biscuits. We were given two blankets one to lie on and one to put over us. I had bottles filled with hot water put all over me and I soon got a bit warm, until then I was very cold as I only had half a pair of pants and a singlet on, my puttees and socks were taken off and I had my tunic for a pad for my leg. The 14th went ashore next day and we started for Alexandria and now here we are in Cairo again . . . Ken Walker is well and training again . . . Well lads I am fairly tired so I will close, love to all.*

I remain Your old cobber Tina.

A later letter from Ken reads in part: 'Poor Teena will be too bad to be able to go to the front again, he was shot through the leg but is as cheerful as possible. He is the whitest little fellow I know and have ever met.'

Ellis, ever insouciant, had gone into battle with his camera around his neck. The bullet that hit him rebounded from his oar, scything huge splinters into his left leg up to the groin and tearing through his knee to blast away the upper part of one bone and take most of the flesh, sinew, nerves and muscle behind the kneecap. As he was dragged ashore his rescuer grabbed his camera and shoved it in behind the remnants of his knee, doubling up his leg to hold it there as a hastily improvised tourniquet. A quick twist of the camera strap and the worst of the bleeding was staunched. His family recalled that he was more than a little peeved that the film inside was so blood-soaked it couldn't be developed.

On arrival the men were taken to Cairo's First General Hospital, in the Khedive's Palace at Heliopolis, a splendid residence not long vacated by the Turkish Sultan's representative in Egypt. When Ellis found himself semi-conscious on an operating table at Heliopolis he sensed the surgeon shaking his head and muttering that the leg would have to come off. A nursing sister looked on aghast. 'Can't you save it?' she pleaded. 'He's so young!' At that moment Bert Sutherland came into the theatre. A doctor from Ascot Vale near Essendon, he knew the Stones family. 'Isn't that Teena Stones?' he asked. He put in a word for the leg, and it stayed on. Ellis's superb physical condition also helped, the doctors said.

Probably this was a blessing. To be sure, the leg sorely troubled Ellis for the rest of his long life. It forced him in and out of hospital. On the job it caused unceasing inconvenience, and constant pain that at times was all but unbearable. He saw it as a handicap, particularly in the early years, but as he grew older and further operations helped for a time with the pain, he did not find it insupportable (although his family could always tell by the drawn expression on his face at the dinner table when he had had a particularly bad day). But he acknowledged that had he come home, still a teenager, on a peg-leg, his world would have contracted and he might well have lived as a cripple for the rest of his life. His whole attitude would have been affected because he would not have been able to keep up with other people, nor do the active work he thrived on. He would not have set up as a builder nor been able to spend time and crucial formative years working in the Australian countryside, which he had loved since those boyhood rabbitting trips, and absorbing its forms and atmosphere. Nor would his path have crossed that of Edna Walling, the inspirational landscape designer who, in the mid-1930s, encouraged him to give up building and to devote the rest of his life to landscape.

THREE

'Wounded leg Bill gone'

The Stones family received two telegraphs, and one can imagine that the messenger-boy caused a stir as he cycled past the rows of sedate Victorian and Edwardian houses in Nicholson Street. The first came from Heliopolis on a now indecipherable date, and read: 'Wounded leg Bill gone Ellis'. The Ministry of Defence message, dated 14 May, was marked urgent and said: 'Regret reported Private E. A. Stones wounded will advise you receipt further particulars Secretary Defence'.

Ken Walker, back at Gallipoli, died in action on 12 July, leaving Ellis the surviving 'musketeer'.

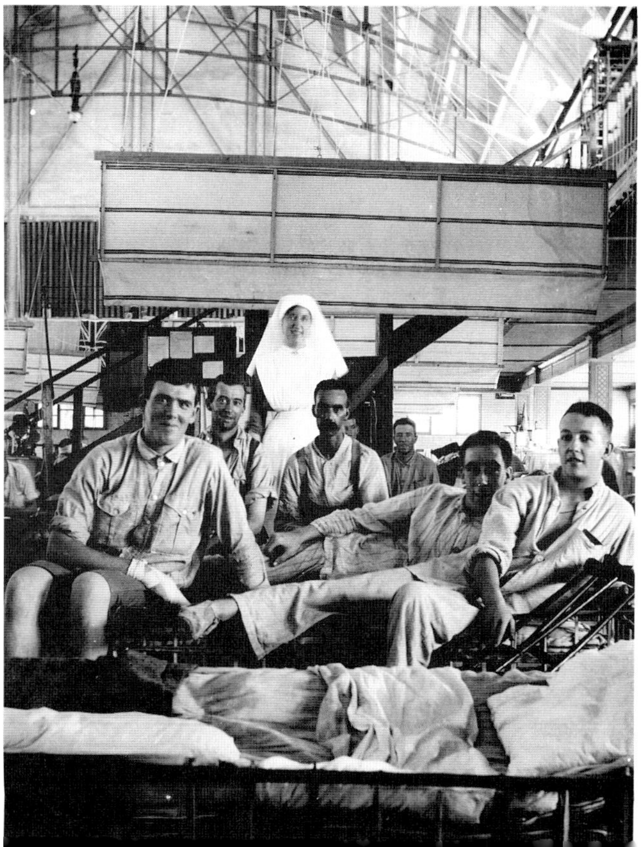

A hospital ward (Ellis, front right).

His wound became infected and he spent almost three months in hospital in Egypt. His photographs show a resurgence of his old spirit, with groups of grinning, pyjama-clad patients and smiling nurses, as well as views of the intricate facade and superbly decorated palace 'wards'. Some soldiers with similar injuries were sent to England for further surgery and complex nerve sutures but Ellis, it was decided, would return home. Perhaps his wound did not seem as bad as some; perhaps, like many other injured boys, he was desperate to get back to familiar

*W*ounded soldiers on the long trip home.

places and people. He re-embarked on 28 July, again on the *Hororata*. The voyage was monotonous, with little conversation and none of the anticipation and horseplay of the trip out. The men – boys no longer – had plenty to think about. A powerful photograph taken by Ellis and inscribed by him 'wounded soldiers' shows a group leaning on the ship's rail. One man is forcing a smile, but generally the grim-faced soldiers, dressed in a motley mix of uniform and pyjamas, bare feet and boots, some leaning on crutches and sticks, appear as grey and cold as the tilted horizon of the chilly sea behind them.

The ship docked at Port Melbourne to be met by the press and by anxious relatives. Thomas Stones, still working at the wharf as a customs officer, was appalled at the sight of his thin, pale son, dressed in pyjamas and hobbling on crutches, with his bad leg bent up behind him from a kind of halter around his neck. He whisked him straight home. From there he went into the base hospital set up in the police barracks in St Kilda Road, Melbourne, and on to the Melbourne Hospital for the first of several operations. He spent his twentieth birthday in hospital.

Had Ellis recorded his impressions of those first months back, probably he would have described them as nightmarish. Not only was he in constant pain and having to suffer the indignity and discomfort of having one leg telescoped behind him while hopping, stork-like, on the other, he was also very lonely. In July 1915, the month he re-embarked for Australia, some 36,500 Australians enlisted for service abroad, in August the figure was almost 26,000. (These were the peak figures for this war, never again approached.) Essendon was a close-knit community. All his friends had gone, many were already dead. And his memories of his one day in action must have been frightful. He was by no means battle-hardened, a condition that allowed some soldiers to view the carnage with, if not equanimity, at least a degree of detachment. Patsy Adam-Smith's book *The Anzacs* records this comment from a First World War soldier who fought in France: 'You asked me how these sights affected me . . . well, I wouldn't have known at the time, we never talked to one another about it. Mark you, I reckon each of us had learnt from the first shock not to register (the sights) again.'

Ellis never talked to his wife or family about what he had seen or felt as he watched the fighting. But like many other Gallipoli veterans, until he died he suffered from dreadful nightmares after Anzac Day, or whenever he met any of his Seventh Battalion mates. Despite his leg, whenever work commitments allowed he marched on Anzac Day, being driven part of the route and joining in towards the end. When both his age and handicap conspired against him he would try to go to the Shrine of Remembrance and sit through the service.

Ill and bored, then, the teenager veered between his home and hospital, in a climate from which the first flush of patriotic fervour had worn off so that many people remained ignorant of the experiences of the men at the front, or were even contemptuous of them. At home he found little to do. His two older sisters were working and the youngest girl, Eva, was still at school. She remembered that his temper remained even and that he never complained about his wound. But his father's health was indifferent and his mother was devastated by her once athletic son's general condition, although she tried to hide it. The backyard gymnasium equipment was put away. A photograph of Ellis and a friend in uniform, standing lop-sided in the Stones's backyard, was wryly captioned by Ellis 'Australia's Last Hope'.

Ellis and Eva Stones in their parents' garden after Ellis was invalided home.

For a while Ellis, pictured with his sister 'Gus', was forced to use a walking stick.

He underwent three major operations in the space of twelve months. He suffered from acute pain, a lack of sensation in part of the injured leg and his foot, and – once he was off crutches – a pronounced limp, which he never lost. At one stage he had weights suspended from the dropped foot on the wasted left leg so that he would be able to straighten it enough to walk. For the rest of his life he was unable to put his heel to the ground and had to take his weight on the toes of his left foot. Some doctors gave relatively optimistic reports, others were gloomy about his prospects. Twice he was discharged as medically unfit, in November 1915 and again twelve months later, having enlisted in the Home Service in the meantime. Medical opinion was that he would never again be fit to do strenuous work but that given easy conditions, he might be able to support himself. Early in 1917 he did get a job, but it meant long periods of standing, and he could not manage it. He remained at home with his parents, paying them board and receiving almost a full pension. He bought a holiday house in Fourth Street, Black Rock, to which he, his sisters and their friends – including Olive Doyle – would travel at weekends by horse tram. His photographs show smiling faces as well as a remarkable degree of imagination – a sensitively posed group between the twining skeletons of the coastal tea-tree that masks the beachfront in that part of Melbourne, a row of grinning heads and feet projecting from a sunny, calm sea. This must have been a welcome change of scene.

To the immediate problem of his leg was added that of headaches and recurring nervous attacks. In contrast to his young sister, Olive Doyle remembered that he was terribly tense after his return home – perhaps he put on a brave face for his family. Olive had kept in touch with the Stones family after the death at Gallipoli of their boarder and her great

Summer in the sea at Black Rock (Ellis, second from left).

*E*llis photographed a group of friends amid the tea-tree in the garden at Black Rock (Olive Doyle, second from right).

friend, Bill Elliott (whom she had planned to marry after the war), so it was logical that once Ellis was fit enough she would go with him on outings to the pictures or the hills, or simply to spend the day. People then felt some responsibility for returned soldiers, and she was sorry for him as he was so obviously lonely.

There was the added involvement of a friendship between one of his sisters and her own sister, Ann. Her father, James Doyle, was a prominent grazier, owning several large properties in New South Wales and Victoria. Of these, 'Woodsome Leas' at Tocumwal was Olive's favourite, a lovely spot with a rambling pioneer homestead (James Doyle had bought it from the original owner) and a freehold frontage to the Murray River with its fringe of venerable river red gums. The family went there for holidays and on one occasion Ann Doyle asked her father if her friend's soldier brother might come as well, since he was on crutches, had nothing to do and loved the country. So Ellis and his father joined the party. Encased in plaster to the hip, Ellis went for daily spins with Olive in a buggy and pair. On the first such trip the horses bolted. The diminutive Olive wasn't scared since she was used to such situations, although it did cross her mind that the harness might break as she fought to bring the horses under control. Ellis, despite his love of horses, was scared stiff. It was during this holiday that Olive got to know him better and to see 'what a fine chap he was'. The relationship between the two slowly deepened.

As the war ground on, Ellis's leg became comparatively less difficult and in April 1917 he re-enlisted in the Home Service, doing clerical work. Two years later he moved to the service's passport guard, then to the intelligence section of the Department of Defence, when his responsibilities included surveillance of interned prisoners and 'spies' under deportment orders.

He was worried about the future. He hated working at a desk job – most of all he enjoyed nature and the outdoor life – but what else was he to do? Some doctors suggested he should take a full pension, but this he would not consider. Since he volunteered for active service, he maintained, Australia didn't owe him a living. And he said he would have gone out of his mind if he had not been allowed to work, as would have been the case had he settled for the TPI (totally and permanently incapacitated) label. Never mind that one doctor had told him he would be a cripple for life, and that another had pronounced him unfit for any strenuous work. Building was his training, and he decided on that. Working for his cousin Fred O'Neill, he contracted to erect houses at first in Melbourne, where he also began work on a house for himself in Essendon, and then in the country.

He and Olive became engaged in 1920, just before Christmas. No date was set for the wedding. He was still in and out of hospital, with regular checks needed on the leg, which was numb in parts and extraordinarily painful in cold weather (on very cold days he sometimes collapsed with the pain). An engagement photograph shows two cheerful, unclouded faces. Not surprisingly, Ellis has lines that weren't there in 1914, but he still appears absurdly young. Despite going prematurely grey, he never looked his age, and always it was assumed that Olive was the older of the two.

Olive and Ellis at their engagement, c.1920.

FOUR

'You're a natural'

Ellis and Olive – who called each other 'Sam' and 'Sue' in a parody of two popular wartime songs – were married on 15 March 1922, at St John's Church, Essendon. They lived at Olive's parents' house in Moonee Ponds while Ellis was building their own house, in between commitments in city and country. A child was due around Easter 1923 and Ellis, who was working on two farmhouses at Beulah in the Mallee, came home briefly for the birth. Like most first babies, this one was late. 'Can't you hurry it up?' he fumed. 'I've got men waiting up there and if I don't get back they'll go off.'

A son duly arrived and was named William James ('Billy'). Both parents were thrilled. But when the baby was about four months old, Olive was sitting one afternoon feeding him when Ellis, who had been watching, went to the kitchen for a glass of water and collapsed. He did not regain consciousness for a worryingly long time.

After his marriage, Ellis continued work as a carpenter.

He had a complete breakdown. The combination of his war experience, his painful leg, and the effort of forcing himself to carry out work that was a great physical strain, had taken its toll. He had to stop work. 'With a leg like that', said the family doctor, 'he just can't manage what he does'. A specialist recommended a stay in the country. Ellis was to have a complete rest, he said, and he must no longer climb ladders. Olive fretted because he no longer took the initiative in anything, a stance quite foreign to his nature. She was told not to worry. He would recover, as long as no-one pushed him into anything.

Ellis didn't object to the idea of living in the country. But while his wife planned a move to an uncle's house in the Goulburn Valley, he suddenly spoke up, and at this stage it was so unusual for him to offer an opinion that everyone listened. He wanted to go to Nevertire in western New South Wales, where Olive's sister and brother-in-law were living on her father's large property 'Oxley Park'.

The young family arrived there at a time of drought. Ellis drifted around like a ghost. He went out on the property with his brother-in-law Jack Williams – sometimes down to the Nine-Mile paddock, so called because you had to drive nine miles from the homestead to reach it. He wandered off by himself and would disappear only to be found asleep. As the year progressed the drought worsened, the heat intensified, and in December, two days before Christmas, the baby became very ill. Mother and baby were taken to the little hospital at Trangie, thirty miles away, where the doctor diagnosed heat exhaustion or meningitis. They were put in isolation, and left alone. As night fell a dry thunderstorm blew up and the lights went out. Billy whimpered, cried, suddenly screamed, then died in Olive's arms. Even more than fifty years later, her re-living of this experience darkened a sunny suburban living-room with anguish and incomprehension.

Burial took place hastily at the Trangie cemetery, because of uncertainty about the cause of death. Ellis did not come into town for the funeral; he never again talked of his son to anyone except his wife and family, and that rarely. Olive and her sister went to Sydney, where their parents were then based. The men stayed at 'Oxley Park'. Olive's weight dropped to six and a half stone, but despite her heartbreak she did not blame Ellis for his lack of reaction. Instead, she worried, because she knew he was so unwell that he simply hadn't comprehended what had happened.

She returned to Nevertire the following May. Her brother-in-law had gone to Melbourne and Ellis was left in charge. While he was not yet fully capable of organising the men working at 'Oxley Park', he had begun to take more of an interest in life, responding to the wonderful sunsets, the vast horizons and empty plains of that part of Australia, likening it to Dorothea Mackellar's 'sunburnt country'. He stopped his aimless fiddling around and began to use tools properly again. And he invented a sheep-drafting gate, the ingenious 'improved collapsible gate'. Made of T-section and L-section angle iron, it was secured on one side to a gate post, and used pivoting cross-rails and a loose ring and peg to retain the rails when the gate was in the collapsed position. It could be operated manually on the spot, or from a distance with a draw rope and pulley. Ellis developed his design over the next few years, and patented it. Goldsborough Mort acted as agent and, Olive recalled, 'sold all that were made'. (The patent eventually was taken over by the manufacturers of a different drafting gate.)

A year after Billy's death, Ellis and Olive returned to Melbourne and lived for a short time with the Doyles in Moonee Ponds. Although Ellis was taking more interest in life, his wife still had to egg him on. He found building work in Horsham, where they lived in a boarding house. Then they moved to 'Forest Holme' in the small town of Avenel north of Euroa. This fourteen-room house, owned by Olive's aunt, was their base for five years. It saw the birth of three daughters – Lesley, Patricia and Elizabeth – in 1926, 1928 and 1931, and the establishment of family life. Echoes of the Stones parents' Essendon houses recurred as 'Forest Holme' came alive. The local theatre group rehearsed there; Ellis was active on the progress association, the local committee to get electric light and other facilities in the town. He played tennis and football with friends. And he was busy working, sometimes on his own account, sometimes with carpenters from the nearby town of Seymour, building shops and houses, doing repair jobs or alterations. His brother-in-law, Jack Williams, came and worked with him for a time.

Ellis, c.1930, with Lesley, Patricia and Olive.

A beach outing, c.1930 – Olive, Ellis (wearing hat), their two eldest daughters and friends.

On a property just outside the town he built a house, 'Winterfold', for Mr and Mrs Dick Webster, to a design by architect H. Raleigh. He was head carpenter on a wage of twenty-two shillings a day. Construction began on 4 October 1929 and finished on 11 February the next year – a speedy job, more so when one considers that builders usually take time off over Christmas. Perhaps the onset of the Depression provided an incentive. More likely Ellis's enthusiasm fired his fellow workers.

At 'Winterfold', apart from the basic carpentry, Ellis laid rosewood flooring from the nearby Seven Creeks estate in the dining room and sitting room, and panelled the walls of these rooms with Pacific maple. Then the Websters said they would like a granite fireplace. 'I've never

'Winterfold', Avenel, built 1929–30 with Ellis as head carpenter.

Ellis Stones's first rockwork – a fireplace of local stone in the living room at 'Winterfold'.

handled stone before', said the man who was later to make his name through it, 'but I'll take it on'. He and Marjorie Webster went out into the paddocks and chose pieces of stone from the property, bringing them in on a spring cart. Everyone was delighted with the job. The design included two gently projecting flat slabs of stone, one each side of the hearth and about halfway up the fireplace surround, on which the clients could rest their feet as they sat by the fire in their leather armchairs – typical of the concern Ellis always showed for a person's comfort. The Websters remembered him as 'a lame little man, always cheerful, very reliable and an excellent hard worker'. He did a beautiful job with the fireplace, they said proudly. It was the first of its kind in the district.

But not for long. A year or two later Ellis was working at Chateau Tahbilk, the historic winery near Avenel, and while doing odd jobs he told the owner, Eric Purbrick, that he could build him a stone fireplace. This was done in the sitting-room of the old homestead, again using Avenel stone, with a mantelpiece of old, worm-eaten, grey box that Ellis cut from a tree on the property – an idea which he had wanted to try at 'Winterfold' until it became clear that a piece of dressed timber would better suit that living-room. Eric Purbrick was so pleased with his fireplace that five years later, when the noted architect Roy Grounds designed a new homestead for Chateau Tahbilk, he moved the fireplace stone by stone and re-erected it in the winery office.

Ellis was busy during the years at Avenel. His latent creativity meant that, work and leisure activities aside, he occupied himself with inventions. He lodged the papers to patent his sheep-gate, and, troubled by the country combination of hot summers, dusty roads and closed car windows, he developed a type of ceiling fan for cars, similar to the ventilators used on public transport. Olive was not only a tiny woman but an inveterate smoker. To the amazement of their friends in the small country town, he would install her, smoking furiously, in a large packing case on the verandah of their house, to check the way the air currents moved. He went to Melbourne for expert advice, but did not proceed with the idea. (Later he developed a blowfly guard for chimneys, operated with weighted wires from the hearth beneath – a great improvement on the contemporary practice of stuffing the chimney with newspaper once the weather turned warm.)

But by the end of 1931 his nervous condition came back in force. An injury on the job, when a pipe was dropped on him while working on a tankstand, left him unable to use his right arm properly for a time, which did not help matters. Work opportunities dried up as the Depression gained momentum; there was nothing for him to do in Avenel, where local people still remember how, at this time, lots of people 'of good education' would pass through and ask for food. Not being a businessman at heart, he lost track of details of jobs and money owing (a problem that was to plague him all his working life). Early in 1932 'Forest Holme' was put on the market, with the family moving back to Melbourne and renting a house in suburban Heidelberg. Ellis suffered from severe headaches and occasional blackouts, which medical opinion ascribed variously to financial worries or to his war experiences. For the bare necessities, he knocked on doors and patched flyscreens – threepence for a small hole, sixpence for a larger one, carefully weaving small pieces of flywire into the holes. He made superbly crafted little wooden boxes for sale, and travelled by bicycle to do any building work that came along, sometimes with Jack Williams, sometimes for Fred O'Neill, who now lived in Eaglemont. But although times were tough there was always humour. His worries were kept from his daughters, who remember endless jokes between him and 'Uncle Jack'. (During the 1950s and 1960s while building gardens, Ellis would have co-workers in stitches whenever he started on his fund of 'Depression stories'.)

Doctors continued to tell him that he was not fit enough for building work – but his response was: 'That's what I'm trained for. What else am I to do?' Appearances were kept up. Ellis's photographs show three beautifully dressed little girls in floral party dresses and pretty bonnets, sewn by their mother. (While the children were always immaculately turned out, Olive could not manage many changes in her own wardrobe. Her daughters vividly remembered the smart new clothes worn by friends who came to afternoon tea – and the old yellow and black dress in which, year after year, she dressed for old girls' day at the Presbyterian Ladies' College.)

As a result of his war injury, Ellis was meant to wear a heavily built-up surgical boot on his left foot. Although he drew a pension in the early years, once he began earning his own living he didn't inquire about any form of Government help – he volunteered, he said, so the country wasn't bound to support him – and for years he paid for his own special boots. During the 1930s he consulted an orthopaedic surgeon, seeking relief from the pain that troubled him so, and he went in ordinary boots. 'Why are you wearing those?' asked the surgeon. 'Because I can't afford the new ones', came the reply. He was, in fact, entitled to free boots, and the doctor immediately despatched him with an order. (He was also meant to wear a caliper from the hip, but always found it most uncomfortable.) Despite his disability he played weekend cricket with a Returned Services League team.

'Three beautifully dressed little girls . . .'

He was a devoted father. Even when the girls were older, he would clean their shoes for them before they went out; he often took them to school (Olive never being an early riser). Their friends would comment: 'He isn't grumpy like our fathers'. And despite his lack of education, he adored reading them stories at bedtime. His favourites were C. J. Dennis's *The Moods of Ginger Mick* and A. B. Paterson's epic poem 'The Man from Snowy River'. Asked for a story, he would visibly preen himself. He would read several pages with the girls hanging on his every word, then slowly, deliberately, close the book at the most exciting part, declaiming: 'Tomorrow night, girls!' When the family moved in 1937 to Locksley Road, Ivanhoe, only a stone's throw from the Yarra River, on summer weekends he and the children almost lived in the river. Their friends might be at the pictures but if the sun was shining you would know where to find the Stones kids. The Yarra then boasted clean, sandy beaches, and if you were quiet there was often a platypus to be seen. These fun-filled days with his children were the start of Ellis's love for the river that was to prove the major spur for his determined anti-pollution stance in the mid-1950s.

In 1934–35 his carpentry business began to pick up, and he found work at a house in Hawdon Street, Heidelberg, belonging to the Donaldson family. The large house was set on a double block, half of which originally was fenced off to serve as a cow paddock. During the late 1920s Mrs Gertrude Donaldson had become interested in acacias, planting many different species in part of her large garden (measuring some 50 metres by 150 metres) with the help of a local nurseryman who shared her interest. As her sons grew up, her husband decided a tennis court was required, and had this placed on the cow paddock with what Mrs Donaldson described as 'an ugly straight drive' excavated alongside, through the area where some of the acacias were planted.

Edna Walling, the 'name' landscape designer of the day, was called in to sort out the garden. A spreading oak tree stood next to the new drive and she designed a curved stone wall to enclose it. She loved designing walls – a stone wall was the feature that had first sparked her interest in garden design – but getting them built the way she wanted them to look was not always easy. One day on the Donaldson job she wondered aloud who she could find to build the 'oak tree wall'. 'I can do it', offered Ellis, who was working nearby. Somewhat sceptically, she asked him to do a small section.'You're a natural!' she exclaimed as the wall arose. 'Throw away those carpentry tools and come in with me. I'll find work for you.'

FIVE

'It is a rare thing this gift for placing stones...'

Ellis, aged forty, decided to do as suggested – at a stage when the convention was that men of his age should be firmly established in their career. He contracted for no more building jobs, although in his first years of working on gardens, if a client had small building work to be done at the same time as the garden, he was happy to oblige. He concentrated first on garden construction, then gradually on design and construction. Years later he wrote, with masterly understatement, that making his living at landscaping turned out to be difficult at first 'as I was not a gardener'.

His family and friends were stunned. 'I don't believe it,' said his mother. 'If there's one thing Ellis hates, it's gardening.' Olive tried to explain that her husband wanted to design and make gardens rather than work as a gardener (and that she didn't mind if he made no money as long as he was doing what he wanted) but, like most Australians of the day, Mrs Stones didn't see the difference. Ellis's cousin Fred O'Neill summed it up. 'Nobody's going to pay to have a garden designed – people do that themselves', he said. 'You'll starve.'

They didn't starve, although the first few months were difficult. This kind of work was seen as a 'sticky thing' and a woman's job – even Edna Walling was referred to as 'the woman gardener'. But there was plenty to be done at the Donaldsons in Heidelberg, where Gertrude Donaldson was an inveterate alterer of both house and garden. Ellis was there off and on for many years, creating a charming small pool near the tennis court, putting stepping-stones and occasional boulders in the front garden and small outcrops here and there, crazy-paving the rear patio, building stone walls round the tennis court and on the front boundary. His walls in this garden (now demolished, although part of the front wall remains) did not have the timeless quality of some of those he was to build in later years, but they were more than competent, streets ahead of similar

The 'oak tree wall' that Ellis built in the Donaldson garden, Heidelberg, after a chance meeting with Edna Walling.

Slate steps and occasional boulders added interest to the sloping lawns at the Donaldson house in Heidelberg. The stepping stones are flat, rounded rocks lowered into the grass.

A small pool and outcrop in the Donaldson garden at Heidelberg. Note the *Agonis flexuosa* (or willow peppermint, an Australian plant) that overhangs the pool, and the patch of Ellis's favourite *Erigeron karvinskianus* to one side.

walls illustrated in garden journals of the time in terms of sensitivity and handling of material. And the boulders he placed showed the sureness of touch of a 'natural'.

True to her word, Edna Walling gave Ellis work. Under her direction, in 1935 he built a stone fence and gateposts, topped with flat pieces of slate, in a garden she designed in Toorak, Melbourne, for the Beattie family. She and James Beattie were great friends, having collaborated earlier on the building of a thatched cottage-cum-clubhouse at a nine-hole golf course he laid out at Doncaster. They sat down together in 1943 over a copy of her first book, *Gardens in Australia*. 'Ellis Stones did very good work there', she commented as they looked at the book's photographs of the entrance to the Beattie garden. Mr Beattie's son recalled that being a carpenter, Ellis 'knew his lines and squares – his work was very precise'.

*E*llis built the front fence and gateposts at the Beattie house as part of an Edna Walling garden design. He used random stone, topped with roughly squared slate. The elegant wrought iron gate was designed by the client.

Ellis travelled to the Bickleigh Vale subdivision of 10 hectares (18 acres) that Walling had established in 1928 at Mooroolbark just outside Melbourne. Over several years he did rockwork in some of the gardens, including her own, and worked on several of the quaintly named cottages – possibly Walling's own cottage 'Sonning' after the first 'Sonning' had been destroyed by fire in the winter of 1935, and in 1938–39, two-storey extensions and a stone chimney at 'Winty'. This must have been a profound learning experience at the beginning of his career. Walling's decision to lay out her own subdivision, and to control rigidly the design of its English-style cottages and their gardens, had no precedent in Australia (except for elements of Walter Burley Griffin's earlier work at Heidelberg in Melbourne, and Castle Crag in Sydney). Ellis absorbed the way Walling used plants and manipulated space around the cottages, and he appreciated some of her innovative touches in their architecture, particularly the way she used fibrous plaster wrong-side-out to impart a textured finish to internal walls. She joked about this technique in her column in *Australian Home Beautiful*, writing of 'Sonning 2':

> *The wall with a wooden frame has been lined with fibrous plaster sheets, used back to front, joined up with plaster, of course, not those conventional strips that look so dreadful in an unconventional structure. The first time I used these plaster sheets with the finished surface inside, in one of the cottages on the Bickleigh Vale Village scheme, the manufacturer was horrified at the bare suggestion, and applied every argument to persuade me to change my mind, and his last card – but it was not the trump – was 'They'll catch the germs'. The thought of these acrobatic little fellows doing stunts on my walls so tickled me that the slight trepidation that I must confess I felt at the experiment, departed, and the plaster went up back to front. About six months later another cottage was built, and the same manufacturer was called in to do the lining. One of the first things he asked was, 'Would you like the random finish?' Somewhat mystified, I asked for a description, and was informed that this new rough finish was produced by using the sheets back to front. One does forget in six months!*

Sometimes the trips to Bickleigh Vale were made complete with family. It was a long trip for the Stones children, quite an adventure. Ellis's daughter Patricia found 'Sonning' different to any other house she had seen, retaining a vivid image of the blue and white checked curtains in the kitchen, setting off a lovely old dresser arrayed with blue and white crockery. Edna Walling she recalled as 'wearing jodhpurs and terribly abrupt – a strident sort of person'.

Abrupt she may have been, but she set Ellis on his feet. She was very particular about how rocks were used in gardens – as early as July 1935 she had advocated 'great restraint' in their placing – maintaining that a modified rock garden idea was a delightful note for a permanent picture in a small garden. 'Even one or two large weathered boulders with a rock plant tucked in beside and a tree close by will make a delightful little scene', she wrote. Her encouragement and patronage were crucial, but she quickly saw that she had a 'find' in Ellis. From the outset she, and people working with her, noticed his rare sensitivity, the fact that

'Winty', at Bickleigh Vale, Mooroolbark, photographed in the late 1930s.

A fine outcrop executed by Ellis in the mid-1930s. This photograph was found in his study; a handwritten note attached to it read 'My first rock garden, Darling 1935'. Gwynnyth Taylor (née Crouch), who worked for Edna Walling at this time, also identified it as the Darling garden, but members of the Darling family do not recognise it as part of 'Warrawee'.

he seemed incapable of placing a boulder or building a stone wall in any but the 'right' way. This was an instinctive talent; more than one onlooker likened his ability to the wonderful handwork done by simple, skilled workers in earlier times. Having watched him work at Bickleigh Vale and in smaller gardens, Edna Walling began to let him go ahead in his own way in a particular section of a garden, and she showed her confidence in him by asking him to build a rock outcrop in a 'wild' section of the Harold Darlings' magnificent seven-acre Toorak garden, 'Warrawee'.

The basis of this garden had been laid many years earlier by the noted architect Walter Butler, and in 1933 Walling had been commissioned to work on part of it. She wrote about it in *Australian Home Beautiful*, telling readers of the retaining wall, the stone-pillared pergola, the graceful flight of steps and wrought iron rails that she had imposed upon what was formerly 'an impossibly steep earth bank' on one side of a valley. She added a stone-paved pathway, a new flower bed planted with foxgloves, irises and yellow *Germanica* to flower with the wistaria on the pergola, and she envisaged plantings of cistuses and echiums beside the steps as a grouping with the native plants for which, she wrote, this part of 'Warrawee' was a sanctuary.

*T*he 'little woodland scene' presented by Edna Walling, working with Ellis Stones and Gwynnyth Crouch, for the Arts and Crafts Society at the Lower Melbourne Town Hall in December 1938.

Ellis's outcrop was near the boundary and was as far removed in flavour from Walling's formal pergola and steps as could be imagined. The date of construction is uncertain. Joan Law-Smith and Elizabeth Baillieu (both née Darling), who were small girls at the time, did not recall Walling doing any major work after the pergola and steps, but they remembered Ellis Stones working with rocks in the garden 'a while later', certainly before 1936. In his study after his death was found a black-and-white negative and photographic print inscribed in his hand 'My first outcrops, H. Darling 1935'. Walling had first published this photograph in *Australian Home Beautiful* in 1941 as part of a column on the subject of stonework. This began:

> *Now stones . . . what on earth shall I say about stones? Well first I will enclose a picture of a rock garden which was built by a man called Stones. You can say what you like about it, he won't hear you, but I think it is rather lovely and hope you will too . . .*

This is rare praise indeed from a professional who was not given to publicly recognising others' excellence in the field. The photograph later appeared in her book *Gardens in Australia* (1943) in a chapter on the natural rock garden, wherein she quoted the English expert Reginald Farrer: 'Rock garden building is one of the sublest of high arts, all the subtler for seeming so simple and natural in its results'.

She had applauded Ellis's work in print once before this, in her Home Beautiful column of December 1938. That year the Arts and Crafts Society of Victoria's exhibition in the Melbourne Town Hall had included a landscape section, and Edna Walling had been asked to create a garden for it. Her aim was to suggest a rock garden drifting into woodland, and she wrote of this 'little woodland scene':

> *Ellis Stones, who did the 'out crop', certainly excelled himself. The little mountain track which wandered up amongst the large boulders gave Gwynnyth Crouch and myself some exciting spots to plant, and whilst I busied myself with the trees and shrubs, Gwynnyth tucked in her beloved rock plants, and hey presto, the landscape was complete.*
>
> *It is a rare thing this gift for placing stones and strange that a man possessing it should bear the name Stones – it should be easy to memorise. Lovely as formal gardens can be, it is these informal schemes, in which boulders form so important a part, that appeal so tremendously for the reason, perhaps, that they give us the atmosphere of the country, and the refreshment of mind derived from such.*

Construction of this garden was not simple. The town hall authorities insisted that the pool should not leak; Ellis had a special galvanised tank made to hold the water. Moss, boulders and plants were wheeled in from Collins Street in rubber-tyred barrows, down the steps to the lower hall. In an uncharacteristic move Ellis – who never pre-planned outcrops – had mocked up this one at home, carefully numbering the stones and boulders before taking them to the town hall. He then found that it would not come together satisfactorily, so had to improvise on the spot. In an unpublished manuscript Edna Walling skilfully conveyed the atmosphere of conviviality and fun that accompanied the venture:

We really enjoyed the preparations, pools, rocks and all . . . To our joy we noticed that the ceiling of the basement was comparatively low and our birches were tall and slender so we asked Mr Stones to cut them to the length of the distance between ceiling and floor. 'Just a wee bit longer so that we can jam them up?' I said. Well it was a good idea until I noticed we had pushed a hole in the ceiling! However off went the offsider down town to buy sponge rubber to make shock absorbers for the tops of the trees; as far as the trees were concerned they looked just right. From then on the ground cover, the rocks and the shallow pool (painted black to give reflections) presented no problem, though we did find ourselves still making that little garden at midnight on the day before the opening. It was a very happy and excited trio who piled into the car that night . . .

Participation in this exhibition was an important step and a potential source of future work for Ellis. ('The contractor who was doing the constructional work of my designs was very keen to be in on such an enterprise', Walling had commented.) He attached his name to the rocks, and he or his wife came in daily to man the display. One day two passers-by stopped short. 'Ellis stones – now whereabouts do *they* come from?' mused one. 'I'm not sure', said the other, 'but I'm sure I've heard of them . . .' Another night, at home over dinner, Olive asked whether there had been any inquiries. 'Oh, a couple of old dears', he said. Olive pressed him. 'Well, who *were* the old dears?' A trifle reluctantly, he said: 'One was Lady Huntingfield, and she thinks Lady Gowrie might be interested when she comes back in March, for me to do something in Canberra'. (Lord Huntingfield was Governor of Victoria; Lord Gowrie was Governor-General of Australia, based at the time in Melbourne, and he and his wife were in England making preparations for a State visit by the Duke and Duchess of Kent.)

The 1938–39 summer was long and hot. At the end of it, Lady Huntingfield herself telephoned, saying she would like to bring Lady Gowrie to see the Stones's garden. Olive glanced outside at her parched plot, and was temporarily speechless. 'Is it a case of the shoemaker's children, then?' asked Lady Huntingfield. 'Exactly.' 'Well, please ask your husband to nominate some of his work which I could show Lady Gowrie.'

Since meeting Edna Walling, Ellis had not only done construction work in gardens of her design, but had picked up a job or two on his own account. For this vice-regal visit he nominated the large rock outcrop and beautiful ornamental pool he had built under Walling's direction in a garden at a new house 'Hillsborough' in Balwyn; work done in another Walling garden, for Essington Lewis; and a garden he had designed and built in Domain Road, South Yarra, for a Mrs Flack.

The visit began in South Yarra and then moved on to Malvern, where the group was delayed over afternoon tea, so did not get to the Balwyn garden (owned by Douglas George, of Georges department store). This

An early garden, which may be that designed by Ellis in the 1930s for Mrs Flack in South Yarra. Note the pebbles, rocks and the ground-hugging plants – and the way in which the whole picture is viewed from inside the house.

Ellis Stones's photographs, c.1938, of his work at the Douglas George garden in Balwyn, which was carried out to an Edna Walling design.

A tiny pool and waterfall built by Ellis in the long outcrop at the former George garden, Balwyn (above). The pool (below) that Ellis built to Walling's design at the far end of the garden remains a dominant feature. His outcrop adds its own atmosphere.

The 'sneak track' at the corner of the outcrop in the George garden, seen from below. Some of the original planting survives, notably the maple and the conifer.

The same track in the George garden seen from above.

Ellis built this pool and outcrop at Benalla around 1938.

A handpainted signboard for a newly established business.

was a pity, because the new house and garden would have been well worth the long drive to the highest part of Melbourne, then an area of paddocks and open country, dotted with a few large Victorian and Edwardian houses. Now known as 'Silver Birches', the two-storey house is set towards the front of a wide, deep, sloping block. House and garden were designed in conjunction, and built concurrently in 1938 (although the garden design itself was begun in 1936). It is believed that before she planned the garden, Edna Walling consulted with architects A. S. and R. A. Eggleston on positioning the house, which runs almost across the 100-metre-wide block, and is only one room deep for the most part so that each room has expansive views to front and back gardens.

The slate paving and low stone wall at the garden front, illustrated in *Art in Australia* in 1939, is the most conventional part of the garden. Ellis's undated photographs of his construction work, taken when the house was nearing completion, display something very different – a bold, extensive, curving outcrop bisecting the back garden and allowing a spectacular change in level. Slate stepping-stones form winding paths to either side of the outcrop, and meander through it at one point, eventually curving round behind the ornamental pool right at the bottom of the garden. This is free-form with boulders seeming to grow out of the ground at intervals around the edges. The newly planted garden is studded with trees, including cherries and silver birches, while several small conifers can be distinguished at one end of the outcrop.

Walling's garden plan outlined the pool and outcrop but indicated no detail of rock work. Perhaps she again let Ellis have his head? The outcrop includes some massive boulders most sensitively placed, and is an extraordinary achievement for someone who had begun this kind of work only a year or two previously. Most of it survives today, with parts of the original planting. Particularly notable is a small waterfall tumbling over a projecting flat rock and down the face of a large boulder into a tiny stone-edged pool. Further along the outcrop, a cunningly concealed path giving access to the higher part of the garden is so typical a piece of Stones's later work that it is tempting to assume it was his own contribution to the design. (Walling's plan shows a more regular flight of steps.) Always Ellis liked to provide what he called 'sneak tracks' in his gardens, no matter whether he was working in a city courtyard or on a country property. A previous owner of 'Silver Birches', who took it over in 1943 when it was overgrown and drought-affected, remembered her husband bursting inside just after they had moved in with a broad grin on his face, exclaiming: 'You'll never guess what I've just found – the most gorgeous little path!'

The huge ornamental pool is still there, too, although somewhat modified. Pieces of slate were set around its edge by this same owner, to accommodate his children and their friends who would spend hours hanging over the water trying to catch fish, tadpoles and frogs. A group of students from Burnley Horticultural College who visited during the late 1940s were loudly disapproving of this modification to a Walling design. But knowing Ellis's love for children and his sympathy for their absorbing pursuits, one feels he would not have been too displeased.

The Flack garden in South Yarra, where the vice-regal party had called first during that afternoon visit in 1939, set off a narrow house by the architect Marcus Martin. It included a stone wall, an outcrop of large rocks to mask the side entrance, and a small stream against the wall, edged with pebbles, mossy boulders and native plants. Double doors opened from the dining room onto this vista. Ellis was delighted with Lady Gowrie's enthusiastic reaction to it, and with her comment that his stonework reminded her of the instinctive, natural techniques of old English craftsmen. Later, she asked him to obtain bulbs for the garden at Yarralumla, the governor-general's residence in Canberra where Edna Walling designed part of the garden – Olive Stones phoned nurseries all around Melbourne to find enough daffodils, bluebells, hyacinths and the like.

In the spring of 1939 Ellis prepared a display for a Garden Week in the Treasury Gardens, at the south-east corner of the city. Again, his scheme included native plants, as well as a rock outcrop with alpine plants. Lady Gowrie, in Melbourne on an official visit, stopped to ask him how he was progressing with his ideas of rock outcrops, natural finishes and Australian plants. Quite well, he said, but slowly. She left the Lord Mayor and his party standing while she continued talking. 'Keep trying', Olive remembered her saying, 'you must get through because your way is the answer for Australian gardeners'. Gwynnyth Taylor (Crouch) recalled this display garden as 'quite an extensive scheme – very lovely and simple'.

Among Ellis's other work during the late 1930s was a small ornamental pool in Heidelberg for Mr Rupert Anderson, a local identity and well-known builder. The geometric, stone-edged pool is still a valued part of this suburban garden, whose ownership has changed only once since then. He was responsible, too, for a stone path and an oval pool at 'Moralla', a property near Skipton, as part of a Walling design, and for an outcrop in the Heidelberg garden of Mrs Blanche Marshall. A pharmacist, Mrs Marshall had lived at 'Sonning' in Bickleigh Vale village for a year in the mid-1920s, helping Edna Walling with her accounts. She married in 1929 and in the late 1930s Walling designed her Heidelberg garden, using Eric Hammond as contractor for the stonework and planting, and Ellis Stones for an outcrop. Mrs Marshall remembered Walling saying she didn't give Stones instructions, because of his natural affinity for rockwork . . . 'I just tell him what we want done, and that's it'. He manhandled in 'about ten enormous stones'. As well, she wanted a small 'garden room', which Walling designed and Ellis built. (It included sheet plaster hung wrong-side-out.) There was a disagreement over the size of the ventilator he put into the gable of the garden room, Mrs Marshall saying it was too large, and that it looked dreadful, while Ellis maintained that it had to be that size to draw out stale air near the ceiling. He installed smaller ventilators as directed, but Mrs Marshall soon realised he had been right. He was a practical man as well as an artistic one.

In 1938 Ellis helped position a statue in an ornamental pool at 'Miegunyah', the Toorak home of Russell Grimwade. It is thought that Edna Walling may have introduced Ellis to this huge inner-suburban garden, although no documentation for work there by her survives. Nor does it for Ellis's work, apart from his own writing. But several of his employees

A flight of steps in a seaside garden, built in the early 1960s to unite two blocks of land at differing levels.

Rockwork by Ellis Stones at the front of Ben Schubert's nursery for native plants in the Melbourne suburb of Noble Park.

*T*he Thornthwaite garden (1949–1950) has been 'an endless source of interest and pleasure' to its owner.

(whom he took there to show them what he had done over a period of years) say it led to a solid working relationship with Russell Grimwade, the noted philanthropist, industrialist and conservationist. The two were streets apart in terms of education and social standing, but they had common interests. Both loved native plants, with Russell Grimwade's all-consuming practical and aesthetic interest in eucalypts being far ahead of its time; both were fiercely nationalistic and aware of the need to protect Victoria's natural heritage. Both were interested in how things worked; one of Ellis's employees recalled that they 'used to get together in the toolshed'. Both loved fine woodwork, and were keen photographers. Russell Grimwade made a present to Ellis of a small wooden bowl he had turned, and although not one for lending his possessions, he once loaned Ellis a camera lens. Given her husband's absent-mindedness, Olive did not rest easy until it was returned.

Ellis illustrated his work at 'Miegunyah', and wrote about it, in his book, *Australian Garden Design* (1971):

> *. . . statuary is always difficult to place in a garden. On one occasion I was given the task of placing and installing a Spanish well head in a rather large garden. I selected a position in the centre of a rose garden, where the well head could be a focus for the eyes from a long way off. Some years later the client produced a small nude figure, and instructed me to install it in the garden. I decided that it should be mounted in a pool, in the vicinity of the well head, and what more appropriate than a couple of boulders as a base.*

In fact the well head, which is Italian (not Spanish), was given to Russell Grimwade in 1945, so could not have been placed in the garden before the statue, which had been installed in 1938. The model for the statue was the Grimwades' young niece, Amanda, and that year her uncle wrote a charming account of its commissioning and installation, which he titled 'Gosh! said Amanda'. This mentions Ellis neither by name nor scarcely even by implication among the protagonists in an affair which was clearly an 'event' for all concerned, but Ellis always spoke proudly of how he placed this statue on its rock, and for some forty years a fine photograph of it, captioned 'Ohmigosh!' and signed and dated on the reverse: 'W. Russell Grimwade October 1938', hung in pride of place on the timber panelling in the entrance of his home.

Ellis was called back to 'Miegunyah' several times more between 1945 and the early 1950s – to place the well head, to lay squared slate paving (using original slate from the pavements of Collins Street in the city, some pieces almost two metres long) around the house, and to convert the disused tennis court above the rose garden to a glade of silver birches. Between the glade and the rose garden he built a generous, broad flight of shallow slate steps, allowing the tiny daisy *Erigeron karvinskianus* – one of Edna Walling's favourites – to ramble through the joints. To place the trees he used another Walling technique, tossing out handfuls of potatoes and planting a birch where each fell. Beside some of them he half-buried an occasional flat, lichen-encrusted boulder.

As Ellis's professional career stabilised, so did his family life, with the purchase of a house in Locksley Road, Ivanhoe. They moved there

'Amanda' giggles from her perch in the pool in the rose garden at 'Miegunyah' in this signed photograph by W. Russell Grimwade, dated October 1938 and owned by the Stones family.

Ellis taught workers who carried out paving for him to use the biggest and best pieces of stone on the treads of steps.

In 1949 Ellis was asked to create a garden in a paddock at Narre Warren where the only existing trees of any note were a row of pines. He added generous swathes of densely planted shrubs, and created longer vistas of grass and trees.

*E*llis built a picturesque tea-tree enclosure to screen service buildings in the Walters garden at Narre Warren.

*T*he shrub borders at Narre Warren offered contrasts in colour and texture.

'*W*ide steps unite two sections of a large garden – the area illustrated was once a tennis court and has been planted with silver birches', read Ellis's caption for this photograph of the steps at 'Miegunyah' in his book *Australian Garden Design*.

in Christmas 1937. A polio epidemic was raging, and Ellis had insisted the three girls be taken out of school – all started at the local state school before attending private schools – to have lessons at home. 'I don't want any of them crippled – I've had enough of that myself', he said to Olive. At first they rented the house, a modest timber bungalow set on a deep block in a curving street running down to the bush-shrouded Yarra River, but they were able to buy it when the owner's wife refused to consider living 'in the country' (few houses had yet been built in that part of Ivanhoe). The river became Ellis's 'other garden' as with friends and family he took his recreation there – swimming, walking, or simply looking at the water and soaking up the atmosphere of the billabongs and the bush. In the house itself he panelled the entrance hall and living room with mellow timber, giving the effect he had achieved years before at 'Winterfold' in Avenel. And he began working on the typical suburban, featureless front garden, installing a few carefully placed flat rocks on either side of the path to the front door. But his main concern was design, and Olive and the girls were responsible for the garden's maintenance.

Ellis and Olive Stones at home, in their own garden. Ellis is sitting on a folding chair that he designed, using the locking mechanism he devised in the late 1920s for his 'improved collapsible sheep-gate'.

'Olive and the girls were responsible for (home) garden maintenance.' Betty Stones mows the front lawn during the 1940s.

Fallen autumn leaves enhance the natural appearance of the small pool in the Stone garden, Ivanhoe.

'A feeling of immense generosity' in the curve of the steps in the Stone garden, Ivanhoe, designed and built in 1956–58.

Autumn colour, more bluestone steps and rock walls in the Stone garden.

The swimming hole in Deep Creek, 'Glenara', Bulla.

Ellis enjoyed swimming in the creek at 'Glenara'. He is pictured with Prudence Rundle, c.1960.

SIX

Walling: teacher, employer, colleague

The association between Ellis and Edna Walling had begun as one of employer–employee; all his life Ellis referred to her as 'Miss Walling' while she called him 'Andy'. This name was bestowed at their first meeting, when his offer to build the wall in the Donaldson garden was received with: 'All right, I'll give you a try. What's your name?' 'It's Ellis.' 'That's too fancy. What's your second name?' 'Well . . . Andrew.' 'Much better. I'll call you Andy.'

He wrote to her in April 1971 in Buderim, Queensland, where she was living, sending a copy of his newly published book, *Australian Garden Design*. His letter read:

Dear Edna

I am taking the liberty of calling you Edna, as I feel we have known each other for a long time, although we haven't seen much of each other in latter years. When I was asked to write a book on landscaping I naturally thought of you, as we know you suggested I might do better at landscaping than building. I will be ever grateful to you for putting me on the right road in those early years, and so I dedicated the book to you . . .

Wishing the best for the future, I am Yours Sincerely

Andy.

(During her professional career the only employee whom Walling had allowed to call her by her Christian name was Eric Hammond, the contractor who built most of her gardens from the 1920s onward.)

But there were further dimensions to the Stones–Walling relationship. What better example could there be for a novice landscaper than working with this forthright, confident woman at the height of her career? Early on she guided him in how much to charge the often wealthy clients (even though some thought his bills far too small). But more important, he responded quickly and intuitively to her inimitable way of organising space in the garden. And knowing little of plants, he picked up a lot of information from her, observing the plants she specified and how well they worked, using her nursery at 'Sonning' as a source, not hesitating to ask for advice. Documentation for his design work in 1946 at the Gippsland garden 'Strathfieldsaye' includes a list in Edna Walling's handwriting of thirteen different plants, headed by her 'got from Sonning'. Among them are Walling signature plants like *Pyrus ussuriensis* (Manchurian pear), *Brachycome multifida* (the small mauve Australian daisy that she liked to see planted in sheets) and Westmoreland thyme. His 1971 letter to her includes the generous acknowledgement: 'I hope you are satisfied with your pupil's work'.

As well, Edna Walling's respect for his innate ability with stone (as shown by her exclamation 'You're a natural!' in the Donaldson garden) meant that in this area at least, on a conceptual level they could talk as equals. As noted previously, as he became more experienced she usually gave him free rein with stonework. Gwynnyth Crouch, working for Walling in the late 1930s, remembered that 'Edna would mostly allow him to go ahead in his own way on a particular section'. And during the 1940s, 50s and even the early 60s, when Walling's garden designs called for outcrops, walls or small pools, often she would simply direct the clients to Ellis Stones to carry these out. One longtime acquaintance of both described theirs as a firm and friendly professional relationship, distinguished – because both were strong-willed – by heated arguments on site or on the telephone. 'Children and fools shouldn't see things half-finished.' 'Too bloody pigheaded.' 'I don't want to work on tizzy gardens . . .' Olive Stones marvelled that the telephone didn't sizzle up with some of their rows. 'By Jove, we had a ding-dong go', Ellis would say as he came back into the room. Then there would be silence for weeks or even months, until Edna phoned again; 'I've got the most interesting new job and you can do what you like . . .' And they would resume as though the last argument had never been.

There is some evidence that Ellis's background in building helped Walling with practical problems. The outstanding example is the beautiful stone swimming pool that he built under her direction in 1939–40 at Olinda, in the Dandenong Ranges behind Melbourne. Ellis always maintained, in print and in conversation, that he played a major role in this pool. Walling, he said, had been baffled by the steep slope and inaccessibility of the site, but he assured her that the informal effect she wanted could be achieved, and worked out how to build it. According to Olive Stones, when Walling drew, photographed and described the pool in *Australian Home Beautiful* in April 1941, and in her book, *Gardens in Australia* (1943) without giving any credit to the man who felt it was as much his creation as hers, there was an argument that outdid all previous disputes. Perhaps Ellis's expectations had been raised by Walling's earlier printed praise of his work. At this stage of his life it was not often that he put pen to paper but this time, his wife said, he sat down and wrote her a letter of complaint.

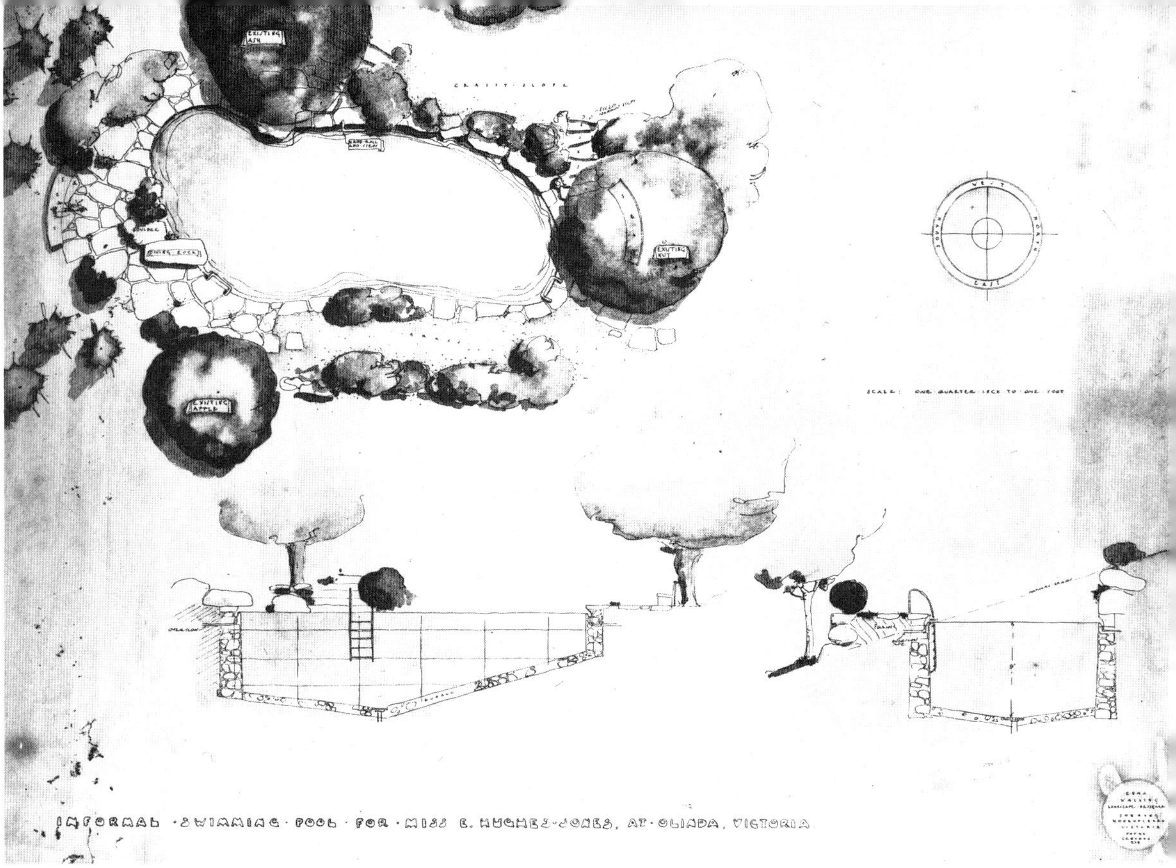

*E*dna Walling's plan of the Hughes-Jones pool at Olinda, as reproduced in the *Australian Home Beautiful* and in *Gardens in Australia*.

More than thirty years later he described the building of the pool in his own book:

> *Years ago I was commissioned to construct a swimming pool in the garden of a private home in the hills just out of Melbourne. The owner wanted an informal pool and I agreed that this was ideal for the area. I was particularly pleased with this pool because it presented all kinds of difficulties which were eventually overcome by teamwork and common sense. The excavations gave some trouble because it was impossible to get any mechanical equipment onto the site. The team consisted of one good horse, a plough, scoop, three good local men and myself. After the excavation was completed to a depth of 10 feet the construction was started. The pool was constructed entirely of stone, most of which was obtained on the site. The bottom was of stone about 6 inches deep; the sides, also of stone, were 3 feet thick at the bottom, tapering to 1 ft 6 in thick at the top, reinforced every 1 ft 6 in with galvanised hoop iron. When this was done, the whole surface was rendered with a strong mixture of sand and cement with water-proofing added . . .*

The sheer physical labour involved in excavating to a depth of more than three metres on such a site almost defies the imagination. But achieve it they did. A photograph in *Gardens in Australia* shows a deep corner of the excavated pool, an outcrop of large rocks already in place at its verge. In the shadow beside the outcrop sits a woman, plan open on her knee, talking to a singlet-clad worker whose features cannot be made out; two shovels lean mutely against an internal wall that is probably some two metres high. Walling used a large existing hazelnut tree to set the finished level, thus entailing more excavation than some of those

'Preliminary excavation for swimming pool', from *Gardens in Australia*, shows the cascade of rocks defining the slope to one side of the retaining wall of random stone.

involved felt necessary. But she maintained that the end effect justified the extra work. Nothing similar had been attempted before, and she advised the client, the nursing identity Miss Edith Hughes-Jones (then the matron and proprietor of Windermere Hospital), that after conferring with Mr Stones she believed the advice of an engineer would be 'most profitable' after excavation was complete. 'We could then tell him how we proposed to proceed and secure his approval of this.'

An engineering specification was duly prepared and refined over the next six or seven weeks as construction proceeded, necessitating a large volume of correspondence. Walling had to ask the meaning of the engineer's specified 'batter of 1 in 3' for the walls; when the term 'batter' had been defined for her she managed to have this requirement altered as it would have meant adding a further three feet all round to the already huge excavation. (Did the workers complain?) The engineer also designed a handrail for the narrow terrace set into the side of the hill above the pool 'from which', Walling wrote, 'onlookers may enjoy the graceful actions of some swimmers and the ridiculous antics of others'.

Howard Gay, one of the 'three good men' who worked with Ellis on the pool, remembered the fun of the job. 'Ellis Stones's attitude to life was all different. You couldn't see him serious.' The stone and rocks were manhandled on potato sacks and sledges, yoked by chains to the medium-sized draft horse that, to Ellis's amazement, went up and down the precipitous slope on its own. When it came to the above-ground work, Howard Gay was stunned at his ability. 'He'd put in a rock as if it grew there, not as if it were thrown there.' His ingenuity was recalled, too, in conversation forty years after the event. The engineer had suggested using a ready-made 'scum gutter' to catch leaves floating on the surface of the water, but Ellis improvised, using three-ply and the bottom of a beer bottle to trowel the necessary 'lip' into the rendered wall. For the grass that ran down to the edge of the pool, Ellis rolled up and lifted inch-wide strips of roadside grass that had been nibbled flat by rabbits. 'We put it down', said Howard Gay, 'and in three weeks you couldn't tell the difference between it and regular lawn'. Edna Walling approved of this technique, writing in *Gardens in Australia*:

> *Roots of the natural grass growing wild in the district have been planted around the pool, forming a close thick turf demanding much less attention than sown areas of refined lawn grasses. The creeping bents . . . are extremely valuable as drought-resisting turf-makers, browning off in summer, when water is not available, and springing into vigorous growth of a rich, soft, velvety-green, fine-textured sward after the first autumn rain.*

She was not completely happy, however, with another aspect of the finished pool, as she noted in her Home Beautiful column:

> *In this pool we have not been entirely successful in concealing the scum gutter, which undeniably ruins the natural effect of the pool. Obviously, flat stones which could have overhung the gutter would also have appeared artificial if they had followed the pool right around, but I do think we should have very carefully introduced some to break the continuity of the cement line; that is, in addition to the boulders which appear at the water's edge in the pictures.*

Ellis's later photograph reveals beautiful reflections of the landscape into which the pool was fitted.

A comparison of contemporary photographs taken by Stones and by Walling with Walling's beautiful drawing of the pool shows a discrepancy in treatment at the edge of the pool. On the drawing, flat slates or stones overhang the edge to conceal the gutter, in a line broken only by the huge diving rock, whereas photographs show that, as built, the pool was edged with occasional boulders or flat rocks, interspersed with grass running to the water's edge so that the gutter is visible in places. Clearly this was an instance when Ellis Stones went ahead on his own initiative. Was it in the absence of regular site visits from Walling, or was it because he felt that he should have the final word? Over the years some of these carefully placed boulders have vanished or become overgrown so that the offending gutter shows even more. But this is not to minimise the overall achievement. In terms both of design and construction this pool is recognised as a pivotal work in the history of Australian landscape design.

The pool in the early 1980s.

(Ellis always applauded the fact that it 'had never shown any signs of a leak'. But ironically, occasional leaks in the pool – as well as its invariably freezing temperature – were remembered by a friend of Miss Hughes-Jones who was a regular visitor to the beautiful garden in its heyday. Ellis, too, never forgot how cold the water was, because after it was first filled the rest of the team threw him in, fully clothed, to christen it. Thirty-five years later he could still raise a chuckle about this.)

Walling's magazine column about this pool was headed 'Swimming Pool that fits into the Landscape'. The relationship of gardens to their natural surroundings was another area where she and Ellis Stones agreed; they were very much in the minority in a country where for decades, the architect Robin Boyd wrote in *Australia's Home*, there had been general dissatisfaction with nature, the average home builder destroying every native tree, planting one or two 'disciplined English plants', trimming grass, hedges and shrubs into geometric shapes. Walling's early gardens had been distinguished by their use of exotic trees and shrubs, but with time she became progressively more enamoured of the natural landscape. The development of her design ideas is best documented through her columns in *Australian Home Beautiful*. These began in 1925 when the magazine was entitled *Australian Home Builder* and continued, sometimes monthly but more often in fits and starts with gaps of as much as six months, until July 1950.

In April and May 1925 in a two-part series on planting 'little trees' she advised readers to choose exotics like golden and Lombardy poplar, Persian plum, Roman cypress, crepe myrtle, purple-leaved crab-apple, double-flowered hawthorn, Judas tree and liquidambar – the last of these she describes as 'comparatively small-growing'! But the following month she observed: '. . . everyone can learn from nature how to plant his garden', and she suggested gardeners use 'red flowering ti-tree (*Leptospermum nicholii, L. chapmanii*)' to give the same soft effect as varieties commonly found in the bush in Victoria. By 1938 she was suggesting that readers consider Australian trees for their gardens, and from the early 1940s repeatedly she sang the praises of native plants, eulogising about 'the quiet perfection of nature's planting':

> *Walks into the country are the best lesson in landscape gardening. Notice how the trees are naturally grouped, how the ground-covering plants grow in drifts of different species round their feet, how boulders help to make up the natural scene . . .*

Of course, this is how Ellis Stones did his apprenticeship (albeit an unwitting one) in landscape gardening – in the boulder-strewn hills around Euroa as a child, in the harsh plains of outback New South Wales where the flat open land provided a kind of healing in the aftermath of his breakdown in 1923, on building jobs in the Victorian countryside in the 1920s and early 1930s. He wrote in *Priority Landscaping* (c.1973):

> *These country jobs gave me a close contact with nature and an opportunity to use natural materials. It didn't make sense to me to cart bricks great distances to country properties when on many occasions you have stone on the site which was much more attractive. I used stone whenever the opportunity arose . . .*

The type of gardens I wanted to make were to remind people of nature. I realise now the reason I was so interested in landscaping was that my occupation and physical disability made it necessary to live most of my time in the city, when I wanted to live with nature. So unconsciously I was trying to bring nature to the cities . . .

Edna Walling thought similarly. In her Home Beautiful column of March 1945 she said it was a serious reflection upon our sense of the fitness of things that we had not yet begun to realise that 'the recreation of the natural scene is the only way to deal with quite a considerable amount of the landscape work surrounding any city'.

In the absence of documentary evidence one can only speculate on the effect the thinking of each practitioner might have had on that of the other. Did Ellis Stones learn from Edna Walling's example in this area, as in so many others? Or did the effect created in her gardens by his simple, evocative outcrops crystallise her own ideas about creating 'natural' gardens? 'I have found that in landscape gardening a few weathered boulders, especially those that are large and somewhat flat, will give stability to a design that might otherwise be rather dull . . . it would have been better had I said naturalness instead of stability, perhaps', she wrote in 1941.

In later life, however, she came to disapprove of rock outcrops, and in 1965 she wrote:

The time came when clients could no longer afford such expensive gardens as I was designing, and I found myself trying my hand at outcrops as a comparatively inexpensive way out of the difficulties of contours. Having found someone excellent at this type of work I was happy enough to hand it over and say FINISH to gardens now that the trend was away from the architectural garden – the only kind I like designing.

In the margin her friend, the landscape architect Mervyn Davis, who was acting as editor, noted '?? Ellis Stones' beside the last sentence, writing at the bottom of the page:

7.6.65. Discussed this last paragraph with Edna this morning because I can't read her writing. What she wishes to say is that she beleives [sic] *that gardens of 'rock outcrops' are not gardens that will 'live'. They will alter and lose their architectural concept.*

Perhaps Walling's attitude at this time was coloured by her general opinion of Ellis's ability as a garden designer, which she disparaged, despite her enthusiasm for his ability with rock. But whatever her sentiments in 1965, she had not thought this way originally about rockwork. 'This cult of rock gardening is not likely to be a mere passing fashion', she commented in 1943, having been happy already to incorporate Ellis's outcrops into two of her most ambitious and extensive 'architectural' gardens of the 1930s. The first as we have seen, was 'Warrawee' for the Darling family, where she described his work as 'an informal rock garden that reproduces a bit of natural landscape'; the second, also in Toorak, 'Churston', for Dr and Mrs Ringland Anderson. Designed by architect Marcus Martin, 'Churston' (1936–37) was surrounded by a Walling garden

Ellis's photograph of his rockwork at 'Churston'.

of heroic proportions with formal stone walls and steps, slate paving, iron balustrading, creeper-hung pergolas. Behind the house the back garden was almost completely taken up by two tennis courts, side by side, one grass and the other en-tout-cas. Between them and the house ran a rectangular colonnaded swimming pool, beyond which steps led down to a mellow slate-paved path, flanked by herbaceous borders running to the very end of the tennis courts and planted in season with massed Japanese iris, lupins, delphiniums and Michaelmas daisies. Eric Hammond did the construction work, but Ellis was called in to add an extra dimension to the extensive treed 'side' garden next to the house, where Walling's plan showed stepping-stones meandering through the lawn, and through new and existing trees. Probably around 1939, Ellis added two small pools and a rock outcrop and put in occasional boulders, creating an atmosphere of planned informality. Near the back boundary he made a small dry creek with boulders, to solve a drainage problem.

The side section of the garden was subdivided and sold off, with the hard tennis court behind, during the 1970s. But luckily Dr Anderson, a renowned amateur photographer, took a series of colour transparencies in the mid-1940s that include one or two of Ellis's work. Ellis returned to work at 'Churston' after the war (his daughter Patricia helped maintain the garden from 1945 until around 1950) and he, too, recorded the garden in a series of memorable photographs. Several atmospheric shots of the borders, the birch trees and winding paths, and the swimming pool are a masterly evocation of the spirit of Edna Walling's design while showing – once again – his artist's eye for beauty and his skill in composition.

In the late 1930s, probably in 1939, he travelled to Benalla in north-east Victoria to build a small outcrop at 'Wooleen', a garden designed by Edna Walling for Mr and Mrs Laurie Ledger on an allotment running down to the picturesque lake in the centre of town. The plan had been drawn and partially implemented a year or two before the Ledgers looked up Ellis, whom Walling had recommended for rockwork. The outcrop marks the second of the garden's three levels; it incorporates cunningly placed boulder steps that thread their way almost imperceptibly up beside small alpine plants tucked into the crevices and spreading over the rocks.

*P*arts of the Edna Walling-designed garden at 'Churston' photographed by Ellis, probably in the mid-to-late 1940s: lupins in the herbaceous borders; and a trodden earth path running between birch trees.

Ellis suggested Mrs Ledger put in primulas and similar low-growing plants, but left the planting detail in her capable hands. The outcrop has given its owners enormous pleasure. Today, embellished by several of Walling's hand-made pots, it remains a favourite corner of this important garden, even though increased tree growth has removed the play of light and shade that enlivened the rocks, and reduced the range of plants that can be grown there. If change such as this is what Walling meant by a rock garden's propensity to alter over time and 'lose its architectural concept', then surely the change is one imposed by the very nature of gardens and gardening, rather than by any deficiency in the structure as such?

Work under Walling's aegis – in terms both of her direction and the cachet afforded by her reputation as the 'name' landscape designer of the day – was more than welcome. But Ellis's aim was to succeed in his own right. The representative of the Melbourne classified telephone directory called to suggest he advertise as 'Stones the stones man', but this was too gimmicky for him. Describing himself on his letterhead and beautifully painted signboard as 'rock garden constructor', eagerly he took on any new clients who came his way. He built up suppliers of the lichen-covered rocks he loved: a farmer in South Morang just outside Melbourne, who was clearing land for cropping and let him have the rocks first for the price of the cartage, then for one pound a truckload, and a widow at Tullamarine, just past Essendon airport. Like him she had a gammy leg, and with delight he adopted her phrase – 'I've got one and a swinger' – to describe his own uneven gait.

Late in 1939 he was commissioned to design and build a garden in South Yarra near the Royal Botanic Gardens for the prominent businessman, Ross Grey Smith. In a handwritten specification dated 15 January 1940 he undertook to landscape the front garden, drive and back garden for the sum of £112, including lawn, rock outcrops, stepping stones, a 'ti-tree' fence, paving slabs, agricultural drains, shrubs, creepers, soil, manure and extra trees. With it he sent a note asking for £30 on account 'to tide me over a lean time' and, according to his letter, 'a rough sketch' that he undertook to draw up if it was satisfactory. He added: 'I will not be on your job for a couple of days, but my man will be there, and Miss (Gwynnyth) Crouch is to start planting on Wednesday'.

This commission came to an abrupt end with a stiff letter dated 29 April 1940. Mr Grey Smith wrote to Ellis that he had for some time been most dissatisfied with the way the garden was coming on, but that as he knew nothing about gardens he had accepted his assurances that the work had been properly done. However, he had decided to seek independent advice on its suitability. He had been told (by another garden designer called in by his architect, Marcus Martin) that the lawn was never likely to succeed, the beds had not been properly prepared and the shrubs were far too small. The work done was valued at less than the amount already given in progress payments. He continued:

I have definitely decided to determine your contract and have the work completed or redone by someone else . . . I am not being influenced in my decision by the numerous delays which caused great inconvenience or the fact that the price quoted by you was a gross overcharge, but which would not have been questioned if the work had been even reasonably well done.

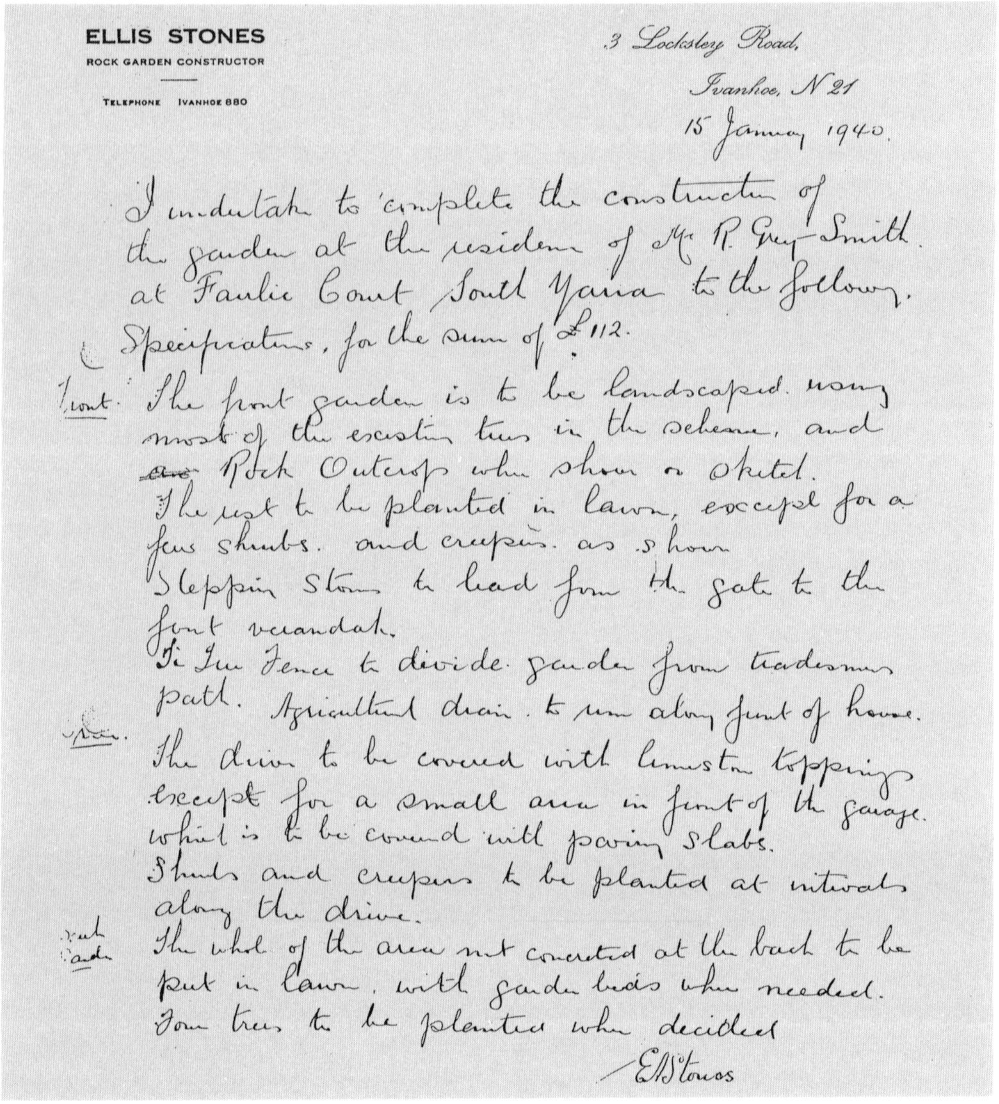

ELLIS STONES
ROCK GARDEN CONSTRUCTOR

TELEPHONE IVANHOE 880

3 Locksley Road,
Ivanhoe, N21
15 January 1940.

I undertake to complete the construction of the garden at the residence of Mr R. Grey-Smith at Fairlie Court South Yarra to the following specifications, for the sum of £112.

Front: The front garden is to be landscaped using most of the existing trees in the scheme, and Rock Outcrops where shown on sketch.
The rest to be planted in lawn, except for a few shrubs and creepers as shown.
Stepping Stones to lead from the gate to the front verandah.
Ti Tree Fence to divide garden from tradesmens path. Agricultural drain to run along front of house.

Drive: The drive to be covered with limestone toppings except for a small area in front of the garage which is to be covered with paving slabs.
Shrubs and creepers to be planted at intervals along the drive.

Back Garden: The whole of the area not concreted at the back to be put in lawn, with garden beds where needed.
Four trees to be planted where decided

E.E. Stones

The specification for the Grey Smith garden.

This letter must have caused great disappointment, and no doubt Ellis learned a lot from it. But leaving aside the question of the competence of the work, which cannot be measured at this distance, it raises points that remained constant throughout his career.

First, clients often thought the shrubs and trees he put in 'too small'. He always maintained that small plants – particularly native plants – grew better and got off to a stronger start than did large ones. Often he asked jokingly why clients were in a rush for effect. Wasn't most of the fun in watching the plants grow? In 1973 when Ellis was making a pilot programme on small gardens for ABC television, the interviewer commented on the length of time such a garden would take to grow to maturity. Ellis, normally mild-mannered, retorted: 'The trouble with you young buggers is you're always in so much of a hurry!' 'Keep it going!' exhorted the director, delighted at such spontaneity. But Ellis, ever the gentleman, clapped his hand over his mouth in horror at what he'd said, and clammed up.

Second, usually he was more interested in the beginning of a job and its general execution than in the finishing touches, particularly when he was very busy. In later years his office diaries were liberally sprinkled with phone messages 'Mr D wants the camellia you promised.' 'Mrs R rang back to know when you are going to finish their job.' Most clients put up with this for one reason or another. From time to time, one didn't.

SEVEN

Building a career

Ellis's family noticed a change in him after his change in career. It was obvious that – perhaps for the first time in his life – he really enjoyed his work. 'He loved landscaping', said his eldest daughter, Lesley. 'You could see it when he came home each night – he was just full of it.'

His sense of humour, which was never far from the surface, bubbled up constantly. One weekend Olive was away and Patricia did the ironing. He walked into the pavilion for the weekend RSL cricket match with an exaggerated bow-legged gait. 'What's up with you?' asked a team-mate. 'Oh, nothing really', said Ellis. 'I'm just following the creases my daughter put in my trousers.'

Weekend cricket with the Returned Services League (Ellis, bottom right).

There was no laughter, though, when his nephew, Bruce Williams, was drowned in 1941 on HMAS *Sydney*. Ellis had planned that Bruce, an accountant who was also a competent artist, would work with him after the war was over – he badly needed someone to keep track of office finances and to send out and chase up accounts. He was extremely fond of his nephew and this bitter blow sent him to the recruiting office, not once but several times. He felt there must be something he could do. (Bad leg notwithstanding, he was fit and very agile. During construction of the Hughes-Jones pool at Olinda, fellow worker Howard Gay remembered how Ellis, using his 'good' leg, would hop unaided from the ground onto the back of a tip truck.) Not surprisingly, he was not accepted for military service but he did join the local Volunteer Defence Corps. His developing knowledge of landscape design was a help in a night-time exercise when his company had to infiltrate a local park without another company's knowledge. He located the main stormwater drain and crawled through. It was the tightest fit imaginable and the prospect of meeting a tiger snake on the way through was not pleasant. But to everyone's amazement he made it unharmed and undetected to a spot behind the 'opposition' lines.

Around this time, with growing fears that Australia could be invaded, he became involved in designing and making an armoured car. The group of like-minded men (among them a businessmen and a journalist) struck problems in making the odd-looking vehicle bulletproof; Ellis came up with the idea of bending the steel covering so that bullets would ricochet off. They believed it would be the salvation of the civilian population in a Japanese invasion. The army tested the car at Williamstown, after which it was driven home by way of Collins Street, past incredulous passers-by. The group then took it to Canberra for demonstrations. At Albury they encountered General MacArthur and his entourage; undeterred, they bailed up the American commander and asked him to have a look at it. Nothing came of this presentation and the concept lapsed when Ellis decided in July 1942 to leave the VDC and volunteer for the Civil Construction Corps. (He had wanted to sign up with the Red Cross, but decided on the construction corps because it offered an allowance to his dependents.) Before leaving, he dug an air-raid shelter for his family in the vacant block opposite their house.

*T*he home-built armoured car.

They missed him dreadfully. Like the Stones houses in Essendon a generation earlier, the house at Locksley Road was a hive of activity for the girls and their friends. Lesley, Patricia and Betty had swimming lessons with the local Sea Scout group on the river at nearby Wilson Reserve, and firm friendships were made there. The Stones's door was always open; you were sure of a welcome at any time. After Ellis left to join the construction corps, local boys continued to call in, helping with odd jobs, chopping wood, relishing the convivial atmosphere. One night Olive, who stood perhaps four feet ten inches in her stockings, braved the throng. 'Come on boys, you're causing too much noise', she protested. The largest among them scooped her up and sat her on the mantelpiece, from which perch she joined in the party.

Ellis was sent to the Northern Territory as a carpenter, to do construction and camouflage work at Katherine and Darwin, learning a precept he was to advocate thereafter – the painting of 'service' buildings in dull green so as to make them merge into the landscape. He moved on to Queensland, preparing sites for military camps near Maryborough. He was particularly interested in one site that had to be slotted into virgin forest, with positions for buildings being chosen to avoid unnecessary cutting down of trees. Here he is said to have camouflaged one installation so effectively that searchers at first could not find it. During this time he was introduced to the bulldozer, which he regarded henceforth as 'man's new weapon of destruction'.

Much further south, 1943 also saw the publication of Edna Walling's first book, *Gardens in Australia*, illustrating several gardens in which Ellis had executed the rockwork that created so much atmosphere. But in northern Queensland this must have seemed a world away. Ellis hated the climate; problems with his leg recurred and he spent most of that November in hospital in Maryborough with acute pain at the back of his left heel (the toes on his 'bad' left foot had been causing pain for some years previously). Then early in 1944 he came down with an extreme case of tropical dermatitis. He was invalided home in February.

Back in Melbourne and struggling to pay school fees, Olive had gone out to work. She held a sales job at Myer Melbourne, a department store with which she had had dealings some years earlier when, during the Depression years, Ellis applied his collapsible sheep-gate design to a hinged canvas and timber folding chair. Olive had lugged the heavy home-built chair – which was almost as large as she was – into the city, to show it to the Myer outdoor furniture department, whose representative wanted to place a bulk order. Ellis and Olive did not see how they could fill this and went no further.

He came back covered with an angry skin rash, bandaged from head to toe with masks across his face. Bran baths were needed to clear it and plenty of recovery time – including spells in hospital – but although he was very depressed and times, once more, were hard, his family remembers that 'he always had a smile'. And he never complained.

Soon he was landscaping again. He returned to the Harold Darling garden in Toorak, where his daughter Lesley put in six months' maintenance work for him in order to earn the money for the uniforms she needed to train as a nurse. And Edna Walling introduced him to a client in Kew,

'An elegant, curving flight of granite and slate steps . . . the focal point of the garden.'

as 'a man who had great feeling for the use of moss-covered boulders'. He brought boulders from Whittlesea to define paths through this large front garden, masking some with prostrate junipers. He built a rustic country-style rock wall to separate the front and back gardens, then opened up an existing trellis fernery to make a little creek settling into two small ponds, which he stocked with goldfish. As well, he put a small, square pond into the glasshouse, and stocked this with fish. He was paid on a daily basis.

The clients were well pleased with him and his work, and were struck by his obvious love of what he was doing. Edna Walling they remembered as rather high and mighty, one who came and walked around the garden, made a few suggestions, left and sent a bill for £5. Most of all they appreciated her putting them in touch with Ellis Stones. Cuttings for some of the new plants came from Ellis's own garden; his daughter Patricia maintained their garden for some years thereafter.

Twenty-five years later the same clients were to use Ellis in a new garden near the sea, where he solved the knotty problem of linking two blocks of land at vastly differing levels. He built an elegant, curving, flight of granite and slate steps between the two blocks, with occasional boulders beside the steps embellished with small rock and alpine plants. This neatly turned a potential disadvantage into an advantage and remains the focal point of the garden. (Ellis wrote in notes for a 1971 article that any well-designed garden should always have some permanent framework to give character to the area and build a floral display around; steps added interest, he said, to areas that otherwise would have to rely solely on plant material for effect.) In neither the Kew garden nor the seaside garden for these clients was a plan drawn – ideas were discussed, a daily wage agreed and work done. The upper block in the seaside garden was rich in native eucalypts, tea-tree and melaleucas. Typically, Ellis saw no point in tampering with these and simply added near the far fence a broad patch of the blue agapanthus so typical of coastal resorts near Melbourne.

Immediately after the war Ellis embarked on a job that was a personal favourite. 'Strathfieldsaye', on the northern shore of Lake Wellington near Stratford in Gippsland, is one of the oldest properties in Victoria and probably the earliest Gippsland building still standing. The part of the homestead dating from 1848 is built of hand-sawn red gum boards, and mounted on an ivy-covered plinth in the garden is a cannon souvenired from the 1841 wreck of the steamer *Clonmel* on the sandbar at Corner Inlet. (In 1842 the government gave the cannon to William Odel Raymond, who pioneered 'Strathfieldsaye', as protection against the aborigines who were preying on his flocks and herds.) In 1869 the then huge grazing property came into the ownership of the Disher family, so that some plants in the garden today probably date from the 1870s. In 1945 Dr Clive Disher asked Ellis to redesign part of the garden.

Dr Disher was a well-known medical identity and oarsman, a friend of Russell Grimwade, and of Dr Ringland Anderson, who is thought to have recommended Ellis to him. Station diaries at 'Strathfieldsaye' record the delivery of a load of stone on 31 August 1945, while Dr Disher's daily memo book for that year notes the arrival of 'Mr Stones landscape gardener' on 17 September, and his departure eleven days later. Ellis returned by train the following July for a nine-day stay, bringing with him Patricia Stones, a Miss Brennan and Mrs H. Stephens. During this stay, plants were bought in Stratford nearby. He came back briefly in October, with Patricia and Miss Brennan, perhaps as a final site visit.

'Strathfieldsaye' is now owned by the University of Melbourne, whose archives contain copious plant lists for its garden. Some are in Ellis's well-rounded hand (which throughout his life remained as clear and firm as the writing in the letter he sent home from Gallipoli as a teenager). Others list a variety of exotic and native plants with possible sources – Hodgins Nursery in Essendon, the garden of Miss Brennan, nurseryman R. V. Prichard (for herbaceous perennials), Edna Walling's nursery at 'Sonning' (for perennials and Woodend bent lawn seed), the State Nursery at Macedon. There is a very rough pencil sketch of part of the garden, annotated and perhaps drawn by Ellis, showing the approximate location of boulders, and positioning plants like alpine phlox, thrift, creeping thyme, prostate veronica with taller plants behind these – Michaelmas daisy, iris and lupins.

The flavour of Ellis's work in this garden was old-world, perhaps in response to the historic nature of the site. A report on the garden, prepared in 1983 by Carrick Chambers (then professor of botany at the University of Melbourne, now director of the Royal Botanic Gardens, Sydney), describes it as primarily one of introduced domestic species, with a rich variety of trees, shrubs, perennials and bulbs, lying on either side of a central axial gravel path with sensitively placed broad stone steps at intervals. Other gravel and grass paths run parallel to this and intersect

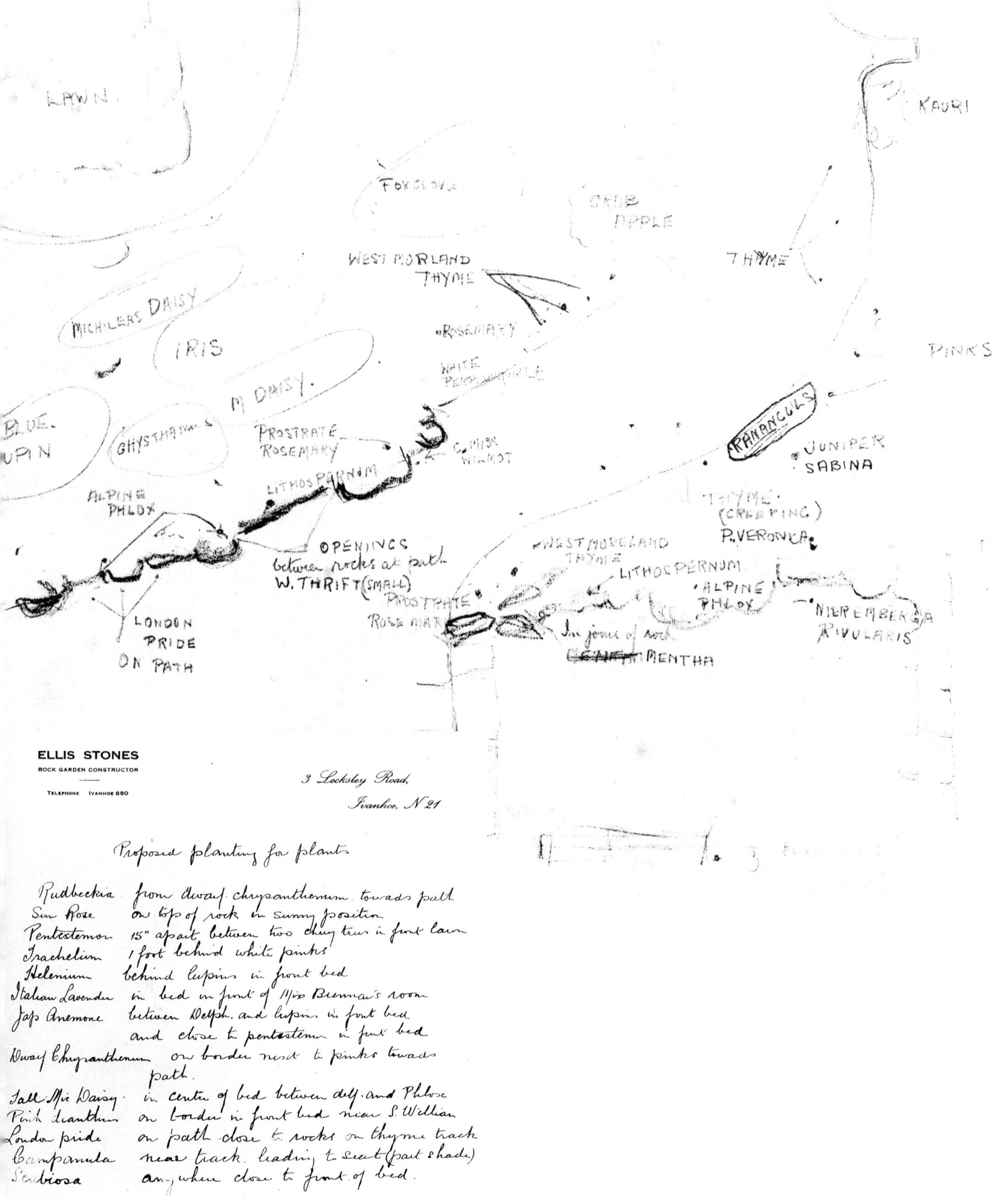

ELLIS STONES
ROCK GARDEN CONSTRUCTOR
TELEPHONE IVANHOE 880

3 Locksley Road,
Ivanhoe, N 21

Proposed planting for plants

Rudbeckia — from dwarf chrysanthemum towards path
Sun Rose — on top of rock in sunny position
Pentestemon — 15" apart between two cherry trees in front lawn
Trachelium — 1 foot behind white pinks
Helenium — behind lupins in front bed
Italian Lavender — in bed in front of Miss Brennan's room
Jap Anemone — between Delph. and lupins in front bed and close to pentestemon in front bed
Dwarf Chrysanthemum — on border next to pinks towards path.
Tall Mic Daisy — in centre of bed between delf. and Phlox
Pink dianthus — on border in front bed near S. William
London pride — on path close to rocks on thyme track
Campanula — near track leading to seat (part shade)
Scabiosa — anywhere close to front of bed.

A planting list and plan for the garden at 'Strathfieldsaye'.

with a series of informal curved contoured paths through shrubberies and small gardens, sloping gently down towards the lake. Professor Chambers's report reads in part:

> *We know this garden dates from at least the 1870s . . . However, the garden form as we know it today is basically a later design redeveloped by Dr Clive Disher in the immediate post-war years . . .*
>
> *(A sequence in the station diaries, and other entries) almost certainly proves the truth of the story that the very skillfully built broad steps on the central axial path were completed by Ellis Stones and party, except for the bottom step . . . I have not been able to find definite documentation that proves Edna Walling influenced, in a major way, the design of this garden but it can be reliably stated that Ellis Stones constructed much of it into its present form.*

Looking up the stepped area of the central path towards the house at 'Strathfieldsaye'. Ellis laid the stone steps.

A break in the gardening at 'Strathfieldsaye'. (Ellis, third from right, Patricia Stones, third from left.)

Patricia Rice (the 'Miss Stones' of Dr Disher's diaries) said her father received this commission in his own right, independent of Edna Walling. It was a particularly happy job. Ellis's photographs show a group of smiling workers, men and women – 'the men on the property did a lot of the manual construction work', Patricia recalled – arranged in a carefully positioned semi-circle with wheelbarrow and tools at the ready. Ellis took one photograph then, in characteristic style, handed over the camera and had himself recorded with the group. His undated photographs of the garden show well-established low planting along the major gravel path, and the cannon set on a lawn among trees and shrubs. These may have been taken during his two-day visit in October 1946.

*E*llis's photograph of 'Strathfieldsaye', c.1946, shows planting and boulders beside a gravel path with Lake Wellington in the distance.

*E*llis's curving driveways of crushed gravel edged with occasional boulders and soft ground-cover plants were different for the time, as were his informal pools and garden beds. These photographs are thought to be from the late 1940s.

So in harness again, gradually he was building up a strong following. Some new clients were attracted by his ideas, which were so different for the time. Potential clients saw or heard about Ellis's rocks, his walls, his curving driveways of crushed gravel edged with soft ground-cover plants instead of the ubiquitous concrete kerb – and wanted this effect in their own gardens. Helping a keen gardener in her move from a large and beautiful old house and garden to a new villa set on a small, flat, featureless block in Hawthorn, for instance, he created a space in which the paths were not straight (as was the norm then) but gently curving, where the irregularly shaped fish-pond was positioned in the bend of a path for maximum impact, and where occasional rocks set off to perfection the client's beloved rhododendrons and azaleas. Word-of-mouth recommendations kept him busy. There was plenty of opportunity locally, as land was coming onto the market in Ivanhoe and Heidelberg and, despite shortages of building materials, new homes and gardens were springing up, particularly in the East Ivanhoe area. Ellis's photographs of an unidentified garden in Ivanhoe, perhaps from the late 1940s, show the front garden of a sparkling new two-storied house where he has done his best to soften the effect of the work already done by others – a hard-looking stone front fence, a rigid central driveway of unyielding cement – by introducing long, low bold outcrops at intervals down the grassed slope on either side of the drive. Gravel toppings around each free-form outcrop blend into the lawn grasses, and it is obvious that when the newly planted shrubs, ground-covers and trees mature, the effect of the garden will be far from ordinary.

A bold treatment for a suburban lawn in a garden belonging to a neighbour (presumably the plaster gnomes were added after Ellis had finished his work).

(These photographs were found in a box of unlabelled glass plate negatives that document some of Ellis's work from the period immediately before and after the war. They include the Donaldson garden in Heidelberg, what is thought to be the Flack garden in South Yarra, 'Strathfieldsaye' on Lake Wellington and his own front garden.)

At this time Ellis also maintained large old gardens around Toorak, including some in which he had done work for Edna Walling before the war. He was always busy. From 1946 he employed a full-time helper, Bob Crosbie, as well as his daughter Patricia, who did some part-time study at Burnley Horticultural College, and local boys – some of them former Sea Scouts – who laboured during school and university holidays and who thus developed a life-long appreciation for stone walls and mossy boulders. Other occasional helpers included a couple of ex-navy men who had a local trucking business, and a Burma railway veteran, 'Wild Jack' McIntyre, who lived in Heidelberg. 'They were real hard cases', says Bob Crosbie. 'Oh, there were plenty of laughs on the job, that's for sure. We had a ball.' But there was a positive side to the fun. Crosbie, who still works in the field, looks back on his years with Ellis Stones as the major learning experience of his life. 'He was such a good man at his caper, one of the best. Unfortunately he wan't a very good manager on the books side. But then this was not what he was there for.'

From the outset of his long career (and, indeed, throughout it) Ellis undertook a wide range of work. He would as soon turn his hand to a job for the man around the corner as he would lay out gardens and build walls and outcrops for the wealthy. Everything was a challenge. Jobs recalled by Crosbie from this period included a flight of curving stone steps at a new house in Mornington; post-war rejuvenation at 'Churston'; a stone wall and steps for the Ringland Andersons at their country house, 'Culraven', Olinda; a large new garden around a house in the outer Melbourne suburb of Heathmont. There was, too, a garden for a cream brick house in Balwyn, one of the first built by A. V. Jennings, in which Collins Street slate was used to line the driveway, and to create a paved area around a fish-pond. In 1950 a memorable commission took

*T*he garden around a large house in the outer Melbourne suburb of Heathmont included a curving entrance path, low stone walls and steps, an outcrop and a fish-pond.

*S*late lifted from Collins Street in the city was used to pave the driveway of a brick veneer house built by A. V. Jennings, to form steps and to edge a fish-pond.

*E*llis's work at the historic South Australian house 'Padthaway' included low walls of local stone and an expanse of random paving.

*T*he day's work done at 'Padthaway', rabbitting proved a favourite recreation. The haul was invariably a good one.

Ellis to the border of South Australia and Victoria to rejuvenate the garden around the historic house 'Padthaway'. The job lasted several weeks. The picturesque two-storied house sat in a flat expanse that he broke up with formal steps and low limestone walls. The stone came off the property, and was mixed with lime burnt on the site. He laid a long expanse of random slate paving along one side of the house, beneath a pergola laden with wisteria. At the request of Mrs Keith Lawson he laid out a formal rose garden on the site of an old tennis court. Patricia Stones was in charge of the planting; Ellis chose the plants and Olive despatched them from Melbourne. 'One or two' native plants were used, but the Lawsons wanted a predominantly English-style garden. At the day's end recreation came in the form of rabbitting, with Patricia and the two men he took to help him build the garden. The piles of carcasses in his photographs show that the property must have been alive with rabbits – and that the skills he acquired as a child were still well-honed. Mrs Lawson remembered Russell Grimwade recommending Ellis for this job on the strength of his work at 'Miegunyah'.

By 1946 Ellis had felt sure enough of what he was doing to go into print with his ideas, contributing articles to *Australian Home Beautiful*, edited by W. A. 'Bill' Shum. Writers for this monthly magazine then included leaders in their fields – among them Edna Walling, of course, whose articles now dealt almost exclusively with Australian plants and the natural landscape, Marguerite Mahood on pottery, John Mockridge on architecture, Mavis Thorpe Clark on house design. The magazine was popular. In March that year, Mr Shum noted with enthusiasm that the removal of restrictions on newsprint would allow – for the first time in five years – printing of enough copies to satisfy public demand.

Ellis's first article appeared in 1946 and dealt with boulders and borders. Illustrated with photographs of parts of the Donaldson garden, his own front garden and the garden in front of a new white brick villa, it crammed a wide range of ideas into only a few hundred words. Shum summarised it in his editorial as 'a plea for the use of undressed stone in the development of our gardens as a break away from the formal quarried stone-and-cement walls, paths and other "features" . . . (showing) . . . how natural are the effects to be obtained with basalt boulders of varying shapes and sizes'.

More thought had to be given to the planning of gardens in relation to the houses they surrounded, Ellis wrote. Why not let lawn, or gravel, run up in places to the wall of a brick or cement house, rather than making garden beds all along the walls? If using rock, he wrote, take care. Make sure it blends with the house. Instead of the foreshortening effect of a rock wall, consider an outcrop of selected boulders. 'But place them carefully or you may finish with one of those awful rockeries we see so often in our gardens.' Consider, too, the area in the vicinity of the back door and plan it so that you have a back garden instead of a 'yard'. Treat a small area as an extension of the living-rooms of the house, for relaxation. Why not add a 'summer room' in a small part of the garden? This, he wrote, could be made as attractive as any of the rooms of the house, and more restful – and it could be done on the smallest allotment.

Two months later another Stones article appeared entitled 'Pools – Formal and Natural; notes on the use of water in the garden'. Here he emphasised the 'endless' ways in which water could enhance the beauty of a garden. Even an uninteresting blank space could be made a charming spot with a wall fountain, he wrote (the title block of the article was illustrated with a sketch of an elegant, simple wall fountain, based on an unidentified photograph found among his papers). Other illustrations showed his own tiny, informal backyard pool edged with shrubs, grasses and one or two boulders, a formal square pool within a fernery, and a rocky glade with slate paving beside a small pool (the garden made in 1938 for the Arts and Crafts Society's exhibition at the Lower Melbourne Town Hall). He stressed that the designer/builder should not compromise.

> *Exactitude in measurement, proportion and workmanship are important in constructing a formal pool. Good workmanship is no less necessary in making the informal pool, but it is even more important to conceal the worker's hand and make it appear that nature did the job! Thus all evidence of the use of concrete should be covered up or disguised. Water should be led in over a curved rock or some such device.*

Advice was included on the optimum water depth for growing water lilies, and on keeping goldfish. Bill Shum noted in his editorial that in making such pools the amateur was strongly advised '(a) to conceal the evidence of his craftsmanship and (b) to avoid the cactus at all costs!'

Like Ellis's gardens, the ideas in these articles were novel. They spoke directly to the ordinary man with an ordinary suburban garden, and their strength was that they confined themselves to effects that could be achieved in a small space. They showed that even at this stage, he wanted to tell his readers how to do it. He and Edna Walling argued about this. You shouldn't tell them *too* much, she would say. But they did think along similar lines. The following year Walling's (by now) irregular Home Beautiful column, 'Letter to Garden Lovers', introduced the idea of an out-of-door living room, while the month after that she wrote about natural-looking pools.

Ellis's family remembered Bill Shum pursuing him for more articles during the late 1940s, but writing did not come easily to him, he never had any spare time, and deadlines meant little. (The undated, unsigned typescript for a long and technical article on building stone walls, with pencilled annotations by W. A. S. – presumably Bill Shum – remains among his papers, but does not appear to have been published.) And gradually Home Beautiful's gardening coverage, which had been so influential, became more prosaic, less inspired. The major writers in the late 1940s and early 50s were Thomas A. Browne, introduced to readers as 'one of the most widely known authorities on practical gardening in Australia', and garden designer Olive Mellor, who provided plans for readers. Edna Walling's column appeared more and more infrequently. Its subject-matter and approach – best summed up as consciousness-raising for native flora – was a mile away from that of the splashy spring gardening supplement for 1950. Compiled by Browne and Mellor, this contained factual articles on vegetables, annuals and perennials, garden planning, soils, lawns, trees and shrubs, fruit trees and was introduced by a cover photograph of huge magenta rhododendrons, captioned: 'Rhododendrons like these in Thomas A. Browne's own garden in Melbourne's Dandenongs are flowers that most amateurs dream about'. The emphasis on thoughtful garden design, nurtured by Edna Walling over more than two decades with the magazine and echoed briefly during 1946 by Ellis Stones, was giving way to a concentration on matters horticultural and on 'performance' in the home garden. It was not until 1970, when Ellis began contributing a monthly column on garden design, that the pendulum was to swing back.

EIGHT

Towards an 'Australian' garden

Edna Walling's magazine contributions may have become less frequent, but her writing went from strength to strength. More than 11,400 copies of her books were sold between 1943 (when *Gardens in Australia* appeared) and 1950. *Cottage and Garden in Australia*, published in 1947, described the building and fitting out of the cottages at Bickleigh Vale, and the principles behind the design and planting of their gardens. *A Gardener's Log* (1948) was a compendium of extracts from her columns in *Australian Home Beautiful*, arranged by seasons and with a comprehensive index, which added to the book's usefulness. By 1950 *Gardens in Australia* was in its fourth edition. This was an achievement, given the general public's lack of interest in the topic. 'Unfortunately for her she was operating when landscaping was not considered very important', Ellis Stones wrote in an unpublished tribute to Walling after her death in 1971 – but if her name, at this stage, still was not a household word among the broad mass of gardeners in Victoria, certainly she was increasingly well-known and popular, with a reputation second to none.

Edna Walling, 1925.

She was not the only garden designer of note in the professional scene that Ellis entered in the mid-1930s. In New South Wales, Jocelyn Brown was designing elegant gardens on sites ranging from cramped city allotments to country properties, and from 1939–42 she wrote regularly in the up-market Sydney-based monthly magazine, *Home*. These influential and thoughtful articles on gardening, garden design and plantsmanship, often were illustrated with her own artwork; her flower-filled gardens were based on strong structure and formal architectural elements – carefully planned vistas, steps, fountains and the like. Brown's biographer, Helen Proudfoot, finds similarities between some aspects of her style and output, and Walling's, although she was nothing like as prolific as Walling.

Other garden designers in Walling's home state of Victoria were mainly women. Peter Watts in *The Gardens of Edna Walling* acknowledges the role of Olive Mellor, who during her long career claimed to have designed more than five hundred gardens – even more than Walling. (As a young woman Mellor is remembered for having persuaded the then Minister for Agriculture to allow her to study full time at Burnley Horticultural College, which at the time allowed women to attend lectures but not to engage in the practical component of the course.) Watts pays tribute to Emily 'Milly' Gibson as a designer of some note who 'probably deserves more credit than anyone else in Victoria for promoting large-scale industrial landscape design'. Mrs Gibson worked at one time in the office of Walter Burley Griffin and Marion Mahoney Griffin, and in England. Not only did she teach at Burnley College over a thirty-five year period, she managed a private practice and wrote a garden page for the *Argus* newspaper. At Burnley she inspired a succession of eager students, many of whom later made their mark – among them were the ex-servicemen who flocked there to study after the Second World War. During the early 1950s she encouraged her students to enrol in new courses in landscape design being established in England; among them were Erica Ball, Mervyn Davis and Margaret Hendry. In their earliest days of practice Walling, Olive Mellor and Emily Gibson had been part of a group of enthusiastic women designers who charged £1 per garden design, plus ten per cent of the cost of plants.

Another practitioner of the time was Nerine Chisholm. A friend and associate of Mrs Gibson, she was a tall, gaunt woman of ascetic appearance, named after a flower. (The story goes that her father, continually disappointed in his hopes for a son, resorted to whatever flower he noticed blooming in his garden to christen each of his four daughters.) Little information survives about the nature or extent of Nerine Chisholm's practice, but she is to be seen in a photograph of staff at Burnley Horticultural College taken in the late 1930s, and her book *Australian Gardens*, published in 1949, can be found still on second-hand shelves. Even today this is a useful and quite imaginative manual for anyone considering making a new garden or rejuvenating an old one, with an emphasis on garden design and planning rather than on matters horticultural, which was outside the mainstream of its time.

Ellis Stones would have agreed with her statements on rock gardens. Rock gardens, Chisholm wrote, should never be obtrusive, and must be in scale and keeping with their surroundings. They should be carefully planted; haphazard planting could ruin their beauty. She suggested that readers should use their neighbours' trees and views to make a 'distant picture' – one of Ellis Stones's favourite maxims – that they should guard existing large boulders and make note of natural dips for use in a sunken garden or pool, and that they should retain existing native trees and shrubs, at least for a temporary purpose in the initial stages of garden-making.

> *Until your garden is made, that natural shrubbery, that native growth so wild and scrubby, will be your place of retreat . . . A wandering track through it, some ground cover to keep down the weeds, some water to start the growth, and you will have a wild nature-garden into which your main garden may lead. Who knows but that you may find some of our native plants more interesting, at least in part of your grounds, than many exotic plants?*

Indeed, by the time Chisholm's book was published, broader interest in Australian plants was beginning to develop, having been promoted through the 1940s mainly in magazine and newspaper articles – in particular by Edna Walling and by the naturalist and author Jean Galbraith, who wrote (over a fifty-year period) as 'Correa' in *Australian Garden Lover*. Ellis was pleased to note this, as he used these plants where possible in his designs – such as the *Agonis flexuosa* he planted in the late 1930s to overhang a small pool in the Donaldson garden in Heidelberg. During the 1920s and 1930s, however, native plants had been more peripheral, the preserve of a hardy few. Edna Walling had begun to observe and collect them in the bush in the 1920s, propagating some in her nursery at 'Sonning', but this was a small-scale effort. In the early 1930s Arthur Jones of the Department of Agriculture gave well-attended illustrated lantern lectures around Melbourne on wattles, wildflowers and similar topics, and from around 1930, gardening journals like the *Home Gardener* and *Australian Garden Lover* reported items such as Mr Jones's lantern lectures, and the annual wildflower show of the Field Naturalists' Club. At this show there was eager demand for table-growing (potted) specimens of native plants; Jean Galbraith helped on the identification table from around 1925 until the war years, and she scarcely found time to draw breath for the press of people wanting advice, and specimens brought in for naming. As 'Correa' – it was not accidental that her pen-name was that of a native plant – she wrote often about native plants in bush settings and about those in her own garden, while from time to time through the 1930s C. B. Frond in his regular articles in *Australian Home Beautiful* described private gardens where 'wildflowers' were grown, and directed readers to nurseries where they could be bought. There was an element of nineteenth-century plant-hunting mania in the heading 'Taming the Wildflower' given to Frond's September 1930 account, 'Native Plants in Nursery and Garden'. Illustrating the newly introduced Geraldton waxflower as well as the old standard, *Thryptomene*, he wrote: 'The growing interest in wildflower cultivature [*sic*] is reflected in an increasing demand for plants that will adapt themselves to local conditions . . .' In the same year he noted that for the first time in Australia a trophy was to be presented at a gardening show for the best specimen of a cultivated wildflower, shown either as a single spray or a bunch.

Obviously Frond was an enthusiast. He referred to his own garden where, he said, it was easy to imagine that one was in the bush rather than in a suburban garden, and which boasted tea-trees more than thirty feet high. In 1933 he described in glowing terms the Heidelberg garden of Mr and Mrs Harold Jenkins, 'successful horticulturalists and winners of prizes at flower shows', who had converted nearly half an acre of their land into a forest of native trees and shrubs, some of these brought from the bush, others acquired at nurseries and markets. (This gentle and appreciative appraisal was in stark contrast with an article published the following year in *Australian Home Beautiful* in which architect S. C. Meyer, in collaboration with 'a lady who has achieved a large amount of success with her garden', designed a garden to meet the needs of the average householder on an average block of land. He allowed what he described as a large area for native trees and shrubs – in fact, a pocket on the back fence between the toolshed, the incinerator and the compost bin! – because, he wrote, these plants needed only 'poor soil, little water and no digging or hoeing', they demanded a minimum of labour, gave a maximum of effect, were easily grown and made 'a glorious background for green lawns'.)

Edna Walling, for her part, wrote in 1933 about the vegetation that she hoped to preserve on her newly established subdivision at Bickleigh Vale. 'The remaining land has grey or woolly tea-tree and white swamp gums scattered about in picturesque groups. It is already "landscaped" for someone . . .' Two years later C. B. Frond continued her theme, noting changes in garden style to a more naturalistic look.

> *Australian plants are so familiar in gardens now, we scarcely remember the time when only a few kinds were cultivated instead of scores. The Australian flora has won the hearts of garden lovers; even the crusty old conservative who once looked upon acacias as weeds finds room for wild flowers tamed.*

It should not be assumed, though, that this early support for native plants constituted any kind of ground swell, and the gardening press – both magazine writers and correspondents for daily newspapers like the *Argus* – still concentrated on exotic plants and 'traditional' gardening information. Olive Mellor noted in *Australian Home Beautiful* in 1938 that only twice in her twenty or so years of practice had she been asked to design a native garden. Her chapter on 'Planning a Native Garden' in the 1939 publication, *Australian Gardening of To-Day Illustrated*, is notable more for its cramming of almost eighty different species around the perimeter of a standard suburban block than for any great design achievement. She wrote of this garden plan: 'The word native always brings to mind something free and restful, with nothing prim or formal, so the lines are generous and the planting random . . .'

This book's editor, W. A. Shum, noted in his introduction that it should prove 'of world-wide interest, for it includes . . . the widest and most accurate description of native flora obtainable'. The first section comprised forty-four articles dealing with every imaginable phase of domestic gardening and written by 'Leading Authorities'. As noted, Mr Shum edited

Australian Home Beautiful and it was a measure of the esteem in which the magazine's gardening coverage was held that he was able to attract for his book 'name' contributors like E. G. Waterhouse, A. S. Thomas, P. Crosbie Morrison and Edna Walling. Apart from the Olive Mellor article referred to above, only a handful of these writers dealt with native plants (Edwin Ashby on shrubs, C. B. Frond and W. H. Nicholls on orchids), but accounting for more than half the 768 pages was a comprehensive garden encyclopaedia. Bill Shum proudly noted that this brought together for the first time the known genera of Australian plants, although not all the species. These were included with their botanical names as part of the full range of gardening lore, listed alphabetically with exotic plants, pests and diseases, garden equipment and techniques.

Inadequate and uncertain supply was a problem for native plant enthusiasts, as Ellis found when he began looking for these plants for his own garden. As early as 1930 the Coburg nurseryman James Railton had been quoted as saying native plants offered 'an untilled and very promising field for the hybridist', yet complaints were heard throughout the 30s about the paucity of plants available to gardeners, compared with the almost untapped wealth growing wild and not yet brought into garden cultivation. Olive Mellor commented in 1938 on the home gardener's 'limited field' of native flora, and Edna Walling also bemoaned this:

> *We do seem to have rather an unfortunate genius for propagating the least attractive of the native plants, and of allowing hundreds of treasures to go unseen in the wilds . . . Of course all that can be done to protect and help their increase in the bush must be done, but one would like to see some of the best of them more frequently propagated by some enterprising nurseryman. Again and again one hears 'I did try a few natives, but they were left on my hands'.*

Two years later she commended two unnamed nurserymen in New South Wales and in Kew, Victoria – 'blessings upon their heads!' – who were propagating and making available 'two of the most beautiful plants in the world', the natives, *Callitris collumellaris* (cypress pine) and *Eriostemon obovalis flore pleno* (the double fairy waxflower).

Probably one of the nurserymen was George Althofer at Dripstone, near Wellington in New South Wales. He had begun growing native plants in his garden in 1932, establishing his Nindethana nursery in 1938 as a local industry, under primitive conditions using only dam and tank water. It grew quickly, and from the 1940s he found an expanded market, introducing many species and sending plants Australia-wide and to New Zealand, the United States, England, Ireland and to countries in Europe. His early contacts with local enthusiasts included notable names like Edwin Ashby and William Burdett in South Australia, and Ivo Hammett, Bill Cane and the Lindner brothers in Victoria. At this stage these enthusiasts were growing Australian plants out of botanical interest or for conservation reasons, as was Althofer, rather than for any nationalistic or aesthetic sentiment.

His initial one-page catalogue quickly swelled, so that by 1954 he was producing a sixty-two page illustrated catalogue including thousands of species, many of which he described as 'one of the best'. Using a

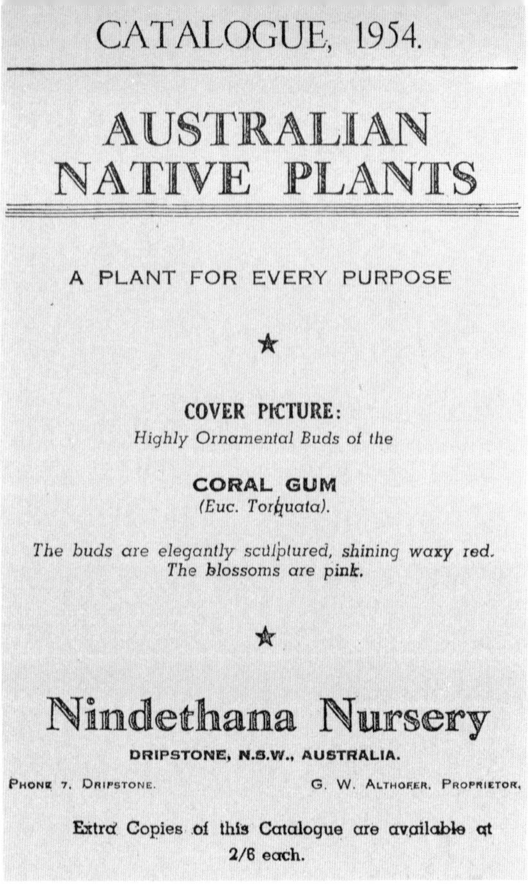
CATALOGUE, 1954.

AUSTRALIAN NATIVE PLANTS

A PLANT FOR EVERY PURPOSE

★

COVER PICTURE:
Highly Ornamental Buds of the

CORAL GUM
(Euc. Torquata).

The buds are elegantly sculptured, shining waxy red. The blossoms are pink.

★

Nindethana Nursery

DRIPSTONE, N.S.W., AUSTRALIA.

PHONE 7, DRIPSTONE. G. W. ALTHOFER, PROPRIETOR.

Extra Copies of this Catalogue are available at 2/6 each.

George Althofer's illustrated 62-page catalogue for 1954 included a wide range of native plants and advice for growers.

statewide 'SOS' section in his catalogue to solicit plants he wanted, from towering trees to small, scrambling shrubs and rare lilies, he collected seed Australia-wide and even in Europe. He once noticed a strange acacia listed in a French seed catalogue, and ordered it – to find to his surprise, when the resultant seedlings grew to maturity, that he had hundreds of the same species almost on his back doorstep. An acacia native to the Dripstone area had travelled to Europe, where it had been given a garden name! Ellis ordered several packages of plants during the 1940s and 1950s, mostly single plants of eucalypts, grevilleas and hakeas. George Althofer remembered him as 'one of several hundred customers' during that time, and corresponded spasmodically with him.

Althofer's pre-eminent role was acknowledged by the wildflower expert Thistle Harris in her second book, *Australian Plants for the Garden*, which was published in 1953 (fifteen years after her *Wild Flowers of Australia*, and two years after Jean Galbraith's invaluable handbook, *Wild Flowers of Victoria*). She wrote: 'For assistance in the technique of cultivation I have called on the knowledge possessed by several of my friends and acquaintances. To my old friend George A. Althofer . . . I owe the greatest debt in this regard.' Her new book was predominantly practical, introducing gardeners to native plants suitable for conditions from bog gardens to window-boxes, for 'special uses' like windbreaks, avenues and gardens large and small, and advising them how to grow the plants. But its philosophy was wide-ranging and its focus clear. She aimed at the average garden-lover –'that legion that knows the joy of planning and planting and arranging the garden of dreams'. To help the dreams along, she provided (with a little help from Edna Walling, who contributed 'base garden plans') no fewer than seventeen different garden plans for a range of sites, with extensive planting lists, each keyed to soil type and to situation in terms of aspect and prevailing winds. The plans were on simple lines, she wrote, for gardeners of only slight experience; they made no allowance for exotic plants nor even for a small kitchen garden 'for this book deals only with Australian native plants'. Throughout, she stressed the need to consider the plants' natural habitat, and she warned that gardeners could be in for surprises and disappointments. 'You must be prepared to take some chances with your native garden . . . But it is only in this way that you will come to know the potentialities of our extraordinarily diverse and beautiful flora.'

Despite the overall paucity of information about native plants which bothered Edna Walling, by the late 1930s she was not only writing about them and praising the way they looked in nature, but beginning to use them in her gardens. Her motive was design rather than horticultural interest. She used them in 1937 in an Ivanhoe garden for Fred and Peggy Grassick, the brother and sister-in-law of Emily Gibson. The Grassicks asked for native plants in one section of the garden, because Mr Grassick felt they would require little upkeep. Edna Walling had already prepared a beautiful plan in traditional vein for the garden as a whole, but she jumped at the chance of specifying native plants – 'she was beginning to think that way', Mrs Grassick recalled – and she suggested leptospermums, hakeas, prostantheras and the like, with occasional larger acacias and eucalypts. The native plantings were combined with some typical Walling effects; Mrs Grassick remembered masses of daffodils ('Queen of the North', 'Buttercup', 'Emperor') growing through the grass and blooming in a shout of gold beneath a grove of *Acacia longifolia*. She said Edna Walling, however, never considered this garden 'one of hers'. And it was not an unqualified success, because most of the plants failed to thrive. Some came from George Althofer, a sure source, but plants bought from local nurseries – 'they never knew how to handle native stock' – proved pot-bound.

Walling's enthusiasm was well and truly kindled. 'Let's talk about Australian trees and shrubs!' she wrote in *Australian Home Beautiful* in April 1938. 'Let us see what there is in the local catalogues that we could plant with a reasonable hope of enjoyment.' And she listed *Baeckia plicata, Eriostemon myoporoides, Leptospermum laevigatum, Prostanthera ovalifolia* and *Tristania laurina* – although she was not sure whether or not *Tristania* was a native (a reader put her right the following month). At the same time she altered the signature below her column, which for some years had read 'Yours deciduously', to a simple 'Yours'. When, that year, Thistle Harris's book *Wild Flowers of Australia* was published, Walling is said to have driven in one day from Melbourne to Sydney to talk to her about it.

Australian Home Beautiful reported in 1940 on a garden Walling had designed for a new house in Toorak, planted mostly with Australian shrubs and trees; the writer (John Seymour) described this as unusual 'because so few home lovers give Australian flora half the use it deserves'. In 1944 she designed a native garden in the Melbourne suburb of Kew, where she used acacias, callistemons and *Eucalyptus citriodora* as well as 'lots of little creepy crawly things' that didn't survive the client's young children. (She also planted up to three trees in one hole, a technique that Walter Burley Griffin had used twenty years earlier when he landscaped a subdivision in Heidelberg with Australian plants.) And as noted, from the mid-1940s her Home Beautiful column – her major journalistic outlet, influential and widely read – looked almost exclusively at the merits of Australian plants both as a design feature in the home garden, and in the wider landscape. In a column entitled 'Recipe for a Native Garden' (reprinted in 1948 in her book *A Gardener's Log*) she suggested:

> . . . *a regular sheet of* Thryptomene mitchellii, *prostantheras behind and adjacent to them, then clumps of the lemon scented tea-tree,* Leptospermum citratum, *and* Eriostemon neriifolium *in the foreground, masses of* Eriostemon *in front of the coastal tea-tree* (Leptospermum laevigatum) *in the dry spots, with* Callitris cupressiformis *at the very back. This will be a lovely native garden. Many a half-acre could be delightfully treated in this way, and be easy to maintain when once established.*

1947 saw the opening of Bernhardt Schubert's nursery for native plants – Melbourne's first such nursery – in the suburb of Noble Park. Previously he and his wife Dulcie had operated from their backyard in Oakleigh, and from the Grampians in Western Victoria. In the nursery's first years of operation public reaction was apathetic, but native plant enthusiasts offered encouragement, while as Ben Schubert's beautiful display garden grew up and matured, it provided an object lesson for landscapers who sought to use the plants for aesthetic effect, including Edna Walling, Ellis Stones – he carried out rockwork there in the mid-1950s – and, later, Glen Wilson. Soon after Schubert had set up at Noble Park, Edna Walling took him to Holbrook in New South Wales to advise her on native plants for use at 'Kildrummie', where she was designing a garden for Douglas and Margaret Carnegie. Eric Hammond did the initial building work, including a ha-ha wall constructed under Walling's supervision, but she took Ellis Stones with her, too, to build a series of lyrical sweeping low stone walls. This was an instance where she did not allow Ellis to go ahead in his own way – she decided exactly where he should put the walls, and their height and width. Ellis is remembered continually asking questions about the Australian plants being used in the garden – 'he was obviously learning' observed the clients, Douglas and Margaret Carnegie. No doubt Walling was too, else she would not have had Schubert there as a consultant. By the early 1950s she had almost completely rejected exotic plants in favour of native plants in her garden designs, a change that is said by Eric Hammond to have occurred almost overnight. Perhaps it did, but obviously it had been brewing for some years prior to that.

Much later, in 1965, Walling recalled with fond amusement how she had hated working on the Australian border during her student days at Burnley Horticultural College . . . 'The one lady instructor was so crazy about this particular border that it put me off it, I think. How little I knew that I was to live to appreciate native plants so much . . .' It was about this time, after a period of almost one-eyed devotion to native plants and only six years before the end of her life, that she became reconverted to the merits of exotic species.

As for Ellis Stones, he had begun using Australian plants where possible in the late 1930s, in the garden commissions that he gained independently of Edna Walling (where he was responsible for the whole garden, and

Low stone walls at 'Kildrummie', Holbrook, NSW – designed by Edna Walling, built by Ellis Stones.

not just walls and outcrops). Native plants were tucked into crevices beside the pebbled stream he created in the Flack garden in South Yarra (c.1938), and into his display garden in the Treasury Gardens (c.1939). In later life he told a friend and colleague that when he started to work on rock gardens he found the exotic plants he placed beside the rocks somehow unsatisfactory, and remembered instead his childhood experiences around Euroa, and the look of the plants that grew naturally around the rocks there. (Thistle Harris advised in *Australian Plants for the Garden* that because introduced rockery work must be made to look like part of the landscape, gardeners seeking to build rockeries or outcrops should first study natural rock formations. 'Rock gardening is an important aspect of Australian landscape architecture', she wrote, 'for many of our plants grow naturally in rocky formations . . .')

In his early days of practice, Ellis found it hard to locate a wide enough range of native plants. Always he would stop at any nursery he passed, to see what was in stock. As well, he would ask Olive to phone round the nurseries to check what they had. 'It was ring, ring, ring . . .', she recalled. One source was the fine, now defunct, nursery of Sparks and McAlpine in Box Hill, which advertised in September 1942 that it specialised in Australian native shrubs, trees and climbers. The same year an article in *The Home Gardener* extolled Sparks and McAlpine's wide range, including five varieties of *Prostanthera* and several unusual grevilleas. Later, Ellis bought from Althofer, Schubert, and Boddy's Eastern Park nursery at Geelong, and during the early 1950s he stocked some native plants in the small nursery he ran in Ivanhoe. From the outset, Olive Stones said, people would resist his arguments in favour of native plants, because they were thought to lack flowers. His usual response was: 'Give me a chance, and I'll give you a native garden which has flowers all year round'.

Debate is heard often on whether it was Edna Walling or Ellis Stones who first promoted Australian plants in designs for domestic gardens. Since both began to use them at about the same time, in the late 1930s, it seems probable that they were responding more or less spontaneously to a trend emerging from the background of limited, horticulturally based 'special interest' that had been building in the years prior to that, and to their own independent observations of nature and the Australian bush. But there is no doubt that Walling's acknowledged position as an authority on garden design – and, increasingly, landscape – made hers the major influence. Ellis affirmed this in 1971 in his unpublished tribute to her:

> *When I first met her she was designing . . . along the lines of the English cottage gardens . . . but she changed to using mostly Australian native plants. At that time there was not the demand there is now. I think her influence helped to alter the approach to plants, with a switch to Australian natives.*

In 1949 he travelled to Ocean Grove near Geelong to lay out a garden around a new house for Mrs Inez Thornthwaite. This was not an easy job as there was a big fall across the block, but to this day the drainage and rock work are perfect. He laid a clay foundation along the winding paths and across the backyard; the stone walls are cemented rather than

Ellis clowning 'on the job' at the Thornthwaite garden, Ocean Grove, c.1950.

The garden was fitted onto a bare site around a new house.

dry. (He preferred to build dry-stone walls, but Mrs Thornthwaite was afraid that snails would hide in the cracks.) A feature is a lovely set of circular stone steps, which grow in beauty year by year. Originally he planted most of this garden with native plants – tea-trees of different colours, kangaroo paws, grevilleas – set in shrubberies to protect the garden from the prevailing easterlies, but he also used birch trees.

He did the job quickly, with immense enthusiasm, and the client felt at completion that it had been properly done, and her money well spent. 'He often came back to look at it, he was always interested to see how things were going. Once, quite a few years after he had finished, he came down and most of the native plants were looking pretty sick. He told me I'd better take them out and put in something else, perhaps hydrangeas. I did keep a lot of the tea-trees though, for shelter.' Ellis had been recommended to her by Russell Grimwade. 'He and Mab came one day while the house was being built and I said I was in a daze about what to do with the garden. He told me I ought to get hold of Ellis Stones, who had a great future and tremendous skill with native plants. The garden has been an endless source of interest and pleasure to me ever since.'

The circular stone steps have become lovelier with the years.

Construction photograph of the Thornthwaite garden shows stone walls and circular steps.

NINE

Of paving and planting

The years immediately after the Second World War saw great creative expansion in Australia. In Victoria the designer Alistair Knox was making his presence felt as he designed mud-brick houses in and around Eltham, on Melbourne's outer fringe. He employed returned servicemen, struggling artists, and members of Justus Jorgensen's artists' colony at Montsalvat to build his houses while he worked as a bank clerk, and studied building at night classes at the Royal Melbourne Institute of Technology.

This view looking down from the second level of the Busst house (1948) demonstrates Knox's use of heavy timbers, rendered surfaces, unusual window apertures and paved floors.

Knox's houses were different not only in the material used for their construction – which had been used first in Eltham by Peter Glass, in a cottage built in 1938 – but in their design methods. The mud-brick walls rose from concrete slabs said to be the first in Australia; the bricks proved a stumbling block for local shire engineers and councils, who in Eltham issued Knox with a building permit for his first house only after he found and presented an expert pamphlet validating this centuries-old method of building. The roofs of his houses were flat, the walls thick, the windows placed to admit uninterrupted light, and he incorporated natural materials like heavy, untreated timber and stone flooring to give an effect that was new for suburban Australia. They demanded gardens very different from the accepted suburban versions of the day, which Knox categorised as:

> *. . . guided by nurserymen who concentrated on horticultural gardens featuring asphalt or concrete drives, herbaceous borders, hollyhock corners with torulosa and lambertiana hedges rising darkly green behind them. Flower beds of azaleas, rhododendrons and other Himalayan exotica, surrounded by edging of lavender and forget-me-not occupied the centre of lawns. These were complemented with cannas, snapdragons and giant petunias to provide 'colour'. Oaks and chestnuts were for bigger gardens with branches of 'triumphant' palm rustling together in the wind, accompanied by the raucous Indian mynahs squabbling in the midst of the half-ripened dates. Only a rare eucalyptus was allowed to flourish because of their continual shedding leaves and the English lawn-destroying habits.*

No doubt this was why so often he was to suggest to his clients that they use Ellis Stones (or Gordon Ford, who trained with Ellis in the early 1950s before starting on his own as a landscaper) for garden design.

In 1949 he asked Ellis to work on the surrounds of a new house and garden on a twenty-five acre site fronting the Yarra River at Eltham. The simple mud-brick house was a weekender; not a lot of 'landscaping' was needed, because the clients, 'Dick' Downing and Dorian Le Gallienne, had a deep love of the natural bush, which was allowed to run almost to the walls of the house. But it was the start of a long and fruitful working relationship. Ellis and Alistair Knox had met that year through Alistair's future wife, Margot. Eighteen years old and an art student, she lived in a bungalow in Ivanhoe behind a house owned by a local identity who was a keen gardener. Perhaps worried about how regular an impecunious art student might be in paying the rent, the landlord suggested to her tenant that she would be good at gardening, and inquired about job opportunities at a nursery around the corner from her house. This led Margot to Ellis Stones. Immediately he began to teach her the rudiments of stonework and paving – he told her women had an instinctive feeling for working with stone. Always he liked to employ women, explaining once to Alistair Knox that they were easier to hire part-time, they cost less – cash flow, as ever, being a problem – they were uncomplaining and often superior to men at the work, in particular being very careful with planting. It has been said that he and Knox (whose foreman during the

A large expanse of random slate paving, with retaining walls, at a garden near Eltham (1951). The Warrandyte stone for the walls was quarried on the property.

1940s was the redoubtable Sonia Skipper) were the first male employers in Victoria to use women on building sites.

In 1951 Margot Knox laid a vast terrace of random slate for Ellis outside a large old house near Eltham. The house had been added to several times and Ellis felt a broad expanse of paving would help unify the disparate styles of architecture. He found long stints at this task difficult, due to his painful knee, so it fell to Margot to do the bulk of the work while Bob Crosbie built the associated retaining walls and advised on the paving. It was winter, and she froze on the high, exposed site, which commanded views of the mountains on one side and the sea on the other. She was starving as well, having left home usually after only a meagre breakfast.

This was not the only job on which she found herself hungry and working alone. Generally Ellis would collect her in his old bull-nosed Morris Cowley, fitted with a tray on the back, he would deposit her and get the day's work under way, then head off round the corner to buy buns for morning tea. Waylaid at other jobs, more often than not he did not return until evening, and then without the buns. Margot put up with it because she was young and eager, she enjoyed the work and his company, and was fascinated with the effects he could achieve.

She watched him 'sculpt' the landscape, shuffling around dragging hoses behind him to delineate planting beds and put some interest into the predictable contours of flat, ordinary suburban blocks. His ideas were in advance of their time, she later realised. 'He was so much ahead of people in his thinking that either he had to beg and plead to get them to accept small but important features of his designs, or he had to relate these to aspects of daily living which they could understand. For instance, he was keen on seats in gardens. "Wouldn't you like somewhere to sit in the garden and do the beans?" he would ask. They absolutely loved that.' Margot Knox admired his talent for discovering simple features like these that clients instinctively wanted in their gardens, little things that would delight them but they wouldn't have thought of unprompted. 'They would ask him to bring the path in at a particular spot. He'd inquire: ''Which way do you ordinarily walk?'' They'd say: ''We usually come up here but we're going to . . .'' And he'd say: ''You'll usually *always* come up here''.' He would plot the path so that it provided the most logical route from one point to another, then effortlessly he would introduce features to turn it into a natural walkway, full of interest and variety. His maxim, she recalled, was always that gardens were for people. He adored his work, he had a simple way of talking to clients to which they instinctively responded, and most of his clients loved him, particularly the women. 'They thought they'd found a gem in this little man. He often took ages to get round to a job, but most people were prepared to wait until he could come.'

To this day she remembers Ellis's lessons about random paving (he didn't use the popular term 'crazy' paving). 'Break your joints – long cement joints between slabs look dreadful. Use your biggest and best pieces of stone where the treads go – coming out of a door or up a step – for maximum impact. Make every piece of stone work for you; don't hunt round for a piece exactly the right size but cut the one you pick up to shape.' He was particularly firm about initial blocking out of the *whole* site, and about levels. 'I lived in fear of having a puddle in the paving.'

Margot Knox, c.1951.

The jobs during her three or four years' employment usually involved small gardens, with a steady flow of work: the clients were a varied lot. As well as local clients there was a complement of what she called interesting eccentric women, chief among them Mrs Donaldson in Heidelberg, 'an incredible person who loved altering her house and garden and who used to rush round with a three-foot rule singing out for "Sto-o-o-nesy"'. There were several gardens in Fairfield, running down to the Yarra River; there were jobs for wealthy clients in Toorak. Margot describes herself in those days as scruffy on the job: 'I was dark and a bit grubby and gipsy-looking, terrible really, and his daughter Pat, who also worked for him, had beautiful tidy blonde hair and immaculate blue clothes. I remember Rocky saying once in the nicest possible way but a bit plaintively: "Try and diddle yourself up just a little bit for the clients?"'

He was using native plants at this stage, she says, but she felt this was instinctive rather than a matter of philosophy. He neither talked to her about it, nor explained why, it was simply a question of choosing certain plants because they achieved the effects he wanted. But he was not rigorous, often mixing native and exotic plants – and this she does remember him discussing, saying he didn't want to be a purist. In the same way, he liked to use certain exotic plants for particular effects. Cinerarias, for instance, were planted boldly to brighten up dark corners of the garden.

Native plants were his immediate solution in the garden at Mt Pleasant, near Eltham, where Margot had proved such a sterling paver. His client remembered him as 'a darling old thing, a really good egg who worked terribly hard, madly enthusiastic about his work, particularly natives, which weren't popular then. We had a dam, but not big enough for watering the garden, and he said the obvious solution was to plant natives.' She had thought in terms of rhododendrons and azaleas and roses. He wasn't keen but he capitulated to a degree, confining these plants to curving

Ellis retained several large eucalypts in the Eltham garden, adding timber sleeper seats nearby (and a curved stone seat near the barbecue). His characteristic low planting beds, with occasional boulders, also typified this garden.

beds off the terrace and near the house. The rest of his planting here was native – except for a weeping elm installed in the middle of the terrace to provide a shady sitting spot (at the owner's request, he noted in *Australian Garden Design*). A bed of natives around the new fish-pond included a decorative *Melaleuca encara* that hung out over the water. A long, low stone sitting wall curved around the lawn. The client recalled: 'He did a gorgeous job on the garden. I was fascinated by the way he mulched all the new plants, I'd never seen anything like that. He was always trying to get some atmosphere into the place; he gave us a hitching-post for all the people who, he thought, would be visiting us on horseback. No-one ever did!' (Margot Knox says fondly that he was 'as corny as Kelloggs' Corn Flakes'.) He is remembered, too, for his gentleness when a small daughter of the house pulled off her fingernail in an accident – he calmed the agitated mother and daughter and rushed them to the doctor in his own truck – for his cheerfulness and the way he 'never stopped working', and for his renovation job in 1956 when the garden opened to raise money for the Olympic Games. He arrived with truck-loads of flowering potted plants and buried them in the garden beds for instant effect – a technique he had learned years earlier while working at the Harold Darling garden in Toorak. 'Doing a Rocky Stones' quickly became the family description of a quick clean-up.

Another paving job for Margot Knox was the interior and terraces at 'Stella Park', a house built in Templestowe in 1952 for Guelda Pyke and her sister, Polly. The sisters and two fellow artists, also women, had acquired part of the first property in that traditional orchard area to be sold for subdivision. At that time it was seen as particularly daring to move to what seemed like the country; they found it hard to get used to the lack of city lights at night. Each chose a five-acre patch and built a house designed by Alistair Knox. Unlike later subdividers, they cleared

Random paving carried out by Margot Knox, under Ellis's direction, inside the house at 'Stella Park', Templestowe, c.1952.

only enough trees for construction of their houses, so that to this day their land still boasts some original windbreak pines – planted by the early orchardists – and fruit trees. Building was an expensive process and, strong-willed and independent women, they were exacting clients, knowing exactly the effect and the decor they wanted. When it came to the garden their funds were almost exhausted. They tried to landscape it themselves with little success, then called in Ellis Stones. 'He was very much in vogue then, everyone wanted him.' Trying to pin him down was difficult, but eventually he turned up and created a simple environment of flowing curves, occasional boulders and pebbled terraces around the house that, the sisters maintain, taught them a great deal about garden design. They were struck by the way the rocks he placed looked as though they had been there for ever. He observed that it was a pity people usually sank all their money into their houses, leaving nothing for the garden; he told them that the garden belonged to the house and the house to the garden.

A year or two earlier Ellis had had the chance to lease a small piece of land in Lower Heidelberg Road, around the corner from his own house. He thought he could grow native plants there, then decided to begin a small nursery, seeing it both as a handy source of plants for the gardens he was designing, and as a kind of shopfront. Olive manned it most days (even on the morning of their daughter Lesley's wedding), but on Saturday mornings when he was not busy on a job or working in the country, Ellis made a point of being there to help, to answer questions and meet prospective clients.

It has been said that at this nursery Ellis stocked a better-than-average range of native plants. Some clients of the day recall it as an ordinary general nursery, offering a bit of everything, while the teenager who worked there on Saturday mornings, public holidays and occasionally after school remembers no special emphasis on native plants. But it could be argued that this reflects a general lack of awareness of native plants among suburban gardeners in the early 1950s. A friend with whom Ellis used to go camping in the country and who shared with him a love of the Australian bush said the nursery stock included 'a lot of natives'. Another friend whose tastes ran to azaleas, rhododendrons and camellias remembered Ellis as 'always pushing the natives. At first I wasn't keen on them but he would say "Look at the delicate flowers" and he did teach me to love them.' ('Our flowers are modest; they do not swagger', Betty Maloney and Jean Walker were to write fifteen years later in their fine book, *Designing Australian Bush Gardens*, '. . . be endeared by their gentleness, their wild charm and untamed loveliness'.)

A cyclone fence ran across the front of the narrow, sloping block, set back to allow for footpath display of plants and seedlings. A picturesque crab apple tree grew to one side, against the wall of the neighbouring garage. Wide, shallow steps edged with typical Stones boulders led down past the plants for sale towards the back of the deep block, where Ellis installed a small garden shed-cum-office. Behind this he and Genevieve Poulter, his teenage helper, potted up and propagated slips and cuttings. (Ellis, she said, grew some of his own stock. More was brought in by a fellow nurseryman, Jack Blakey, who owned a delivery truck. Since Olive did not drive and Ellis did not have the time, Jack Blakey – who later worked for Ellis as a driver and labourer – would collect orders for him from the Victoria Market, as required.) The daughter of friends and neighbours, Genevieve had expected simply to serve and not to learn, but Ellis taught her a great deal and she remembered him as 'companionable and nice to work with – you didn't have to talk, we would stand alongside each other and he'd explain what we were doing, crocking, the different grades of sand for potting and so on, and if there were silences it didn't matter'. All the stock was good and healthy; broken plants had to be rejuvenated and tidied up before they went on display. Ellis was always concerned to carry a wide range and, unlike many nurseries, would have plants in stock out of their flowering season. Always he was willing to search out a special plant for a customer.

Saturday mornings were the busiest time, with a steady stream of customers asking for plants (vegetable seedlings were always in demand) or for general advice. Some of the latter came because they had seen and liked gardens that Ellis had designed for friends – a large percentage of his work was still local, in Heidelberg and Ivanhoe – others because they had seen his signboard on jobs and wanted to talk to him. For the helpers there were cream puffs for morning tea, the money coming out of the till.

Order books from the nursery for 1952–54 are an indication of what was being planted then in suburban gardens. Most orders included a couple of native plants, usually listed at the end, perhaps a tea-tree or an acacia. A Hawthorn gardener ordered a burgundy gaillarda, which Ellis marked 'unobtainable'. There were variegated weigelas, boxes of annuals, roses, lupins, delphiniums and 'snaps'. For one gardener a large order included hypericums, eriocephalus, helianthemums and 'ferny things'; another gardener from Clayton wanted birches (silver and cut-leaf), luculias, *Camellia sasanqua*, orange and lemon trees, golden laburnum and hibiscus. By contrast, a Dr Monk in Heidelberg put in a large order for native plants – among them *Eucalyptus torquata, E. preissiana, Cassia, Hypocalymma robustum, Melaleuca fulgens*, native pomegranate and weeping callistemon. (Several of these names were misspelled, a common occurrence.) Planting was continuing at Mrs Thornthwaite's garden at Ocean Grove with an order for 'torquata gum, 20 ghost gums and banksia'. And a very large mixed order for H. Walters at Narre Warren listed alpines, and a Geraldton waxplant.

Ellis had met Harry Walters, a Prahran licensed grocer, in late 1945 when Mrs Walters, a keen gardener, engaged him to renovate the garden of their house in Lower Malvern Road. A receipt for this job from Haydocks cartage contractor came to £15 for six yards of rockery stone, twelve yards of Morabin [*sic*] soil, sand and screenings. For the back garden, Ellis invoiced Mr Walters for these plants; 'Amelancia', fifteen bearded iris at one shilling each, hydrangea, rudbeckia, daffodils, crocus, 'Erigion', black bamboo at £1 5s, twenty-four roses at two shillings each, and rocks. Three years later Harry Walters bought a dairy farm at Narre Warren North, where both house and garden needed attention. He had the house extended and, since the area was very wet, put in a concrete drive and pathways around the house. Then Ellis was asked to create a garden in the one and a half acre house paddock where the only planting was grass, a lemon tree and a distant row of pines.

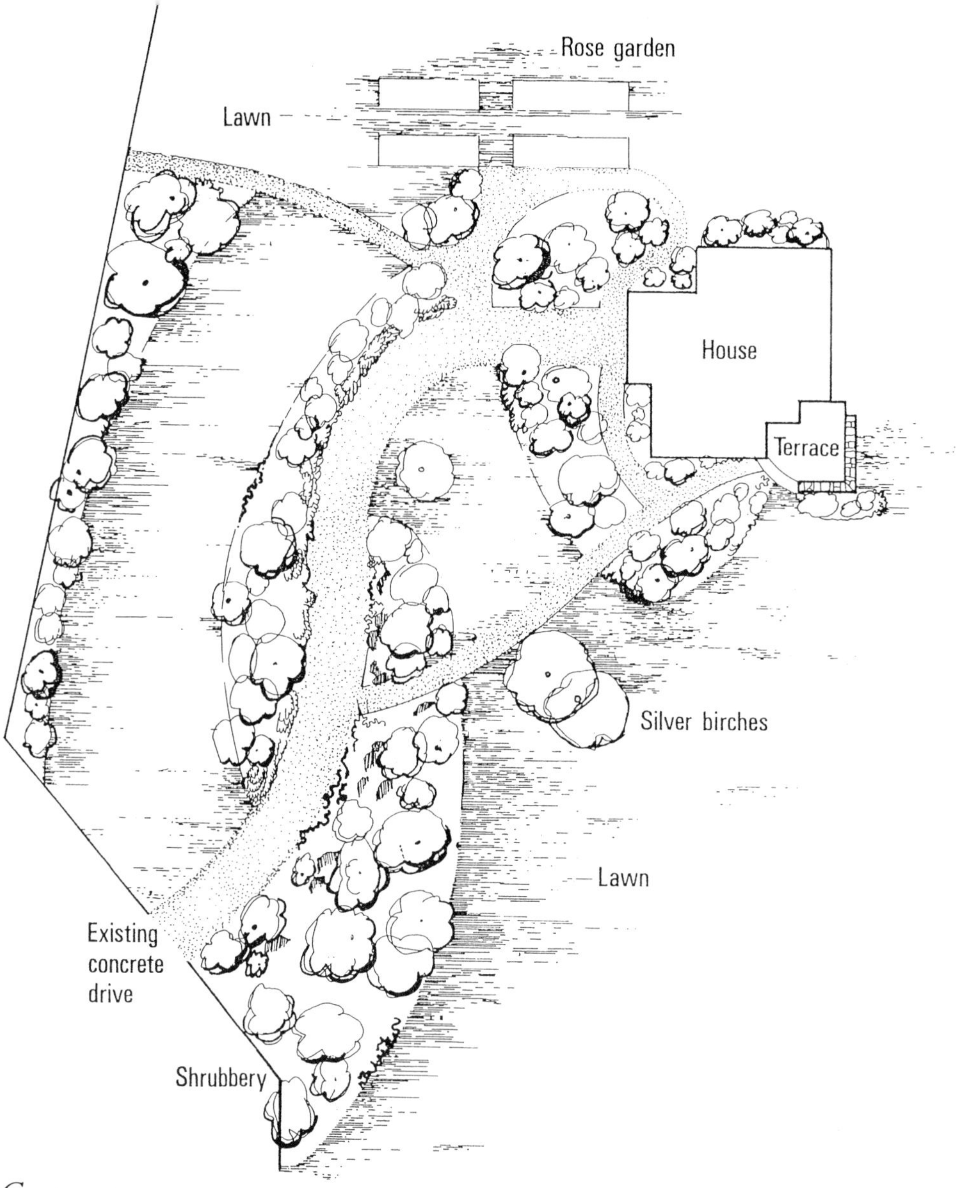

Garden plan at Narre Warren (c.1949) showing how dense planting was used to camouflage the existing ugly concrete drive and paths.

Some years after planting, the ugly concrete drive no longer stood out.

Ellis was keen on 'before and after' views of his jobs, and this was one of his most graphic. His book *Australian Garden Design* includes bald black and white photographs of the 'ugly and depressing' drive and pathways and a description of them as an additional problem for the landscape architect. He writes: 'When the designer is confronted with an ugly feature which cannot be removed or totally hidden, remember that the eye is attracted to a beautiful as well as an ugly object'.

He solved the problem with lawn, shrubs, and carefully placed trees to create a changing landscape where generous swathes of densely planted shrubs and occasional outcrops gave way to longer vistas of grass and trees, in which the concrete paths and drive no longer stood out. The 'lawn' was not lawn as such, but the paddock grasses regularly mown. Low shrubs hung over the verge of the paths and taller shrubs extended over these at head-height, softening the hard lines. Some shrubs were lifted from the Malvern Road garden and replanted, many others were bought in. Mrs Walters wanted a formal rose garden, which Ellis laid out in the only part of the garden he levelled, but perhaps in mute protest, the entrance to the grid of standard roses ran down through a subtle rock outcrop whose steps and large boulders he planted with low-growing alpines. Rock for outcrops was excavated from a hill on the property one hot, hard-working summer. Ellis, his men and the Walters (Harry and his son Max, home on school holidays) levered huge moss-covered rocks out of the ground, transporting them to the garden with a horse and sled. The making of the garden was happy and fun-filled. 'Father was a great one for good-natured banter and he and Ellis bounced off each other.' A photograph shows him seated, grinning, beside the house with Harry Walters and two workmen. On the job he bobbed up constantly, camera in hand.

Not only was Ellis required to create an overall landscape; he was asked to 'make something' of the front entrance to the house, a bare pergola over a concrete and wooden porch floor. He tore up the floor, enlarged the area and paved it with random slate, extended the pergola

Smoko by the front door – Harry Walters second from left, Ellis seated next to him.

*E*llis enlarged the patio, paving it in random slate and building low stone 'sitting-walls'. Careful planting transformed the scene, as shown in photographs taken around 1957, and in the late 1960s.

and planted wisteria at its base. Then he built a small stone sitting-wall to enclose the area, planting beyond it a white *Prunus serrulata* 'Mt Fuji' and a strong-growing *Euphorbia*. 'When in bloom', he wrote twenty years later, 'this combination of green and white delights the eye' – and he used it in several other gardens. Utilising his skills as a carpenter, he also built for Harry Walters a picturesque tea-tree enclosure to screen an outhouse and the woodshed – a simple, eloquent piece of bush carpentry. To set it off he knocked up a rustic garden seat of the kind that today makes antique dealers salivate.

A reporter from the *Australian Women's Weekly* visited the garden in 1957, after some five years' growth, and was favourably impressed. Her article, illustrated with colour photographs, described it as an object lesson for home-owners faced with the problem of beautifying a bare site. She wrote of a wilderness transformed, describing the parkland garden as 'a colourful inspiration':

> *. . . the house is set in picturesque surroundings, featuring a slate terrace, formal rose garden, sweeping lawns dotted with shrubs to block out unattractive views and highlight others, and 'outcrops' of granite boulders to give a touch of rugged beauty.*
>
> *Undulating land provided a good basis for landscaping, so Mr Ellis Stones, landscape gardener of Ivanhoe, decided to follow the natural contours even though the concrete paths presented a problem.*
>
> *Since removing the paths would have been costly, he left them and planned the garden to make them less conspicuous.*
>
> *His three reasons for keeping to the natural contours were that the garden is easier to keep than if it were terraced, it is economical, and terracing foreshortens the views . . . The garden has a parkland character with vistas between concentrated shrubberies and silver birch specimen trees dotted over the lawns . . .*

In 1954 Ellis was having such troubles with his bad leg that a major operation – a sympathectomy – was performed on it, in order to increase its blood supply. (This achieved some immediate relief although the old problems of cramp in the calf and pain behind the knee remained.) While he was convalescing Alistair Knox wanted landscaping work done on the new courtyards created by extensions to the Le Gallienne/Downing house on the Yarra, where he and Ellis had begun their professional association. Because Ellis was on crutches it seemed that his physical involvement would be limited, so Gordon Ford was put in charge. But Ellis was not to be suppressed. Knox wrote in his book *We Are What We Stand On*:

> *I coerced him onto the site and placed him in an armchair and told him to direct Gordon (Ford) and another to place the boulders according to his directions. He used to call the heavy work of placing boulders 'the cavemans' annual sports day' and with a series of well-known jokes encouraged them on. When they got one in position, after considerable grunting and bending of crowbars, he could restrain himself no longer. 'That's it!' he would shout and leap up and hop on one leg over to the scene and start ramming earth around the boulder with his crutches.*

Gordon Ford, today one of Melbourne's longest-established landscapers, had worked as a clerk for the Forests Commission before the Second World War. After the war he developed a taste for the outdoor life as he built himself a mud-brick house in Eltham, and worked on similar houses for Alistair Knox. Knox described him as – in those days – the king of the mud-brick makers; a photograph in *Australian Home Beautiful* (June 1948) showed a tow-headed, youthful-looking Ford stamping mud into a mould in front of a half-built mud-brick house, watched by Knox and his co-workers.

At the Downing/Le Gallienne house on the Yarra River, Ellis's landscaping had to complement the surrounding natural bush.

Alistair Knox (left), Tony Jackson and Gordon Ford making mud bricks for a Knox-designed house in 1948.

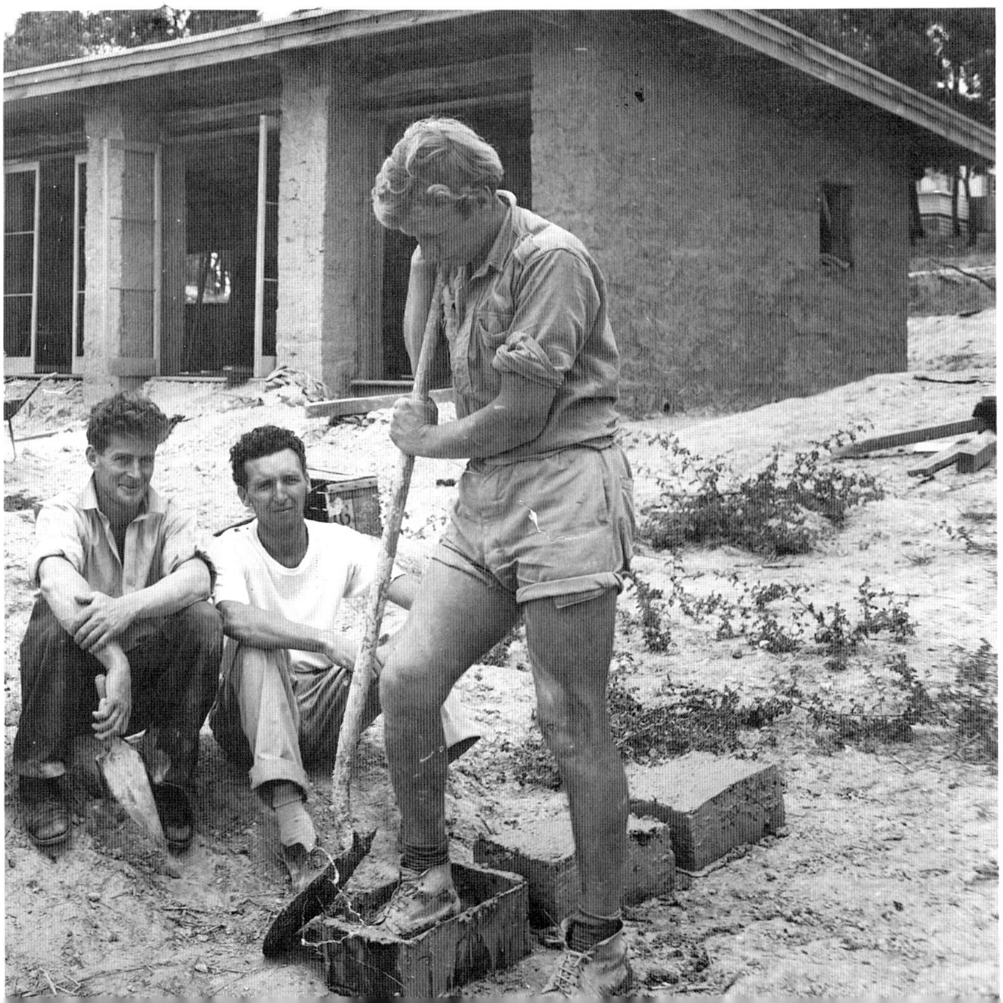

Also working on the Le Gallienne/Downing house was Clifton Pugh, who was employed to help lay and render the mud-brick walls. Pugh was beginning his career as an artist and would call on Alistair Knox for casual employment when times were hard. In this way he, too, came to work for Ellis Stones, digging and moving rocks. For him this was 'spasmodic but pleasant work, quite inspirational. I mean Rocky would talk, he'd get the excitement in his voice, you'd get all inspired and you could turn this back into your own work. Gordon and I were like apprentices, Rocky would organise it and we'd do the manual work. And in doing it you got a visual appreciation – that is something Rocky gave me.'

At the time Clifton Pugh was building his own house at Cottles Bridge, beyond Eltham. Ellis used to visit him there and, Pugh recalls, 'he would talk about things I might be able to do when I'd made some money'. Now known as 'Dunmoochin' and donated to the people of Victoria through the Victorian Conservation Trust, the property was dubbed 'Hunger Ridge' by Alistair Knox because he maintained it ran about a lizard to the acre. Whether a tall tale or not, this Knox story from *Living in the Environment* bears repeating:

> *Cliff had a really good athletic figure. He took to wearing a strong man's leopard skin garment and sandals, ostensibly for natural living and also possibly from justifiable pride in his condition. He would stride through the bush carrying a long-bow with a leopard skin quiver thrown over his shoulder to shoot rabbits. It was an interesting sight. Subsequently he put his leopard skin away for two reasons. The first was that he couldn't hit any rabbits with the bow and arrow. And the second and final blow came when on one of his treks through the scrub he came upon two shooters . . . they caught sight of Cliff with his curly hair, beard, leopard skin clothing, sandals, and bow and arrow. With a gasp of horror they turned simultaneously and ran off at high speed . . . They are probably today regaling their grandchildren in the suburbs with stories about the twentieth-century Wild Man of Cottles Bridge.*

In his two books, Knox told similarly hilarious tales about Gordon Ford – for instance, he had him running naked across a paddock, carting mud bricks six at a time in a wheelbarrow from one building site to another. What an era this must have been at Eltham, which was home to a wide range of artists, musicians, writers and other free spirits! While she was working for Ellis Stones, Margot Knox moved there from Ivanhoe and lived in a converted cable tram, cedar-lined, with a primus stove at one end. How did Ellis react, being in his mid-50s, simple and comparatively conservative? 'Rocky was a bit dumbfounded, but he coped with it because he really liked me. He used to ask occasionally, rather bemusedly, "What's going to happen with your life?" But all that mad mob at Eltham loved him, particularly his basic simplicity.'

Gordon Ford began working for Ellis by chance. He lent him a hand one day to build a dry-stone wall in a garden in Rosanna, and knew immediately that this was how he wanted to spend the rest of his life. 'It was as quick as that. I loved the free form of it. Rocky was just my style of person, too. We clicked right from the jump.' Wisecracking was part of the daily routine. There were hilarious scenes as they met at Ellis's house to begin the day's work, with one having to tow the other around the block to start whichever battered car was refusing to co-operate that day. There were jokes, too, about the clients. 'I mean, some of them were still talking about England as home! This certainly inhibited Rocky's vision of the Australian landscape.'

Both enjoyed physical work, and loved the natural landscape. Gordon says Ellis taught him everything he knows. He showed him how to shape the ground, how to manipulate space and juggle the second and third dimensions, how to obliterate boundaries, how to use timber sleepers – which Ellis introduced in his gardens from the early 1950s – and, most of all, how to place rocks. Gordon learned by example, because Ellis did not often theorise about his work. 'He was intuitive, not a great talker, more of a doer. I wanted to know about landscape principles; he lent me some marvellous books about "Capability" Brown, Humphry Repton, rock and alpine plants.' He remembers two maxims. Ellis would say: 'When in doubt, plant *Spiraea*'. And again and again he would insist: 'Be bold' – when making design decisions and particularly when placing rocks.

Plant nomenclature, however, was an area where Gordon did not find him much help. '"What's that?" I would ask when I saw something I liked in one of his gardens. Rocky would say: "Oh I don't know, can't remember the name now, one of those native things". Shapes is what he was interested in.' So he learned his plant names after hours, taking cases of specimens from Ellis's gardens into the city to Ernest Lord's night classes, and asking that expert to identify them.

Gordon Ford is generous in his praise of Ellis Stones's achievement. His best gardens have a subtle quality all their own, he says. They have unmistakeable style and spirit, engendered by the sculptural quality of the rocks, developed by his handling of space. 'Oh, he knew how to make a bit of mystery in a garden. Go into one of his old gardens and still you can feel the spirit of the old Rocky around.'

TEN

Conservation begins at home

*I*ncreasingly, the Yarra River was a special place for Ellis. His children had grown up splashing in its shallows, he loved its quiet beauty and varied wildlife. He identified with the peace and tranquillity of the river valley that Alistair Knox, living nearby at Eaglemont in the late 1930s, had experienced as 'a place of great light and atmosphere. There was hardly a house to be seen. In the mornings it would be bathed in sunshine except where the mists still lay to mark the meandering course of the Yarra.'

After his daughters had grown up, Ellis continued to spend time at the river with local boys in the First Ivanhoe Sea Scouts (a troop formed in 1908 by 'Skipper' Wilson, who was to train 2000 local scouts in the ensuing thirty-six years); donating a flagpole when the troop's new 'den' was opened in 1944, executing the stone work for a drinking fountain erected immediately after the war in memory of one of the boys who did not come home. Twenty years later he was delighted when his grandsons became members of the troop in their turn.

*M*embers of the First Ivanhoe Sea Scouts pictured in the early 1940s by the Yarra River.

His awareness of the valley's natural beauty was heightened in 1949, as he worked on the surroundings of the Le Gallienne/Downing house on the banks of the Yarra at Eltham. The landscape around this house was magical, with platypus, black wallaby and other animal life, and a great range of bird species, including gang-gang cockatoos. The clients were erudite men with a strongly formed philosophy on the environment. Alistair Knox wrote that around their house they wanted 'no lawns, herbaceous borders, non-indigenous growth or suburban formality. Their tree planting consisted of the concealment of planting, the creation of instinctive masses and voids merging back into wilderness. Natural informal growth came right up to their doors . . .' The building of this house and garden extended in stages over several years and always there was time for exchange of ideas on the job. Knox credited Dorian Le Gallienne with encouraging him to stop being 'clever' in design and to slow down, think simply, and try to relate to the Australian landscape, rather than outdo it. No doubt, Ellis, who instinctively thought this way, would have made his own contribution to the discussions.

He was pleased to be asked in 1951 to work on a garden in Fairfield that ran down a steep slope to the Yarra. The narrow site was some six metres wide; he allowed his design for the deep garden to gradually peter out as it merged with the natural cover towards the water's edge. The client's children had learned to swim in the Yarra almost as they began walking, and the sight of a platypus at the bottom of this garden was not unusual. But as Ellis was working here the environment of the Yarra was altering. Rubbish was beginning to permeate the natural setting – floating down the river from industry upstream, being dumped in the billabongs in Chelsworth Park, one of his favourite haunts – and this greatly perturbed him.

He shared his concern with a dentist, Ken Johnson, who lived locally. Ellis had designed and built a small front garden the previous year at the Johnsons' new house on The Boulevard. It was a pleasing blend of random paving and lawn, with informal planting around the edges and

By the early 1950s the quality of the water in the Yarra River was no longer what it had been when these sea scouts enjoyed a swim in the early 1940s.

a rock retaining wall. The planting was mainly exotic, crab apples (*Malus* 'Gorgeous' and *M.* x *eleyi*), forsythias, ceanothus and abelia, with a patch of tea-tree in one corner. 'He suggested putting in bluebells and snowdrops under the trees', Ken Johnson recalled. 'He brought the plants from his nursery, I thought there weren't enough but he said "You'll have a few holes for a while but it will fill up". He was right.' Noticing the family Christmas tree was growing too large for its pot, Ellis suggested installing it in the garden. The large blue spruce has proved a rich source of memories.

Ivanhoe residents liked to swim in the Yarra at two spots in Chelsworth Park – at Horseshoe Bend and at the '440', so called because it was 440 yards from the other swimming spot. There were sandy beaches, dressing sheds and a local swimming club. When Ken Johnson came to Ivanhoe in 1949 the river water was still relatively clear and three or four untouched billabongs were to be found along from the '440' beach. But after a golf course was created beside the river in the 1940s, golfers complained of losing their balls in the billabongs. Eventually rubbish-dumping began in a dry billabong, bulldozers stripped off topsoil to cover the rubbish, trees died, and local protest began to mobilise.

Heidelberg City Council, which had assumed control of the park (the one-time Chelsworth Farm), had been involved in the rubbish-dumping exercise. Then it began filling more billabongs. Suddenly, access to the '440' was fenced off, and a group that included Ellis Stones and another local protester, Chris Bailey, went out one night to pull down the wire fence. Ellis was involved in drawing up petitions, and when Frank Pound,

Ellis's photograph by the side of a billabong shows a piece of unspoiled bushland.

a family friend and former sea scout, returned to Ivanhoe after several years in the United States, Ellis rushed him down to the river with his new camera and colour film, to photograph the existing trees, billabongs and wildlife. A well-attended protest meeting was held at the town hall and the road re-opened (at the meeting Ellis organised a showing of a film about the effects of pollution on the Potomac River in Washington DC). Then one weekday a local resident noticed a machine digging a trench almost two metres wide from the end of the billabong towards the river. Volunteers, among them Ellis and Ken Johnson, spent the next weekend trying to fill in the trench by hand; eventually the local council was persuaded to bring a bulldozer and help them complete the task. This billabong still exists (although there is little or no water at the end where the trench was dug, and the scar remains). These episodes led to the formation in 1955 of the Ivanhoe River Parklands Protection League. Ellis Stones was its first president.

In August 1954 a letter from Ellis had been published in the metropolitan daily newspaper, the *Argus*. Headed 'Save our bushland', it read:

Are we in the city losing all love of our Australian bush? It seems in this age of hustle very few have time for appreciation of natural beauty, of which there is still a small area left close to Melbourne.

There once existed a beautiful strip of virgin bush along the River Yarra at Ivanhoe, known as Chelsworth Park, with billabongs and gum trees. Unfortunately this is gradually being destroyed. A few years ago the Heidelberg Council, which owns the land, decided to use a dry billabong as a rubbish tip, killing all the trees in that particular area.

The latest move is to use a large portion of this land for golf. Bulldozers have already cleared part of the area of trees right to the river bank. The council already owns a full eighteen-hole golf course adjoining the park. Originally there was a lovely bush track along the river's edge of about two miles, from the swimming pool to Burke Rd bridge. The council has decided to take a large area between two billabongs to put down four golf holes, and use the area containing four existing holes for sports arenas.

Surely with all the present interest in green belts for cities, something can be done to preserve this park in its natural state. The proposal is to plant the Olympic Village with native trees – while at the other side of the city they are busy destroying trees which have been growing in a natural setting for many years.

Is there no way of awakening our councils to the beauty and value of our native flora? Unfortunately those of us who appreciate Nature are made to feel we are sub-normal and should be treated as such. If the State Government could see fit to take it over as a national park, Chelsworth Park could with very little outlay be restored to its former beauty, though minus some of the lovely old trees which have already been destroyed. It has long been a recognised sanctuary for native birds, and there have been platypuses there for many years. It is certainly worth a visit by everyone who enjoys the quiet of the bush.

Surely it is time we, as a nation, began to preserve rather than destroy.

Ellis addresses a protest meeting by the river, c.1954.

This letter appears to be the first public exposition of Ellis's views on conservation, which for the next twenty years he was to promote with occasional fury or with a touch of wistfulness, but always with unshakeable sincerity. He used the spoken and the written word. He gave lectures to audiences ranging from kindergarten parents' groups to service clubs, he was interviewed on television, and he talked to anyone who would sympathise with his point of view – or who he felt needed convincing of its correctness. From time to time he alluded to conservation in his regular *Australian Home Beautiful* column from 1970–75, and he promoted it in articles for and interviews with newspapers, both metropolitan and local. Towards the end of his life he prepared a manuscript on the subject. This did not find a publisher, but he regarded its message as far more important than that of his highly successful book, *Australian Garden Design*, which sold 50,000 copies.

In Ellis's letter to the *Argus*, it is notable that after exploring the specific issue he moved easily on to the wider view. His concern shone through for nature, for 'the beauty and value of our native flora', for the overall good of Australia. This was unusual. Certainly in the mid-50s, even as late as the early 1970s, when a conservation or environment-oriented viewpoint was aired at all it tended to be confined to the local issue from which, invariably, it had sprung. But Ellis Stones had the whole picture in mind.

Ellis's letter was followed in 1955 by an article in another metropolitan daily, the *Herald*, written by architect Robin Boyd. It described the 'ravage of a beauty spot' as Chelsworth Park on the Yarra was being 'unsystematically reduced to a wasteland'. A billabong had been filled with surplus earth from a railway cutting and part of it used as a household rubbish dump, Boyd wrote; trees had been blasted or bulldozed out for a golf course, the river had been fenced off from public use and building blocks cut in from the Ivanhoe side. In short, he said, Heidelberg City Council was following 'the Melbourne tradition of using the river as a dumping ground'.

It is easy to surmise that through their professional contact, Ellis may have alerted Robin Boyd to the issue. In 1953–4 Ellis had landscaped the garden for one of Boyd's most innovative houses, the 'Bridge House', built in coat-hanger shape across a creek valley in Toorak. The owners remember him as a 'charming, shortish man, most interesting to talk to', and were impressed with the way he used large boulders to retain the soil on the steeply sloping site. This was the first of several gardens that Ellis designed and built for houses by the 'name' architects Grounds, Romberg and Boyd. Alistair Knox knew Frederick Romberg well, and had introduced Ellis to the partnership. Professor Romberg did not believe the firm's use of him was a careful selection, rather it was a case of Ellis doing 'the sort of thing we were looking for'. At the time, he said, the choice in the field was not wide, and Ellis could be trusted to do a proper job. Robin Boyd's wife, Patricia, remembered that her husband 'liked Ellis very much', appreciating his use of native plants – Boyd was fiercely nationalistic – as well as the stone and timber in his gardens. (Alistair Knox maintained that it was only after Ellis began designing gardens round houses by Grounds, Romberg and Boyd that he began to use timber for construction work as well as stone.) Certainly Ellis's naturalistic style meshed as well with Boyd's designs as it had earlier with Knox's houses. It did not intrude nor seek attention for itself, but set off Boyd's work to perfection.

In 1956 Ellis laid out a garden for a Boyd-designed house, built in Ivanhoe on a steep site above the Lower Heidelberg Road cutting. The clients, Dr and Mrs Victor Stone, started on the landscaping themselves before realising they would need properly built retaining walls. They approached several garden designers who produced solutions they did not like for prices they could not afford. Then a friend arrived one day with Ellis and Gordon Ford in tow. Mrs Stone said that as soon as they began talking they found they spoke the same language. 'What we wanted was a very natural, rather romantic, wild garden without being completely native. The garden had to be terraced, and we needed a terrace leading out from the back of the house, with a wooden bench around to seat people if we had a party. Everything he suggested I agreed to, and vice-versa. We confronted him with a slippery pile of clay – my husband had dug out a room under the house – and he turned it into a garden.'

Ellis built stone retaining walls, and flights of stone-edged steps. He and Mrs Stone collaborated on the planting; surviving plants include a Mexican hawthorn, double flowering cherry and wintersweet. From time to time over the ensuing years he would turn up with plants from large gardens he had been engaged to renovate. 'He would say, a bit apologetically: "Don't feel you have to take these but I had to pull them out and I knew they were the kind of plants you like" . . . and he'd heave out an iris, a guava, nice bushy things.' He found a spot in the garden for the family's pot-bound Christmas tree, which grew to impressive proportions. He left the bottom part, where there had been a formal rose garden, for Mrs Stone to plan herself.

Bluestone borders a terrace Ellis built in the Stone garden, Ivanhoe, in 1956. Built-in seats are set at the far side to take advantage of the view.

She said the initial making of the garden was one of the happiest periods of her life. 'Rocky had a couple of Sicilian labourers, they would sing dark Sicilian songs as they worked. Sometimes when the baby cried one of the men was up with her before I could get there. Nobody ever handled boulders like Gordon Ford – he held them like children. Rocky was so lively in his laughter and his movements; he had such brilliant eyes, always sparkling and twinkling. You felt that if he didn't have that rotten leg he'd be running.'

*V*isitors to this garden descend a flight of shallow gravelled steps, then pass a tiny pool.

Ellis returned twice to this garden, in 1958 to add a pond and steps at the top, and in 1960 to site a carport and build a tea-tree fence. The pond and steps are particularly skilful; the area involved is not large but there is a feeling of immense generosity in the curve of the steps, while the materials of trodden earth and bluestone are at one with the simple glass and timber of the almost unaltered Boyd house. Beside the lowest step and beyond a cleverly placed small maple, the tiny pond – it measures one metre in every dimension – sits beneath a gentle outcrop-cum-retaining wall. Even though set well back, it is the focal point for the small clearing that leads to the front door. Peggy Stone told Ellis she would love a pond, but that she was sure there wouldn't be room. 'Rocky said: ''Oh, you've got to have one, no garden is too small to have water in it. I'll make it so you have a little rill, with water trickling down from the rocks above''.' Since then, whenever it rains heavily or when the sprinkler is on, the sound of falling water delights the owners. Ellis had a simple answer, too, for Mrs Stone's concern that visitors would veer off the path into the pond. 'Just plant something prickly next to it.'

Never was there a dull moment when Ellis and his men were making a garden; the fund of humour proved inexhaustible. 'There goes another load of poison', Ellis, who was allergic to milk, would reflect as a milk-cart trundled past. Singing and whistling enlivened the day. (Several employees noted that when his leg was painful Ellis tended to whistle, but he would never discuss it.) 'Vintage' assignments at this time combined Ellis's irrepressible good humour with the knockabout comedy of Gordon Ford, the jokes of Jack Blakey, and the quieter, but no less penetrating, wit of Bob Grant, his foreman from 1956 to 1965. Repartee was developed to a fine art. At times the hilarity on the job was such that neighbours would peer over the fence and ask to share in the joke.

Equally, never was there an idle moment. 'It was the blokes who rolled a cigarette on the job that annoyed him. You worked hard for Daddy, everyone did', said his daughter Patricia. Ellis left home at 7 a.m. and was rarely back before 6 p.m. He got through the day without a cooked breakfast and with a lunch consisting largely of fruit, and he didn't take a full hour for lunch. Part of his lunch-break involved stretching out flat on his back, after he had had eaten, for a fifteen-minute nap.

This snapshot from the late 1950s shows Bob Grant (leaning on shovel) and Ellis (in hat).

All his life he had done this, and he liked to tell people that on board ship going to the war he had even taught himself to sleep in the rungs of a ladder. Wherever he was he found a spot – along the top of the new stone sitting-wall at the Walters job in Narre Warren, on the lawn, on a large piece of cardboard or plastic if nothing else was to hand, once on a windy, cold day cocooned inside a roll of paper. He tried to convince his men what a good idea this was and from time to time they'd try it. 'He'd tell us to relax every muscle, away we'd go, then he'd start to snore and that would be the end of it', recalled Bob Grant.

At this time all the hard physical work was done by hand. Rocks were manoeuvred out of paddocks, into the truck, out of the truck again and into their resting-place on site with crowbars, sacks, sledges and wheelbarrows. 'He had it worked out to a fine art', said Tom Garner, who worked with Ellis in the late 1940s (and with whom he was briefly in partnership in 1960–61). 'You'd lie your barrow down and roll the rock in, with one fellow on one side and three on the other as you brought it up.' Digging was done with spades; rotary hoes were not used even for lawn preparation. Here Gordon Ford's great strength was valued. Alistair Knox wrote in *We Are What We Stand On* how in 1949 Ford and a co-worker had poured and screened a concrete slab for a house in one day with no mechanical help, mixing more than twenty tons of material (including fifty-two bags of cement).

> *They first placed the materials in a dry state at the top of the slope and stood opposite each other with the heap between them. They drove their shovels into it and turned it over twice . . . as it rolled down the hill, the process was repeated after it had been wet down. By the time it reached the edge it was ready for placing. Underlying this vast physical effort were the inflexible wills of two strong men who would have died rather than admitted to each other that they could not have continued.*

Gordon Ford moved on, more mechanical equipment became available, but Ellis clung to the methods he knew. David Leech, who worked for him between 1958 and 1963, persuaded him eventually to use a crane for loading boulders on and off the truck, instead of planks, sacks, and crowbars. 'But then, of course, the rocks were larger and we still had to place them on the job. I had seen a trolley used for heavy loads and I insisted that we should have one. After much pestering he allowed me to buy one and it was put to excellent use, impressing even Ellis with its ease of operation. It became known as "David's trolley" and the last time I saw it, it had almost collapsed through continual use.' Jack Blakey vividly recalled the effort involved in filling the window-boxes for an office building in St Kilda Road. 'Ellis asked me to go to Cranbourne and get a truck-load of soil, then he told me to take it home, tip it out, turn it over three times and mix in tanbark and manures. Then I had to shovel the six tons back into the truck and take it to the job. Then it had to be put into five-gallon drums and shouldered up two floors of stairs into those window-boxes.' Bob Grant helped with this Herculean task and he, too, shuddered slightly as he recalled it. Former employees said they wouldn't have laboured like this for just anyone. 'Landscaping can be dreadful work, and really boring. Other landscapers I'd worked with were more into just shifting dirt around', said David Leech. 'But with Ellis it was fun – he got pleasure out of his work, you see – and because he taught you such a lot it was interesting and rewarding as well.'

Through the 1950s job followed job, larger engagements coming through word of mouth, while locally Ellis was known as the person to get if one's garden needed doing. In this way he came to work for Peggy Grassick at 'Appledore' in Eaglemont, at the garden where Edna Walling had planned a native section in 1937. The large block was subdivided in 1957, Alistair Knox designing three houses to go into the far part of the garden. Ellis came to do small but important work – altering the fall of the land and the shape of a path, carrying out stonework around the new houses, making small changes to help the Grassicks adjust to the cut-back in size. 'We all knew him, he lived nearby and he was a grand person', Mrs Grassick recalled. 'He was so helpful; whenever we had a problem about where to get manure or where to get stones we would contact him. When we were doing the levels for the new houses he worked by the day. I don't think he ever sent us a bill for the little bit of alteration to our garden.' In 1969 a fourth house was built on the site and Ellis came to advise on altering the line of a flowerbed. He stayed for an hour or two and would take no money for it. 'Don't be silly', he said to Mrs Grassick. 'You know as much about this as I do.'

For a man in business this self-effacing generosity was perhaps acceptable between friends, but it lost him opportunities as well. Ellis was not skilled at selling himself, so sometimes he was passed over by potential clients who were in a hurry, or who did not recognise his innate qualities. One such was F. M. Norway of Langwarrin, better known as the writer Nevil Shute, who wrote to Ellis in August 1956:

Dear Mr Stones,

After our telephone conversation yesterday Mr Swanson arrived bringing with him unexpectedly a stone expert with whom he is accustomed to work in the neighbourhood. This put me in a considerable quandary because I had told Mr Swanson at the start that he would be responsible for doing all the work of laying out the garden according to Miss Walling's plan. And I am convinced that he could do it to my satisfaction. However Miss Walling, not having worked with him before, was rather doubtful of his capabilities and insisted on calling you in.

After seeing Mr Swanson's stone expert I am certain that he could do the job very well, and he is also able to provide ample supplies of rock and stone without delay.

My chief interest is to get the garden made as soon as smoothly as possible. You are a very busy man, and it is difficult for you to fit in this small job among your more important commitments. I have therefore decided to stick to my original plan of leaving all the construction work to Mr Swanson. I am very grateful to you for your help and interest, and would be glad if you would send me your account.

There was plenty more work, however. One of Ellis's favourite jobs resulted from another referral from Edna Walling. Eric and Ruth Rundle owned a house on a five-acre block running down to the Yarra River at Eltham. Walling, consulted in 1954, advised the Rundles that the land was so lovely it should be left alone, but she suggested building a dry stone wall along the curving driveway, and gave them Ellis Stones's name. He and Gordon Ford built the long, low wall, then he carried out rockwork around the house, created a barbecue area lower down the slope, and floored a new glassed-in breezeway with random slate paving. His leg caused problems while he was paving. Mrs Rundle remembered: 'He didn't ever hurry things and he never charged enough. But it was a very pleasant association.' So, three years later, in 1957 when the Rundles acquired the beautiful Bulla property 'Glenara' where Alister Clark had bred his famed roses and daffodils, they asked Ellis to make small alterations to the garden. Well before the days of awareness of historic gardens and of interest in their restoration, he did this with rare sensitivity.

A little way past Melbourne Airport, 'Glenara' is regarded now as one of Australia's most important historic gardens. The elegant 1857 house is set on a steep site sloping down to Deep Creek, a tributary of the Maribyrnong River that runs through a rocky gorge, and surface water was a problem on the winding driveway leading down to the house. To handle the pelting stormwater Ellis introduced subtle small run-off channels along the length of the drive, which thirty years later remain effective and unobtrusive. The gravelled turning circle in front of the house was too small for cars – it had been designed for carriages – and he extended this, re-siting the original sundial and marking the corner with a half-buried flat rock and a clump of wild iris. So deft was his touch that it exemplified Edna Walling's dictum: 'The secret of all landscape work . . . is to conceal one's hand. Success is only ours when the finished job looks as if it had "just growed".' At 'Glenara' Ellis was entranced by the whole property – the way the old garden (where teams of gardeners were employed last century) tumbled down the hill to the river, the wild outcrops of rock, the superb natural swimming-hole in the gorge. Often he used photographs of it in his lectures, to demonstrate the virtues of nature's landscaping. Again and again he sang its praises to friends and associates. He would call in when passing, simply to sit and look. During one such visit he noticed Mrs Rundle stumbling across uneven ground to the clothes-line. 'That's dreadful', he said. 'Why don't I make it nice for you?' He levelled the piece of ground and put in a few rocks, simplifying and giving a touch of pleasure to a mundane, everyday chore.

Meanwhile on the conservation front, the River Parklands Protection League had been keeping a watchful eye on the Yarra while focussing also on issues like converting a plantation near Ivanhoe railway station to a car-park. 'This means despoiling a park for the sake of a few people', Ellis told a reporter from a local newspaper. 'It is a nice shady spot; people walking from the station use it a lot. They would have to pick their way through cars instead of leafy trees and shrubs if it was converted to parking.' But affairs on the Yarra began to simmer, and in 1957 Stanley Korman tried to subdivide the historic Banyule estate beside the river. With the local council seemingly unwilling to contest the action, local opinion mobilised, leading to a public meeting in August 1958 to form the Save the Yarra League.

The meeting was held on a Sunday at Wilson Reserve, on the banks of the Yarra just below Ellis's own house. Rain-spotted attendance lists show that despite inclement weather, 117 people turned out. A prime mover was local parliamentarian Vernon Christie, who served damper and billy tea on the river bank in the driving rain; Ellis was elected one of two vice-presidents. Quickly it became obvious – perhaps Ellis had his say here – that concern was not confined to the Ivanhoe/Heidelberg area. Along the length of Melbourne's major river, banks were being eroded, sewage was discharging into the water, and – most alarming – land was being re-zoned from rural to residential. It was decided that the Save the Yarra League should consider 'the larger task of creating a National park within the valley as a whole'. Meeting at Ellis's house in September the following year, the committee was shown a plan that appears to have been produced in his office, entitled 'Paradise Lost' and graphically illustrating re-zonings from rural land. These ran from the outer suburb of Warrandyte through Eltham, Lower Plenty, Templestowe, Rosanna as far in as Ivanhoe and Heidelberg.

Despite initial interest in the League, the early meetings were not regular and in April 1960, at a committee meeting held at Ellis's house, the minutes record the following:

> *E. A. Stones spoke on the future of the League and felt that we were not sufficiently active in seeking a membership which really represents the people's feelings and in seeking publicity to hammer home the alienation of the river valley which is going on all the time. Although our League started with a lively meeting and good attendances we had done very little since then to hold the interest of the people concerned or to inform them of the League's activities. He felt that we should have an intensive drive for active membership, public meetings to hold the interest and publicity through the local press to widen our field. Dr Allen, supporting Mr Stones, said he felt we should be more active and instanced the feelings of land-holders in the valley who thought our policy was to acquire their agricultural properties . . .*

Dr Len Allen, a foundation member and long-term president of the Save the Yarra League, remembered that in its early days Ellis was very active. But he was not seen as a good committee-man, being impatient, intolerant of the authorities and the time it took to achieve results. He favoured 'soap-box stuff' on the river bank – years earlier his family had had to restrain him from throwing the local mayor into the river at a protest meeting, so irate was he at that worthy's point of view. He urged drum-beating and strong attacks, and he did not always understand the need for research and negotiation, which increasingly became necessary in the league's dealings with bodies like the Melbourne and Metropolitan Board of Works (MMBW). On a personal level, however, his honesty, sincerity and conviction had a considerable effect on people, and he was always given a hearing. He is remembered stumping into meetings from his utility – and sometimes giving the blunt impression that sitting round and listening to others air their views was a waste of time when he believed

*L*ocal MLA Vernon Christie was not deterred by driving rain from making billy tea and damper at the river bank launch of the Save the Yarra League, in 1958.

'*P*aradise Lost' – a 1959 plan prepared by the Save the Yarra League to show riverside areas being re-zoned from rural to residential or other uses.

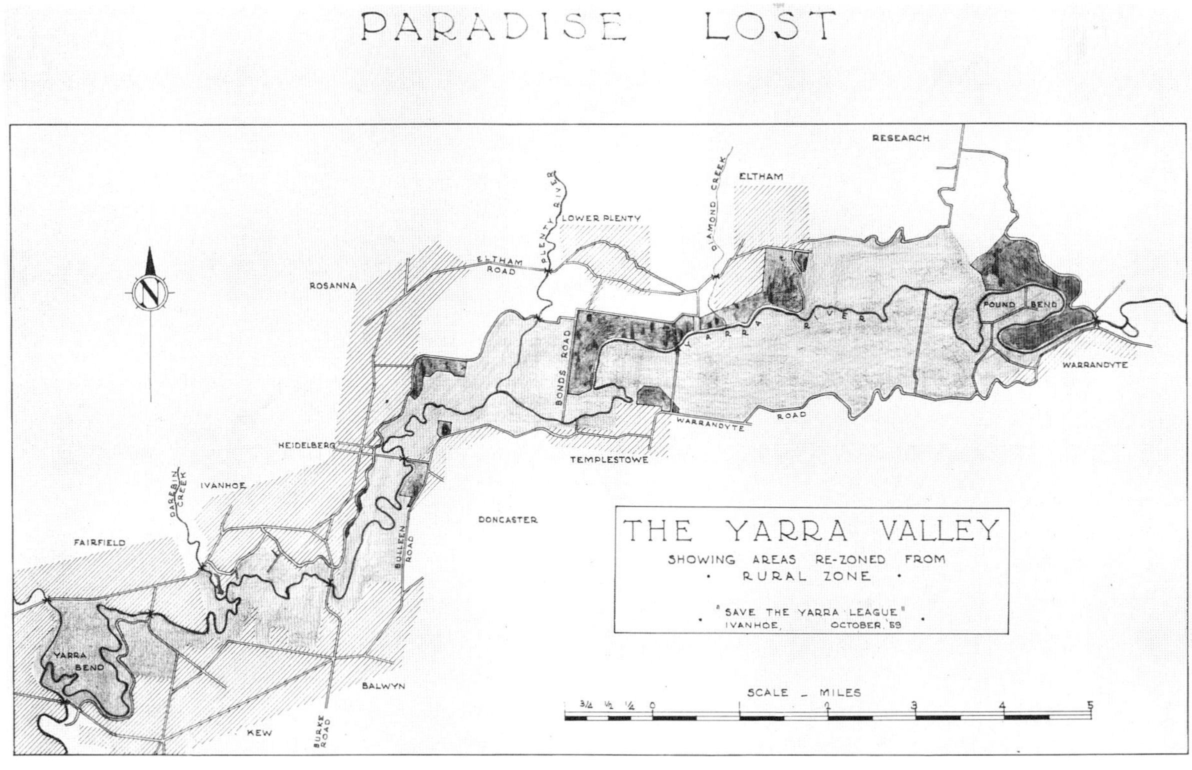

immediate action could be undertaken. Although the kindest of men, when angry he could be scathing. A member of the Save the Yarra League recalled the discomfiture of Heidelberg City Council staff at a meeting on the Yarra bank as Ellis, the advocate of natural planting, took out a tape and demonstrated the mathematically identical spacings between trees newly planted by the council.

During the next seven years he served intermittently on the Save the Yarra League committee (which became known in 1966 as the Yarra Valley Conservation League). Mentions of him crop up from time to time in the minutes. In March 1963 he advised that he would be meeting Heidelberg Council representatives to inspect the Chelsworth Park area. In May 1966 he suggested that some areas along the Yarra could be fenced off temporarily to allow regeneration of river red gums. In February 1967 the newsletter was offered an item of special interest from Ellis Stones on 'the importance of open areas and trees as appreciated in overseas countries'. The following month he retired from the committee, at the same time warning that rubble was being tipped into the river along part of the Greenacres Golf Links boundary. On New Year's Day he had noted in his office diary: 'Tipping brick and rubbish into the Yarra at Ivanhoe. Green Acres Golf Club Kew a large gum tree has been felled into the river.'

In his manuscript *Priority Landscaping* Ellis wrote that, while in garden-making he had wanted always to bring nature to the city, he had tried also to protect areas of virgin bushland.

> *After the War . . . I was among a handful of people who were very conscious and concerned by the needless destruction of our landscape. It was hard to get the story through to the authorities that one day we would need as much as we could get of the virgin bush, that in many cases was being needlessly destroyed in the name of progress. It seemed strange to me that Australia is acknowledged as the driest continent in the world and here man in his ignorance and greed does not hesitate to destroy not only the beauty of rivers and swamps but interferes with their normal function.*

His interest in the Yarra never wavered, and this extended to its tributary creeks. He campaigned ceaselessly against the MMBW's policy of diverting creeks underground so that they ran in concrete drains, in the name of flood control, and he saved newspaper cuttings on the subject from the mid-1950s onwards. At the time of his death he had just completed work for the Yarra Valley Freeway Action Group on a report entitled 'The Yarra Valley in Melbourne for People'. Published in 1976, this report's dedication reads: 'To Ellis Stones, a pioneer in the vision of Australian landscape, who valued the Yarra Valley'. It is a pity Ellis never knew that not long after this, the MMBW was to preserve parts of the remaining natural land along the valley and create a series of metropolitan parks that today are enjoyed by tens of thousands of city-dwellers each year.

ELEVEN

Living with landscape

'The only skilled work on the project, apart from planting, was the slate paving and rock walling', wrote a reporter for the *Australian Women's Weekly* in 1957, about the Narre Warren garden that Ellis designed and built for Harry Walters. And she referred to him as a 'landscape gardener'.

At this time the average Australian still had firm ideas about the two elements, 'landscape' and 'gardens'. The landscape was something viewed from a distance, most commonly in the country. A garden was what you had around your house, created and maintained usually by the householder. Little or no connection was drawn between the two; unless you were wealthy or you had perception out of the ordinary, you did not have a 'landscaped' garden. In the field, no government department took responsibility for protection or maintenance of the broader landscape, while employed gardeners still were seen as not much more than labourers in terms of prestige and salary. Only in 1940 had the Melbourne classified telephone directory introduced a category for 'gardeners' in which the names of garden designers were to be found – Ellis was among the first group so listed, along with Olive Mellor and Eric Hammond.

But slowly, attitudes to this entrenched situation were changing. By the late 1930s, Edna Walling's employee Gwynnyth Taylor (née Crouch) noted, although the ordinary working person couldn't have afforded a grand garden, there were the glimmerings of a change of attitude to the area of land around the house, with some journals (notably Home Beautiful) encouraging readers to plan their gardens. After the Second World War increasing numbers of graduates from Burnley Horticultural College began to make their presence felt in areas associated with the broader landscape, as did graduates of the school of botany at the University of Melbourne under Professor John Turner. In the early 1950s new books encouraged the average Australian to open his eyes and look around him, as did Thistle

'The quiet beauty of roadside scenes in Victoria' was illustrated in Edna Walling's photograph of part of what she called 'the enchanted mile' along the Mount Donna Buang Highway (from *The Australian Roadside*).

Harris's work with schoolchildren through the Tree Wardens' League of New South Wales. *Australian Treescapes* (1950), in the Ure Smith miniature series, used masterful photographs by Harold Casneaux and an eloquent essay by Elyne Mitchell to put the case for 'the subtle beauty that is Australia's'. *The Australian Roadside* (1952), by Edna Walling, illustrated the quiet beauty of roadside scenes in Victoria and New South Wales. Walling's photographs, most of them taken on major highways of scenes easily accessible to the travelling public, showed stands of saplings and majestic forest giants, mountains and valleys and sheep peacefully grazing in paddocks, wave-tossed oceans, still rivers, delicate wildflowers. She asked:

> *Could any excitement surpass the thrill of discovering the exquisite and elusive beauty to be found on the roadside, in the open country and through the forest? . . . The thought of any journey to a place where the trees and natural ground cover are still unspoilt is thrilling to me. Nothing can equal the exhilarating joy of these exquisite pieces of landscape in which the plant groups are still happily joined together.*

It did not require a large leap of the imagination to make a connection between this, and the atmosphere that could be aimed for in local parks and suburban gardens.

Since 1917 Burnley College had offered a full time course in horticulture, but although after the Second World War some of its instructors promoted awareness of the broad landscape, generally graduates interested in landscape design had trouble finding opportunities for further training. Frank Keenan, a former parks and gardens superintendent for the Melbourne City Council, finished the Burnley course in the late 1930s then, seeking to continue his studies, found that the only landscape-related course he could do was agricultural science at the University of Melbourne. Neither this nor botany appealed, so he wrote to Harvard University in the United States where the school of architecture offered three streams – architecture, planning and landscape architecture – and asked if he could study landscape architecture by correspondence. This was not possible; but he was sent a reading list.

A degree in agricultural science proved the starting-point, however, for John Stevens, the first landscape designer to establish a professional office in Melbourne. He had graduated from Burnley in 1938, then did design work with a firm of landscape contractors. Enrolling at the university on his return from war service, he settled for agricultural science rather than pure science because it covered the vital subjects of soil and climate. Loving plants, he majored in botany. Towards the end of his studies in the late 1940s, a turning point for him was a meeting with Professor John Turner, who on his arrival from England ten years earlier had set about building the university's botany school into one of world repute. John Turner was immediately struck by the tall, softly-spoken Stevens and they became firm friends and associates. Professor Turner noted: 'John really knew something about plants. He had aesthetic appreciation and in those days it was rare to find this. Once he was in practice for himself he badgered nurserymen. You'd go into a nursery and ask for one of his favourite plants and they'd say: "Oh you're from that man Stevens I suppose". But eventually, and thanks largely to him, some of the nurseries stocked more unusual plants.'

Professor Turner's introductions, as well as encouragement from the architect Roy Grounds, led Stevens in 1952 to set up an office in St Kilda Road. There his clients included Melbourne's leading architects, who utilised his skills in large-scale industrial, commercial and institutional projects. While he also designed private gardens, through the 1950s and early 1960s his commissions included the grounds of the Royal Children's Hospital; city office buildings like ICI House and Mobil House; universities – the campus at Monash University and landscaping around Wilson Hall at the University of Melbourne; refineries – Shell at Corio Bay (with Emily Gibson) and Vacuum Oil at Altona; as well as work for various municipal councils. By contrast, Ellis Stones appears not to have designed anything but private gardens until 1959, when he began to receive the occasional commission for commercial or institutional work.

John Stevens and Ellis had common interests, one of which was a love of the natural landscape. There were happy, friendly dinners at Ellis's house in Locksley Road, preceded by a stroll along a section of the Yarra River. 'I always looked forward to these', Stevens recalled. At these meetings Ellis talked enthusiastically about river and creek valleys in the Melbourne landscape, a subject in which Stevens already had a keen interest. He credits Ellis with at least some of his education in the subject. At a parks and recreation conference during the 1950s he gave a paper on the possibilities of stream-side parks, and he tackled with great care a commission to landscape a golf course beside the Yarra (on the opposite side of the river to Ivanhoe!).

As well, there was professional involvement, with John Stevens employing Ellis to carry out rock work or paving for some of his designs. These included landscaping around new multi-storey city office buildings

*E*llis placed rocks and laid paving outside this St Kilda Road office building in 1957, to John Stevens's design.

like the ICI building, and Hume House in William Street. In 1957 he asked Ellis to install exposed aggregate paving and to place rocks in the forecourt of a new St Kilda Road headquarters building for the architects Bates, Smart and McCutcheon. Ellis took great pains with the paving; he would pick up and consider half a dozen pebbles before settling in the pebble that best matched the one he had placed previously. Osborn McCutcheon, senior partner of the firm, was not impressed. 'That fellow's taking a long time', he remarked peremptorily one day as he left the office for lunch. He also queried the positioning of a large rock – something none of Ellis's associates ever dared to do. 'Ellis always said there were twenty way of putting in a rock and nineteen of them were wrong', remembered Tom Garner, who was working for him at the time. 'With a big rock we would use crowbars and mattocks and we'd work it around a foot, even an inch until he said "Stop it . . don't touch!", then we didn't dare touch it again. On the St Kilda Road office job we had just got a rock placed to his satisfaction when this fellow walks out of the office and tells us the rock is too low, to jack it up a bit. Well, you should have heard Ellis.' It says volumes for 'Os' McCutcheon's commanding personality that Ellis *did* raise the rock.

*E*llis became most eloquent when discussing the proper placement of rocks (c.1970).

John Stevens took landscape design to the wider community as well, writing for newspapers, appearing on television, lecturing at the University of Melbourne. In 1964 he left Melbourne for a two-year appointment as landscape architect to the Australia National University in Canberra, where he stayed for thirteen years. The citation for his Medal of Australia, awarded in 1988, described this campus as the most serenely beautiful university setting in Australia, one that 'like all his works, bears witness to his sensitivity to the land and the people who use it'.

Meanwhile Ellis's practice continued along the lines established in the early 1950s. He had sold his nursery business late in 1954. He was never short of work, usually having one or two permanent helpers and a number of casual workers. He designed and built gardens for some 'name' clients, and many smaller ones. He loved what he was doing but he did not make big money; instead, he agonised over his inability to keep track of the minutiae of the jobs. When it came to sending out accounts, to his great concern, he simply could not remember for whom he had bought this load of sand and cement, or that truck-load of rocks, so that often he could not bring himself to address the problem and would end up paying for materials himself. Olive Stones was a driving force at home. 'She kept him sorted out', recalled their youngest daughter, Betty. (Like

A wall of local stone is created in a country garden in the mid-1950s.

Lesley and Patricia, she had married in the early 1950s, but whereas the two older girls settled in New Zealand, Betty and her family lived in Ivanhoe, not far from her parents.) Olive manned the telephone, kept an appointment diary, marked up street directories for Ellis – he hated driving more than ever – and chivvied him into following up loose ends. His physical disability continued; after the initial relief of the sympathectomy operation in 1954, again his leg caused great pain. He would wear a caliper to help out, although he disliked this intensely. He tried to build extra support into his boot but in 1958, struggling to keep upright on a particularly bad day, his ankle gave way and he fell awkwardly, breaking an arm. This was the year when he employed Louise Landale in his office. She found herself doing anything from digging and planting to driving Ellis between his jobs, and producing the occasional plan. Thereafter he was rarely without a 'girl' to help out.

Louise had met Ellis in 1953–54 when he travelled to Deniliquin in New South Wales to design gardens for her parents and her brother on the recommendation of a family friend (and Louise's godmother), Mrs Thornthwaite of Ocean Grove. The Landale garden at 'Netherplace', on a two-acre site on the Edward River, proved exceptionally fast-growing. No rocks were available on the featureless Riverina plain; Ellis used timber sleepers for retaining walls while the planting for the garden, now subdivided, included poplars and a number of pretty, small brooms. For the low-maintenance garden required at 'Mundiwa', he suggested a ha-ha wall instead of a front fence – a device which Edna Walling sometimes used on country properties. This, too, was built of timber rather than stone. Over the years he returned to this district for new commissions, usually homestead gardens. During one visit he was asked by the shire council to suggest design improvements to the local memorial park. On his recommendation clumps of lemon-scented gums were planted, and the various scoreboards, office and changing rooms repainted in dirty green-black so that they did not stand out in the surrounding landscape – another application of his experiences in northern Australia during the Second World War.

With constant demand for his services, Ellis's ideas on design of the home garden were consolidating. He never talked much about why he tackled problems in a particular way; his design solutions usually appeared instinctive but they were buttressed by practical experience and deep thought. 'I believe, for I talked to him often about it, that the principles and truths Ellis discovered he found for himself', said his friend, the businessman David Yencken, in a lecture given in Melbourne in 1977. 'He did some things and he liked them, and he did other things and he didn't like them, and he worried out a principle . . . Ellis's ideas seem not to have come from books but from his own experience.' Perhaps this is true up to a point, but in fact Ellis was a student of the 'greats' of landscape history. He read about the work of Le Notre, of 'Capability' Brown and Humphry Repton, while in later life he was fascinated by the rockwork executed by Chinese and Japanese landscapers. And during the late 1950s, when there was not a lot of local reading matter available in Australia for the student of garden design except for books by Walling and Nerine Chisholm, he seized enthusiastically on what the eminent American landscape architect, Thomas Church, had to say.

*L*ike Thomas Church, Ellis did not advocate heavy planting around the base of a house. His treatment for this Merchant Builders house, c.1968, allows the house to speak for itself.

Church's classic book, *Gardens are for People*, was published in 1955. It was not long before Ellis acquired a copy, and he must have been pleased to see that Church emphasised factors dear to his own heart like the sensitive use of rocks, the provision of intimate spaces in gardens for outdoor living and for doing household chores and, above all, the need to carefully control the relationship between house and garden. Church wrote:

> *Too much enthusiasm in planting at the base of a house can do a garden in quicker than anything else. It is a shame to veil any house in shrubbery when the house itself is well designed.*

Ellis had written in *Australian Home Beautiful* (July 1946):

> *If the house is brick or cement finish, the lawn or gravel drive should be allowed to run up to the wall in places, and the garden beds not made along all the walls as though there were something to be hidden.*

Church went on to say:

> *With most of the planting moved further out into the garden, it can also be enjoyed from inside the house, and the home will make its full contribution to the garden composition . . . a tree, placed to frame the house or cast its shadow on it, does more softening than a forest of shrubs.*

Ellis had thought the same way in 1946:

> *A finely designed house should be enhanced with a few well-placed, carefully chosen trees and shrubs in the foreground to soften hard lines and create a sense of distance.*

'Note the feeling of distance (achieved) by having a few large trees to cast shadows', Ellis commented about this photograph of the Ridge garden (c.1968).

Thomas Church's book spoke to Ellis with an immediacy lacking in the distant expositions of Brown, Repton and their colleagues, and on the job he talked to his employees about what Church had to say, bringing out his copy of *Gardens are for People* to underline his points. 'Landscaping is not a complex and difficult area to be practiced only by high priests. It is logical, down-to-earth, and aimed at making your plot of ground produce exactly what you want and need from it', Church wrote. Reading these words and remembering how he had argued with Edna Walling during the 1940s about the need to tell Home Beautiful readers about the reasoning behind landscaping decisions, Ellis must have felt more than a little vindicated.

One client who aimed to make his plot of land produce exactly what he needed was Zelman Cowen, then professor of law at the University of Melbourne and later, Australia's Governor-General. He was a busy man who loved football and he felt that one day a year was all the time he could reasonably devote to gardening. His 'one-day-a-year' garden became one of Ellis's favourites. The Cowens' new house, in Kew, had been completed in 1958 to Robin Boyd's design; the space available for garden-making comprised a nicely sloping area at the back, and a formidably steep incline at the front. Robin Boyd sent Ellis to see the Cowens – 'This is the man to get', he told them – while recommending that the areas behind the house should be terraced. Sir Zelman recalled: 'Ellis immediately said "No, don't do that, put in a bank of shrubs to make a place where the children can go to get away from you". He talked to us about rocks and native plants. Our immediate impression was that we liked him, we liked him very much.'

Ellis prepared no plan although the Cowens remember a rough outline sketched on a lunch wrapper. They were struck by his unerring judgment for summing them up and for getting things right. He spent time explaining the reasons behind his design. He turned the cliff at the front into a cascade of native plants, a 'waterfall garden' with a brick path winding up to a courtyard by the entrance to the house. He installed boulders to retain the slope and provide planting niches, and he laid the path himself with the aid of the Cowens' three-year-old son who acted as works supervisor, brick-examiner and trowel-snatcher – this Ellis did not appear to mind. After putting in the native plants he suggested planting low-growing annuals the first year to provide some colour against the rocks 'just to lift your spirits'. By the second year, he said, the native plants would be making their own impact. The ugly flat roof of the street-level carport stood out in the view down from the house, so he planted the swift-growing native creeper, *Kennedia nigricans*, to cover it with a carpet of green. From other people's gardens he brought plants – little pieces of iris for the back garden, for instance – returning to the Cowens in later years to 'borrow' pieces of theirs.

*E*ventually Ellis began to describe himself as 'garden designer' – a step forward from the 'rock garden constructor' of the 1940s.

Two years later he was to use native plants again in a garden for a new Robin Boyd house for the Clemson family on another vertiginous site in Kew. Even before the plate glass was fitted into the large windows that looked onto the natural bush of the Yarra Valley, Ellis, who was in partnership with Tom Garner at the time, was on site to design slate steps on either side of the house, and to install an outcrop of rocks and native plants. It is easy to see why Boyd brought in Ellis, because conventional means of retaining the slope would have negated the dramatic impact of the house in its encircling bushland, while exotic plants would have been out of place.

As Ellis worked on the Cowen garden in the late 1950s, most of all the Cowens observed his concern for the environment. Then, and during visits in later years, he talked about what the authorities were doing to the Yarra and to Melbourne's creeks, and about the concrete drains he abhorred. He asked advice on getting support for his point of view, and seemed unsure how to go about this. Discussing this twenty years later, Sir Zelman still remembered the passion with which Ellis spoke, but also he recalled his inner conviction. 'There was never this frenzied approach that you would get with the environment in, say, the late 1970s. This was a good-humoured, determined commitment. He didn't see the damage to the environment as a ghastly plot, but as the result of tragic indifference.'

He impressed the Cowens as a plain man, not particularly educated and with 'none of the external trappings of the aesthete', but with great artistic sensibility. He was down-to-earth and warm, with a strong sense about people. He spoke to them of his belief that hospital gardens should not be great grassy swards with a few rose trees, but friendly places offering little nooks and crannies to which visitors, patients, or staff could escape for a few quiet moments – an idea that he advocated without success years later at the Repatriation Hospital in Heidelberg, but which he was able to implement in the grounds of an old peoples' home, the Judge Book Memorial Village at Eltham. Beginning this job in 1959 and continuing for several years, he created individual corners for the residents (who, sadly, did not always agree, with one small pool having to be filled in after the inhabitants of the adjoining unit complained about the noise from the frogs that had arrived to live in it). During a conversation with the Cowens in the 1960s he told them about a corner park that he was designing for a municipal council. Onlookers had asked, he said, why he was making such an effort when the local vandals would only destroy it. He went straight to the local coffee shop and told the assembled teenagers what he was doing, in these terms: 'They tell me you chaps will rip it up. You won't do that, will you?' Ellis Stones liked people. And he trusted them.

During the 1950s other landscape designers were showing concern about destruction of the natural landscape – particularly Edna Walling, a furious correspondent to the letters pages of newspapers and periodicals, John Stevens, and Grace Fraser, who had trained at Burnley Horticultural College in the early 1940s. (Grace Fraser remembered most of her fellow students as 'devoted to being Edna Wallings', but her main interests were plant pathology, Australian plants and the bush.) On her return in the mid-1950s from overseas study, Miss Fraser was appalled to see that natural areas like Ashburton Park, which she remembered as full of red gums and native orchids, were being taken over for housing. 'We were absolutely passionate about what was happening to the landscape, in the parks and on the roadside. But no-one was doing anything much about it and we had to struggle on and teach ourselves.' She joined John Stevens's office, where she worked in the late 1950s and early 1960s. In subsequent years her own design work included the Australian plants garden in Royal Park for the Melbourne City Council, and landscaping around the administration block of the BP refinery at Hastings, where she used native plants. She had difficulty in obtaining indigenous coastal species for the extensive stand of trees she felt was needed to block views of the refinery from the water; she remembered with some amusement the reaction of the English engineers who had done the site planning when she invited them to come and see the native orchids in flower near the foreshore. 'Yes, they said, we'll just hop in the car. Can you imagine trying to look at tiny little native orchids from the *car*?!'

Clearly, then, for some designers environmental awareness was becoming a key element in successful landscape design. In Ellis's unpublished manuscript *Priority Landscaping* he wrote with passion about the destruction in the name of progress of trees and natural areas in cities, and about the nibbling away of parks for freeways and the like; he discussed, too, the role of the tree – 'a unique chemical factory' – and the pollution that follows the destruction of natural areas. He wrote: 'there is one thing certain, we must take advantage of what is left to landscape and introduce more parks and trees wherever possible. Number one priority: Landscaping.'

TWELVE

Birth of a profession

From the early 1960s onwards, in print and in lectures, Ellis bemoaned public lack of appreciation of the landscape architect, who, he said, usually was brought onto a site only when the engineers and architects had finished with it. He wrote in *Australian Garden Design* that the ideal way to design a garden was in consultation with the architect or builder before work began '. . . so that the building may be sited in a way that will give plenty of scope for the garden, preserve some of the existing trees if the area is a wooded one, or emphasise any other strong features that may be evident in the natural contours'.

The same held, he believed, for public landscaping. In a 1970 report to the Housing Commission of Victoria, he wrote:

> *We have reached the stage in our cities where landscaping is, or should be, one of the most important aspects of 'density living' projects and I would suggest you seriously consider following the pattern practised in Europe where the Landscape Architect is called in at the beginning of any project so that he can consult with the Engineers on the position of car parks and drives and thus try to avoid cutting up the areas with masses of concrete . . .*

Edna Walling always complained about being called in at the tail-end of proceedings, although sometimes she managed to arrive early on the scene. We have seen how around 1936 she was asked to consult on siting the new house 'Hillsborough' (or 'Silver Birches') in Balwyn, where Ellis was to build such a splendid outcrop and pool to her design in 1938. The generous, airy atmosphere in this grand house, with garden views from both sides of almost every room, must owe a lot to her early intervention. There was co-operation of the kind she enjoyed, too, with the Ringland Anderson house and garden, 'Churston'. In May 1937 she commented of 'Churston' in the *Australian Home Beautiful*:

> *. . . the garden and the house are a unity, so much so one scarcely knows where one begins and the other ends. The place indeed provides evidence of the intelligent co-operation of building architect and landscape architect . . . too often the garden is merely an irrelevant frill around the house.*

During the late 1940s Broken Hill Associated Smelters asked her to help site several houses for its coal-mine at Mount Kembla in New South Wales. Peter Watts wrote in *The Gardens of Edna Walling*:

> *The design required four houses to be placed on a hillside backed by dense rain forest with a view over Lake Illawarra. Within hours of arriving at Mount Kembla Edna had abandoned the house plans she had been given, had won over the mine manager, and was directing a front-end loader to shift giant boulders around the house sites she had chosen: 'I soon realised that here was an opportunity not to be missed. It was such a treat to have men and machinery so geared to carry out one's ideas instead of a whole gang of men standing limply around waiting for a slow-witted boss to make use of them' . . . Returning to Melbourne she had the general manager employ a young lady architect to redesign the houses. Together they pushed around small models of the houses on a contour plan until a satisfactory result was achieved. Passing through that country some years later Edna found 'it was most gratifying to see how pleasantly the little gardens were nestled up to the huge boulders we had placed, and how well those houses looked'.*

Like almost all her colleagues, Walling had had no formal training in her profession save the course of instruction at Burnley Horticultural College. The rest had been learned on the job. However, aspiring landscape architects in the 1950s could travel to England for further study at Kings College, Durham University or at the University College, London. (An early Durham graduate from Australia was Erica Ball, who on her return home was asked to design the surrounds for the 1956 Olympic Village at Heidelberg – her plan was only partially implemented.) During 1956–57 Mervyn Davis, a Melbourne landscape designer and diplomate of Burnley College, took the Durham course, moving on to further study in the Netherlands. In 1958 and in 1960 she attended the conferences in Europe of the International Federation of Landscape Architects (IFLA), but as an observer only, since Australia had no official representation. In 1959 she was appointed an individual member of IFLA, sharing the position with John Oldham of Perth. They were then asked to set up a professional institute for landscape architects in Australia. This Mervyn Davis regarded as a huge task but a signal honour. 'I nearly died, but I set to', she said.

Mervyn Davis sealed her professional reputation during the 1960s, when she was responsible for the landscape around major airports at Melbourne (Tullamarine), Perth, Canberra and Launceston for the Commonwealth Government's Department of Housing and Construction. Ellis could never understand why she had designed extensive rose gardens around

*P*reliminary work for the Dickie garden, 1962. By now Ellis's men are using a front-end loader to collect rocks.

Melbourne airport. Miss Davis's explanation for the roses was that she thought weary travellers should be offered something familiar. But surely, Ellis said repeatedly, visitors should be greeted by beds of native plants instead? Among his papers are these notes, presumably for a speaking engagement:

> *First impressions are very important . . . at our airports we should make every effort to impress visitors with the fact that they are in Australia. I am afraid this approach is not always considered . . . we so often see exotic gardens that are inferior to those in other countries that we are copying.*

Mervyn Davis also designed private gardens, and during 1961–62 she and Ellis worked together on an extensive garden in the Melbourne suburb of Hawthorn. The site, beside Fairview Park, ran down to a bend of the Yarra River; she described her design as 'a flowing, changing series of areas with easy-to-maintain, yet intimate, detail' in which she aimed to enhance the feeling of a house floating above the landscape. She engaged Ellis to carry out the stonework necessitated by the sloping site. The house was cut into the slope so that the entrance was along an elevated walkway; beneath this Ellis installed huge boulders and a pebble-strewn stream leading to a small pool, the stream being fed by a copper jet at footpath level whose flattened end was concealed beneath a rock. (He was particular about camouflage of this kind; his 1972 diary includes a note to chase up the contractor who had installed a similar feature for him next to a swimming pool, but had forgotten to place a rock cap over the copper pipe outlet.)

Ellis also built a dry stream and outcrop in this Hawthorn garden and while Mervyn Davis was pleased with his work – except for a small grated drain that he installed by the large rocks below the entrance, which she felt destroyed the scale of the area – there was no doubting her general attitude to him. She regarded him not as a landscape designer but as 'a contractor – a marvellous dependable man for his subject, which was stonework'. It was a source of initial difficulty for her that as she sent out a questionnaire in 1962 to canvass landscapers around Australia for their views on setting up a professional institute, a large percentage of the interest and response should come from practitioners who were either self-taught or lacking what she felt the international parent body would deem acceptable qualifications. She did acknowledge the need to involve from the outset all people who had done acceptable work, mainly because landscaping in Australia was such a fledgling field with its practitioners few and scattered, but she held firm on the need for potential members to have professional qualifications.

Around the same time John Duncan, a lecturer in architecture and interior design at the Royal Melbourne Institute of Technology (RMIT), had been developing a series of landscape design-oriented lectures to cater for what he felt was a ground swell of interest among the wider community. Duncan had watched the growth of newspaper advertisements calling for landscape practitioners to work on large-scale public projects, and he was concerned that few professionals qualified to carry out this important work were to be found in Australia. Indeed, as late as 1967, when the professional institute was formed, the Melbourne classified directory still had no listing available for landscapers save that of 'gardener'. (That year, however, it did introduce a section for 'land developers'.) With a long-standing awareness of landscape design and a real commitment to it, John Duncan believed a post-graduate course in the subject should be started in Melbourne – post-graduate, he maintained, 'because landscape architects worked in public places concerning the community, so should be people of relative maturity'.

The Dickie garden, Hawthorn.

In the winter of 1960, in a theatrette at the State Library, he ran a 'preliminary' series of lectures on landscape design. The speakers were Mervyn Davis, Eric Littlejohn (then head of Burnley Horticultural College), Alistair Knox, Gordon Ford, and Wallace Ruff (a visiting landscape architect from the University of Oregon). So successful was this venture that a larger venue had to be found for the 1961 series, attended by around 140 people – predominantly architects and horticulturalists, but also engineers, doctors and other professionals. The series was booked out. Speakers at the RMIT Radio Theatre included Mervyn Davis (on three topics – relating house and garden plans, paving and garden walling, open spaces and their relationship to changing land uses), and Ellis Stones (on exploiting natural contours and indigenous materials). There were technically oriented lectures, too, but perhaps more notable was an emphasis on the broader landscape, with Alistair Knox speaking about the principles of landscape, and about the landscape and regional building, while Ann Taylor, an architect, discussed landscape and architecture.

Winter 1962 saw a repeat series with more speakers and more lectures. Again the Radio Theatre was booked out. Margaret Hendry, who later lectured in landscape design at Canberra College of Advanced Education's school of environmental design, was a new face among the lecturers. Ellis Stones spoke twice, his subjects being an integrated landscape, and the practice of landscape. In previous years each lecture had been followed by animated open discussion; this time James Earle served as rapporteur, summing up findings and conclusions, and developing a policy and aims for the establishment of a landscape design course at RMIT. The public mandate was unmistakeable. John Duncan then asked Ellis to arrange a meeting at his home with people interested both in the lecture series and the profession. Margaret Hendry, who was there with Alistair Knox, Mervyn Davis, John Duncan and Peter Glass, remembered this as the *first* meeting of people interested in taking steps to set up the profession and, later, the institute. 'Not only did Ellis and his wife host this first meeting, they supported and encouraged all our moves', she said. (Twenty years later, Mervyn Davis's friend and associate, Daphne Pearson, vividly recalled Ellis's enthusiasm at this and subsequent informal meetings, and his habit of quietly leaving money on the host's mantelpiece 'to help pay for the sandwiches'.)

A landscape design course was set up, beginning at RMIT in 1965 (as did a similar course in New South Wales). Ellis Stones was a foundation lecturer at RMIT. He talked about landscape design and construction with an emphasis on field work; he did not give many traditional lectures as such, but simply took his students out on site for three-hour sessions, usually on summer evenings, explaining problems and solutions as they walked around various jobs. One regular port of call was his own front garden, to underline the effect that could be achieved by removing a front fence and putting in a sweeping driveway. He was in the habit of setting small design projects, then discussing the students' work during the site visits, which proved most instructive for all. He kept up the lectures until the late 1960s, but he found they tired him, and pressure of work intervened. Many students remember Ellis's lectures as the most interesting – and relevant – part of their course, the practical sessions being

*E*llis took students of landscape design to his front garden for on-site lessons. The evolution of his thinking can be seen in the mid-1940s, 1950s and 1960s with – in each case – a major transformation.

inspirational although, since he himself was such an intuitive worker, his technical explanations often left something to be desired.

Further meetings to discuss the proposed professional institute for landscape architects had been held in Canberra and Adelaide in 1963 and 1964, the so-called 'landscape group' holding meetings during annual conferences of the Royal Australian Planning Institute, under its auspices. Ellis did not go to Canberra, but he and Olive were there in Adelaide when the landscape group decided a landscape institute, separate from the planning institute, should be formed. Thirty-two practitioners travelled to this meeting, from all states of Australia. The formal vote for the establishment of an institute was finally taken in Sydney, in 1966. Then came the knotty problem of deciding exactly who should belong to it. Peter Glass and Alistair Knox, who attended the Sydney meeting, recalled more discussion about the need for formal professional qualifications – until the chairman, Peter Spooner, 'saved the situation' by pointing out that the numbers of qualified people in Australia were too few for a viable institute, and that this line of thinking would exclude people, like Ellis Stones, who already had made a considerable contribution and whose input was valued.

An interim committee met at Burnley College in Melbourne throughout 1966–67, when categories of membership were the main concern. Among those who attended were Beryl Mann, Grace Fraser and Mervyn Davis, and from interstate, Richard Clough, John Oldham and Alan Correy. It was agreed that the initial offer of corporate membership should be made to people who held formal academic qualifications in landscape architecture, and to people who were unqualified but were in private practice or teaching and not deriving income from landscape contracting. Applications for consideration for affiliate membership should then be invited from people with practical experience who were engaged in landscape design and construction but who did not derive their whole income from landscape contracting. Practitioners in the affiliate category included Ellis Stones as well as names like Alistair Knox, Bruce Mackenzie in Sydney, Peter Glass, Gordon Ford and Eric Hammond.

Edna Walling stood apart. She had written to Mervyn Davis in June 1962, while formation of the institute was being discussed, that she felt she would be an anachronism in any institute. Later that year another letter read: 'the one who rather cheekily said it was "my duty to belong to the association" might have had something, so I am getting on with a revised edition of *Gardens in Australia* with all speed hoping that this will be better – far better – than my membership'. Two years later Mervyn Davis had not given up hope of persuading her to join, but Walling remained firm. A letter of August 1964 read in part: 'how very kind of you to continue to send invitations to the meetings of the Landscape Association, but I hope you will excuse me and understand when I tell you I am really no longer interested in landscape work and find it quite impossible to stir up any enthusiasm for anything but conservation and the natural scene'.

The decision to have two categories of membership caused considerable dissension and ill-feeling, even though it was based on the model of the Institute of Landscape Architects in the United Kingdom. Alistair Knox was particularly outspoken. He did not agree with the two categories – 'everyone who had done *anything* was missing from the proposed list of corporate members', he said. At one meeting he aired his views, as did several other design-and-construct practitioners. Tempers flared. Ellis had been sitting quietly, but when he stood up to speak, the edgy atmosphere was suddenly subdued. Knox recalled: 'It was heart-rending really, Rocky got up and in a plaintive voice put his case. I forget just what he said, but it was sad. I mean, he'd almost introduced the whole Australian landscape business; all these other people had done a little, but had not left and never would leave a mark like Rocky . . . they were all ensconced within, looking out.'

Ellis was accepted as an affiliate member of the institute in 1967. It is important to reiterate that he was wholeheartedly behind the establishment of the institute, no matter how its organisers viewed him and his credentials. He felt that landscape design *must* be given professional standing, in order to gain recognition for a form of creativity that, in the eyes of the general public, was still mostly the domain of eccentrics and maintenance gardeners. This attitude shows the same broad vision as his early stance on conservation. (For his own part, he believed his early experience as a builder and carpenter stood him in stead as good as any professional training, but as always, he had the overall picture in mind.)

He was offered a fellowship in March 1975, the month before he died, in recognition of his contribution to landscape architecture in Australia. At this time ten other practitioners had been so honoured. He responded in these terms:

> *I am in receipt of your letter informing me of the Council's decision to make me a Fellow of the Australian Institute of Landscape Architects. I accept with pleasure this honour, and I am naturally very thrilled and happy and trust I am able to still help to improve the standard of landscaping in Australia . . .*

Is a successful landscape architect born or made? Consider this comment from Ellis's introduction to *Australian Garden Design*:

> *In order to become a landscape architect today it is necessary to go through a long period of specialised training from which a man of talent benefits, but if he does not possess that inborn artistic imagination necessary to visualise his designs, then his training may have been in vain.*

THIRTEEN

'Gardens are for people'

It is fascinating to discover how much of Ellis's best-loved work related directly to the Yarra River. In 1961 he designed a garden on a block of land that overlooked the river in Fairfield for Dr (now Professor) and Mrs Kenneth Cox, who moved there from Locksley Road where they had lived only a few doors from the Stones family. Libby Cox's father and Ellis had been boyhood friends in Essendon and had gone to the war together; Ellis often reminisced about how sixty years earlier they had kicked a football on the vacant block in their street.

The Coxes had not long lived in Locksley Road before Ellis persuaded them – as he persuaded several other neighbours – to pull down their front fence in the interests of the street's overall appearance. 'Just look down any street with front fences and you will realise how ridiculous all the different kinds of fences of varying colours appear', he wrote in 1970. 'You design your fence as a special unit. It is your contribution to an ugly street . . . to those who must have a front fence, have a shrubbery, with an inconspicuous fence among the shrubs and trees.'

He had removed his own front fence some twenty years earlier, indicating the street boundary of his property with shrubs and a few boulders, and later putting in a picturesque silver birch salvaged from a development site. (Ellis was always ready to try and move mature trees, saying that if these were excavated properly and replanted swiftly and with care there was no reason why they shouldn't survive. In the late 1940s he successfully moved a five-metre silver birch to a new garden he was making around a brick veneer house in Balwyn, built by A. V. Jennings.) Eventually he encouraged one of his next-door neighbours to agree to take down the first few panels of their common side fence as well, using shrubs and boulders again to divide the two properties. By the early 1960s he had done away with his small lawn and front garden almost entirely, replacing them with a broad, curving sweep of gravelled drive which gave an illusion of much greater space; he often advocated this treatment for an undistinguished front garden. He was not the first to do so. Robin Boyd writing in 1951 in *Australia's Home*, had spoken approvingly of the way 'something of the air of a community park' had been achieved in Western Australia in the 1930s, when often in Perth's inner suburbs all front fencing was removed so that private gardens and nature strips merged in one sweep of lawn and shrubs. He noted that around this time some municipal councils in the eastern states, like Camberwell in Victoria, had tried unsuccessfully to persuade their citizens to eliminate front fences for the sake of general appearance.

The Ellis Stones Garden Book, published posthumously in 1976, explained that decisions like removing a fence sprang from the landscape design maxim of never defining one's boundaries. Ellis wrote that people who lived in outer suburbs, away from the noise and bustle of the heavily developed inner suburbs

> *. . . may find that there is no particular reason why a front boundary should be denoted by a fence . . . If you can do without a front fence you will find that a thick planting of trees and shrubs and flowers gives you privacy and looks most attractive. But vary the area of planting – if you plant in a perfectly straight line it will look almost as bad as a fence or brick wall.*

Kenneth and Libby Cox had spent some years in suburbia in the United States, where front fences were not the norm. They liked this effect, so were more than happy to remove their fence when Ellis suggested it. As they were planning their move to Fairfield, Ellis offered his services to beautify their old garden for the sale; then he recommended his friend,

In front of Ellis's house a sweeping gravel drive replaced a standard suburban lawn, the front fence was removed, and boulders and shrubs defined the first few metres of the side boundary.

*E*llis combined bluestone blocks, rocks, gravel and low-scale planting to enliven and disguise the steep ascent to a house in Fairfield whose living quarters had to be raised above the Yarra River flood level.

the architect Peter Hooks, as designer of their new house. The new block was ony a stone's throw from the river, almost hidden by eucalypts and dense undergrowth and accessible along a dirt track. Because the site had been flooded in 1934, the house had to be elevated by three metres. This was a source of anxiety, but Ellis reassured them that problems like this often made for the most interesting landscaping.

Working closely with architect and client, he advised building the wall beneath the house – whose understorey was to be used as a workshop, play-room and plant-room – of bluestone blocks, grouted so they stood out in low relief (he supervised this work, and later planted a yellow climbing rose there that gave great delight to the neighbours). The Coxes were still worried about what they described as the 'house jacked up in the air look', more so when Ellis ordered that all the rubble and excavated material be put in a pile directly in front of the house. 'He kept reassuring us that though it might look like an upturned pudding basin not to worry, all would be well', Mrs Cox recalled. 'When he produced his plans, though, I was disappointed as I thought they looked too formal – not like us at all – and I really couldn't visualise what he was talking about. However we'd seen so much of his work that we completely trusted him.'

Ellis built dry bluestone walls on either side of the 'pudding basin', interspersed with lichen-covered rocks, then constructed a gentle pathway that went up three shallow steps, turned through ninety degrees, up three more steps, turned in the other direction, then up three more steps to link with the stepped ramp that gave access to the house. 'You wind your way up', he told the Coxes, 'so you can stop and look at the view'. Planting was in small patches of yellow, orange, mauve and white. Mrs Cox likened his positioning of the rocks to painting a three-dimensional picture – two men maneouvred them while he gave minute directions for adjustments. 'No, roll it a little to the left, no, tip it back a bit, rotate that corner in . . . stop!' Reluctantly she objected to the position of one rock, feeling it would be dangerous for anyone in a hurry. He concurred, and moved it. Gardens were for *people*, he said, and so were the steps. Some months later he was thrilled to hear that the Cox children loved climbing on 'his' rocks, calling them the sun, the moon and the stars.

Mrs Cox noticed that when Ellis explained his ideas for garden design he did not push or 'sell' them; rather, he threw up a concept in an off-hand, take-it-or-leave-it manner, and was delighted when the client took it. 'Usually it was so right you wondered why *you* hadn't thought of it.' Likewise around this time Edna Walling, who was soon to retire to Buderim in Queensland, was not as dogmatic about design ideas as she once had been. Mrs Mac Cuming, for whom she had designed a superb garden in Toorak in 1938, called her in again in 1960 when she moved to a smaller property in the area. She walked around the new garden while Walling no longer told her to 'Do this . . . do that' but instead made gentler comments: 'It would look nice if you did this'. She prepared a design, and told the Cumings Ellis Stones was the only person to get for the rockwork. He put in a small outcrop and steps in the sloping front section. Mrs Cuming's sister then asked him to do some work in her garden nearby. One day he was labouring alone there, close to the street frontage, using a crowbar to worry a large boulder into a position he had chosen partly beneath the exposed roots of a mature tree. A passer-by stopped and watched. Ellis, concentrating on the job at hand, continued to heave and push, moving the rock around in infinitesimal stages. Finally the onlooker could stand it no longer. He tapped Ellis on the shoulder. 'You know, you'll *never* get that rock out of there', he said.

During 1960–61, Ellis was in partnership with Tom Garner, whom he had once employed. They undertook a range of work: large projects like landscaping the Watsonia army camp, many private gardens, some commercial jobs like the Judge Book Memorial Village at Eltham and the Mason Firth McCutcheon printing works in Moorabbin, and maintenance such as lawn-mowing, rotary hoeing, and resurfacing driveways. Advertisements were lodged in local papers, time-sheets had to be filled in and the outside workforce sometimes numbered as many as ten men, often with Ellis's workers laying out a job and Garner's men completing it – in all, not quite the style of work Ellis knew.

Ellis had begun work at Mason Firth McCutcheon in 1959, having met Bob Eggleston, the architect who designed this unusual building on the Nepean Highway, some years earlier through Alistair Knox. He had worked on the Egglestons' garden in Heidelberg, and had employed their son, Peter, as a casual labourer during university vacations. Bob Eggleston thought it 'a natural thing' to ask him to do the landscaping around the new building. 'The client wanted an effect of the sort Rocky had to offer, we didn't interfere, just left him alone to work with the architectural envelope.'

'A well-designed factory in beautiful surroundings is as much a visual asset to a community as the best-designed park.'

This may well have been Ellis's first commercial commission – it is difficult to be sure, since no office diaries exist for earlier years – and he approached it with gusto. He wrote later that neglected designed input into the environment of warehouses and factories had led to eyesores that unpleasantly affected the whole community.

> *One of the reasons for this is perhaps that it is not generally realised that a well-designed factory in beautiful surroundings is as much a visual asset to a community as the best-designed park . . . Another reason for landscaping the environs of a factory or warehouse is that a large number of people are accommodated there daily, all of whom would benefit to a greater or lesser degree, depending on their aesthetic sense, if their surroundings were well landscaped.*

Because he regarded parked cars as 'the largest blot on both city and landscape' and conspicuously placed car-parks as environmental disasters, he was delighted to find that staff cars at this place of work were to be parked behind the building.

> *The owner did not want cars defacing the view of his building, therefore the landscape architect made provision for all cars (including the owner's) to be parked out of sight . . . A large gravel area was included in front of the warehouse for clients' cars only, but even in this area a few boulders, half-buried at strategic positions, were placed. These rocks have since been covered with ground-covering plants, but still serve as a deterrent to fast driving.*

Asked to landscape the grounds of a factory in suburban Notting Hill, he found a similar situation. The low building stood on high ground sloping down to the street, so that he felt it would have been 'fatal' to allow cars to park in front. Again he exiled them to the rear of the building. He terraced the front lawn in broad, shallow grades and installed large concrete stepping-stones in a direct line from street to front door. He did not usually like stepping-stones, but an entrance for pedestrians was needed and he felt a solid path of any kind would have detracted from the clean horizontal lines of the building. This simple treatment extended to the plant material. Against the Mason Firth McCutcheon building, whose facade was a dominating white-painted pierced screen, he had used the strong texture of rice plant (*Aralia papyrifera*) as a plant that he felt could stand up in effect to that building's 'busy' appearance. But at Notting Hill he simply put a small shrubbery to one end of the building, and planted a few lemon-scented gums (*Eucalyptus citriodora*) on the lower stretches of the lawn. These trees, he wrote, gave the height necessary when the building was viewed from a distance, and also cast shadows over the lawn on a sunny day. (As Thomas Church said, a tree framing a building and casting shadow achieves more softening than a forest of shrubs.)

In 1960 Ellis began work on another garden for the partnership of Grounds, Romberg and Boyd, around a Robin Boyd-designed house in Berwick. His treatment of the driveway recalled that of the Walters garden in Narre Warren ten years earlier, with a curving drive – here covered in Lilydale toppings – edged by clumps of shrubs and expanses of lawn to create unexpected vistas and a sense of distance. There were camellias and other exotic shrubs around the house, but on the lawn, with its glorious views across farmland to Mt Donna Buang, he made bold plantings of callistemons and melaleucas – as well as putting in several Queensland bottle trees! Further across the large garden he planted a grove of birches, and in the far corner of the garden, an extensive thicket of native trees and shrubs – a special joy for both Ellis and his client. He added a sweep of rocks and pebbles in front to accommodate an occasional drainage problem. 'I selected this portion of the garden for an Australian native section but discovered it was too wet in winter owing to excessive seepage', he wrote in 1970. 'I turned to nature for the answer. What does nature do under such conditions? The answer is construct a creek, and fill it with pebbles of various sizes.'

*H*e built a dry, pebbled 'creek' to cope with a seepage problem in that part of the Berwick garden devoted exclusively to native plants.

As this garden was being built, demands on Ellis's time were increasing. A typical couple of months during 1961 brought a range of telephone calls, noted in a diary filled in irregularly by his wife. The *Age*, the *Herald* and the ABC news were seeking him – possibly due to his aggressive stance on the alleged discharge of untreated sewage into the Yarra at Heidelberg near the Burke Road bridge. (Ellis was among local protesters who continually complained without success to the Melbourne and Metropolitan Board of Works; eventually, in 1963, dramatic proof was obtained by one of their number who was lowered into a concrete drain to find it, and more protest meetings led to a promise from the state premier that a new trunk sewer would be built.) There were calls about speaking engagements from groups including the North Balwyn Garden Club, the Red Cross, and the Beaumaris Tree Group ('if lost, phone . . .', read Olive's message, because Ellis was notoriously bad at following directions). The architects Robin Boyd and Peter Hooks and the landscape architect Mervyn Davis left messages. There were meetings to attend of the National Trust, the River Parklands Protection League and the Returned Services League. 'Ring Jean E', read a note in Ellis's handwriting (Bob and Jean Eggleston's son, Peter, had died suddenly; Ellis then encouraged Mrs Eggleston to help him one day a week, planting and maintaining rockeries, in the hope that this might help heal the wound). A worker phoned to say he was going home, because 'polythene at Berwick no good'. A client wanted to get in touch about rotary hoeing. A furniture store in Prahran wanted 'a Japanese setting' and the caretaker of St John's Hall, Toorak, rang 're display'. And an initial call was noted from a new client in Templestowe, giving directions to her house for an early-morning meeting: 'Go up Ruffy Street over bridge up steep hill bearing to right turn left first turn left bear to right first left go to left'. It is to be hoped that Ellis was not driving himself to this meeting! Probably his chauffeur would have been Beverley Hanson, who had begun working with him in 1960 after completing a course at Burnley College. She stayed full time for four years, and helped him out – particularly with planting, maintenance and as his driver and projector-operator for evening speaking engagements – from time to time for the rest of his life. Today her own landscape designs, which owe more than a little to Ellis's teaching and example, are widely acclaimed.

The Templestowe house sat at the top of a block of almost one hectare, part of an old peach orchard sloping steeply to the Yarra River. The owners had bought the block in 1958, built their house and laid out the garden. Then, somehow dissatisfied, they had asked a friend for advice. The friend was Alan Blazey, chairman of the garden products firm Hortico, in whose own garden Ellis had worked for some years installing outcrops, generous sweeps of squared slate paving, and a decorative small pond. 'Get in touch with Rocky Stones', was his answer.

When Ellis arrived there he saw that paths had been laid from side to side of the deep block, and that drainage was a problem, with water rushing down the slope and cutting runnels through the gravel. Immediately he brought in truckloads of boulders. However predictable a solution this may seem, his installation was masterful. In the beds the rocks anchored the paths and gave focus to the planting, while at changes of gradient

Colourful random planting in a garden at Templestowe.

they formed steps that were not only beautiful to look at but easy to negotiate, even on such a steep slope, so that the visitor almost imperceptibly wound his way down to the river bank on the narrow gravelled paths, all the while finding opportunities to stop and admire the wide range of plants. A friend who saw the garden in its heyday described the atmosphere of this section as 'romantic'. From an emphasis on annuals and perennials – delphiniums, Russell lupins and the like – it was agreed to alter the planting 'more or less' to a native garden, with some exotics being allowed to remain for colour. Ellis moved an almost full-grown acacia up the slope and successfully replanted it by the front gate. Melaleucas were put in along the side boundary, and more tea-trees, grevilleas, kangaroo paws and many other native plants were added to the established shrubs already there, along with some of Ellis's favourite plants like *Loropetalum chinense* with its lacy, white, grevillea-like flowers, and clumps of *Dietes grandiflora*. Little or no work was needed on the approaches to the river bank where eucalypts – manna gums, spotted gums and river red gums – and kunzea grew naturally. Natural growth on river banks should be left alone,

Ellis said. He simply built a barbecue and some heavy timber seats in a small clearing near the bank with a good view of the water.

He described the making of this garden in *Australian Garden Design*:

> *The land was well wooded with natural bush, and fell quite steeply from a level area at the road to the river flat. The house was built on the level part at the top . . . but this area was so narrow that there was no space for a garden around the carport and entrance, thus the first difficulty to be overcome was how to make the entrance generous and inviting. To compensate for the lack of garden space, a white wisteria drapes the garage, and tubs of camellias, which are attractive all the year round, occupy part of the drive.*
>
> *A delightful view of the garden . . . is obtained from the main rooms of the house, which open onto a terrace set with tubs of geraniums, not high enough to obstruct the view but providing a necessary foreground.*
>
> *Steps from this terrace lead to a rather formal lawn, which is the only level part of the garden. The owners . . . had a bronze brolga which they wanted incorporated somewhere in the garden. As I find it difficult to place statues in an informal garden, I created a realistic setting for the bird by placing it near a large flat boulder which contained a natural basin that held a little water and a few rushes . . . The remainder of the garden is constructed of gravel paths or tracks which are contoured for easy walking and at the same time create interesting planting over a wide area . . .*

Ellis was pleased with the solution he found for a 'hot spot' in the garden where a clay bank extended for a considerable distance from the junction of two paths. He was reluctant to use rock, having already built a shallow rock outcrop as steps there. Instead, he turned it into a spot for displaying succulent plants (luckily, being on a hill, the drainage was good). 'The blending of the different shades of greens and yellows in an apparently uncontrolled mass is a most pleasing sight most of the year, apart from solving a difficult problem', he wrote.

In detail and breadth of conception this beautiful garden – which still exists, although altered by subsequent owners – was only equalled in Ellis Stones's achievement by a garden he made in 1963–64 on another deep block sloping to the Yarra. The clients were Mr and Mrs David Hawthorne, whom he had first met in the early 1950s. Joy Hawthorne is a gardener of extraordinary dedication and ability who has always loved 'the bush, beautiful stones and the way Nature places them'. After the Second World War she bought a piece of hilly land at Lilydale that she thought would best suit native plants. She asked Edna Walling to look at landscaping it; Walling appeared 'rather old' and not particularly interested. 'Who would I get, then, with the same feeling you have for natural things?' she asked. Walling recommended Ellis. He did a little work there in 1952–53. Mrs Hawthorne remembers an obvious place for a pool, where water always gathered; he chipped out a pool from the natural rock, and planted his favourite native violets (*Viola hederacea*) around it.

Seven years later the Hawthornes built a small block of flats in South Yarra. They were living in Kerang, their builder organised the landscaping, and Mrs Hawthorne did not really approve. 'There was a retaining wall that looked all right after it had been planted, but I wanted more. I rang Ellis. "Can you come and fix this?" He did a lovely, simple, small-scale job in the narrow piece of land – perhaps four metres wide – adjoining our ground-floor flat. There was a pool, an outcrop and the water-washed pebbles he loved, a beautiful tea-tree fence and he planted bamboos and maples. We looked out on it from every window. It was beautiful.'

Then in late 1963 Mrs Hawthorne, looking for a gardening challenge, found an acre of river-front land in Hawthorn, where the old house and equally old garden were just what she wanted. 'I phoned Ellis and asked him if he would be interested. He was so enthusiastic, just like a big kid. The very day we got possession he arrived with a couple of boys and started work. He didn't do a plan. "No, no, I don't like working that way", he said.'

Simplicity in a South Yarra courtyard for the Hawthorne family (1959).

The garden – which no longer exists, having been subdivided – had a difficult two-way slope, down and away from the house. It widened as it sloped past an old tennis court to eucalypts and willows on the river bank. There were some old exotic trees – a magnolia, a tulip tree, a birch and a mistletoe-infested prunus. The prunus was in dreadful condition and Ellis felt it should be removed. Mrs Hawthorne asked him to give it a year's reprieve; she cut it back and cleaned it out to reveal lovely billowing lines. It flowered the following spring in a burst of palest pink blossom, and Ellis said she had been right – it was the loveliest tree in the garden.

The key to this magnificent garden was a largish informal pool, placed where the magnolia overhung it, and stonework that is generally acknowledged as the finest Ellis ever did. This included several rock outcrops – one positioned to protect the roots of the birch tree – all the rocks, some of which were huge, being brought in by hand and rolled down the slope. There was a flight of informal bluestone steps luxuriantly planted with alpines and ground-covers, and a beautiful double retaining wall, dry-built of bluestone and supporting a wide range of rock plants and perennials. The double wall was dictated by the steep slope and had two benefits – twice the amount of stonework for the viewer to admire, twice the amount of wall space for Mrs Hawthorne to plant out. (This technique is not seen often in Ellis's gardens. A precursor was a double stone wall that Ellis built to Edna Walling's design in 1935 at the Beattie garden in Toorak. Behind the front wall on the street boundary stands another, set back perhaps two metres down the slope towards the house. This allows space for bold planting facing the house, both between the stone walls and against them. It is more than just a planting bed, although it has less impact than the Hawthornes' splendid double wall.)

A flight of bluestone steps in the Hawthorne garden in Hawthorn during construction (1963–64).

Trickling water enlivened the large rocks that retained the slope at the entrance to the Dickie garden.

Native trees – which have grown prodigiously – were planted around the perimeter of a Berwick garden to frame country views.

*I*n a large Templestowe garden (1961) narrow gravelled paths edged with rocks and a variety of colourful plants wound down to the river.

*E*llis preferred not to tamper with plants that grew naturally near the banks of a river, as in this Templestowe garden.

The pool was made by removing two small existing ponds and enlarging the depression. 'Because of the slope on the land', Ellis wrote, 'it was possible to use a few selected rocks projecting over the side and under the water'. The rocks under the water he placed to shelter fish from marauding birds; those above the water hid the concrete edge. One very large rock was anchored with a 'sling' of thick steel reinforcing rods, hooked beneath it and bent back over the pool edge. Ellis used neither spirit level nor theodolyte, the levels were set with the naked eye. Mrs Hawthorne occasionally pointed out to him that the pool overflowed at one end in times of rain. His reaction was: 'Oh, well . . .'

The old tennis court came in handy at first as a spot for dumping and burning rubbish from the house and garden renovations, then it was broken up and buried. Ellis scooped out and contoured the terrain to make a vast sweeping expanse of lawn down to the river. He seeded it himself by hand. He worked there, on and off, for about twelve months, sometimes alone, sometimes with helpers when the rocks were being placed. Mrs Hawthorne moved rocks, drove a rotary hoe – 'We had a wonderful time, I don't think I've ever had so much fun' – and did most of the planting that, she said, Ellis was happy to leave to her. After the garden was finished he was a regular visitor. So sure was he of the way it would be maintained that he would come with friends, associates, potential clients and overseas visitors. She remembers him standing in the garden in his bib-and-brace overalls in characteristic pose, favouring his bad leg, one hand on hip, the other on his head unconsciously tipping forward his old felt hat as he talked.

A hat was daily attire for Ellis; there were working hats and hats for going out in. As absent-minded about his possessions as he had been when he was a cadet soldier in camp at Broadmeadows, it was not unusual for him to attend an evening meeting wearing his 'good' hat – and to return with one that was either too big, too small or too battered, and that, of course, was someone else's. On the job, he found a hat had uses beyond sun protection. If he was late or overdue for an appointment, he would knock at the kitchen door, open it and skate his hat across the floor – a technique aimed at disarming the sometimes aggravated client. One woman, however, was equal to this. 'I'm a bit late', he muttered to David Leech as he shied his hat through the door. 'I was meant to be here two years ago, I hope she won't be upset.' 'Oh, hello, Mr Stones', came the reply. 'We've built on a room since we saw you last. I'm afraid we don't need you now.'

FOURTEEN

A master in small spaces

Ellis finished the major work on the Hawthorne garden towards the end of 1964. He did it against the odds because despite his bright-eyed, fresh-faced appearance, increasingly he was prey to ill-health. He was in hospital regularly for check-ups on his bad leg, and from time to time he suffered from fierce allergic reactions. Exposure to concrete caused dermatitis, for instance, and he could not tolerate penicillin, sulpha or morphia. One staff member at Heidelberg Repatriation Hospital, being asked by Ellis on admission not to prescribe these three substances, scratched his head and said: 'What do I do with you, then? Poultice you, or put on leeches?' In 1964 Ellis's appendix was removed, the following year he was diagnosed diabetic. As well, he begun to suffer from occasional chest pains and angina attacks. Perhaps such complaints are not unusual for a seventy-year-old. But then, few seventy-year-olds carry the workload he did.

Over the years Olive had become more used to Ellis falling ill, although this always disturbed her, particularly when it was related to his leg. When she said she couldn't stand to see him suffering, one doctor told her that the pain from the leg, with its damaged nerves and inadequate blood supply, would be like constant pressure on an exposed nerve in a tooth. As usual, Ellis simply coped with it, and with other illnesses, as they occurred. He would succumb, then bob up again, and his employees became used to his absences. 'We would see him in bed and assist if we could, not really expecting him to regain his incredible energy ever again – but sure enough within a few weeks he'd be pushing and shoving rocks and timber as usual', David Leech recalled. In the office diaries are occasional notes: 'Please phone . . . when you are up again', '. . . sends best wishes for your stay in hospital', 'Mr S. sick in bed but came to . . . and planted from 11.30 a.m. until 3 p.m.'. Paradoxically, although Ellis was stoical about any major illness or injury, his family knew him when he was suffering from a cold or the 'flu as 'the sickest, most ill-used man in the world'.

The ornamental pool was the focus of the Hawthorne garden.

The garden sloped to the river in a series of rolling lawns.

*M*asterful rockwork beneath spreading trees.

*A*ttention to detail and form is vital in successful planting of any rockwork – as in the Hawthorne garden.

The large gardens described in the previous chapter had offered him great scope in generous areas of land, and he responded magnificently to these challenges. But at the same time his touch in small areas – in courtyards and in sections of larger gardens – was ever surer. During the early 1960s he used lichen-covered boulders to great effect in corners of two gardens in bushland near the outer Melbourne suburb of Warrandyte. In a garden running down to the Yarra river, and owned for many years by the Osborne family, he seized with delight on a huge kauri said to have been planted by Ferdinand Mueller, making its many-branched trunk (the result of a bushfire in 1939) the focal point for several intersecting paths. So simple and effective is his rockwork and associated planting around this noble tree that there is no sense of this part of the garden having been 'landscaped'. For Miss Kathleen Jepp he used boulders, alpines and native plants to transform a steep bank of fill thrown up behind a new house. The embankment creates a generous feeling of enclosure, a fine counterpart to the extensive views across country on the other side of the house. At one end the delicate apricot flowers of a spreading grevillea make a splendid foil for a huge flat boulder, set vertically, that marks the turning-point out of the driveway, while further along, a cunningly contrived 'sneak track' of rocks up a mountain-goat incline is both decorative and useful. (Most of the original planting in this garden, built in 1963, was native, as was subsequent planting carried out, with rockwork, in the Osborne garden in the mid-1960s.)

In 1961 Ellis began work, which was to extend over several years, on a garden in suburban Canterbury for Mr and Mrs Eddie Baitz, who commissioned him initially because they wanted a natural garden with a bush-like flavour, requiring little maintenance. They designed their new house themselves to give extensive garden views, but because the site was small and the house covered most of it there did not seem to be much immediate scope for landscaping, particularly outside the main living area. The Baitzes felt a little alarmed when Ellis proposed using a heavily planted rock outcrop to fill almost half the outdoor living-space between the rear part of the house (which held the kitchen and living areas) and the side fence. But when the work was complete and the virtues of a

A small pool, an outcrop and a gravel mowing strip contributed to a feeling of space in a narrow section of the Baitz garden (1960–61).

meandering path through the outcrop became evident – there is even a hidden seat behind the outcrop, reached by another 'sneak track' – they were amazed not only at the resultant feeling of spaciousness, but that Ellis had managed also to fit in a rock-edged pool, an expanse of random paving, a stretch of lawn and an elegant sitting-wall of cut bluestone.

In two courtyards associated with this house – an entrance courtyard and a miniscule, enclosed central space between the living-room and kitchen – Ellis achieved similar triumphs. The main feature of the formal entrance courtyard is an L-shaped reflecting pool edged with slate and river-washed rocks and pebbles, and the planting is deliberately spare – azaleas in tubs, ground covers, and leafy plants like *Moraea* and bamboo. Ellis wanted to create a generous, inviting, first impression of the house, so he provided a wide expanse of grey slate paving for easy access, and let the simple colour scheme of 'black, grey and green in relief against the white of the walls and the house' speak for itself. Similarly, the tiny inner courtyard evokes a feeling of calm and simplicity. Two centrally-placed black stones sit like a piece of sculpture, surrounded by pebbles and a symmetrical border of concrete slabs; the planting is understated. Ellis wrote that spaces such as this one, which was really only a light well, had primarily aesthetic value, and should always be tranquil and uncluttered:

> *Small shrubs which flower gloriously once a year and look bare and scraggy for the rest of the time are not for this kind of courtyard. Colours and materials, too, should be kept to a minimum. In this area the colour scheme was restricted to black, grey and green against white walls. The black is provided by* Phyllostachys nigra *(black bamboo) and the piece of natural sculpture, black basalt rock. I believe that all courtyards of this type have to be sat in to be fully enjoyed, so I always like to provide some kind of seating, although this is of secondary importance to the aesthetic quality. In this case the owners stipulated that they wanted to sit out in suitable weather, and even do some of the kitchen chores outside, therefore a rough black-stained timber seat was included in the design. The stepping-stones are simply mellowed concrete slabs set in water-worn grey pebbles. The only plants present are* Aralia papyrifera *(rice plant), a prolific grower which adds a rather tropical flavour, and* Anigosanthos flavida *(kangaroo paw)*

Ellis was very conscious of outdoor living – man's need for it in an urban setting, and its benefits, describing it as 'one of the great pleasures and privileges of the Australian way of life'. He believed that courtyards, patios, and all outside intimate areas close to the house were ideal spots for children playing, for adults entertaining or sunbaking, for the elderly sitting, relaxing or reading the paper – in fact, for family life. Try using your courtyard as an impromptu breakfast room, he wrote. 'Breakfast out-of-doors is a most pleasant experience and puts you in a great frame of mind to face the day.'

He was concerned that most outdoor living areas, whether courtyards or other small garden spaces, were not well enough integrated with the buildings they adjoined nor with the surrounding landscape. Such areas, he wrote, should be more than just an extension of building and landscape,

*E*llis's selection of long pieces of sawn bluestone for steps, and building blocks for an adjoining retaining wall, perfectly complemented the symmetrically placed stone heads embellishing a wall at the Hawthorne garden.

A double bluestone wall retained a steep slope.

A 'sneak track' offering a route up a steep slope in the Jepp garden near Warrandyte, designed in the early 1960s.

Rockwork in the Osborne garden, Warrandyte: below double flowering cherries in springtime; around the base of a venerable kauri; marking a change of level on a lawn.

*I*n an inner-suburban garden Ellis used a staggered series of tea-tree screens to enclose and create space.

they should be a part of both – particularly when not fully enclosed. Structural materials should be carefully considered; paving should be kept neutral, as should screening materials. From the late 1940s onward Ellis used tea-tree screens with great virtuosity, both to provide boundary fencing and to block unwanted views. For an enclosed South Yarra garden built in the late 1960s he constructed a raised, staggered series of screens that successfully obliterated the prospect of tall apartment blocks looming on either side, and also created pleasant nooks for planting and outdoor living. He loved tea-tree not only for its natural softness and neutral tones but for its open aspect, which made it a fine backdrop for creepers and shrubs.

In small spaces he regarded colour – or the lack of it – as a key to success. He paved one courtyard with large, square slate slabs, then had the outdoor furniture and a built-in bench seat painted a deeper charcoal grey to create a restful effect. Try to think of plants and flowers as background material in courtyards, he would say. Remember the potential of people for adding colour and movement in such spaces.

Ellis did not have garden plans drawn up on a regular basis until 1966, when he stopped doing construction work and had to rely, generally, on contractors to build his gardens. His courtyard designs from the late 1960s for which drawings exist follow a basic pattern, but each has a subtle variation. Components that crop up repeatedly include gravel, river-washed pebbles and boulders, sometimes slate paving, and usually a built-in seat – 'in the matter of furnishing I am inclined to go mainly for built-in seating because this will enable you to move more easily and naturally into your courtyard area when entertaining', he wrote. Often there would be a small pool, either set into the ground with a rock or two at its edge, or with a raised surround of timber, brick or stone for seating. (An excellent example is the square, timber-edged pool in the courtyard of a Merchant Builders development in Toorak, pictured on the back cover of *Australian Garden Design*, and owned by John Ridge.) For courtyard plants, almost always he would specify small-leafed ivy, blue grass (*Festuca glauca*), *Juniper sabina* and *Moraea*. Black bamboo was a favourite, as was *Azara*, and *Nandina domestica*. If the clients were inclined, there would be Australian plants – a grevillea or two, native violets, kangaroo paw, a small banskia or callistemon or, in a larger space, perhaps a *Eucalyptus caesia*. If native

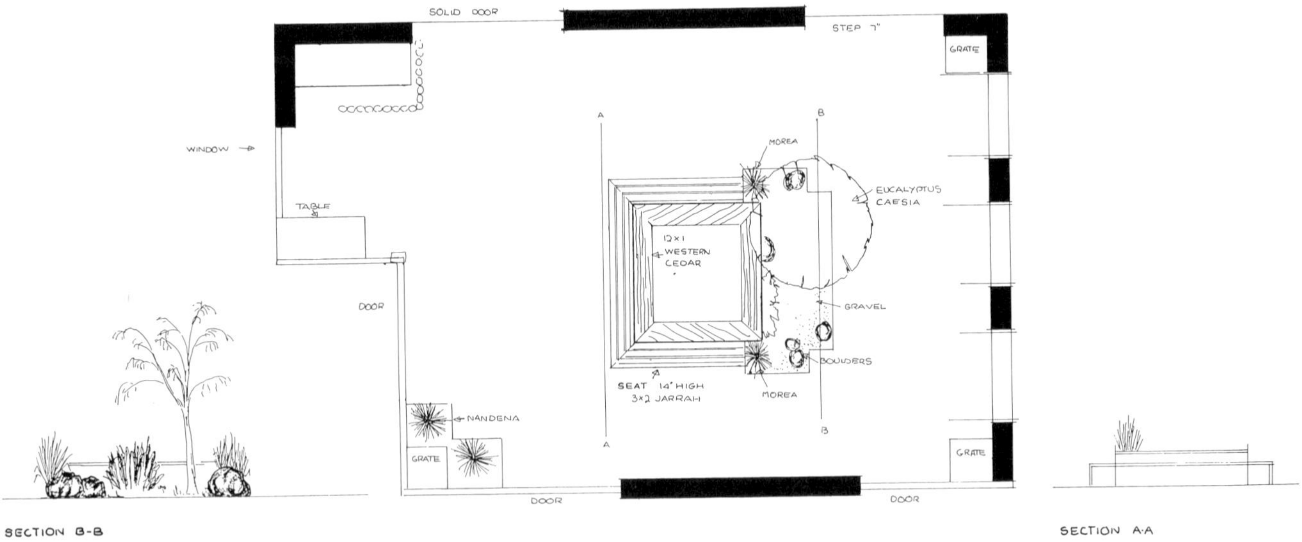

A typically simple courtyard design from the late 1960s included a specimen tree overhanging a timber-edged raised pool, with a built-in seat around it.

A small pool with a timber border (1968).

plants were not wanted, then he might include a camellia or a *Loropetalum*, or a rice plant. (Ellis had what some regarded as an unfortunate predilection for the tropical exuberance and strong texture of rice plants. Employees during the 1960s remember him keeping an eye out for mature specimens in any nursery they visited.)

Sometimes he is criticised for his 'limited palette' of plants. It is more to the point to emphasise that he knew what would give an effect, and specified accordingly, often playing safe because he never could be sure of the amount of maintenance his gardens would receive. Admittedly many of the native plants he chose outgrew their boundaries and later had to be removed, but in part this may have been due to the mistaken idea, given great currency in the late 1960s and the 70s when native plants surged into popularity, that a native garden is a no-maintenance garden. He would choose a plant not so much because he liked it, as for its texture and shape, and for its ability to reveal or conceal, to highlight or to provide a backdrop.

Courtyards at the Baitz garden in colour schemes of black, white, green and grey: an entrance courtyard with a reflecting pool; and an internal courtyard with two sculptural pieces of rock.

A 'sneak track' in the Baitz garden.

*H*idden from view at the end of this inviting path, Ellis placed a rough seat to which his client could withdraw to read quietly or enjoy the garden.

He could make a successful courtyard anywhere. In 1968 Robin Paisley, an accountant in Tumut, New South Wales, asked him to landscape the rooftop of a new office building there. Mr Paisley wanted to be able to walk out of his upper-floor office into a garden setting and to use this space for business entertaining, and had had the building designed accordingly. In Melbourne for a visit, he heard about Ellis's work from a friend. He flew him to Tumut in a small plane for advice, meeting him for the first time only that morning and not knowing about his bad leg. Ellis found the trip in the confined cabin agonisingly uncomfortable, but predictably did not complain.

He looked at the space available, some twelve metres by six metres, and said immediately that he wanted to pave it in grey river pebbles. At that time the Snowy Mountains Authority was damming the Tumut River for the Blowering Dam, so plenty of pebbles were available, and the Paisleys undertook to get them. 'We didn't quite understand, we got 200 or 300 and thought we'd done well but that wasn't enough, he wanted thousands! They had to be the right shape and the right size and the right colour. Sunday after Sunday, we went out with the station wagon and sifted pebbles. It was quite a job, but we had to be prepared to do it.' Robin Paisley and his staff used the courtyard for morning teas, lunches and entertaining after work. He remembers the sun, the pleasant feeling engendered by the black bamboo, the rock outcrops and massed shrubs and grasses, the varied spaces – from big areas to little nooks and crannies where if you wished, you could eat a sandwich or drink a cup of coffee in private. Ellis wrote:

Because (the roof garden) was planned for relaxation, heavy timber seats were placed along a couple of the walls and a large portion of the 'floor' was set with cobblestones (the river pebbles). A tea-tree fence was erected to block out concrete and brick walls and so create more of a garden atmosphere. The section of the fence was taken up high enough to screen adjacent buildings without interfering with the view of the distant hills. Careful consideration had to be given to the type of plants which would stand up to these conditions, particularly in summer owing to the reflection of the sun from the surrounding buildings and the lack of any depth of soil.

He added the useful advice that anyone planning a roof garden should consult the designer when construction of the building began. Heavy material could then be put in place while there was space to bring in appropriate machines. Manhandling at a later date would be much more expensive.

Later, working on the Paisleys' five-acre country garden, he designed a private courtyard adjoining the master bedroom. Completely enclosed by tea-tree screens, this was paved in old bricks, with a rock outcrop, a few shrubs and small timber seats in the sun. There was provision for the owners to shower outside on fine, warm days. So secluded was this space that it could be used for showering even when a gardener was working on the other side of the screens.

One of Ellis's finest courtyards was built in 1971 for Jane Carnegie, a dealer in oriental art, who lived and worked in a two-storied shop in Malvern. She wanted the narrow five-metre-wide space behind the shop to offer pleasant views from her ground-floor gallery, as well as providing a relaxed area for outdoor living, and parking space for her car. She wanted plants that could be easily maintained with once-a-year attention, and she asked that the garden have an Australian flavour, with some oriental influence. Initially the back yard appeared 'a dreadful space', with the only plant worth retaining a prunus with pale pink blossom. Ellis wrote that the courtyard was created:

> *. . . in a cramped area and from a mess that would have deterred all but the most enthusiastic garden planners. Privacy was essential, and this was obtained by putting screening strips on timber poles, which were set slightly out from the actual boundary line to enable planting behind and in front of them. The area was brick-paved for ease of maintenance, and despite the lack of space the little garden was given a small rock outcrop as a point of interest . . . An area at the bottom of the garden had to be given over to housing the car, but this has been screened off in such a way that the garden does not visually lose space, the screen suggesting merely that there is more garden to see beyond it, around the corner.*

Two huge boulders for use in the garden were sent from 'Kildrummie' at Holbrook, Jane Carnegie's childhood home, where Ellis had built stone walls to Edna Walling's design some twenty-five years earlier. It was this happy association with her family that led her to contact him for her own garden – 'and he was so helpful and willing to do it that I didn't hesitate'. The oriental influence she requested took the form of a pebbled corner, opposite the carefully shaped prunus tree and illuminated at night by the gentle glow of an antique Japanese lantern. Here the two 'Kildrummie' boulders – one with a flat top, the other gently pointed, like a small mountain – were favourite sitting spots. Native violets crept around the base of the boulder that marked the corner of the brick paving, while *Juniper sabina* made a feathery green screen behind it. Black bamboo and blue grass grew against the rear wall of the shop, and among the river-washed pebbles. Along the wall beyond the prunus, Ellis specified several grevilleas ('Dargan Hill', 'Pink Pearl', and 'Poorinda Queen'), and *Hakea purpurea*. Narrow slatted timber seats were built in an L-shape against the opposite wall and against a tea-tree screen, set halfway down the small yard and running almost across its width to hide the parked car. Beyond this screen were planted a small gum tree (*Eucalyptus torquata*), a grevillea, two callistemons and a melaleuca, all of which eventually were visible either above the screen, or to one side of it.

Installation of the 'screening strips on timber poles' gave Ellis great satisfaction. He used reverse-side-out panels of Stramit, the straw-like ceiling lining material – he had been longing to try this for years, he said, but no client had given him a free hand. The strips were raised perhaps two metres from the ground, braced with sawn timber, and set in from the boundary fence, a bold move in such a constricted space. Beneath this elevated screen he planted bamboo, with the idea that this would grow up *behind* the screen and create an illusion of depth. The scheme was a great success, the only problem being arresting the march of the bamboo (for economy reasons, the less invasive black bamboo was not used over this length).

*B*oulders for the Carnegie courtyard came from the client's childhood home, where Ellis had worked twenty-five years earlier.

For Jane Carnegie several aspects of her association with Ellis Stones remain vivid. One was her surprise at the size of his fee – he charged only some $50 for design and supervision of the work. Another was a kind of unspoken communication occasioned, perhaps, by her own battle with the pain of an impaired leg. She was touched by his helpful attitude, his courtesy and the alacrity with which he tipped his hat every time he saw her. And she remembers her courtyard with great fondness, not only as a place of calm and beauty but as a skilful response to her brief.

What is notable about Ellis's design principles is that in general, and particularly where small spaces are involved, he speaks a similar language to the American designers, Garrett Eckbo and Thomas Church. In 1937 Eckbo had put the view that gardens were places in which people lived out of doors, that their boundaries were backgrounds, their features accessories, for life. People were important, 'every garden a stage, every occupant a player'. But the garden had to be something more than an 'outdoor living-room' if it was to be worthy of its name. 'It must have scale, it must have enclosure, it must have a third dimension.' (As noted, landscape designer Gordon Ford regarded Ellis's tuition in 'juggling the second and third dimensions' as invaluable.)

These ideas already had currency in Australia. In October 1944 a local architect, one L. W. Jackson, wrote in *Australian Home Beautiful* that outdoor and indoor living should be linked and that garden designs of the future would be determined not by plants but by the activities of their users, especially children. In 1946, in the same magazine, Ellis suggested that in one's back garden

> *. . . at least a small area should be treated as an extension of the living rooms of the house, for relaxation on suitable days. We Australians pride ourselves that we are outdoor people, but are we? The average city and suburban family lives in the house every day and night, and never thinks of adding a summer room – a small section of the garden.*

Nine years later, in his best-selling *Gardens are for People*, Thomas Church sent this dictum around the world as he emphasised the importance of the garden as a setting for people, maintaining that successful garden design depended on unity (of house and garden), on the functional integration of practical and decorative requirements, on simplicity and scale. He believed a guiding principle of the designer should be the provision of easy access between house and garden, creating a feeling of intimacy. Features like 'small, quiet places to read the morning paper . . . or shell the peas', retaining walls wide enough to sit on, permanently built seats, screens to allow service features to be part of the garden yet not constantly in view – all added to this effect. He wrote:

> *The new kind of garden is still supposed to be looked at. But that is no longer its only function. It is designed primarily for living, as an adjunct to the functions of the house. How well it provides for the many types of living that can be carried on outdoors is the new standard by which we judge a garden.*

In 1962 the English designer Russell Page noted the west-coast American trend whereby climate conditions transformed gardens into pieces of 'humanised landscape', with horticulture taking second place to the pleasures and needs of out-of-door living. As antecedents he cited historic movements ranging from Babylonian and Persian civilisations to Pliny's gardens, while acknowledging twentieth-century determinants like car-parking, swimming pools and play equipment. These, he commented in *The Education of a Gardener*, were no longer seen as necessities infringing on precious garden space but as a legitimate form of landscaping. Hard surfaces were proliferating, while grass and flowers, trees, shrubs and hedges were becoming 'like islands, and as precious as them'.

Because of similarities in life-style and in climate, one would expect contemporary Australian gardens to have more in common with their counterparts on the west coast of the United States than with the English-style gardens that always have been the standard here. This potential relationship, however, continues to elude many of our landscape architects and garden-makers, as it does home gardeners who seek to emulate the English model while failing to understand that, except in certain areas of gentle climate (the Dandenongs, Macedon, the Blue Mountains), it is not really suited to our conditions. Ellis Stones wrote in 1971:

> *Even today the English influence is seen in our domestic gardens and in many of our public parks, although our climate is not exactly suited to this type of garden. Perhaps some day we will design our parks and gardens to suit our climate and display our native flora.*

Always he tried to give his clients the plants they yearned for, like roses and perennials – 'a garden is a very personal thing', he said – and because of this his gardens sometimes appeared more 'English' in style. But in terms of their relationship to the houses they surrounded and their integration of facilities suited to our way of life, they had a lot in common with the west-coast American model.

FIFTEEN

Success in town and country

Merchant Builders advertisements did not hesitate to mention Ellis by name.

It was Ellis's skill in handling small spaces that sealed his successful association with the project-home company Merchant Builders. This began in 1965. Excluding Edna Walling's initial encouragement and continued referrals, the commission to design gardens around the Merchant Builders houses was the biggest single influence on his career, and it was to bring the kind of public acclaim and recognition of his ideas for which he had yearned. Press advertisements over a period of several years mentioned him by name, with phrases like 'Merchant Builders homes are landscaped by Ellis Stones'. Had any other land-scape designer in Australia received such publicity?

The Merchant Builders product – architect-designed houses at project-home prices – was a great leap forward from the unimaginative stereotypical brick veneer boxes that for almost two decades had been the pinnacle of ambition for most suburban home-owners, and all that was available to them. Eric Wilson wrote in *Australian Home Beautiful* in 1965 that Merchant Builders' first three houses broke with the traditional approach to project building and sales. In Melbourne their approach was not absolutely new – some years earlier Robin Boyd had designed a project house for Contemporary Home Industries, while word had filtered south about a range of houses of similar character designed in New South Wales from 1963 on by Ken Woolley, for the firm of Pettit, Sevitt and Partners. But the Merchant Builders houses had enormous impact. They offered flexibility, variety, innovative use of space and easy maintenance. Their vocabulary of large expanses of glass, natural brick walls and exposed timbers was as unusual for the project market as was their emphasis on well-thought-out design and an easy flow between indoors and outdoors. Town planner Howard McCorkell's first sight of the houses remains vivid, and typified the reaction of potential buyers. 'I was out driving around. I came across them by chance. What an inspiration! I was struck in particular by the freshness of the architecture and the total presentation – the harmony of the whole package.' Among buyers flocking to the display centre in outer-suburban Springvale Road, Glen Waverley, were young professionals, tradespeople, salesmen, people from all walks of life. The common denominator was that they realised something was lacking in the established new-home market so pitilessly summarised by Robin Boyd in his book *The Australian Ugliness* – and that in the mid-1960s, they had some awareness of the importance of design.

Merchant Builders had its beginnings in discussions between the Melbourne businessman David Yencken and Robin Boyd about the need for architect-designed project houses that were available to the average home-buyer. David Yencken had a background in motels – in the early 1960s he had built the Mitchell Valley Motel in the Victorian country town of Bairnsdale, to a design by architect John Mockridge, then he built and operated the Black Dolphin Motel at Merimbula on the south coast of New South Wales, for which Robin Boyd was his architect. Working on this project as a member of Boyd's staff was a young architect, Graeme Gunn, and he and Yencken developed the idea of project houses, feeling sure there was a market for the product they had in mind. John Ridge, a Melbourne timber merchant, and Yencken then set up Merchant Builders. Graeme Gunn was their architect. To complete the team they sought a graphic designer and a landscaper: Bruce Weatherhead of Weatherhead and Stitt was signed up to do the graphics, then Gunn suggested they approach Ellis Stones for the landscaping.

Gunn had first met Ellis in 1961. Not long graduated as an architect, he was working for Robin Boyd while also carrying out some private commissions. In those days, he said, only rarely did architects consider landscape as integral to their architecture. He felt boulders and native planting might be an appropriate landscape treatment and had tried this out around one or two of his own houses, but with limited success. Then Ellis Stones turned up in Boyd's office one day to talk about his work,

*J*ohn Ridge, Graeme Gunn, David Yencken and Ellis (left to right) in the courtyard of a new Merchant Builders development.

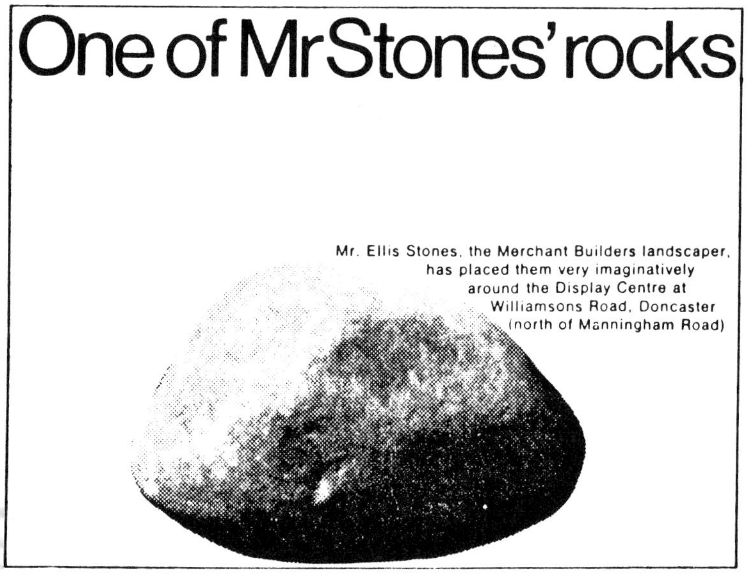

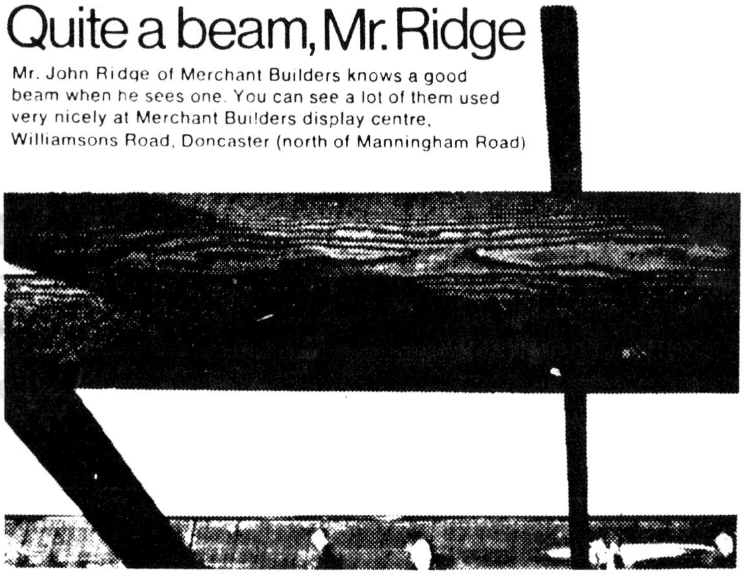

*B*ruce Weatherhead's advertisements were as lively as the product they promoted.

and Gunn was captivated. 'Here was this comfortable, gentle old man with beautiful slides of almost Japanese-type gardens, of a delicacy which I hadn't seen before. It persuaded me that the components he used could work well with new housing.'

After that Gunn – now one of Melbourne's most respected and successful architects, and a past dean of architecture at the Royal Melbourne Institute of Technology – kept in touch with Ellis. They worked on projects together from time to time, Gunn even labouring for Ellis for a day or two in 1965. They talked. 'He brought a sense of sanity', Gunn recalled. 'I was about thirty then, I'm sure a lot of my education was simply talking to him about the way things ought to be. He was a kind of paterfamilias in the benign way he talked about the environment, the landscape and general human morality. He stressed the need to integrate houses with the landscape.'

Likewise, Ellis made an immediate impression on David Yencken. Here was a seventy-one-year-old man, well past the age at which most people retired, yet whose energy was equal to – if not greater than – that of the businessmen around half his age with whom he was working. 'The overwhelming thing about Ellis was his remarkable enthusiasm', Yencken recalled. 'We were delighted with him, his exuberance and interest. He was always excited about anything I took to him. This was so infectious and warming! You were rarely conscious of his age because he was always so interested.'

In terms of professional achievement, Yencken, Ridge and Gunn felt Ellis was so clearly the right person to carry out their landscaping that there was no point in looking further. He had covered a wide range of work, he was proficient with native plants – which they wanted – and he had a sure, skilled touch in confined spaces. This last was particularly relevant with new houses set on small, regular suburban blocks where courtyards assumed increased prominence. 'He did a superb entrance area to our "Terrace House" – it really needed something since it didn't have a formal approach. He had to create a kind of outdoor lobby and a sense of entry so that people were led in', David Yencken recalled. His firm was ahead of its time in realising that the overall appearance of a house set in a complementary landscape could prove a selling point. Even the journalist Eric Wilson commented in *Australian Home Beautiful* only on the bricks, mortar and internal finishes and planning of the Merchant Builders houses. He gave little attention to site planning or landscape treatment beyond remarking in March 1966 that in terms of colour and form, the Studio House was tied intimately and sympathetically with the landscape 'a quality that seems more prized in Melbourne than the other capital cities (of Australia) if the success of the designer Mr Alistair Knox . . . is any criterion'.

The company's aim was to build houses to order, and to give buyers a total package, so Merchant Builders provided an on-site landscape interview for clients once Graeme Gunn had met them and sited their chosen house on the block. Ellis did these interviews initially, but being a practical man he found it difficult simply to give advice. He would become lost for words; his habit of forgetting the names of plants didn't help. 'Apart from the days when that awful wound in his leg troubled him so, these on-site interviews were the only time we would recognise his age', said David Yencken. Better for him were the situations when he was called in to actually build the garden. Following the Glen Waverley display houses, the first Merchant Builders house to be constructed was in Lower Templestowe, for the then chaplain at the Brotherhood of St Laurence, Canon Peter Hollingworth (now Anglican Archbishop of Brisbane) and his young family. The Hollingworths had been living in North Melbourne, in a cold old vicarage that did not lend itself to the demands of two babies. They needed to move out, but they couldn't bear the idea of something 'suburban'; they wanted a house that was 'environmentally good' and inexpensive. A friend told Peter Hollingworth about the new project houses designed by Graeme Gunn. 'My heart sank. I thought we would never be able to afford one, but I went to see him. He showed me a sketch plan on his drawing board and it was just what we were looking for. "What's the price?" I asked tentatively. "Five thousand pounds", he said. We ordered a Terrace House immediately, and David Yencken said we must get Ellis Stones to do the garden.'

It was a difficult job; the block sloped away more than the Hollingworths had realised and the long, narrow house sat on it rather awkwardly. Ellis saw this as a challenge and completed the work in one day. He maximised the amount of level space with clusters of large boulders, extending the sitting area under the pergola. Ann Hollingworth was struck by his young co-workers' long hair, and by their good humour. 'In those days you didn't really come across long-haired chaps – they were gorgeous. And there was such a marvellous spirit and atmosphere about the way they worked, sitting down on the boulders for their morning tea, their dirty hands plunging into the sugar bowl and dishing out sugar and dirt. There were jokes, and laughter, and jovial discussion. Ellis Stones was much older, of course, but he was very much one of them, and he did all the physical work with them.' Ellis provided a plan for plants to be bought as finances allowed, including a flowering cherry beside the pergola, and a range of native plants that the Hollingworths got from the nursery run by Peter Glass's wife, Cecile, at Eltham. For them this was the beginning of a 'tremendous interest' in native plants that has inspired subsequent gardens in city and country.

Peter Hollingworth met Ellis only twice – once when he went to his house to discuss the work to be done, once when the garden was being made. But to this day he retains an indelible impression of 'a very simple man, with a grasp of the earth and what it was about. I sensed he came from a Methodist background. He had an unerring sense of what you had to do to recreate an environment with simplicity, a minimum amount of fuss and a fine sense of design.' After Ellis's death Peter Hollingworth wrote a letter to the *Age* newspaper, praising not only his achievement in the design of domestic gardens, but his quest to re-establish the beauty and dignity of the Australian environment in places where it had been destroyed by concrete and bitumen. (He commented with some sadness that of all the letters he had written to the *Age* over the years, he believed this was the only one to go unpublished.)

As Merchant Builders houses grew steadily in popularity, and as the field became more crowded – with only five such builders Australia-wide in 1965, the following year there were eighteen – David Yencken and John Ridge decided to tackle town-house developments. Changes to the Strata Titles Act enabled them to build town houses with self-contained garden spaces, which proved a fine vehicle to display their commitment to landscaping. In 1967–68 Ellis found himself working not only on the gardens of individual Merchant Builders houses in outer suburbs – 'we always recommended him to clients looking for a landscape architect', said John Ridge – but on large town-house schemes in prosperous, established suburbs like Brighton, Toorak and Malvern. Yencken and Ridge discovered early on that with these speculative developments there was no point in trying to landscape to an exact budget, as Ellis had no real feeling for this. They reconciled themselves to the fact that the landscaping would cost whatever it cost, and left him to it, much as decades earlier, Edna Walling had let Ellis go ahead in his own way on a particular section of a garden. They had to put him under considerable pressure, however, to meet completion dates.

They struck the occasional problem, finding that his measurements – often jotted down on the back of an envelope – sometimes were inaccurate in terms of levels and falls. If the plans that emerged from his office did not seem to match up with the site in question, then they would have to return and check the measurements. It took some time for Ellis to become used to dealing with plans, because until now he had preferred simply to discuss concepts with a client, then to move into the garden with his team, beginning work at a key point and taking it from there. In those earlier days, sometimes his workmen would have no idea why they were carrying out certain tasks until the day when suddenly the garden 'came together' and Ellis's design objectives were revealed. Occasionally a client had insisted on a plan; over the years Louise Landale prepared these when asked, as did Beverley Hanson in the early 1960s, on good-quality art paper, using pen, ink and watercolour. 'They weren't up to much', Beverley says. One such plan for a suburban back garden survives from 1962, with an accompanying letter that displays a blend of mild enthusiasm and exasperation:

Dear Mr Stones

Thank you for your draft plan. We have examined it closely and would like you to consider the following comments. We liked your suggested arrangement of porch and steps and toppings on the northern side.

It is hard to criticise the plan of the north-western section as

1. *the garage is not drawn to scale,*
2. *provision for trailer is not shown at the side of the toilet as specifically asked for,*
3. *incinerator has been shown where there is an existing Hawthorn tree which we wish to keep, and*
4. *Lilly Pilly tree shown in wrong position and the clothes-line is not shown at all.*

As regards 'perennials' shown under the Hawthorns, I was looking to you for specific recommendations. As already stated I feel I would like some screen for the back fence and I do not feel perennials are the solution. I do understand that some of the shrubs placed nearer the house are to act as a screen, but I would like something instead of, or in addition to these, about 6–8 feet high near the Hawthorns.

In the northern sideway you have shown:

1. *A* Grevillea rosmarinifolia *where the oil drum is, and*
2. *the Cumquat tree outside the laundry window and the Coprosma outside the kitchen window have not been shown, both of which we wish to keep. Would this alter shrubs 27, 28, 29, 30, 31?*

I presume that in the shrubs where you have mentioned generic names you mean to give us advice as to what species, eg. Melaleuca. *To conclude, I understood from our conversation that you would come again and discuss the plan, and I feel that in view of the comments above this will be essential . . .*

If Ellis had been able to get on with the job in the way he preferred, would these problems have arisen?

For Ellis's part, with the Merchant Builders work he sometimes found himself having to cope with situations where the excavation and site preparation were not what he would have hoped. Here his years of construction experience stood him in good stead, as did his facility with retaining materials like boulders and timber sleepers. One such case was a series of town houses in Malvern where an owner who moved in before Ellis had started work remembered that a change in level indicated on the plans as one metre was actually a three-metre drop. Ellis did a beautiful job of disguising the resultant bank with sleepers, she said, but even this did not dispel the feeling of 'living in a well'. However, for her 'the rocks were the thing, and they were lovely'. She admired the way Ellis created perching spots around the small garden with built-in seats and low walls – she retains an enduring mental picture of her five-year-old daughter sitting in the middle of the rockery 'folded up like a little frog' – and she was thrilled with the way the garden settled in so quickly once he had completed his work. She was disappointed, however, that despite regular cups of morning coffee and her own interest in native plants, she could not seem to get him talking on the subject. '"What would you put in there?" I'd ask. He'd smile and say rather vaguely: "I'm sure you'll find something that pleases you".' (Perhaps he could not remember the names.)

Throughout his professional career Ellis's costings were low. He prepared a plan for an old peoples' home in 1966 for a fee of £10 a day; an average fee for a garden plan, including a site inspection and discussion, was around £30. But his 1966–68 receipt book shows that some clients jibbed at this. Charging a client in Heathmont £35 for 'detailed plan of garden as quoted', he was sent five guineas. He didn't submit an account for the balance owing. This attitude persisted. In 1972 a $95 account for an interview, inspection and plan was marked simply: 'Refused to pay'. The following year he noted on another $95 account: 'Paid only $45. Will accept this and close the deal'. An accountant and old friend who helped Ellis with his tax returns commented that although Ellis's bad debts were always considerable, he could not persuade him to follow them up. 'Money was a secondary item to Ellis; he loved his work, he was keen to get onto a job and do it. And he had some very shrewd clients who could pick this.'

By 1965 he was being sought for a range of work in the public arena. This had started in a small way some years earlier. As president of the Ivanhoe River Parklands Protection League, in 1960 he joined the National Trust's landscape preservation council, formed, according to a newspaper article of the time, 'in lieu of any official consideration of aesthetic control over our environment'. The council had come into being after a meeting held late in 1959 in Professor John Turner's office at the University of Melbourne's botany school, to discuss forming a tree preservation society along the lines of a similar group in Western Australia. Professor Turner suggested broadening the charter from 'trees' to 'landscape'; Dr Norman Wettenhall, who attended that meeting, remembered that many of those present were surprised to find other people interested in conservation 'which at the time was not the burning issue it is now'. Members of the council, drawn from conservation groups throughout the city, came and went as various groups and interests were topical. They tried to protect existing landscape features – early battles centred on mining at Mt Sugarloaf, clearing for dairying in the Heytesbury forest, installation of a 'scenic road' in a sensitive part of the South Gippsland coast. They tried also to restrain bodies like the Board of Works and the State Electricity Commission from destroying or damaging landscape features in newly developed suburbs. Meetings with government authorities, politicians and other influential people were held with the aim of educating and preventing, rather than confronting; one topic discussed was the siting of power lines in the Yarra Valley. 'Victoria must grow and change', read a promotional leaflet for the landscape preservation council, 'but we believe that its growth should be planned in such a way that life in our more crowded State will remain pleasant for us and our descendants . . . we need to learn to care for the property we hold in common – our beaches, river banks, mountain tops and bushland. And surely we are interested in preserving something of our specifically Australian heritage – our native plants and animals . . .'

This, of course, was the message Ellis had been promoting for years, and from there it was but a short step for him to a much more major involvement with the National Trust (and thus with the public) as its honorary landscape architect. Sometimes this workload extended to fetching and carrying – a telephone message in his 1965 office diary read: 'Miss Adamson (Como) wanted to know if you could pick up an old sewing machine donated by a Mrs Wood in High Street Preston . . .' but later there were more complex assignments for which he always found time even though they ranged from one end of the state to the other. (His pool and rockery, built for the Trust in 1965 at Como, South Yarra, was not done in this honorary capacity.)

There was 'public' work for friends and associates. In 1961–62 he created an outcrop and dry watercourse, embellished with native plants, near the administration block at Burnley Horticultural College. This is remembered as 'outstanding' by a lecturer who was a student there at the time, and was done voluntarily. 'I seem to remember him saying that

Burnley had done a lot for horticulture and he wanted to do something for us', said Eric Littlejohn, past principal at the college. Around 1963 he designed a delightful small pool at Chris Cross, a garden supplies outlet in the suburb of Deepdene from which he bought rocks and other materials. He was good friends with the owner, Mrs Rana Plowman; often he called in, when passing, for a cup of tea and a chat. Mrs Plowman spoke of his rosy cheeks, his hands – 'very small and narrow' – the effortless way in which he handled rocks, and his bushcraft. 'Once I had in a load of beautiful stone and I rang him. He came round to choose and he said; "I bet there's a snake under there". We pooh-poohed him, but there was. He quickly picked it up, whipped it back through the wire by the tail and killed it.' The small, kidney-shaped pool – much admired by clients and visitors – was edged with random slate, pebbles, river-washed stones and one or two carefully chosen boulders. 'Simplicity is the answer to installing a pool in a small garden. Focus must be kept on the pool by using neutral colours, plain materials and sparse planting', Ellis wrote.

Mrs Plowman supplied the rocks for an unusual project that Ellis carried out in 1965 at Monash University, at the CSIRO's division of physical chemistry. The calibration of delicate instruments in an underground laboratory was being upset by pedestrians walking across the large courtyard above, and it was felt that rocks piled on the ground might deaden the vibrations and divert foot traffic. Architect Allan Anderson, working with the Department of Construction, decided to telephone Ellis 'on the off-chance that he might be able to do something'. (His own interest in Edna Walling's work meant he knew a little of Ellis's background.) He expected

A small pool built for a garden supplies firm.

that the job might appear too mundane and was pleasantly surprised at Ellis's friendliness, and his immediate interest in helping solve the problem. Access was difficult; a crane couldn't be used because of the surrounding buildings, then Ellis consulted an expert in heavy machinery who suggested building a concrete ramp (which had to be covered in sand) and driving in the rocks by machine. This worked perfectly, and he completed the 'keep off' treatment by installing prickly plants around the rocks, as he had done a decade earlier next to the small pool in the Stone garden at Ivanhoe.

Most of Ellis's work through the 1960s was for gardens in the city and suburbs, but he continued to enjoy country projects. In 1962 he travelled to Millicent in South Australia to help lay out a garden for Louise McDonald (née Landale), his former staff member who was newly married. This was a joint venture where his broad sense of design and Mrs McDonald's love of plants combined to form a superlative garden (almost destroyed in the 1983 bushfires but since rebuilt). The site was studded with huge stringybarks, which he loved, and the entrance gate was positioned so that two stringybarks framed the first view of the house. Ellis wrote:

> *After entering the property the drive passes another fine tree. I took advantage of this tree by using it as a starting point to make a low outcrop of the local limestone which formed an area for guests' cars. The tree supplies the shadows necessary to complete the picture . . . The owner who is responsible for the lovely garden has been able to keep a balance between the native area and exotic trees, shrubs and flowers.*

The entrance to the McDonald garden in South Australia was sited between two stringybarks that framed the first view of the house.

*E*llis used gravel and a small outcrop at the base of a particularly eye-catching tree.

The exotic flowers would have shrivelled up had Ellis not installed a series of tea-tree screens to break the strong prevailing winds that made it almost impossible to use one section of the garden except for lawn. He wrote:

> *Sometimes a windbreak is necessary in a very large garden where it is difficult to get results with planting alone. Under these conditions a fence or screen is the best solution and can make a most attractive section of the garden. The exact siting and angle of the fence or fences is most important, as another feature is being added to the garden. In this garden both sides of the fence were visible from the house on the windward side . . .*

*T*ea-tree screens served as windbreaks in the McDonald garden.

Ellis's masterful handling of these screens is reminiscent of Thomas Church's work in its sense of proportion and direction, and its awareness of light and shade.

In another large country garden, built in 1965 for Mr and Mrs John McIlwraith near Violet Town in north-east Victoria, Ellis was given a free hand with the garden, the only proviso being that the client did not want to spend all her time in it. He travelled into the nearby Strathbogie Ranges, taking the McIlwraiths with him, and gathered rocks, including thin granite 'caps' that he levered off with his crowbar and that, skilfully placed in the garden, looked like solid boulders. He planted black bamboo and rice plant around the fish-pond in the courtyard, as well as a little clumpy plant that he had noticed in the creek. Liking its form, he dug it up and tucked it in next to the pond. It was nutweed, a dreadful pest, and Mrs McIlwraith pulled out its progeny for years thereafter.

He put down slabs of rock around the swimming hole, built a stone wall, dragged in logs as seats and planted *Azara*, crab apples, japonica, kangaroo paws and other native plants thickly clustered at one end of the garden. A little way from the house he placed two quince trees on the curving creek bank. 'No large site in the country is complete without a couple of old quinces', he said. Except for the courtyard there was no great sense of enclosure in the garden. He said to the McIlwraiths: 'You want to look out over those burnt paddocks'.

Two years later he returned to the district to create a garden for Mr and Mrs Barry Nolan around 'Mogolimby', a new house outside Euroa.

On a country property near Euroa, the new house was sited near a large eucalypt and an existing dam that was extended to form a lake.

He was involved from the outset in the siting of the house, designed by Graeme Gunn. The Nolans had picked a spot where they thought the house might sit well, but Gunn suggested consulting Ellis first, and a new site was chosen. Later he wrote:

> *When planning the approach to a country property, remember that visitors who have travelled long distances have become accustomed to wide horizons, therefore it is necessary to think on a large scale . . . the entrance to the property was chosen because of the large* Eucalyptus microcarpa *near the road. The house . . . is hidden from view at this point by the larger of the hills, which is partly circled before the building again comes into view.*

He told them that he didn't want the surroundings of the house to be a 'garden' – he wanted the planting to merge into the paddocks. For the

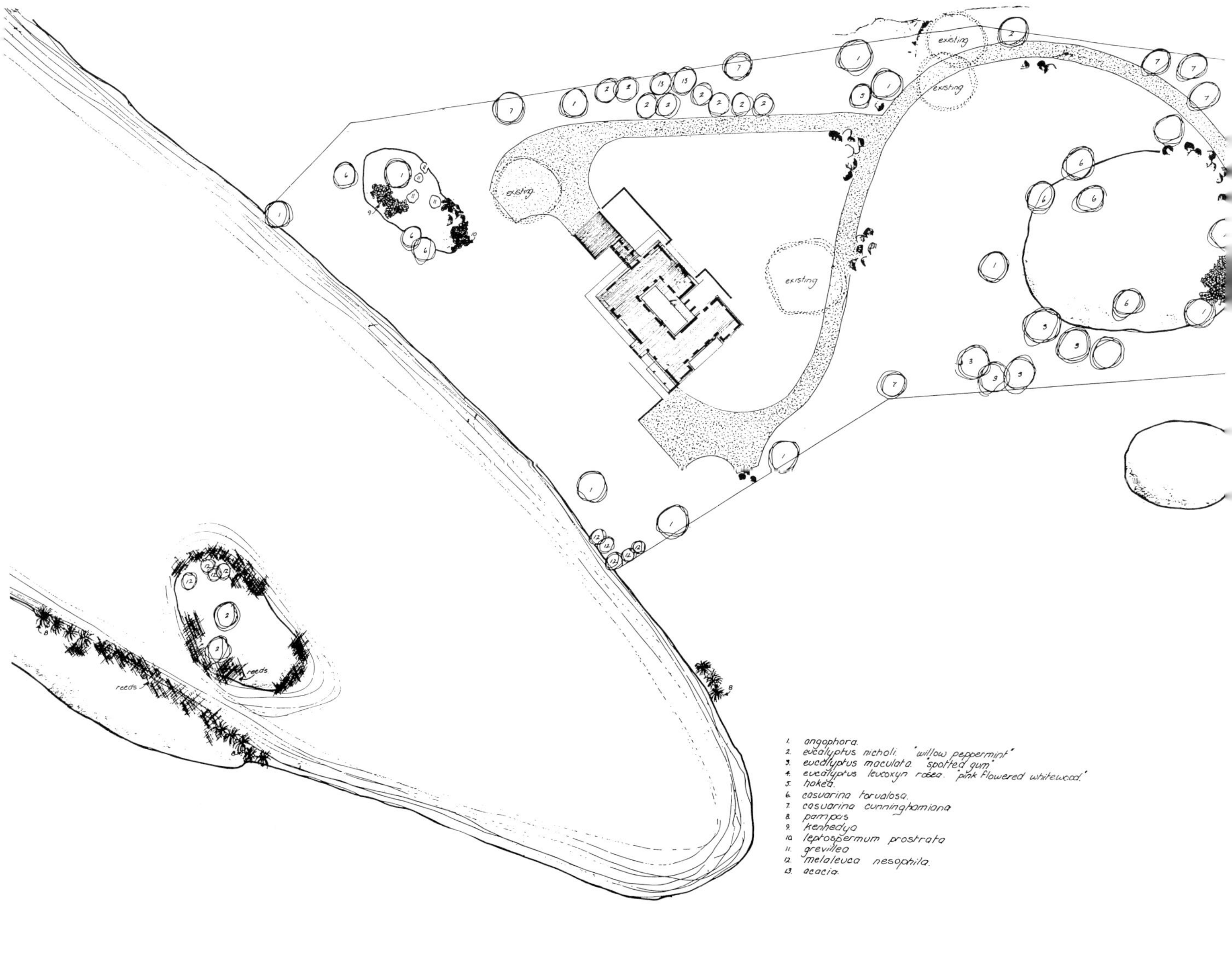

*T*he broad landscape plan of the Euroa house demonstrated a confident use of mounding, and only a few species of native plants.

area immediately adjoining the house he prepared a detailed plan, using many different exotic and native plants, but for the broader landscape – the drive, the front paddocks and around the dam – the plant schedule was short and simple. It comprised three kinds of eucalypt (*E. nicholii, E. maculata, E. leucoxylon* 'Rosea'), *Casuarina torulosa* and *C. cunninghamiana, Melaleuca nesophila, Leptospermum prostrata* and 'angophora, grevillea, kennedia and acacia'. (He also specified pampas grass – one clump on the dam edge.) The native plants were dispersed boldly yet sparingly, with repetition a key element of the scheme. He chose, and carefully placed, a special diving rock for the dam.

All his life Ellis spent time sitting in the bush, or in natural surroundings, and simply looking. He liked to take a tent to the country and camp in the open. (His bushcraft skills were considerable; he taught his grandchildren how to spot lizards and snakes in rocky country and how not to get lost in the bush by knotting seedling trees to mark their path.) He would make the forty-minute trip from his home to 'Glenara' near Bulla, to look at the rocks and the river and recharge his batteries; he did the same in 1966 during a visit with Graeme Gunn to John and Cicely Fenton's Western District property near Branxholme. Today John Fenton is one of Victoria's premier conservationists, with his schemes for native planting and wetlands acclaimed Australia-wide. But when Ellis was there the property was bare except for an 'embryonic recreation of a swamp', and the Fentons were formulating ideas about how best to cope with it. Ellis sat, sketching, on a little platform at the edge of the swamp, attended by the Fentons' four children aged under six. John Fenton then took him on a five-hour walk through nearby sand dunes. He observed that Ellis was having a difficult time with his bad leg, but Ellis stayed with the two much younger men as they strode across the dunes, and kept them busy listening to what he had to say about the native sedges, the water plants and how wonderful their delicate forms would be in domestic landscaping, about the broad-acre countryside and the way that the backs of dam banks should be blended into the surrounding land and appropriately planted.

John Fenton took a lot of heart from what Ellis said, and sees him as a formative influence on his own beliefs and the way his life has developed. He still thinks of him and of his capacity for observing the landscape, and learning from it. Ellis wrote in the Fentons' visitors' book: 'Lost in the swamp'. He meant that he was lost emotionally, not physically.

SIXTEEN

Of street trees, pools and pollution

Ellis's interest in streets and the city environment received a major boost in 1965 when Nunawading City Council asked him to prepare a layout for a trial section of the median strip in Springvale Road. This commission came through the Blackburn Tree Preservation Society. Ellis knew this group through its membership of the National Trust's landscape preservation council; as well, he was a regular customer at Rock Plant Supplies, a fine nursery in Blackburn run by two of the society's members, Robin Conran and Audrey Scott. (This nursery specialised in alpines and unusual perennials at a time when such plants were very hard to find, and was a mecca for Melbourne's more knowledgeable gardeners.) At the time the section of Springvale Road in question comprised a wide reservation with dirt roads on either side of a strip of natural bush that included mature eucalypts, acacias and native cherries. As Melbourne's suburban sprawl extended and the area's orchards and paddocks were taken over for housing and light industry, sealing the road became a priority. It was planned to clear the reservation from kerb to kerb, a proposal that alarmed local residents and the tree preservation society.

Ellis Stones had given an illustrated talk to the society in May 1964 about his approach to landscaping, before being called in as consultant. His suggested treatment for this part of Springvale Road was revolutionary at a time when much street planting in Melbourne involved geometrically exact lines of elderly plane trees, or of alternate melaleucas and bright-pink-flowered cherry plums. He came up with the idea of bold clumps of Australian plants within the median strip and staggered on either side of it, thus deflecting the headlight beams of oncoming cars at night. Set in beds between twenty and forty metres long and half the median strip in width, these were to include remnants of the natural bush, some existing trees, and new shrubs and trees.

Soft native planting at the Nunawading Civic Centre.

Initially the council officers resisted the proposal. But after three months' consideration, and lobbying by councillors who were in sympathy with Ellis's plans, permission was given to go ahead. The original planting stretched from south of the railway line below Whitehorse Road, to Canterbury Road, and was later extended through to Waverley Road. It became a model for subsequent planting of median strips throughout Victoria. And it encouraged Nunawading City Council to use Ellis again – in 1968 to landscape around its new municipal offices, and in 1974 to design part of the median strip in Canterbury Road (from east of View Road to the intersection of Boronia and Mitcham Roads). Here he broadened his original concept, using rock outcrops and low bluestone walls.

In Ellis's library at his death was a copy of *Landscape of Roads* (1960) by the English landscape architect Sylvia Crowe. He referred often to this important book and suggested it to his RMIT students for further study. He was influenced, too, by the dictum of the English designer Russell Page, that roadside planting should be bold in scope and concept, so that it has an impact on motorists passing at speed. Heavily underlined in Ellis's personal copy of Page's *The Education of a Gardener* is the comment that planting along arterial roads should be determined by an executive authority because in the past this had been seen only as a 'garden problem' to be viewed on foot or at leisure. But for motorists, Page wrote: 'A mile of one kind of planting is almost the shortest effective length'. Ellis's interest in street planting was intense. In the late 1960s the then Minister for Local Government, Mr Hamer, suggested that avenues of trees, grassed areas, garden beds and flowers should be planted to beautify nine major roads into Melbourne. Ellis toured some of these roads with a reporter from the evening newspaper, the *Herald*, and the resultant prominently placed article noted his ideas under the heading 'How to put on a better front – trees, shrubs for roads'. He suggested clumps of slender gums on the eastern side of the Tullamarine Freeway to give motorists a good view under high foliage, and gums with low foliage on the opposite side to screen views of 'flat and uninteresting' country. On the Hume Highway near Campbellfield Ellis advocated planting large trees and low shrubs on the median strip, with gaps to display occasional interesting features like the old bluestone Scots Church.

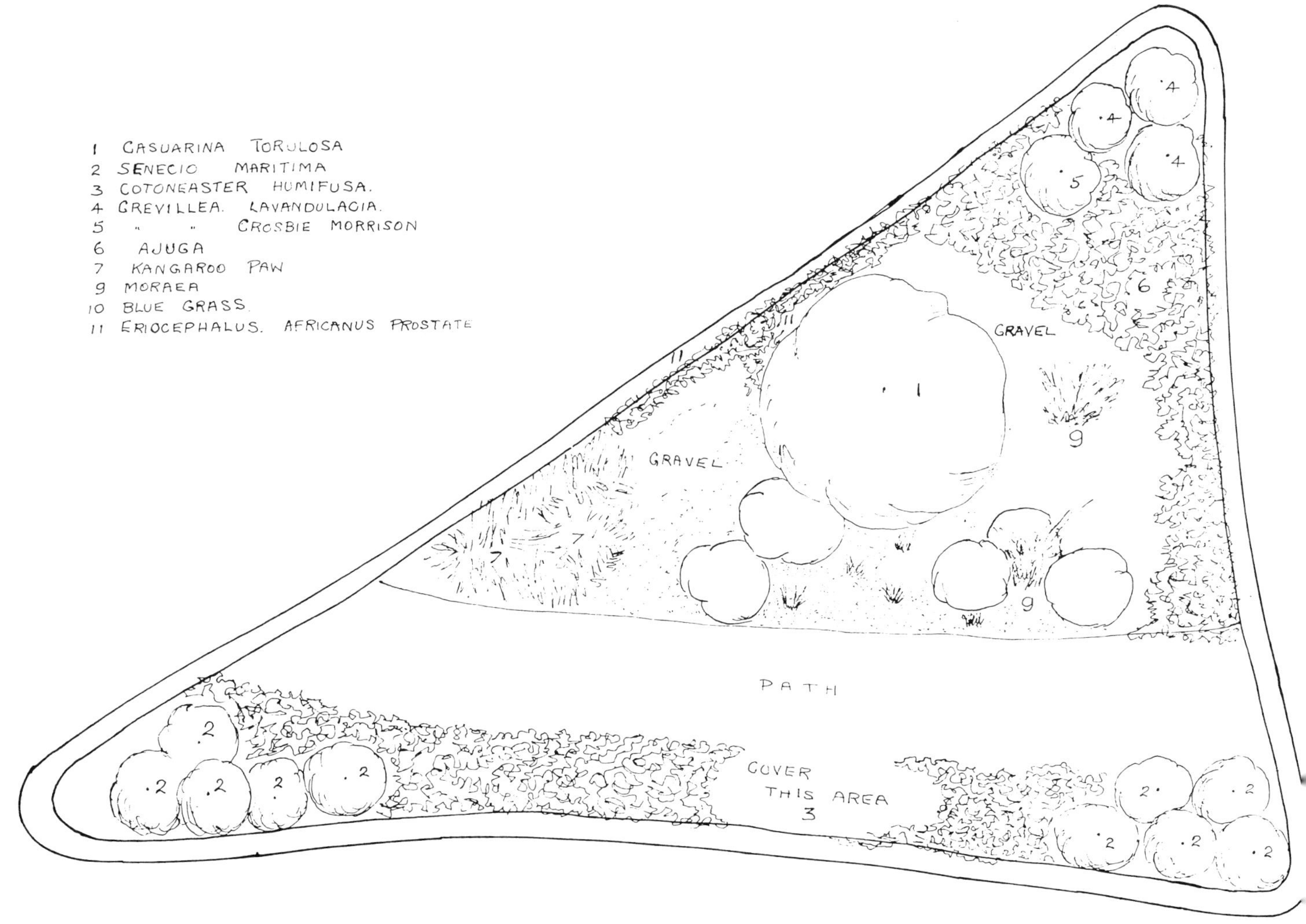

Ellis's own drawing (undated) for suggested replanting of a roundabout in Keam Street, Ivanhoe.

During the drought of 1967–68 many street trees in Melbourne were under stress. The trees on either side of St Kilda Road were cared for by different municipal councils; one side appeared to be dying while those on the other looked healthy. Ellis maintained that this was due to lack of water, and organised a bucket brigade of friends and concerned citizens to prove his point. Subsequently some were removed. A newspaper cutting of the time quoted Ellis as saying the sprinkler system for watering these trees was all wrong; that the trees were dying from starvation because the watering did not reach their roots. A hose should be left running on each for about eight hours so that the roots were properly soaked, he said. 'The public was told the trees were diseased and had to be taken out, but if they were watered properly they should live for years.'

In *Australian Garden Design* he wrote at some length about street planting, maintaining that of all the living material in the landscape trees were the most important, and in many cases the most neglected. He continued this argument in *Priority Landscaping*. His well-founded sentiments appear prophetic in the light of today's nationwide tree-planting drives:

There is a greater awareness of the value of trees in one's street today than there has ever been before, yet in spite of this we see cases of people in power at Council level ignoring the wish of the people and the value of street trees. This is the level where education should start. We must make sure that people standing for election to councils are aware of the value of street trees and will see that these trees are cared for, and wherever there is a chance, plant more trees.

It is not always possible to plant trees in some streets. Under some circumstances, where roads and footpaths have been established for some time, it is very difficult to introduce more trees. Therefore any existing trees . . . should be cared for, and provision made for getting water and fertiliser through to their roots, even at the expense of breaking up some of the bitumen if necessary.

The care of these existing trees above ground is as important as it is to feed them. The chief value of our street trees is their beauty. In spite of this, in many suburbs, we see trees mutilated each year. The plane tree seems to be singled out for this treatment more than any other tree, and yet this is a beautiful tree if allowed to grow naturally, giving that height which is needed in street trees.

When new areas that have no trees are made available for housing, provision should be made for a generous amount of trees, both in streets and wherever there is an area where they can be planted. Nothing looks worse than rows of houses packed closely together where large shrubs or small trees are planted in the streets. Trees should be large when planted in streets.

Where the area already has trees established, the roads should be planned to retain the best of the trees. The planners should remember that they are planning for people as well as motor cars, and if the road has to go around trees, does it matter?

The design and function of the suburban street has not altered in my lifetime except in a few cities where the value of trees is appreciated. On most occasions councils insist on constructing standard hard surface footpaths, destroying native trees that encroach on the line of the footpath, when a simple gravel path or even taking the hard surface around the trees would serve the few pedestrians and enhance the whole street.

The case for maintaining and establishing street trees is in your hands . . .

Meanwhile, still more work in the public domain was coming into the small back-room office at Locksley Road. Ellis, already busy with Merchant Builders and with domestic garden jobs, took it all on with gusto. But to friends and family he confided: 'This is coming at the wrong end of my life. I should have been born twenty years later.'

For some time Professor John Turner of the University of Melbourne had felt Ellis's skills should be displayed to a wider public. The opportunity arose in the mid-1960s at two properties where Professor Turner played an important role – the National Trust property 'Como', in South Yarra, and the Royal Botanic Gardens.

John Turner had been involved with the acquisition of 'Como' in the mid-1950s. (He went with Daryl Lindsay to talk to the owners, the Misses Armytage. 'Wearing hats, they gave us tea in their own drawing room. Then one said: "I think father left a little bottle of sherry in the cellar. Go down and see if there's any left." There was, and it was fine.') He headed the Como garden committee, whose members included Eric Hammond and John Stevens. When Stevens left in 1964 to work in Canberra, Ellis took his place on the committee. He was then commissioned to build a rockery and informal pool on a site below the main gate and adjoining Como Park, on the side of a hill, draining toward the park. Ellis chose the lowest point for the pool. He wrote:

There are many factors to be considered when siting an informal pool. Unlike the formal pool which can be placed almost anywhere, on level ground or even on raised ground, an informal pool should look natural and nestle into the landscape, which means that it is nearly always sited at a low level. The only thing to remember is to keep the materials – plant as well as structural – in proportion to the size of the area.

Excavation was carried out by Bob Grant and Como's head gardener, Chris van Riemsdyk, until a layer of ironstone was reached, hard and almost impenetrable, on which picks and even a pneumatic drill made little impression. So the pool was built on top of this with a concrete shell poured to be on the safe side. At one end Ellis made a dry wall, over which water flowed to form a bog section, later removed, for water-loving plants. He decided not to install drainage pipes. ('Agricultural drains – specify *where necessary*', read a student's notes from Ellis's RMIT lectures.) Grant and van Riemsdyk placed huge rocks by hand, working under Ellis's supervision; generally the planting around the pool was left to van Riemsdyk. Visiting children clambering on the rocks meant that any small-scale rock plants – dianthus and the like – did not survive; some years later an assistant gardener grew an impressive amount of dahlias from seed and planted them out among the rocks. When Ellis saw them, he was furious. He wrote that this pool showed:

. . . lack of consideration to detail in the planting of the pool and surrounding outcrop. In this type of pool I always try to hide as much of the concrete edge as possible by growing low plants between the over-hanging boulders, thus hiding the ugly edge of concrete and at the same time uniting the boulders. Unless the designer's ideas are followed through after the project is handed over, the plan will lose a lot of important details, as has happened with this pool because of the failure to cultivate the low plants . . . and by even planting dahlias in among the rocks.

The planting remains sparse today, and probably would please Ellis not much more than it did twenty years ago, but his beautifully controlled rockwork continues to create an atmosphere of calm reflectiveness that is rare in any public garden.

In 1966 Ellis was commissioned to design and build a rock garden in Melbourne's Royal Botanic Gardens, on a patch of lawn below the Australian border running down to the Nymphaea Lily Lake. This was funded by the Maud M. Gibson Gardens Trust, which Professor Turner

*R*ockwork around the 'Como' pool.

headed. The gardens' then director, R. T. M. Pescott, saw this as remedying the 'lack of a representative rock garden' in these historic gardens and described Ellis as 'probably the greatest exponent of this kind of work in the country'. This site was chosen because it was thought to be cool, and protected from the drying north winds of summer, but in the event it was found to be a 'hot spot' where few small rock plants of European origin flourished, and during the 1970s it was restocked with native plants. At the same time, drainage pipes had to be installed. Here again, and presumably taking into consideration the sloping site, Ellis had elected not to carry out preparatory drainage work, but in the years after the rock garden was completed the century-old pipes further up the slope subsided, and the need for remedial work became evident.

This was a job of major importance for Ellis. He used several workmen and a crane to help place the rocks, while the planting was left to the gardens staff. Mr Eddie Nelson, a senior gardener there, was fascinated; this concept was new to him, his previous experience with rockwork having been with formal bluestone or the cement 'grotto' work seen in other parts of the gardens. He found it most satisfying to watch the creepers and small plants clothing the rocks, and to see the garden 'grow on'. (Today the planting is shrubby and relatively sparse.)

This commission brought one amusing interlude. During construction one morning Ellis and his workmen were confronted by a naked young woman who appeared, her only attire a loudly blaring transistor radio, on the newly placed rocks at the top of the outcrop. Jaws fell, tools were dropped. Ellis instinctively took off his hat, then angrily hurled it to the ground and, ever the gentleman, said simply: 'That'll be enough. Go home, miss. And you boys get on with your work.' On a more serious note, in 1966 immediately after accepting the commission, he travelled to Germany to attend an International Federation of Landscape Architects meeting, taking letters of introduction from Mr Pescott to the directors of six botanic gardens in England, Scotland and France. These described him as 'a landscape designer of considerable repute in this state' who on his return from overseas would be undertaking the construction of a substantial rock garden. Ellis visited the Royal Botanic Gardens, Kew, on 28 June and examined the rock garden with Sir George Taylor, the director. A month later he spent four hours in the Royal Horticultural Society's garden at Wisley with the director, noting: 'Inspected Rock Garden with Mr Knight, had construction fully explained'. He also went to the rock garden in Edinburgh's Royal Botanic Gardens and the Jardin des Plantes in Paris.

There was time for sightseeing, fitted in between the conference and professional engagements. Ellis did not find England to his taste; he thought it too green and 'soft', but he loved the bare, rolling landscape of Scotland. And in Europe itself he found plenty to interest him, so that he returned home fired with new determination to convince Australians of the evils of pollution and the necessity for tree-planting and careful landscape design. Hardly was he through the door at Locksley Road when he sat down and wrote a letter that he sent to the town clerks of twenty-one municipalities in Melbourne. A handwritten draft reads:

Just recently I attended a world Congress of L. Architects, at Stuttgart in Germany. One of the aspects of the Congress was landscaping for Survival, and the proper use of land.

The air and water pollution in the largest cities is alarming, and both Germany and America are planning to combat this as much as possible with the use of trees and careful siting of housing and industrial projects to allow a free flow of air with the main (illegible).

I have slides showing the approach to this problem and would be pleased to show your council . . .

More than half the councils did not reply, or showed no interest. There was a range of responses: 'Water and air pollution are matters which are beyond the province of this council'; 'We would be pleased to view your slides on a date to be arranged'; '(We will) show your letter to the reserves, foreshores and properties committee'. Others put the matter in the 'too hard' basket, sending the letter on to such worthies as the chief health inspector, the city engineer or the parks and gardens chairman. Nevertheless Ellis did address several councils and felt he was getting his message across. The local newspaper also interviewed him on his return, when he emphasised that natural landscapes around Australian cities should be preserved, particularly existing pockets of bushland that were 'drastically being wiped off the map'. He compared Australian conditions to those he had observed in Germany, where parks and gardens abounded and factories offered special facilities for their employees' open-air recreation, where as much thought was given to the design of gardens around buildings as to the cost and materials of the building, and where children's playgrounds had a background of trees and shrubs growing naturally. He was thrilled at the 'unanimous acceptance' he observed in Germany of the importance of parks and gardens to everyday living, and at the way growing trees were given continual care – in comparison to Australia, where he said 'thousands of trees were slowly dying because of neglect'.

This trip to the other side of the world was of inestimable importance to Ellis. No doubt he learnt plenty in a professional sense. But more important was the realisation that he was not alone in his point of view on conservation, that others thought the way he did. This rekindled his energy, and he was ready to try and encourage Australians to follow their example. We should have the will to learn from other countries and do something *now* to put our house in order, he wrote.

It must be remembered that by 1966 Ellis had been promoting conservation for at least twenty years, with most of his energy being directed to a largely disinterested audience. 'My friends called me Rocky because of all the rocks in my gardens . . . the others did so because they said I had rocks in my head as well', he once commented wryly. And he explained in *Priority Landscaping*:

> *After the War (the Second World War) the uncontrolled destruction of my country started. There were large building projects appearing in all directions and roads started pushing out to serve these new areas, irrespective of what was destroyed in the process. I was amongst a handful of people who were very conscious and concerned by the needless destruction of our landscape. But the power of destruction was too strong, politically and financially . . . It was easy at that time to kill any attempt at conservation. We conservationists were just plain 'Cranks!'*

SEVENTEEN

Of publishing and playgrounds

Writing never came easily to Ellis. He would sit down reluctantly with scraps of paper to prepare for public lectures, writing out a page or two in full, then tailing off into note form and brief headings. When he was commissioned by the Macmillan company to prepare a book about his approach to garden design, initially he was thrilled. But committing his ideas to paper was a different matter.

Robert Cross, an Englishman who headed Macmillan in Melbourne, had met Ellis in 1967 when he landscaped his small inner-suburban garden. Confronted with a 'dust bowl' overlooked by rather grim flats on both sides, Ellis designed an ingenious series of raised, staggered tea-tree screens that effectively deflected one's eye from the flats while creating an attractive courtyard space. His client had never liked rocks in the garden, but Ellis's mastery of this medium quickly converted him. The relationship grew into friendship and Ellis took Robert Cross to look at other gardens he had designed where stone and timber were used with great flair, and where the emphasis was on native plants. It was immediately obvious to the publisher, who had worked in England on Russell Page's *The Education of a Gardener*, that here was a talent that should be recorded, and a style of landscape design about which nothing significant had yet been written. *Australian Garden Design* was the result. (It helped, too, that for some years Alistair Knox had been urging Ellis to write a book.)

Family, friends and favourite clients were thrilled, but the book did not happen overnight. Ellis was sure of the approach he wanted to take: he felt it should explain and illustrate his ideas on the value of the natural landscape and his philosophy of garden design, and that it should tell people how to achieve certain effects (he liked where possible to emphasise the 'before and after' aspects). But although he was in the habit of photographing all his work he did not always record or remember the names and addresses of clients, so he had trouble coming up with a range of locations for the photographer, Ted Rotherham. And the actual writing was a nightmare. 'It's the hardest thing I have ever done', he told a journalist. Help was provided by the publisher in the form of Pat Thomas, then editor of general books at Macmillan. She did an old-fashioned desk-editing job to get Ellis down on paper (an occurrence, the Melbourne *Herald* was to note in reviewing the book in 1971, that was long overdue).

Pat Thomas found the job long and hard – 'no publisher nowadays would do it that way' – but she enjoyed it. 'He'd come in to the office, or I'd go to his house, a whole afternoon at a time. The first time he came with a bundle – scrappy bits of paper and photos. We'd sit down and begin. "Now what do you want to say, Ellis?" I had to try and catch his tone of voice. The book had to be in very simple English, it had to be readable and it had to give information. It was fiddly, much harder than editing a novel. He was no good at the names of plants, but he had such a feel for his subject! He was a natural designer – he used to just know where things went.'

Pat Thomas was struck particularly by Ellis's interest in playground design. This was innate, springing from his deep-seated love of children and his memories of his own happy childhood. He believed passionately that playgrounds should be attractive, that the equipment in them should be natural-looking, that it should create challenges for the children who used it and, above all, that it should be safe. (Driving round Melbourne in the late 1950s with Louise Landale, he would exclaim not only at the mass-produced equipment but at its danger. 'They'll hurt themselves there', he would say.)

For some years he had been agitating for the establishment of a children's playground at Wilson Reserve on the Yarra river, near his home. Named after 'Skipper' Wilson of local Sea Scout renown, and acquired for public use in 1924, this was a picturesque natural area where vandalism had become enough of a problem for an 'honorary vigilance officer' to be appointed in 1963. Heidelberg City Council minutes record that around this time 'Mr Ellis Stones and the committee for the development of Wilson Reserve be invited to meet the Parks and Gardens Committee'. By mid-1967 the Ivanhoe Progress Association was petitioning the council for 'improved park facilities' at Wilson Reserve, asking that 'Mr Ellis Stones be consulted about preservation of the natural bush setting and planting of native trees and shrubs', and requesting picnic tables and play equipment. At a public meeting that month there was a unanimous vote for retention of the bushland setting, with which suggested amenities had to blend. Ellis's offer to prepare a playground plan as a basis for discussion and submission to the council was 'gratefully accepted', the council allocating money for construction of the project early in 1968.

Ellis charged no fees for design and supervision of this playground. Like so much of his work, it was new and different. His drawings show clusters of logs, sawn to different (child-size) heights or stacked one on the other, timber-framed see-saws and swings, log fences – the material for these was second-hand telephone poles – and a huge old fallen tree for climbing on. The treatment was simple yet imaginative. At a time when the average children's playground was crammed with metal equipment, often rusting, the only metal to be seen at Wilson Reserve was the steel

ELEVATION: VAULTING LOG.

PERSPECTIVE: VAULTING LOG.

LARGE LOG FOR CLIMBING.

ELEVATION OF CLIMBING LOGS.

PERSPECTIVE: CLIMBING LOGS.

ELEVATION: SEE-SAW.

PERSPECTIVE: SEE-SAW.

*E*llis's carefully detailed play equipment at Wilson Reserve was designed with children in mind, and used natural materials.

slide, set into a hillside with timber climbing stumps beside it. Ellis used timber for its beauty as well as its utility. Generally, he liked it unpainted – he believed timber when painted became just another construction material, with the colour of the paint the dominant factor. He wrote:

> *It was easy to decide what material to use when asked to design a children's playground which needed a strong fence to keep cars out of the area – a beautiful natural flat near a river bank, fairly well covered with eucalypts. As the fence had to be strong I couldn't help turning my mind back to my own childhood, and remembering how, as children, we loved climbing on stock yard fences. Children are no different today, except that many have never known these pleasures; they resent being organised, and the uninviting steel equipment that is erected in some playgrounds would tend to keep them away. It is a well-known fact that children prefer timber, and if it is possible to give them this material to build with and play make-believe, so much the better. As the area where this playground is situated is not under supervision, everything had to be made as foolproof as possible against vandalism. The log fence, as well as serving as a barrier, turned out to be one of the most popular parts of the equipment. Children derived as much pleasure from climbing over it as they did from any of the other pieces of equipment.*

Several years later the eminent Sydney landscape designer, Bruce Mackenzie, was to comment in a letter to Ellis that the extensive timber pole work in a new park he had designed in Balmain was 'undoubtedly inspired by seeing your bush playground in Melbourne'. Heidelberg City Council repaired the playground in 1977, replacing some of the equipment and the telephone-pole fences. It remains a lovely place but sadly, the vandalism that Ellis tried to avoid has taken its toll, as has the passage of time.

Wilson Reserve attracted wide attention, and Nancy Dexter, the redoubtable women's editor for the *Age* newspaper in Melbourne, took up Ellis's ideas in print. She noted that twenty-nine children had been admitted to one district hospital after being seriously injured in playground accidents, mainly involving metal playground equipment, and she surmised that there must be hundreds of similar injuries throughout Victoria. Why not replace these dangerous, sterile pieces of equipment with something to stimulate children's imaginations? She quoted Ellis: 'Instead of a ladder on a slide I use a heap of heavy rocks . . . Children don't like being organised. Playgrounds should be an adventure workshop. The kids should play with junk.'

It was newspaper publicity that led two Footscray doctors to Ellis in 1968 after their six-year-old son died, falling accidentally from a second-storey window. Seeking to perpetuate his memory, they hit on the idea of creating a playground and park on a vacant piece of Crown land next to their house. They telephoned Ellis after reading about him in the *Age*; he came immediately to see them and produced a design that featured timber play equipment and seats, occasional rocks and native plants. Ellis was deeply touched by the circumstances of the commission; always he seemed to have time to talk over a cup of morning coffee or over lunch,

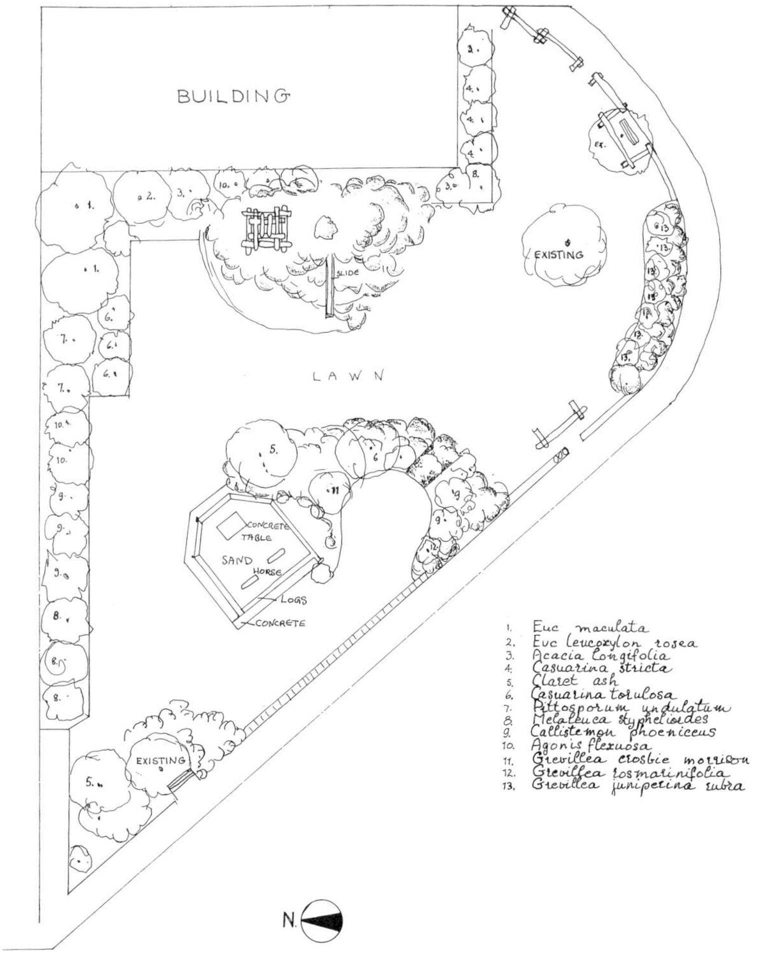

*E*llis took special interest in the McCoy playground in Footscray, drawing the plan himself.

and the bereaved parents found this a great consolation. (He even wrote a poem about their son.) They looked forward to the sound of his car pulling up at 7.55 in the morning. He had to be pushed hard to accept a fee for his work and even though he had given up construction, he supervised this job from beginning to end, joining in the physical work where necessary. Some of the play equipment in the Michael McCoy Reserve has been altered or removed over the years and vandalism has become a problem, but the family continues to maintain the park, which is a well-loved spot in Footscray.

Meanwhile Ellis was designing a playground at Churinga in Greensborough, for use by retarded children, and another at Yooralla, Balwyn, the school for physically disabled children. Yooralla's was no ordinary playground. It had to accommodate children in wheelchairs and calipers, children with imperfect bones, children with the uncontrollable movements characteristic of cerebral palsy. Ellis met the staff and the children and spent time at the school, watching them move around the expanse of asphalt that served for their recreation. He designed a timber pole pyramid upon which they could climb with safety, winding paths so that wheelchairs did not have to go in a straight line from point A to point B, strategically placed low slate-topped tables with timber legs – one with a chess board inlaid – where passers-by could stop and play games. Ellis went to Yooralla at weekends and attended working bees there with boy scouts, technical college students, and other community groups. He charged no professional fee for this work. The playground opened in 1969 and was enthusiastically received, particularly by the resident children who could use it after school hours. The staff commented that the equipment would give the children a new sense of achievement.

A youthful Andrew Peacock was pictured at the 1968 opening of the Yooralla playground. Here (as at Wilson Reserve) the low log boundary fence was a popular part of the equipment.

He also designed two playgrounds in Invercargill, New Zealand. Invercargill had been a regular port of call since the early 1950s, when his daughters Lesley and Patricia settled there after their marriages – in all, Ellis and Olive made twenty-four trips to New Zealand, often taking with them their youngest daughter, Betty, and her sons. Even though on holiday, when asked, Ellis would help his daughters and their friends with their gardens. Sometimes he built single features like a fish-pond or a barbecue, sometimes he created whole sections of a garden – flights of steps or outcrops – in a short-term, madcap working bee involving large numbers of family and friends. Or he prepared plans for execution by others, as was the case with the timber playgrounds at Gladstone Scout Den (1969), where his great-grandchildren play regularly today, and at Waihopai School (1969). At Waihopai he specified native plants in the schoolground – something different for the area, and later emulated in schoolgrounds throughout New Zealand. Some of his work in and around Invercargill remains almost unaltered – in particular a formal fish-pond (below) that he built with his own hands in 1953, and both the playgrounds.

*P*layground, Waihopai, Invercargill, New Zealand (1968).

Ellis suggested a flying fox for the Waihopai playground, a feature he was to incorporate in a 1970 design for a sloping site at Travancore Children's Home in the inner Melbourne suburb of Flemington. Here the users were older children, so as well as the flying fox he provided for a challenging climbing platform, a rope ladder climb, a billycart track and a workshop. This last feature was also part of his design for the vast new Ministry of Housing (then Housing Commission of Victoria) estate in Lennox Street, Richmond, a project for which he was delighted to be commissioned and on which he worked throughout 1969 and into 1970, incorporating modifications required by Commission staff. ('How long to do House Comm job?' reads a telephone message in Olive's handwriting in his office diary for November 1969. 'How long to finish design with all amendments?')

Between four tower blocks and their associated car-parks, concrete drives and pathways, Ellis's amended design, dated 24 January 1970, inserted four small timber playgrounds, each with slightly different equipment – vaulting logs, a slide running down from a mound some two and a half metres high, a log stack, swings, a climbing platform. There were large-scale sporting facilities and several other carefully positioned mounds with seats adjoining, to create variety and interest in the landscape. His aim

Rock garden in Melbourne's Royal Botanic Gardens (1967).

Part of Ellis's outcrop at the University of Melbourne, installed in the early 1970s.

was to provide as much space as possible for gardens and for unrestricted children's play; he dispersed the play areas over the site (perhaps he was aiming to give the children somewhere to play away from their parents, as he had suggested years earlier at the Cowen garden in Kew).

He had also proposed an underground 'cave' or workshop for teenage boys, but this idea was quickly vetoed. He was fully aware of the amount of vandalism that could take place and had always had this in mind, he wrote in the report accompanying his initial sketch plan of the playground. 'But we have to take certain risks, and accept the fact that some damage may be done.' No risks were allowed. The 'cave' was not approved (although work benches were proposed in a more centrally-placed shelter shed that was to be built, however, without walls).

Nancy Dexter took up the matter of the 'cave' in the *Age*:

> *Something nasty in the woodshed is nothing to what the Housing Commission decided could happen if a covered workshop and play area were built into the grounds of the new Richmond high rise flats.*
>
> *When landscape architect Mr Ellis Stones was asked to plan the grounds of the flats, he says he was thrilled to do something that would give people pleasure. 'Landscaping isn't just planting a few trees and shrubs', he says. 'That is a minor part of planning for people.'*
>
> *Mr Stones appreciated that children came from houses that, tumbledown as they were, still had sheds and backyards in which they could mend a bike or nail pieces of wood together. To take the place of these, he planned an extensive concrete workshop with heavy benches and a play area partly under cover for use on wet days. These were to be covered by a mound rising from the street, and the mound planted with shrubs and trees as a barrier against street noise. The idea, he says, was promptly ruled out by the commission on the excuse that the workshop would be a place where boys and girls might go at night although the building was completely open at the front facing the flats.*
>
> *Mr Stones, a man who has been talking about the quality of life long before it became a catch phrase, says: 'Have we the moral right to take away people's freedom without making some real attempt to give them something worthwhile in the place of the homes they have left? Responsible authorities should consider not only how many people can be accommodated in the building but how many can be accommodated outside. Looking at some of our housing projects it seems they were planned solely for motor cars. Land is too valuable to be used for cars. They can easily be parked underground. The official reaction to this is that the cost is too high. To hell with the cost. Dispense with the top floors and spend the money where it will be of some positive value to the people in the flats and ultimately to the community. Social workers everywhere have found that children with nowhere to play and pursue hobbies are frustrated and tend to become vandals as an outlet for their natural energy. We will only have ourselves to thank for the unrest of youth in these flats and also for the mothers who break down under the strain of coping with children with no place to play.'*

Ms Dexter concluded that Ellis was a real twentieth-century Don Quixote. Fancy, she wrote, even thinking of trying to buck the fact of life that well-parked cars were of more value than well-adjusted children.

A landscape architect who worked then with the Housing Commission remembered Ellis's concept as a series of little cameos, reflecting an 'innocent, if not naive, view of the way children play together'. It was felt he did not understand the types of people thrown together on these large estates, and the way in which they could abuse the facilities. Housing Commission policy was to allow no opportunity for such misuse – which, of course, completely negated Ellis's own views. And his plan was thought to harbour potential problems. Was the unusual timber equipment structurally proven? Because the landscape treatment was so different, would it create problems of estate management? Ellis is said to have resigned early in 1970 (although this is not indicated in Housing Commission files nor in those office papers that survive), and friends and family said afterwards that they had rarely seen him so angry. In the final plan for the site the Commission did incorporate certain of his ideas, like the mounding that brought much-needed variation to the landscape beneath the tower blocks, and the log fences; these features reappeared in later large-scale Commission projects.

While such failures were disappointing his enthusiasm did not waver; each commission was new, fresh, exciting. There was honorary work for the National Trust, often done at weekends; this included the landscape around Woolaston Bridge at Warrnambool, the garden at 'Lake View', Chiltern, work at Portarlington and in Gippsland and the Western District, and general advice ('Mrs . . . rang re. McCrae homestead, strip of garden near house unplanted, wants names of a few plants also suggestion for a tree to shelter from sun'). The work often involved travelling, like this assignment in 1968: 'Left early a.m. for Warrnambool for N. T. inspection to Woolaston Bridge, car broke down in Terang, back to Melbourne by train' – but the following January it proved easier: 'Caught train to Warrnambool, spent day selecting rocks, returned that night'. At 'Lake View', the country house associated with author Henry Handel Richardson, Ellis prepared a design for the garden, car-park and log fencing. There was some dissatisfaction with the simplicity of his treatment, while the earthiness of the log fence upset some architectural purists. His wife recalled that some of the committee wanted the garden 'tizzied up', but, she said, he had tried to plant it back to what the older people in the district remembered.

Ellis had become a member of the Town and Country Planning Board's advisory committee on preserving places of historic interest, he attended meetings of the National Parks Association and kept up his membership of the National Trust's landscape preservation council, as well as being a regular at meetings of the Australian Institute of Landscape Architects. He never said much at meetings – in a group setting he tended to take a back seat, unless the subject under discussion really rankled, and then he would put his point of view. But his quiet presence was always noted. His interest in environmental matters continued unabated. 'Mr Stones went to a meeting in the Botanic Gardens to protest about the building of

*P*rojecting 'bays' of boulders and low planting added interest in the wide driveway of a Malvern town-house project.

*E*stablished eucalypts, timber steps, low planting and boulders at Winter Park.

*I*n the parkland at the core of Winter Park, Ellis let the mature eucalypts and rough-cut grass speak for themselves.

A sylvan landscape in the Rosanna Parklands – old pines, with native trees in the distance.

*A*n exercise in communal space – the 'ride' that ran between the first two groups of houses built at Elliston and extended to the park.

the restaurant', read a diary note for December 1968; in October 1970 he was guest speaker at the inaugural meeting of the Warringal Conservation Society (in Ivanhoe/Heidelberg) on the topic of pollution in Melbourne suburbs; in his 1971 diary he scrawled the address in Canada of a group calling itself the Conservation Research and Natural Knowledge Society. Increasingly, municipal councils and community groups, particularly parents' organisations from kindergartens and primary schools, sought him out for speeches, advice, or design work. And there were almost more commissions for private gardens than he could manage. These were from clients both long-established and new. He turned nothing down, darting around Melbourne, travelling to the country and interstate – during the late 1960s there were jobs in Sydney, Perth, Adelaide.

Ellis now contracted out construction of his designs. Chief among the contractors whom he used regularly was John Jackson of Devon Gardens. John Jackson, a nuggety Scotsman, had met Ellis in the mid-60s, and while their relationship was professional – Jackson always referred to Ellis as Mr Stones – they became good friends. Jackson built many gardens at Merchant Builders jobs; he did a range of domestic gardens and commercial and institutional work for Ellis, as well as landscaping around swimming pools. He greatly enjoyed working with him. 'We just clicked from the start. If I couldn't understand the drawing, I'd ask "What are we aiming at here? Remember the job we did for Mrs X – do you want it like that?" He always liked it right, and once you got the feel of where he was going he was very relaxed. He was part of the team, the boss, but of course it didn't seem like that. Even though he was old he'd want to get on the end of a crowbar. He liked to come on the job, grab a couple of blokes and direct them, and we used to just let him go.' At the end of the day Jackson would sometimes drive Ellis home and stay for a drink while the busy Stones household hummed around him – television and magazine commitments being juggled with friends and family dropping in, queries about photographs for 'the book' and telephone calls from clients. 'Mrs B . . . has been waiting at house since 9.30.' 'Mrs L . . . rang as you didn't show up.'

John Jackson says the successful landscape contractor must adapt to every design style. As he works, he learns more skills, tricks he can get up to. From Ellis he gained valuable knowledge, particularly about rock placement, and about working in a confined space. 'He really had the knack of making a little tight corner come alive. He could pull things out of the hat – raising a pool above ground level, putting a seat around the top.' And Jackson, unlike some others, admired Ellis's way with plants. 'He was not a botanist, but he knew what he was doing. When you planted, you thought there wasn't enough but three or four years later it was perfect. He knew exactly the size the plants would grow. When his gardens were finished they were balanced and full – and not overplanted.' ('Landscapers finished at Black Rock', read a telephone message from an architect, 'and owner disappointed – planting too sparse'.)

Jackson remembers, too, Ellis's 'natural gift' for using ground-cover plants, which in the late 1960s were not as fashionable as they later became. Ellis wrote in *Australian Garden Design* that he placed great value on the

*E*llis enlivened this tight corner of an inner-suburban garden – viewed here from the kitchen window – with a vine-covered pergola and a small, raised brick pool into which a jet of water played.

Ellis's courtyards at Winter Park – an example of the nationalistic style in Australian landscaping.

A corner of the McLennan garden at Narre Warren, showing part of the fine Victorian house with its sweeping driveway.

Colourful detail on a rock wall at the McLennan garden.

Another 'trick' – a gently winding gravel path, a few steps, some native plants and boulders, and the back entrance to a suburban garden looks like a piece of bush. This is Ellis's own garden (a tea-tree fence behind the shrubs to the left concealed a service yard where his equipment was kept).

relationship of plants one to another and their role in furnishing areas where structural elements, rather than floral display, were being relied on for effect – an important aspect often neglected in landscape design. Cecile Glass, who sold native plants from her home at Eltham, found always that Ellis was less interested in the form or flower of a particular plant than in its habit, and how he could make it fit into his landscape concept. (A Frenchwoman, she had come to Australia in 1960 after marrying the Eltham-based artist and designer, Peter Glass. She was fascinated by the native flora and began growing it from seed, much of it obtained from George Althofer at Dripstone. Ellis noticed this when visiting the house and suggested she go into business.)

'He never charged enough', John Jackson maintained. When Ellis was asked in 1967 to design a new garden in the country for Sir Ian McLennan of BHP, Sir Ian also was surprised at how little he asked for fees.

Here Ellis was faced with a dilapidated garden where overgrown shrubs obscured views in all directions. His idea was to open it up and 'bring the farm into the garden'. (He wanted to build a ha-ha wall but this proved impractical because the rock on the site was too close to the surface.) He designed and built a steep rock outcrop winding round two sides of the fine Victorian house, to display a range of interesting rock and alpine plants that he brought up one bitterly cold spring day, to be planted by Lady McLennan and his assistant of the time, Quentin Madden. He specified native plants in other parts of the garden, and along the drive, but told the McLennans he didn't want any in the rockery. They remembered him as a perfectionist. His grandson Barry Rice, who worked for him during university holidays, was struck by how fussy he was about methods of planting. 'You cut a hole to a generous depth, put some loose soil back in, watered the hole, spread out the plant's roots, put it in, very firmly pressed soil on top, watered it again, then added old leaves or something similar for mulch. It had to be done right.' Contractors who built walls for him, including Tom Garner and Don Weston, knew he would insist that 'dodgy' bits be pulled out and redone. While he was still building his own gardens his supervision of his workers was regular but not constant, but Bob Grant said: 'You knew darn well it had to be right for him'. Some family and friends ascribed his occasional frustration towards the end of his life to the fact that he no longer had full control over the way his gardens looked.

Ellis returned to the McLennan garden some years later to design a swimming pool. Before that he had carried out landscape work at BHP's new research laboratories in Clayton, where the original planting had suffered badly in the 1967–68 drought. Some BHP staff members of the time remembered Ellis calling in at the laboratories for a couple of hours one morning and suggesting that a few different types of eucalypts be planted, not seeking a more major input because another designer had been there before him. However, his 1969 office diary – which, like all his diaries, was not filled in regularly – indicated repeated 'BHP' sessions and site visits between February and August that year, and discussion about a contractor for the work (he asked Eric Hammond, who could not fit it into his schedule).

A natural swimming pool in a beautiful garden setting.

A pool (1971) finished with a black lining in the Morgan garden.

A quiet corner of the McCubbin garden at Sunbury (1973–74), which Ellis supervised closely. The planting is to his specification.

*E*llis's innate talent and absolute affinity with stone is expressed in these photographs of the Downing/Le Gallienne garden, Eltham, (1949–54) above left; the Hawthorne garden, Hawthorn, (1963–64) above right; the Morgan garden (1971) below.

Ellis's achievements were sometimes underestimated because of his modest demeanour and gentle manner, the essential simplicity of much of his work, and his unwillingness to spend time talking about it. 'He did nothing really. Just put in a couple of trees' (the director of a firm whose office grounds were landscaped in 1965 for the sum of £340 – one of Ellis's larger accounts for that year). 'I found him so unimaginative, rigorously native, rocks and nothing but . . .' (a leading architect who used him in 1961 for landscaping around a block of flats in Parkville).

A drystone wall formed part of an outcrop sloping up towards the house at the McLennan garden, Narre Warren. The top of the outcrop was planted with azaleas, camellias and rhododendrons and the lower part with rock plants, alpines and perennials.

'I wanted to tidy up my garden. I made the mistake of complaining about the way the children played cricket in the back in summer, and football in winter, and how the lawn wouldn't grow. He said it was just nice and that I must have a garden for the children. He suggested I plant a lemon-scented gum in the front garden. I felt somehow disappointed. Certainly I had expected more enthusiasm' (a woman who consulted Ellis in the early 1960s).

Perhaps such clients expected a full symphony orchestra when the occasion merited only a solo instrument, or a sweep of strings. As Edna Walling had written almost thirty years earlier: 'It is a most elusive thing this matter of design in the garden . . . we all have different ideas about how the ground should be dealt with'. Restraint came naturally to Ellis. Sometimes he was predictable, occasionally a little hackneyed, but rarely was he obvious.

*T*he Yarra River – for generations a symbol of Melbourne – photographed at dusk from the bank below Wilson Reserve, Ivanhoe.

*R*ockwork at Salt Creek in the Rosanna Parklands, newly completed in 1975, and today, somewhat overgrown.

EIGHTEEN

Elliston – the importance of landscaping

The advertisements for Merchant Builders' most ambitious project, a large housing estate on the site of the old Rosanna Golf Links, promoted both an achievement and a new way of living. 'At Elliston, trees are built around, and birds still sing. Underground wiring and fifty acres of natural parkland provide a perfect setting for Merchant Builders houses . . .' they read. 'Visit unorthodox Elliston.' 'Magnificent Elliston – nationally acclaimed as a superb example of natural planning . . .'

The forty hectares of land had been a farm originally, then a golf course. Subsequent subdivision plans by its owners had caused heated local protest, but a compromise was reached whereby Heidelberg City Council agreed to buy the golf course, selling half for housing development to pay for the retention of the other half as a park. Merchant Builders was the successful tenderer. They asked four architects – Graeme Gunn, Charles Duncan, and the firms of Jackson and Walker, and McGlashan and Everist – to come up with fifty related but different basic house designs available to people who bought land on the standard subdivision. The open-ended form of this was already set, and its combination of loops and culs-de-sac giving onto the park was most attractive to Merchant Builders. Ellis Stones was in charge of site planning, of the landscape around the houses and – in a separate commission from the local council – of the adjoining Rosanna Parklands, through which ran Salt Creek. This was to link the two elements, housing and landscape, on a scale not attempted before, creating what was described as a garden suburb of character and harmony. At the opening ceremony in July 1969 the Minister for Local Government, 'Dick' (later Sir Rupert) Hamer, said Elliston was 'a glimpse of homes of the future, which won't have a view of bitumen and power lines'. Some 250 houses were planned at a base cost of between \$23,000 and \$31,000. In the event about seventy were built before Merchant

Builders made land available to other developers so that the original concept lapsed – for buyers, this had included contractual conditions such as landscaping by Ellis Stones to each house, and safeguards against out-of-scale development (two-storey additions and the like). It is a pity the response from the buying public was not better, because the whole idea was ahead of its time.

In Melbourne an earlier scheme had met a much harsher fate. In 1966 the Lend Lease Corporation engaged Robin Boyd's firm, Romberg and Boyd, to design some 400 houses at a new development in Glen Waverley called Appletree Hill. *Australian Home Beautiful* noted that this was to be 'a garden suburb where the gardens grow into one another rather than standing out in stiff and formal array as competitive monuments to the industry of their owners', where front fences would be abolished, native trees and shrubs planted and existing trees retained, while wiring from street poles to houses would be put underground. Appletree Hill did not last long. While 10,000 visitors trooped through the first display houses over a two-month period, only six orders eventuated and Lend Lease aborted the project.

It was Graeme Gunn who suggested that Elliston be named after Ellis. On the way to a job one day, David Yencken asked Ellis how he would feel about this. '"You're joking", he said. We drove along for a while. Then he said: "Are you really serious?" "Yes, quite serious." "That's wonderful, bloody wonderful."' Thereafter he threw himself into the project with even more than his normal enthusiasm, working there at weekends, calling in to plant trees and creepers and to talk to the residents. But he never lost sight of the overall significance, writing in 1971:

> *They were kind enough to call Elliston after me. I like to think that this was not merely a tribute to a person, but a recognition of the role of landscaping, firstly, as the total unifying element in the park and throughout the development; and secondly, as a vital aspect of a personal environment . . . I hope that this is a sign of the beginning of a new appreciation for landscape.*

Ellis knew what he wanted to achieve in design terms. Even though constrained by the subdivided format, he wanted the gardens, streets and park to flow into and through each other, with the pervading influence being the feeling of the old landscape – *Eucalyptus maculata* and *E. botryoides* and the old pines planted by the early settlers. Luckily, all the streets except one had almost direct access to the park, and the first group of houses was designed to give onto a common 'ride' of shared land at the rear that also led down to the park. Where two houses were being built at the same time, fence lines were able to be juggled so that a 'dead' space beside one house was taken in by the neighbour, and vice-versa. Side fences were planted in depth with the types of shrubs and trees also used in the park, so that they would 'virtually disappear . . . with no sense of visual interruption at the fence line'. Low log fences separated gardens looking onto the park from the park itself.

Knowing what he wanted was one thing – 'the landscape must be strong and simple, with one continuous flowing feeling'. But getting there was another. By now Ellis was seventy-four years old and although he was to work for other developers (like A. V. Jennings and Stocks and Holdings) this was the first time he had encountered anything on this scale. Co-ordinating the development was Robin Edmond, a young architect newly returned from England, where he had been involved in similar projects. It soon became apparent to him that Ellis was a little out of his depth. 'It wasn't that he couldn't do it – he had a wonderful touch, absolutely fantastic – but that he had never worked the way we now needed to work. I would say "Ellis, we need a grading plan" and he would reply "I don't work like that – I just tell the bulldozer driver what to do". He realised quickly that he had come to the limits of his technical ability.'

A typical garden plan at Elliston included boulders, gravel drive and paths, and native planting.

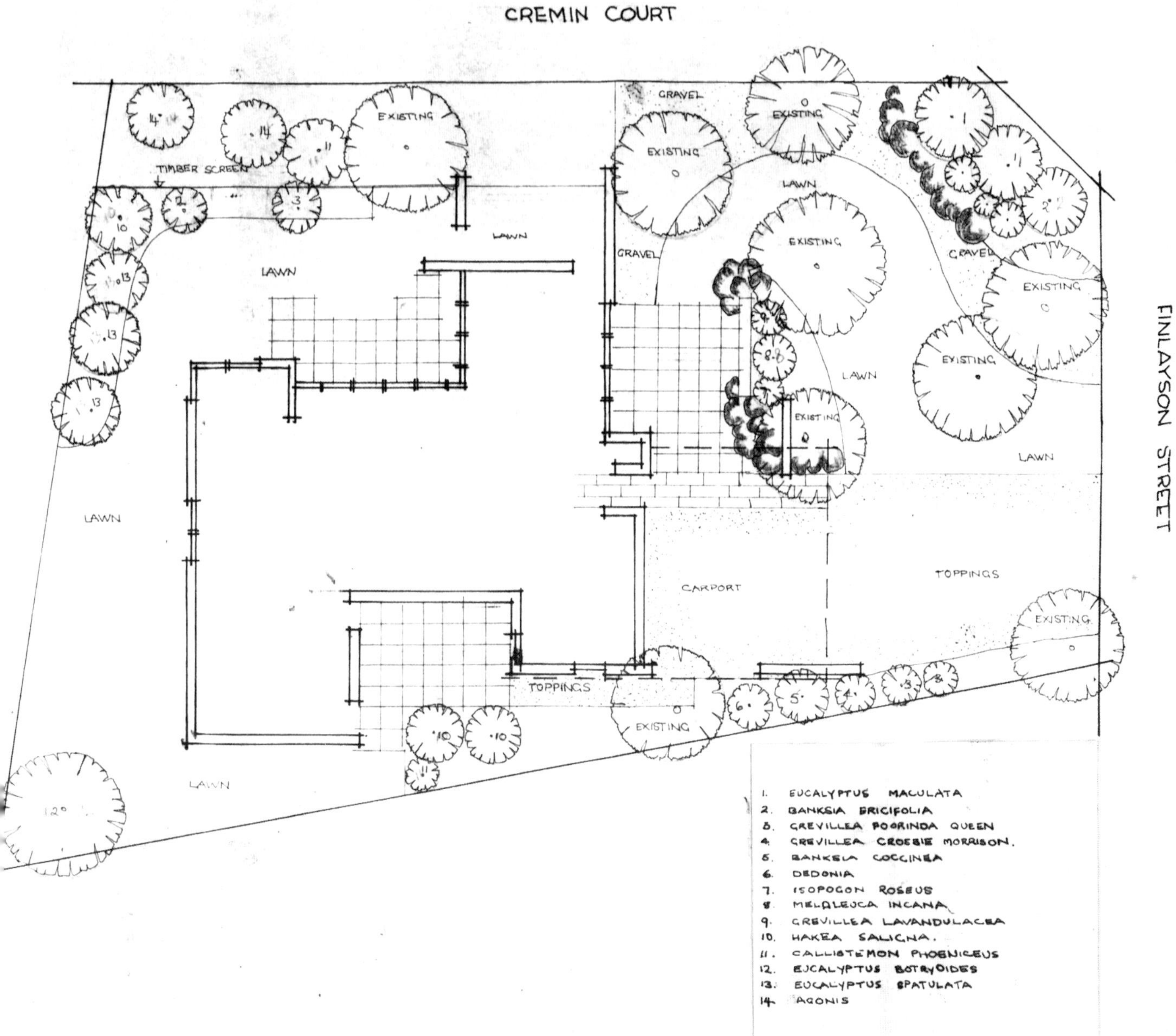

Robin Edmond (who is now a landscape architect doing large-scale work in Australia and Hong Kong) had long sessions with Ellis, so that he fully understood what Ellis wanted, and so that Ellis would trust him not to muddy the design themes. Chief among these was the use of only a few elements, and of simple materials. Edmond prepared drawings, discussing them with Ellis either on site or – when Ellis was suffering one of his bouts of illness – at Locksley Road. He developed short-cuts; a way of drawing rocks so that the contractor (John Jackson) would know how to place them without Ellis's supervision, and a way of identifying different types and shapes of rock so that they could be ordered easily. (This involved visits to farmers on rock-strewn properties near Melbourne, photographing what was available.) With systems like these in place, the process of developing the site was speeded up while quality was maintained.

For both it was a learning experience. Robin Edmond helped Ellis understand and accept the methods now required of the landscape architect working on large-scale projects, and he encouraged Ellis to communicate his own methods more closely. For his part, Edmond said working with Ellis was one of the special times of his life. 'He was very modest but very determined. He pointed out aspects that I hadn't observed properly before, he taught me important early lessons. I learned that rocks should be used only where appropriate, I learned how to use them as a material in the landscape, how to arrange them so that they looked natural, to bury them so that it seemed they were emerging from the earth rather then having been dumped off a truck. Ellis had read widely about the way Japanese landscapers used rocks, and before them the Chinese, he had absorbed all this and he was fascinated by it.

'He taught me that in order to be a landscape architect you don't have to know every plant in the world. He didn't claim to be a horticulturist or a botanist or an ecologist, but he did know how to utilise plants in an urban environment. He knew as much about plants as he needed to know, and I've used that principle ever since. He taught me, too, that for special jobs, whether broad-scale or of intimate detail, if you don't know it all yourself then you find someone who does, not just anyone but someone with a feel for the task.'

Robin Edmond watched the women who planted for Ellis, who would come onto the job with 'rubber gloves and trowels and baskets of small plants'. One such woman worked with a friend during the late 1950s to plant and maintain outcrops he installed, and she remembered Ellis directing in terms like: 'Something big here, something smaller there and something flowering in between'. He then let them do more or less what they thought right, and he was not too proud to learn from them details about the behaviour of plants in certain situations. In 1967–68 he asked Bill Molyneux, the native plant expert, to undertake planting for him on several jobs, instructing: 'I want something narrow there, to go up the wall . . . and something low here, but don't allow it to cover the face of the rock'.

He would say occasionally to colleagues like Grace Fraser and Glen Wilson that he wished he knew more about plants, but although hazy on plant names, he did his homework. His small but select personal library included two fine old books on alpine plants – Jenkins's *The Rock Garden*, and T. C. Mansfield's *Alpines in Colour and Cultivation*. The latter was marked with pencilled ticks, presumably listing plants he liked, or that he knew he could obtain, among them *Androsace lanuginosa, Campanula isophylla, Dianthus x* 'Highland Fraser', *Iberis sempervirens* and *Santolina chamaecyparissus*. During the 1960s Ellis's office assistant Beverley Hanson, knowing the plants he liked and the effects he preferred, would talk to him about his designs and what he had in mind before preparing detailed planting lists and heading off to buy at the nurseries. He taught her not to do 'spotty' planting with one of this and one of that, but to 'repeat and repeat'; to put a drift of a plant in one place, then reintroduce it further away. A surviving list for Ellis's Burnley Horticultural College outcrop and dry creek bed (1962) includes a broad array of Australian plants, among them some of the reedy plants that Ellis loved but are only now being widely used in gardens (like *Orthrosanthus multiflorus, Stypandra glauca, Dianella tasmanica*). Beverley chose these from the catalogue of Boddy's fine specialist nursery, Eastern Park in Geelong – perhaps from the 1958 catalogue, which was still in Ellis's office at the time of his death.

Today the orginal part of Elliston (centred round Bachli, Cremin, Ferrier and von Nida Courts) is leafy and secluded, a far cry from the cluster of ten stark new houses, surrounded by bare dirt and fences, to which engineer Robert Dunster came as one of the first residents. He remembered Ellis's contagious enthusiasm at a group meeting, when he discussed his landscape plans. Most early purchasers were married couples with small children so that the common 'ride' that extended between the backs of the first two rows of houses quickly became a hive of activity. A dry, pebbled watercourse ran down the centre of the ride; it was not long before back fences were demolished and the exercise in communal space took on real form. One resident asked that his funeral service be held there (which it eventually was); another, whose child was physically handicapped and confined to a small cart, built a wooden crossing over the pebbles so that the child could move easily from house to house. Ellis suggested installing a barbecue at the low point where the ride led into the park. Surrounded by sleeper seats, it developed into an informal meeting-place to which residents could gravitate at any time. If you took a cup of coffee out there it was an invitation for someone to join you.

Ellis's work in the adjoining fifty-three acre linear park, which is bisected by Salt Creek, was extraordinarily subtle. He used native trees and shrubs to soften both the broad openings of what used to be fairways, and the lines of planting that had divided the fairways; he made mounds to create and enclose vistas; he installed outdoor seats, low tables and play equipment. The park still has a 'Hampstead Heath' feel to it – 'kites, dogs and children', to quote one regular user. It is a very Australian space, alternately verdant and dusty, where the rattle from the train that runs along one side is almost drowned out at dusk by the sound of frogs and birds, and where the undulating terrain creates a feeling of space that is rare in any large city. Originally the Melbourne and Metropolitan Board of Works had wanted to put the creek in an underground drain through the park, because it feared the adjacent council subdivision would cause increased stormwater run-off and – given the nature of Salt Creek's bed and banks – accelerated erosion. To Ellis's delight the council opposed this suggestion and asked that it be left as a natural creek. Thereafter the Board generally left responsibility for the creek up to Heidelberg Council, while still requiring permission for new work, and holding the council responsible for expenditure and safety precautions.

Ellis's treatment of the Rosanna Parklands might have been subtle, but not all clients were as appreciative of his restrained touch in public spaces. Invited to Ballarat to talk about converting a couple of paddocks along a creek into a park for a local service club, his solution was extremely simple – a fence, a few seats and trees. The client envisaged the park as more of a showcase. Ellis did not receive the commission.

But at Winter Park, a Merchant Builders cluster housing project in (then) outer-suburban Doncaster, he had free rein. The result was deemed by many to be some of his finest work, particularly the combination of elegant brick-paved courtyards, generous timber steps, and outcrops, which showed the benefit of previous years of experience working around Merchant Builders houses. The project involved clusters of houses (twenty in all, built and landscaped between 1970–74) with common entrances and private garden courtyard spaces. In the courtyards Ellis's delicate planting and cleverly placed built-in seats received much acclaim, while his juxtaposition of brick paving, rockwork and gravel toppings provided appealing solutions in the public spaces – visitor parking, driveways and the like – that receive little attention in most medium-density developments. The clusters were set around a large shared park, whose broad spaces and picturesque native trees would have been engulfed in a conventional subdivision. Today this park is quite heavily planted, but twenty years ago Ellis's treatment was spare and restrained. He cleaned up the slightly scraggy existing eucalypts and did not plant much else, letting the mature trees and sweeping rough-cut grass speak for themselves. Tim Colebatch wrote in the *Age* in April 1975 that the whole place conveyed 'a quite beautiful sense of ease and freedom'. During the first weekend that Winter Park – Victoria's first cluster housing project – was open, seven thousand people inspected it, and on subsequent weekends they kept coming in their thousands.

In 1987, in an article on design directions in Australian landscape architecture in which he concluded there was not an 'Australian style' as such but a range of 'contextually appropriate solutions to different situations', the landscape architect Rodney Wulff singled out the Winter Park courtyards as a fine example of what he called the nationalistic/naturalistic style. 'Rocks, sleepers and native plants are the dominant feature of this direction', he commented, hailing Edna Walling, Ellis Stones and Bruce Mackenzie as 'high quality' practitioners of the genre (though whether Edna Walling ever would have used timber sleepers in her gardens is a moot point). He added: 'While this design direction has a considerable history in Australia, its application has not always been well handled. In many cases this treatment has been used on sites that are flat and where retaining of earth is unnecessary or inappropriate. In some cases the choice of rock types and plants has totally disregarded the physical, ecological and social context.' Ellis's permanent framework (rocks, timber seating, paving) in the Winter Park courtyards seemed exactly right, but his original native planting outgrew its boundaries and has been largely replaced, so in these terms perhaps its contextual appropriateness is open to

The enclosed gardens at Winter Park provided pleasant living spaces, with an easy flow between indoors and outdoors.

question – although it must be noted that the developers wanted the courtyards planted heavily for immediate effect, expecting purchasers either to thin out the plants later, or to maintain them with care. (Edna Walling had warned as long ago as 1938 that even those Australian trees and shrubs suitable for the average suburban garden would grow straggly if they were not regularly pruned at the right time.)

At the same time as he was busy with Winter Park, Ellis was making television appearances on a weekly Channel 0 programme 'Building Today', presented by Murray Jones. So popular did this half-hour programme become that after its first year it was extended to an hour, and was replayed each week. (It ran from 1969 to 1973.) Jones had met Ellis through his work at a project-house 'village' near his home. He recalled: 'Ellis would never appear with me in the studio to do a live interview, insisting that we must *show* people on film the right way to landscape. No-one could equal his mastery at matching, even improving nature. He could stand and look at a "nothing" layout and in minutes develop a beautiful layout. When filming, if we didn't have plants to show an effect he used to improvise with grass and bush to give an idea of highs and lows in the landscape.' Murray Jones, although not a landscaper, continued to use the principles Ellis taught him when making gardens – as did many other clients and friends. It is one thing to be capable of designing a beautiful, natural-looking garden or landscape, but it is quite another to excite others to comprehend, even implement your philosophy. This was one of Ellis's strengths. Those who sought to landscape in his fashion may not have reached the heights he did, but they understood what he was aiming at, and tried to make their own contribution. To him this was of the utmost importance. Again and again he stressed the importance of observing nature, the best teacher.

Another avenue for publicising his point of view opened up in December 1970, when he became gardening writer for *Australian Home Beautiful*. He succeeded Olive Mellor, who had taken over in the early 1950s as principal columnist for this national monthly magazine. Seeking to build circulation, John Morgan, then the magazines manager for the Herald and Weekly Times group, thought of approaching Ellis, and Home Beautiful's editor, Tony Hitchin, was given the task of convincing him to write a column. This was not altogether easy. The magazine itself was emerging from a 'low' period; Ellis's work commitments were heavy, he was unsure of his ability to express himself, and felt a monthly deadline would be an additional burden that he didn't really need. But when Tony Hitchin offered to 'ghost' the articles, he agreed to take it on.

Thus began four and a half years in which Hitchin would travel each month to Locksley Road, notebook and tape recorder in hand, to enjoy Ellis's company and Olive's superb cooking. 'He was always very courteous and pleased to see me – bluff, hale and hearty. Then we'd go into the front room and he'd sit down with this terrible air of resignation, as if I was about to extract his teeth. Previously I would have pumped him for addresses of gardens where we could take photographs, and I would have a batch of pictures in hand – courtyards, entrances, fences and so on. Either he would have prepared one or two quarto pages of handwritten notes, or he would talk about the photographs, I would prod him a little, take it down in shorthand, record it as well. In conversational asides I would pick up a little more. I don't believe I got anywhere near the essence of the mán, but I think the job was reasonable.' Although his topics included 'safe' subjects like annuals in the garden, swimming pools, lawns and paving, many were more challenging. 'Shadows in the garden' was one such; among others were 'Adjusting your garden to suit changing conditions' and 'Gardens without lawns'. Most were decided on after discussion with Tony Hitchin, but some were vintage Ellis, like 'Odd corners', and 'The value of trees'.

Tony Hitchin introduced him to the magazine's readers in glowing terms:

> *Who is Ellis Stones? He's a well-established garden design expert whose gardens exist in New South Wales, Victoria, South Australia and New Zealand. He is seventy-four, is so busy he can't find time to retire, lives in Melbourne and has spent much of his life as a one-man-band trying to interest people in garden design based on a 'natural' look . . . His admirers (and he has many) think he is a genius . . .*
>
> *If you are proud of your garden you will find his comments and advice invaluable. He likes a garden to have an air of permanence about it in the same way that the bush seems to be permanent. For that reason he is inclined to favour the use of handsome rocks and chunky logs where*

they are appropriate. But he is not fanatical about them. 'It's no good going to extremes', he says. 'I like the bush and I try to give my gardens a bit of what nature is all about. But you can't put a bush garden in George St, Sydney, or Collins St, Melbourne, and it's no good trying . . . He doesn't promise to improve your garden but he is sure he'll give you something to think about. 'Landscape gardening and garden design are phrases that sound expensive and are inclined to put a lot of people off', he says. 'But it doesn't have to cost a lot. It can be fun. And it will almost always be rewarding'.

Just as *Australian Home Beautiful* had changed course in the early 1950s, its gardening articles concentrating on practicalities rather than ideas, so in 1970 Tony Hitchin's promotion of Ellis signalled another reverse in direction. Hitchin wrote that gardeners seemed increasingly interested in planning their gardens rather than in making them up as they went along, and that most of the magazine's gardening queries now sought advice on what to do *with* a garden, rather than on *how* to do it. This was why Ellis Stones, 'the man who many feel is Australia's best landscape designer', had been asked to take over the gardening column.

Such changes, of course, have come and gone through the recorded history of gardening; without them, would it not be boring? *Australian Home Beautiful*'s variations in direction are not unlike those which occurred in English magazines in the early nineteenth century, only to be reversed some sixty or seventy years later with the advent of the aesthetically oriented William Robinson and Gertrude Jekyll. The English author Derek Clifford, in *A History of Garden Design*, indicates that John Claudius Loudon, publisher in the 1820s of the *Gardener's Magazine*,

. . . put his finger on the essential change of outlook between the eighteenth and the nineteenth centuries. He pointed out that the stream of books on the aesthetics of gardening had narrowed to a trickle, dried up, and been replaced by a flood of gardening literature which was almost solely concerned to introduce new varieties of plants to its readers and to instruct them how they should be grown. This is the period . . . when the type of cheap gardening magazine written by professional gardeners for enthusiasts of the artisan and middle classes first appeared . . .

Possibly Clifford's book, published in 1962, was acquired as a result of Ellis's involvement with John Duncan and the landscape design course at the Royal Melbourne Institute of Technology (RMIT). Clifford's sparkling arguments on the evolution of garden history must have appealed to Ellis. Changes in gardening style should not be considered only as fluctuations in fashion, Clifford wrote; the ebb and flow of history was important, too, and gardens could not be viewed apart from the people who made them.

As has been noted, while Ellis was not a great theorist, he knew his garden history at a time when it was not a subject of great popular interest. He talked at length to Robin Edmond about the subtle use of rocks in Chinese and Japanese gardens. Graeme Gunn had found, around 1960, that Ellis's work had an almost Japanese-style delicacy – Ellis designed several specifically 'Japanese' gardens when asked to by clients, but he did not regard his work as the genuine article. 'The Japanese gardens belong to Japan, and I admire them very much, but they are constructed by artists and craftsmen with generations of tradition behind them. Learn from them, but don't try and copy them', he wrote. As well, Ellis liked to discuss topical landscape matters with people of like mind. A letter survives that John Duncan, of RMIT, wrote to him in October 1969, about published comment by others on Walter Burley Griffin's design for the Australian capital, Canberra. It reads in part:

> *Thanks for letting me read the enclosed. I think (the writers) are a bit hard in claiming that Griffin copied Le Notre. Of course we tend to be influenced by earlier great masters and this is not necessarily a bad thing. But let us be realistic and ask, how many basic geometric forms are there? No matter what we design on this scale it is sure to bear some similarity to something which has been done before. And every major plan has its axes and focal point or points . . .*

It was through the RMIT course that Ellis met Ron Rayment, with whom he worked in partnership for fifteen months in 1970–71. Rayment had been among Ellis's first group of students. He was fascinated by Ellis's philosophy, and he appreciated the practical exercises Ellis gave the students, when simply being asked to explain one's drawings would generate spontaneous advice full of good sense, valuable experience and know-how. In the late 1960s Rayment took over from Mervyn Davis as lecturer in landscape history at RMIT; then John Duncan retired and asked him to assume responsibility for the course. Seeking to keep his own practice going while sharing the workload, he asked Ellis to form a partnership with him.

The Stones and Rayment office was based at the Rayment house in Hawthorn, at first in the living-room, then in a newly built studio block. Two assistants drafted plans – Ron Rayment noted that Ellis's documentation 'needed support', and that he seemed to find going to the office 'a bit of a bind'. The partnership worked fairly well, he felt, finding it marvellous in terms of personal relationships – 'he was just such a lovely guy, gentle and enthusiastic'. But keeping track of Ellis's finances was another matter altogether! As well, the partners' approaches were fundamentally different. Rayment was a trained architect who had worked always in formal office set-ups, and to whom correct documentation and concern for professional liability were of paramount importance. Ellis was a hands-on man, happiest out on the job, and his irrepressible enthusiasm for whatever work was current sometimes led him to discount more pragmatic concerns.

There was a large volume of work but the partners worked side by side rather than always together, each tending to take care of the jobs that he brought in. Ellis was busy with Elliston, Winter Park, National Trust work, several playgrounds and a range of private gardens, some of which were beginning to flow from inquiries to his magazine column. Ron Rayment's work came in the main from municipal councils, institutions and fellow architects; it included the landscape along the new South-Eastern Freeway. There was occasional collaboration. At Sovereign Hill, the

Part of a Japanese-inspired garden in Toorak (1967). 'Learn from Japanese artists and craftsmen, but don't try to copy them', Ellis wrote.

Some of Ellis's early work had an almost Japanese delicacy, like this small pool in the Blazey garden (c.1959).

recreated gold-mining centre in Ballarat, Rayment did the landscape plan while Stones designed and helped build, with rocks he chose himself, the creek (subsequently altered) where each day, delighted children still pan for gold. At the University of Melbourne Rayment designed and planted the south lawn that sat atop the new underground car-park; Stones was responsible for the massive outcrop that retains this lawn near the heavily trafficked Baillieu Library.

The creek at the Sovereign Hill gold-mining township at Ballarat, pictured in the late 1970s. Ellis designed and helped build it.

Carrick Chambers (who was then a member of the university's grounds committee) said Ellis was the logical choice for this work, which was installed and planted in 1972–73. He is remembered perched on a boulder in his suit and hat – always he was neatly dressed, whether the appropriate garb was a pair of overalls or a collar and tie – making sure that everything was done as he intended, supervising John Jackson's men as they used bulldozers and cranes to manoeuvre the enormous rocks into place. Contemporary photographs show the breadth of his original concept and its fine execution, but the outcrop today is sadly overgrown; shrubs are sparse and woody while huge trees, some of them self-sown, have dwarfed the rocks. There were what Carrick Chambers remembers as 'lovely touches', like wooden seats backed with rosemary, thyme and other prostrate, aromatic plants, which released gorgeous scents as one leaned back on them. During 1974, Ellis was asked to give advice on problems of pedestrian traffic and drainage in the area and his replies combined practicality and aesthetic sense. Pedestrians were cutting corners at strategic spots on the lawn, creating undue wear, and the university's buildings department wondered whether strategically placed rocks would stop this. No, said Ellis, just fill in the corners with pebbles and let the foot traffic continue. And treat the drainage problem near the medical library with rocks and pebbles to make a small dry creek.

The outcrop near the underground car-park at the University of Melbourne, photographed by Ellis in 1973, soon after planting.

'Be bold', Ellis often said. Indeed it was a bold decision to complete a large-scale, muscular, rock outcrop with a delicate detail like thyme-lined wooden seats. But in the field of landscape design Ellis was absolutely sure of what he was doing, and if he judged a course of action right, then he would follow it. 'Be bold . . . and be patient', he wrote in 1966 across a plan that he prepared for friends building a new garden in Invercargill, New Zealand. 'Be bold. Don't fiddle, don't be petty', he told Bob Grant when he began work for him in 1956. 'BE BOLD', he wrote in *Australian Garden Design.* 'When working with rocks this does not necessarily mean the use of very large stones . . . as a rule of thumb, when spacing rocks in an outcrop I find it quite safe to double the distance first decided upon.'

Did he have to tell himself to 'be bold' when he went back to work as a carpenter despite his war injury, or when he decided as a middle-aged man to give away building and devote himself to landscape design? Probably not. Boldness, where required, was part of Ellis's personal make-up and it stood him in good stead all his life. His readiness to argue for what he believed in kept him active right to the end of his life while around him, others became frail old men. He never liked to miss an Anzac Eve reunion with his mates from the Seventh Battalion, but in his last years he did fail to attend several. Of course, he wasn't the only one, but while excuses from other non-attenders published in the battalion magazine included phrases such as: 'can no longer see to read or write', 'very much an invalid now', 'slowly picking up in the Alfred (hospital)', Teena Stones's apologies were of a different kind. In 1969 he was 'on a job', in 1970 he was 'overworking himself' while in 1974, aged seventy-eight, he phoned through this message: 'I meant to come, but just have to be out superintending an important developmental job'.

Ellis (bottom right) at an Anzac Day march in the 1970s.

NINETEEN

'I can't slow up – they won't let me'

Fulsome reviews accompanied the publication in April 1971 of *Australian Garden Design*. These noted that Ellis saw gardens as a source of relaxation for people forced to live in densely populated cities, and included comments such as: 'An excitingly different book on gardening . . . Getting Ellis down on paper was a long-awaited event and Macmillan did the job . . . He caters for all tastes, from the anti-gardener to the person who would gladly spend every spare minute working with plants and flowers.'

Ellis's masterful use of railway sleepers showed this timber was a marvellous medium for landscaping, whether for seats, steps, retaining walls or even paving.

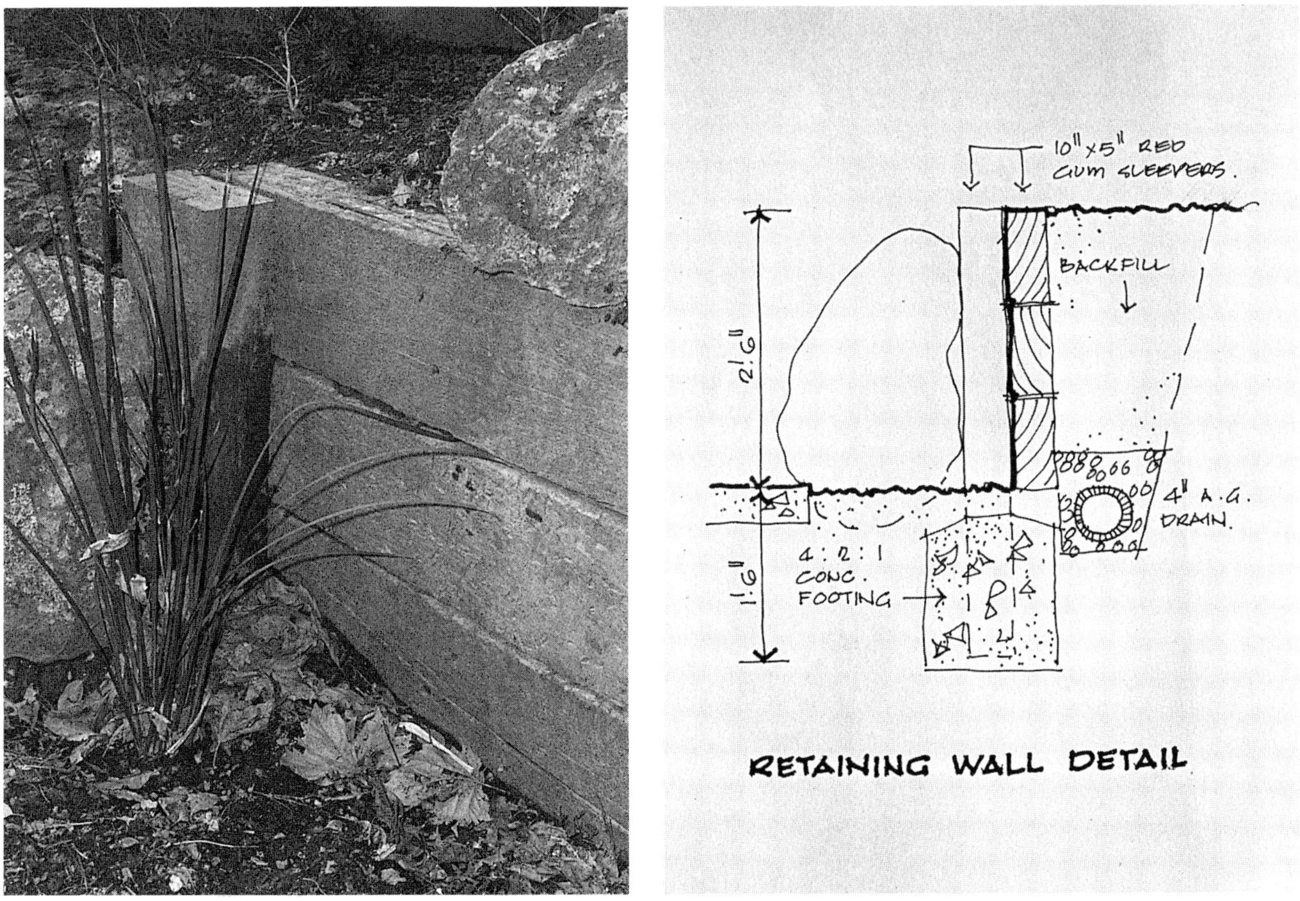

*T*imber retaining wall, with construction detail.

The *Australian Women's Weekly* gave invaluable nation-wide coverage, with three colour pages devoted to illustrations from the book. Its review stressed the book's message that a garden was more than a collection of growing things; rather, it was a blending of features seen in the natural terrain – stone, wood, contours – with trees, shrubs and low-growing covers to form an harmonious whole. The Herald/Sun group offered the book at a special price, and the publisher's records show that it sold 50,000 copies in two editions – a remarkable achievement. (It has been out of print for years, despite its pre-publication description in a booksellers' and publishers' journal as 'a absolute mine of information . . . a book that will have tremendous appeal and wide and continuing sales'; but can be found still in specialist second-hand shops.)

With Ellis's emphasis on the creative use of natural timber for retaining walls, steps and seats in the garden, an unusual consequence of publication was a steep rise in the price of railway sleepers. Ivan Stranger, whose landscape contracting firm built gardens for Ellis from 1967 onwards, had been able to obtain these with no difficulty for around 20 cents each – but after *Australian Garden Design* appeared, he noted that demand increased and the price went up to $2 or $3. (Ellis, of course, had his own sources of supply. A note in the 1967 office diary read: 'Road foreman from Geelong railway station rang. Good sleepers coming from Gheringhap in about two weeks.')

The book was launched by Professor John Turner at an evening party outside a new Merchant Builders town-house development. Ellis was thrilled to see it in print at last, and delighted at its immediate success, but already he was working on something new. There was no ghost writer for his manuscript on the general topic of pollution, first titled *My Country*, later *Priority Landscaping*; he penned it himself and had it typed in his own office. Even though only some thirty-five double-spaced quarto pages long, he felt he put more work into it than into his other two, much larger, books. The response to *Australian Garden Design* meant that various publishers were eager to look at the new manuscript, but no offers emerged, and the consensus was that its contents would be better suited as individual articles in a newspaper. He submitted it to the *Herald* in May 1972 – 'more power to your elbow', replied John Morgan, 'and let us see it in proof form with pictures' – but in the event it remained unpublished.

The manuscript, written in simplistic vein that occasionally obscures its important message, touches on his childhood days and beginnings in landscape architecture, but moves quickly on to the topic of conservation and pollution. It looks at issues like clean air and water, the value of trees, uses for vacant land along railway lines, town planning. Central to its argument is Ellis's belief that landscape elements of natural beauty should be saved for future generations, and that this would be achieved best through establishing a landscape authority to control all important landscape features, both constructed (like the Royal Botanic Gardens) and natural (river and creek valleys). 'There is no department with any authority to deal with the landscape of our country and cities', he wrote. 'There are numerous boards and committees nibbling at the problem but no authority with power to override all opposition.' An undated, handwritten note in the Stones files held at the Australian National Library, Canberra, underlined this 'urgent need'. In it Ellis described the way topsoil had been stripped from acres of land – a much greater area than was necessary, he said – in preparing runways for the new Tullamarine Airport outside Melbourne, then dumped beside Deep Creek nearby, destroying some of the bank and spilling into the stream. Objections were lodged, and as a member of the National Trust's landscape preservation council, Ellis was present when the government departments involved were brought together. Sadly, he wrote: 'The usual outcome was that while admitting there was damage done, it would be rectified and the area beautified . . . one government department will not override another, and so the destruction continues'.

'Pollution of the Eye', a feature article published in 1971 in the *Herald* newspaper, had a related theme. Landscape must be given priority, Ellis wrote, because we in Melbourne had taken all and given little, despoiling the Yarra River, our only natural landscape feature, and the 'beautiful and generous' St Kilda Road. Common sense had been left behind in the race for progress. Future expansion in Melbourne should be carefully planned, parks safeguarded, more trees planted and properly cared for. Why not do this on bare, unsightly railway embankments? . . . 'that would be a start, it would be fairly easy and it wouldn't be expensive'. There was some response from readers. One correspondent asked that all municipal councils employ at least one gardener trained in tree pruning – Ellis's article had been illustrated with a picture of a badly pruned elm tree – while Preston City Council advised that recently it had planted 20,000 street trees, with 6000 more to go in, and that its schoolchildren were receiving 'junior tree warden' certificates.

A measure of Ellis's increasing public exposure was that his clientele was more widely dispersed. A veterinary surgeon and his wife from the outer Melbourne suburb of Preston contacted him after reading an article he had written about black pebbles in *Australian Home Beautiful*. He chatted at length on the telephone, telling them where to buy the pebbles; they were thrilled that he would give them so much of his time. Several years later, in 1974, they decided to install a swimming pool and adjoining rockery, and again phoned to ask for advice. Ellis drove to Preston, suggested altering the proposed rectangular shape of the pool so that at least one side was curved, and brought his grandson, Stephen Junghenn, to place the rocks. He described Stephen as 'the only man I allow to do my rock outcrops without supervision'. And even though he was then seventy-eight years of age, he picked up a shovel and joined in the physical work.

He had tremendous skill with swimming pools, preferring them to look as natural as possible. He found there were two types of pool clients, those who wanted the pool to be the focal point of their garden and those who sought an unobtrusive treatment. 'Needless to say the people who take the latter approach are the ones that win me!' In 1968, asked to site and design a pool on a country property in Victoria's Western District, he elected to cut it in below a projecting piece of land so that it was not visible from the weekend cottage it adjoined. (Significantly, before beginning work he had taken this client to Olinda to inspect the Hughes-Jones pool he had built there in 1939–40.) He didn't like predictable shapes. He liked to use rocks at the pool edge, for their intrinsic beauty and for a natural effect, for their usefulness as a place to sit or to drape a towel, and for safety reasons – a diving rock was safer for children than a springboard, he said, and carefully placed rocks slowed up children who wanted to race around the pool. A 1974 pool in Toorak, now demolished, showed this to perfection. 'He was in tune both with our visual needs and, as we had young children, with the use to which the pool was to be put', the client recalled. 'He was very firm about design features which he thought inappropriate – for instance, he would not use standard tiles. I remember him sitting there directing where all the rocks should go. He was most exacting about this.'

A pool built in 1971 for Elizabeth and Hugh Morgan was irregularly shaped and, at the owners' request, was finished with a black lining – a technique that Ellis had not tried before, but that he found he liked. John Jackson carried out the landscaping around this pool, installing slate paving and bluestone retaining walls that set it off to perfection, as well as a beautiful flight of slate steps leading up to the house – 'garden steps . . . should always be as wide and shallow as possible; eighteen inches is a nice width for the tread, with a rise of no more than six inches and if the steps are to be a feature remember Be Bold!' Ellis wrote in 1971. These features have grown in beauty with the years, as have the occasional flat boulders at one end of the retaining wall, which drift off subtly into the lawn. Ellis chose these, and placed them himself. The pool he designed at 'Glenara' in 1973 also exhibits splendid rockwork incorporating stone seats, and a pebbled watercourse running behind it, adding to the atmosphere of a ruined nineteenth-century stone winery on a rise just above the pool.

A curving flight of steps in random paving.

'A pool can be made to fit into its surroundings to some degree', he wrote, adding that one advantage of a free-form pool was that the landscape design could be taken right to the edge in at least one spot, often with one or two really big boulders. As a practical suggestion, he noted that the concourse should be sloped 'ever so slightly' down and away from the pool edge, to keep dirty rainwater from running into the pool. Plant material should be considered very carefully, he said, even virtually abandoned in favour of other natural materials. His beautiful pool at 'River Gums' in the Melbourne suburb of Alphington was a case in point. The Yarra River flows at the bottom of this garden, with the grey-green mass of the Yarra Bend National Park on the opposite bank – a more dramatic natural landscape would be hard to find. Ellis made the concourse from selected red gum timbers and placed occasional very large boulders. He installed a timber seat and tea-tree screens of varying heights to block an unwanted view to one side and provide shelter on another. These blend perfectly with the mottled trunks of the tall eucalypts in the distance. (The timber surround, having rotted, was replaced in 1989 with a more conventional paving material.)

Ellis continued to battle ill-health, having a minor stroke in 1971, from which he made a quick recovery although his impatience was the despair of therapists at the Heidelberg Repatriation Hospital. The stroke left him with impaired movement on his left side. While physiotherapists

A pool designed to blend with the surrounding bush in a garden in Alphington, running down to the Yarra River.

regarded this as a permanent condition he was convinced it was temporary, and that he soon would return to normal. They would stand him in front of a mirror, explain to him how to button his shirt with one hand, and leave him to get on with it; he would call out to passers-by until one stopped to help him finish dressing, then stalk off grumbling 'A man could freeze without his shirt'. Simply, he couldn't see the point of wasting time learning a technique that soon he would not need. He hated the forced inactivity of hospital and its routines, and invariably discharged himself early. When confined to a strict diabetic diet he would get other patients to order forbidden food for him. Once, seeing a nurse laying down the law to a seriously ill cancer patient, he asked innocently: 'What's the joke?' 'There's no joke', the nurse snapped. 'Oh', said Ellis. 'That's funny. I thought I saw a smile on your face.'

As the 1970s progressed he occasionally seemed tired. Olive was struck down by meningitis – for a few worrying days her life was in danger, which greatly perturbed him – and he had back trouble in 1973. 'I'm out of action with a cracked spine', read a note to a client. Yet usually a day or two's rest would revive him enough to continue the daily round. He carried a workload that would have made much younger men quail, with consultation after consultation for private gardens as well as continuing work for developers, commissions from public bodies, and small work – usually done free of charge – for kindergarten, school and community groups. One day in 1970 saw him all over Melbourne for appointments at 9.30 and 11 a.m., 12 noon, 2, 6.30 and 8 pm. No job was too small. He designed a letterbox for one client, a garbage tin enclosure for another.

'Why don't you slow up?' friends and family kept asking. 'I can't', he replied. 'They won't let me.' The card file for his 1972–75 jobs is 120 cm thick, some of the cards (for clients like Merchant Builders or Stocks and Holdings) listing up to eight different jobs, while the numerous 'free' jobs were additional to this, not even being given a card. 'Sincere appreciation for your contribution to the planning of the school site recently and for the time and knowledge devoted to preparation of drawings', read a letter from the advisory council of a local high school. 'Sincere thanks for your assistance . . . a motion has been passed by council to allocate money to the project . . . please accept our invitation to view the results when there is something worth seeing', wrote a representative of the Keilor Civic Group. Towards the end of 1974, this group asked Ellis for a beautification scheme for the Calder Highway as it passed through Keilor, once a country town but at the time developing into an outer suburb of Melbourne. Ellis's suggestions included log fences of selected used electricity poles, and bold rock outcrops planted with grevilleas and similar shrubs. He wished the civic group luck in trying to maintain the town's distinct character, feeling sure that the shire council 'wouldn't want to lose this by doing anything tizzy'. So ubiquitous has the low log fence become as an edging for anything from large housing estates to council playgrounds that it is easy to forget it was Ellis Stones who popularised it.

Among people asking him to design private gardens during the early 1970s were an increasing number of young married couples, many of whom got in touch after seeing his work in friends' gardens. Ellis enjoyed these clients. He recognised that they hadn't a lot of money and that, setting up house, they were heavily committed, so he would give them what he called a 'seven-year plan' in which he staged the work that would be needed to fit their budget. According to Pam Reynolds, his assistant at the time, he would suggest that initially they should spend money on getting the form of their block right, contouring and shaping it. Then he would advise them to complete and plant out one area at a time, perhaps an intimate corner outside the living room window – he believed garden views from inside a house were as important as external vistas – or the area around the front door. The entrance, he said, was a vital part of any garden. 'It can say "welcome" and "stay out" better than any sign, and if you are going to be proud of your house and garden this is where you must start . . . first impressions are the most lasting.' Don't buy little things in pots now, he would say to these young clients, wait until you're ready to plant them – and then why not go to Coles and buy them small, in a tube? Small plants usually got a better start, and tubes were cheaper.

Always, Pam Reynolds said, Ellis himself would take a completed garden plan to his clients (unless they lived too far away for this to be practicable), discussing it thoroughly and explaining every aspect, making sure they understood it and that they were happy with it. At this time his average charge was around $120; this included the initial visit and measure-up, the design, and presentation of the plan.

Because by now Ellis had worked on private gardens for almost forty years he had developed a sense about whether he and new clients would get on. He didn't want any undue pressure, so he was not as interested in working for people who contacted him simply because he was fashionable – although he certainly enjoyed the feeling of being in demand – or for people who, on first meeting, showed themselves to be not in sympathy with his basic principles of garden design. One client whose garden he had made in the early 1960s phoned him in 1974 to ask for help in a new garden. 'He told me he was no longer doing private gardens, just articles for Home Beautiful, lectures, and housing projects in the outer suburbs. "That's as busy as I want to be now – I'm too old", he said. But we chatted on and then he said "As I recall we got on pretty well. I can't do the work but if I do the design and get the rocks can you organise the rest?" Of course, I said.' This garden, which Ellis inspected the day before he died and was well pleased with, included a small Japanese-inspired courtyard and a flight of beautiful bluestone steps, ideal for perching on. It had no front fence. 'I suppose you want roses', he had said before starting on the plan. 'Yes . . . a lot.' 'All right, but they're not going in the front, you know!'

Late in 1973 Graeme and Pam McCubbin contacted Ellis to ask for help on their two-hectare block of land at Sunbury, half an hour's drive north-west of Melbourne. The steep block was heavily timbered with native eucalypts, had no topsoil worth speaking of, and bore the brunt of fierce prevailing winds from the north. The new house had been cut in near the top of the hill, with the spoil pushed out in front. 'It was just a dust bowl. We wondered what on earth we could do', said Mrs McCubbin. 'My father had died and left me some money so we decided to have the garden properly designed, in his memory. We had read Ellis Stones's articles in Home Beautiful, and telephoned him. I couldn't believe how friendly he was! He drove up here and looked, and said it was a challenge that he'd like to take on.'

Ellis left the front part of the block untouched; today the numerous gum trees, with dusty grass beneath, make a pleasant introduction to the property as the gravelled drive winds through them. Close to the house he suggested lawn, with heavily planted outcrops to retain the slope. At one corner he designed a gentle flight of timber-edged gravel steps – a place of quiet repose where, because of the steps' shallow gradient, the change in level is almost imperceptible. He planted wisteria on the posts of the deep timber verandah behind the house, making a shady 'outside room' in hot weather, and put rough timber seats and tables onto the verandah and around the adjoining barbecue. Immediately behind the rear service areas of the house a nicely built rock wall, with niches for planting, retained the slope and enlivened what is usually a 'dead' area in similar houses. He hid the clothes-line with a tea-tree screen. The owners later added a swimming pool in the top corner of the garden, mainly as water storage against bushfires in this dry, harsh part of Victoria, but bearing in mind Ellis's ideas, they made it as inconspicuous as possible.

They left everything to Ellis. The planting was mostly native, into imported topsoil; over the years a lot succumbed to the prevailing winds. John Jackson's men were on site for some three months, and Ellis and Olive made regular visits with Pam Reynolds. The McCubbins enjoyed the pleasure of his company over cups of tea, the enthusiasm with which he worked, the lively interest he took in their children (particularly the new baby). And they recalled with some amazement the size of his bill. They had braced themselves for a big one, given the number of site visits. Ellis charged $150.

He asked no fee at all for a large garden in Ivanhoe that he designed in 1974 on a long, very narrow, previously vacant block of land opposite his own house (the spot where he had dug an air-raid shelter for his family before leaving for service in the Second World War). Sloping steeply away from the road and down, the land was right on the level of the 1934 Yarra River flood; a stone-lined stormwater drain ran through it. The owners, Alan and Yvonne Clark, knew Ellis Stones by reputation, because he had designed a friend's garden. Mrs Clark hesitated to contact him because she had heard he'd retired – her surprise was immense when she finally looked up his telephone number to discover he lived across the street. The next night the Clarks and Ellis were outside at the same time. 'I was delighted when I saw your roof tiles were going to be black', he called out. 'We were afraid they'd be orange. And it's good to see a house going up there. For years we've been looking at people tipping rubbish over the edge.' 'Well', said Alan Clark, 'it'd be better, wouldn't it, if you could look across at your own work instead?' Ellis rubbed his hands together. 'How marvellous. I didn't know how to approach you.'

He placed huge rocks, brought in with cranes, to give form to the sloping land. Bluestone was used for paving, for walls, and, with the joints raked out, for the steep drive leading under the house to the garage. Away from the house ran a long, low stretch of native plants, interspersed with boulders and sleepers. For the walled front courtyard he designed a beautiful small pond, overhung by two trees – *Hakea sericea* and *Eucalyptus caesia*. Because the new house had to be long and low to fit the strangely shaped site, he suggested planting low-maintenance ivy along its street frontage, to soften the severe line. There was to be no boundary fence. Ellis greatly enjoyed this garden and regularly popped in, delighted when he would glimpse Mrs Clark reclining on the sleeper seat – 'that's why I put it there' – and looking guilty if the Clarks came home on a hot night to find him watering their newly planted trees and shrubs. 'Well, I just gave them a bit.' No fee account arrived after the garden was finished, and eventually they asked for his bill. 'Oh, no', he said, surprised. 'That was a moving-in present.'

Ellis's rockwork in this garden showed that, despite his advanced years, his touch was as sure as ever. His colleagues agree that rockwork was his great strength; no Australian landscape designer before or after him has displayed such virtuosity.

John Stevens recalls the 'transcendental feeling' that Ellis had about rocks and stone and describes his use of the medium as an absolute aesthetic expression. Gordon Ford, whose own rockwork is highly regarded, speaks of the evocative quality of Ellis's work, its delicacy and restraint, and says that while building walls or outcrops he still often thinks of 'the way Rocky would have done it'. Thistle Harris has described Ellis as 'that superb worker in rock', writing: 'Rock and boulder outcrops demand the highest of skills because of their dominant nature: errors and deficiencies will be obvious because lavish planting cannot be allowed to camouflage them . . . Few people have the innate ability to use rock in the superb manner (Ellis Stones) did.' Ellis was no prima donna, he was not selfish with his ability, always being happy to advise or guide his fellow workers. Such lessons stood them in good stead. When Bob Crosbie left his employ in the early 1950s to work for Eric Hammond, he found he was asked often to place rocks on jobs. When the time came for him to move on, Hammond commented: 'Sorry to see you go – I like your style of rockwork'. 'I learnt that from Ellis Stones', replied Bob. 'Yes', said Hammond. 'I thought you would have.'

Ellis set out his philosophy on rock work, and his 'ground rules', in *Australian Garden Design*.

> *I always consider weathered boulders one of the most valuable materials for use in the garden, or the natural landscape. In my youth, while hunting in the hill country, I was impressed by the beautiful rock formations, and was amazed to note how each outcrop, although entirely different, was always pleasing to look at. I was so impressed with nature's grouping of these boulders that in later years I studied rock formations; the principle I learnt from nature I follow in the selecting and placing of boulders in the garden. When boulders are used to form an outcrop in a garden, the idea is generally to raise part of the garden without terracing; the boulders then should appear as natural as possible.*
>
> *There are no hard and fast rules to follow, but if the gardener remembers some of the principles and experiments in his own garden, he will discover how interesting natural boulders, properly placed, can be.*

Observe how the rock was placed in its natural state, as this will nearly always look right in a domestic garden. Do not be afraid to bury a large part of the stone if necessary . . . Above all do not create a rockery by using too many rocks. Another point to remember is that natural outcrops nearly always follow a line or strata, even if they are some distance apart.

It is also important when working with rocks to be bold, and this does not necessarily mean the use of very large stones. Do not use too many rocks of roughly the same size together, or the outcrop will lose character, and remember that the person constructing the outcrop looks at the work from close up, while other people will see it, at least for the first glance, from a distance . . .

He tended to differentiate between rockeries, which he saw primarily as show-places for plants, and outcrops, which he said were built (apart from their practical purpose of retaining ground) to display the innate beauty of the component rocks. He recommended treating boulders as steps, in conjunction with planting; he used them to give a feeling of distance in a small space or a focus in an ugly area – 'beauty attracts the eye where all the surroundings are unattractive', he wrote. He warned that local stone was always preferable, and that rocks should never be ordered in bulk over the telephone – rather, one should speak directly to a cartage contractor about the desired size, colour and shape. (He would not work with rocks he thought were unsuitable. In 1967 he rejected in these terms a load delivered to the site for construction of a memorial gateway at the Natural Resources Conservation League in Springvale: 'You can cart the whole lot away. They're just no good.')

In a paddock strewn with rocks, his ability to pick out exactly the pieces he needed for a particular job was uncanny. Friends and clients who went rock-getting with him recalled that the stone seemed almost to speak to him (or he to it). He spent weeks trying to find a piece of stone to set off a bronze statue of a bird in the large garden that he designed in the early 1960s at Templestowe, on the Yarra River. 'I walked and walked in the paddock', he told the client, 'and when I found it I could have got down on my knees and hugged it'. He liked to make presents of special pieces to people whom he knew would share his enthusiasm. In the late 1930s he gave Edna Walling a stone trough that Gwynnyth Taylor (Crouch) recalled as 'a beautiful lump of basalt with a natural depression in its centre'. Chris Bailey, the Ivanhoe chemist at whose side Ellis fought many conservation battles for the Yarra River, received from him a slab of sandstone patterned with myriad subtle colours, with the quiet comment: 'I think you will appreciate this'.

Ellis summed it up himself. 'I love rocks. They have a naturalness, an air of permanence, a beauty all of their own. They add to the solidity, the serenity, of a garden layout. They belong.'

TWENTY

Achievement, acceptance, fame

Heidelberg, only six kilometres from the GPO, has more natural green space than almost any other municipality in Melbourne. The Yarra River, joined by the Plenty River and the Darebin and Salt Creeks, loops diagonally through the city, cutting a lazy swathe from one corner to the other. Along much of its length it is bordered by parks or bushland.

Of course it looked far different last century, when open country stretched as far as the eye could see, and when McCubbin, Conder, Streeton, Roberts and the other painters of the Heidelberg school were based at the semi-derelict Mount Eagle homestead, on a Heidelberg hilltop overlooking the Yarra. It was here, in 1888–90, that Sir Arthur Streeton produced the 'Golden Summer' canvas that Lionel Lindsay described in 1920 as the cornerstone of the 'Australian' vision of the Heidelberg artists. Here, too, he painted the famed 'Still glides the stream, and shall for ever glide', described in the catalogue of the 1985–86 art exhibition 'Golden Summers, Heidelberg and Beyond' in these terms:

> *. . . the stream is the Yarra as it meanders through the flats near Heidelberg which are half in light and half in shadow; with the uplands beyond catching the last rays of the declining sun, and the full moon rising from behind the ranges, which detach their misty blue silhouettes from the still warm sky.*

The painting's title came from a sonnet written in 1820 by William Wordsworth. The exhibition catalogue explained that Streeton intended his canvas to be not so much a depiction of a particular place (even though he inscribed it 'Heidelberg') as a general statement about a *type* of place and the feelings it evoked. 'Like Wordsworth, he recognised that Nature persists long beyond the lives of individual man.' Ellis Stones felt exactly the same way. Arthur Streeton and his contemporaries had painted Nature.

Ellis saw that it was in danger, and he fought for it, recognising the special place the Yarra River holds in Melbourne, loving its grey-green fringe of native vegetation and the ribbon of still, brown water that brought a whiff of the bush to the streets and houses that, even in the early 1950s, were beginning to hem it in. If individual man had his way, he felt, this facet of nature would not last much longer.

Over the years his relationship with Heidelberg City Council had been strained, with the battle lines drawn at a time (thought to be in the late 1940s) when the then mayor had proclaimed his intention to pull out eucalypts that grew naturally along one part of the Yarra bank, replacing them with pine trees. From the mid-1950s, as president of the Ivanhoe River Parklands Protection League, he kept a constant and critical watch on the council's stewardship of those parts of the Yarra under its control, particularly Chelsworth Park, abutting the river near his home. Activities like rubbish dumping in billabongs, closing of public access to bathing beaches, discharging by others of raw sewage into the river, were anathema to him and he campaigned long and hard against them, as did other conservation-minded locals (most notably the chemist, Chris Bailey and later, Dr Len Allen of the Save the Yarra League). But despite disagreements, communication between Ellis and the council continued so that by the mid-1960s, as we have seen, it accepted his design for Wilson Reserve playground, and later commissioned him to design Rosanna Parklands.

It was around this time that Ellis came into contact with Vern Henderson, a surveyor and local councillor who is widely credited with helping ensure preservation of much of the municipality's natural landscape. Henderson was a dynamo whose concerns ranged from Wilson Reserve across the Banyule Flats to View Bank and the Warringal wetlands, and who was aware also of the potential of the Darebin and Salt Creeks. In the early 1970s he and Ellis worked closely with the council's new city planner/architect, John McInerney, with the result that Ellis was consulted on almost all the council's work where this involved 'natural' treatment or fitting in with the natural landscape.

In 1972 he wrote to the town clerk:

> *The plan that I have submitted for the landscaping of the Golf Links Estate Park at Rosanna could have been much more undulating, especially in the vicinity of the railway; but I was led to believe that the council was not in favour of this approach . . .*

The following year he again contacted the town clerk, asking the parks and gardens committee to meet him on a Saturday or Sunday at a local reserve 'to discuss careful thinning of badly placed trees'; in 1974 he carried out rockwork at Macleod railway station and prepared a cost estimate for a total landscape treatment in Chelsworth Park. He consulted on various council pavilions, including a changing shed in Chelsworth Park initially designed in brick by council staff and sited in the middle of open space. Ellis suggested tucking it back under the trees, and that Graeme Gunn should be brought in as architect. This led to a disagreement with council officers who thought Gunn's timber construction might burn down, and who criticised its lack of downpipes; in 1976 this building won an award from the Royal Australian Institute of Architects. A Henderson/Stones initiative was the acquisition from a Country Roads Board excavation of a pile of huge rocks and boulders. Ellis was overjoyed because he rarely had access to rocks of this dimension. 'Where are we going to put them?' Vern Henderson asked. 'In Rosanna Parklands at the top end of Salt Creek', said Ellis, who was busy implementing his overall landscape plan there, and who had plans for that waterway.

John McInerney was imbued with landscape philosophy, having come to Heidelberg from four years' work in Canberra with the National Capital Development Commission. Soon after his arrival, Vern Henderson took him to Locksley Road to meet Ellis, about whom he had heard from other landscape designers, notably Bruce Mackenzie. He was immediately charmed by Ellis and excited by his ideas. 'In those days it was hard to talk about landscaping to anyone, but we hit it off straight away', he said. 'Even though he always made you feel you were more important than him, you knew you had a common purpose. The thing I remember about Ellis was not his work – this was easy for him, quite natural, bread and butter – but his absolute dedication to the future of large-scale land-use planning. He had a deep understanding of the relationship between water and land use. He believed in sensitive handling of water run-off, the development of flood basins to handle excess flow and using these for public recreation, rather than piping it straight to the sea. Few people comprehend this properly.' (Significantly, Ellis's early plan for Salt Creek in the Rosanna Parklands had involved creating small occasional lakes to accommodate higher flows in the creek, but these were disallowed on the ground of safety.)

Ellis's strong convictions on the subject inevitably led him into conflict with the drainage authority, the Melbourne and Metropolitan Board of Works. He had crossed swords with the MMBW in the early 1960s over sewage discharge into the Yarra; now he geared up for more argument over the city's radial creeks. In the natural landscape, creeks were great assets, he said, so why not treat them as such in an urban context? Increasingly, MMBW policy was to set such creeks into underground or above-ground concrete drains, but he believed they should be retained as natural waterways, landscaped so as to provide ponding basins for occasional flood control, and beautified for much-needed useable green space and recreation areas.

Heading the Board was the redoubtable Alan Croxford. In 1966, when Croxford was a councillor in the neighbouring municipality of Doncaster–Templestowe, he and Ellis had been pictured together on the front page of the local newspaper as Ellis enthused about his plan to create a 100-acre garden and park area along Ruffey Creek. But by the early 1970s Ellis was not quite so complimentary about Mr Croxford and the planners under his control, particularly in 1972–73, when plans were well advanced to run part of Glass's Creek into a partially underground concrete drain. The badly eroded creek, in Kilby Reserve, Kew, crossed an area known as Hay's Paddock, used then for agisting horses and cows; the work was seen as necessary because of construction of a new freeway nearby, and because Kew City Council wanted more open space for playing fields.

Glass's Creek as it looked in the early 1970s, and with Ellis's concept for its beautification superimposed.

More than 1300 local residents signed a petition to the MMBW, asking that the creek should be landscaped rather than put into a drain, and the paddock developed for passive recreation. The Kew Natural Environment Group asked Ellis to help it draw up a submission. His suggestions included creating mounds and treating the creek with large rocks, to give a natural effect, to absorb energy in times of flooding, and to stop erosion. The MMBW did not approve of some details, but it was not against the concept in principle and agreed that it might save money. But while it was deliberating, an article by Ellis appeared in the *Herald*, with the inflammatory title of 'Vandals in Grey Flannel Suits'. His ghost writer did not mince words:

> *The longer I live the more I become convinced that some of the worst louts and vandals in this country wear grey flannel suits, a collar and tie and carry some fancy title that says they are experts at town planning.*
>
> *I've been watching them at work in and around Melbourne for many years now, systematically destroying the natural beauty and gradually whittling away the beauty created by those who founded the place. And sometimes I wonder why I am daft enough to go on trying to stop the rot.*
>
> *Take a fairly simple example like the many little creeks around our suburbs. Before we got here they were pretty things, some of them quite beautiful. Nowadays we are full pelt into the task of ripping them all out and turning them into concrete courseways . . .*

He could weep with rage, he said, at some of the stunning decisions reached by the MMBW's planners. They might be honest, well-intentioned men but unknowingly, they were villains.

> *Their job is to make the city work better and they have neglected making it look better. Let us keep our picturesque creeks instead of turning them into concrete tunnels. Heavy rains and the occasional flooding will keep them clean . . .*

And he referred to his plan for Glass's Creek. This, he said, was a positive landscape response and would cost much less than the Board's proposed treatment. Ellis's attitude did not endear him to the authorities. 'Mr Ellis Stones needs to be put right on several matters', retorted a letter to the *Herald* from the MMBW's chief planner. But the following year the MMBW did allow him to go ahead with his long-cherished proposals to beautify a similar stretch of Salt Creek, Rosanna. In 1974 he suggested further rockwork in an upstream section of Salt Creek. At a meeting to discuss the idea, the Board's planners were not impressed and told him why. Mr Stones, a spokesman said, 'quickly understood the problems and withdrew his proposal', and this part of Salt Creek was put underground. In 1976 his Glass's Creek plan, partially modified, was implemented over a short stretch of that creek.

By now the MMBW was not the only public authority with which he was dealing. Late in 1974 and early the following year he was delighted to be asked to design the surrounds of five new railway stations and two tramway interchanges. The railway commission came through Yuncken Freeman architects, who sought him out because staff members working on the new station design thought 'Well, who else would you have but Ellis?' In 1975 VicRail appointed Ellis a judge for its competition to redesign Heyington station. The tramway projects, involving the bleak, busy St Kilda Road/Park Street terminus and exchange near the Shrine of Remembrance, and the extension of the Burwood Highway route, were interrupted by Ellis's death.

He worried about his advancing age; he would try to work even when ill and flat on his back, agitating that every day was precious – 'I can't waste one'. During 1973 he continued to travel, accepting jobs in Adelaide, Deniliquin, Ocean Grove, Wangaratta; he gave his usual round

Ellis worried about his advancing age, but he was all smiles as he and Olive celebrated their golden wedding.

of talks to community and school groups. Development companies sought him out for jobs from the central city to the outer suburbs. The Stocks and Holdings company asked his advice on planting greenfields housing development sites; he loved these assignments, which were carried out in advance of subdivision, feeling that through them he was making a real contribution to the broad landscape. He continued to work for Merchant Builders, advising in similar terms on new projects, scrambling up and down rough terrain and sketching out in simple terms the early planting – 'trees here, scrub there'. Howard McCorkell, today a leading town planner, drove him on these occasions, an experience from which he said he learned a lot.

By now, with sophisticated technology being brought to bear in landscape architecture, David Yencken and John Ridge found they needed more trained knowledge for Merchant Builders projects than Ellis could give them. Rodney Wulff returned from the United States to join their team; nevertheless the firm's new planning arm, Tract Consultants, advertised its landscape service as 'an association of Tract's specialist skills in analysis and design with Ellis Stones's wealth of experience as a landscape architect'. According to Tract's publicity brochure, its skills in site and landscape design solved practical problems (drainage, soil retention, etc.), safeguarded environmental quality, and promoted 'precious qualities' like the relationship of plants and other materials, the placement of trees, the suggestion of continuing space, and illusions of distance – qualities, of course, that Ellis had made his own.

Ellis took Rodney Wulff around Melbourne after his arrival and showed him some of his work, from the grounds of the APM factory in Fairfield to plantings at Yooralla special school's new headquarters in Glenroy. Wulff was struck by Ellis's mastery of his techniques. 'What he did, he did beautifully. I particularly remember his use of *Eucalyptus maculata*, and those delicate little courtyards at Winter Park.' Later they travelled to South Australia, where Tract was preparing a report on the proposed Rocky Gully–Narrinyeri Hills recreation park at the new town, Monarto. The report, for which Ellis was a consultant, pointed to the need in the park for mass planting – Rod Wulff remembered it as 'difficult country' – and for the re-creation of a natural environment. Ellis was particularly taken with an old farm within the park boundary. His notes read:

> *One section of the area to be set aside for wild life. A suitable rugged area would be a wonderful home for rock wallabies* etc . . . *walking track designed to pass natural features . . . any car-parks to be disguised so that they do not offend. My first impression is that it would be better to retain farm as a farm rather than a museum, as they are everywhere, but the area around should be in a real farm setting with perhaps a few old implements thrown in . . . but avoid overdoing it by getting gimmicky.*

As his reputation grew, so researchers sought him out. Margaret Hendry wrote from Canberra in 1974, looking for material on his early work. In his reply, Ellis simply listed a few of his more important consultancies – Heidelberg City Council, the National Trust, and so on – and for pictorial material, directed her to *Australian Home Beautiful.* The Sydney architect Howard Tanner came to Melbourne in the same year to talk about including an example of Ellis's work in a new book he was preparing on major Australian gardens. He got nowhere, he said, 'because Ellis did not feel his work was in this category. He was such a modest man. He and his wife entertained me to tea and cake in an unpretentious cottage at Ivanhoe . . . while he would confess that his later work at "Winter Park" was of some interest, perhaps he felt that I was some nut looking for works of his comparable to those by, say, Guilfoyle. He wished me well and I went on my way.' (Several years later Tanner was to put together Australia's first major exhibition on historic garden design.) However, an interested student at Preston Institute of Technology, inquiring about Ellis's work, fared better. 'I look on it as a pleasure to assist the younger generation in any way if I can', Ellis said, directing the student to Winter Park, playgrounds at Wilson Reserve and Preshil school, and the Baitz garden. In early 1975 the noted architect Daryl Jackson suggested Ellis begin a new project at St Paul's School, Woodleigh, by visiting the school and talking to students. 'I am looking forward to this approach to landscaping', Ellis wrote. He was involved with several buildings designed by Jackson and Walker; meetings with these architects usually were scheduled for late afternoon and held in the office's 'conversation pit' so that interested members of staff could listen in and learn from what Ellis had to say. Most took advantage of this opportunity.

Towards the end of 1974 the National Trust asked Ellis to attend a meeting about a proposed book on historic gardens in Australia. He replied politely enough that he would be interested, but he could have been excused for being a bit terse, because two months previously, at a meeting of the Australian Institute of Landscape Architects' meeting, he had been surprised to hear read out a letter from the Trust asking for the services of a landscape architect for the grounds of the Portarlington Mill. He wrote to the Trust's chairman, Rodney Davidson, that he had already prepared a plan that could be carried out there using voluntary labour, adding 'Had the plan not been according to the Trust's requirements I think you might at least have discussed it with me before taking this action'. There were copious apologies; no discourtesy was intended, Mr Davidson wrote, but it had been assumed he no longer wished to be active in his original capacity since the landscape institute as a body had agreed to help the Trust . . . 'however, as you notice, we still show you separately in our annual report as a courtesy to the days when you were our original and only adviser . . .'

Ellis had been late in replying to the Trust's invitation to talk about the proposed new book because it had arrived while he was holidaying in New Zealand. His last project there was an outcrop at a new house at Wanaka, below the Cardrona snowfield. Invited to lunch one weekend by the owners, John and Jocelyn Mills, he was extremely enthusiastic about the ten-acre site, but discovered that they were worried about coping with the huge pile of soil from the basement excavation that was sitting against the house. Ellis called for a front-end loader and set to work. The machine was available for only one hour but in that time, using rocks that were already on the property, he transformed the mound and the swimming pool, and explained how to complete the work. The loader driver would have made a fortune in Melbourne, he said. 'He handles that thing like a teaspoon.' Some years later the Mills built a lovely flight of timber and gravel steps in this garden with occasional boulders at the edge, taking their lead from examples shown in Ellis's books.

Work executed with this precision and speed showed Ellis's complete command of his profession. Ten years earlier he had done a rather similar job in Melbourne at a garden on a very steep, bare site in Pascoe Vale. 'Where's the wheelbarrow?' he said as he arrived for the one-day contract. The weather was blazing hot and the rocks were waiting; working with Bob Grant and the writer, Frank Kellaway, he set to with vigour, placing them all by hand, laying out the paths and building several walls for good measure. The client, Robin Ottrey, was well pleased with the job but what really struck him was the 'human relationship'. They were real comedians, he recalled, 'a riot, once they got going'. Helen Clemson, whose parents followed Robin Boyd's advice and commissioned Ellis to design part of the garden around their 1959 Boyd house in the riverside suburb of Kew, recalled similar camaraderie. 'I was a teenager then and to me Ellis Stones seemed middle-aged, even old, but he was so warm and vigorous and rumbustious with the two or three young guys working for him that the whole project was a delight. Oh, they had a lovely sense of fun!' More than thirty years on, Miss Clemson retains a vivid memory of waking up on a warm spring morning in the new house to an almost impossibly sweet scent that she had never encountered before. It was brown boronia, which Ellis had directed should be planted below her bedroom window.

Good fellowship permeated the Yarra Valley project on which Peter Glass and Ellis were involved in the last months of Ellis's life. Hoping to promote reasoned use of the valley and increased awareness of its attributes, the Valley Freeway Action Group had asked them to carry out a landscape assessment as part of an overall plan for a two-hectare stretch of the valley, between Heidelberg and Doncaster–Templestowe. This was threatened by a highway reservation and by expansion of industry and private clubs; it included places of major historical importance, swampland, billabongs that still were being filled in, golf courses and farmland. The two walked the length of the study area, a day at a time. Peter Glass took his sketchbook with him; Ellis took his bad leg, his years of experience and absorption of the Australian landscape, and his sense of humour. Together they produced detailed maps with suggestions for landscape treatment – for example, 'plant nursery should be removed', 'plant heavily here' (beside a drive-in theatre), 'no cycling or horse riding on foot track'. This work, done on a voluntary basis, was a delight for Peter Glass. 'I enjoyed being with him so much. We got on terrifically well. Afterwards we would sit down, talk it over and write it up.' The report, dedicated to Ellis, appeared after his death and its conclusions are vintage Stones.

There has not been any grand scale planning of parks and public gardens since Melbourne's original planning. There has never been the urgency there is today to conserve our landscape. The coming generations will have enormous problems to solve; it is now up to our generation to preserve what open space is still left in and around our cities.

Peter Glass felt Ellis thoroughly enjoyed this work because once again, it gave him the chance to make a large-scale contribution. Other activities during the previous year had demonstrated Ellis's continued desire for this. In mid-1974 he had chaired a session at a landscape symposium at La Trobe University, when one speaker talked about the necessity of approaching landscaping on a large scale instead of taking small areas at a time. Ellis contacted this speaker immediately to let him know he had been conscious of the deterioration of the landscape and had been fighting against it, and for the development of alternate parklands in Melbourne. But he felt he had started off on the wrong foot with 'the authorities responsible for the destruction of our landscape . . . I am afraid I have been too outspoken in condemming [*sic*] their action'. The speaker's remarks strengthened his efforts to keep trying and fighting, he wrote, but he needed help. This was not forthcoming from the landscape architects' institute 'as I am afraid that they look on me as a rebel'. Would it be possible, he asked, to contact some of the students at the university where this speaker worked, to present his plan of action 'and see if they are enthusiastic enough to join in the fight . . . ?'

Later in 1974 he fired off a letter to Melbourne's new Lord Mayor, Cr Ronald Walker, who had been quoted in the press as wanting to beautify and enliven Melbourne. Ellis's subject was the Tullamarine Freeway, 'the present gateway to our city . . . and a modern eyesore and disgrace by anyone's standards'. The Lord Mayor, he wrote in a letter drafted with Tony Hitchin, was the first person of any importance that he had come across in years who had given any indication of loving the city and wanting to do something for its betterment. He noted that Melbourne's formal parks were beautiful but that opportunities to create new ones were being missed. The Tullamarine Freeway offered such a chance, at comparatively little cost.

> *I envisage the whole length of the freeway as a beautiful bushland setting, with the statuesque river red gums a main feature, the ugly concrete open drain returned to the attractive creek it once was, and a full range of our Australian native trees and shrubs screening the suburban sprawl from the eyes of our visitors. Newcomers would be at the top of Elizabeth Street before they knew they had even arrived . . . What a welcome!*

He was not looking for a job, he added, but he would be happy to contribute anything if it could help the city 'of which we are both apparently so proud and which has given me much pleasure over the years'. A year earlier Ellis had noted on a newspaper clipping describing the erection of plywood and steel barriers against traffic noise on this freeway: 'Three years for trees to grow. The alternative for sound barrier.' He continued to agitate, too, for re-use of vacant land. An article in the *Age* (December 1974) showed his plans for the low-cost conversion to a bushland park of a dismal strip of treeless, unused railway land in the western suburbs. Dozens of similar pocket-handkerchief sites generally regarded as useless were crying out for this treatment, he said.

He travelled to Queensland in 1974 in response to an invitation to lecture at the annual 'Green Fingers Week' held by Binna Burra Lodge in Lamington National Park. He suggested three topics – domestic landscaping ('which is always popular, and is mainly based on natural gardens'); public parks, streets and recreation; designing the native garden ('the designing is very important so that plants of all sizes are shown to advantage') at a fee of $10 per lecture. A snapshot shows Ellis and Olive walking in the gardens of Binna Burra, Ellis smiling broadly, his trusty Rollei camera around his neck. He travelled on to Brisbane, where Sir Zelman Cowen, then the vice-chancellor of the University of Queensland, arranged for him to speak about landscape design to students in the school of architecture, among them Ellis's grandson Barry Rice. (It is interesting to note that Ellis's grandchildren enjoy a wide range of creative occupations: acting and stage direction, pottery, architecture, garden design [particularly rockwork], art.)

In the last two years of his life Ellis had regular contact with a new residents' group that was fighting to preserve a former tip site on the Heidelberg side of Darebin Creek. The Rockbeare Park Conservation Group, formed in 1973, found him readily available whenever advice was needed. There were plenty of requests – at the time the group had no idea how many demands there were on his time, seeing him simply as an expert and willing helper. He told them he approved of what they were attempting. Better by far, he thought, to take immediate action to preserve a park than to put time and energy into fighting bureaucracies or preparing lengthy studies. The MMBW donated 300 trees for planting on the site: Ellis helped the group chose these from the Board's list of available plants. As he could not negotiate the steep slope a four-wheel drive vehicle was provided, from which he directed the positioning of coloured stakes on the creek flats to mark where each tree should grow. The following day he came for several hours while forty volunteers planted the trees. He designed the entrance to Rockbeare Park, running along a walkway between private houses – a simple, understated treatment with casuarinas, a boulder or two, low shrubs. He had agreed to prepare an overall landscape plan for the Darebin Parklands and had promised to sit at the park entrance for the group's first guided walk in April 1975 – but he died the night before it.

In March–April 1975, working happily in the Rosanna Parklands only a stone's throw from Elliston, he was busy installing rocks at the mouth of Salt Creek around the spot where it emerges from an underground drain. This work was part of his landscape plan for the parklands, and as noted, it had the hard-won, qualified approval of the MMBW. The huge boulders he was using came from the pile he and Vern Henderson had gathered years earlier (some of which still sit heaped up in the parkland). Along the creek verge today, tall grass has grown up to almost mask the shrubs and trees that are part of Ellis's landscape treatment,. and to obscure some of the boulders, but once the water's edge is reached the atmosphere is that of a country stream, light years from the noise and clatter of the city so close at hand.

Peter Glass visited Ellis on site the day before he died, and found him 'leaping around those rocks like an antelope'. He came home for dinner on the night of 9 April, tired and happy. 'Oh, I've had a good day', he said to Olive. 'There's a boy on the job who really understands

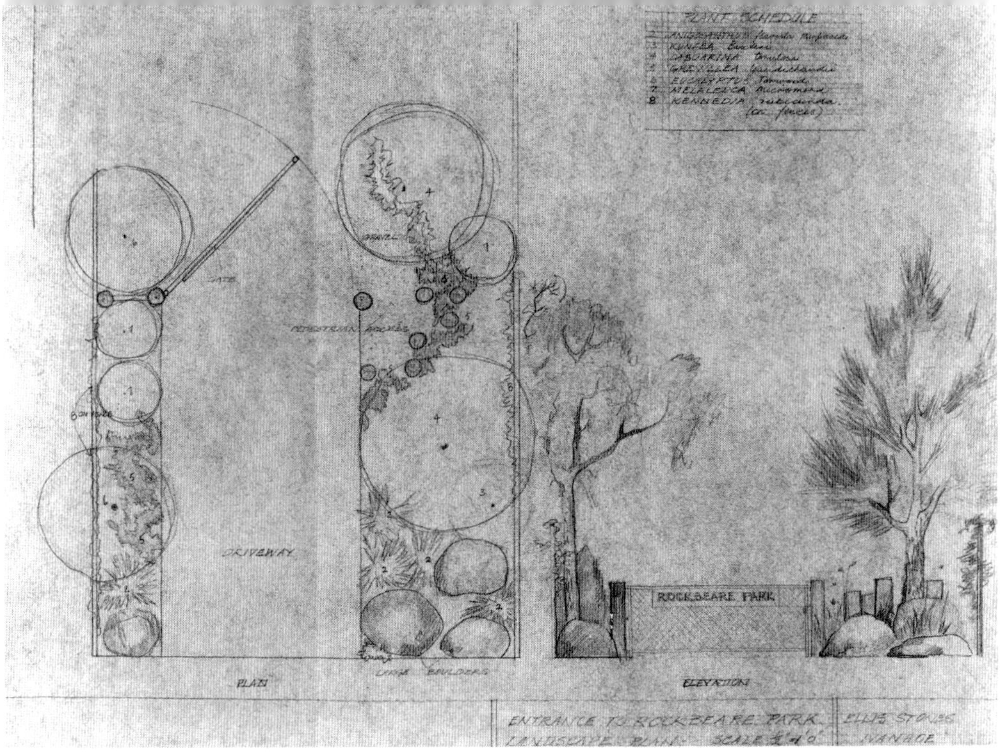

*T*he entrance to Rockbeare Park, Ivanhoe. Today the planting is sadly depleted.

what I'm talking about.' He went for a short lie-down before the evening meal, and did not wake. He died in harness, quickly and quietly, as he wished it.

His funeral at the Heidelberg Methodist Church was crowded. The minister (who had not known him) spoke of his achievements and hymns were sung, but the service was quite devoid of the vitality and enthusiasm that had typified Ellis's whole life. As it drew to a close several of the congregation shifted in their seats. 'We can't send him off like this', thought a friend from Merchant Builders. 'Isn't anyone going to say something?' Then as the organist began to play, signalling the close of proceedings, Chris Bailey jumped to his feet. In a few heartfelt words he conjured up the early days on the riverbank when barriers were pulled down overnight and breaches in billabongs filled in. He spoke of Ellis's contribution to conservation and landscape design, and of his effect on his friends. Everyone heaved a sigh of relief.

There were to be other memorials. The week after Ellis's death 'This Day Tonight', the ABC evening television programme, produced a segment on his life and work which encapsulated his philosophies. He inspired the young unconsciously, said the commentator, Kate Baillieu. And his recipe for unhappiness or ill-health was simple. 'You'll feel better if you go outside and hug a gum tree – it's so much stronger than you are.' Later that year, the Victorian chapter of the Royal Australian Institute of Architects awarded Ellis its Robin Boyd environmental medal. 'We see this as a once-in-a-lifetime opportunity to recognise qualities that the environmental movement is all about', read the award citation. *The Ellis Stones Garden Book*, an illustrated compilation of Ellis's *Australian Home Beautiful* articles on which he had been working for some time with Tony Hitchin, appeared in 1976 – its foreword written by Thistle Harris who concluded: 'I really cannot do justice to the work of a man I admired so much, but I appreciate being given the opportunity to try'. The book quickly sold out its first edition and was reprinted.

As well, in 1976 an appeal was begun in Ellis's name to raise funds for a chair of landscape architecture at the University of Melbourne. It was said that this would be an appropriate memorial to him as well as a major step towards adequate recognition in Victoria of the importance of landscape architecture. The first drive languished; the appeal was relaunched and the resultant chair subsequently named after the major donor, Dame Elisabeth Murdoch. Ellis's name is perpetuated in the 'Ellis Stones Memorial Award', offered biennially to a landscape student for an outstanding piece of research – ironically, an area that was not Ellis's great strength as he preferred practical work and tangible results. The first such award was made in 1985.

Plaques commemorating Ellis Stones's work are to be found here and there around Melbourne. For those who knew him, his abiding memorial is less official but more enduring. 'The two gardens that he made for me will remain a bright and happy memory', a client wrote to his wife, Olive. 'This weather calls me into the garden all the time, and wherever I turn I feel his presence.'

Bibliography

BOOKS

Boyd, Robin. *Australia's Home: Its Origins, Builders and Occupiers.* Melbourne University Press, 1961.

Cassidy, Darien. *Strathfieldsaye: A Historic Structures Report.* University of Melbourne, October 1983. See in particular Carrick Chamber's app.

Chisholm, Nerine. *Australian Gardens: Their Planning and Making.* Georgian House, Melbourne, 1949.

Church, Thomas, with Hall, Grace and Laurie, Michael. *Gardens Are for People.* 2nd edn. McGraw-Hill, USA, 1983.

Clifford, Derek. *A History of Garden Design.* Faber & Faber, London, 1962.

Dixon, Trisha and Churchill, Jennie. *Gardens in Time: In the Footsteps of Edna Walling.* Angus & Robertson, North Ryde, NSW, 1988.

Ebury, Sue (ed.). *Proceedings of the First Garden History Conference: Melbourne 28–29 March 1980.* National Trust of Australia (Victoria), 1980.

Harris, Thistle Y. *Australian Plants for the Garden: A Handbook on the Cultivation of Australian Trees, Shrubs, Other Flowering Plants, and Ferns.* Angus & Robertson, Sydney, 1953.

Hetherington, John. *Witness to Things Past: Stone, Brick, Wood and Men in Early Victoria.* F. W. Cheshire, Melbourne, 1964.

Knox, Alistair. *Living in the Environment.* Mullaya, Canterbury, Victoria, 1975.

———. *We Are What We Stand On: A Personal History of the Eltham Community.* Adobe Press, Eltham, Victoria, 1980.

Maloney, Betty and Walker, Jean. *Designing Australian Bush Gardens.* Horwitz, Sydney, 1966.

Page, Russell. *The Education of a Gardener.* Collins, London, 1962.

Patrick, John. *Australian Garden Designs.* 2nd edn. Penguin, Melbourne, 1989.

Proudfoot, Helen. *Gardens in Bloom: Jocelyn Brown and Her Sydney Gardens of the 30s and 40s.* Kangaroo Press, Kenthurst, NSW, 1989.

Shum, W. A. (ed.). *Australian Gardening of To-Day*. Sun News-Pictorial, Melbourne, 1939.

Stones, Ellis. *Australian Garden Design*. Macmillan, Melbourne, 1971.

———. *The Ellis Stones Garden Book*. Nelson, Melbourne, 1976.

Ure Smith, Sam and Morton Spencer, Gwen (eds). *Australian Treescapes: A Photographic Study*. Ure Smith Miniature Series, Sydney, 1950. See in particular essay by Elyne Mitchell.

Walling, Edna. *Gardens in Australia: Their Design and Care*. 3rd edn. Oxford University Press, Melbourne, 1946.

———. *The Australian Roadside*. Oxford University Press, Melbourne, 1952.

Watts, Peter. *The Gardens of Edna Walling*. National Trust of Australia (Victoria), Melbourne, 1981.

Watts, Peter and Barrett, Margaret (eds). *Historic Gardens of Victoria: A Reconnaissance*. Oxford University Press, Melbourne, 1983.

ARTICLES, PAMPHLETS, UNPUBLISHED WORKS

Australian Women's Weekly. 'From rough paddocks to parklands: a wilderness transformed'. 9 October 1957.

———. 'Landscaping: blends the themes of nature'. 12 May 1971.

Colebatch, Tim. '"Pocket" park plan urged'. *Age*, 6 December 1974.

———. 'A pioneer landscape architect'. *Age*, 26 April 1975.

Dunk, Gillean. 'This man who's changing Melbourne'. *Sun News-Pictorial*, 27 January 1977.

East Yarra News. 'Chelsworth Park History'. 24 February 1956.

Eckbo, Garrett. 'Small gardens in the city: a study of their design possibilities'. Publication unknown, September 1937. In possession of Prof. Michael Laurie, University of California, Berkeley.

Frond, C. B. 'A wilderness garden'. *Australian Home Beautiful*, February 1933.

———. 'Wattles in the garden'. *Australian Home Beautiful*, July 1934.

———. 'Changing fashions in our gardens'. *Australian Home Beautiful*, March 1936.

Grimwade, Russell. '"Gosh!" says Amanda'. Melbourne, 23 May 1938. Grimwade Family Collection, University of Melbourne Archives.

Hitchin, Tony. 'Gardening: the rocky road to success'. *Australian Home Beautiful*, December 1970.

Hendry, Margaret. 'The life and times of Mervyn Davis: a brilliant strategist and advocate for landscape architecture'. *Landscape Australia*, vol. 1, 1986.

Jackson, L. W. 'Tradition in landscaping: let us find a new approach to garden design'. *Australian Home Beautiful*, October 1944.

Landscape Preservation Council of the National Trust of Australia (Victoria). *Proposed Yarra Valley National Park*. National Trust of Australia (Victoria), n.d.

———. *Safeguarding the Victorian Landscape*. National Trust of Australia (Victoria), n.d.

Melbourne Times. 'Turn our concrete drains into natural creeks'. 19 June 1974.

Pearce, Sandy. 'Gambling on togetherness'. *Bulletin*, 11 July 1970.
Spackman, Michael. The Art of Ellis Stones. BLArch. thesis, University of New South Wales, 1984. See in particular ch. 11.
Stones, Ellis. 'Boulders and borders'. *Australian Home Beautiful*, June 1946.
———. 'Pools: formal and natural'. *Australian Home Beautiful*, September 1946.
———. 'Save our bushland'. *Argus*, 13 August 1954.
———. 'Pollution of the eye'. *Herald*, 27 February 1971.
———. 'Vandals in grey flannel suits'. *Herald*, 17 October 1972.
Turnbull, Jeffrey. 'Robin Boyd: visions of living'. *Building Ideas*, vol. 5, no. 5, March 1973.
Turner, John. 'Ellis Stones 1895–1975: a tribute'. *Trust Newsletter*, National Trust of Australia (Victoria), vol. 3, no. 11, July 1975.
Valley Freeway Action Group. *The Yarra Valley in Melbourne for People*. Valley Press, Melbourne, 1976.
Walling, Edna. 'The planting of little trees'. *Australian Home Builder*, April 1925.
———. 'Uses of little trees'. *Australian Home Builder*, May 1925.
———. 'The Italian influence in our Australian native gardens'. *Australian Home Beautiful*, December 1933.
———. 'The use of boulders and the choice of rock plants'. *Australian Home Beautiful*, July 1935.
———. 'The building of Sonning 2'. *Australian Home Beautiful*, January 1936.
———. 'A swimming pool that fits into the landscape'. *Australian Home Beautiful*, April 1941.
———. 'Letter to garden lovers'. *Australian Home Beautiful,* 1937–1950. See in particular April 1938; December 1938; September 1939; January 1941; September 1944; March 1945; August 1945; August 1946.
Wulff, Rodney. 'Contextually appropriate?: some interpretations of design directions in Australian landscape architecture'. *Landscape Australia,* vol. 4, 1987.
Yencken, David. Edna Walling and Ellis Stones. Lecture for the National Trust of Australia (Victoria), given at 'Illawarra', Toorak, December 1976.

Acknowledgements

So many people have helped me make this book that is is very difficult to pick out individuals. But special thanks are due to Ellis Stones's family – the late Olive Stones, Lesley Frampton, Patricia Rice and Elizabeth Anderson – and to my husband, Peter, all of whom have remained cheerful, interested and helpful over a long period.

I received valuable help with research from the late Anthea Staveley, and from Sue Course. At the *Age*, Greg Taylor and the late Nancy Dexter allowed me time off in office hours in the early stages of research, and many years later, Ray Blackburn arranged for printing of the First World War negatives. Ian Smith of Custom Colour coped skilfully with printing old negatives.

Unstinting help and enthusiasm came from many of Ellis's employees, in particular Beverley Hanson and Bob Grant. Ralph Neale and Ruth Sanderson of *Landscape Australia* passed on a box of valuable old files from Ellis's later years with *Australian Home Beautiful*. The Ministry of Housing, the Melbourne and Metropolitan Board of Works and Heidelberg City Council kindly allowed me access to their records.

Sections of the book were read, with critical comment, by Jean Galbraith, Margaret Hendry and David Yencken. I am most grateful to them, and to Peter Watts, who read the whole manuscript. Thanks are due also to Theresa Janssen and Leonie Stott, for editing and design.

Without co-operation from owners of gardens where Ellis was involved in design and/or construction, the book could not have been written. Many thanks to all those who welcomed me in, provided information or lent photographs – particularly Mrs Joy Hawthorne – and to the following people who allowed photography in their gardens: Mrs Shirley Mayes, Mrs Inez Thornthwaite, Mrs Ruth Rundle, Dr and Mrs Victor Stone, Mrs A. M. Webb, Mrs D. Forge, Mr and Mrs Eddie Baitz, Mrs Beryl Osborne, Miss Kathleen Jepp, Sir Ian and Lady McLennan, Mr and Mrs Hugh Morgan, Mr and Mrs Graeme McCubbin.

PHOTOGRAPHIC ACKNOWLEDGEMENTS

The author thanks those listed below who kindly supplied illustrations, or who gave permission for them to be reproduced (page numbers in italics refer to colour illustrations): Mrs E. Sutton 2, 18; the late Mr and Mrs R. Webster 25; Gwynnyth Taylor 33 (top); Barbara Barnes 33 (lower), 55, 78, 191; Mrs E. Ledger *39* (lower left); Glen Wilson *42* (lower); Elizabeth Anderson 45; Max Walters *46* (lower), *47*; Jean Eggleston *51* (lower); State Library of Victoria, La Trobe Collection 54; Peter Watts 57; University of Melbourne Archives 63, 69 (Strathfieldsaye Estate collection), 70 (T. C. [Carrick] Chambers collection); National Library of Australia (MS 5188) 65, 124, 195; Bob Crosbie 74, 88; George Althofer 83; Margot Knox 90, 93, 95, 101; Mrs P. Harrison 94; Frank Pound 105, 106, 109; *Age* newspaper 114; Daphne Pearson 133; David Yencken *151*, 192 (top), *201* (lower right), *209* (top left), *212* (lower left), 232, 241, 249; Mrs J. Hawthorne, *154* (top right, lower), *155* (lower), *158* (top, middle), *Bulletin* 170 (top); Bruce Weatherhead 170 (lower); Ron Rayment 183, *197* (lower), 228; Heidelberg City Council 192 (drawings); Tract Consultants *201* (top), *204*; Ballarat Historical Park Association, Sovereign Hill 224.

As far as can be ascertained, Ellis Stones took the photographs on pp. 8–12, 16, 17, 19, 20, 27, 30, 31 (top), 37, 56, 60–1, 67, 71, 73–74 (lower), 75, 89 (lower), 92, 98, 100, 107, 148, 177–8, 223, 225. Those on xi, 4, 6, 7, 18 (lower), 21–2, 24, 34, 49, 64, 99, 111–113, 115, 135 (top two), 143, 156, 161, 179–80, 184, 194, 215, 226, 242, 248 are from family sources or from the Ellis Stones collection now lodged at the State Library of Victoria (La Trobe Collection). Illustrations on pp. 48, 95 (lower), 98 (top), 100, are reproduced from Ellis's book *Australian Garden Design*. Photographs on pp. v, 126–7, 134, 135 (lower), 140–1, 144, 146, 149, *150* (top), *151* (top), *154* (top), *155* (top), 176, *200, 205* (top), *208* (top), *209* (top right), 160, 162, 166, 187, 203, 205 (top), 206, 209 (top right), 210, 219, 227, 231 and the front cover were taken for *Australian Home Beautiful* by the late Leslie Runting. Other photographs are by Prue Carr pp. *38, 39, 50, 51* (top), *162–3, 197* (top) and the back cover; Sandy Scheltema pp. 31 (bottom), *159, 201* (lower left), *208* (middle), *209* (lower), *212* (top and lower right); Jennifer Wilkinson pp. 42 (top) and 46 (top); Mark Strizic 57; Ursula Powys and the Touring Camera 94; Ray Blackbourn 105–6; Wolfgang Sievers 123 (top); Kurt Veld 123 (lower); and Peter Latreille pp. *39* (lower right), *43, 86,* 89, 127 (lower), *150* (lower), *158* (lower), *205* (lower), *208* (lower).

Index

Numbers in italics refer to photographs.

Adam-Smith, Patsy 18
Age 172, 193, 198, 246
Allen, Dr Len 117, 239
Alpines in Colour and Cultivation 217
Althofer, George 82, 83, *83*, 84, 87, 207, *and see* Nindethana
Anderson, Allan 176
Anderson, Elizabeth *see* Stones, Elizabeth
Anderson, Dr and Mrs Ringland 59-60, 68, 132, *and see* 'Churston' and 'Culraven'
Anderson, Rupert 41
Anzac Day 18, 226
A. P. M., Fairfield 243
'Appledore', Ivanhoe 84, 115
'Appletree Hill', Glen Waverley 214
Argus 13, 81, 108
Art in Australia 40
Arts and Crafts Society 35, 76
Ashby, Edwin 82
Australian Garden Design 44, 52, 95, 109, 131, 147, 160, 184, 190, 202, 226, 227-9, 236
Australian Garden Lover 80
Australian Gardens 79
Australian Gardens of To-Day Illustrated 81
Australian Home Beautiful 32, 35, 53, 57, 58, 75, 77, 84, 109, 120, 126, 132, 166, 169, 171, 214, 220, 221, 230, 234, 235, 243, 248
Australian Institute of Landscape Architects 132-3, 137-8, 199
Australian Plants for the Garden 83
Australian Roadside, The 121
Australian Treescapes 121
Australian Women's Weekly 101, 120, 210
Avenel, 'Forest Holme' 24, 26

Bailey, Chris 107, 237, 239, 248
Baillieu, Elizabeth *see* Darling family
Baillieu, Kate 248
Baitz, Mr and Mrs Eddie 156-7
Baitz garden, Canterbury 156-7, *156*, *162*, *163*, 244
Ball, Erica 79, 132
Bean, C. E. W. 7, 13
Beattie, James 31
Beattie garden, Toorak 31, *31*, 149
B.H.P. research laboratory, Clayton 207
'Bickleigh Vale', Mooroolbark 32, 53, 81
Blackburn Tree Preservation Society 182
Blakey, Jack 96-97, 113, 114
Blazey, Alan 145
Blazey garden, Balwyn *223*
Boddy's Eastern Park Nursery 87, 217
Boyd, Robin 58, 109, 110, 127-9, 140, 144, 145, 169, 214, 245
Broadmeadows army camp 5, 6
Brown, Lancelot 'Capability' 104, 125
Brown, Jocelyn 79
Browne, Thomas A. 77
'Building Today' 219
Burdett, William 82
Burnley Horticultural College 120-1, 129, 145, 175
  outcrop 175, 217
Butler, Walter 34

Cane, Bill 82
Carnegie, Douglas and Margaret 85, *and see* 'Kildrummie'
Carnegie, Jane 164-6
Carnegie garden, Malvern 164-6, *166*
Chambers, Professor Carrick 68, 225
Chateau Tahbilk, Avenel 126
Chelsworth Park, Ivanhoe 106, 107, 108, 109, 119, 239
children's playgrounds 2, 189, 191-9, 211
Chisholm, Nerine 79, 125
Chris Cross pool, Deepdene 176, *176*
Christie, Vernon 117, *118*
Church, Thomas 125-7, 166, 167, 179
'Churston', Toorak 59, *60*, *61*, 73, 132
Civil Construction Corps 65
Clark, Alan and Yvonne 235
Clark, Alister 116
Clark garden, Ivanhoe 235
Clemson garden, Kew 129, 245
Clemson, Helen 245
Clifford, Derek 221
Clough, Richard 137
'Como' pool, South Yarra 175, 185, 186, *187*
Contemporary Home Industries 169
Conran, Robin 182
Correy, Alan 137
Cowen garden, Kew 127-8, 198
Cowen, Sir Zelman and Lady 127, 128, 247
Cox garden, Fairfield 139-41, *141*
Cox, Professor and Mrs Kenneth 139-41
Crosbie, Bob 73, 92, 236
Cross, Robert 190
Crouch, Gwynnyth 35, 41, 53, 62, 120, 237
Crowe, Sylvia 183
Croxford, Alan 240
'Culraven', Olinda 73
Cuming, Mrs Mac 142

Darebin Creek, Heidelberg 238, 239, 247
Darebin Parklands 247
Darling garden *see* 'Warrawee'
Darling, Harold and family 34-5
Davidson, Rodney 244
Davis, Mervyn 59, 79, 132-3, 135, 137, 145, 222
Designing Australian Bush Gardens 96
Dexter, Nancy 193, 198
Dickie garden, Hawthorn 133, *133*, *134*, *150*
Disher, Dr Clive 68, 70, *and see* 'Strathfieldsaye'
Donaldson garden, Heidelberg 28, 29, *30*, *31*, 76, 80
Donaldson, Mrs Gertrude 28, 29, 94
Downing, 'Dick' 91
Downing/Le Gallienne garden, Eltham 91, 101-3, *102*, 106, *209*
Doyle family 20
Doyle, Olive *see* Stones, Olive
Duncan, Charles 213
Duncan, John 134, 135, 221, 222
Dunster, Robert 217

Earle, James 135
Eckbo, Garrett 166
Edmond, Robin 215-6, 221
Education of a Gardener, The 167, 183, 190
Eggleston, Bob 142, 145
Eggleston, Jean 145
Eggleston, Peter 142, 145
Elliott, Bill 4, *4*, 5, 6, 7, 8, 14, 20
Elliott, H. E. 'Pompey' 8
Ellis Stones Garden Book, The 140, 248
Ellis Stones Memorial Award 249
Elliston, Rosanna *201*, 213, 214, *215*, 216-17, 247

Fenton, John 181
Field Naturalists Club 80
First Ivanhoe Sea Scouts 66, 73, 105, *105*, *106*
Flack garden, South Yarra 36, 41, 87
Ford, Gordon 101-4, *102*, 110, 111, 113, 114, 116, 135, 137, 166, 236
Frampton, Lesley *see* Stones, Lesley
Fraser, Grace 129, 137, 216
Frond, C. B. 80, 81

Galbraith, Jean 80
Gallipoli 13
Garden Week display (c.1939) 41, 87
Gardener's Log, A 78
Gardens are for People 126, 167
Gardens in Australia 31, 35, 53, 66, 78
Garner, Tom 114, 123, 129, 142, 207
Gay, Howard 55-6, 65
George, Douglas 36, *and see* 'Hillsborough' ('Silver Birches')
Gibson, Emily 79, 84, 122
Glass, Cecile 172, 207
Glass, Peter 91, 135, 138, 207, 245-6, 247
Glass's Creek, Kew 240-2, *241*
'Glenara', Bulla 116, 230
Gowrie, Lady 36, 41
Grant, Bob 113, *113*, 114, 186, 207, 245
Grassick, Mr and Mrs Fred 84, 115, *and see* 'Appledore'
Green Fingers Week 246
Grey Smith garden, South Yarra 62-3
Grey Smith, Ross 62
Griffin, Walter Burley 32, 79, 84, 222
Grimwade, Russell 41, 44, *45*, 68, 75, 88, *and see* 'Miegunyah'
Grounds, Romberg and Boyd 110, 144
Grounds, Roy 122
Gunn, Graeme 169-71, *170*, 181, 213, 214, 221, 239

*H*amer, Sir Rupert 213
Hammett, Ivo 82
Hammond, Eric 41, 52, 60, 85, 120, 137, 186, 207, 236
Hanson, Beverley 145, 172, 217
Harris, Thistle 83, 87, 121, 236, 248
Hawthorne garden, Hawthorn 148-52, *149*, *154*, *155*, *158*, *209*, *front cover*
Hawthorne garden, South Yarra 147-8, *148*
Hawthorne, Joy (Mrs David) 147-52
Heidelberg City Council 107, 110, 119, 191, 193, 213, 239, 240, 243
Heidelberg Repatriation Hospital 153, 232
Heidelberg School artists 238
Heliopolis, Egypt 15
Henderson, Vern 239-40, 247
Hendry, Margaret 79, 135, 243
Herald 109, 183, 191, 229, 241
'Hillsborough' ('Silver Birches'), Balwyn 36, *37-9*, 131, *back cover*
History of Garden Design, A 221
Hitchin, Tony 220, 221, 246, 248
Hodgins Nursery 68
Hollingworth, Ann 172
Hollingworth, Archbishop Peter 172
Home 79
Home Gardener 80, 87
Hooks, Peter 140, 145
Housing Commission of Victoria 131, 199
estate playground, Lennox Street, Richmond 196-9
Hughes-Jones, Edith 55
Hughes-Jones pool, Olinda 53-58, *54-7*, 65, 230
Huntingfield, Lady 36

*I*vanhoe River Parklands Protection League 116, 145, 175, 239
Ivanhoe Sea Scouts *see* First Ivanhoe Sea Scouts
Invercargill playgrounds, New Zealand 195-6, *196*

*J*ackson and Walker 213, 244
Jackson, John 202, 207, 216, 225, 230, 235
Jackson, L. W. 166
Jenkins, Mr and Mrs Harold 81
Jennings, A. V., Balwyn house 73, *74*, 139
development work 215
Jepp garden, Warrandyte 156, *158*
Jepp, Kathleen 156
Johnson garden, Ivanhoe 106-7
Johnson, Ken 106-8
Jones, Arthur 80
Jones, Murray 219
Judge Book Memorial Village, Eltham 129, 142
Junghenn, Elizabeth *see* Stones, Elizabeth
Junghenn, Stephen 230

*K*eenan, Frank 121
Keilor Civic Group 233
Kellaway, Frank 245
Kew City Council 241
Kew Natural Environment Group 241
'Kildrummie', Holbrook, NSW 85, *86*, 165
Knox, Alistair 90, *90*, 101-3, *102*, 105-6, 114, 115, 135, 138, 171, 190
Knox, Margot 91-5, *93*, *95*, 103

*'L*ake View', Chiltern 199
Landale gardens, Deniliquin, NSW 125
Landale, Louise 125, 172, 177, 191, *see also* McDonald garden, SA
landscape architecture 78
training available 120-2, 132, 134-5
development of profession in Australia 131-8
overall importance 214
Landscape of Roads *183*
Law-Smith, Joan *see* Darling family
Lawson, Mr and Mrs Keith 75, *and see* 'Padthaway', SA
Le Gallienne, Dorian 91, 106
Le Gallienne/Downing garden *see* Downing/Le Gallienne garden
Le Notre 125
Ledger, Mr and Mrs Laurie 61, *and see* 'Wooleen', Benalla
Leech, David 114-15, 152, 153
Lindner brothers 82
Littlejohn, Eric 135, 176
Lord, Ernest 104

*M*cCorkell, Howard 169, 243
McCoy Reserve, Footscray 193-4, *194*
McCubbin garden, Sunbury *208*, 234
McCubbin, Graeme and Pam 234
McCutcheon, Osborn 123
McDonald garden, Millicent, SA 177-9, *177*, *178*
McDonald, Louise *see* Landale, Louise
McGlashan and Everist 213
McIlwraith garden, Violet Town 179
McIlwraith, Mr and Mrs John 179
McInerney, John 239-40
McIntyre, 'Wild Jack' 73
Mackenzie, Bruce 137, 193, 218, 240
McLennan garden, Narre Warren *205*, 207, *210*
McLennan, Sir Ian and Lady 207
McNicoll, Brigadier-General W. Ramsay 13
Madden, Quentin 207
Mahood, Marguerite 75
Mann, Beryl 137
Marshall, Blanche 41
Martin, Marcus 41, 59, 62
Mason Firth McCutcheon building, Moorabbin 142, *143*, 143-4

Melbourne & Metropolitan Board of Works 117, 119, 145, 217, 240-2, 247
Mellor, Olive 77, 79, 81, 82, 120, 220
Merchant Builders 126, *160*, 168-74, *168*, *200*, *201*, 202, *204*, 213, 218, 233, 243, 248
Meyes, S. C. 81
'Miegunyah', Toorak 41, *45*, *48*, 75
Mills garden, Wanaka, NZ 244
Mills, John and Jocelyn 244
Mockridge, John 75, 169
'Mogolimby', Euroa 179-81, *179*, *180*
Molyneux, Bill 216
Monarto, SA 243
Monash University, outcrop 176-7
'Moralla', Skipton 41
Morgan, Hugh and Elizabeth 230
Morgan garden *208*, *209*, 230
Morgan, John 220, 229
Morrison, P. Crosbie 82
Mueller, Ferdinand 156
Murdoch, Dame Elisabeth 249
Myer Melbourne 66

National Parks Association 199
National Trust of Australia (Victoria) 145, 175, 199, 243, 244
landscape preservation council 175, 182, 199, 229
native planting 58, 78-88, 96, 144, *144*, 146, *180*, 181, 218-19, 247, *and see* Stones, Ellis, ideas
natural landscape *51*, 58, 59, *102*, 104, *107*, 116, 129-30, 181, 220
Natural Resources Conservation League 237
Nelson, Eddie 188
Nevertire, 'Oxley Park' 23
Newton garden, Toorak *223*
Nindethana nursery 82
Nolan, Mr and Mrs Barry 179, *and see* 'Mogolimby'
Norway, F. M. *see* Shute, Nevil
Nunawading City Council 182-3, *182*

Oak tree wall, Donaldson garden 28
Oldham, John 132, 137
O'Neill family 3
O'Neill, Fred 21, 27, 29
Osborne garden, Warrandyte 156, *159*
Ottrey garden, Pascoe Vale 245
Ottrey, Robin 245

'Padthaway', Naracoorte, SA *74*, 75, *75*
Page, Russell 167, 183, 190
Paisley gardens, Tumut, NSW 164
Paisley, Robin 164
Pearson, Daphne 135
Pescott, R. T. M. 187, 188
Pettit, Sevitt and Partners 169
Plowman, Rana 176
pools, ornamental 29, *31*, *34*, 35, 36, *38*, *39*, 40, 41, *50*, 60, *72*, 76, *112*, 113, 133, 149, 152, *154*, 160, *161*, *162*, 186, *187*, *195*, *203*
pools, swimming 53-58, *55*, *56*, *57*, 208, 230, 232, *232*
Poulter, Genevieve 96-7
Pound, Frank 107-8
Preshil school 244
Preston City Council 229
Prichard, R. V. 68
Priority Landscaping 3, 58, 119, 130, 184, 189, 229
Proudfoot, Helen 79
Pugh, Clifton 103
Purbrick, Eric 26
Pyke, Guelda and Polly 95, *and see* 'Stella Park'

Railton, James 82
Rayment, Ron 222-4
Repton, Humphry 104, 125
Returned Services League 27, *64*, 145
Reynolds, Pam 234-235
Rice, Barry 207, 247
Rice, Patricia *see* Stones, Patricia
Ridge garden, Toorak *127*, 160, *161*
Ridge, John 169, *170*, 172, 243
Riemsdyk, Chris van *see* van Riemsdyk, Chris
'River Gums', Alphington 232, *232*
River Parklands Protection League *see* Ivanhoe River Parklands Protection League
Rock Garden, The 216
Rock Plant Supplies nursery 182
Rockbeare Park 247, *248*
Rockbeare Park Conservation Group 247
rocks *30*, *31*, 32, *33*, 35, *37*, *38*, *39*, 40, 41, *42*, 51, 55, 59, *60*, 62, 67, 76, 79-80, 87, 99, 104, *123*, *133*, *134*, 149, *155*, 156, *159*, 165, *166*, 176-7, 186, *187*, 190, *197*, *209*, *212*, 216, 221, *223*, 225, 236-7
Romberg, Professor Frederick 110
rooftop courtyard, Tumut, NSW 164
Rosanna Parklands *212*, 213, 217-18, 239, 240, 247
Rotherham, Ted 191
Royal Australian Institute of Architects 248
Royal Botanic Gardens outcrop, South Yarra 185, 186-8, *197*
Royal Melbourne Institute of Technology 134, 135, 221
Rundle, Eric and Ruth 116, *and see* 'Glenara'
Rundle garden, Eltham 116
Ruff, Wallace 135

St Kilda Road, Melbourne 184, 229
St Paul's School, Woodleigh 244
Salt Creek, Rosanna *212*, 213, 217-18, 240, 242, 247
Save the Yarra League 117, *118*, 229, 239
Schubert, Bernhardt and Dulcie 85
Schubert nursery, Noble Park *42*, 85, 87
Scott, Audrey 182
Seventh Battalion AIF 5, 13, 226
Shum, W. A. 75, 77, 81, 82
Shute, Nevil 115
'Silver Birches' *see* 'Hillsborough'
'Sonning', Mooroolbark 32, 53, 68, 80
Sovereign Hill, Ballarat 224, *224*
Sparks & McAlpine nursery 87
Spooner, Peter 137
Springvale Road, Nunawading 182
State Nursery, Macedon 68
'Stella Park', Templestowe 95, 96, *96*
Stevens, John 122-4, *123*, 129, 130, 186, 236
Stocks and Holdings 215, 233, 243
Stone garden, Ivanhoe *50*, *51*, 110-13, *111*, *112*
Stone, Dr and Mrs Victor 110-12
Stones, Elizabeth 24, 27, *27*, *49*, 66, 124-5, 195
Stones, Ellis
  as committeeman 117,199
  Australian Institute of Landscape Architects
    membership 138-9
    attends international conference 188
    attitude towards 138, 139, 246
  begins work as builder 21
  begins work for Edna Walling 28-9
  birth 1
  birth of children 22-4
  books/manuscripts/articles
    for *Australian Home Beautiful* 75-7, 220-21
  newspaper articles 229, 241, *and see Australian Garden Design, The Ellis Stones Garden Book, Priority Landscaping*
  concerns
    conservation and environment 107-8, 116-19, 129-30, 189, 239, 246
    controlling authority needed for landscaping 229
    radial creeks 119, 240-2
    pollution 188-9, 229
  consultant work
    Heidelberg City Council 239
    Merchant Builders 168-73, *and see* Elliston, Winter Park
    National Trust 175
    Royal Melbourne Institute of Technology 135
  costings 166, 174, 207
  death 242, 247, 248
  design methods 92, 148, 160, 173
  'Elliston' named after him 214
  engagement and marriage 21-2
  enlists in AIF 4
  first outcrop 35
  first use of stone 24-6
  health problems 19, 26, 153, 232, 233, 242
    with leg 15, 17, 19, 27, 101, 125, 153, 164, 171
  ideas
    courtyard design 157-61
    factory surrounds 143-4, 189
    gardens as response to climate and life-style 166-7
    gardens for people 142, 167
    importance of landscaping 131, 214
    land-use planning 240
    native plants 85-7, 94, 96, 144, *144*, 146, *150*, *151*, 156, 160, 161, 165, *180*, 181, 218-19, 247
    paving 46, *92*, 93, *95*, 231
    play space for children 2, 128, 193, 198-9, 211, 230
    removal of front fences 139
    stone, rock in gardens *see* rocks
    street trees 182-5, *184*
    tea-tree for fencing, screening *47*, 160, 178-9, *178*
    timber in gardens 104, 110, 193, *161*, *200*, *227*, 228, *228*, *232*, 233
    use of plants 94, 104, 161, 202, 207, 216-17
    water in gardens 76, 113, *and see* pools
  invalided home 17, 66
  inventions 23, 26, *49*, 65, *65*, 66
  love of bare countryside 23, 179, 180, 188, 238
  love of natural landscape 58, 116, 129-30, 181, 239
  new ideas on garden design 72, 76
  nursery proprietor 96-7
  on site
    difficulties 124, 171, 173, 174, 215
    enjoyment of work 111, 113-14, 115, 172, 222, 245, 247
  partnerships
    with Tom Garner 142
    with Ron Rayment 222
  photography 8-13, 17, 57, 60, 71, 73, 190, 247
  posthumous honours
    Robin Boyd environmental award 248
    University of Melbourne appeal 249
    Ellis States Memorial Award 249
  publication *Australian Garden Design* 190, 227-8
  relationship with Edna Walling 52-9
  restrained style 210-11
  stops constructing gardens 202
  wounded at Gallipoli 13

Stones, Eva 18, *18*
Stones garden, Ivanhoe 135, *136*, 139, *140*, *206*
Stones, Hannah 1, 7
Stones, Lesley 24, *24*, 27, *27*, 66, 96, 125, 195
Stones, Olive 6, 7, 19, *20*, 21, *21*, 22, 23, *24*, 27, 36, 41, *49*, 53, 66, 75, 96, 124, 125, 138, 145, 153, 220, 233, 235, *242*, 246, 247, 249
Stones, Patricia 24, *24*, *27*, 32, 60, 64, 66, 67, 68, 71, *71*, 73, 75, 94, 113, 125, 195
Stones, Thomas 1, 7, 13, 17
Stones, William 22, 23
Stranger, Ivan 228
'Strathfieldsaye', Stratford 53, 68-71, *69*, *70*, *71*
Streeton, Arthur 238

Tanner, Howard 243-4
Taylor, Ann 135
Tayor, Gwynnyth *see* Crouch, Gwynnyth
'This Day Tonight' 248
Thomas, A. S. 82
Thomas, Pat 191
Thornthwaite garden, Ocean Grove *43*, 87, 88, *88*, *89*, 97
Thornthwaite, Inez 87
Thorpe Clark, Mavis 75
Tocumwal, 'Woodsome Leas' 20
Town and Country Planning Board 199
Tract Consultants 243
Tullamarine Freeway 246

University of Melbourne 68, 120, 122, 175, *197*, 224, *225*, 249

Valley Freeway Action Group *see* Yarra Valley Freeway Action Group
van Riemsdyk, Chris 186
Volunteer Defence Corps 65

Walker, Ken 4, 7, 8, 13, 15, 16
Walker, Councillor Ronald 246
Walling, Edna 28, 31, 32, 34, 35, 36, 40, 41, 44, 52-63, *54*, 66, 75, 76-7, 78, *78*, 79, 80, 81, 83, 84, 116, *121*, 125, 127, 129, 131-2, 137, 142, 147, 149, 165, 172, 211, 218, 219, 237
Walters gardens
  Malvern 97
  Narre Warren *46*, *47*, 97-101, *98*, *99*, *100*, 113, 120
Walters, Mr and Mrs Harry 97-99, *99*
Walters, Max 99
'Warrawee', Toorak 34, 66, 95
Warringal Conservation Society 202
Waterhouse, E. G. 82
Watsonia army camp 142
Watts, Peter 79, 132
Weatherhead, Bruce 169, *170*
Webster, Mr and Mrs Dick 24, *and see* 'Winterfold'
Weston, Don 207
Wettenhall, Dr Norman 175
Wild Flowers of Australia 83, 84
Wild Flowers of Victoria 83
Williams, Bruce 65
Williams, Jack 23, 24, 27
Wilson, Eric 169, 171
Wilson, Glen 85, 216
Wilson Reserve, Ivanhoe 66, 117, 191, *212*
Wilson Reserve playground 191, *192*, 239, 244
Wilson 'Skipper' 105, 191
Winter Park, Doncaster *200*, *201*, *204*, 218, *219*, 243, 244
'Winterfold', Avenel 24, 25
'Winty', Mooroolbark 32, *33*
Woolaston Bridge, Warrnambool 199
'Wooleen', Benalla *39*, 61
Woolley, Ken 169
Wulff, Rodney 218, 243

Yarra River 28, 48, 105-10, *106*, *107*, 116-19, *118*, 139, 145, 147, 191, *212*, 229, 232, 237, 238-9, 240, 248
Yarra Valley Conservation League *see* Save the Yarra League
Yarra Valley Freeway Action Group 119, 245
'Yarralumla', Canberra 41
Yencken, David 125, 169-73, *170*, 214, 243
Yooralla, Glenroy 243
Yorralla playground, Balwyn 194, *195*